Gaston County, North Carolina,
in the Civil War

Gaston County, North Carolina, in the Civil War

Robert C. Carpenter

McFarland & Company, Inc., Publishers
Jefferson, North Carolina

LIBRARY OF CONGRESS CATALOGUING-IN-PUBLICATION DATA

Names: Carpenter, Robert C. (Robert Claude), 1951– author.
Title: Gaston County, North Carolina, in the Civil War / Robert C. Carpenter.
Description: Jefferson, North Carolina : McFarland & Company, Inc., Publishers, 2016. | Includes bibliographical references and index.
Identifiers: LCCN 2016008320 | ISBN 9781476662442 (softcover : acid free paper) ∞
Subjects: LCSH: Gaston County (N.C.)—History—19th century. | North Carolina—History—Civil War, 1861–1865.
Classification: LCC F262.G2 C37 2016 | DDC 975.6/77303—dc23
LC record available at http://lccn.loc.gov/2016008320

ISBN (print) 978-1-4766-6244-2
ISBN (ebook) 978-1-4766-2330-6

BRITISH LIBRARY CATALOGUING DATA ARE AVAILABLE

© 2016 Robert C. Carpenter. All rights reserved

No part of this book may be reproduced or transmitted in any form or by any means, electronic or mechanical, including photocopying or recording, or by any information storage and retrieval system, without permission in writing from the publisher.

Front cover images © 2016 iStock

Printed in the United States of America

McFarland & Company, Inc., Publishers
Box 611, Jefferson, North Carolina 28640
www.mcfarlandpub.com

In memory of my parents:
Claude and Georgie Carpenter,
who taught me Christian values,
a strong work ethic,
a belief in the American Dream,
and an appreciation for our heritage

Table of Contents

Acknowledgments ix
Preface 1
Introduction 3

1. Life in Gaston County 7
2. Dallas, Iron and Gold Manufacturing and Cotton Mills 30
3. Gaston's Fighting Confederates 52
4. Soldiers, Wives and Mothers 75
5. Family Life 91
6. Unionists and Deserters 106
7. Gaston Violence and Lawlessness 128
8. Changing Politics During the Civil War 144
9. The African American During the War 166

Concluding Thoughts 189
Appendix: Gaston County Tax List of 1863 193
Chapter Notes 283
Bibliography 307
Index 313

Acknowledgments

Completion of a book of this magnitude cannot be undertaken without the assistance of many persons. I am deeply indebted to various people and institutions for assisting with this project. It is impossible to succeed in naming everyone individually, but I will attempt to do so.

The personnel at the North Carolina Department of Archives were especially helpful, as they provided me with numerous manuscripts and advice and answered my many questions about records available. The Southern Historical Collection at the University of North Carolina at Chapel Hill and the Rubenstein Library at Duke University provided me with necessary materials upon my visits and through email requests. The University of North Carolina at Charlotte's library allowed me access to their newspaper microfilm collections. The Brevard Station Museum and Joyce Handsel were especially supportive of my research and aided significantly in locating sources. All were gracious and helpful hosts.

No depository was more helpful to me than the Lincoln County Historical Association. Jason Harpe allowed me access to their vast holdings, would troubleshoot with me on finding resources, and acted as an advisor in the project. Together we visited numerous persons with private papers, many of which ended up in the association archives to be saved for posterity.

A number of persons read the book and offered much helpful advice. To Ann Dellinger and Steve Huffstetler, your advice has made this a more effective book. Rachel Eickemeyer has been my conscience and my advisor. Her insightful advice, edits, and suggestions transformed my research into a readable and organized book. I thank her for taking so much of her personal time to assist me.

I advertised my project locally so that I could access private papers and collections. To the *Gaston Gazette* and *Charlotte Observer* and writers Wade Allen and Joe Depriest, I thank you for publicizing the project, which resulted in numerous contacts. Jason Harpe at LCHA, the Gaston Lincoln Genealogical Society, and the Gaston County Historical Society also spread the word. Numerous civic groups, like the Brevard Station Museum, Crouse Community History, Mt. Holly Historical Society, genealogical seminars, and DAR groups, allowed me to present my research and motivated persons to contact me with help and advice.

These efforts resulted in contacts to offer their papers, research, and advice to me: John Eddleman, Mike Sumner, Martha Parks, Darlene Levernier, Anita Roberts, Cheryl Mauney, George Moore, Violet Bumgardner, Martha Wilson, Morris Jenkins, Janice Bentley, Farrell Mauldin, Edward Phifer, Hugh Wilson, Daphne Friday, Margaret Hill, Mildred

Newton, Lynda Hancock, Joyce Handsel and Brevard Station Museum, Gale Benfield, Fred and Mark Goodson, John and Wylma Monteith, Lucy Penegar, Gerald and Suzanne Deal, Jim Love, the Gaston County Museum of Art and History with Jeff Pruitt and Stephanie Elliott, Bill Beam, Mike Stroupe, Kitty Thornburg Heller, Elizabeth Carpenter, Wade Carpenter, Dr. Ed Anthony, Steve Huffstetler, Corinne Puett Gianitrapani, Anne Gometz and the Gaston County Library, Mike Peters, Greg Payseur, Danny Wilson, Mary Alice Carmichael, Rudolph Young, Rachel Eickemeyer, Daphine Peach, Charlie Rhyne, Kathy Gunter Sullivan, Len Clemmer, Bruce Cloninger, Gaston County Register of Deeds, Lincoln County Register of Deeds, Randy Thomason, and Lewis Carpenter. Even though this list is long, I fear that I have omitted someone and for that I apologize. This has been a community effort.

I wish to thank Melany Dawn Crouse for taking the pictures included in the book and for her technical expertise. Jason Harpe also assisted with scans, pictures, and computer assistance.

To Brenda Beard-Bostian, thank you for making my attempt at a Gaston County map to come alive as a legible and attractive map. Your professionalism and expertise is greatly appreciated.

To my children I especially want to express thanks for offering advice, helping with my computer questions and issues, and helping me finalize the research—Candace Hester and Michael and Marcus Carpenter. They, especially Candace, agreed to help their technology-deficient father and spent much time doing so.

To my wife, Sue, I thank her for once again allowing me to be consumed with a publication project of this magnitude, which too often took me to my computer and papers in the basement. She helped me transcribe the tax list on a "vacation" to Raleigh and Chapel Hill, managed my speaking engagements, and suffered through those long phone calls, often taking messages for me. Her support, assistance, and quiet suffering are greatly appreciated.

To Jason Harpe and others who assisted with the Index, I thank you for your hard work. Indexing is never easy, but your assistance has been invaluable.

Finally, even though I have labored to limit misspellings, mistakes, and omissions, I accept full responsibility for any which may have occurred. I hope you will enjoy this book!

Preface

All history is personal and local. Exploring an area, time period, or event requires the discovery of details and events, which correlate into a broad picture. With this perception, I have created *Gaston County, North Carolina, in the Civil War* to tell the story of a previously unstudied Piedmont area. This history is written in the words of county residents, inclusive of everyone—politicians, soldiers, manufacturers, wives, mothers, slaves, Free Blacks, and children. Using their own words and deeds, all aspects of life have been analyzed and transported into a seamless journey of discovery.

This book is not a simple accounting of battles and generals, political leaders, and only the wealthy, but rather it tells the story of poor farmer, wife, child, Unionist, slave, and soldier. Efforts to solicit previously unpublished letters, diaries, and accounts not in public repositories have resulted in the inclusion of a significant amount of new historical documentation.

I combined these unpublished accounts with materials from archival collections, newspaper accounts, census records, letters to Governor Vance, public documents at the state and local levels, oral histories, and the 1863 tax list to create an inclusive journey into Gaston's Civil War past. The journey represents the attitudes, struggles, and opinions of much of the state and the South. Over 90 percent of the sources utilized are contemporary, many outside archival collections, and the narrative and the tax list complement each other in providing descriptions of people, their life and conditions.

As you read, be aware that the words of Gaston Countians include inconsistent and phonetic spelling, poor grammar, sometimes no punctuation, unique colloquial phrases, and sporadic capitalization. Their words convey the limited literacy of individuals but yet the overall literacy of the people. We are reminded of Alexis de Tocqueville's observations in the 1830s that Americans were highly literate, read vociferously, and were well informed. These letters and writings document that Gaston County also had a highly literate population, female and male, wealthy and poor, even if they deviated from academic English.

The book is topically divided into chapters. Chapter 1 and 2 creates the backdrop for the book by delineating the county's formation, its economic foundations, and social class structure. They explore the iron and cotton manufacturing operations, Stoneman's Raid, and the development of Dallas. Chapters 3 and 4 involve the writings of Confederate soldiers and their families. They describe the horrors of battle, forced marches, food and provisions, and anxiety the war brought them, providing a poignant accounting of food shortages, inflation, and home front fear without husbands and sons. Chapter 5 describes family life with an emphasis upon children. School, church, recreation, romance, and gossip are captured in the writings of adolescents, adults, and young soldiers.

Chapter 6 and 7 explore the often ignored topics of Unionists and deserters. These citizens expressed their support for the United States, their disdain for the Confederate goals, and Chapter 7 describes how the community devolved into lawlessness and anarchy as the war ground to a close. Chapter 8 discusses local politics, disclosing virulent disagreements, vigilante activities and the rush to secession, the peace movement, and how the county distanced itself from the secession and Confederate viewpoint after the war. Chapter 9 employs a variety of sources to document the role and significance of slavery in Gaston County, to describe the lives of slaves and Free Blacks, and to convey how whites and blacks related to one another during the war years.

The book also includes a transcription of the 1863 Gaston County tax list, a unique and informative document, detailing taxables with land, slaves, and luxury items. My discovery of this marvelous record motivated this book and my further research. The complete tax list allows historians and genealogists to explore life in Gaston County from a socioeconomic and a personal perspective. The data further expose slaves by name, age, and monetary value with the listing of luxury items such as "pleasure vehicles," pianos, and investments. The book creates a comprehensive portrait of life in Gaston County during the turbulent years of war.

Introduction

I embarked on this fascinating journey into Gaston County's Civil War past after discovering a tax list[1] in an old tattered brown book with detached binding which had been tucked away in the stacks at the State Archives in Raleigh with little use over the years. The 1863 record described the normal tax listing information of landowners, land quantity and value, and geographic location. What captured my attention was unique data with a fuller description of taxable income including slaves by name, age, and value; luxury items like pianos, "pleasure vehicles," and furniture; investments such as stock and bonds, cotton, and other valuable commodities such as leather, gold and silver items; and, of all things, dogs. The detailed account of people and their social and economic status rivaled anything previously encountered and, as future research would disclose, was required by state law to provide a cash-strapped Confederate state the necessary funds to conduct war and manage its affairs. I vowed to transcribe this complete listing for the county because of its value to historians and genealogists.

If I had stopped there, the data would have benefited researchers dramatically. However, the details and valuable insights of the tax list appeared as a skeleton needing skin, face, hands, legs, and feet; so began the process to accumulate and communicate the story of a typical, often atypical county, during the tumultuous conflict for Southern Independence. I advertised the project to local historians and the public, seeking contemporary, unpublished sources. After five years of research and writing, my collaboration of soldier letters, letters to Governor Vance, newspaper articles, laws and governmental documents, diaries, and privately held papers collectively creates a personal story of people living through difficult times and decisions, wartime stresses, battlefield adventure, emotional appeals to arms, political conflict, economic entrepreneurship, Unionism and desertion, lawlessness, survival of slaves and Free Blacks, and the struggles of women, children, and families. These accounts depict a comprehensive Civil War story not previously told.

The research findings contradict many of my perceptions of the war based upon my educational background. I was in elementary and high school in Gaston County and loved history. Teachers imparted upon me and others the traditional southern view of the Civil War, which they usually called the War Between the States.

I learned that slavery had little to do with causing the conflict; that slaves were not treated badly; that all southerners supported secession so that they could preserve their rights; that southerners supported the war effort unanimously with most volunteering for the Confederate army. My historical understanding of Gaston County was that it was a small farmer-oriented county with few plantations and few slaves. I took this concept of local and southern history to college.

When I took courses at Lenoir Rhyne College (now University) in Hickory, North Carolina, not all my professors were southern but some were. When I got my master's degree in history at Wake Forest University, most of my professors were southern gentlemen. Yet, southern history at college varied significantly from my early years. For example, I learned that North Carolina refused to secede originally and was known as a Unionist state. I learned that not everyone in the state supported secession or the war effort and that most historians considered slavery and its extension to be the primary factor in causing the war. The litany of antebellum issues—Missouri Compromise, Wilmot Proviso, what to do with Mexican Cession lands, the Compromise of 1850, the Kansas-Nebraska Act, "Bleeding Kansas," John Brown's Raid, and the Dred Scott Case—precipitated the war because our politicians failed to compromise concerning the extension of slavery into western territories. I also learned that soldiers joined the war effort for various reasons.

Most historical writings about Gaston County and similar Piedmont North Carolina areas reflect the dominant viewpoint of southern Confederate support, the limit of divergent opinions, and a benign effect of wartime challenges.[2] The in-depth study of Gaston County, North Carolina, a previously unstudied geographic area, explores all aspects of people's lives.

In this study I decided that Gaston County residents should speak for themselves, describing their lives, motivations, and battles. Fear, loss of property, uncertainty, entrepreneurial "speculation" and profiteering, and governmental interventions impacted lives and often affected Confederate soldiers as they read about dire circumstances on the home front. The research also examines how slavery positively affected slaveholding families during the war while the lack of slave manpower negatively impacted poorer farmers or farm laborers. The book discloses the war, its challenges, and people's opinions in their own words:

William Groves Morris volunteered as a Confederate soldier, was promoted from a private to colonel, fought in numerous battles, scaled the fortifications at Gettysburg where he was captured, and spent the remainder of the war as a prisoner. He knew and understood why he made those sacrifices and from the battlefield wrote to his wife at home, instructed his children, and attempted to manage his 301 acre Dallas farm, while providing agricultural instructions and allowing his slave Randall to make major farming decisions. He grappled with the sudden death of his father-in-law and whether to remain in the army or return home.

Caleb Senter, Morris's neighbor, enlisted as a volunteer and received a $50 bounty; he harbored little support for the war, read his wife's letters of food shortages and despair, deserted, returned to his unit, and died in Confederate service. Landless Senter was not even listed in the 1863 tax list. His wife's struggles to feed the family affected his service, and his daughter's death brought grief and regret that he was away from home.

James Hillhouse White, a Democratic politician, wrote Governor Vance letters on behalf of his constituents, offered him political advice, assisted with the formation of Gaston County and Dallas, supported economic incentives, and witnessed the rise, decline, and defeat of the Confederate states. He supported secession and the Confederacy.

Wesley Mauney was born a slave, experienced separation from his family, upon emancipation returned to his parents in northwestern Gaston County, and eventually overcame all to become a successful lumberman, constructing churches and schools. He and his family's labors created much of the area's progress, but most historians know nothing about him and slaves like him.

Harriet R. McIntosh, a girl of fourteen, corresponded with her friends and relatives discussing death, destruction, romance, chores, church and school activities, and fear. Her life was stretched and strained as the war took a physical and emotional toll on everyone. The war altered her young life as she and her friends attempted to live a normal life during abnormal times.

Morris, Senter, White, Mauney, McIntosh, and others left a historical trail of their lives, thoughts, and emotions as thousands of Gaston County residents experienced the Civil War. Their personal experiences, survival, and motivations convey a portrait of the war, unique in detail but representative of others in the South.

The book quotes liberally from various sources, regardless of social class or station in society, as most are contemporary to the events they experienced and many come from local attics and personal files. Gaston County's Civil War story conforms to some previous historical research but also challenges some conclusions about the war and its participants. It chronicles the race to secession, use of vigilantism, and political support for the Union and, as the war progressed, documents increased Unionism, desertion, and local violence. The research adds perspective as to why Colonel Morris, Lieutenants Lemuel Hoyle and "Willie" Linebarger, and others exhibited strong support for the Confederacy and the war effort, while Senter, Franklin Hanna, Larkin Thornburg, Newton Sellers, and others felt disconnected, with some deserting, and others defiantly impeding Confederate efforts. What motivated some Gaston Countians to support the Confederacy unequivocally, while others did not? The tax list offers social and economic insight as soldiers made decisions affecting the rest of their lives.

Historians have documented dissent, social class and economic disparities, and political disagreements in the North Carolina mountains and Quaker Belt. This project exposes these issues in a county which embraced the loyal Confederate viewpoint in 1860–61. An increase in anti-war dissent to a majority opinion as the war ended is a unique and unusual journey. Gaston County citizens became conflicted as they realized wartime struggles, inconsistencies of the war administration, and increased governmental involvement in their lives. Gaston residents often challenged Confederate authority, as the war was not quickly won. These variant opinions, an understanding of how they arose, and their overall effect challenge the historical interpretation that residents consistently supported "the cause" with little dissent and opposition. That a seemingly loyal Confederate area could dissolve into violence, theft, and fear is another unexpected discovery the research project conveys.

The tax list, helpful to historians and genealogists, portrays a microcosmic study of the county's residents, examining social class and its implications, and provides clues about how socioeconomic and political considerations impacted resident's actions, opinions, and decisions.

Using contemporary sources, the tax list explains slavery's dominate role in economic, social, and political affairs. The tax list correlates slavery with economic success and political domination. Even in a county where about 70 percent of the taxables owned no slaves, slave ownership delivered clearly defined economic advantages and ascendancy. The narrative also documents the lifestyles of slaves and Free Blacks. The dominant theme of lack of control over one's future dictated a lifestyle which undermined family life, religion, education, economic productivity, and marriage. These despicable conditions certainly contrast with the now discarded view of happy Negroes devoted to their masters. The despair of family separation, sexual exploitation, and poor living conditions are exposed as are collaboration with Union soldiers and slave runaways.

The journey is long and complex, beginning as the state legislature created the new county of Gaston in 1846. Within twenty years, residents experienced a new county seat and government, economic prosperity, political upheaval, and the war—War Between the States, War for Southern Independence, War of Northern Aggression, the Civil War.

1

LIFE IN GASTON COUNTY

The area known as Gaston County began with the settlement of Scotch-Irish, English, and German pioneers starting around 1750. Political designations changed until 1779, when it was named Lincoln County, after Revolutionary General Benjamin Lincoln. Old Lincoln County, which embraced present Gaston, Lincoln, Catawba, and eastern Cleveland, was dismantled over a period of six years. In 1841 the General Assembly sliced portions of Lincoln's western lands to create Cleveland County; the next year a new county, Catawba, was formed north of Lincolnton. In late 1846 the legislature created Gaston with its borders being South Carolina to the south, the Catawba River and Mecklenburg County to the east, Lincoln County at the north and Cleveland County to the west. The South Fork River runs southeast through the center of the county and fast moving streams, which hindered water transportation, enhanced manufacturing.

By 1863 Gaston County included the county seat Dallas, three cotton factories, grist and saw mills, iron and gold mines, iron manufacturing north of Dallas at High Shoals and near Kings Mountain, and local store-post offices. The railroad from Charlotte to Lincolnton crossed the Catawba River north of present Mt. Holly, stopped at Brevard Station (present Stanley), and dropped back into the county with a stop at Cherryville on a path to Shelby, which was not completed until after the war. Roads and horse paths crisscrossed a largely rural landscape of small farms.

There was no Interstate 85 or Highway 321. A few churches dotted a landscape of cornfields, grain fields, and free range livestock. Poor farmers often lived in humble log homes with some log outbuildings. A few grander homes existed and slaveholders provided humble dwellings for their slaves. Contemporary sources communicate a county involving politics, slave culture, economic progress, and differing attitudes about sectional disagreements.

Gaston County's story began with political intrigue, as the new county ushered in economic possibilities and a new county seat.[1] Gaston's citizens held familial, economic, social, political, and traditional connections with citizens from Old Lincoln, Cleveland and to a lesser degree, Catawba. To create the new, leaders and citizens relied upon past knowledge, modeling their county, county seat, mills, mining operations, and other enterprises on Lincoln County, its county seat Lincolnton, and the economy of the past.

In 1860, of the state's 87 counties, Gaston ranked 39th in white population and 58th in slave population, slightly above average for whites but significantly below average for slaves. Of its bordering neighbors it exceeded only Lincoln in white population—6,997 to 5,999 and in its slave population—2,199 to 2,115. It also outnumbered Cleveland's slave population—2,199 to 2,131.² Gaston was typical of other Piedmont counties in white and slave population.

The 1863 Gaston County tax list divided the county into eleven militia companies, a localized national-guard system which had been in place since colonial times. German-speaking people's unique culture, different language, specific religions, and separateness contrasted with English and Scotch-Irish families. An analysis of the German contingent in each militia company provides an ethnic snapshot of the county illustrated with the following chart:

Taxpayers in Each Company Identified as German

	Percentage	Number
Cherryville	44%	41
Crowders Mountain	2%	2
Dallas	55%	60
Duharts	38%	23
High Shoals	42%	41
River Bend	22%	17
Roberts	44%	48
Rudisill	72%	49
South Point	2%	2
Tanyard	7%	9
Woodlawn	17%	18
Total	30%	310

The county's German population in 1863 was based in the northwestern, western, and central portions of the county. The companies of Rudisill, Cherryville, Dallas, High Shoals, and Roberts, comprised about 77 percent of Gaston's Germanic heritage, and also held fewer slaves and slave owners.³

Examining Gaston's creation and antebellum history provides the foundation for its war experiences.

"A new county, to be called Gaston"

On December 12, 1846, Lincolnton's *The Lincoln Courier* exclaimed: "A new county, to be called Gaston, is to be established off the Southern part of Lincoln—a county town to be established within 3 miles of the Baptist Church on Long Creek." The new survey for the county would occur in January with Andrew Love and I. Holland representing Gaston. "Lincoln has to part with strong and faithful friends, as well as Catawba, as well as Gaston." A new day dawned. Gaston citizens created their county and county seat while national political issues involving the acquisition of Texas and the coming Mexican War occupied citizen's attentions. On February 27, 1847, a meeting in Gaston County resulted in the raising of "a Company of Mounted Volunteers" for the Mexican conflict.⁴

The Court of Pleas and Quarter Sessions, also known as the County Court, managed administrative and minor judicial issues. Creating a new county required electing and selecting various officials, planning for a courthouse and jail, creating the new county seat of Dallas, and countless other matters. Many of the Gaston leaders had been influential Lincoln County politicians—Andrew Hoyl, William Joseph Wilson, James H. White, A. W. Davenport, Larkin and Jasper Stowe, and others. They simply shifted their political influence to the new county.

Leaders created the county seat of Dallas, and the courthouse infrastructure in a similar geographical configuration as Lincolnton, locating the courthouse in the middle of the town, which is also how Newton (Catawba County) and Shelby (Cleveland County) had been planned. The following discussion reflects the tenor of the times, issues people faced, and everyday life as the country moved toward an unexpected war with itself.

On March 1, 1847, *The Lincoln Courier* reported a "Meeting in Gaston" with Isaac Holland as chair and James Quinn as secretary, which formulated resolutions including opposition to Mexican treatment of the United States and to the North Carolina Whig Party's legislative endeavors which were termed "aid and comfort afforded the enemy," support for "Senator Larkin Stowe," and volunteer military units. James H. White, Larkin Stowe, John F. Hoke, and Henry Cansler offered speeches in support of the volunteer company. "There were many Whigs on the ground, who confessed themselves in favor of the war, and were willing to contribute." The paper also advertised "Town Lots For Sale in Dallas, in Gaston County."[5] Even though Gaston expressed independent opinions, the presence of Hoke and Cansler exposed a Lincoln County influence.

By June 1847 "Inspectors for the next Congressional Election" for Lincoln and Gaston were posted. Later county officials sought "Proposals ... for building a Courthouse and Jail." On August 11, *The Lincoln Courier* announced that "The first County Court in Gaston will commence to be holden at the location near Jesse Holland's, on Monday next." Official business was conducted in a "temporary log house" until the new courthouse could be constructed.[6]

Meeting in Gaston

Leaders of the new county sought economic development. On October 9, 1847, Dallas hosted a "Meeting in Gaston" to select delegates to attend a "convention" in Shelby supporting a railroad route through the area. Charlotte leaders had proposed a railroad, and western counties competed for a connection.[7] When the meeting convened on October 26, none of the delegates attended and only "John Harmon" was listed from Gaston, as Gaston County held court on that day. The convention appointed commissioners from all the counties and Gaston's group included: "Wm. J. Wilson, James H. White, Andrew Hoyle, L. Stowe." That same year the County Court paid Adam Cloninger $150 for building the poor house and "Henry Setser" $1,625 "for putting public Bridg across South Fork near A. Hoyls."[8]

By 1850 Gaston County had more residents than Lincoln County but fewer than Catawba and Cleveland. In February, Paul Froneberger had been elected county sheriff, one of the few elective county positions.[9] The County Court, whose justices were appointed by the governor, appointed almost all other county positions in North Carolina. At the August 1850 Court, William J. Wilson requested that the tax assessment for his "Kings Mountain Gold Mine" be reduced. It was reduced by $15,000, which left its value at $20,000. The County Court also authorized E. A. McArthur and J. F. Plonk to retail liquor. "A Notice" in 1851 concerned filing Gaston County taxes and listed the militia companies with a date for persons "to examine said lists and give information of all such as have failed to make return of their taxable property." L. A. Mason, county sheriff, would attend to the task at the "muster grounds" of each company.[10]

In 1855 the County Court authorized others to sell liquor in locations throughout the county—Richard T. Cansler at "Cansler Old Stand"; Robert Beaty "at Woodlawn"; Thomas J. Ferguson "near Kings Mountain Gold mine"; Hezekiah Rumpfelt "at the Lattimore place"; Larkin B. Gaston in Dallas—as other communities experienced economic growth.[11]

During the 1850s nationally, the country lost prominent leaders to death: Henry Clay, John C. Calhoun, Daniel Webster, and Andrew Jackson. Similarly, Gaston County also lost William Joseph Wilson, Andrew Hoyl, and Larkin Stowe. Wilson and Hoyl were Whigs while Stowe was a Democrat, and the loss of these Whig leaders helped shift county political allegiances toward the Democratic Party.[12]

In February 1856 the County Court created the Board for the Common Schools, which included Col. Richard Rankin, William Reed, James M. Hanna, Christian Eaker, James McNair, James Ferguson Esqr., Amos Morris, Ephraim Friday, L. A. Mason, and Wm. H. Johnston and also authorized Robert Holland, Jonathan Rhyne, and Jonas Hoffman to construct a "Bridge across Big Long Creek at Robert Hollands."[13] In August 1857 the Court listed merchants who paid taxes for the year. The list provides a picture of economic development:

Lineberger & Co—$25.22	J. Froneberger & Co—$25.90
Froneberger & Co—$19.81	And Hoyl & Co—$16.99
C. W. Hoyl & Co—$3.31	M. Nathans—$18.66
Wm. M. Holland—$19.15	Eli Pasour—$1.60
Wm. H. Johnston—$9.96	T. R. Tate—$6.66
S. W. Craig—$5.00	J. & E. B. Stowe—$2.10
J. G. Marks—$.33	R. T. Cansler—$5.86
L. A. Mason—$6.17	

Whether the above merchants operated a comprehensive mercantile operation, a store in conjunction with a cotton mill, or a modest business with a post office, trade provided profits and opportunities. Taxes were also assessed on "Peddlers" Messrs Myers & Co; Kohn & Co; "Liquor Traffice" upon J. G. Marks, R. T. Cansler, Black & Co, Wm. H. Johnston, And. Hoyl & Co, L. M. Summitt, Boyce & Co, Lineberger & Co, Wm. M. Holland. Sheriff Paul Froneberger reported the tax revenue to the Court.[14]

In April 1858 the Court appointed justices to list taxes in ten militia companies and also appointed "Inspectors of the Elections" at nine precincts: Sandifers, Stowes, Canslers, Rhynes, Mauneys, Blacks, Decks, Ferguson, and Dallas. Entrepreneurs, Melchi and Caleb Rhodes, applied for and received permission to create a toll bridge across the South Fork River north of Dallas with toll rates ranging from $.01 for hogs to $.35 for a six horse wagon.[15]

By February 1859 the Court established tax rates per $100 land valuation and for poll taxes: County—$.15 and $.45; School—$.06 and $.20; Poor—$.04 and $.15; State—$.20 and $.80. The May Court appointed inspectors for the electoral precincts and in August appointed assessors for taxes.[16]

By the 1860s Dallas emerged as the center of activity in the county. Boarding houses, the Hoffman Hotel, sellers of alcohol, merchants, carriage and harness makers, grocers, and skilled craftsmen conducted business. Citizens visited on county business, to shop, and to attend political activities or attend to legal matters. Three county cotton mills created jobs for young ladies, men, slaves, and children and spawned mill villages. In 1860 the iron and gold mining operations were in decline. But as the war began, manufacturing of cotton, iron, and gold would rebound dramatically.[17] The war affected all life in Gaston County.

On April 14, 1861, citizens read newspaper reports that Fort Sumter had been captured. Soon after that and Lincoln's call for troops, North Carolina and the county dissolved political divisions and the emotional tide for secession swept the area. Gaston County military units began forming and drilling in anticipation of conflict. At least three Gaston military companies had formed by the time readers learned on July 13 that North Carolina's Ordinance of Secession had been approved.[18]

Brevard Station

Secession fever and war captivated citizen attention. On May 1, 1861, the first Gaston military unit, Company M of the 16th North Carolina Regiment, organized in Dallas with ironmonger Benjamin F. Briggs as captain. "Miss Jenny Johnston" gave the "Kings Mountain Grays" a flag as a send-off from the Brevard railroad station. On June 12, Captain Elias M. Faires created the "Gaston Guards," Company H of the 23rd. On July 30 a third unit, Company B of the 28th, the "Gaston Invincibles," organized under Captain Thomas H. Edwards. On October 6 Captain William Rufus Rankin created the "Gaston Blues," Company H of the 37th. On March 22, 1862, Charles Q. Petty captained the "Gaston

Gaston County Courthouse in Dallas, completed in 1848, was built in the middle of the square, centering county life where political speeches were heard and court business was conducted. A 2015 restoration is visible. This is the front view where Confederate soldiers mustered on their way to catch the train at Brevard Station (now Stanley) (courtesy Melany Dawn Crouse Photography).

Rangers," Company H of the 49th.[19] Countless other Gaston citizens served in other units, either as volunteers or conscripts to replace fallen brethren, and served in various other capacities during the war.

Recruits were ordered to Dallas, where they organized into companies, received some equipment, and then proceeded to Brevard Station, now Stanley, where soldiers boarded trains to Charlotte, then Greensboro, and then to the nearest training camp. When the Confederacy approved conscription, the militia, called the Home Guard after 1863, had duties to contact and assemble the men and to find and capture deserters and "outliers," persons avoiding the draft. The flow of men made Dallas and Brevard Station busy places.

As the war fever burned, Dallas and Gaston County once again supported running a railroad line through the county. On March 23, 1861, Dallas hosted another meeting regarding constructing a railroad, as commissioned in the last General Assembly. The railroad would connect Yorkville, South Carolina with Dallas and, hopefully in the future, to Lincolnton and Newton, crossing the Charlotte and Lincolnton railroad line. Charlotte's *Western Democrat* reported that the road would "prove to be the most lucrative in all this region of the country." On June 1, 1861, the "Dallas and Kings Mountain Railroad" commissioners met in Dallas to satisfy the state statute's requirements. Commissioners included "Edward Whitesides, Lawson Wilson, Moses H Rhyne, Jacob Froneberger, J F Pegram, Samuel Jarrett, and J G Lewis." Fifty thousand dollars in stock had been subscribed, satisfying the law. Commissioners appointed White, Lewis, and Wilson to meet with representatives of the "Kings Mountain Railroad Company."[20]

The war effort ignited Confederate patriotism and brought economic opportunities. Examples of Confederate purchases document how the Confederate States of America sought initially to fight a war without soldiers and matériel. During October 1861, Confederate agents needed horses and bought from J. P. Alexander of Lincoln County a "Bay Horse" for $50 and a "Black Horse" for $150. Gaston County residents also sold horses: "Robt. Ormand" sold "one brown mare" for $140; "Saml Rankin" sold "a Bay Horse" for $150; Samuel Black sold "one Bay Horse" for $130; A. R. Henderson sold "two Bay Horses" for $325.[21]

Later, North Carolina Confederate authorities hired "agents," like E. D. Ramsey, to purchase needed items from the community. Lincolnton's Ramsey kept a journal, which documents his visits to various parts of the community, most likely stopping at a store or post office, where citizens came to sell. Ramsey purchased the following commodities from individuals: rifles, pairs of socks, shotguns, lead weights, blankets, padlocks, wool and cotton, barrels, axes, muskets, lead, and other items. He purchased metal, most likely to be melted, and the socks and blankets were most likely homemade. His travels began on March 19, 1862, and while not all persons listed may be positively identified, the buyers' names establish his routes.[22]

For example, on March 19, 1862, he visited western Lincoln and Gaston County, the Cherryville area, and the Hokeville cotton factory at present Laboratory, where he purchased from "N. H. Pixly" two rifles, one shotgun, 23 pair woolen and 13 cotton items. Most commodities purchased on that day included rifles and shotguns. In the next dated entry, April 15, Ramsey was in the Cherryville area and traveled south toward present Bessemer City and Kings Mountain. An increase in the variety of purchases is observed, which included blankets, barrels, and socks. However, of the commodities recorded that day, twenty-two out of thirty-seven purchases were for rifles or shotguns.[23]

On May 2 he traveled into Cleveland County north of Shelby and west of Cherryville. Again a majority of his purchases are for guns, 27 out of 35. During the period he made a trip "to Charlotte & back with check." His purchases were modest. For example, the largest amount he paid on the May 6 entry was $44 for a rifle, shotgun, powder, and an axe from Samuel Wilson. The lowest amount was 75 cents for an axe from Miss Jane Dalton.

Apparently, he boxed the matériel and sent it to military leaders. Each box itemized the enclosed items and included their specific and total values. On May 12 he continued into northern Cleveland and western Catawba County. By May 22 and 23 he was in the Jugtown area of Catawba and Lincoln County. On June 1 he traveled from that area to the Shelby area where he purchased "3 old axes" from cotton and woolen mill operator, A. B. Homesly, and purchased commodities around the Cherryville area. Ramsey also listed his expenses for "lodging" and "board." Later he returned to the Catawba County area, most likely around Newton. On June 20 he remained in the Catawba County area and also purchased paper and stamps. The pattern comes to an abrupt end with a number of purchases of paper and envelopes most likely in 1863. At the bottom of the page "Dec 1–1866" begins a new entry.[24]

Ramsey's journal provides a unique insight into economic opportunities in the Confederate South. Citizens of various economic means could sell to Ramsey, generating unexpected income. Ramsey clearly negotiated with each person for the gun or blanket. For example, a rifle may sell for $17, $14, $8, $16, or $16.50. A large sale of $35 involved a rifle and "S Gun" purchased from Isaac Houser, and lower prices included 35 cents for a pair of wool socks from Mrs. Price. Ramsey scoured the countryside west of Lincolnton from Catawba County to Gaston County and west to Cleveland County.

The Confederate Citizen file for E. D. Ramsey corresponds with many of the purchase amounts in his journal. On July 17, 1862, the Ordnance Department recorded the total of $2,302.64. On December 2, 1863, a $30 purchase of paper was recorded. By November of 1863 Ramsey is recorded as employed at the Confederate Asheville Armory,[25] having ceased his purchases in the area.

The North Carolina Ordnance Department forwarded "cash" to Ramsey to make his purchases: $250, $500, $1,000, and $1,000, which totaled his credits of $2,500.[26] Securing supplies challenged the Confederacy, but its greatest challenge involved recruiting an army and maintaining a stable economy.

Conscription

War conditions dominated the newspapers as the voracious need for troops motivated the governor to offer a bounty to volunteer. The Confederate Congress's approval of America's first draft, enacted a year before the Union's draft law, would result in the dramatic increase in Confederate troops and eventually dissent and desertion.[27]

For southerners and Gaston County citizens, one of the Confederate Congress's most necessary and yet disruptive legislative acts involved the Conscription Act in April 1862. Approved to add troops to a numerically declining army, the law reached into the homes of area citizens and solicited significant dissent, as it created inequities by exempting citizens, like blacksmiths and shoemakers, cotton and iron manufacturers, militia, and government workers. The "20 Nigger Rule" motivated dramatic dissent, as it exempted slaveholders or their overseers, if they possessed over 20 slaves. Since the law allowed governmental officials to exempt persons they perceived to be "essential," many poor southerners viewed the law's application as highly discriminatory. The perception continued as the law allowed hiring substitutes, of which wealthier citizens often took advantage.

Understanding how men were exempted from conscription is confusing since few records survive. The law exempted "Militia Officers ... for the purpose of aiding the authorities at home in arresting deserters and inforcing the conscript and other laws." One local exemption notice documents that "Melchi Rhodes" received an exemption because of "being Militia officer" on March 28, 1864.[28] As the war progressed into 1865, even exempted persons like Dallas merchant Jacob Froneberger and cotton manufacturer Jasper Stowe lost their exemptions and became involved militarily.

In August 1864 Jacob Froneberger observed that "all the men at home as Blacksmiths Shoe Makers & Co. will have to leave for the Army. It is a hard call but exempts none and there will be a great deal of trouble among their families when they leave. I see no prospect for the war to close soon." By October, Froneberger reported that the U.S. government had drafted 500,000 troops and the Confederacy "has ordered out all classes of men from 17 to 50 years of age excepting a few State officers heretofore exempted. This will materially increase the Southern Army." As 1864 ended, contemporaries observed that "there is no men in the neighborhood except 3 or 4 old men."[29]

Many North Carolinians believed that the Conscription Law and later Confederate Congressional actions such as the Tithing Law, revocation of the writ of habeas corpus, impressments, and logistical decisions, seemed to discriminate against its state and citizens, further promoting dissent and fueling desertion. Governor Vance and state judges supported personal freedom against Confederate mandates, and newspapers reported North Carolina's opposition to the Confederate revocation of the writ of habeas corpus and what they perceived as unfair conscription practices.[30] Calls for more troops, Confederate monetary inflation, food and commodity shortages, lawlessness, and violence further undermined home front support for the war effort.

"to incorporate a Toll Bridge, near Vestals Ford, Gaston County"

The war also fueled entrepreneurial opportunities. On August 13, 1862, C. J. Hammerskold of Iron Station in Lincoln County advertised 1,400 acres of land near Sharon railroad depot as "a safe and profitable investment." The land included a "Flouring Mill," dwelling houses and outbuildings, and a productive wheat producing area. A young lady from Virginia offered her "Educational" services in Shelby, and William Richards of Brevard Station (now Stanley) offered "Ready Made Clothing" to the public "cheap for cash." The "Charlotte Gas Light Co." enticed customers to light their homes using gas. The Conscription Law promoted "Substitute Wanted" headlines, and the paper advertised "Equity Land Sales" which included 500 acres of Edward Lonergan at Lonergan's Ferry on the South Fork River in Gaston County. In January 1863 *The Daily Bulletin* informed their readers of a "Large Sale of Whiskey," 1,000 gallons of mountain whiskey for sale in Shelby, that William Tiddy continued to sell leather, and that the internal civil war in Madison County, N. C. continued. On January 28 T. R. Tate of Mountain Island Mill "Wanted" 8,000 pounds of good soft soap.[31]

The Melchi Rhodes Account Book provides historians a unique glimpse of period economic entrepreneurism. Rhodes diversified his business interests with relative, Caleb, and others. Rhodes and partners produced brick, grain, and partnered in the "Quartz gold mining company" at Vestal's Ford north of Dallas. Employees included slaves, rented slaves, and white laborers, where they operated grist and saw mills. The 1860 census lists Melchi and Caleb with seven slaves each. Melchi Rhodes had benefited from a gold-seeking journey to California, returning home to pursue interests in the Rhodes Gold Mine.[32]

By 1857 Melchi and Caleb Rhodes operated a toll bridge across the South Fork River near present Philadelphia Lutheran Church. Investors were needed to make improvements. On November 12, 1862, Caleb advertised that "Applications will be made to the Legislature at its next Session to incorporate a Toll Bridge, near Vestals Ford, Gaston County."[33] The North Carolina General Assembly endorsed the idea on February 10, 1863, with "An Act to Incorporate Vestal's Ford Toll Bridge." The law allowed Caleb Rhodes and his associates to "make a body politic and incorporate ... for the purpose of erecting and keeping up a toll bridge over the south fork of the Catawba River, at or near Vestal's Ford." The common stock for the incorporation "shall consist of one thousand, divided into shares of one hundred dollars each." The law also established set tolls.[34] County citizens took advantage of the investment opportunity. The 1863 tax list in Dallas Company specifically taxed Jacob Plonk Esq. $25 and Henry Setzer $125 for "Cap in Toll Bridge." By April 1, 1863, Melchi Rhodes recorded his investment of five shares of "Bridge Stock," valued at $125.[35]

The Melchi Rhodes Account Book documents yearly profits during the war. A profit of $107.28 in 1857 compares with $6,541.48 in 1862; $3,300.74 in 1863. While inflationary Confederate money contributed to some differences in profit margin, Rhodes was clearly doing well for himself. On April 7, 1862, he recorded being owed $4,034.11 "at Interest," $252.22 for "Co[mpany] amount"; $600.00 "Confederate bonds," $2,215.15 "Cash on hand," for a total of $6,541.48. By April 1 of the next year, he recorded $3,300.74 in assets and profits. By April 1864, interest owed him totaled $7,847.55 with $26.85 in gold and silver, and $90 in "Co[mpany] notes," as he served his neighbors as a banker.[36]

In the 1863 tax list "M & C Rhodes" was assessed $1,000 for the one acre mill tract; Melchi Rhodes $3,000 for 420 acres; and Caleb Rhodes $5,000 for 416 acres. Caleb was also assessed for 9 slaves at $5,873, $300 cash, $3,300 solvent debts, $121 "toll bridges," and $105 for furniture. A family enterprise, infused with investment capital, resulted in profits and financial success during the Civil War. A grist and saw mill with a brickyard, mining, and mineral processing operations could be very successful when located near a toll bridge.

The Rhodes enterprise was a truly homegrown operation. Other examples of wartime entrepreneurship included the Edgecombe County investors who profited from the war by bringing money, slaves, and political clout to revive the iron and gold operations of High Shoals and Crowders Mountain. Their investments provided jobs, circulated money, and facilitated trade.

Economic opportunities near the county's borders also impacted Gaston residents.

Long Shoals, Hokeville/Laboratory, Cleveland County

Gaston citizens frequented Long Shoals and Hokeville, both located on the South Fork River, near the Gaston-Lincoln county line. Long Shoals was the site of a paper mill, store, grist mill, and shops of other skilled artisans. About a mile farther upriver at Hokeville/Laboratory was the cotton factory of Hoke and Childs which was operated by N. H. Pixley, another paper mill, an axe and box factory, a grist mill, an oil mill, the Confederate Laboratory, and an even greater concentration of skilled craftsmen. Cotton and wool products, paper, and corn meal and flour were produced.

Another example of the role of business during the war involves an 1863 letter from J. C. Whitson to Governor Vance soliciting support for a bucket factory in Lincolnton. He asked that Ephraim Cauble, a millwright, be exempted from conscription "to work in the factory" and solicited government contracts for his new business. He also wanted assurance that his "five hands" would remain free from the army at the factory.[37] Business along the northern boundary of Gaston County enticed residents, who received exemptions from conscription.

Hokeville's "A. C. Wiswall & Co" paper mill's business records demonstrate a viable business operation with a regional scope, selling to vendors in Statesville, Charlotte, and Greensboro. For example, from March through December 1862 the company purchased commodities valued at $4,151.84, while sales ranged from $200 to $1,300 or bartered rags valued at $1,395.40 in lieu of payment in currency.[38]

The most unusual business in the Hokeville complex was Dr. A. Snowden Piggot's Confederate Laboratory. In collaboration with the Charlotte Nitrates operation, it created medicines with a number of local employees, all of whom were exempt from military duty. Other manufacturing facilities were rumored to be hotbeds of Unionists, where they could avoid the draft while supporting the Confederate war effort. The Confederate Laboratory produced various drugs for Confederate use, grew opium poppies in the area, and found itself in the middle of a strong Unionist community, whose employees often applied for Union Loyalist Claims.[39]

Other manufacturing and business operations west of Gaston in Cleveland County also impacted Gaston because the Cherryville depot served as a critical hub for economic activity and travel. A. B. Homesley operated a profitable woolen mill on Broad River with a Shelby address. In May 1862 he sold North Carolina cashmere and cloth valued at $1,707.50. From August through December he and partner T. M. A. Oates sold products valued at $13,779.92.[40] Homesley's operation posted additional income until October 2, 1863, when he wrote Governor Vance that "on last Thursday night I had the misfortune to have my woolen Mill destroyed by fire." The fire began as an accident when a lamp dropped into "some loose cotton." The loss was "about $35,000. No Insurance." It caused a number of "poor people" to lose employment and hurt the government since "all the woolen cloth manufactured was sold to the Government."[41] Nearby, the Fronebarger family operated an iron works and paper mill. "D. Froneberger & Co" advertised for "Hands Wanted" at Buffalo Paper Mills. The company hoped to hire 20–25 "able bodied hands to chop wood. Fair wages paid." Froneberger's Iron Works produced "rolled iron," with the hope to complete construction of the railroad from Cherryville to Shelby.[42] While the railroad was never completed, the Cherryville depot created Gaston-Cleveland connections of economy, kinship, politics, and mutual benefit.

As business opportunities flourished and the local economy expanded, Gaston citizens craved newspaper accounts of the war, political activities, advertisement, and commerce.

"The True Pedigree and Early History of Abraham Lincoln"

Contemporary newspapers interspersed articles of local interest and business advertisements with war news. Through these articles and ads, one can see the arc of wartime moods and conditions as Gaston County swings from patriotic enthusiasm at the war's onset, to the scarcity of food and commodities, to the collapse of civil order as the war dragged on.

On July 4, 1861, nearly two months after the firing on Fort Sumter, Capt. Robert A. Brevard of Lincoln County donated $100, a "Liberal Contribution," to each recently raised military company. Within two weeks, readers learned that Gov. Ellis had died and then, only days later, the North Carolina Ordinance of Secession had been approved.[43]

In 1862, John Tate of Mountain Island Cotton Mill donated $100 to the Soldiers Aid Society in a very public manner. "The Ladies of Catawba" appealed "to the lovers of their country and friends of humanity" to oppose the manufacture of whiskey. In Newton "Ladies" fired pistols, "'cussed' heroically," marched to the depot, and broke open about 900 to 1,000 gallons of whiskey barrels. But war conditions dominated the news. "Catch the Deserter," a column authored by Capt. John F. Hill of Lincoln County and W. O. Harrelson of Gaston County, sought David Reid of Caldwell County. Inflated prices for commodities and goods were publicized, and the cost of newspaper subscriptions escalated due to the price increases of "Paper and other material." Newspaper ads involving runaway slaves had increased over the past few months, and Capt. C. Q. Petty of Gaston County offered $30 rewards for the return of deserters, Aaron Costner, Zimri Costner, R. A. Molton, and W. G. Massey.[44]

In early 1863, Gaston newspaper readers closely followed the controversy of three Gaston county textile mills accused of price speculation. Governor Vance threatened a shut-down if they did not adhere to governmental regulations and within a month all three mills had complied. Newspapers reported on the scarcity of corn, corn meal, and other food stuffs. This "selfish" hoarding of food was condemned by the governor and the news tabloids. "A Citizen" offered contrasting examples of Confederate patriotism. A "Good Example" involved a Stanly County resident selling flour at $10 per barrel to soldiers instead of the current rate of $30. The "Bad Example" involved a Catawba County administrator's sale where a speculator outbid a "poor woman" for wheat.[45]

In March 1863, conscript substitutes were sought and locals read a most interesting article about Abraham Lincoln's ancestry. "The True Pedigree and Early History of Abraham Lincoln" contended that Lincoln's mother was a single woman having from one-eighth to one-sixteenth "negro blood in her veins." The article further asserted that Lincoln's father was "Abraham Inlow" and that when Lincoln was four years and six months old his mother married Mr. Lincoln. Inlow and Lincoln fought one another which caused little Abe to be sent away from home for a number of years. The article's author emphasized that Abraham Lincoln's supposed African ancestry was where he "obtained his notions of negro equality." The author further contended that cruel treatment by his stepfather caused Lincoln to be a "fit tool for carrying out the Hellish purposes of the Abolition party." The *Western Democrat* offered an abbreviated version, describing the "whole family, Inlow, Lincoln and Abe's mother [being] of bad character and low habits."[46] The story that Abraham Enloe fathered Abraham Lincoln continues in the Rutherford

County area with stories, a historical site, and published books.⁴⁷ Other news items informed readers.

In late June 1862, Salisbury's *Carolina Watchman* announced "COTTON FACTORY BURNED." The fire "supposed to be accidental" destroyed "one of the oldest factories in the state," and owners L. D. Childs and W. J. Hoke suffered a "$40,000" loss. Another news report boasted that Childs, who owned cotton factories in South Carolina, was "proprietor of the old 'Lincoln Factory,'" in then Hokeville and now Laboratory, and produced cloth for the Confederacy "at exceedingly low prices," contrasted with "those miserable land-sharks, called *speculators*." Samuel N. Stowe of Gaston County had been promoted to major in the "Gaston Invincibles" Company of the 28th NC Regiment, as Stowe and his company "held their position till a number of them were bayoneted" at the Battle of Fredericksburg, since they heard no order to retreat even after running out of ammunition.⁴⁸ The next month, W. H. Michal of Lincolnton advertised selling "Snuff" either wholesale or retail, "High Shoals Iron Company of Gaston Co., N. C." offered "Nails For Sale," and "Col. Wm. A. Stowe," "a gallant and able officer" of Gaston County, was in fair condition from wounds received at the Battle of Chancellorsville. Jasper Stowe traveled to Virginia with Dr. Sloan of Dallas to transport his brother by train to recuperate at home. J. M. Roberts, another "brave soldier" from Gaston County, was also "improving rapidly" from his Chancellorsville wounds.⁴⁹

Only two months after the untimely death of General Thomas Jefferson "Stonewall" Jackson, newspapers informed patriotic southerners that they could buy a biography of the famous Confederate hero.⁵⁰ More bad news in 1863 included Confederate defeats at Gettysburg and Vicksburg, increasing desertion, higher taxes, and more serious economic strains on the home front. Confederate defeatism and optimism competed as local citizens sought to survive. The collapse of the southern market economy became evident as more businesses offered to trade goods instead of accepting inflated Confederate money.

On March 4, 1864, Samuel R. Oates of Lincolnton advertised to trade in-kind: "Farming Iron for Corn and Bacon" and could fill orders for "Hollow Ware and Molasses Mills, large Cast Iron Kettles and Paste Boards," which he could also exchange for corn and bacon. He also sought to hire "50 able bodied NEGRO MEN." The newspaper provided extracts of Governor Vance's speech at Wilkesboro, as he sought reelection.⁵¹

Deserters and fear of lawlessness pervaded much of the news. On April 28, 1864, Gaston's W. A. Rankin offered a $90 reward for the return of deserters from Company H, 49th NC Regiment—"W. G. Massey, Jas. Hope, and J. W. Casiner." On July 7 readers learned that five "Yankee prisoners" had escaped in Mecklenburg County and were headed toward Beaty's Ford Road, and P. Z. Baxter declared for the Lincoln County House of Commons.⁵²

Business, politics, and desperation continued in the news. On June 28, 1864, the Shipp & Reinhardt Company of Iron, NC advertised: "Cane mills, Kittles and Hollow ware on hand and for sale at Rehoboth Furnace." In the same newspaper William T. Shipp of Gaston County announced his candidacy for House of Commons running against Lawson S. Mason and Capt. John H. Roberts, and it publicized Governor Vance's most recent proclamation concerning deserters.⁵³

Gaston County and the surrounding area suffered from home front concerns and soldier issues but had not experienced actual combat until 1865. For the first time citizens experienced the fear of Union soldiers, travel disruption, and further disintegration of civil order as General William T. Sherman and his soldiers converged from the south, the Union Navy attacked Fort Fisher on the east coast, and General George Stoneman swept down from the mountains.

Stoneman's Raid

Prior to the arrival of Stoneman's raiders, rumors created panic. On February 19, 1865, W. D. Glenn characterized himself in his diary as "rather gloomy and low in spirits [because] both Columbia and Charleston, SC have both fallen into the hands of the hated Yankees." On February 23, 1865, he observed that "the people of our town [Dallas] woke up at two oclock with the unwelcome intelligence that the Yankee calvary were within 8 mile of us. We heard in a few hours that this was false."[54] On March 3, Violet Ann Sifford wrote "Cousin Hariet" McIntosh, who resided in Mecklenburg County, with news and rumors: "I suppose you have been in a state of fear about Yankees," she wrote, "I was so troubled about you all thinking you would be in a hearing of a battle which we heard was to be fought near Charlotte." She also heard the rumor that "the right and left of Shermans army was in Lincolnton."[55]

Violet Ann continued to describe the panic among "the rich people," "Mrs [W. P.] Bynum came running," and "among the rich people there was agreat hiding their provisions gold and silver &c.." Even though the rumor resulted from Confederate "Wheelers Cavalry ... came to Gaston," Violet Ann and others would "yet look for raiders." On March 5, 1865, Isabella Sifford commented to "neace" Harriet McIntosh that "the Horse men are Coming in here thick thare is 80 Horses camp[ed] blow A Sifford At the nance School House And thay say there is Hundred More coming on I think Thay will eat the cuntrey out."[56] Soldiers from both sides foraged the countryside for food and provisions.

David Schenck heard the same rumors in Lincolnton. He noted that "confusion" pervaded. "[R]efugees from the South, ... Government property, officials, and guards; fleeing negroes, and frightened speculators" filled the town. He feared that Sherman would invade Charlotte. He then heard that Union raiders were in Gaston County, the truth being they were Confederate foragers. Schenck buried his silver plates, hid food, and sent off a load of valuables to the west.[57] While he did not mention the famous diarist Mary Chestnut, her flight to Lincolnton and brief comments about the town personalizes persistent fears as the war ground to a close. She arrived on February 18, to be "somewhat dingily lodged" opposite from the cotton manufacturer John Phifer's residence. Phifer, whom Chestnut described as "the rich man *par excellence* of Lincolnton" predicted the end of the war and that "'The raiders will come, you know.'" Describing worthless Confederate paper money, lodging for the cost of $20 per week for firewood, and the generosity of cotton manufacturer L. D. Childs, she joined her husband by late March in Chester, South Carolina, repeating rumors of Sherman's march through South Carolina and imminent threats.[58]

On April 8, 1865, "Isa Sifford" wrote "neace" Harriet that "there was 14 Hundred Calvry cross the river At Beaties forde Just Fryday there was 4 of them Here to day and one of them Was the strongest war man you ever saw. He made out Like he could whip the yanks Him self." She "Herd that Chermun [Sherman] had tuckin Rola [Raleigh] but I recon that ant so."[59] This time the rumor was true, Sherman had captured Raleigh and dispersed the state government, as Grant accomplished the same feat in Richmond, setting the scene for Confederate surrenders.

These immediate threats forced authorities to conscript previously exempt Home Guard units. Jacob Froneberger, as a member of "the third class of Home Guards," left "home on the 19th Decr as ordered," and deployed with his unit to eastern North Carolina, where they helped defend Fort Fisher. They were "disbanded" and reached home by early January. On March 14, 1865, his unit "struck for Lancaster" in response to Sherman. On "the 27th March" his unit marched to join the army. After the surrender he "left for home on the 15th April. Reached home Monday the 17th and told the people that the war was over." On that same night it was reported that the "Yankees reached Dallas." On Tuesday "the Yankees passed through Dallas," and on Wednesday Froneberger "was captured." He reported that "the Yankees remained in Dallas for six days—took a great many horses and some negroes, then went in the direction of Shelby," marching to Rutherfordton.[60]

In early April 1865, General George Stoneman led his cavalry units through the North Carolina Mountains into the Piedmont. His original objectives were to disrupt the countryside, create a western threat to Generals Lee and Johnston, destroy bridges and military matériel, and to create a western buffer against Confederate retreat. Other objectives included capture of the Confederate prison at Salisbury and control of rail, water, telegraph, and land transportation. After marching to Salisbury, Salem, Statesville, Taylorsville, Hickory, and Newton, Stoneman departed for Tennessee and divided his forces with General Alven Gillem in command. Gillem headed north toward Asheville, and Stoneman ordered Colonel William J. Palmer to secure the river crossings to the south.[61]

By April 16, Schenck noted in his diary that Colonel William J. Palmer's brigade of Stoneman's army arrived. On April 17, 1865, Union records document that the 15th Pennsylvania Cavalry reached Lincolnton, traveling from Hickory and secured the town by nightfall. As Colonel Palmer led the main force into town, a shot rang out. The cavalry quickly found the "bushwhacker," a "beardless boy of fifteen or sixteen," whose mother pleaded for her son's life. Palmer allowed the mother to take her son home to "keep a better watch over his actions." Lincolnton was "a pretty town, of about 1000 inhabitants; they are extremely rebellious—bitterly so, but with it all are refined and intelligent." The Yankee captors received "invitations to dinner, … while the colored people are eager to help us by baking biscuits and cakes for our men."[62]

"a small keg of sorghum molasses"

Palmer created his base of operations in Lincolnton at the home of John Phifer, cotton mill owner, suspected Unionist, and father of three Confederate soldiers, two of whom had died in Confederate service. In Lincolnton, L. C. "Cass" Payseur recalled his actions when the Union army arrived: hiding "a small keg of sorghum molasses" in a hole in the ground at the family barn and "hiding hams" on the back porch between the weatherboarding. He also described how he and "the boys" would ride Union horses to get water, would "hide them and walk back." He and other boys would often "sell the laboratory roots and herbs" and described how Confederates "knocked the heads of the barrels," emptying "a lot of whiskey" after they poured some into their canteens. Payseur also recalled that the Federal soldiers "stayed all the winter," using "Child's woods—Southwestern part of town" as their quarters and Memorial Hall as their hospital. He described only a few incidents of gunfire or conflict within Lincolnton. He also described how the "Confederate Government had the Armory and machinery moved to Lincolnton from Columbia, S. C., to keep Sherman from destroying it." Eventually the six to eight railcars carrying equipment was sent to Cherryville where "the yankees destroyed everything."[63]

Union recollections included a sojourn at Sherrill's Ford, incorrectly placed on the Yadkin River. A slave suggested that the men go "down the river" to "Factoryville" where they made "cloth down there for the rebel soldiers." The description suggests that "Factoryville" was Tate's Mountain Island mill in Gaston County. The raiders took as many horses as they could find, threatened to "destroy the factory," and captured a few Confederates in the area. They told the people to take all the cloth and they did. At least two slaves were freed and accompanied the Union soldiers.[64]

On April 18 the Union lost their last soldier in Lincolnton, "Corp. Geo. J. French," who had been shot on picket duty by a "bushwhacker." The townspeople allowed French to be buried at St. Luke's Episcopal Cemetery in town "with military honors" and they laid "wreaths of flowers" on his coffin. Palmer ordered Major Wagner's battalion to ride to the Catawba River, where they burned a bridge and "destroyed a splendid railroad bridge, over the same river." They noted that they were the first Federals seen by the locals and found it "comical" to witness their "fear." Palmer's forces remained in Lincolnton until the 24th where they captured and paroled "over 800 Confederates." A more accurate figure of 2,000 Confederate parolees includes the entire area west of the Catawba under the command of Palmer. As they departed town for Rutherfordton, they reflected upon Lincolnton as a "pleasant place to be in."[65]

From his base in Lincolnton, Colonel Palmer sent out raiders into the countryside, seizing horses, securing river crossings, and destroying bridges. He dispatched a portion of his force to Dallas, where they were also to threaten Charlotte. Union raiders captured Sherrill's, Cowan's, Beatty's, and Nation's fords on the Catawba. By April 18 W. D. Glenn learned that the "Yankee Raiders" were in Lincolnton and soon arrived in Dallas where they seized horses. By April 20 Glenn recorded that the "Raiders" traveled "through [his family's] neighborhood" in southern Gaston County. When he returned to Dallas, he found a "state of confusion." Palmer had ordered Major Erastus Cratty Moderwell to destroy the Catawba River bridge at Nation's Ford in South Carolina, which took him through the southern portion of the county. The Dallas contingent also occupied Tuckaseegee Ford near present Mt. Holly, where a notable skirmish occurred and where they burned a railroad bridge crossing the Catawba. Possibly during this mission the Union raiders destroyed the gunpowder mill and Acid Works on the Mecklenburg side of the Catawba. On April 21 troops stationed in Dallas occupied Armstrong's Ford in Gaston County with no resistance.[66]

Local stories have circulated about Palmer's venture into Gaston County, including reports of "confiscated horses, raiding smoke houses, and burning barns and sheds." One story describes a Union raiding party approaching Lineberger's Woodlawn Mill near present Lowell. They had planned to burn the mill but the foreman, German William "Bill" Sahms, responded that he too was a Yankee. He renewed a past friendship, and the story concludes that they left the mill standing.[67]

Few reports of damages from the Union cavalry have been documented, reflecting loyal Confederate Schenck's and Froneberger's positive assessments in their diaries. They acknowledged that the Union army brought stability and order to a lawless area and avoided widespread conflict or destruction. In Dallas, Froneberger believed that "under

Federal rule ... they will do all they can to restore order and quiet in our country. Our place has been troubled several times this week by a mob of several bad men. We will adopt measures to surpress them."[68] Schenck was also gracious to Palmer's forces as they protected the population from "violence or molestation." While southerners had to feed their conquerors, he was aware of few instances of Union theft. Schenck hid his own horses and observed that "[s]everal negroes went off with the Yankees." He accused former slaves of being "idle, refusing to work, lounging around the street by the hundreds and acting as spies to discover hidden horses or food" while the Union army was in town.[69]

I calculated the amount of property claimed by Gaston County citizens to the Loyalist Southern Claims Commission to get a general idea of documented civilian losses. They included 22 horses, 17 mules, two hams and bacon, two revolvers, two claims with a total of 45 gallons of whiskey, one cow, 40 pounds of corn, five bridles and one saddle, and one buggy. These numbers only represent Unionists, as loyal Confederates were not eligible to apply for a claim. Clearly a number of materials were taken, which primarily involved horses, mules, and paraphernalia.[70] Yet, it is impressive that Palmer's raiders left all three cotton mills, two iron manufacturing operations, the town of Dallas, and countless stores, homes and outbuildings without damage. Their presence instilled fear among many citizens but also maintained stability.

Palmer's units were present in the area while Generals Lee and Johnston surrendered and President Lincoln was assassinated. These events created uncertainties for both Union soldiers and southerners. Leaders pondered whether to continue fighting and under what circumstances. Issues were further confused by Johnston's surrender, Sherman's acceptance, and the invalidation of the armistice. These circumstances added to the stress and uncertainty of the times. Schenck had learned of Confederate army surrenders and reported his thoughts in his diary: "This was the sudden, and to the people, unexpected downfall of the cause for which so many sacrifices of life, pleasure, property and peace had been made, and we found ourselves at the mercy of our foes."[71]

Most of Palmer's men did not cross the Catawba River, choosing to allow Confederate strength in Charlotte to remain unchallenged. The proximity of Palmer's forces to Jefferson Davis's fugitive Confederate government in Charlotte during April 1865 is a unique irony of history. Palmer's failure to march into Charlotte allowed Davis and his Cabinet to escape. At least some residents west of the Catawba knew about Davis's whereabouts. On April 8, 1865, Lincolnton's Jasper Stowe invited "General J. C. Brockinridge," Confederate Secretary of War, to reside with his family in Lincolnton when Breckinridge and Jefferson Davis's Cabinet evacuated Richmond and fled south to Charlotte. It is not known whether Breckinridge moved any of his family there. For one week Charlotte served as the "last capital of the Confederacy." By April 26 Davis fled farther south toward Georgia, where he was eventually captured. Breckinridge is also credited with advising Governor Vance to remain in North Carolina instead of fleeing with Davis.[72]

With Lee's and Johnston's surrenders, the war may have been over but uncertainty remained. On May 23, 1865, Jacob Froneberger noted in his diary that "Federal forces under Col. Wheeler came to Dallas on the 19th and yesterday some 15 of them went to Shelby under Captin Purinton. There is over 200 here yet. They have come to restore order and institute civil law, which is very much needed in this community."[73] The same month Gaston Court Clerk W. D. Glenn complained of "having nothing to do."[74] Union sources document that by May 20, a portion of Sherman's army, commanded by Colonel Wheeler, marched from Greensboro through Charlotte to occupy Dallas, "a small place of 3 or 4 hundred inhabitants. The country is very poorly formed. Butter is 15 cts per lb." Dr. Alonzo Garwood, a surgeon for the 28th Michigan Infantry, wrote in his diary that he "[a]ttended the Presbyterian church when they took sacrament." He commented that the "citizens are coming in and having the situation explained to them ... what is expected of them." In Dallas he "visited the place of punishment of criminals, the stocks, whipping post and pillory" and by May 25 observed the "justices of the peace" taking the "oath of allegiance." Union forces moved to Shelby, Lincolnton, and Charlotte. Dr. Garwood "Commenced at dinner boarding at hotel." The occupying army replaced the Confederate government. By June 1 Clerk Glenn noted that "Federal troops" had been in Dallas "for some 12 days. [He] had but little to do these days," and by July 10 he had been "ousted as clerk."[75] By June 22, 1865, Dr. Garwood accompanied the Union soldiers to Lincolnton, which would become their base of operations. His stay in Dallas included anecdotes about sick soldiers, "a colored man" who wanted to "have [a] Sabbath school," a soldier who accidentally shot himself in the hand, transporting sick or wounded by "ambulance," "established hospital," observed the swearing in of the "police force," observed "A Negro was arrested for attempted rape," attended to "a sick woman" and a "Negro ... brought in from the country very sick" who later died, "took a ride to a grist mill," and described the flow of provisions and supplies. He understood his history. As he crossed the Catawba River, he noted that Cornwallis had crossed it chasing General Nathaniel Greene. He proudly observed Kings Mountain, site of the Revolutionary battle.[76]

Palmer's and later Union occupation of Gaston County, Dallas, and the surrounding area was disturbing to the local population. Yet, the overall picture, as described by both southern and Union sources, suggest a smooth transition, stability, and continuance of normal routines. There was no burning of courthouses, towns, destruction of cotton mills, stores, or other buildings. The area fared much better than Atlanta, Columbia, Asheville, Morganton, or Salisbury. Palmer's leadership played a role in Union leniency.

The preceding history of Gaston County forms the basis of our study. To learn more we must consider the 1863 Gaston County tax list, which provides unprecedented insights into the social class and economic means of the citizenry.

Social Class in Antebellum and Civil War Gaston County

The tax list is complete for the county, and it fosters an understanding of social class and social mobility.

I utilized Paul D. Escott's *Many Excellent People Power and Privilege in North Carolina 1850–1900* to identify social and economic class. Escott, former professor at UNC-Charlotte and presently at Wake Forest University, states that two groups maintained economic, political, and social power in North Carolina. The elite or gentry were white males who owned over 20 slaves. Instead of the romanticized vision of cotton, tobacco or rice plantation owners, Dr. Escott describes the Piedmont elite as being prosperous merchants, doctors, lawyers, and manufacturers, who were entrepreneurs, dabbling in various economic activities. The elite often married one another, were well educated, and understood their social, economic, and political role in the society. The North Carolina elite owned one-eighth of the state's slave population in 1860, comprised about 12 percent of the white population, and accounted for 36 percent of the legislators.[77]

Escott defines the middle-class as the second most powerful group, owning land and fewer than 20 slaves. He defines them as small farmers, merchants, manufacturers, aspiring entrepreneurs, and professionals like doctors and lawyers. They were upwardly mobile, often political leaders in the county and state legislature. The middle class and the elite formed the governing class of North Carolina.[78] The data also described yeoman and landless whites.

Escott's research delineates that 72 percent of white North Carolina families owned no slaves, and that, in 1860, 69 percent of North Carolina farms consisted of fewer than 100 acres. Further, 42 percent had fewer than 50 acres. Yeomen were landed small farmers with no slaves. Most were subsistence farmers, highly independent, primarily farming corn, wheat, oats, hay, and vegetables, and who sought to accumulate no debt. They raised hogs, cattle, horses, using cash to pay their taxes or to purchase store items by selling excess crops, distilling brandy, practicing a trade, hauling commodities, or assuming other financial activities outside their local farming operation. They often sought upward mobility and assumed social superiority over slaves and Free Blacks. The keys to their life style involved immediate and extended family and their religious activities.[79]

Escott describes landless whites as farm or town laborers, who owned no slaves or land. Some worked as tenants and others were farmer's sons, who had not yet accumulated land. Escott states that in 1860, thirty-six thousand or about 30 percent of the adult white population in the state are included in this group. They hunted for their food, herded livestock, raised crops for their landlords, or worked at a trade. Some have been described as "poor white trash" with poor health and few possessions.[80] Together with the yeomen these two groups represented what the elite or middle-class defined as the "unreliable lower class" of almost 50 percent of the adult white population.

The status, living conditions, and health of all white classes usually exceeded those of the African American population. While some Free Blacks were able to accumulate land and possessions, most were caught in a proverbial catch-22, as state laws, starting in the 1830s, restricted their freedoms and potential success. Slaves remained in a perpetual caste without social, economic, or political influence. All whites assumed race-defined superiority over African Americans.[81]

In antebellum North Carolina, "wealth in slave property was highly concentrated." In 1860, 85 percent of North Carolina legislators owned slaves. The governor appointed justices of the Court of Pleas and Quarter Sessions, who served for life and controlled county government. They constituted "virtuous citizens," the elite and middle-class, who formed a power structure of economic and social dimensions, extrapolating these privileges into political power.[82]

Virtuous Citizens

"Virtuous citizens" opposed reforming the status quo fearing that if the "unreliable lower class," yeomen and landless whites, ever banded together they would be out-voted. A common strand, which bound all classes together, was the evangelical Christianity practiced throughout the state and the South. Devout Christians, Baptists and Methodists primarily, found common ground.[83] The other common strand of course was race.

Gaston County is representative of a Piedmont county as defined by Escott with some deviations, as the following comparisons will present. Since the 1863 tax list fails to assess landless white laborers consistently, the number of county laborers has been estimated by subtracting the number of heads of household in the 1860 Gaston census from the taxable citizens in 1863 (1,272–1,016=256). The figure of 256 or about 20 percent of Gaston's white males approximates the number of farm and town laborers and is likely a low estimate. The data suggest that 71 percent of the white male population in Gaston County belonged to yeomen and laboring classes, a higher estimate than Escott's statewide research. Gaston also had significantly lower numbers of gentry, about 2 percent, and middle-class, about 27 percent.

The following chart delineates social class with the number of taxables and percentage in the county and within each militia (tax) district:

	Elite	Middle	Yeomen	Laborer	Total
County	27/2%	345/27%	645/51%	256/20%[84]	1,273
Cherryville	0/0%	18/19%	74/81%		91
Rudisill	0/0%	21/32%	45/68%		66
Roberts	2/2%	35/32%	72/66%		109
Dallas	2/2%	33/30%	74/68%		109
Crowders Mtn.	1/1%	36/38%	58/61%		95
Duharts	1/1%	19/32%	40/67%		60
High Shoals	6/6%	23/24%	68/70%		97
River Bend	4/5%	34/44%	39/51%		77
South Point	4/4%	52/55%	39/41%		95
Tanyard	1/1%	40/30%	94/69%		135
Woodlawn	6/7%	34/41%	42/51%		82[85]

An examination of assessed land value further defines social and economic influence. The predominant role of slave ownership will be discussed in another chapter, but the data clearly show that assessed slave value exceeded land values by about 15 percent. Considering the county's total assessed land value of $1,626,087, the twenty-seven Gaston elite citizens owned land assessed at $409,262 or about 25 percent of the total; Middle-class taxables possessed land values of $660,192 or about 41 percent of the total, which left the remaining 34 percent of assessed land valuations of $558,833 to the yeomen. To explain another way, of Gaston's 1,016 tax-paying citizens, 372 slaveholding citizens possessed about 66 percent of the total land value. Yeomen, about half of the county's population, owned assessed land value of only ⅓ of the county's total.

The differential between elite and middle-class land values indicates that the middle-class held an advantage of $250,930; however, elite taxpayers averaged land assessment of about $15,158 per taxable, while middle class averaged about $1,914. The clear losers in the land assessment were the 645 yeomen, whose average assessment was about $867.

When slave assessed values are functioned into the equation, the prosperity of elite and middle-class jumps exponentially. Elite total assessment of $1,110,222 and middle-class total assessment of $1,864,244 equals a grand total of $2,974,466 (land plus slave values). Yeomen tax value of $558,833 was $2,415,633 less than the combined land and slave valuation of the elite and middle-class. Clearly, the 372 elite and middle-class Gaston County citizens held significant economic advantages. Of the almost $3 million assessed value of land and slaves, non-slaveholders barely mustered over $500,000 in assets. These economic realities were consistent with Escott's research with the caveat that Gaston County actually had fewer gentry and middle-class than the state as a whole.

The Elite

Gaston County's gentry, 2 percent of the taxables, differed considerably from the state average of 12 percent.[86] Of the 27 Gaston gentry, 12 resided in the three eastern districts; nine owned cotton mills or gold and iron operations; two owned stores or hotels; at least two were doctors; two resided in Mecklenburg County, being absentee landlords. Of the eleven farmers listed, at least three also held county positions. Some examples illustrate.

Some elite citizens inherited their wealth. Lawson Wilson of Crowders Mountain Company, assessed for the "L & E B Wilson" partnership, owned 22 slaves and 676 acres and was the son of antebellum leader, William Joseph Wilson, longtime Lincoln County Register of Deeds, who had built a solid economic and political base with a farm, a grist mill operation, and a gold mine. The 1863 tax list further discloses that Lawson had $2,900 in cash, $300 in county bonds, $10 in Railroad dividends, a silver watch worth $20, a "pleasure carriage" worth $100, furniture valued at $50, and was taxed for one dog. Interestingly his partner and brother, E. B. Wilson, had $31 in cash, $800 in county bonds, $20 in railroad dividends, and a silver watch worth $15.

Caleb Wilfong Hoyle of Dallas Company, son of prominent antebellum citizen "Rich" Andrew Hoyl, was a deaf mute whose assessment included inherited wealth of 31 slaves and 850 acres. He also was taxed for $5,774 in cash, for studs and jacks, for gold watches worth $100, and for a silver cane worth $1. His father, a state legislator and justice of the peace, at one time owned four stores, controlling interest in the High Shoals Iron Manufacturing Company, and over 14,000 acres of land. Two gentry from High Shoals Company were relatives Ephraim and John N. Friday with 21 slaves and 483 acres and 23 slaves and 624 acres. Their total value was $8,750. The Fridays were farmers with inherited land and slaves.

Economic prosperity varied throughout the county. The affluence of the Gaston's three eastern districts eclipsed economic prowess of the rest of the county. River Bend Company had four elite.

- Dr. S. H. Johnston with 36 slaves and 1,763 acres, valued at $12,300. Johnston possessed some of the most valuable items in the county: $1,816 in cash, $2,544 solvent debts, $1,200 county bonds, $100 in silver watches, $65 in cotton, $525 in railroad bonds, $225 in gold and silver plating and jewelry, a piano, $500 in bond dividends, $1,605 railroad capital, a carriage worth $250, furniture worth $1,000, and cattle worth $4,120.
- J. W. Moore had 33 slaves and 500 acres, valued $5,000. Moore was taxed for $300 cash, $1,200 solvent debts, $75 in silver watches, a carriage worth $150, furniture worth $100, and one piano.
- Robert McDowell, an absentee landlord with no personal items, owned 22 slaves and 1,334 acres, valued at $13,000.
- Finally, Thomas R. Tate owned 63 slaves and 1,245 acres, valued at $150,000. He operated the successful Mountain Island Cotton and Woolen Factory. Tate was taxed for $39,200 cash, $10,002 in solvent debts, $900 worth in carriage or carriages, $178,840 in cotton, profits of $85,475, 5 dogs, gold watches worth $300, $150 worth for plating and jewelry, and $1,000 worth of furniture.

South Point Company also had four elite persons.

- Milton Gullick owned 21 slaves and 490 acres, valued at $3,416 and was taxed for a carriage worth $75.
- Moses H. Hand owned 18 slaves and controlled 13 slaves as Leeper Executor and for M. Neagle. He only owned 70 acres, valued at $1,400, a carriage worth $105, and silver watches worth $20, and was the colonel of the militia and Home Guard during the war.
- John D. McLean owned 38 slaves and 957 acres, valued at $7,052. He was also taxed for $22,484 cash, silver watches worth $100, furniture worth $50, and two dogs.
- The Stowe family operated Stowesville Cotton Factory or as it was officially known, "J & EB Stowe." The company owned 12 slaves outright and apparently rented 8 others from various individuals. Other Stowe family members in South Point or Tanyard Companies likely hired slaves to the milling operation. The Company land tract included 745 acres, valued at $50,000. Jasper Stowe, one of the investors, resided in Lincolnton in a prominent house and had served as a state senator and in other various political positions. The tax list compiled taxes for the company at $20 in silver watches, $3,500 profits from manufacturing, 1 piano, 1 silver cane, furniture worth $800, and 1 dog.

Woodlawn Company had six elite citizens.

- J. S. Davison owned 26 slaves with 1,079 acres, valued at $7,500. He was also taxed for gold watches worth $150, gold plated worth $53, a carriage worth $300, and cattle.
- A. W. Davenport owner of 20 slaves and 500 acres, valued at $4,000, served in the state legislature during the war. He was taxed for $150 cash, $200 solvent debts, and furniture worth $100.
- C. L. Hunter owned 19 slaves with 520 acres, valued at $3,000 but had no personal property taxed, and resided in Mecklenburg County.
- J. D. Rankin owned 28 slaves and land totaling 1,354 acres, which was valued at $8,300. He was taxed for $200 cash, $4,000 solvent debts, a carriage worth $100, furniture worth $150, $200 railroad capital, and 2 dogs.
- Abram Scott owned 21 slaves and was listed as administrator for Moore heirs with 15 slaves. He was not taxed for any personal property.
- William T Shipp owned 19 slaves and 842 acres, valued at $5,900. He was also taxed for $1,000 solvent debts, carriages worth $250, furniture worth $150, bank capital worth $14,000, railroad capital worth $400, $500 in county bonds, 1 piano, and gold plates worth $30. He figured prominently with the militia and as a legislator during the war.

Consistent with Escott's research, the Gaston County's gentry were entrepreneurs and manufacturers, owning mills, iron and gold mining operations and holding wealth in slaves, railroad stock, cash, and gold and silver items. They could afford expensive furniture, carriages, and pianos.

The Middle Class, Yeomen and Landless Whites

Middle-class citizens composed 27 percent of the taxables with varying degrees of affluence. Upwardly mobile, all understood that slave ownership was critical to future economic success. James H. White, Richard Rankin, Moses H. Rhyne, and Jacob Froneberger are examples of middle-class citizens. All held political positions and were exempt from the Confederate draft.

- James H. White of Dallas Company was a prominent legislator prior to and during the war, whose assessment included 515 acres valued at $2,675, four slaves at $4,552, $1,785 cash, a $60 carriage, $100 in furniture, and was a guardian for three other citizens.
- Richard Rankin of Woodlawn was taxed for 825 acres assessed at $4,900, 11 slaves, $50 cash, $1,600 solvent debts, $55 furniture, and one dog. He was an early supporter of secession.
- Moses H. Rhyne also of Woodlawn owned stores in Dallas and Woodlawn and had invested in the Woodlawn Cotton Mill. He was assessed for 607 acres worth $4,500, 12 slaves, $50 for a gold watch, $75 for carriage, $100 furniture, one piano, a stud, and a dog. His possessions approached the affluence of the elite. In Dallas he was taxed for the Rhyne Store, which still stands.
- Jacob Froneberger also owned a store and boarding house in Dallas. He was taxed for 192 acres worth $2,325, 6 slaves in his name and 5 for whom he was guardian, 9 town lots, $7,000 cash, and a $60 carriage. He served in the militia and Home Guard and held other governmental responsibilities at home during the war.

Other middle-class citizens owned less. E. E. Boyce of Crowders Mountain owned 346 acres valued at $2,000, 6 slaves, $100 solvent debts, and $100 carriage. Robert ? Boyd also of Crowders Mountain owned 408 acres valued at $2,500, 9 slaves, and a $100 carriage. Confederate Colonel William Groves Morris of Dallas was taxed for 301½ acres for $1,800, 2 slaves, and a $60 carriage.

Specific economic comparisons of middle-class with yeomen demonstrate major differences. Some yeomen examples include:

- From Dallas: Berryman Jenkins who was taxed for 54 acres at $375 value; Andrew Long whose tax obligation included 160 acres valued at $1,450, 1 white poll, $108 for tobacco purchase, $75 for a carriage, and 3 gallons of brandy.
- From Duhart's District: John W. Davis was taxed $250 for 70 acres and 1 white poll; H. H. Floyd for 105 acres at $525 and 1 white poll; Thomas M. Hanna 100 acres at $500.
- From Cherryville Company: James Carpenter was taxed for 722 acres valued at $2,500 and one dog; M. J. Craft for 133 acres at $540; D. Crouse for 69 acres at $200; David Eaker for 100 acres at $300 and 11 gallons of brandy.
- In Roberts District: Wm. Clark was assessed for 100 acres at $300 and one white poll; George Dameron for 52 acres at $150.
- In Rudisill's Company: Edward Baker was assessed for 188½ acres at $940 and 85 gallons of brandy; David Crouse 114 acres at $798.
- In Tanyard District: Nathan Mendenhall, a militia captain, was taxed for 200 acres at $1,200 and $3,117 cash; Dr. J. L. Neagle for 73 acres at $350.

County yeomen owned land of less value, held no slaves, often manufactured brandy, and owned fewer possessions than their middle-class neighbors with only a few being in the county government. Yet, they also aspired to middle-class status, which mandated acquiring slaves.

No landless laborers were identified in the first portion of the tax list and only a few in the second. In High Shoals Company, John Hovis, John Lancaster, and John Nance were assessed for one white poll each. Of the three farm laborers whose war letters were examined in the project, only Franklin S. Hanna appears in the tax list from Duhart's with no entry beside his name. In Cherryville District, J. N. Harvey has no information beside his name. Little to no information about farm and town laborers indicates their lack of property, possessions, and influence.

Socioeconomic status varied between geographic regions of the county. A review of the map of the militia districts may enhance one's understanding. Cherryville and Rudisill, located in northwestern Gaston, had no elite and few middle-class citizens. Of the 157 households taxed in the two districts, almost 76 percent were yeomen without slaves. Only 39 middle-class citizens had slave totals ranging from one to 11 with the majority of the slaveholders owning one slave.

Eastward along the Catawba River, yeomen from South Point numbered 41 percent, Woodlawn, 42 percent; and River Bend, 44 percent. These figures contrasted with elite and middle class taxables of Woodlawn (48 percent), South Point (59 percent), and River Bend (49 percent). But the county as a whole was a land of yeomen. Of the eleven tax districts, seven were assessed with over 65 percent yeomen. Wealth was concentrated in the east and increased as one traveled from west to east in Gaston County.

Documented sources offer an optimistic future for Gaston County. They looked with pride upon their new county and county seat, fledgling cotton mills, grist mills, and iron furnaces. The Civil War impacted all citizens in various ways. Soldiers left home for war; wives and children survived the best they could at home. Politics and differences in opinion were sometimes violent and strained, as African Americans played major roles. But the story begins with cotton mills, iron manufacturing and Dallas.

2

Dallas, Iron and Gold Manufacturing and Cotton Mills

Gaston County's creation in 1846 dawned a new era for area citizens. Three issues dominated the county's early history and impacted its citizens as the Civil War raged: the county seat of Dallas; iron and gold manufacturing operations; and cotton mills.

"In a dull town"

The area of Gaston County had no towns; from 1785 Lincolnton had been the only area municipality in Lincoln County. Hoylesville, a post office established in 1817 in present Gaston County, revolved around postmaster and store owner Andrew Hoyl, who operated stores at three other locations. Hoyl, a wealthy political leader and his son, Eli, invested heavily in the High Shoals Iron Works.[1] Hoylesville was a prominent place until the creation of Dallas.

With the formation of Dallas, the Hoylesville post office and accompanying store moved a few miles south as it prospered on Jesse Holland's "donated" land.[2] Young, ambitious lawyer and Lincolnton native, David Schenck, set up his law practice there in "pretty comfortable quarters in a dull town."[3] Dallas was no Lincolnton but would become critically important to the new county.

Once legally established, *The Lincoln Courier* advertised "Town Lots For Sale in Dallas, in Gaston County," as commissioners, "Isaac Holland, Andrew Love, Richard Rankin, A. W. Davenport, Ephraim Friday, Robt. Beatty, Christian Aker," offered lots for sale on April 6 and 7 with "credit of one to two years." On June 24, 1847, the newspaper advertised "Proposals will be received by the undersigned until the 4th of August, 1847 for building a Courthouse and Jail at Dallas, Gaston County (N. C.)," which specified construction "be of Brick, except the basement, which or a part of which, is to be of Granite: its size is to be 40 feet by 60 feet." The Jail, "30 feet by 40 feet," should be completed in 14 months and the Courthouse completed in two years. Proposals will be opened on the date stated by the committee, "Larkin Stowe, Wm. J. Wilson, James H. White, Andrew Love."[4] The County Court promoted the new town by authorizing to Wm. Edwards and Amzi Ford licenses to retail "Spirituous Liquors" and placed Jacob Plonk in "charge of the publick Square and all the land belonging to the Town of Dallas not otherwise appr and make use of all timber necessary for enclosing the publick Square."[5] Within a few years Dallas took shape with churches, internal road improvements, shops, and taverns.

In April 1848 the County Court appointed a committee to "Lay off five Lots for the purpose of Erecting Churches thereon for the Babtist, Presbyterian, Soseder or Social Reform & Methodist denominations to worship in."[6] "ENTERTAIMENT AT DALLAS," *The Lincoln Courier* publicized, as Mr. Kruse leased "the Establishment known as 'Jesse Holland's Brick House,' ... put the building in complete repair, and furnished it anew with bedsteads and bedding" with the "table [to] be well supplied.... Of generous wine and food.... His STABLES are commodious and well supplied with Grain." "[C]harges" for his Boarding House, "will be moderate, and his endeavors to please, he hopes, will give him claim to a fair trial."[7]

On September 1, 1848, three Gaston County citizens, Jacob Costner, Jacob Plonk, and Andrew Hoyle solicited bids to construct a "Bridge across the south Fork at A. Hoyle's ford" with specifications of five stone pillars, twenty two feet high, twelve to fourteen feet long, six feet thick, "strong Bannisters" and with the river 160 feet wide.[8]

In February 1849 the County Court issued Lewis Clemmer a "Licence to Retail Spirits at his grocery on the west Square of Dallas for 12 months" and in October paid William E. Rose, proprietor of High Shoals Iron Company, $20 "for putting a bridge Acros Long Creek near the Furnas on the Shelby road." The Court paid John H. Roberts for creating the "Publick well" in Dallas and authorized him to "Sell the Old Court house [a temporary log structure] in dollars as Soon as the New Court house is reveived [sic]." In April the Court paid James and Edward Lonergron, "Contractors of the Public Buildings in the Town of Dallas," $1,135.90; however, no subcontractors were listed.[9]

Commercial development surrounded the newly built courthouse: James H. Oates located "in the Town of Dallas, one door South of Quinn & Holland's store, where he is in receipt of the latest Fashion, and anxious to accommodate his friends and the public for reasonable compensation"; "Thomas Bordley, Saddle & Harness Maker, Dallas, Gaston, N. C." located his store on the main street and would repair harnesses and paint and do trim work; "Hoyle & Stowe, Dallas" sold Dr. LeRoy's pills; J. J. Lawing advertised as a Tailor.[10]

In August 1850 County Court ordered that "Andrew Hoyl Furnish the Courthouse with a suitable Chair for the judge to Sit in and report to next court" and by April of the next year paid him $5 for it.[11] By 1850 Dallas had taken form: a brick courthouse, jail, and Hoffman hotel adorned an organized town square; residents included attorneys, merchants, grocers, and governmental officials including a sheriff, clerk of Superior Court, clerk of county court; and 31 town lots had been sold, valued at $5,275.[12]

Consumers could shop at new businesses surrounding the courthouse: "DELLINGER & Co Dallas, Gaston, NC" offered "Johnston's Tetter Ointment.... Salve.... Pain Extract"; "A HOYLE & CO" advertised "FALL AND WINTER GOODS.... Staple and Fancy Dry Goods, Groceries, Hardware, Cutlery, Crockery, Dye Stuffs, A large stock of Paints &c." to be sold for cash or credit, and "[a]ll kinds of country produce taken in exchange for goods at market prices"; "ADOLPHUS P. HARRIS CABINET-MAKER ... re-opened his shop" in Dallas "south-west of the Court House." On March 8, 1851, A. E. Michaels advertised the "Dallas Tailor Shop," located conveniently "at the buildings opposite the Court House."[13]

On June 6, 1851, the last known copy of *The Lincoln Courier* documents Dallas and county events, publishing "Inspectors of the Congressional Election" for Gaston County and gossips that Gaston residents, Jasper Stowe, Dr. William Sloan, Ben Briggs, and Jacob Rhom, were guests at "B. S. Johnson's Hotel" in Lincolnton. Dallas's "A. Hoyle & Co" advertised "a complete stock of FOREIGN and DOMESTIC Fancy Dry Goods" for spring and summer and "*Ladies and Gentlemen's Wear....* SILKS, BARAGES, MUSLINS, GINGHAMS." The store's variety included "A complete stock of **Groceries**, together with Hardware, BOOTS, Shoes, Caps, Bonnets, Hats, Hosiery, and every other article usually kept in stores in the up-country." The April 12, 1851, ad invited customers to "call and examine for themselves."[14]

In September 1851 citizens elected Lawson A. Mason their new sheriff, and in the next year Henry Summitt, R. J. Hand, and "A. & E. B. Holland & Co" were licensed to sell liquor in Dallas and John F. Glenn to "pedal goods." By August 1853 the Court appointed Amos Morris, Daniel Hoffman, Winchester Pegram to serve as a committee to repair "the prison fix doors and Run Partition and make Sufficient Door in Partition."[15]

Early 1854, additional persons were authorized to sell alcohol in Dallas—John McLelland, James Nolen, and John McLurd. Voters re-elected Paul Froneberger the county sheriff. In 1856, L. & A. Groner were licensed to retail liquor in Dallas, and John H. Roberts was appointed both Coroner and Deputy Sheriff.[16] In a few short years, citizens in Gaston County could shop, attend Court, and spend the night in a hotel or boarding house.

"I am sick of this little village"

On June 25, 1857, David Schenck, began his law career "in my new house snuggly stowed away in a quiet little office in the village of Dallas, where I am to commence my career in life." He had received his license on June 9 and came to Gaston County with "a corps of strong and influencial friends from the county who promise me both patronage and influence." He had been in Dallas since the 22nd and "find the citizens extremely kind and they continually express to me their gratification that they have a young lawyer among them."[17]

However, within two years, Schenck had soured on Dallas. On May 7, 1859, he returned from his Spring Court circuit to "his own little room" in Dallas, having been in Newton with little success because of the "slow Dutch there." Later on July 4 upon his return from Lincolnton, Schenck confided in his diary that he planned to remain in Dallas one year before moving away. He commented: "I am getting awful tired of this miserable little sink hole of iniquity. Our land lady is not as agreeable as she has been and I have many misgivings about boarding here." Later he referred to Dallas as that "dull and cheerless town."[18]

After his August 1859, wedding, Schenck and wife found themselves "sitting in our own room in Dallas—boarding with Mr. Pegram, have a comfortable room, a bounteous table and plenty of business to support us." In January 1860 Schenck commented in his diary that he was "sick of this little village, and I want my wife to have a home."[19] This "little village" would be his home until the third week in November when he took his new bride to Lincolnton. Schenck's description of Dallas exposes his cynical attitude while also illustrating the town's social and cultural limitations.

"Town Property"

By 1863 the "little village" embraced forty town lots under "Town Property" in the tax list. At least five other town lots have been identified in Dallas Company and other town lots were taxed throughout other companies in the county. Thirty six slaves were specifically identified within the "Town Property." However, since so many persons owned farm land in addition to town lots, the total number of slaves within the town is difficult to determine.

Dallas brought new economic dynamics to Gaston County. While white farm laborers had historically rented agricultural land, a new breed of town worker appeared. Governmental officials, tradesmen, storekeepers, and other urban workers owned a town lot or rented their home. These workers formed a new social and economic vitality, and hotels and boarding houses often met their needs.

In 1860, Winchester Pegram operated a boarding house and had four persons with dissimilar last names in the household, plus "Merchant" William W. Pegram and family. In 1863 Winchester Pegram's son, J. F. Pegram was listed with three town lots but also with 11 slaves for himself, 13 as executor of W. P. Pegram, and a town lot representing "Hoyle & Co.," the mercantile operation of the deceased Andrew Hoyl. J. F. Pegram headed a household with apparent wife and three children. His boarding house included nine other persons including a school teacher, clerk, physicians—Dr. William Sloan and E. B. Holland— two medical students, and previously mentioned David Schenck.[20]

In 1860 Daniel Hoffman, "Hotel Keeper" of the Hoffman Hotel, with apparent wife and two grown children, one of whom was a "Dentist," also housed a "Gardner" and two Mulattos, which included a bound servant and a "Rail Road Hand." In 1863 he was taxed for five town lots, 428 acres which was described as the "mill tract," 270 acres described as "Tuckasge," and an apparent town lot, described as "Tan Yd." The Hoffman Hotel was valued at $4,000.[21]

Jacob Froneberger, whose diary has been a major source for this project, called himself "one of the first citizens in the place," and was involved in "merchandising." His store lot was taxed for $3,000 and his renters included a "Clerk," a "Farm Laborer," two persons with "(S. C.)" beside their names, a "Mill wright," a "Mulatto," an "Agent," and Jasper Stowe, the cotton manufacturer, who apparently rented a room while owning a home in Lincolnton.[22]

Dallas mercantile establishments included Froneberger's store, the Hoyle Company store, Pegram's store, and the Rhyne Store of Moses H. Rhyne, a brother-in law to hotel owner, Daniel Hoffman. Rhyne's Store was taxed for $1,400 and still stands on the Dallas square.

Diverse occupations contrast considerably with the redundant farmer or farm laborer throughout most of the county's 1860 census. Town residents included attorneys, merchants, school teachers, physicians and medical students, grocers, tailors, a painter, a wagon maker, a dentist, a hotel keeper, a "Ditcher," machinists, a shoe maker, and carriage makers. Other tradesmen included tanners, blacksmiths, carpenters, seamstresses, millers, and farmers. Apprentices often resided in the master tradesman's home. Governmental officials also resided in Dallas, including Amzi Ford, Clerk of Court with two town lots in Dallas and five acres of land on Catawba Creek and John G. Lewis listed as a Clerk of Court with at least two lots in town and as estate administrator of Paul Froneberger, the former sheriff.[23] John H. Roberts, a former county official, was listed without land or town lots but with eight slaves.

Lawson Summitt, "Grocery Keeper," was assessed for one acre and four slaves; Austin Groner, another "Grocery Keeper" was taxed for one town lot. Dr. Sloan, boarder of J. F. Pegram, was taxed for two tracts of land outside the town and eight slaves, S. P. Pasour for two town lots and served as a "Master Blk Smith" with white and black apprentices, and George Clemmer, a farmer in 1860, for a lot worth $1,800, which implicates an establishment based upon the Court-issued 1849 liquor license to Lewis Clemmer.[24]

Two persons, S. D. Holland and Eli Pasour, held the occupation of "Note shaver,"

The Rhyne Store was built about 1850 by Moses Hoffman Rhyne as Dallas assumed its role as county seat. Rhyne also owned another store in the present Mt. Holly area, stock in various cotton manufacturing and mining operations, other property and numerous slaves (courtesy Melany Dawn Crouse Photography).

which was a local note and bond speculator, and received special taxation under the 1863 tax law. Pasour was taxed for one town lot, and the house, in which he later taught school, still stands on the town square.[25]

"Wagoner" was another important "urban" occupation. Lawson A. Mason, who may have owned a town lot, held the occupation, as did the "Mulatto," Mansfield Chambers, living next door, apparently without land. Racial diversity also proliferated in Dallas with the presence of Free Blacks. The 1860 census enumerated sixteen "Free persons of color," of which all but one were mulatto. Many were listed as bound servants. Their occupations included "Wagoner," "Rail Road Hand," "Miner," "Cook," and "Black Smith."[26]

While page after page of the 1860 census lists persons being born in Gaston County, diversity of origin is readily apparent in Dallas. Thirteen persons were born in Mecklenburg County, eleven in South Carolina, two in England, one in Cleveland, Ohio, one in Hartford, Connecticut, one in Ireland, and one in Prussia; three were born in Catawba County, one in Cabarrus, one in Davie, one in Rutherford, one in Anson, and one in Burke County.[27] The assimilation of these racial and geographical entities created a small but vibrantly diverse courthouse town.

While Dallas had existed since 1847, it was not formally incorporated until 1863. "An Act to Incorporate the Town of Dallas in Gaston County" passed the North Carolina General Assembly during the 1862–63 sessions, empowering Dallas to govern and tax its residents.[28]

To describe Dallas as "cosmopolitan" may be an exaggeration. Yet, the town's population contrasts dramatically with the rest of the county, as it maintained a dynamic political atmosphere, hosting meetings and speeches, and was a destination for shopping and trade. Dallas' proximity to the High Shoals Iron Company provided economic opportunities during the war.

Iron and Gold

After the American Revolution one of the most significant economic engines west of the Catawba River had been iron and gold mining and manufacture, which accompanied the rich mineral vein running northeast to southwest, including eastern Lincoln, western Gaston, and southeastern Cleveland Counties. J. Peter Lesley noted in 1859 that the rich iron ore belt ran from eastern Lincoln County to "the King's mountain range of Gaston County" in a southeasterly direction. The belt continued "to King's mountain where Briggs vein is 40 feet thick." He noted that iron had been made there for "half a century" and that "a spectacular vein 6 to 7 feet wide" was near the top of Crowders Mountain. He also described the iron works in Cleveland County and noted that "Brigg's Yellow Ridge Bank" furnished much of the ore for those operations.[29]

High Shoals Iron Works in its heyday operated a foundry, nail factory, a string of blast furnaces, thousands of acres of land and a cadre of white and black workers. Timber had to be cut and processed into charcoal, and skilled black and white artisans performed complex tasks such as molder, collier, and hammerman. John Fulenwider, a German-speaking Revolutionary War veteran from Rowan County, began the operation. Upon his death, he bequeathed the company to his heirs, and the family-dominated business became a corporation with local investors. Financial uncertainty, lag in productivity, and competition resulted in lower income and significant drains upon the company's capital.

By the mid–1840s hard economic times and squabbles among company stockholders limited income.³⁰

By 1850 investors leased the company to New Yorker William E. Rose, owner of 38 slaves. The operation had a net worth of $60,000, operating an ironworks and forge, a rolling mill, nail factory with three machines, a blast furnace, and a "feedling furnace." He averaged working 50 hands, and the value of his product was $27,810. The Industry Schedule also lists the High Shoals Gold Mining Company, valued at $25,000, which averaged working 60 male hands and 2 female hands with an overall product value of $10,136. On the agriculture schedule, he utilized 600 acres of improved land and 16,000 acres of unimproved land. The farm value of $50,000 included ten horses and 44 mules or asses, four milk and four beef cows, 16 sheep and 35 hogs with livestock valued at $6,000. His farm produced 60 bushels of wheat, 1,000 bushels of corn, 500 bushels of oats, and eight pounds of wool. It grew 20 bushels of peas and beans, 12 bushels of Irish potatoes, 35 bushels of sweet potatoes, 150 pounds of butter, and 20 tons of hay. The value of livestock slaughtered was $1,150.³¹ His farming operation fed his large slave population.

A tangled web of lawsuits, out of state investors, leases, and foreclosures challenges an understanding of the business operations. Whether owners from New York could own slaves in a southern iron manufacturing and mining company also became an issue. Rose's business failure resulted in foreclosure and the mortgage transfer to Philip Groot, yet another New York investor.³² By 1860 bad economic times and business disruptions rendered the High Shoals Company ineffective, and it was not listed on the Gaston County Industry Schedule, boasting only one slave. In 1859 Lesley's book on iron making listed the once glorious company "in ruins."³³

Various lawsuits were appealed to the United States Supreme Court, which detailed a convoluted, circuitous trail of transactions and owners.³⁴ Philip W. Groot lost the property in foreclosure to Andrew Hoyl who held the mortgage; the executors of Hoyl's estate, William P. Bynum and Thomas Grier, sold the entire tract to Aaron E. Hoovey of Gaston County who was a "straw man" for Olcott and Stephenson of New York; and Hoovey thereupon transferred lands to Olcott and Stephenson and provided Bynum and Grier a deed of trust. By April 28, 1860, the High Shoals property was sold to Dr. William Sloan of Dallas, who served as an "agent of the High Shoals Manufacturing Company." By 1861 the Civil War had interfered with the New York investors. By March 1862 the property was sold to R. R. and J. L. Bridgers for $65,000 of which $30,000 was paid in North Carolina bank notes. The Bridgers brothers and investors "immediately took possession, and worked the property until their sale to Admiral Wilkes in 1865." No deed to the Bridgers group has been found in the Gaston or Lincoln records.

After the Supreme Court decision Wilkes recorded a legal transaction which established the Edgecombe investment group's ownership. On May 24, 1873, Admiral Charles Wilkes of Washington, D. C., created a deed in which he acknowledged indebtedness to William P. Bynum and Thomas Grier in the amount of $30,000. The document further states that "Robert R. Bridges [sic] of New Hanover, John L. Bridgers as Executor of the Last Will and Testament of Joseph A. W. Powell of the County of Edgecombe, & Frederick Phillips as Trustee of B. B. Barron & also as Trustee of J. L. Bridgers also of the County of Edgecombe," were of a "third part" of the transaction. Wilkes also owed the third group various amounts of money and payment plans were specified. The transaction further conveyed to Bynum and Grier "all those several Tracts, pieces, and parcels of land Known as 'High Shoals lands' in Gaston, Lincoln, and Cleaveland Counties ... containing

… 14,873 ½ acres," based upon the mortgage deed from the "High Shoals Manufacturing Company to Philip W. Groot" written February 24, 1854.[35]

The 1873 transaction clearly proves that the Edgecombe County, North Carolina, investment group owned the High Shoals property through a lease agreement.[36]

Four factors influenced the renewed High Shoals operation. The demand for iron and steel products needed to conduct war, and gold to support the southern currency spurred production, as the war and the Union blockade significantly restricted trade.

The Civil War provided ample opportunity for profits, as Robert R. Bridgers and his brother John L. Bridgers, B. B. Barron, and Joseph J. Powell acquired the company so that by 1863 the reorganized High Shoals Company was selling products to the Confederate government.[37]

A third factor involved the affluence and political connections of the investors. Both Bridgers brothers were successful attorneys in Tarboro and owned extensive lands. Robert R. Bridgers was a leader in the Bank of North Carolina's Tarboro branch and became president of the Tarboro branch of the Wilmington and Weldon Railroad. He served two terms in the Confederate Congress from North Carolina. John L. Bridgers also served as director of the Tarboro Bank of North Carolina, as the first University of North Carolina escheator, as a military Captain, and in the state legislature. He lived at "The Grove," a plantation in Edgecombe County, built by Thomas Blount. The house still stands (2015) and is a museum.[38] B. B. Barron, a business associate, also served as a "Receiver" during the war and in 1863 was taxed as a resident of Gaston County. In 1860 Robert R. Bridgers was living in Tarboro and was worth $78,000 in real estate and $125,000 in personal estate.[39] J. W. Powell was deceased by 1863 with assets invested in the company.

Finally, the Edgecombe investors protected their slave investments as they moved them inland while Union forces invaded the Outer Banks, the New Bern area, and challenged Tarboro itself, as their political connections gave them business advantages.

High Shoals Iron Co.

With new proprietors the High Shoals Company became fully operational. In 1863 the tax list revealed that "High Shoal Iron Co." held 14,750 acres which was valued at $90,000. The company was assessed for 14 slaves, eight of which appear to be rented. The total valuation of the slaves was $14,783. The tax list enumerated R. R. and John L. Bridges[40] as owning no real property but with their 169 slaves assessed at $123,390. Partner B. B. Barron was assessed for 61 slaves, valued at $38,569. "J. W. Powell Est." for 57 slaves with a value of $39,456. The tax list discloses that 301 slaves, valued at $216,198, were directly involved in the High Shoals Company operation of iron and gold mining and processing.

On August 6, 1863, "Robert R. Bridgers, Bolan B. Barron, and John L. Bridgers in right of the estate of Dr. J. J. W. Powell of the county of Edgecombe" expanded operations by purchasing about 420 acres from Melchi Rhodes for $5,500. The land appears to be in the High Shoals area on "both sides of Hoyles Creek."[41] Rhodes and brother, Caleb, operated a grist mill and saw mill and a toll road in the area, also being involved in mining and processing minerals.

Government contracts provided significant revenue to the High Shoals proprietors.

Extant documentation reveals that in 1863 the company sold the North Carolina government nails, horseshoes, rolling iron, and wagon boxes totaling $13,528.73.[42] The next year revenue increased, selling nails and performing technical bloom work including rolling and cutting iron, mining nitrates, refining iron, and working with railroad steel, earning $75,606.41.[43] No government revenue was listed for 1865.

Governmental contacts for two years totaled $89,135.14. Proceeds for nail production accounted for $20,305 of that total. The price of nails inflated over the war years from $60 per keg in 1863 to $170 per keg by the end of 1864, almost a 300 percent increase.[44]

High Shoals Iron Company also sold to private citizens and businesses as well. Some documentation of these sales has survived. Private citizens J. H. Chapman, T. D. Gay, Rev. M. Bennette, and Cicero Green, purchased kegs of nails and other items like a forty gallon "kettle."[45] The company also retailed its products through agents at various locations. Henry Moore of Columbia, South Carolina sold products in Augusta, Georgia, and J. C. Wolfe of Columbia also served as a company agent. "Rountree & Company" of Wilson, Andrew Baker and Company of Goldsboro, and Alex McRae Jr. & Company of Wilmington also purchased nails and other iron items for resale, while Wilcox and Hand of Augusta and J. Thomas & Company of Burneysville also placed orders.[46] The company catered to a regional customer base.

Some examples of private sales include sales of $516.35, $2,100, $660, $9,378, and $4,900. The total of $17,554.35 from extant sources, most likely does not include all their sales to private individuals or companies.[47] Obviously governmental sales of $71,580.79 were critical to their success.

While the company conducted business in North Carolina and the southeast, expenses for food stuffs like bacon, salt, molasses, and flour limited their profits. Other expenses included hides for shoes and clothes, railroad freight costs and the cost of "drayage," and transportation of products by wagon or other conveyance. For example, the company owed $8,239.25 to a vendor in Columbia in 1863. By February 2 the next year 25 kegs of nails were applied to the debt to lower it to $4,339.25. Another example involves a debt of $4,829.45 to two railroad companies. A third railroad expenditure from 1863 cost the company $14,738.95.[48]

Doing business during the war was challenging, as Confederate money lost its value. At least one purchaser of nails in 1864 reminded B. B. Barron to "take in consideration the small value of Confederate money," and the season and war conditions limited the sale of iron products. For example, iron did not sell in Augusta, Georgia as General Sherman marched through the state. One vendor found it "impossible" to sell iron but expected sales would improve in the fall when farmers needed to plow, and High Shoals found that they were in competition with other businesses.[49] Confederate monetary issues caused one purchaser to agree to trade 100 shares of the Bank of Cape Fear in Wilmington for nails. By 1864 the company owed M. C. Dial $4,339.75, and Dial agreed to take nails for the debt. Documents also indicate the trading of salt for iron.[50]

The High Shoals operation stimulated other economic activities. At least two citizens wanted to sell mules to the company. Another offered to trade mules for commodities.[51]

Communication, transportation, and the ability to fill orders posed challenges during the war. Wm. T. Worth complained that his nails had not been delivered even though he ordered them "some months since." Two customers, Wm. H. Jones of Granville County and Andrew Baker & Co, only received part of their orders. Jones ordered 1,000 pounds of iron but only received 446 pounds and had "waited 10 long months." Mr. Boone of

Sumterville paid "Mr. H. Dellinger" for nails, but since they had not been delivered he questioned whether Dellinger was a company agent. John B. Winthrop expressed some concern about shipping of the product and payment of the bill.[52] As most of these issues are documented in late 1864, war conditions exacerbated the Company's operations and profits.

Another issue for the High Shoals Company involved the labor force. Iron making required significant numbers of laborers, and maintaining the slave laborers was a challenge. The Company received many offers to hire slaves. B. B. Barron spent much time managing and trying to locate the hired slaves who ended up in the Wilmington and the Asheville jails. Managing slaves meant providing them food, shelter, and other amenities, while providing them passes for travel. By 1864 runaways were a major concern for the company with doubts of their recovery. An advertisement placed in the Richmond *Daily Dispatch* sought the Kennedy hired slaves: "Run Away from High Shoals Iron Works $75 Reward … negroes Ammon, Jake Whitehurst, and Bob Clarke, hired of Messrs. Kennedy and Ellison of Beaufort Co."[53]

Yet as late as 1864 the need for more slaves, especially ones with specialized skills, like a blacksmith, required discussion. Slaveholders opposed the impressment of their slaves to work on Confederate fortifications, and pressures to grow more crops to feed the slave labor force required discussion. By 1864 with Confederate monetary inflation the Company accepted in-kind payment. As late as February 17, 1865, the naval yard in Charlotte ordered "Flat iron for the Navy Yard at Charlotte" as soon as possible.[54] For the High Shoals Company the need for more slaves increased and business remained active.

A thorough examination of the High Shoals Iron Company operations provides a unique picture of a successful yet stressful business enterprise during the war. Clearly the war motivated it and provided economic opportunities for the High Shoals investors and others in Gaston County. Other Edgecombe investors found Gaston County a lucrative business opportunity.

The Garrett Brothers

Edgecombe's "Garrett Brothers" acquired the Crowders Mountain mining and iron works of B. F. Briggs.[55] In 1859 J. Peter Lesley reported that "Brigg's Iron Works" was a bloomery built in 1853 on Crowder's Creek six miles south of Dallas. He noted that Benjamin F. Briggs of "Yorkville P. O., Gaston County, South Carolina" operated the bloomery which had three fires, water providing energy for one hammer and had produced "336 tons of blooms" in 1857.[56] While Lesley was unaware that the bloomery was in Gaston County, he provides specific details of the operations but failed to mention the gold mine.

The 1850 Gaston County Industry Schedule indicated that Briggs mined and processed 46,000 pounds of gold ore. He owned 53 slaves and worked 100 male and 10 female workers, which included white laborers. He mined both gold and iron as gold was valued at $82,800 and the iron at $2,850. Briggs owned 47 horses, 10 mules, five improved acres of land for farming and 5,080 acres of unimproved land. On the farm, he possessed seven milk cows, 13 beef cattle, 25 sheep and 70 hogs with all livestock totaling $2,800. He also grew 400 bushels of corn, 100 pounds of butter, ten tons of hay, and $120 worth of animals slaughtered.[57]

By the 1860 census Benjamin F. Briggs had suffered significant financial losses. He had only 18 slaves, a decline of 35. The Industry Schedule listed him as an "Iron Master" with $70,000 capital invested. He worked 2.1 million pounds of iron ore and used 8 males with no pay, all apparently slave. He also mined gold and cut wood.[58]

Briggs's operation continued losing money. By the Fall Court Term of 1861 through 1862 creditors sued Briggs and received judgment on his property, slaves, horses and mules, and other business assets.[59] On May 4, 1861, Briggs mortgaged his lands and operations in two deeds to Samuel R. Oates, A. R. Homesley, and Peter Z. Baxter for $20,000 and $40,000. On February 9, 1863, B. F. Briggs sold 5,100 acres of land to Edgecombe County investors, "Joseph G. Garrett, Charles W. Garrett, Richard H. Garrett, Francis M. Garrett, & Isaac W. Garrett Partners in trade and Style & name of Garrett Brothers" for $2,000. On May 14, 1863, Briggs' creditors, A. R. Homesley, Samuel R. Oates, and Peter Z. Baxter, sold machinery to the same Garrett Brothers "of Gaston and Edgecombe County."[60] Briggs transitioned out of debt and into military service as the captain of a locally raised company.

The 1863 tax list provides a snapshot of the Garrett Brothers operation. They were assessed for 93 slaves valued at $64,221 and owned 10,342 acres in 11 tracts valued at $42,770. E. W. Garrett was assessed for one white poll, $8,450 cash, $4,439 in cotton, $150 for gold watches, $125 for gold and silver plated items, and $150 for a carriage. Brother R. H. was assessed for one white poll.

Few financial records have been located for the Garrett Brothers enterprise. In April 1863 the government paid them $1,925.64 for blooms; the following year, $4,732.07. The

This trough was used at the Kings Mountain Gold Mine to grind ore, producing gold. It was transported to the farm of William G. Morris after the enterprise stopped operation (courtesy Melany Dawn Crouse Photography).

Garretts' farming operations in Edgecombe County also provided commodities to the Confederate government. From 1862 to 1864, J. J. and F. M. Garrett sold corn and fodder and allowed the Confederate army to forage on their land. Dr. J. J. Garrett also charged the government for medicines and prescriptions.[61] In the absence of private papers, local transactions cannot be determined. As with the Bridgers investors, the war prompted the Garrett investment in Gaston County. It is likely that their operations were as profitable as High Shoals, as moving their slaves inland also protected them from Union intrusion.

Another gold mining operation, the Kings Mountain Gold Mine, continued to be productive. Lawson Wilson, the youngest son of William Joseph Wilson, became the primary manager. The 1863 tax list assessed Lawson with 445 acres worth $7,000, $2,900 cash; $300 in county bonds, $10 in railroad dividends, $20 for silver watches, $100 for a carriage, $50 in furniture and one dog. "L. & E. B. Wilson" was listed with 678 acres valued at $698 and 22 slaves of $13,191 assessed value. E. B., Lawson's brother and business partner, was taxed for 676 acres valued at $3,376 and 9 slaves with $6,343 value and $31 cash, $800 county bonds, $20 railroad dividends, $15 silver watch. Their inherited wealth provided a significant impetus for success.[62] No Confederate government pay vouchers have been located.

"An Act to Construct a Railroad"

Because of the restored and thriving iron industry, the Edgecombe investor's influence, and local leaders' dedication, constructing a railroad was once again pondered. The legislature approved "An Act to Construct a Railroad from Dallas in Gaston County, by way of Lincolnton, to Newton in Catawba County." Enacted December 17, 1862, the incorporation allowed for $500,000 in stock divided into "shares of fifty dollars each." A list of commissioners were specified in the law and included: Dr. William Sloan, John L. Bridgers, R. R. Bridgers, J. F. Pegram from Gaston; William Lander, L. E. Thomson, Jacob Ramsour (M. W.), Melchi Rhodes from Lincoln; Franklin D. Rheinhour, George Setzer, Major Joseph Bost, Elisha Ramsour, Capt. L. McCorkey, Joseph Fry, Moses Hewet from Catawba. The commissioners had authority to: appoint a chairman, facilitate subscribers, appoint a board of directors, and hold meetings of stockholders once sufficient capital was raised.[63] The legislation was similar to previous attempts to construct the railroad from York, South Carolina through Kings Mountain to Dallas.

The Gaston railroad investors were an equal mix of Edgecombe-High Shoals leaders, Bridgers and Bridgers, and local Dallas leaders. Dr. William Sloan had taken possession of the High Shoals Company after the New Yorkers abandoned it, and J. F. Pegram was a Dallas merchant with a boarding house. The Rhodes Toll Bridge project[64] and railroad project underline the serious transportation limitations of the time, which affected profits, availability of materials, and sale of commodities. The railroad would facilitate transporting iron from High Shoals to Newton and connect to the rail link in Lincolnton financially tying the communities together. The rail line was never constructed until after the war.

Gaston's iron works coexisted with eastern Lincoln County businesses where it remained a prominent economic force. In early 1861 Jonas W. Derr managed the operation of the Spring Hill Forge and produced "Soft Pig Iron" and "Cooking-ware, Machinery, &c" throughout the war. He also sought "Moulders" and in 1864 "wished to hire twenty good able-bodied Negro men" and "two good carpenters." "Vesuvius Furnace Iron Works" manufactured pig iron north of the Sharon railroad station, creating "Machinery, such as Mill Gearing, Thrashing, Maching Irons, &c; also Hollow-ware and Salt Pans." The Rehoboth Furnace also operated three miles "East of Iron P.O.," selling "Pig Iron."[65] The war enhanced iron making operations.

A third wheel of economic development during the Civil War involved cotton and wool manufacture. Three Gaston County cotton manufacturers reaped financial benefits.

"a large couton factory is building"

The fast-flowing streams of the Catawba River basin had served industrial purposes from early settlement. From localized grist and saw mills and iron works to early cotton mills—Schenck-Warlick and Hoke's Factory—the land provided the opportunity for manufacturing profits. Cotton manufacturing developed in Gaston County around 1850.

Tate's Mountain Island mill was the earliest and largest. The 1850 census documents Mountain Island mill and enumerated John Tate, a Greensboro investor as "Manufacturer," with about 20 community persons, either single or with small families, who held occupations such as "joiner," "carpenter," and "bricklayer." The Industry Schedule confirmed the first cotton mill being built: "Thomas Tate & Co." was listed as operating a saw mill with the notation, "a large couton factory is building" on the Catawba River.[66]

In 1860 Mountain Island Mill, capitalized at $100,000 with 500 spindles and 52 looms, consumed 800 "bails" of cotton and worked 40 males and 80 females. It produced "Cotton Factory Shirtings," annually producing 2,306 bushels of yarn and 232,254 yards of shirting. The overall value of the operation was $23,069.[67]

By 1860 two locally invested cotton factories operated on the South Fork River. "J. & E. B. Stowe" was the legal name of Stowesville Factory, which was capitalized at $16,000 with 1,284 spindles and 26 looms. The factory produced yarn and "shirting" from 120,000 pounds of cotton. Stowesville worked 8 males and 30 females and produced 42,900 yards of shirting, valued at $4,075 and 23,000 bushels of yarn, valued at $20,700. The Stowes continued their lumber production at the saw mill and shelled corn for farmers, also creating plows, iron castings, and charcoal.[68]

Prior experiences contributed to their success at Stowesville. A March 31, 1849, *Lincoln Courier* newspaper article exposes their experience at the Long Shoals location: "The Cotton Factory of Mesrs. J. & E. B. Stowe, young men of the right sort of enterprise, continues its operations night and day, with two sets of hands; (and some right pretty girls among them, but, we have nothing to do with that part) the machinery is the latest improvement, and besides usefulness is very pretty. We hope our young friends of the Buena Vista factory will prove as successful as Old Zack, himself, for their *yarns*, are said to be relished as inferior to none in the market. A Saw-mill, Blacksmith, Tinner shop, Store, Carpenter, Plumbers, Painters and every thing else for a little village is all on the hill. If the road were made a little better at some places, we would recommend the public, and strangers, generally, to visit to pay our Lowell a visit, and give Lincoln county, and her citizens the credit to which they are justly entitled, for industry and enterprise— *native* at that."[69] The article also pointed out that George Mosteller's paper mill was nearby.

The Stowesville Factory was most likely completed about 1853 on property owned by Larkin Stowe on the South Fork River, as his sons, Jasper and Edwin B., operated the mill. Jasper learned the cotton mill business from Lincoln County pioneers, L. D. Childs and John Hoke, and the Stowes moved the machinery from the Long Shoals mill to the Stowesville location. A description of the Stowesville Factory includes a three story, 35 feet by 70 feet structure with an attic. The mill had nine cards, nine spinning frames, 24 looms, and a "Rail way & Trough." Producing 1,000 lbs of cloth required running day and night. A "picker? House," which was 50 × 20 and three-stories high, had been added to the mill. The wood and rock mill dam was 800 feet long and 4 feet high with a race 500 to 600 feet long. There was a fall of 16 feet at the wheel.[70]

The Stowe Family Account Book documents hiring slaves from 1856–1858, banking at Charlotte and the "State Bank," paying railroad freight costs, purchasing corn, flour, and other commodities and purchasing cotton from local growers . They also loaned money to private citizens and borrowed money from individuals and banks. The accounts include local area people and companies, and those from outside the area like Charlotte, Rutherfordton, and Winnsboro.[71]

The census records Woodlawn Mills also known as "Pinhook" as the third "Cotton Factory" and another locally invested enterprise. It held $17,000 in capital with 1,000 spindles and 26 looms, used 160,000 pounds of cotton, and produced 249,000 yards of shirting and 9,340 bushels of yarn. They worked 7 males and 40 females. The value of their shirting was $2,246 and $934 for their yarn. The enterprise also operated a grist mill and saw mill.[72] Further examination exposes Woodlawn's evolution.

Woodlawn originated as a quasi-agricultural and industrial enterprise, funded by local investors, many of whom held familial relationships. As early as 1835 Valentine Clemmer and his brothers Andrew and John secured land on the South Fork River. About 1834–35 the Clemmers formed a partnership and erected a saw mill, probable grist mill, and iron forge. The iron works produced iron but by 1844 only John Clemmer survived in the family business. On February 17, 1848, Clemmer and Moses H. Rhyne contracted to manufacture iron. By December 3, 1851, Lewis Lineberger, Moses H. Rhyne, John Clemmer, Caleb Lineberger, John L. Lineberger, and Jonas Hoffman formed the company known as Woodlawn. By 1860 the Linebergers owned controlling interest in the cotton mill.[73]

All three mills—Mountain Island, Stowesville Factory, and Woodlawn—were water powered and boasted mercantile stores.[74] All three proprietors also owned slaves. Thomas Tate had increased his Gaston County slave holdings from 1850 to 1860 from 12 to 30 slaves and by 1863 his slave totals increased to 63. In 1850 "E. B. Stow" was listed with 3 slaves; in 1860 he owned 9. By 1863 "J & E B Stowe" owned 12 slaves, valued at $8,766, and operated their "Cotton Factory & C" on 745 acres with property worth $50,000. The company was taxed for eight rented slaves, assessed at $8,250. The Linebergers of Woodlawn Mill also owned slaves. In 1850 Caleb owned 3; Jonas owned 11. In 1860 J. Laban Lineberger owned 11 slaves and Caleb J. Lineberger owned 9.[75] By 1863, C. J. Linebarger was listed with 12 slaves, J. L. Linebarger with 15 slaves, and L. Linebarger and Co. with 8 slaves. The total 35 family and company slaves were valued at $22,570.

By 1860 all three cotton factories had developed mill communities surrounding them. According to the 1860 Gaston County census the largest cotton factory, Tate's Mountain Island, employed at least 66 persons as a "factory hand." Of the 66 persons listed, 54 (82 percent) were female and 12 (18 percent) were male. A total of 29 or about 44 percent were under the age of 18. The Stowesville mill village employed about 40 persons, as a "factory hand." Thirty or about 75 percent were female and ten (25 percent) were male. Seventeen (43 percent) were under age 18. Less specific was the Woodlawn factory mill village, as no "factory hand" was identified in the Woodlawn post office. Seventeen persons listed as a "Factory Hand" were mentioned in the Dallas post office and one in nearby Erasmus. Fourteen (78 percent) were females, four were males (22 percent) and six persons about 33 percent were under 18.[76] It appears likely that the census taker under reported factory workers for Woodlawn.

The data suggest a sizable mill village near each factory, whose workers were primarily female and under age 18. The 98 female workers at all mills extrapolated to 78 percent of the total workforce. Fifty-two workers were under age 18, about 42 percent of the total.

While the data confirm the existence and significance of these mill villages, the Stowe Family Ledger books document everyday life. While none of these ledgers delineate the Civil War years, entries for 1860 serve as examples of how the villages and company stores operated.

Workers held accounts at the store where their purchases became debits and their wages became credits. "Mrs. Mary Wallace," "Alexander Millen," "John R. Long," "Bolivier Lovelace," "A. M. Tucker," "J. P. Sellers," "John Nicholas" (Nichols) and other members of the family, "Mrs. Webb," and "Mrs. Gray" are identifiable on the 1860 census.[77] They typically bought flour, corn, peaches, waste cloth, sugar, bacon, coffee, ribbon, "spools thread," yarn, shoes, "plug Tobacco," potatoes, paper, "Tin pan," "box pins," "Loads Wood," and "Combs." John R. Long, "Factory Hand" who was married with a wife and children, accumulated debits from January through February 13 of $110.67 for items above plus "Butter," beef, "Postage on newspapers," "Calico," snuff, "Cash," "Shirting," nails, and "Pepper, Spice & Ginger in Charlotte." His "Wages" of $39.50 only slightly reduced his overall indebtedness. As of April 7, he still held a bill of $89.27, even when being paid $2 "By Painting Waggon."[78]

In February "Bolvier Lovelace," a younger member of the Allison Lovelace family, accumulated a $40.23 debt minus wages of $29.26, leaving a balance of $10.97. By March his expenses of $33.43 was offset by wages of $33.83. Eight members of the Lovelace family were listed as "Factory hand." A. M. Tucker headed a family of a wife, child, and others in 1860. He purchased soap, fish, "1 pair small negro shoes," silk scarves, a bushel of salt, a "wash tub," peas, and other items for a debt of $427.33 from January through February, only receiving $4 "By Retta," a member of his household.[79]

"J. P. Sellers," a "Molder" with wife and family, received January wages of $32 for himself and $6 for "Daughter" in February to cover January expenses of $48.03. His March expenses left him owing $15.35. In February "Mrs. [Mary] Gray," whose large family included five listed as "Factory hand," accumulated expenses of $10.33, and "wages for hands" of $26.89; and for March her expenses were $41.84 with wages of $30.60. "Miss Mary Tucker" paid $4 "To Board" and received wages of $3.14 in one month. "Mrs. Webb," most likely Elizabeth Webb, with a large family including a "Seamstress" and three factory hands, accumulated expenses prior to May 1 of $132.21 and wages for April of $34.33 for a total indebtedness of $97.88. She was also paid $3 "By making of 12 pr pants" but her debt grew to $108.93 by the end of May. John Nichols, "Nicholas," farm laborer, was able to employ six members of his family in the mill and in January only had a debt of $28.33.[80]

Mill workers found comfort and convenience in the company town: housing, a store and the factory were in close proximity. Though some special occupations like "Moulder" and "Seamstress" brought additional monies into the household, workers perceived that with more family members working, they could acquire more wages to reduce their debt to the company store. Yet, the evidence clearly shows how workers remained indebted to the factory.

Mill owners concerned themselves with keeping their workers from being drafted during the war. On September 19, 1862, John Tate wrote Governor Vance because one of his "principal hands" at the woolen mill had volunteered for the army. He asked Vance to allow his worker to return to the mill. Tate conveyed his concern: "unless I can retain my hands at my Cotton & woolen mills they will have to stop." Tate bragged that he had "furnished more goods to the state N. C. in proportion to the woolen machining than any other mill in the state."[81] The war facilitated further demand for employees. On July 7, 1863, Tate advertised for "250 WOMEN," who "[c]an get constant employment in making Soldiers' coats, by applying this week at Mountain Island Mills (Tate's Factory)."[82] Like iron manufacturing, maintaining a quality workforce remained essential for success.

Of the Gaston County mills, Tate's Mountain Island Factory produced the most cotton and wool material. Documentation reveals that in 1861 Tate's Mountain Island produced $15,396.63 in shirting, cashmere, cadet, jeans, rope and sacking for the government.[83] In 1862 company receipts increased to $48,668.99, due most likely to greater demand for soldier uniforms.[84] In 1863 documented sales included $29,809.90. This drop may involve both the lack of documentation and disputes between Governor Vance and the Gaston mills, which will be discussed below. In 1864 only $647.50 has been documented.[85] Contemporaries commented on the quality of Tate's cloth. On September 2, 1863, *The Daily Bulletin* reported the quality of a bolt of cloth from "T. R. Tate of Mountain Island Mills." Calling Tate the "Prince of Manufacturers," the article compared his "beautiful suit of dark Cassimere" to the best of German, French or English productions.[86]

The pressures of producing cotton and wool cloth and making a profit became evident early in the war. In 1861 Tate and the Confederate government agreed to $1 per yard for cotton and $2 per yard for cashmeres. However by December, Tate notified authorities, that increases in materials would require him to increase his prices to $1.50 and $2.50. By March of 1862 Tate sought to receive payment in bank notes instead of Confederate money.[87]

Documented Stowesville Factory governmental sales are sparse and include: On May 10, 1862, Jasper Stowe of Lincolnton sold lime to the state for $23.76.[88] On November 27, 1863, J. and E. B. Stowe Company sold 240 bundles of yarn to the state of North Carolina for $2,400. On October 26, 1864, the company signed a contract with S. R. Chrisman, representing the state, to furnish cotton yarn and sheetings.[89] No documentation of sales to private citizens has been located.

Determining the success of Woodlawn Mill also remains challenging because of few records. The assessed documentation suggests a small operation primarily producing yarn and cotton cloth. From June 15 until July 20, 1863, the state of North Carolina purchased approximately $2,255 of yarn and bales of cloth. Only one purchase exceeded $300. At least one order from this period would be delayed because of problems with machinery.[90] The mill owners experienced other hardships.

On March 8, 1863, the Lineberger family suffered a serious loss. Jacob Froneberger noticed a "light in the east" from his Dallas home. He discovered that "several hundred bales of cotton" "belonging to Lineberger & Co. was set on fire by lightening." Charlotte's *The Daily Bulletin* reported that about 600 bales of cotton were lost, "supposedly accidental," and the *Western Democrat* reported the loss at "six or eight hundred bales of Cotton." As the war wore on commodities became scarcer, which interfered with business productivity. On two occasions in 1864 the company requested "card cotton" from Governor Vance. On September 29, 1864, J. L. Lineberger and Company contracted with S. R. Christman, Major and Quartermaster, to furnish the North Carolina government cotton yarns.[91]

The significance of the Gaston County and area cotton manufacturing cannot be under-estimated. One source, most likely 1862, indicates that three of the state's eight woolen mills were located nearby, Tate's Mountain Island mill, A. R. Homesley's mill in Shelby, and N. H. Pixley & Co in Lincolnton, 38 percent of the mills. Of the forty-six state "cotton factories," five or about 11 percent, were from the area: T. R. Tate at Mountain Island, "Lineburger & Co" or Woodlawn Mills, Stowe & Brother at Stowesville, Phifer & Allison in Lincolnton, and High Falls Company without location but listed with the others from the area.[92]

The Gaston County cotton mills benefited financially from the war, as North Carolina endeavored to clothe all its soldiers. A mixture of capitalistic opportunism and blatant speculation facilitated confrontation and conflict.

"Speculation and Extortion"

As early as 1862, David Schenck claimed that "Extortion and speculation are the besetting sins of our people." He provided examples of cotton mill speculation: "the manufacturer is giving only 8 cts for Cotton he is selling Yarn at 30 and 35 cts a pound, and shirting at 30 cts a yard." He complained that the stores were empty and that the price of "Jeans" went from 50 cts to $1.25. Deploring poor wages for lawyers, he noted that "manufacturers are making immense fortunes, their profits are almost incalculable." Many Confederate citizens had to wear homemade clothes.[93]

Contemporary newspapers also noted price gouging and profiteering in salt, food stuffs, and by November 1862 Charlotte's *The Daily Bulletin* communicated that "Speculation and Extortion" in cloth production was a problem. One writer opposed a "pointed attack" on cotton and woolen factories, which were charging high prices for their goods.[94]

By early 1863 Governor Vance executed an "Executive Order" which specifically addressed illegal speculation by Gaston's three cotton factories. He ordered "Stowe & Co, Lineberger [splotch], and T R Tate" to stop selling their products above the "75 percent on cost" allowed by Confederate law. Such excessive profit making contravened Confederate legislation, and he would arrest all workers and employers "ages of eighteen and forty" and send them to the army.[95] The Confederate government had set commodity prices and profit margins during the war.

It is unclear how Governor Vance learned of the local mills' activities, as no letters were located reporting the described practices. Governor Vance ordered the Adjutant General to communicate with Gaston officials. On December 23, 1862, the Assistant Adjutant General "instructed" Col. M. H. Hand of Stowesville to "arrest and send to Camp all white males between the ages of eighteen (18) and forty years of age." The governor ordered the directive executed against "the Factories in Gaston County," naming them, because "they are selling their goods at a price much beyond what is allowed by law."[96] All three Gaston County cotton factories were on the verge of shutting down.

Vance's proclamation had the desired effect. On January 7, 1863, Adjutant General J. G. Martin directed Colonel Hand: "you will not arrest those men subject to conscription who are employed in the woolen factory of Mr. Tate." Two days later, he also notified Hand to "not arrest Lineburgers factory hands as conscripts."[97] Tate and the Linebergers would comply with Governor Vance's order. But Hand's orders remained in effect against his neighbors, the Stowes of Stowesville.

In early January, Jasper Stowe of Stowesville Factory responded with a war of words in an article printed in at least two area newspapers. Printed initially in *The Daily Bulletin* but reprinted in other newspapers, Stowe angrily attacked the governor for the "unauthorized suppressive measure." He accused him of inaccurately acting upon "mere rumor and hearsay" and of incorrectly accusing Stowesville Factory. He argued "price allowed by law" was an overreach of legislative price setting and contended that "cotton and woolen factories" were specifically exempted from price controls. He charged that the governor "plainly transcended his authority in the premises and has assumed to himself powers he does not rightfully possess, and has committed an official usurpation." Stowe considered the proclamation "arbitrary, illegal, and oppressive." He attacked Vance as possessing "intense devotion to States Rights" to the point of placing himself in "direct conflict with the Confederate government." Stowe insinuated that Vance's proclamation had preceded any conscription in Gaston County and "might tempt us to indulge the suspicion that the Governor was particularly *alert* and active in regard to the *Gaston* factories." Closing the cotton factories in Gaston County, he contended would cause a monthly loss of not less than 75,000 yards of sheeting, 25,000 pounds of cotton yarn, and all woolen goods produced by T. R. Tate. He pointed out that about two hundred mostly female "hands," who supported numerous children and older persons, would lose their jobs, and the measure would not result in many new military recruits. At Stowesville only two persons would be conscripted, a carder and a spinner. Stowe contended that the measure would financially harm the community and accused the governor of an overreach in his judgment and authority: "his zeal in the public cause has mislead his judgment."[98] Colonel Hand's involvement in Stowe's letter suggests insubordination of the Adjutant General's orders.

"No one, in the present crisis, can serve his pocket and his country at the same time"

On January 21, 1863, The *Standard*, printed in Raleigh by W. W. Holden, delineated a point-by-point rebuttal of Stowe's contentions. The paper contended the governor could enforce price supports just as he had enforced the highly unpopular conscription laws. The *Standard* ridiculed Stowe's analysis in comparing habeas corpus cases to price controls and then the newspaper attacked Stowe along political lines. While acknowledging that he was an "ardent original secessionist," it suggested that he had opposed the election of Vance and that he endeavored to profit from the war. "[L]ike thousands of others who entertained the same views, he has remained quietly at home, exerting all his energies to amass a fortune, and has not seen, much less fired, the first gun at a Yankee." With this sarcastic personal attack, the paper congratulated Tate and Lineberger for accepting the governor's conditions, supported the 75 percent profit margin, and complimented Governor Vance for restricting "the manufacturers of cotton and woolen goods to this profit." With patriotic fervor and editorial license the *Standard* closed the article: "We have but little patience with any man who seems to be more intent on amassing a fortune than he is in aiding to provide for the wants of our people and in repelling the foe. No one, in the present crisis, can serve his pocket and his country at the same time."[99]

On the same date as the *Standard* article, the Adjutant General confirmed that Stowe's employees remained under orders to be arrested. The letter specified "J. & E. B. Stowe, factors, are selling or having recently sold their goods at a higher rate than Seventy-five per centum on the cost of manufacture." Hand was to "enroll as conscripts and send to the Camp of instruction near this city at once all persons" between the ages of 18 and 40 who were "engaged in said factory of J. & E. B. Stowe, whether owners or employees."[100] The governor had decided to arrest and conscript both owners and their employees.

No further response by Jasper Stowe has been located, and Stowesville Factory continued to operate which indicates that he apparently abided by the governor's order. No further communication about the issue has been found between Hand and the Adjutant General's office.

A family member, Minnie Stowe Puett, offered an oral tradition that Jasper Stowe offered to volunteer to serve in the Confederate army at the beginning of the war. The story goes that Governor Vance needed him at home manufacturing cloth: "Stowe you shall not go to the army. No man in the South can take your place of where you are."[101] Contemporary documentation offers a different version. Vance was not the North Carolina governor when the war began. In early 1863 Governor Vance's proclamation threatened to force Jasper Stowe into the army unless he and the other Gaston County mills stopped charging prices higher than approved by the government. Apparently, Stowe joined the Home Guard near the end of the war when almost all exemptions were eliminated.[102] On October 1, 1864, his name appeared as a Lieutenant Colonel from Stowesville in a letter to Charlotte. The ambiguous record listed him as either a Detailed Man or Junior Reserve. Some sources intimate that he was a Senior Reservist.[103]

Contemporary sources confirm that Stowe accumulated significant wealth during the war. In Stowe's obituary in the *Charlotte Observer*, Mr. M. P. Pegram of Charlotte related that upon visiting Mr. Stowe near the end of the war, he observed $300,000 in Confederate money. Stowe told him that he refused to use Confederate money to pay his debts but would pay them with "good money."[104] Clearly wartime cotton manufacturing was very profitable.

Price speculation remained in the press. On March 3, 1863, the *Western Democrat* suggested that Governor Vance had not been able to "regulate the profits of the Cotton Factories," quoted other newspapers about the practice in other parts of the state, and surmised that the mills traded cloth for "corn, wheat, bacon &c."[105]

Local cotton manufacturing also spawned other economic opportunities. "L. Mulinix" of "Stowesville, Gaston Co., N. C." advertised his services in Salisbury's *Carolina Watchman*. His attractive advertisement—"Another Great Victory!"—offered his services to produce black, red or blue inks and "shoe blacking." He also advertised "welding cast steel" and "varnishing iron." He was a "Headdle-maker,[106] for the cotton mills." He first advertised his services October 5 and they ran in most issues through December. He was also quick to point out that he had amassed his materials and knowledge from the north prior to the war.[107] Many citizens worked in the mills or in collateral enterprises.

The research discloses that the war brought significant economic progress to Gaston County. With an influx of investments, the High Shoals and Briggs Iron Manufacturing operations evolved from bankruptcy into thriving profitable companies that spurred collaborative economic opportunities, as war-induced out-of-county investments stimulated an otherwise stagnant and provincial economy. Government contracts and local sales also revitalized the county's three cotton factories. These opportunities, investors' leadership, and newfound optimism catalyzed erecting a toll bridge, discussions of a railroad, and Dallas' incorporation. Dallas became the home of numerous retail businesses, craftsmen, and other economic opportunities. It may be argued that, without the war, these economic opportunities and profits most likely would not have occurred or at least not as quickly.

Manufacturing enterprises altered Gaston County, creating mill villages and motivating entrepreneurs. As unlikely as it might seem, the Civil War actually brought significant economic development to Gaston County.

The economic success of Gaston County and the surrounding area is similar to the dramatic prowess of Charlotte and Mecklenburg County. Michael C. Hardy conveys how Charlotte acquired Confederate investments, trade, and opportunities. The "Naval Yard," "Mecklenburg Iron Works," the railroad, a "General Hospital" and wayside hospitals, the "Rock Island Woolen Mill," a company for the "manufacture of small arms and ordnance," the "North Carolina Powder Manufacturing Company," "Sulphuric Acid Works" to make saltpeter, and mining activities are a few examples of enterprises created or expanded during the war. Hardy summarized its effect upon Charlotte: "Wartime industry expanded the commercial district of Charlotte, while bringing hundreds of new people, laborers, and other refugees to the Queen City."[108] While the area west of the Catawba may have experienced less dramatic investment and economic growth, clearly the war effort brought opportunities.

Dallas Lots

The plat of the town of Dallas is dated February 23, 1852, but it was not recorded in the Gaston County Register of Deeds until November 9, 1973. The original was apparently in the hands of private citizens, and they made notations on the original plat over the years. The preceding Town Lot Map was found in the Gaston County Register of Deeds, Plat Book 28, page 70. I thank Lucy Penegar for alerting me to its existence.

I used the 1863 tax list to align town lot owners with the plat. The following is my attempt to align the two documents and provide a fuller understanding of life in Dallas in 1863. I will list the town lot number and corresponding owner. It is very apparent that a number of the lots were rented

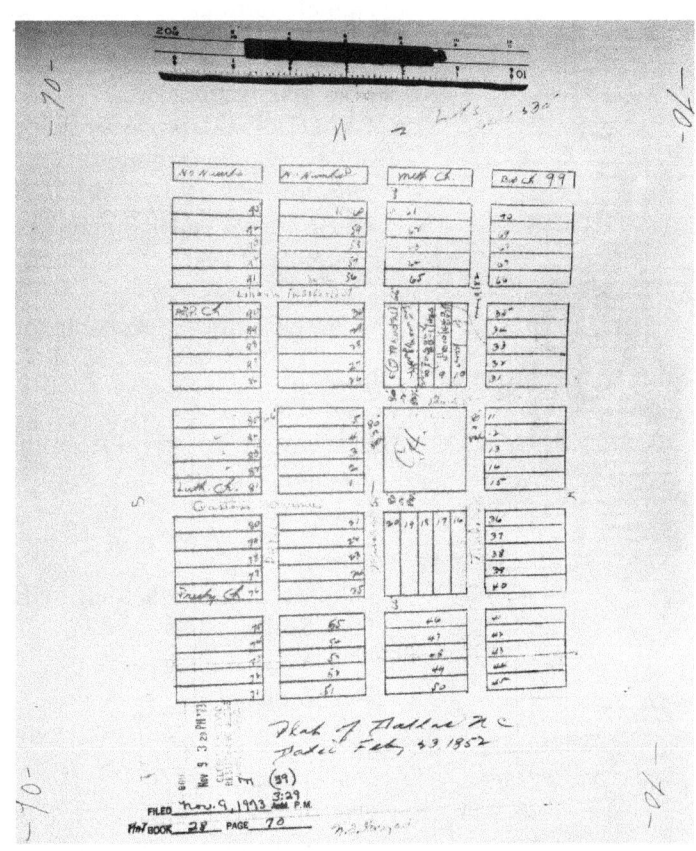

Plat of Dallas (Gaston County Register of Deeds).

as businesses or residences. Unfortunately the tax list only lists the owner, and it appears that some lots were omitted. It is unclear why these omissions occurred unless the owners were not listed in "Town Property" but in another militia company in the county.

The extant records suggest that the northern square was not developed with no taxables listed for Lots 11, 12, 13. I think this doubtful but cannot explain the omissions.

  #14 Caleb Rhodes
  #15 J. F. Pegram Boarding House

East of the square was heavily developed:
  #16 Jacob Froneberger's Store
  #17 Moses Rhyne's Store, still standing
  #18 Austin Groner operated a grocery
  #19 Daniel Hoffman
  #20 Unidentified

South of the square included:
  #1 Unidentified
  #2 S. W. Love Gd.
  #3 either Amzi Ford, clerk of court, or J. D. Rankin
  #4 Daniel Hoffman's "Tan Yd"
  #5 Daniel Hoffman's Hotel, now Gaston County Museum of Art and History

West of the square was well occupied:
  #6 W. M. Holland, probably the "Holland's Store" mentioned in newspaper accounts
  #7 John Rudisell
  #8 Eli Pasour resided in Smyre-Pasour House, still standing, working as a Note Shaver
  #9 J. Beam
  #10 George Clemmer (probably for Lewis Clemmer's grocery)

Northwest of the square:
  #31 J. N. Friday
  #32, #33 S. P. Pasour "Master Blk Smith"
  #34 Mauney
  #35 Unidentified

Northeast of the square:
  #36, #37 Jail; it is unclear whether the Jail was on #37 only or both lots.
  #38 D. B. Smith
  #39 B. A. Wier
  #40 D. B. Smith

Southeast of the square:
  #21, #22 May Morris
  #23, #24 Elis. Bradley (probably for "Thomas Bordley, Saddle and Harnes Maker" from newspaper accounts)
  #25 Rich Rankin

Southwest of the square:
- #26, #27   Unidentified
- #28   Unidentified
- #29, #30   Franas Beattie

Other identified town lots:
- #41   J. G. Lewis for P. Froneberger
- #42   J. G. Lewis
- #46   Jane Holland
- #47   Andrew Long
- #49   A. Hoyle & Company Store
- #50   Jacob Froneberger or Julius Holland (?)
- #57   Jno Rudisill
- #58   Jacob Froneberger
- #59   Jno Rudisill or Wm. Rutledge (?)
- #61   S. W. Love Gd.
- #62   Samuel Jarrett
- #64   Jacob Froneberger
- #66   John G. Lewis, clerk of court
- #67   Jacob Froneberger Boarding House
- #68   Catharine Rhyne
- #82   ?Alj. Dellinger
- #83, #84, #85   Daniel Hoffman
- #91   Alex Wier

3

Gaston's Fighting Confederates

While entrepreneurs, mill owners, and iron manufacturers were accumulating profits from the war, soldiers marched into battle to defend the South and strike a blow for southern independence. Their stories, motivations, and experiences varied but also held many similarities. Gaston County's fighting Confederates, many of whom had never been far from home, departed expecting a brief and successful military victory. They communicated their unanticipated encounters with disease, camp life challenges, and deadly battlefield descriptions to captivated family and friends, who pictured the dead, wounded, and a devastated countryside.

The letters represent three of the most heralded military units from the area. Leonidas Torrence belonged to the "Gaston Guards," Company H of the 23rd North Carolina regiment, which fought at 1st Bull Run, the Peninsula Campaign, Antietam, Fredericksburg, Chancellorsville, and Gettysburg. Colonel William G. Morris, M. L. Holland, and many other county residents were members of the "Gaston Blues," Company H of the 37th Regiment, which fought at New Bern, the Seven Days Battles, 2nd Bull Run, Antietam and Harpers Ferry, Fredericksburg, Chancellorsville, and Gettysburg. James Fulton, James Wellington Linebarger, Robert Newton Wilson, Edward and George Phifer, members of Company G, H, and K of the 49th Regiment, including the "Gaston Rangers," battled at the Seven Days Campaign, 2nd Bull Run, Antietam, Fredericksburg, Wilmington, New Bern, Petersburg, Cold Harbor, and the Crater. Other letters describe events in eastern North Carolina, eastern Tennessee, South Carolina, and other locations.

The tax list identifies the soldiers' social class. Three middle-class soldiers, owning land and slaves—Lemuel Hoyle, William G. Morris, Leonidas Torrence—wrote extensively. No elite Gaston County soldiers, owning over 20 slaves, were identified, and the correspondence of the three sons of John L. Phifer, a Lincolnton cotton manufacturer, was used.

Yeomen, soldiers whose families owned land and no slaves, include A. S. Coon and his brother David and the Daniel Haynes Dellinger family. These soldiers resided in Lincoln County, and Dellinger had relatives in Gaston. James Wellington "Willy" Linebarger wrote extensively and though his young family was of Yeoman status, his father-in-law, Henry Setzer, was middle class.

Soldiers from the laboring class with no land or slaves represent a significant portion of the letters. Caleb Senter and F. S. Hanna composed many letters. Other smaller but insightful collections include those of Thomas A. Davis, J. J. Brown, Newton Sellers, and the five sons of Frederick Lineberger Dellinger of the Cherryville area.

Soldiers from Lincoln or Cleveland County were not identified by social class because of the absence of tax list information. Many Gaston soldier letters emanate from Dallas and the western area of Gaston County with few letters from more affluent eastern Gaston.

Most recruits mustered in Dallas and departed by rail from Brevard's Station, present Stanley. Rufus Carson of Co. B, 28th Regiment, described his departure thusly, "Left home on the 17th of Sept. 1862, in company with brother James Carson. Boarded the train at Old Brevard Station and landed in Richmond, Va. On the 20th of Sept."[1] Numerous young men, boys, fathers, and sons traveled the same route.

Various reasons motivated each soldier to fight. Prominent historians, James F. McPherson and Kenneth Noe, have described soldiers' motivations using a large sample of letters. Noe differentiated motives between early and later enlistees. Utilizing the research of Noe and McPherson, this project analyzed motivations including duty, honor, country, slavery, women, hatred, pay, religion, comrades, nationalism, and patriotism.[2] Noe and McPherson defined later enlistees as being after the 1862 draft, and Noe discovered only one[3] who deserted. Of the more limited survey of Gaston soldiers, four are believed to have deserted, and Gaston soldier letters add to the historical narrative with their motives for going to war.

"throw the shield of His protection around us all"

Early enlistees, William G. Morris, Lemuel Hoyle, Leonidas Torrence, George Phifer, David and A. S. Coon, and Jacob Dellinger, convey personal motivations primarily dealing with dedication to duty, Confederate patriotism, home protection, and protecting the southern way of life. Morris, Hoyle, Torrence, and Phifer owned slaves, and preserving the southern life style inherently includes preserving slavery. Hoyle, Phifer, Torrence, Dellinger, and the Coons were single men, while Morris was married with children. Of the seven early enlistees at least four occupied advanced ranks in the army.

Well-educated Lemuel Hoyle volunteered on June 20, 1861, became a lieutenant, and his letters convey both patriotic and religious fervor. He exhorted God to "throw the shield of His protection around us all and permit us again to assembly around the old homestead and joyfully commune with each other, while our now distracted country shall be liberated and basking in the sunlight of peace and prosperity."[4]

In 1863 he blamed Confederate losses on the lack of faith and moral turpitude of southerners: "I have not much hope for a termination of the war, Mother, while our people remain so proud, sinful and rebellious. We must humble ourselves before God will bless us, but instead of that, it seems like our people are growing worse and worse." In the same letter he expressed "trust that He will cover my head and spare me, as he had done in the past, … I trust that he will, for the sake of His Son, Jesus Christ, who died for guilty sinners such as I, admit me to a resting place at His right hand on high." He then implored, "Pray for me, dear Mother, that He will have mercy upon me."[5]

At home lawyer David Schenck echoed Hoyle's excuses for Confederate failure. After the Battle of Chattanooga, he opined, "The tide of Fortune has once more set heavily upon us. The wickedness of our people has brought upon us again the judgement of an offended God."[6]

As General Grant maneuvered against General Lee around Richmond in 1864, Hoyle hoped that "this fight may end the bloody drama and secure to our Country the blessing of 'Peace and Independence.'"[7] Hoyle and Schenck connected Christian beliefs with Confederate independence. When bad things happened, it was not because God was against the Confederacy, but rather, southerners failed to follow Christian precepts or lacked faith.

"I feele Like I am in the Discharge of a Dewty that Every Patriot Should be Engaged in"

William Groves Morris expressed similar opinions. On November 12, 1861, he confided the reason for his service, "I feele Like I am in the Discharge of a Dewty that Every Patriot Should be Engaged in." In early 1862 he considered resigning his position of captain and returning home following the death of his father-in-law. His explanation to his wife informs the reader of his rationale for remaining: "I Came to the Conclusion that I Could Doo My Country More Good by Stayin with the Co as they had Conferred the Honors of a unanimous Vote ... besides I doo Not believe I could Stay at home & perhaps would have to Go as a private before the war was Ended." After discussing matters of the estate, farming issues, and his appreciation for his slave Randall, he offered, "If I but Doo My Deuty to Man & God I will be spaired to Return home to EnJoy My self with you all."[8] Duty, support for country, and a strong belief in God maintained Morris in the battlefield.

Morris, like Lemuel Hoyle, inter-mingled religious and Confederate patriotic themes: "Simpley Because While Engaged in the cause of our country to Defend our rights as a people We are Sining agains the very Power that is able to Save us from the horrors of war and Misery." He rationalized, "Though we are Engaged in a Just cause in the defence of our country and rights we Must Not Expect Peace Without the proper Respect and Recognition of the divine Power.... [T]hen as Sin is the cause of this war it becomes Necessary to remove the cause," he continued, "As our Cause is Just let us Not Sin against that power. Onley that is able to Save us from the hand of our Enemeys."[9]

In a later letter, Morris sought God to "Give us strong hearts & Steady nerves that we May Defend Our Soil from thos that are So vain and Murderous as to attempt to force us to think & act as they do. God has shown himself always to Be on the Side of freedom if We but put our trust in him." He once again believed that the war continued because of "the Ways of Sin and folly" and man's failure to "Serve him only."[10] Morris believed that God was on the side of the Confederacy and, like Hoyle, believed that Confederate failures emanated not from God but because of southerners' Christian failures.

McPherson observes that Confederate motives of liberty and slavery were intermingled as most southerners understood that they fought for liberty to preserve their way of life, which included slavery. He also describes "Dewty" as a "binding moral obligation" which most men understood to protect their country, family, and home.[11]

"The Company is all anxious to get in to a battle"

Younger soldiers exhibited various motivations. Leonidas Torrence from a slave-holding family failed in his 86 letters to reveal political or emotional motives for his service. The detail with which he described battles, formations, and movements suggests that he found the adventure enticing: "The Company is all anxious to get in to a battle and say they cannot go home satisfied with out a fite." He seldom wrote about being homesick but rather discussed neighbors, relatives, and the need for food, letters, shoes, or clothing. He spent much time as a sick soldier but assured his parents often that he "has got well." He wrote, "I can draw any thing that I need if we ever get settled or Peace being made soon." He experienced the Peninsular Campaign, Chancellorsville, Antietam, and died at Gettysburg.[12]

The limited letters of David A. and brother, Adolphus S. Coon of Lincoln County also fail to reveal their service motivation. David's advance in rank to Sergeant, and his exploits at Pickett's Charge suggests he was a fearless soldier with a youthful desire for adventure.

On October 18, 1861, Jacob Dellinger, an early enlistee from the Frederick Lineberger Dellinger family, encouraged "all the young men will come out with brave hearts" to fight for "Southern independence."[13] Other early enlistees supported Confederate service as an honorable duty.

J. J. Brown enlisted July 4, 1862, after the draft had been instituted. "I want you to send Jacob Heafner word," he wrote to his wife, "to not stay there at home and be lafted at for being a coward for him to come out to the army and see something for I have seen more tha I ever thought I would."[14] For Brown, duty and honor motivated his service. McPherson referred to such motivation as for "manhood."[15]

The Phifer brothers were young men from one of the most elite families in Lincolnton, as their father, John F. Phifer, operated a cotton manufacturing operation. While Phifer considered himself a Unionist, all three of his sons fought for the Confederacy. Their letters are excellent examples of how the war split families along political lines.

His eldest son, George L., volunteered on May 8, 1861, as a 20-year-old bugler for the 1st NC Artillery division. Later on April 26, 1862, he transferred to the 49th Regiment, Company K, where he was elected 1st Lt. by December 20.[16] None of George Phifer's letters have been located, and he was the only Phifer son to survive the war.

An insight into George's Confederate support is suggested in a letter from youngest brother Edward to his mother. Apparently his father had offered to hire a substitute for George. "George says you need not try to get him a substitute for he would not have him," Edward wrote.[17]

Younger brothers Edward and William L. enlisted as the conscription law took effect. Both were between age 17 and 19 and could have easily avoided soldiering.[18] No letters from their father exist among the 106 Phifer Letters in the collection at the University of North Carolina at Chapel Hill. The offer by the elder Phifer to purchase a substitute, his Unionist tendencies, and his ability to acquire exemptions for all three sons suggests they strongly supported the Confederate cause. George and Edward both became officers almost immediately, most likely because of their social status.

The absence of political, motivational, or inspirational discussions in the Phifer letters suggests that the sons refused to enter discussions which might facilitate their father's displeasure. On November 1, 1863, Edward wrote his mother that George planned to write "Pa ... a letter of 3 or 4 sheets as soon as he gets back from Raleigh but he does not expect to get an answer from him. I do not mention him in any letter but I always mean him as much as any other one I say things to you and at the same time mean it for him." While the father and sons may have held philosophical differences, the sons sought recognition and support from their father. In June 1864 when George suffered a wound and was hospitalized, "Mr. Fullendwider" and his father retrieved George from the hospital, whose wound was "very painful." They brought him home where he convalesced during the remainder of the war. Later in June when Edward suffered a wound which would eventually kill him, he requested that his father come "to him immediately" as he was "quite homesick … very patient and prudent, the idea of being cut off from home." Nurse Patterson explained that "his Father not able to get to him has annoyed him a little."[19] The complicated allegiances within the Phifer family suggest that the sons supported the cause and went to great lengths to moderate their views with their father.

The disparities of opinion between father Phifer and sons expose a common, but often ignored, differing of opinions among many families during the war.

"in defense of my Country, friends, Father, Mother, Sisters, & brothers"

Other letters reveal conflicting motivations. The letters of the Daniel Haynes Dellinger family expose the opinions for yeomen and laborers. On March 9, 1862, young P. Frank Dellinger volunteered prior to conscription, and he proudly described drilling and shooting positions he had learned. On April 10, 1863, he wrote that he had been involved in a battle where "we killed a grate many of the trifling Scamps and some of their best officers."[20] Frank Dellinger's letters convey a resignation to fight and to experience adventure.

Other family members hoped for peace. On March 21, 1863, Henry Huss wrote his "uncle" D. H. Dellinger and family about the "hard times" and "fiten going one close heare." He commented on the heavy losses and hoped for "Peace on Some terms or another i don't Mutch care how so they Make Peace." From near Charleston Robert F. Peck wrote about the shelling of Fort Sumter and his hopes that "the war will end this spring." But he offered, "We will never give it up until we are free and our own independence is gained." On September 5, 1864, "Cousin" Thomas Howser wrote Daniel from Petersburg. He had received a slight leg wound but offered to "go meet [the enemy] and stand in defence of our Glorious Cause" because "God had been my Shield and gide and has brought me out Safe." However, Howser was "getting Very tired of this Cruel war but I am still willing to Stand in defense of my Country, friends, Father, Mother, Sisters, & brothers but I fear all will be in ruin, if so I can say I have done my duty." By February 18, 1864, Daniel Haynes Dellinger had been conscripted into the Senior Reserves.[21] He complained little about his fate in his letters home but rather communicated camp circumstances and farming operational needs. Various family members expressed overall support for the Confederate effort similar to Lemuel Hoyle and William Morris, defending their homes, way of life, and duty.

James Wellington Linebarger, later enlistee who achieved the rank of lieutenant, did not specifically communicate his motivation in his letters to his wife. His dedication to battle and company detail, to doing his duty, and to "defend our country" suggests that he held similar views with Hoyle and Morris. His adverse opinions of deserters also convey Confederate patriotism.[22]

Later enlistees of the Frederick Lineberger Dellinger family contrasted their military service with others who were reluctant to go. Relative, W. B. Brown happily communicated that "I am glad to hear that money & hoke carpiner have to come to the war they maid thair brages so big that they wasent a coming,"[23] suggesting support for both duty and manhood.

Other later enlistees of yeomen and laborer status exhibited economic motivations for service. The letters of Caleb Senter and Thomas Davis confirm that they received the $50 bounty to join prior to conscription, and 19-year-old Rufus W. Carson also received the bounty.[24] Farm laborers, especially those in debt found the bounty especially appealing.

Senter volunteered to secure a bounty prior to mandatory conscription, but his letters reveal that he and his wife never fully endorsed the conflict. "[P]ore Solgers and Sogers wives must Be under the rich," Senter noted, as he expressed social and economic frustration. His wife complained about financial opportunism at home: "this is an unjts war any persome can get off By coaling for a Big man an some for cutting wod for the cars an som for haling."[25]

Laborer Thomas Allen Davis offered religious and patriotic images more similar to Hoyle and Morris after receiving his bounty: "I still look forward with a

William Groves Morris, Company H of the 37th North Carolina Regiment the "Gaston Blues," in his Confederate uniform. Morris' letters convey deep religious beliefs, support for the Confederacy, and military leadership and bravery (courtesy Daniel Wilson of Dallas, NC).

joybul hart when God will take our cause in his own hands turn the enmys fase homeward when we will be set at liberty what a joyful time it would be." On August 17, 1863, he remarked, "I would much Rather be at home with you but you all know I cant do that at this time without I do like a grate many is doing Run a way and com [home] and I don't think I will do that yet."[26] He chose duty and honor after his financial reward for volunteering.

"you cannot get off"

Franklin S. Hanna and others waited for the draft to force their service. Landless and from a Unionist family, he sought an exemption as early as October 1862. His father offered that "you cannot get off the mechanic must follow his trade" and that "you cannot get off but you must content your self and do the best you can." But Hanna persisted. He encouraged his wife to secure a petition and attempted to "[s]ee the governor." His efforts failed. He considered the war as an opportunity for "Speculation," and that wealthy merchants and investors would make significant profits. He opposed the Tithing Law and speculated that if the Confederate authorities take "anything that their Familys have made that they are going Home that they come to the Army to fight for their Homes and firesides or that is what they was told and if they cannot do it here they will at Home." They would "as Soon fight to put down Sutch Law as to fight the yankies."[27] Hanna compared the Tithing Tax as similarly arbitrary as the causes of the war and like the Senter family viewed wealthy "Speculation" as the culprit for all ills.

Newton Sellers, an August 16, 1862, newly-married conscript, by 1864 wished "this war would close for I think all the men is Sick of it" and "wount fight as hard as the[y] have don." He predicted, "this Summer will end this war I think the we hain got the men to fight much longer. Old Lee haint got more than forthy five thousand men now." His relative Eli Sellers had been drafted, and he wanted to know how "Eli come out at Ralleigh or whether his mother got him of[f] or not." Newton Sellers eventually deserted and hoped that relatives could avoid military service.[28]

Larkin Thornburg, a seventeen-year-old draftee from a laboring class family, avoided service by hiding out with others. When caught by the "Militia," they forced his enlistment on September 20, 1864. He reminisced later in life that he refused service and deserted because he "followed the dictates of [his] conscience," contending that "slavery as being founded upon wrong principles … was the real cause of the war." He observed "many instances of injustice and cruelty practiced by hard-hearted masters toward their helpless slaves," that "the poor man was fighting that the rich man might keep his slaves," and that slavery "separated forever" husbands, wives, and children.[29]

The Gaston collection of letters exposes some significant differences in motivation between the early and later enlistees. Slaveholding families and early enlistees combined southern independence with Christian motives, adding liberty and status quo preservation as fighting ideals. They acquired higher ranks, and supported their "Dewty," honor and "manhood." These motives are consistent with McPherson's observations. This study's research differs with Kenneth Noe's research, which suggests that later enlistee's motivations varied little from earlier soldiers. Non-slaveholding Gaston area soldiers, enlisting after conscription, appeared less likely to support independence, dedication to duty, or defense of home and hearth. Four are documented deserters. Financial, social, and political differences caused them to view the war very differently.[30] Early enlistees also differed from later soldiers by being younger and unmarried.

All enlisted Confederates encountered similar camp and battle conditions, and their stories begin with sickness.

"confined to My bed for a week"

Upon arrival at camp, disease gripped most recruits. Being from isolated farming communities, many young men had avoided childhood diseases. Early in the war, illnesses, epidemics, wounds, and injuries placed many Gaston soldiers in the hospital, sending some home on furlough.

The poor medical conditions of the day included the scarcity of doctors with untrained young ladies, performing nursing duties. The Confederacy created a hospital system, which included major hospitals and Wayside hospitals along the railroads which offered limited care and prepared men to go home.

By January 7, 1862, about two months after he enlisted, William G. Morris reported about thirty men were "on the Sick Roll" with measles, pneumonia, and yellow jaundice being the main culprits. By January 27 he complained of being sick, "confined to My bed for a week."[31]

Another early volunteer, Lemuel Hoyle whose mother resided near the Cleveland-Gaston County line, reported immediate sickness in camp. On July 29, 1861, Hoyle informed his mother of "a great deal of sickness in our Regiment now" and suggested that "stagnant water" may have been part of the cause. By August he was sick with "the mumps on both sides" but had recovered by September. His mother's hope that sickness would allow Hoyle to come home proved to be false. By October 23 he reported that "Mr. Jonas Rudisill died the 16th Inst. of typhoid fever."[32]

By October 1863 Hoyle was in Lincolnton on furlough because of diarrhea and dysentery, of which he had suffered for several weeks.[33] In May and June of 1864, fighting around Richmond resulted in a "very slight wound in the arm" and time in the hospital. He again suffered from diarrhea and dysentery and was in the hospital from June through August. Hoyle also suffered from "headache and pain in my breast."[34]

On January 9, 1865, Hoyle requested a "leave of absence," which was approved "from Genl Lee," and he traveled to Lincolnton. By March he left "good old Lincolnton" to rejoin his unit. By the time he reached Charlotte, he was sick again. He traveled to Greensboro in an "ugly old car that had no stove in it."[35]

Leonidas Torrence had enlisted by July 1861 and immediately informed his parents that many in camp had contracted the measles. By August 31 he also had the measles. On September 9 Torrence had still "not gained [his] strength." Many soldiers were in the hospitals with mumps, measles, and "Typoid fever." On October 30 Torrence reported that he was "very low with typhoid Pneumonia" and was "able to walk a little now and improving verry fast." By November he informed his mother that his health was improving. But by March 4, 1862, camp life, snowy weather, and exposure contributed to further sickness. He was "verry sick since I wrote to you." First he took "Pneumonia" and as "[he] was getting better of it [he] took Typhoid Fever." He reported that others were also sick.[36]

Later enlistees experienced the same childhood diseases. By May 3, 1862, a sick Caleb Senter opined that "the water" and "measles" contributed to the "Sickness in Camps." On October 23 he reported having "a very hard spell of feaver" and been sick "about five weeks and I have been in the hospitle about 3 three weeks." Cleben Nance wrote Senter's letter, as he was too sick to write. On November 14 Senter penned a letter indicating that he was "geting Sum Beter" but was still in the hospital. He made slow progress: "i Can Begin to Set up a litle and walk a few Steps i have a good stomacke to eate and get plenty of Coffee and tee and mush and milk." By December 1, 1862, he reported that he is "well" and has "Bin looking for a leter." Apparently still in the hospital he related that "my ear has Bin running ... for Six weeks and Still runs yet" and that he had smallpox. While wishing to go home, he hoped to remain in the hospital before returning to the "reigment." On December 31 hospitalized Senter reported that "very near well nothing hirts me ondly the thoughts of staying hear three weeks longer the small pox is Broke oute a gain." Senter remained in the hospital through February 3, 1863, and had returned to his "reigment" in "good health" by February 9.[37]

Continued fighting, physical exertion, and difficult conditions precipitated another minor illness near the end of 1863. On December 3, 1863, Senter reported that "i am not well this morning i am Broke down." By December 18 he reported feeling better. On the first day of January 1864, Senter wrote that his health had improved even though "I have the hart Burn wors than Sum old Breeding woman."[38]

The extended family and friends of Daniel Haynes Dellinger also suffered. Son, P. Frank Dellinger wrote his first extant letter describing sickness and measles in camp. By June 8, 1862, he reported that he had contracted the mumps, and on June 22 he complained that his teeth were "roting out and they ache me very much." By September 15 his unit had moved to Wilmington, North Carolina where a serious yellow fever epidemic raged. It caused quarantines and stopped the mail and rail deliveries. Lt. Lemuel Hoyle also observed the epidemic in Wilmington, which claimed the life of another soldier in his unit, Joseph Carpenter.[39]

"Janders an now i have the mumps"

Other Dellinger family members also suffered. Nephew, John Houser, reported "the chills," "the fever," and "the Mumps." Dellinger's son-in-law, George Rhyne, reported he had "Janders an now i have the mumps." On January 28, 1863, P. F. Dellinger wrote his sister Mariann that he perceived that her husband was at the "Pointe of Deth."[40] On January 23, 1863, Rhyne died in the Richmond Hospital "No 3" of pneumonia. By May 25, estate administrator David Huss collected Rhyne's belongings.[41]

Jacob Jackson Brown, residing near the Gaston-Lincoln County line, was a thirty-year-old newly married man with children. On August 22, 1862, he reported that he "had the feaver and chills." A few days later he reported "very much sickness in Camp now with mumps and chills." On Christmas day he communicated that the "health of our Regiment is very bad now they is sum one or nother dying out of hit every day or too.... Jonas Ryne ... is very low." On January 13, 1863, Brown reported he had "a sympton of the chills." Unfortunately he would not recover. On April 10, 1863, Lt. R. W. Carpenter [probably P. W.] wrote "Mrs. Christina Brown" that her husband "is certainly dead." He died in Lynchburg "of Pneumonia" with "dollars in cash & one suit of clothes ... 3 month & 7 days due him & also some clothing money in all about 50 dollars or near that." He empathized, "he is certainly dead & can but simpathize with you God be thy protector and thy help in time of need. He has paid a debt that we must all pay sooner or latter and we oought all to prepare for it." Carpenter observed, "You[r] husband made a good soldier & fought well in the fight at this place. He died an honorable death. May God by they shield & help in time of need."[42]

On December 8, 1862, Lawson Carpenter wrote his father from Lynchburg, Virginia, where he was in the hospital. He was "very sick with pneaumonia fever," "was taken sick about 10 days ago," and subsequently sent to the hospital.[43] On July 2, 1863, Mary E. Sellers wrote her mother that husband Newton was "weak yet" and "haint ben out of the bed" with a "feaver." She apparently visited him in the hospital in Charlotte. In April 1864 Newton reported "lots of Sickness." He also observed that some men gathered "Sallets," ate them and were "found both ded in their beds" the next morning. Diarrhea and dysentery remained one of the most dreaded illnesses, for which David Eddleman suffered as a prisoner at Fort Delaware after his capture at Pickett's Charge.[44]

"cases of momps and meazels"

Only about two months after James Wellington "Willie" Linebarger enlisted, he reported "cases of momps and meazels" in his company and that "the helth of our Company is bad." By July 4, 1862, he had "command of the Company as the rest are all sick and I hope how soon they may get well," but by the end of the month he was "not able to write ... lying in a private house." He was "improveing but it is very slowly," and W. I. Stowe conveyed to Willie's wife that his condition was not considered "dangerous at all." On November 11 Linebarger reported that he was "tolerable well except Jaundice" and that others were "very low with tifoied fever." His "lite" case of jaundice did not confine him "nary day." Sickness again visited Linebarger's company in April 1863, as many had "a hard spell of meazeles and bilious fever they are about forty five in the Company able for duty." On January 3, 1864, Linebarger described "too more cases of small pox in the regiment last week if they keep brakeing out I would be a fraid to come home." By February he reported "some colds & a fiew cases Phneumonia."[45]

On May 25, 1864, Mary Linebarger received the dreaded letter from Chaplain "P. Nicholson," "[Y]our son was very badly wounded the 14th of the present month." "He was brought to this Hospital & seemed to be doing tolerably well until yesterday. He grew worse gradually & breathed his last this morning between twelve & one oclock. He expressed himself as reddy for the great change awaiting him." Nicholson continued, "He did not seem to suffer much.... I saw him decently buried in Hollywood Cemetery." He then conveyed "the last things he said to me": Linebarger asked Nicholson to write to his mother "& tell her that he wanted his sister to have corn as she wished it" in a previous letter. Nicholson further commented, "Your son was a man of excellent character as far as I knew him." B. S. Gaither informed Linebarger's father-in-law, Henry Setzer that he had been "shot through the breast with a large minie ball passing clear through him & coming out at his back." Gaither further reported that Dr. Warren reported that "the wound was mortal." The "poor fellow," Gaither observed, "he had to give up his life for his country."[46] W. D. Glenn attended Linebarger's funeral at "H. Setzers"; the weather was so cold that the ice was "4 inches thick on mill ponds," and Glenn "walked over Decks pond."[47]

"some sort of blindness"

The story of Thomas Allen Davis of Cleveland County conveys numerous illnesses and an unfortunate demise. Though unable to read and write, his brother-in-law William R. Barnet composed letters for him. On August 16, 1862, he reported that "several of our boys got the measles" and that he was "15 pounds heavier than I ever was." On October 16 Davis reported that his health had been "very bad off." By the 19th he was in the hospital with "Bilious fevar." On October 24 Davis remained "very bad off" with not "much stomack to eat anything" and "cant sit up but very little." On October 27 "Wm R Barnet" informed his sister that Thomas Davis "is very low" and that "he said that he hadnt long to stay in this worl." By November 30 Davis was at home on sick furlough. By February 27, 1863, Davis had returned to his unit, but by March 7 he complained of a "very bad cold cence I have ben hear."[48]

On June 5, 1863, Davis first informed his wife that "once every month on the full moon I have some sort of blindness which last me some hour or hour and a half it takes Place between sun down and dark." He continued, "a kind of a mist comes over them which causes me not to see much." On July 3 he informed his wife from near Richmond that his eyesight continued to deteriorate, "I cant Sea but very litel after nite nor I dont think that I can Se quite as good from an ouer by Sun in the evening." By July 31 he reported that he "cant See any after night but my eyes dont hurt much." On August 6 he reported his "eyes is no better I cant see any after night a tall." He also reported that his Cleveland County friend, W. C. Wolfe, was "at the hospital." On August 27 he complained that he had "not seen a star in a month" and that he also had a "breaking out over me" which caused him to itch.[49]

It is unclear what Davis's malady was, and improvement occurred over time and apparently without doctor's interventions. On September 23, 1863, he informed his wife that he was "the wellest and…. Stouest [stoutest] I have ben cense I was sick." On November 2 he reported that "My eyes has got so that I can Se to get about a rite smart of a nite."[50] No more letters have survived but Davis's physical condition again deteriorated. Rainy weather, exposure, and unsanitary conditions in the trenches around Petersburg and Richmond contributed to his developing dysentery and chronic diarrhea. On August 27, 1864, Davis received a forty day furlough from Winder Hospital and boarded a train for home. Taken off the train the next day because of his weakened condition, he died at Seabrook Hospital. Margaret traveled to Richmond to bring her sick husband home. Unfortunately she learned that he had died but did not discover his burial location. Later, on November 5, 1864, Elizabeth McNeely, a nurse at the hospital, gave Margaret the final account of her husband's life. She wrote at "the request of your husband … while he lay sick at the hospital." Davis "appeared resigned to the will of the Lord … would rather be with his dear wife and children when he died." She recalled, "He said if it was the Lord's will he was willing to die there or between there and home."[51]

Frederick Lineberger Dellinger, who resided near present Cherryville, sent five sons to war. On July 9, 1861, from Yorktown, Virginia Peter Dellinger wrote his "Uncle" that Jacob has been "very sick" with the measles. On October 18 Jacob Dellinger wrote his father from York County, Virginia that "Peter is feeling very low" with typhoid fever as "he don't know anybody scarcely" from his hospital bed. On April 14, 1864, F. W. Dellinger wrote his sister, Margaret Brown, from Virginia informing her that he was "not well at this time." He noted that an apparent relative, Nancy, has the "hooping Cough" and that he expected her husband to end his desertion and return to duty "about the time the Summer campaighn is over."[52]

Soldiers were not the only ones sick. Civilians on the home front also suffered from disease. On May 5, 1862, B. F. Withers of Lincoln County wrote his business associate, "J. F. Goodson Esq.," that there was "sickness in the neighborhood … measles and mumps, fevers flux &c. &c. a number of deaths." He also reported that "Col. W. P. Bynum is very ill in Charlotte." In Gaston's Duhart's District James H. Hanna informed his relative, F. S. Hanna, that there was a "good deal of Sickness in the neighborhood" and provided details of deaths and illnesses. Elizabeth Linebarger informed her husband that "here pople are talken of vaxination about here you be vaxinated it would be better to vaxinate in time they are so mutch sickness and deathe."[53]

"a derangement of the Bowels"

Franklin S. Hanna's enlistment included measles and dysentery. On September 15, 1862, he noted "very mutch Sickness" with "three hundred in the Hospital at Raleigh." On October 30 M. E. Hanna wrote her brother, saying she was "Sorry to hear that you had Been sick." On November 5 his wife Caroline "was glad to hear from you and that you was geting better of the measles." On November 19 she wrote that neighbor "L. M. Holland is in the Hospital and very poorly and wrote his letter a lying on his back." On December 7, 1862, Caroline Hanna sent a letter in collaboration with others to her husband. She worried because she had "not received a letter ... for three weeks" but heard that he was back in the hospital. Other relatives also suffered. "Brother Sam" was infected with "the mumps," and "Brother Thomas [was] sick and in the Hospital at Richmond." On December 14 F. S. Hanna wrote his wife from Fairground Hospital in Wake County, North Carolina, reporting that he was "improving I feel pretty well but I Still have the cough." He also noted that "B G Bradley had the Mumps the last I heard from him." Apparently in December and early January Hanna received a sick furlough and reported back to duty on January 25, 1863.[54]

F. S. Hanna would not remain healthy long. After an unexplained gap in letters, on May 2, 1863, Hanna wrote from Wilmington that he had "a derangement of the Bowels that is common among the men here at present." Food was "pretty Slim and rough," getting "fourth rations of meat ... no Flour Corn Meal all the time and it bran ... it is about Sutch meal as we would feed the Cows on in old Gaston." On May 10 Hanna reported that he had been "Sick for the last week." Gaston acquaintance and soldier "M. L. Holland is in Wilmington a nurse at the way Side Hospital ... [Hanna] had not had any word from home Since he left their." Hanna's bout with diarrhea was not over. On September 9 Confederate records list Hanna in the Hospital in Wilmington suffering from "Diarrhea." On October 2 he received a "Furlough for 30 days."[55] He survived but never returned to service.

"he is dangerously ill"

The Phifer brothers' tragic story exposes the uncertainty of life and death. George Phifer enlisted in 1861 and his younger brothers, William L. and Edward, volunteered the next year. While George and Edward served in Virginia in the same unit, William L. joined the cavalry and served in Tennessee. The letters exchanged between William L. and Edward X. with their mother demonstrates the catharsis of a mother attempting to protect her sons from illness and battle wounds.

William L. regretted his decision to go west: "I wish I was w/Ed and George for I know they have better time then we have." William served in the same unit with Eben Childs, son of L. D. Childs another Lincolnton cotton manufacturer. Sometime prior to October 4, 1863, he and Eben Childs lost their lives. William's mother, Mrs. E. C. Phifer, received a letter from Annie Peck dated October 4, 1863, stating that "Cousin John Hoke" came through the area with the bodies of Eben Childs and "your dear boy Willie." Hoke "had Willie buried in the ? Methodist graveyoard" in "Ringold, Ga.," because he "could not obtain charcoal and without that they will not carry them on the railroad." "Cousin John has some of Willie's hair that a Mr. Connelly cut off soon after he died and a ring that he had on his finger," she continued, "someone had taken his money and other things from him."[56]

"Sympathizing Niece M. E. Lusk" of Hoylesville in Gaston County offered "Aunt Bettie" her "greatest sympathy," as "losing a precious child must be a severe trial at anytime, but to have them close their eyes in death in a distant land with no kind friend to smoth their brow, or receive their expiring words, is truly hard to endure." Lusk assured the grieving mother that he was called "from this world of sinfulness" and would venture to a "land beyond this vale of tears, where friends will be reunited, and sorrow cometh not again." With all the "brave soldier boys spirit," he was "now free from all cares, singing praises to the Lamb that taketh away the sins of all, and when time is no more with those who yet remain, may their spirits be ofted away and dwell once again with sainted Willie on high." Frances Adams reported to "My Dear Cousin," probably Edward, that John Hoke had arrived Saturday with "Willie's hair and a ring that he wore," which Hoke gave to Willie's mother. She appeared "quite well and seems quite cheerful," and a number of guests visited the Phifer home.[57] No evidence of Mrs. Phifer's thoughts on the loss of her son has been located, but her trials were not over as two sons remained in the army.

On July 7, 1862, Edward Phifer wrote his mother that he was sick with the "fever" and a doctor attended to him. While brother George left no letters, his physical condition became a concern of Edward, who shared the same company. In January 1864, Ed Phifer wrote his mother that George had "a painful boil." George's condition was so serious that he received a furlough in February. While in Lincolnton, George went to Morganton but was "quite lame," "suffering a great deal with his leg and some new boils." By May George had rejoined his company but was "quite unwell." By the end of the month he was in the hospital again. By June George was at home convalescing from a head wound. "George and Mrs. Wyche [his nurse] arrived here yesterday," Mrs. Phifer confided, "George is doing well and seems in fine spirits and receives great sympathy—oh! If I only had you here too, I would feel so grateful to the Giver of all good." His mother was "thankful" he was "not killed on the battlefield." In a later letter she conveyed her concerns to Edward: "George is doing finely, that is, his wound is doing well, but he has a bad cold." He "was wounded on the 17th near Petersburg and came home about a week since, a flesh wound in the head he is very bad this morning, delirious and I feel will die."[58]

Soon after receiving news about George, Edward received a wound in his right shoulder in fighting around Petersburg. Julia A. Patterson, a hospital nurse, detailed Edward's wounds and condition in a series of letters. On June 24, 1864, Patterson conveyed a "rather more favorable report of the Lt's condition, … less feverish." He wanted his father to come; she opined, "I think if he could only see his father he would improve very rapidly." He had "some pain in his stomach," received "Morphine which relieved him promptly," and was "comfortable but drowsy." On June 28 she reported that "your son is improving astonishingly in the last two days, we have been very anxious about him, but consider him now fairly out of danger, he has been entirely free from fever for two days past has a very good appetite." Two days later, she reported that he was not "so well this morning" and anticipated a move to Richmond since "the shells have been falling in such close proximity to the Hospitals." Mrs. Phifer had lost son William L., and now faced two wounded sons, "thanks to a merciful Providence, … you are improving," she wrote, "we regret exceedingly to hear you are in danger of the shells, but hope & pray you may have been preserved from all harm. Your father would have gone on for you, but asked Robert Fulenwider to go, he left about a week since and is I hope with you and will bring you home."[59]

On July 11, 1864, Julia Patterson wrote "My Dear Mrs. Phifer … no improvement since I last wrote on the contrary his symptoms for the last week have been decidedly discouraging." He had little appetite, "his cough too is becoming rather more troublesome." She conveyed that the "Dr. told me he was out of danger until it was found necessary to remove the patients from town, I think the excitement more than the removal caused him to relapse, he is in a tent in a very pleasant grove, and I think its possible it is better for him to be there, than in a building as he requires all the air he can get." She encouraged "his Father and yourself" to come visit him. On July 15, Julia Patterson wrote Mrs. Phifer that "Dr. Smith ... informed me that he considers the Lt. very much better, but I have just received a note from Mr. Fullenwider in which he requests that I shall inform you that he is not better, indeed ... he is dangerously ill." He encouraged "Mr. Phifer and yourself should come as soon as you receive this." Upon Edward's initial wound he expressed to Patterson "his perfect resignation to the will of God."[60] Edward did not survive his wounds. The Phifers lost two sons with another wounded, certainly a parent's nightmare. The emotional roller-coaster ride from Julia Patterson certainly took a toll on the Phifers in Lincolnton.

Camp conditions also impacted the young Gaston County soldiers from living conditions, food to eat, and the scarcity of items. They wrote home to discuss comforts and distresses.

"Bilt good little house a Boute the sise of our Shantee ... [with] good Chimney"

Feeding and sheltering the soldiers affected fighting morale. Shelters depended upon battle circumstances, and soldiers had to purchase their own rations. Caleb Senter initially described living in tents, which he had been "left to garde." By September 12, 1862, he resided in "a little house" with other local persons. But a few weeks later, he no longer used his house and had "no tents." On January 1, 1864, Senter and his comrades "Bilt good little house a Boute the sise of our Shantee ... [with] good Chimney ... we sleep warm."[61] In late 1862 Lt. Lemuel Hoyle reported favorable camp conditions: "good bunks to sleep on, and snug little chimneys made of pine poles, daubed with mud and tipped with flour barrels. They make the tents quite warm. I have a cozy little fire burning in mine which reminds me much of home." Subsequently camp conditions near Goldsboro were less favorable with no tents, cooking utensils, or other necessities.[62] Similarly on May 5, 1862, William G. Morris informed his wife that he had not slept in a tent but under the stars for 3 nights "since I left home."[63]

As winter 1863 approached, Hoyle and his company constructed winter huts and were "getting very short rations for several days." He reported to his mother that the "day before Christmas, we got ½ lb. of pickled beef, or 'spiked mule,' as the boys call it, to the man, Christmas day, ¼ lb., and yesterday, no meat at all." The year 1864 brought less food than Christmas day, "some good light bread and some genuine coffee with sugar in it." He reported more bread, but "meat rations are quite light, occasionally a little coffee and sugar, and yesterday and today, a little lard in lieu of meat." Cold weather and snow burdened the troops in Virginia. Visiting relatives and a box of food, butter and sausage, molasses, cheese, fruit, cakes made the declining amount and quality of food rations more tolerable. The end of March brought a fourteen inch snowstorm in Virginia, of which the soldiers amused themselves in a huge snowball fight.[64]

In early 1863, Leonidas Torrence bragged about "a nice little Cabbin to stay in. Our rations are rather scanty but we buy a little of one thing and another." By April, changing locations, he wrote his sister that he was doing well in his "little Collier hut. It is a verry fine House made of Pine Cedar and Poplar poles. It is covered with Pine and Cedar limbs and with sticks and mud. We have verry nice Mahogony Bed steads made of Pine poles and … other fine articles."[65] On January 11, 1864, Edney Hoover informed his wife from Taylorsville, Virginia that it was "mity cold wether here the ground is white with snow." On April 19, 1864, Hoover reported that he had "not drawd no meat for four days" and the men "went out and kild a beef and too geese and then they had plenty to eat."[66]

"we have a pretty confederacy cant Shooe the men"

One of the greatest difficulties southerners encountered was the scarcity of shoes for soldiers and civilians. On August 31, 1862, Frank Dellinger thanked his family for a pair of pants, a pair of slips, and a shirt, which made him "well off with cloths." Yet he needed shoes or "we will be barefooted." As winter approached, he informed his uncle that "we al Moste Froze For None of us Has got no over Coates and Some has got no Shooses."[67]

On March 3, 1864, Newton Sellers "would a rot before now but [the army had] ben on a march." They marched through the rain, sleet, and snow and mud "up to the Shoo mouth." He stated that "about the tenth part of the men was bare footed" as they marched through the snow and mud. "[W]e have a pretty confederacy cant Shooe the men," he exclaimed.[68]

"Willie" Linebarger summarized camp conditions in a number of letters home, when he spoke of "some tents" and having "no haversack," to put his "provision in." By November 1862 he survived "this march [of] four days and it rained on us all the time." Previously "it snoed too days" and "it was tolerable cold wading the rivers and creeks." In May 1863 he "walked twenty four miles" to "ketch" up with his regiment. He "was so tired that [he] could not rite." On August 3, 1863, Linebarger "marched fifteen miles three & half hours that night." In February 1864 the army "had to wade water and mud nee deep for several miles." Eastern North Carolina did not suit Linebarger, since on April 2 he "had to wade water waist deep it was cold travling while in the water and it seems like it raines all the time in this country." On May 4, 1864, he complained after walking "five miles since dark" and "it is bed time but I have no bed to go to." He recalled having "bin marching six days and marched from eighteen to twenty five miles a day."[69]

Lemuel Hoyle described marching on roads in October 1862, which "were awful beyond description: we had literally to wade there through water and bypass swampy mud." On February 20, 1863, Caleb Senter complained that his "feete and leags is sweeld" because of the "MarChing" with great pain.[70] Snow also impacted the young soldiers. On January 26, 1863, William G. Morris reported a "heavy Snow a fiew Days ago," twelve inches deep. Mud also presented a problem for transportation. On March 20, 1863, Morris reported rain, snow and sleet every few days and a six inch snow. On January 18, 1862, Leonidas Torrence reported "a good deal of Snow here this winter. It is raining to day." On April 12, 1863, Torrence wrote that it had once again "commenced Snowing about 8 O clock the nigh[t] we came here." The "wind blew verry hard all night and it was verry cold." On May 7, 1863, he wrote his mother from near Fredericksburg that he had "sore Feet caused by hard marching."[71]

"Preaching Nearley Every day in camp considerable revivals"

Most soldiers expressed strong Christian faith. They often attended prayer or camp services and communicated Christian themes. William G. Morris found solace that Colonel Lee of Mecklenburg County was a strong man of God and conducted nightly prayer meetings. The first of April 1863, Morris reported, was proclaimed a day of "fasting & preyor." He hoped that "a fervent preyor will be offered to God in Behalf of our distracted & polluted Nation" so that "the ritious be united both North & South in asking God to cause all Men and women in America to ask themselves the question am I Guilty of the Sins that are apon us as a Nation." He emphasized, "[t]his war depends on the power of God to Save a Sinfull people" noting that man depends upon "flech and power" but God "will Not use his power in Behalf of a people that ere Land is already Drenched with the Blood of thousands." He closed his letter with "May our hearts be Cleansed from all sin and Guilt."⁷²

Morris enjoyed "Preaching Nearley Every day in camp considerable revivals attend the Meetings." While he reported soldiers were "More Interested in the Salvation of there Souls," "Our officers are Generally very wicked, Moore so Since Coln Lee was Killed."⁷³ 1863 brought many Confederate revivals.

In January 1863 near Wilmington, Wash Dellinger described "a two day meeting here, yesterday and today. The church is in twenty steps of our camp. It is a Baptist Church and the ol' brother preached a first sermon and there was a large congregation."⁷⁴

Some soldiers preferred specific denominational services. George Rhyne wrote his father-in-law, reporting nightly "Prare meetings." Being a good Lutheran he was pleased that Rev. P. C. Henkel was in camp. On November 5, 1864, Daniel Dellinger wrote his wife that he was pleased that Lutheran "old man Goodman" came to the Salisbury prison and "preached as good a sermon for us as I ever heard." A few days later he enjoyed a Baptist preacher. Lemuel Hoyle enjoyed a "Methodist sermon," which he described as a "good, practical sermon."⁷⁵

"a ray of hope sprung up in my bosom"

Lt. Hoyle was very pleased that the regiment had two chaplains, a Presbyterian and a Methodist, and that he had been attending services in the "very large log chapel." After fighting around Richmond, Hoyle implored God to help the Confederate cause: "I trust God will enable us to foil all [Grant's] attempts and defeat his wicked designs." He asked God to "cause discord and confusion in the councils of the enemy" and that God would "give us the victory." Hoyle felt "a ray of hope sprung up in my bosom" at an October 1864 camp meeting.⁷⁶

Staunch Lutheran James Wellington Linebarger, whose family attended Philadelphia Lutheran Church north of Dallas, conveyed a deep religious commitment. On May 17, 1862, he expressed pleasure at attending "preaching last sunday for the first in the 49 our chaplin has been unwell but he has prayer every night know." But he wished to be at his home church with his wife, "I would like to be ther with you to go to church tomorrow.... But my heart is with you and I hope if you go to church you will hears some for me as I cant be there I can hear one sermon a week or two." Lutheran "hinkle was down [in Goldsboro] … and gave us a good sermon." Marching, and the Battles of Antietam and Fredericksburg occupied his time, as he expressed to his wife: "I would a liked to been at home to takin it with you and to went to church for I havent herd but one sermon since I left there." He did not expect services as "we have no chaplin." For six months Linebarger failed to mention religion in his letters. On July 26, 1863, he reported having "too sermons preached today Rev. P. Nicolson he is our Chplin he is a babtist," and in his Lutheran perspective, "they be some diped to morrow." On August 28 he reported "some preaching too" and that "Mr Fosit is holding a meting in the fifty six rgiment but we dont have such meetings as Cansler has in old Gaston." Religious revivals of 1863 impacted Linebarger and others. He indicated there were "fine meetings now in camp by Mr. Andrews a methodist preacher and has had great revivals," and he could "set in the tent & hear the preaching … singing & praying." He believed that "we need some good precher for the men is groing verry wicked and thoutless they dont fear nothing our chaplin does not suite the men but I think he is doing all he can." He remarked they had "preaching every night and they are commenced singing now" and that "the alter is crouded all the time." But he wished "to get home when the meeting is at Philadelphia."[77]

"loosing a great many of good men"

The young Gaston boys and men experienced the fire of battle, witnessing death and destruction to a level unprecedented in the nation's history. Their descriptions, which are offered here in chronological order, were shocking to them and to their readers back home.

In describing the Seven Days Battles of the Peninsular campaign, Linebarger indicated that the Confederate army was "loosing a great many of good men" and that he could "hear the canons every day." "I have been through too battles since I got to ritchman," he wrote his wife, "and how I escaped from the balls I cant tell you for they apperd to bee as thick as hale." He proudly proclaimed that "we have whipt the yankes and I hope they will stay whipt for it isent fun nary time." But sickness grabbed Linebarger and he remained in the hospital as the army moved toward Antietam. By September 11, 1863, he had "started to Mariland," was in Winchester with "sore feet" and "the wont of something to eat," and claimed to have "walked eghty or one hundred miles over the mountains and blew ridg," attempting to reach his regiment. By September 23, he had "caught up with the regment" and had "waded the Potomac twiced that day and night." He had been placed "in command of cpt roberts company as they are nary officer here belonging to it."[78] Linebarger arrived after the Battle of Antietam as the army moved back into Virginia. Others described the Peninsular Campaign.

On July 21, 1862, William Morris described grotesque scenes: "there is Hundreds of the Enemy that was Not Buried besides a Great many they throughed in the River & creaks when convenient." "I Counted 64 Horses in 20 Steps Killed," he recalled, "Strange as it may Seem to you I Never Slept Sounder in my Life. We was so worn out that as soon as we stoped fighting we Could hardly keep awake."[79]

On September 28, 1862, J. J. Brown described the devastation that the war caused, "everything is destored thousands of acres of corn has been cut to peices and what burnt up and the houses torn down and burnt up and that part of the country is worst now there is nobody living there now." "Malvin Hill ... was sightful there the timber was cut to all peices with the cannon balls." He witnessed some shells which "weigh 120 pounds."[80] On November 14, 1862, near "Franklin Depot, Va." F. Wash Dellinger described the fighting: Union "commenceded bummbing this place and they fired two hundred and fifth roundes" while the Confederates only managed "about ten or fifteen roundes."[81]

"The balls were falling around us as thick as hale all the time"

Leonidas Torrence's report on the Battle of Seven Pines included "Federals and Confederates ... both lying thick on the part of the Field that I passed through. It was a verry distresing place." He told his family about "a general engagement" and "some hard fighting." He "came out safe" even though "[a] ball passed my right arm [and] went through my coat sleeve and shirt. The balls were falling around us as thick as hale all the time." He reported others killed and wounded and "saw several trees nearly as thick round as my Body cut down with Cannon balls. There was a ball went through a verry large Pine just over my head. it did not appear to check the ball at all." On July 14, 1862, Torrence communicated that the Union "threw some Bumms verry close to us," and there was a major engagement. "You never heard such moaning and hollowing as was at the Battle Field that night with the wounded." There were a "great many killed and wounded yankeys on it." Another battle occurred on Tuesday, which was "as hard a Battle as ever was Fought. The Balls fell around me as thick as hail for 2 or 3 hours." Only C. A. Fronebarger was seriously wounded as "[t]he ball went in at one Shoulder and Out at the other."[82]

Only a few soldiers described battles around Harper's Ferry and Antietam. On September 7, 1862, Morris reported from "Meriland" that he had been in three battles; "I think I saw fulley three thousand Dead yankeys on the Diffirant Battle Grounds." "My only hope is in Christ our savior to protect Me in the Day of battle & to enable you & our Deare Little Children to beare up in the sore trials you May have to Encounter with."[83]

Extended fighting also took its toll. On September 8, 1862, Jacob Dellinger wrote his father from Frederick, Maryland and reported that he had been in "5 different battles or fights" since fighting around Richmond. He boasted that "now instead of them invading our land, we are invading theirs. And I hope that we may be crowned with success a while longer and I think peace will prevail." He explained, "everything is plentiful here in this State now, but it can't last long.... The health in the camp in general is tolerable good."[84] Death was never far away.

"sad news of the death of our Brother"

On September 28, 1862, David Coon communicated the "sad news of the death of our Brother," who "left me with a smile upon his face." On November 30 despite being a lieutenant, David Coon lamented his inability to "be home at the preaching of Brother Henrys funeral."[85]

Willie Linebarger described the Battle of Fredericksburg: "[W]e are in four miles of the yankes they are on one side of the river and we are on the other side." He happily reported that he had "made my escape again and I am well." "[T]he cannonading commenced last thursday," he wrote, " ... we were in it the holl time day and night but Saturday was the warm time. [O]ur men did slaughter the yankeys for the front line had a position that they wasent exposed," and he estimated "they lost some three or four thousand kild and six or eight wounded if not more."[86]

Many Gaston soldiers were at the Battle of Chancellorsville where they described chilling scenes. Torrence wrote, "We had a verry hard Fight that day and drove the Enemy some 2 or 3 miles with heavy loss on both sides." He described "distressing sights on Battle Fields ... men Killed and Wounded but where we Fought last Sunday the Bums set the woods afire and to look at Killed and Wounded men burned was the worst looking sight I ever saw or hear of." While he suspected that most of "our wounded were carried off before they got burnt," he vividly described a "walk over the Battle Field and see men lying with their cloths burnt off their hair burnt close to their Head their Arms and legs all drawed up with the fire. I never saw such a distressing sight before and hope I may never see such another." He reported that "General Jackson (Stonewall) was wounded," but he hoped only "slightly" with "his arm ... shot off."[87] After the Battle of Chancellorsville a letter fragment in the Dellinger Letters conveys grisly battlefield images. Human remains were "moldering in the Clay more than likely hundreds of their remains are lying upon the ground today and Wild beastes and fouls Devouring their flesh Among them our brave Commander Stonewall Jackson who Dide at Gines Station the other day from the effects of his wondes. his Remains past through heare the other day carrying him to Richmond."[88]

By February 25, 1863, Linebarger was near Wilmington, where he observed "too steamers run the blockade." Moving north to protect the Weldon-Wilmington-Petersburg railroad, he "herd the cannons down to wards newbern they were making the hole earth shake." "[T]hey fond a nother musketeer swamp for us," he sarcastically commented as the unit moved within "forty miles from Petersburg."[89]

Gaston soldiers played prominent roles at the Battle of Gettysburg. On July 1, 1863, Leonidas Torrence's regiment engaged the Union at Seminary Ridge, suffering many casualties and he was mortally wounded. W. J. O'Daniel remained with his friend, who had been "wounded in the head & thigh." While O'Daniel did not believe Torrence's thigh was broken, the "ball in his head went in between his eye and ear ... [and] stopped some place near his brain." "He came to his cesis," O'Daniel conveyed to Torrence's mother, "& told me that he was a going to die & gave me all his things except his testament and his pocket handkerchief. He told me to give his things to you." O'Daniel stayed with his friend until his regiment retreated.[90] On July 20 he wrote "Mrs. Torrence" again. He answered her letter of July 6, describing her son's last hours. Torrence "did not know any thing for several hours." When he did wake up, "He could not eat any thing. He drank a great deal of water but he throwed it all up. I got him some milk but it would not ly on his stomick. When I went to tell him goodby," O'Daniel continued, "he told me that I would never se him again. He said he was a going to die. He also said that he was willing to die. You doo not have any idea how bad that I hated to leav Lon," but the doctor would not allow O'Daniel to stay. Torrence had "$76 dollars in paper money, $1.33 in Silver." Philosophically, O'Daniel commented: "I am sorry to hear that their is another call for more men in N. Carolina. I dont think their is any their to spair. We kneed recruits here verry bad. There is but 7 in our Company. Times are verry disheartening here at present."[91]

On August 10, 1863, O'Daniel again responded to Torrence's despondent mother. He assured her that the doctor tried to assist Torrence but that "he could not do any thing for L wound. The Doctore gave him medicen to make him rest. He did not appear to suffer a great deal." While he would "sleep the most of his time," he also "would throw up and his bowels would get easy." "I do not think that Leonidus could get well," he assured her. "He maid sines for water when he wanted a drink."[92]

"the most obstinate and sanguinary perhaps ever fought upon this continent"

Lt. Lemuel Hoyle's eloquent description of the Battle of Gettysburg belies his involvement in Pickett's Charge on the third day of the battle. On July 12 Hoyle wrote his mother from Winchester, Virginia about the experience: "[T]he most obstinate and sanguinary perhaps ever fought upon this continent." The third day "was perfectly fearful, and the slaughter tremendous. Our men fought with the accustomed valor and determination of Southern soldiers—but in vain—we had to fall back to our original positions." His brigade "suffered as heavily as any portion of the Army engaged. We were cut all to pieces," he wrote his mother. "Of over 500 men carried into the fight by our Regiment on Wednesday, only 110 were left for duty Saturday morning." The loss was even more significant as "[n]early all the field officers of the Brigade were either killed or wounded. Nearly all the company officers of our Regt. were killed or wounded." Hoyle reported that he escaped with a "slight injury, although struck three times. I am nearly well and expect to start in a few days to hunt up the Regt. God be praised for His great mercy towards me." Of the seventy four his company carried into battle on the first day, seventy were killed, wounded, or missing. Hoyle reported that he had been briefly captured but then recaptured in about ten minutes. Hoyle was fortunate that death had not found him. By August 1 only thirty five soldiers in his company were able to serve even though his health remained good.[93] Lt. David Coon also fought at Gettysburg participating in Pickett's Charge.

"Lt. Coon was certainly killed, but a good many of the boys think not"

A nephew wrote "Dear Uncle" that Coon was left "on the field" and speculated that "Lt. Coon was certainly killed, but a good many of the boys think not." He had been "shot three times after he was wounded." The Seagle nephew related that Coon "told me the day before the fight that he did not intend to be taken prisoner without he was killed or mortally wounded.... I think he is dead yet he may be alive." He described Coon as "a good man, he was a Christian. He was also a good officer kind to his men."[94]

Upon receiving that letter the family must have been distraught. It is unclear when the family learned that David had been captured and was alive. On November 18, 1863, brother Adolphus S., also captured at Gettysburg, wrote his sister from the Union prison at Point Lookout that he had "not herd from David." On July 30, 1864, Adolphus had "herd from David he is well and at Fort Delaware."[95]

Colonel William G. Morris did not leave an account of his heroism at Pickett's Charge. Accounts reveal his leading his company and crossing the stone wall at the crest of the ridge with about 20 of his comrades. As Union reinforcements surrounded Morris and the North Carolinians, they surrendered. The story is told that Morris buried his sword within logs of a shed and broke off the end so that he would not be required to surrender it.[96]

Poor communication hindered soldiers and their families. James W. Linebarger's regiment was not at Gettysburg, and he conveyed inaccurate reports home "that gen Lee had cut hookers army all to peaces and kild hooker and wounded meed mortally and if this should turn out to be so I dont think we will be botherd much more." The inaccurate information "anoyed" Linebarger. "[O]ne day we have whipped the yanks all round," he uttered in a second letter, "and then it is a dispatch to the reverse." He concluded "to listen to none of them or but verry little."[97]

Near Garysburg, North Carolina, Linebarger informed his father of Union casualties while fighting near Weldon, "we could see the graves of there dead & they throad some in to wells & I think we had some of the hardest raining that evening & night I ever saw but we took it & grined & stood square up to the rascals."[98]

"Over hundred kild, wounded an taken prisoner"

After Gettysburg loyal Confederates expected to win the war, while the reality of manpower and matériel shortages, coupled with low morale, affected their efforts and their letters home. Their letters describe struggles and attitudes concerning a desperate war.

On October 21, 1863, Cephas Keener wrote his brother Peter from the Virginia battlefield, "Over hundred kild, wounded an taken prisoner." The Union "Ruther got the beter of yus," he wrote. He was in the "front of the Batle as a sharpe shooter." Cephas detailed that "Brother David was Wounded in the hip an the bal Run Don his leg an stopped." Union soldiers captured, medically treated, and left him. Keener's unit fell back and "tore up they railroad to Rhapadan River." The Confederates had captured about "thre thousand Brisners."[99]

Most southerners hated the Emancipation Proclamation and were wary of meeting black Union soldiers. Linebarger described one encounter near Weldon in March 1864, when Confederates decided to take no African American prisoners. As Linebarger's unit charged "there breast works & threw the town [of Suffolk, Virginia] they did not like the game that our boys plaid & broke for shelter." "I cant tell how many they were kiled but they were lying around there in spots … [O]ur men got some in a large house at the fur side of town surrounded it and & shot all that would show themselves & then put fier to it and burned the rest up." He further exclaimed that "I tell you they was nary one taken prisoner they were kiled dead."[100]

Lt. Hoyle wrote his mother about the constant battles around Richmond during the summer of 1864 in graphic details. His chagrin at the persistence of General Grant communicated both disgust and Grant's effectiveness with constant battles.[101]

On May 16, 1864, Edney Hoover, in the middle of Grant's push toward Richmond, reported "an awful time and we are in line of battle now … we hav lost five men out of our company." On June 5 he reported that "we hav had a miserable time for more than an month…. We are inline of battle now about ten miles from Richmond … thar has bin apour of men kild on both sides but I think the yankeys hav lost agrate miny more then we have." Constant battle resulted in Hoover not having "a chance to rite." Instead "we are amarching and afiting every day," he complained, "it seems like this cruel war wold never stop."¹⁰² On June 23, 1864, P. L. Boyd wrote "Mis S. Reinhardt" that "The balls fell around us like hale but non of our boys got hurt."¹⁰³

On August 9, 1864, Henry K. Dellinger communicated details about the Battle of the Crater, "[e]verything remains very quiet between the two great armies since the 30th and ol' Grant made a trial to take Petersburg by mining, but Im am happy to say that he failed efferts. He blew up some sixty or seventy yards of our breast works and then made a charge but did not do much good. He fought all of his Negro troops," who got "the worst end of the bargain." He provided further details of the battle, "[t]hey came hollering no quarters. Well I guess they got what they wanted for our fellows gave them the bayonet and the butt end of the musket They killed some seven or eight hundred and took several hundred white soldier prisoners," another example of taking no black prisoners.¹⁰⁴

On October 6, 1864, Peter Keener from the "Richmond Trenches" wrote his "Wife and Children" that they had "few men her[e] to hold the works." If the Union "Charge our works their will be General Stamped on our part." As a picket Keener can "see the Yankes thick about fifty yards." The Confederate army was "bisey at work [to make] it impossible to Charge." He described the weather as a cold and "clowdy day" with a north wind.¹⁰⁵

Near Petersburg on January 20, 1865, "Jas. Fulton" wrote his daughter, "Rachel Fulton." He indicated that he served "on picket three nights in a week on an average." The conditions around Petersburg were "distressing" as "women and children gather 'round the mills in Petersburg and cry for meal and cannot get it." Since the government ran the mills, meal cost $50 per bushel and flour $1,000 per barrel. On the battle lines there was "occasional shelling" and the "men are deserting and going to the Yankies regular and many more will go if they are not better fed." He wrote up the side of the letter that "The whole seat of my parts is out." His pants were "perfectly rotten. It was ruined in dying."¹⁰⁶

"there is about 30 dise a day"

The letters of Daniel Haynes Dellinger reveal the sad circumstances of North Carolina's Salisbury prison. Official documentation suggests that he was enrolled in the Confederate 4th North Carolina Senior Reserves in June of 1864 in Lincolnton. Family correspondence indicates that the almost 49-year-old 5'10" father and husband with dark complexion, dark hair and blue eyes actually began his service earlier with mixed emotions.¹⁰⁷ The war had been devastating personally, losing a son, a son-in-law, neighbors, other relatives, and observing economic ruin. On February 18, 1864, he wrote his wife from Weldon, N. C. that the army had "Captured 450 prisoners," "it snowed yesterday," and he hoped "this Cruel war would Stop so [he] ... could return home in peace."¹⁰⁸

By October 12 he was in Salisbury "to Gard the Yankees." On October 27 he elaborated that "Wee have to Gard them day & Nite." "Wee have to gard about 10 thousand Yankees. The Yankees dies here from 10–12 a day or every 24 hours. Wee draw beef, flour, & Rice and Molasses tobacco." He wanted George Dellinger to pay his tithe and to check on his "little boys" who were "Sawing Wheat." He needed shoes made and was "Cooking I don't gard any myself." By November 3 the "average" death rate of the prisoners had increased to "25 per day" and disease was rampant. On November 8 he related that a guard shot one of the "Yankeys ... night before last." The prisoner crossed "the line" and "would not stop."¹⁰⁹ Prison guards controlled the prisoners with a line drawn into the earth, no fence or wall.

On November 16, 1864, Dellinger wrote his daughter, M. A. Rhyne, describing the prisoners, "they are about to Perish to death they do not get more than half anuff to eate there is about 30 dise a day and if they do not take them away they will all die for they have nothing to li on and Nothing to Civir up So they will freeze to death this winter." While Union soldiers had little to eat, camp cook Dellinger reported that "I hant Sufered for anything to eat yet but we drawed half rashens." On November 27 Dellinger reported that "We have had a Row with the Yankees. they tride to breakout we had a little fite we killed 16 men and Wounded 40. The Yankees killed 2 men. Is all quiet now." The prison experiences offered plenty of depressing pictures for Daniel H. Dellinger: "lots of them dieing every day … quick as they are dead the others take the Clothes off of them and they have to bury them nude and without Coffins."[110] This observation from the man who insisted that his son, Frank, properly bury a relative in Virginia and insisted upon hearing the details.

As the war effort collapsed around the Confederacy, desperation gripped the prison. On February 1, 1865, Dellinger reported that at the prison "Our old men Keep running off every Night"; thirty left Sunday night and twenty-one last night. Later in February he reported in a brief but happy letter that the prison officials had "orders to go to Greensboro," starting in two hours, where "it is Said that we will take the Yankees."[111] The process of the Salisbury prisoner exchange had begun and the misery in which they lived had ended.

Gaston Countian Rufus W. Carson reminisced about the end of the war. After forced marches "at about 1 o'clock A.M. Sabbath Gen. Robert E. Lee surrenders himself and army to Gen. U.S. Grant at Appomattox Court House Virginia 10 April in fine health only broken down." After stacking their arms, he left Appomattox on the 12th. He traveled by foot to Danville where he "got into an old box car at Danville with friend John G. Lewis and Cephas Bell rode about 33 miles." After a 15 mile march near Greensboro he "got into another old Box car" with Lewis, Bell, and "Gaston Senior Reserves." He rode on top of another "old car" with Lewis, then walked. Most of the remainder of the trip involved "marching" with Lewis; they "crossed the Catawba River at Rock Island factory and the South Fork at Stowe's Mill." He went home with Lewis and walked home from there, arriving "a little after dark" on April 19.[112]

The Gaston County letters describe the war's impact, as it inflicted death, destruction, and unprecedented distress upon soldiers, families, and communities. Other issues, for which soldiers and their families exchanged letters, involve stresses on the home front, feeding the soldiers, letter writing, soldier portraits, furloughs, and the incessant desire for peace. The next chapter discusses these issues.

4

Soldiers, Wives and Mothers

While Gaston county soldiers communicated the horrors of war, difficulties of camp life, and battles with disease and wounds, their concern about home and family consumed many of their letters. Much of the difficulty of soldiers and their families may be summarized in a letter written in 1864 to Governor Vance. S. H. Williams, "a resident of Gaston County," wrote the governor two letters in two days from Langhorn Hospital, Lynchburg, Virginia, where he suffered from an "ulcered leg (Right)" and could not stand. Williams sought a transfer to Greensboro or Salisbury, was a "good carriage and wagon maker," and had a family of ten. Describing his family and friends as "all poor people," he promised in his second letter to provide "certificates ... of my integrity" and certified his "honesty & faithfulness to perform my duty." He informed Vance that the soldiers were "very near naked and shoeless and our rations are awfully short." In an attractive and flowing handwriting Williams closed with a postscript: "I am performing the duties of nurse but am not able to stand it." There is no indication that Vance approved his transfer. Yet, by January 1865 Williams was officially described as being "On detached service at Charlotte, NC." He had spent almost all of 1864 and a portion of 1863 in the hospital.[1] The Williams letter conveys his concerns with his own physical health, performing his duty, and survival of a very large but poor family. His letter is indicative of soldier concerns.

Husbands wrote wives, sons wrote mothers, they often communicated instructions for management, sometimes micromanagement, of the farm. Near Dallas the letters of farm laborer Caleb Senter and middle-class farmer William G. Morris show similarities and differences.

"try and hier sum Body to Cut your fier wood"

With his family residing with Aunt Frances Cloninger, on May 22, 1863, Senter instructed his wife to "go to dalis and Draw your Salt ... too and a half pounds of Salt ... and 9 Dollars for Clothing go to Jacob froneburger." As winter approached, having firewood was essential. "[T]ell Smith MCalister that i thank him," Senter commented, "for halling that wood for you and if you nead eny more halled hier him to hall it dont carry no wood." As 1863 neared its end, Senter was happy to learn that his wife and family "got your Corn all gethered and geting sum oats soad." "[H]ow much oats youe soad and how youe got the reste of the Corn hall[ed] and what youe have to pay for Salt and whether youe get shoos for the Childrn or not," he inquired. As winter 1863–64 approached, Senter worried for his family: "try and hier sum Body to Cut your fier wood. i am Sory that youe hasent got no money But i am in the Saim fix i havent got a Sent and Donte know when i will Draw i Donte get eny thing for the time i was at home i am mity thank full that i havent Bin punished" for his desertion. On February 9, 1864, Senter quizzed "whether the old mear is alive yet or not maby youe Can by a old hors Sum place." On February 13 he continued his farming interests with "whether the cow is with calf or not and whether you are rasing eny more Sheepn or not or eny pigs."[2]

William G. Morris's advantage of having slave Randall Costner becomes evident as 1862 ends. Morris wrote his wife, "as to Hiering Bill you can Doo as you plese. perhaps Randle would rather Not have him there. if Randle wants you to hier Bill perhaps you had better Doo So as we could Not Loose Much by Hiering him.... You will have to Exersise your own Judegemen about our affairs at home as I have but Little time to think of Matters at home.... Tell randle that I am under obligations to him for what he has Done this yeare in My absence. I think he is to bee praised & favered as Much as possible."[3]

Undated charcoal drawing of Louisa Costner Morris, wife of Colonel William Groves Morris. Their correspondence informs readers of battles, life in camp, and the stresses of farm life and the home front (courtesy Daniel Wilson, Dallas, North Carolina).

"Tell Randle to doo the Best he can for Me this Summer"

Spring was a busy time for farmers. "You may read this letter to Randle as I have but little time to Wright," Morris stressfully wrote. "Tell Randle to doo the Best he can for Me this Summer. he can Manage the farm as Well as I can tell him. I think the Hogs Will require Good attention to Make Meet Enough for our family. I hope this Will Be a Good crop year." Morris sought information about wheat and oats. By October as a Confederate prisoner, he became more amenable to the circumstances, "[y]ou can Manage Home affairs without My advice. Show this to randle. tell him to doo the best he can & I will be Satisfied. I feel Myself under obligations to him already for his attention to My affairs." Later, he vacillated between control and restraint, "[t]ell Randle I expected to come to his corn hushing last year but was disappointed so I will Make No promise for this yeare. Tell him to doo the best he can for Me & he Shall be rewarded. dont expect him to expose himself unnecessarily for I think he can Manage to Guet along without so dooing." "Tell Randle I want him to Plant some fruit trees this winter," he instructed, "& a small vinyard." Further, "I think the 3 acre lot on the west Side of the road Next to Smith Jenkinses would be suitable place for an orchard. plant none but choice fruits," he advised.[4] Having Randle gave Morris an economic and logistical advantage.

Yeoman Daniel Haynes Dellinger had managed farm activities as relatives served the Confederacy until the 49-year-old departed as a Senior Reservist, which caused his wife and family to do the work. On September 6, 1864, he instructed his wife to "[s]ave all the fodder you can," not leave the horses "[s]tanding in the grass [as] they might runaway," and to "[s]ow the wheat as regular as you can & plow close as you can" and to "let the hogs live on acorns" not corn. He ordered his wife "[n]ot to sell any Brandy only for Salt or leather dont sell for money at all. You can let it go for yarn if you please." He told her to let P. Z. Baxter have brandy for iron and not to sell it to people "who will get drunck." He encouraged his wife to "draw Your part of the Salt that is on hand for the Solders Wives by paying 40 cents per pound." He advised her to discover the delivery date and "git your part." He suggested that his sons chop wood and care for the stillhouse. He also encouraged them to "take good ceare of our Stock" and hoped "pease will be made" soon.[5]

Colonel Morris was also concerned that his wife exposed herself "unnecessaryally by doing Too Much work." "[Y]ou Doo More work than the Most of Stout woman." Do less work he advised and "[t]ake the world Easier." "Content Yourself with your Condition as well as you can & Doo No hard work that you Can avoid." It is "better To leave things undone than To lose you health." "You can Sow as Much Wheat as you think Best. Henery can advise you.... It May Be best to hier Bill for another yeare."[6]

Newton Sellers expressed concern that his young wife would harm her health through farming efforts: "I want you not to kill your Self a working out you git Some body to help you." He asked about peaches and apples. He wanted to be home to "help you plant corn." He advised his wife not to "Sell any corn for the money unless you nead Some money." He worried, "don't you kill your Self a working out I want to know whether you have planted your water millions patch or not."[7] The loss in value of Confederate money exacerbated the already extreme conditions at home for wives.

"I send some money home"

Newlywed James Wellington Linebarger expressed farming, monetary, and other concerns to his wife and other family members. "Huffstetler owes me five dollars," he wrote his wife in April 1862. Later he instructed "John to take care of my corn and have my wheat and oats soud." "I send some money home," he informed his wife, "and if you need any thing you must let me no." As a new year of farming dawned, he directed his father to "take charge of [my corn] sell it if you think it better than to move it ... [plus] eight bushels of wheat take it." He expressed uncertainty about whether to "cell ... my mewl," which involved subsequent letters. Similar to Newton Sellers and Daniel H. Dellinger, Linebarger instructed "Paw" to "change [Confederate money] off and if he has any of mine I wont him to change it off and he can buy aunt Marys place for me I wont him to do so if he pleases." As summer progressed, he sought "the news in general of the crops" and whether his father had "cut my wheat & are taking care of it & the other stuff." He depended upon his father to manage the farm and directed him to "keep an account," pay "Featherston ... that note," pay "J. R. Rhyne for a piece of leather.... Abernthy starling a little & when ever Liz needs any money let her have it and I would like for you to invest the other in to something in land if you can I would like to have the widows place." He complained "our money is under pare and is not worth much." As 1863 ended, farm workers became an issue, "tell Paw that I think it will be better for [B]rown to work my land than to let Ran Carter move there but he can do what ever he thinks is best for me." Seeing "Jacob cansler on the train," Linebarger directed Cansler to his father to purchase "oats I told him to go to you … they ought to bring half what corn is bringing you trade them to the best advantage and put the money to som youse for it wont do to lay up." The next day, he directed his wife to "Pay to Joseph K. Rhyne $150," which he had borrowed from Esly Rhyne.[8]

J. J. Brown was also concerned about his young wife and about his tools. On November 30, 1862, he wanted his wife to buy "some provisions" with money he planned to send home as "I don't think the war can last much longer." Concerned about his shoemaker tools, he instructed in the last letter he wrote her, "I don't want you to lend out my shoe tools and get them brok up for I am in hopes that I will get home sum time top use them and I want you to take good care of them and your selves too."[9]

Thomas Davis wrote to his wife about money issues and farming. He inquired about "how the mar[e] is doing and if you have a pasture for her or not," and to know "what debts you have paid and how much money you have." By May 1862, he hoped "to come home at harvest if I can get a furlo" with the reality in the June 10 letter that he did not receive a furlough. He triumphantly announced in this letter, "I have got my bounty and will send it home … soon." On August 31 in a letter to Richard Philbeck he requested that he "sel my colts as soon as you can." He feared in October that "you will not make corn enough to do you and keep all the stock" without selling the mule. Following a bout of illness, he advised his wife to, "hold on to that Gold for I hear some saying that they have been offered ten dollars for ounce." He inquired, "write how youre wheate looks and how your winter oates is and how you are makin out getting corn." Farming was never far from his thoughts, "I dont no what to tell you about the wheat on the upper place But you will have to get some one to hall it up for you if you can…. Daniel … write me wether you have any cane seed planted or not." "If you can get them Shoats from Pink and has enough fruit to feed them on I think you had better get them and put them up," he instructed his wife. Again, he recommended, "keep that gold … it is worth 13 dollars that is you can get 13 for one dollar at Richmond."[10]

The newlywed and landless Franklin Hanna also confronted his wife's home front worries. A couple of months after his conscription he advised his wife to "do the best you can for your Self." He inquired whether the "fodder Saved or not." Caroline reported that "the Pig is doing very well it looks like it would make very good eating now…. I think it is fater than our hogs was last year the corn is not gathered yet." Later, Caroline reported that her corn had been "put up but the bottom corn and they gathered it and hauled it this evening." She estimated about "thirty or thiry five bushel of" corn "after the rent was taken out" with her "peas gatered and potatoes dug" but "did not turn out very heavy." She harvested "about 5 bushel of sweet potatoes and three and a half of late irish." She was uncertain about sowing wheat. "[M]y wheat aint fit to Sow and Seed wheat seems to be very hard to get," she exclaimed, plus "I do not know where I can get ground to rent that would bring good wheat." Facing 1863 planting, Franklin inquired "hoe [how] the Wheat crops look … how they are geting along towards a Corn Crop." With Hanna once again sick in the hospital, Caroline confided that she "got my obligeing Sack of Salt I am nearly out of money or Such stuff as they call money I only Paid 17 dollars of it and Father paid the balance."[11] Sickness, a newborn son, and a wife without money contributed to Hanna's decision to desert.

Mary C. Hoover informed her husband, Edney, of activities at home, "hoarses and cows a doing well ... your cow has a nice calf We have cold wether now agin." Hoover responded to the letter being glad "to hear that your stolk [stock] was doing well."[12]

"we dunt get half anuff to eat"

Food was a major topic in soldier's letters with its availability or scarcity depending upon circumstances. On May 22, 1862, Caleb Senter remarked that he was "geting as fat as a pig." He requested "sum onions and taters." By August 24 he reported eating "rost nears plenty" and that the "government has bought a Bout 100 hundred ?? of good Corn for us ... aples and peaches." He got "anuf of meate and Bread." But on September 30 he reported only eating "Crackers and fat BaCon" as his unit was marching. His diet high in fats and carbohydrates caused him to remark, "i way one hundred and fifty four pounds." As the war wore on and armies marched farther from their supplies, food shortages became more common. Senter wrote his wife, "we fare mity Bad hear we get nothing But CraCkers an meate a Quarter of a pound of BaCon and 4 CraCkers and a litle shugar." By October 17, 1863, he found a "good tent," "drawd Sum CraCkers and meat," and thought he would not "Be punishet in the least" for his desertion. Later that month he "DrawD a good pare of Shoos and a Coate Shirt an pants."[13] On September 7, 1862, William Morris reported that the army was in "Meriland" with "[p]leanty of Everything to Eat, Coffee 3 lbs to the Dollar, Sugar 9 lbs to the Dollar, Milk & butter Give to soldiers."[14]

On May 6, 1862, Frank Dellinger wrote his father that he had little to eat, "Goobers," some crackers, and bacon. William W. Haynes reported to "cousin" D. H. Dellinger that he had "half Rashens" near Yorktown and had "no tents attall only our Blankets." Frank Dellinger near Wilmington also reported "half Rashins" with "very little flour and no meat ... plenty of corn mele."[15] In November 1863 Edney Hoover complained to his parents, "we dunt get half anuff to eat." On January 3, 1864, he informed his wife that he ate "corn meal and flour ... but we dunt get but a quarter of a pound of meat a day."[16]

"We Get plenty To Eat but have to pay for it"

Confederate soldiers had to pay for their food. At the beginning of the war Morris summed up the circumstances: "We Get plenty To Eat but have to pay for it," Morris wrote his wife, "20 cts a lb for pickled pork, 4 Dollars pr hundred for Flower, butter is Selling at 60 cts a Point in Newburn." At the beginning of the war chickens cost 50 cents and eggs were free.[17] Soldiers used a portion of their salary to cover these expenses. Privates were paid $11 per month at the beginning of the war and it never increased. Officers like Morris, Linebarger, and Hoyle received higher salaries.

James Wellington Linebarger's letters describe the extremes of camp food. Soon after enlistment in 1862, he noted that the company "would have three meals rasnels by morning and to be ready to march," but the rations "run a little short from sunday morning tell monday evening." Later, he complained that "we have neither blankets nor tents." By September his "diet [consisted] of old bacon and crackers," and he suffered from "sore feet and for the wont of something to eat." By November he fortunately reported getting "plenty of apples and graps ... some that they cauld shugar." He allowed that "a well man can live on the diet we get our men all looks well and are getting saucy." By January he was "feasting on sweet potatoes." Linebarger commented on food and shelter, for which he paid: "my bord and cooking is worth from twenty five to thirty dollars per month now we are living tolerable well know we get Pork and flower." A special treat was "a turkey for dinner ... you just ought to sead me eating," he bragged. Having moved to near Wilmington, his fare declined with "only pickled beef and corn bread we could get some fish but we havent no lard to fri them." As the war progressed the cost of food for the soldiers increased. "[W]e have to pay one dollar and twenty five cents per pound for bacon," Linebarger exclaimed, "we can get some milk and eggs but it is verry high eggs is one dollar per dozen and milk from twenty five to forty cents per quart." By July he estimated "my bard is from fifty to sixty dollars per month" and he desired "something good to eat such as fruit and water melons." As 1863 closed, he reported "drawing good rations Beff and flower plenty." Lt. Linebarger complained that "they issue us rasions now as the privats and we have to make out on it."[18] Soldiers accepted the reality that the Confederate government did not provide food; instead they paid the soldiers and each was expected to pay for their rations. To supplement food scarcity or personal preferences, families sent "Boxes."

This unusual arrangement frequently resulted in limited food, clothing, and provisions. It also more significantly impacted privates, many of whom came from families of limited means. Each soldier preferred certain foods, and most grew tired of the standard camp fare. Wives, mothers, and relatives often prepared "boxes" to send the troops with their favorite food and other necessities.

In 1862 Senter requested "a pare of pants and a pare of Socks." On March 3, 1863, he requested letters, food, and soap, since his clothes were "as Black and dirty as they Can Be and i cant get no soap." When a box arrived on March 24, he "Shead tears when i Saw them apels." He received another box on May 20 "and all the rest of the things." On January 7, 1864, he happily received a box from home and reported that he sold half of the materials to others including his "Chicken for 4 dolars." Later, "[s]end me Sum Sheld Beans or Sum peas," he requested. He offered to make money in the army to send home to purchase a horse for his wife. He sent handmade rings and requested "homaid to Baco." He complained that "money has run out in the army" and suspected that his "Dear and Affectionate Wife" also had a scarcity of money at home.[19]

On September 15, 1862, Frank Dellinger indicated that he got his shoes "Mended" and was sending $30 Confederate money but needed ink and brandy. Daniel Haynes Dellinger and family supplemented their farm income by making brandy. On September 20, D. H. Dellinger informed his son that they were "Nearly over making Brandy" with "about 3 runs to make yet." By January 1863 he promised to send him the lead pencils and socks he requested. He had sold five gallons of his son's whiskey to Dr. Goode for $6 per gallon and wanted to know what to do with the rest. He could get more for his whiskey "by the Speculators" but chose to "keep it in the Neighborhood for the Sick ... for medical purposes." The Dellinger family provided well for their son Frank—sweatbread, pies, butter, sausage, beef, green apples, one chicken, two partridges, potatoes both kinds, onions, two pickels, "Brandy Peaches, soap, jug of brandy, walnut kernels, pair of socks, sewing thread, and pencils." When father, Daniel Haynes Dellinger, was conscripted into the Senior Reserve, his wife, Frances, sent him a box with soap, yeast bread, potatoes and yams, dried beef, a pair of pants, onions, apples, a few peaches from "Uncle George," a gallon of brandy, $10 Confederate money, a quart of molasses, medicine with lambshorn, and a plug of tobacco. Later he received the box his wife sent: three "Tater Pise," sweet bread, loaf of bread, some biscuits, beef, pork, apples, potatoes both kinds, turnips, onions, rice, one head of cabbage, coffee, "Gourd with Soap," and one baked chicken. Unfortunately he did not get the brandy. By January 1865 he still received food, eggs, meat, pies, bread, potatoes "Both Sorts," onions, bacon and pickles , persimmon brandy, and a jug of brandy and tin cup.[20]

Early in the war youthful Lemuel Hoyle requested food and sent his mother "about a quart of Sea Shells" and "two (2) Bushels of Salt" from Wilmington, which cost $8 per bushel. By winter the following year, Hoyle made specific requests: "my scarf, gloves, socks, and one of the over shirts left at Uncle Andrew's, and one more pair of wool socks. I want them colored." Hoyle enjoyed "apples," "cheese," and requested "a pr. Of home made jeans pants for winter."[21]

On February 10, 1862, William G. Morris sent $150 for his wife to use "in case of Immergency." As an officer Morris acquired more money, better sleeping arrangements, and more food. But as the army marched toward Antietam, Morris reported the he had not been paid in "the Last 3 Months but have Money Plenty to answer My Purposes in Camp." Morris was glad to get apples and "Goobers." Captured at Gettysburg, Morris, imprisoned at "Johnsons Island Near Sanduskey Ohio," continued to request and receive items. On July 29, 1864, he reported "plenty of clothing but will Soon run Short of Money." He sought 30 or 40 pounds of tobacco. "Tobacco is verry high heare and cannot be had except for Specie or federal Money." He reminded his wife, "Confederate Money is Worthless heare Except among ourselves." On October 20 he requested "[o]ne coat Pants & vest, Gray or dark mixed would be preferable, coat & vest without button two over Shirts some cotton Shirts for summer two pairs wollin drawers two of cotton three or four Pairs socks."[22] Families supplied much of their soldier's sustenance.

Twenty-five-year-old Leonidas Torrence volunteered by July 1861 and reported the cost of food items in the army: watermelons cost 50 cents, "Rostenears" cost two cents apiece, chickens "the size of a Patridge" cost 25 cents, and a dozen eggs cost 20 cents. "F[l]our is worth $5 per bbl, Corn 60 cts per Bushel, Coffee 40 cts per lb., Salt $7 per sack, Green Peaches from 50 cts to $1 per Peck. Watermelons are not so high. Eggs 20 cts Doz., Chickens 20 to 30 cts, Beff about 12 cts [a pound]. We have plenty of Beff Mutton, Bacon, Cabbbag Irish potatoes, Bakers Bread Tea and Coffee." As colder weather approached, he sought clothing from home including "a pair of Flannel Drawers and Shirt an one pair of Janes Pants, and 3 pair of socks" and "my over coat and close neck't vest peddler." He complained that he could "get nothing here with out paying three times the worth of it ... coarse shoes here bring from $4 to $7 a pair" and wanted a "pair of home made Boots." On February 9, 1863, Torrence asked his "Brother" to bring "Cheese, Butter and Fruit ... some Red Pepper, Whiskey and Soap," plus "some sewing thread." After the Battle of Chancellorsville, he requested "a Pair of Shoes if he has leather and can get them made." Later as Torrence prepared to fight at Gettysburg with a new pair of shoes, he happily received "cheese and Sams meat."[23]

"we don't get nothing to eat but beef and crackers and we are tired out on them"

On August 8, 1862, J. J. Brown sent wife Christina "30 dollars all that I can spare now till I see further along." Brown purchased "some sweet cakes today and I had to pay

40 cents apeice for them." "we don't get nothing to eat but beef and crackers and we are tired out on them." He planned to send the "22 dollars" he hoped to "draw ... in a day or two." On January 13, 1863, he indicated that his box with requested "dried peaches ... dried apples and send some butter ... and a few onions" was apparently lost. He may sell the fruit which "sells here for a dollar a gallon." He also would like some "dried blackburrys."[24]

On October 5, 1862, Thomas Davis requested that his wife "make me a lincy shirt and one cotton one and a pair of pants." On May 10 he sent "twenty dollars by J Grigg." He "heard you got the Bible I sent you and all the childrens names were put down right." Later he sent Bibles, a comb, rings, thimbles, spelling and reading books and primers. By the end of the year, he wanted Margaret "to send me my Shoues."[25]

On May 6, 1862, Frederick Dellinger of western Gaston County prepared a box for his son, "F. W. Dellinger," and others which included "some brandy and each mans name is branded on his jug, also each mans name is on his things" and "one bottle of whiskey for you." On January 9, 1865, Henry Dellinger requested that his father send "peas and dried fruit," "some molasses and some hops and yeast and some onions" to be sent with Zimri Kiser, who would be in Cherryville, and he promised to send "some smoking tobacco" to his father.[26]

On December 14, 1862, Franklin Hanna requested "my overcoat and Gloves ... and would like to have a Comfort to lye on." Early the next year, he sent his wife 4½ "yds Calico ... the black is for a Bonnet," for which he paid $1.75. On May 10, 1863, He paid $1.50 for the tobacco he sent home. It was "verry high here I believe that I will have to quit it for I cannot board myself and get Tobacco Two out of $11 per month." He requested "a couple of Checked" shirts and "I want you to make them with large Seames and press them open and Sew them hard and fast down in the inside for the Lice has got to travling along the Seames of my Shirts Some times and I dont admire the travel of the Animal." A week later he suggested that his wife send "Cotton" pants which are "dark collar [sic] as this is a verry dirty place." Optimistically, "I hope that I will get home before I need anymore Clothes that I have we have to pay 15 cts for washing a Shirt and a quarter for pants or a Coat."[27]

"something to eat from home for there is nothing to eat in this state good to eat"

While yeomen and middle-class farmers survived with provisions from home, upper class soldiers experienced better conditions. Mrs. Phifer of Lincolnton furnished numerous articles for her sons. In November 1862 Edward requested "a overshirt" and "a pair of boots ... one size bigger." Writing around Chrismas, he noted that he had received the shoes but "they were too small for me." He requested "a pair of boots." The overcoat his mother sent "fit very well"; he liked it and the "night cap." On July 8, 1862, W. L. Phifer noted that he received his mother's letter, had socks but requested shoes. He requested "something to eat from home for there is nothing to eat in this state good to eat." On October 3, 1862, he received $50, a "fatigue shirt and shoes but not the boots" from his mother. He also wanted some cloth as he was "ragged" and had nothing "fit too ware in a nice crowd ... please do so if you do not want me to be the worst looking soldier in the company." On May 23, 1863, W. L. Phifer wrote his mother from "Union county,

Tenn." requesting socks, "envelops and stamps." On August 30, 1863, he wrote "My Dear Brother" George that he had lost two horses and needed money to purchase another, a necessity for the cavalry. In the same letter he related that he had "lost all my clothes," leaving them with some "boys" who went home. On June 27, 1863, Edward Phifer wrote his mother requesting a "pair of boots made" and that "George wants a pair of shoes." On October 13, 1863, Edward Phifer requested from his mother a "suit," which would cost "$75 per yard" in Petersburg. A few days later he "received the barrel of apples, ... they are in fine order. I enjoy them so much you know how I like fruit anyhow." Seven days later he acknowledged receiving another box. In November he wanted apples, received chicken and other items, and renewed his request for the new suit as "I am almost clothless I have one pair of pants that is fit to wear, you must have some pants made about an inch longer, than George wore." On December 12, 1863, Edward noted that the box had arrived and "in good order except the chickens which were spoiled." He thought "[t]he candle is very nice." As December closed and January 1864 began, he requested more apples, sweet potatoes, boots, and more candles.[28]

The "Willie" Linebarger letters provide examples of items exchanged. On November 17, 1862, Linebarger requested "a coupple pair of socks" and later promised to "send some money home." His wife responded to his solicitations, "if you hav money or any thing else that you don't nead thare you send it home where it will be taken care of." Linebarger had requested his "over coate" but later responded "I dont need it"; he also did not need the "pair of gloves," which she had made for him. He instructed his wife to inform Catharine, who was "going to make me a coupple of shirts," to "make the colar narrow not more than a inch and a half or too inches wide." He also sought a "gallon of brandy" from Jacob Carpenter. He desired "cloth for a coat," "a pair of socks," and sent his wife "one bible one testament one paper of needles & half paper of pins." After a furlough, Linebarger secured provisions. He got "ten yard of calico in charlotte ... too yards of bleached cloth ... [and] a dress if you will except of it." He was happy that she "was pleased with" the dress. Soldiers received new clothes but "they want shoes plenty," he wrote his father. Linebarger sent home "twenty papers of snuff" and directed his wife to whom they should be distributed. He also "scent cloth to dallas to Franklin Pegrams ... to make me a suite that is for a coat and pants."[29]

Edward X. Phifer, Company K of the 49th North Carolina Regiment. Phifer, son of Lincolnton cotton manufacturer John F. and E. C. Phifer, exchanged numerous letters with his mother and others describing war conditions before dying of his wounds in Richmond in 1864 (courtesy Lincoln County Historical Association).

"i haven't got neary leter from you Since august the 7"

For wartime participants letter writing was essential, and for historians they enrich our understanding of history. The prolific Caleb Senter remarked on August 13, 1862, that "i haven't got neary leter from you Since august the 7." By December 1 he had "Bin looking for a leter."[30]

William Morris communicated his concerns to his wife, "I am very anxious to heare from you." He instructed her: "wright Every week or oftener." On October 4, 1862, Morris reminded his wife that he had not received a letter from her since August 24. He hoped the reason was the "uncertainty of Mail," and on December 6 he indicated that he had not heard from his wife since November 25.[31]

Leonidas Torrence also sought letters. On August 31, 1861, he wanted to hear from home "oftener than I do." On October 30 he complained to his sister that he had received no letter from home since August 24. By November he still wanted a letter in response to his numerous letters home. On June 8, 1862, Torrence chastised his sister that he had not "heard from [her] in a long time."[32]

Lemuel Hoyle persistently encouraged his mother to write: "Write soon" (August 21, 1861); "Write immediately. I am anxious to hear from you" (April 9, 1862); "Write soon Mother and as often as you can" (April 29, 1862); "Write soon" (May 9, 1862). His letters also convey a mature confidence, familial connection, and expressions of love. In the same letter after inquiring whether his father-in-law had departed for the army, he wrote "Tell him to write to me. Heavens richest blessings rest upon you my dearest Mother." Hoyle often infused faith into his letters, "May it please God to continue his blessings to both of us and permit us to meet again on earth in safety, and finally in Heaven."[33]

"i think mite hard that i sent you to School and Learnt you to Rite and you dont Send me no letters"

M. L. Holland wrote his wife: "I want you to write as soon as you get this letter and if you dont get a nother letter from me Soon you may conclude I am gone.... I would like to read a letter from you eery day I have been gone for have nearly one week and have not had any word from home yet I have rote three letters and will write every chance home sweet home I long to see Farewell dear wife and Sweet babes."[34]

Lincolnton's Phifer brothers wrote and received numerous letters. On July 8, 1862, W. L. Phifer noted that he received his mother's letter but had not received a letter in two months. On October 4, 1862, Edward noted that he had not heard from his mother in "four or five weeks." He would have written more but "have not my papper." On December 21, 1862, writing from "Jacksborough, Tennessee" W. L. Phifer wrote that he was glad to hear from his mother but wanted to know "what is the reason that I don't get your letters." On May 23, 1863, W. L. writing from "Union county, Tenn." closed with "give my love to Miss Mamy for me and tell her to write to me and I will write." On August 30, 1863, W. L. Phifer wrote to "My Dear Brother" George that he had not received a letter from home "upward of three months." He started "three letters home and got mad and tore them up because I could not have the patience to finnish them...." On May 12, 1863, Ed Phifer wrote his mother that he had looked "in vain" for a letter from home, and on November 8 he complained that he had written three letters and only "received one I want you to write more frequently." Mrs. Phifer reported to Edward that she received three or four of his letters "at once."[35]

J. J. Brown ended one letter with "saying God be with us all" and another with "if I never see you again the Lord be with us all."[36] Newton Sellers complained that "I haint got but 3 letters yet from home." On April 21, 1864, he had happily received two letters from his wife and three others from home; he was "[s]o glad to hear from home and to hear that you was well and the poor little babe." His wife reported receiving eight letters from him but he contended that was less than "half that I Rote to you."[37]

A few of the letters of the sons and extended family of Frederick Lineberger Dellinger expose the joy of writing and receiving letters. On July 9, 1861, Peter Dellinger expected that "Brother Jacob will write to you soon as he gets from the hospitale. He is not able to write at this time." Jacob Dellinger complained that he had not received "a letter from [his father] in about seven weeks."[38] James W. Linebarger reported that "the mail was robed and the letters throed away and they was found and I got mine back."[39]

On November 12, 1863, Edney Hoover complained about getting "one letter from you in about too monts." After his capture October 13, he lamented that he had "not hurd anything from you since I hav bin in prison."[40] On November 5, 1862, Caroline Hanna "was glad to hear from [her husband] and that you was geting better of the measles." She complained that letters were not always delivered promptly. On December 7 Caroline sent a letter in collaboration with others to her husband. She worried because she had "not received a letter ... for three weeks" but heard that he was back in the hospital. On February 15, 1863, Franklin reported receiving "one letter from home," encouraged Caroline "to write once a week," and had received a "letter from Father." On August 30, 1863, Hanna wrote his wife about receiving her letter, while writing her "4 or 5" and speculating about poor mail delivery.[41]

Clearly the most frustrated letter writer was Senior Reservist Daniel Haynes Dellinger, who had lost a son and son-in-law in the war. On October 29, 1864, he wrote his wife requesting that she "Write once a week at least." An exasperated Dellinger wrote one day later, "i think mite hard that i sent you to School and Learnt you to Rite and you dont Send me no letters."[42]

"to come home at harvest if I can get a furlo"

Another consistent topic of Gaston area soldiers involved the desire for a furlough to go home. On May 25, 1862, Thomas Davis hoped "to come home at harvest if I can get a furlo." His children, Jefferson and Susan, were "still puny." On July 30 he commented "there is no chance to gt a furlow now but if he gets so bad so he looks like dieing you must write and I will try and com home." Davis was unable to secure furloughs either time.[43]

Granting furloughs often was a function of war conditions and soldier numbers. On December 13 David Coon deplored that "an honest man cant get a furlough on account of the many who have gone home and do not return at the end of their time." His request involved attending his brother's funeral.[44] On December 15, 1862, Franklin

Hanna speculated from the hospital, "I do not know wheather I will get a furlow or not I have the promise I spoke to the Doctor about it and he told me that he would send me home if he saw any chance for it but that he had about 20 on furlow and he could not let me go until some of them returned." Hanna succeeded in receiving a furlough but his request for additional furloughs was not successful.[45]

Caleb Senter shared Hanna's frustrations. On May 11, 1862, his hope for a furlough was dashed with the announcement: "no more furlows given to go home." The next year his thoughts returned to home, "i hope to the lord that i will get a furlow." As summer approached, Senter again wrote "they have Stopt giving furlows." His inability to go home, his sickness, his brother-in-law's death, and a frantic letter from his wife caused Senter to go home without authorization.[46]

In January 1864, Ed Phifer hoped to "come home about next month. I think I can get there by then." He hoped to see his girlfriend. Seeing family and a girl friend was good motivation. Brother George had received a furlough home because of boils. On February 9, 1864, Ed Phifer was pleased that George's furlough had been extended.[47]

On January 27, 1863, P. F. Dellinger accused the Confederate authorities of partiality in granting furloughs: "So much Partiality [was] used that I donte think any of us younge men will get to come home."[48] Affluence, even relative affluence, had its benefits. By June 7, 1862, "Mr. Lewis," Lemuel Hoyle's step father who had volunteered a few months earlier, had already received a furlough. By October 1863 Lt. Hoyle learned that Lewis was again home on furlough. By October 19 Hoyle had been furloughed to Lincolnton where he recuperated from diarrhea and dysentery until his return to duty in about two weeks. By early 1864 Hoyle reported that no furloughs were being offered to officers but was possible for "recruits." On October 20 Hoyle hoped that "Mr. Lewis" could get his furlough extended and reported the Confederate desperation to add soldiers. A "Field Board" visited hospitals and were "making a clean sweep, and sending every man that can walk, and some that can hardly do that, to the front for duty." He saw a number "unfit for duty." He opined that "it is perfectly outrageous."[49]

James W. Linebarger often sought a furlough to visit his wife and, later, his son. As early as July 23, 1862, he reported that "no furloughs are to be granted at all under no cinciderations." Sadly on Christmas, he reminded his wife that he had hoped to "be back by christmas with you all but times is no better & I cant ask for a furlow." By February conditions remained "hard and close they are no time for solgiers to be absent from there company." By the end of the month hopes revived, as "they have commenced giving furlough." Finally in October, he requested and received a furlough, because his wife was pregnant. He succeeded in viewing his son with a January to February furlough.[50]

Later in the war to secure more soldiers, the government conferred furloughs to soldiers who brought in recruits. On January 11, 1864, Edney Hoover hoped for a "volunteer and com to this regiment [then] I cold get to come home.... I cold get a fulo for thirty days if you no of iny body.... I just thout it was nothing like trying," he reflected. On March 3, 1864, Newton Sellers wrote his wife that the army gave "a 30 day furlow that fetches a Recruit" and a number of new recruits had arrived. J. R. Dellinger asked his father to bring two recruits, "Henry" and "William Conners son." He would reimburse travel expense and to tell the authorities "they are not eighteen." Do so "as fast as you can for the furlourhs will be stopped soon," he admonished.[51]

"have my likeness taken"

Many soldiers also secured pictures in their uniforms. Some have survived. Thomas Davis indicated that he would "have my likeness taken and send it to you the first chance I have." He wrote, "it cost me four dollars."[52] On September 27, 1863, Edward Phifer planned to go into Petersburg to have his "Photgraph taken" and by October informed his mother that he "had [his] likeness taken. I will send it home by the first opportunity. I think it is a very good one." On October 20 he sent his "likeness."[53]

On June 8, 1862, P. F. Dellinger got his picture made for "Sat is faction of you an the family and olde Grammaw." On June 22 P. F. reported that he had sent "mi likeness" home to his father. On August 18, 1862, Marion Legget Holland wrote his wife that he "went out with some of the rest of [soldiers] to get their likeness taken." On May 29, 1862, James Wellington Lineberger informed his wife that he "had [his] dagaratype taken yesterday and I sent it with Mr. R. Falls." His picture provided reassurance for Elizabeth. She looked "at your likness evry day and some times once a day wont do me."[54]

The Gaston soldier letters reveal many unique stories and anecdotes. Many of these young boys and men saw a world previously unknown to them. One oral tradition involves Frederick Washington "Wash" Dellinger. His third wife, Minnie Cobb Dellinger, was seventeen when she married her husband who was sixty-five. A newspaper interview related the story that Wash was at Ford's Theatre when President Lincoln was shot. Wash and Jonas Hoyle of Lincoln County were prisoners of war housed on the south of the Potomac but were given freedom to work during the day and "were employed at a cemetery." April 14, 1865, was cloudy, and a Union officer gave them his tickets to the theatre for that night. The story relates that both men had just arrived in the theatre and had not taken their seats when John Wilkes Booth "took three steps and shot Mr. Lincoln." Dellinger and Hoyle were "scared. They were Confederate soldiers and they were afraid they might get shot." They "slipped quietly out the iron door and went back across the river to their compound."[55]

David Coon amused "Sister Bob" upon seeing a "blind negro play on a pianno" in Wilmington. His right hand played one tune, "fished Ham pipe," and his left another, "Yankee doodle," while he sang Dixie, "all at the Same time ... with the greatest ease." Coon was amazed that an "idiotic negro having no education at all could perform such wonderful feats."[56]

James Wellington Lineberger communicated some interesting anecdotes from camp. On August 3, 1863, he explained the soldiers' joy at receiving homemade food. "[T]he negroes brought a chicken pie out to camp they pitched in heavy but they found out it was a mixture hog chicken & mostly dog they even had the head of the dog ... some of them said it was good but was awful tuff." Lineberger and his fellow soldiers supplemented their limited rations. In early 1864 "the boys kild another dear the other day and they seam to be enjoying them selves finely hunting." Soldiers "foraged the country ... [and] got a great deal of corn & som too hundred thousand pounds of bacon & pork." Lineberger "only got too squirls and one hair but got a fine diner." He later reported being "out fishing."[57]

On January 13, 1863, P. F. Dellinger wrote his father about the death of J. F. Dellinger: "You wanted me to Rite and Let you Know how [he] was put away." Soldiers carried his body and four others away from the blazing guns. About seven local men carried the bodies to "an olde Mans house to Bery them." With one spade they dug six graves and laid planks on them since they had no coffins. His son offered, "we done the Best we coulde and put his name on the hed Borde," since they were "a fiteing all day and A working all night and travelling all day on one Cracker." He closed with "we done the Beste with pore John that we coulde."[58]

Lt. Lemuel Hoyle, loyal early volunteer from a slaveholding family, penned some of the most eloquent and insightful observations about the war, demonstrating his exceptional education.

On Sunday November 23, 1862, he captured the contradictions of nature and the war: "This is a beautiful morning. The sun is shining in all its splendor and scarce a cloud dims the horizon. All nature seems calm, serene and peaceful. One can scarcely realize, when viewing this lively aspect of nature, that our land is now cursed with war, most dire and calamitous; that even while I write, the work of death may be going on in some place remote—that contending armies may now be engaged in deadly strife, that homes are now being desolated, widows and orphans made, and that this holdy Sabbath Sun may go down upon scenes of blood and carnage. Oh! That this wicked war could cease! That God would turn the hearts of our enemies, and restore our land to peace."[59]

In early 1864 Hoyle speculated on the future of the war: "burden of blood and carnage, suffering and woe, laceration of loving hearts, and desolation of happy homes,"[60] infusing philosophy and reality within the war effort.

From his hospital bed he reflected upon Grant's campaign against Richmond. "One month ago today, this terrible, this awful, battle began—hundred upon hundreds have fallen in the bloody conflict—thousands of loving hearts are now lacerated, torn, bleeding, and the voice of mourning comes up from every quarter of our suffering and afflicted country, and still the work of death goes on—with no prospect of a termination than there was at the beginning. Grant is a murderer and butcher and seems determined to persist in his efforts to take Richmond and 'crush' us out, no matter at what sacrifice of human life." He invoked his Christian beliefs, "I trust God will enable us to foil all his attempts and defeat his wicked designs." He asked God to "cause discord and confusion in the councils of the enemy" and that God would "give us the victory." "My love to all my relatives and friends," he closed his letter. He found Grant to be a formidable general: "Grant is so unlike any other general, that I do not know how to speculate on his movements."[61]

"dear wife I hop this war will end Soon"

Almost all Gaston soldiers communicated their desire for peace. Peace meant an end to hostilities, but it also meant coming home. About three months after enlistment Caleb Senter confided to his wife that "i Cant healp But take a meny a harty Cry when i think of home, home sut [sweet] home o glory mi home if i ondly was thar how hapy i wold feal." Rumors of peace pervaded troops and the home front. On February 24, 1863, he related a rumor, "i was mity oute of hart But But [sic] i have sum news of peas thear is Sum talke of peas and i hope to the lord that this hard times will end Shortly for all the poar Solgers Boath yankeys and our side is getting tired."[62] Later enlistees often hoped for peace.

On April 21, 1864, Newton Sellers expressed hope that the war would end soon: "dear wife I hop this war will end Soon So we can all git home to live in peace one time more." Soon afterward Sellers went home to stay.[63] Reluctant recruit Franklin Hanna, expressed his opinion of the war only two months after being drafted, and hoped "that the time is not far distant when the wicked will cease to truble those who would be at peace." On September 2, 1863, Hanna repeated rumors that England was going to join the Union and France, the Confederacy. He had an opinion: "I believe neither of the forin Powers are comeing in any other way only to help themselves and Conquer the hole and bring us under their Goverment." Following a "very good christmas [meal with] fresh onions and molasses and ... turnips," J. J. Brown hoped for peace in the spring and was "tired ... of camp life."[64]

The correspondence of the Daniel Haynes Dellinger family expresses a deep desire for peace. As early as May 5, 1862, Levi Wacaster optimistically hoped "the Yankeys will giv it up Before long and we all will get home." On March 21, 1863, Henry Huss wrote his "uncle" D. H. Dellinger and family about the "hard times" and "fiten going one close heare." He commented on the heavy losses and hoped for "Peace on Some terms or another i don't Mutch care how so they Make Peace." On January 14, 1864, Daniel Houser wrote his cousin about "Cold weather with a little Snow" near Weldon, N. C. "I hope this Cruel war will soon close," he opined. Senior Reservist Daniel Haynes Dellinger expressed his hope for the end of the war upon enlistment. On February 18, 1864, he hoped "this Cruel war would Stop so [he] ... could return home in peace." On September 5, 1864, "Cousin" Thomas Howser wrote D. H. Dellinger that he was "getting Very tired of this Cruel war" and prayed "God will Speed the day when peas will spread her lovely wings over the glorious land and nation one time more." Dellinger hoped "this war would come to a close for I do not like Camp life tho we fare tolerable well yet but I do not no how long it will last for it Cant last much longer for I think we will eat out before long ther is all the black Smiths and Shomakers to com home and the farmers has to stay here." From depressing Salisbury prison Dellinger hoped "pease will be made" soon. On January 1, 1865, Noah Dellinger wished his "Old Cosin Daniel" a Happy New Year, "O how I long for pece." On January 27, 1865, Daniel Dellinger reported that "there is a White Flag raised in Petersburg and Richmond ... there is little prospect of peace." "I do hope and pray for peace," he opined, "Gods will be done."[65]

Lt. Lemuel Hoyle sought peace with victory: "Oh! That this wicked war could cease! That God would turn the hearts of our enemies, and restore our land to peace." Later in 1864 he encouraged his mother to follow the advice of "some Lady, writing in the Richmond Whig" to pray, "let the heart of evry wife, mother, daughter and sister, in every state in the Confederacy, go to God for peace—an honorable peace." Responding to his mother's "dejected and out of heart" letter, he attempted to assure her "that this cruel war will soon be over and that Mr. Lewis and I will both be permitted to return to you in safety, not to be rudely torn from you again." Fierce fighting around Richmond caused Hoyle to speculate that "this fight may end the bloody drama and secure to our Country the blessing of 'Peace and Independence.'" But after a month of fighting, Hoyle reported "no prospect of a termination than there was at the beginning." By September Hoyle expected both sides would "prosecute the war to the bitter end.... You don't know, Mother, how badly I want to get home."[66]

The Emancipation Proclamation elicited considerable Confederate reactions. On January 26, 1863, Col. Morris was "proud to Say that the North are becoming Disgusted at Lincoln's Emancipation Procklimation and threaten to Lay down there arms and Go home." He reported peace initiatives from the New Jersey and Pennsylvania legislatures but believed that it was "the Most important time for us to Stand firm to our Posts I have a hope of a Peceh Not far Distant." On February 1, 1865, Ambrose Costner from Raleigh wrote his sister, Morris's wife, that "Upon the subject of peace I can only Say that Commissioners have gone on to Washington and I hope something will be done to close this matter." He also hoped for a general prisoner exchange bringing Morris home.[67]

"Some people think Peace will be made soon," early enlistee Leonidas Torrence commented in 1862, "[but] others think the War will continue 5 or 6 years. As for my part, I do not see any prospect of Peace."[68] On September 17, 1862, Thomas Davis optimistically informed his wife that "there is a right smart talk of peace here but I cant tell anything about when it will come about." A few days later he speculated that "the war cant last much longer Some think it wil stop against cristmus," and in October Thomas R. Barnett predicted, "Peace will be maid before Christmas." Davis stopped talking about peace until August 1863 when he expressed rather distressingly, "Oh what glorious news it would be if we could only hear that Peace was proclaimed in our land once more." By the end of the year he lamented, "I long to Se the time com when this war will com to an end for I do think ther has ben anuff blood" and wished "very much to Be at home a[t] Christmas."[69] James W. Linebarger seldom complained in his letters or hoped for peace. On August 5, 1863, he nostalgically longed for "some peaches and water melons" and exclaimed, "I am tired of the solgiers life."[70]

On April 20, 1864, "Em. Houser" communicated that "the Yankee Congress are making peace speeches their is great deal of speech of a speedy peace." David Coon wished "the war will soon end." On March 13, 1863, he dreamed "a very pleasant dream while in Tarboro. I dreampt the war was over." On Christmas Eve he anticipated "a dull Christmas[,] would like to be at home."[71] Edney Hoover communicated the rumor that "north Carolina is a going back in the union and I think if the[y] do that the men will all go home I do hope and pray that they will make peas before long." Later he reflected that "it dunt look much like pease when they are afiting every day." Early 1864 he continued to speculate, "I wold bee the gladest man in the world if I only cold bee at home…. I dunt think that war will last much longer." Again in June, "it seems like this cruel war wold never stop," he complained.[72]

As 1865 dawned, James Fulton expressed his hopes and prediction, "I hope to God this savage war would stop and there seems to be some sign of it at present."[73] The absence of peace discussions by the Phifer brothers is unique. It is very possible that their affluence, education, familial, and community support were effective substitutes for such wishful thinking. While Edward and William Phifer were able to rationalize their service and depravations, their mother was exasperated. After William's death, George's illness, and Edward's eventual mortal wound, she expressed "[h]ow anxious I am to have you with us." "Try to get home if possible," she wrote her bedridden son, "[t]he Lord save and protect you and bring you safely home."[74]

For soldiers and their families, the war altered their lives, as they attempted to maintain normalcy. The story of their families is one of stress and survival.

5

Family Life

Few histories examining the Civil War period explore the circumstances and role of children and the family. When they do, often research involves well-to-do families, political leaders, generals, or businessmen. This project uncovered insightful new information concerning soldier-father communications with wives and children and how the war-created stresses, uncertainty, and disruptions which affected children and families. The story involves ordinary citizens, often of modest means, and the literature contributes to the understanding of how the war affected all people in the South.

The soldiers' absence from home required wives and mothers to assume new roles and responsibilities, as children performed chores as a matter of survival.[1] Other effects included disruptions of school and church, the stress of separation, how fear impacted families, the delaying of adolescent romance, and how the births and deaths of children and other family members impacted them.

In 1860, Harriet R. McIntosh was a 14-year-old Mecklenburg County resident with siblings Juliann and William and parents Alexander and Melinda (Belinda). Melinda's family name was Sifford or Siffert, and the young family resided in Lincoln County in 1850.[2] Harriet corresponded extensively with relatives and friends in both Gaston and Lincoln Counties. She, her family and friends, were of modest means and their spelling, punctuation, and grammar reveal their limited education, but their letters offer unique insight into the mindsets of adolescents, adults, family, and friends during the war.

"I wish the cruel war would come to a close"

The McIntosh letters[3] convey a harsh war: "I wish the cruel war would come to a close," Bettie Little responded in 1864 to a Harriet McIntosh letter, as she lamented missing relatives and friends.[4] Harriet read as relatives and friends shared their experiences.

On June 25, 1862, Isabella Little wrote Harriet that "brother Jim" had been "struck three times with Pieces of bums shells and was Shot one time threw his pants but dident tuck the skin." "Issa" went to see "brother Jim [who] come Home wounded as he was for I never expect to sea him again." He "was hurt so Bad" that she "thought he was dead." She "cant tell [Harriet] my feeling At that time." Bettie Little lamented that she was "sorry to here of Mr. W. M. Martin going to the armie." By September she informed Harriet of the "deth of Brother John" and opined "with as mutch truble As we have seen this cruel war ... brother Jimmie in Heaven." Fortunately "brother William" was at home and "had his furlow Extended for 30 days." Little informed Harriet of the continual deployment of soldiers, "Arch Little leaves to morrow for the armie tho he will not be sent to the field he will be sent to camp home and put on lite dutie."[5]

Soldier disease, battle wounds, and camp conditions negatively affected family members. On September 12, 1864, Elmina L. McIntosh wrote Harriett's father, Alex, that acquaintances had been wounded or killed near where his brother Isaac worked on the railroad. "William," reported Elmina, "is in verry bad health [with] chronic diarrhoea has got verry lean and weak." Her concern for William McIntosh also pertained to "the poor souldiers they haf to go while ever they can walk I think if they would give them a furlow when they get sick to come hom a great many would get well that dies. O that this awfull cruel war would stop and let all the poor soldiers get home." Elmina hoped that Alex would get a furlough soon and would also write. She "saw two souldiers last week that has got home on furlow that has the same disease William has they are nothing but skin and bone," and she advised Alex to "go to hospital."[6]

On October 9, 1864, Bettie Little communicated the "deth of John Nantz and Thommas Hagar.... James Hagar departed this life thursdy last." She had heard that Harriet's "father and his company has to leave ... [and she] Was sorry to here it. I tell you that Air going to take the last man." She continued, "I don't know what Will becom of us all that last man Will hafter go before this cruel war ends."[7]

On December 4, 1864, one of Harriet's maternal relatives Violet A. Sifford of Cottage Home wrote that "Aunt Lizzie is looking for uncle Miles home this week." She anticipated Christmas with mixed feelings, since "there is no men in the neighborhood except 3 or 4 old men." She commented that "little John Bynum has to return to the army again and entirely barefooted and his wife also."[8] Furloughs allowed for recovery and familial support. On December 13, 1864, "aunt Elmina L. McIntosh" wrote that "Isaacs foot is doing tolerable well now the Dr came," who "took out five peaces of bone." Isaac L. McIntosh enlisted at Dallas in 1861 and suffered a wound prior to November 1864, for which he received the furlough. Violet received a letter from William who "will get a furlow sometime this winter." She heard "the other day that brother Alexander got his furlow lenthned thirty days," and she hoped "he will get to stay at home all winter."[9]

On January 15, 1865, "Aunt Elmina" answered Harriet's letter that "there is a good many souldiers at home in this neighborhood some of them are sick." William McIntosh received the box she sent and also enjoyed a "New years dinner" of "loaf bread as would make six small buiscuit, six small bites of turkey and the shoulder of a sheep with all the meat cut of[f] poor [for] dinner." On January 22, "cousine Violet Ann" informed Harriet that she had received a number of letters from soldiers and "uncle [?]Kilen [was] ... disheartened," as he "had not had a letter from N. C. in 2 months." She feared that all men would "have to go and yet be subjugated."[10]

On March 3, 1865, Violet Ann again wrote "Cousin Hariet" that she had "heard nothing from any of our Uncles" and noted that "a great many prisoners came in." She also reported "part of the rail road washing away." As some soldiers came home, she gossiped others "went off in disguise as ladies if is so." She also "heard that Uncle Solomon went with Jennie to the enemies lines. Where is your Pa. has he gone with the [???] I suppose they have all left Salisbury little John Bynum came home last Sunday."[11]

Bettie Little renewed her correspondence on February 12, 1865, and informed Harriett that the war created refugees as "Mr M. L. Dellinger and His wife and Asalger[?] that is staing At unkle green Abernathy." She declared, "I do wish this cruel war could come to Aclose. God hasten the day that peace may be Established.... if every lady new As hard of the war as I am I think Men Would quit." John E. Little had written Bettie that "the men deserting ever day tha Had five left his company." Little used his last "scrap of paper" and wrote all around it. After the surrenders on May 14, 1865, Bettie Little wrote that she was glad "to see Men going home tho I have No Brother to return and but few friends Nearley all my [?] bunnings air kill.... How sad and desolate I feal when I sean Brothers company come."[12]

On June 3, 1865, Violet Ann wrote Harriet "While anxiously waiting uncle Roberts return.... I am so glad your Pa got home safe many boys and men are now at home and others coming which brings fresh to membory my poor unfortunate Brother who longed for the time to get home and stay but we must be reconciled we feel almost that the hand of affliction was more heavy upon us then any others."[13]

"you must be shure to ask me to the weding"

In the midst of wounded, maimed, and dead soldiers, the young McIntosh correspondents attempted normalcy as they gossiped about boyfriends, romance, and flirtation. On June 25, 1862, Isabella Little teased Harriet, "you must be shure to ask me to the weding if you don't I will bee mad huret." Bettie Little playfully discussed marriage with her "ole man" and inquired about how Harriet and "Mr. you Know [were] getting along." On December 27, 1864, D. B. Brown wrote Harriet from Petersburg that he "haint hurd from any of the girls and I dant think that tha air doing their part with me or tha woode righte to me." He bragged, "if you cood Just se my gun in one corner and my haver sack in the other and blanckets folded up in or der redy for in spection. We hav to be up one third of the night and that is hard on us. I woode liken to hav bean with you christmas time."[14]

On June 20, 1865, Charles H. Newbold of Philadelphia, Pennsylvania, supposed that "Cousin Harriet ... [would] have a number of weddings now that the 'boys' have come home. I suppose the secessionists feel too badly yet to go a courting, look out now Harriet & don't get a secesh bean." He wrote that they failed to attend a "wedding, but as Jennie & I received no invitation of course we could not come. I wish the newly wedded pair all success & happiness in life." He speculated, "it will not be long before I shall be called on to congratulate you upon a like event" and flirted about the interests of "Milt" toward Harriet and possible reciprocal feelings, "am I right or wrong in my conjecture?"[15]

Lincolnton's Phifer brothers also flirted and conjured images of marriage in their war letters. W. L. "Willie" inquired about the "pretty ladies at home" in a letter to his mother. Ed Phifer and his mother discussed a potential girlfriend and possible wife. On January 10, 1864, he inquired, "How is Miss Anna Conley getting along. I would like to see her if she is pretty, she is rather young, but that is a small object." Further, "give my love to Miss Anna conley, does she live in Lincolnton now and how long do you expect her to stay."[16] Match-making was a family affair. His mother wrote: "Mamie [his younger sister] had given you to Ada Conley for a sweetheart, she shows her your likeness very often. She is a sweet little girl of 12, I expect you will fall in love with her." "Give my love to Miss Olmstead and Miss C[onley], Kiss mammie and much love to Pa and George," Ed commented among topics of battles, execution of deserters, and food.[17] He closed a number of letters with "Kiss Mamie and Ada, love to Pa"; "Give my love to Miss Connelly

F. Olmstead"; "Give my love to Misses Olmstead, Connelly and Gray and also all of my inquiring friends. Kiss Mammie and much love to Pa." On May 30, 1864, Minnie Gray wrote Edward Phifer from Lincolnton, whom she called her "'Soldier Friend.'" She had communicated a message for him to Ada and she "brightened up immediately." "I feel sorry for a young lady who has a sweetheart in the Army. They suffer more in mind than they are willing to admit."[18]

Minnie Gray believed that Ed Phifer held a tenuous commitment to Ada Conley. She confronted him: "Mr. Ed, I am afraid you do not love [Ada] as much as you make me belive you do. Will you belive me if I tell you that I never did think you loved her, but only tried to make me think you did. I think you admire Fanny Olmstead a great deal more."[19] A few weeks later Edward fell wounded and later died.

"A log roling yesterday evening"

Families occupied themselves during the war as well as they could with occasional entertaining, gossiping, dealing with sickness, and working. Belinda Morris, a fifteen-year-old from Nail Factory, present High Shoals, Gaston County, communicated a glimpse of Gaston life among her friends just prior to the war. Her letters document the common practices of "Cousin Caroline Morris" spending two weeks with Belinda, Belinda spending four weeks with "aunt Mry Sifford," her parents tending to "Mrs. [Moses] Stroup" who had been sick for eight weeks, "A log roling yesterday evening," measles and chickenpox infecting relatives, plans to visit Harriet, and invitations for Harriet and her sister to visit Belinda.[20] On April 14, 1859, Belinda informed Harriet that "mary Jane had the pneumony," "frost has kild" the family apples, and she made a "trip to the mountains for Robert Brevard and the chilren." She also described her mother's garden and discussed writing other relatives. On January 25, 1860, she informed Harriet that she had been "in Charlott last week and Saw uncle Solomons fokes." She reported that "pa has bout more land he bout 8 acors." On February 25 she informed her "cousin" that she attended "A quilting at Mr Hozy Stroups last Saturday" where "ter was 14 girls ther" but they did not "getdun quilting." She reported receiving a "mity fine book" at church "but it wont do it is for the Norten Conference" and also spent time "Colering Some thred."[21]

After the war began, family and neighborly visitation became more sporadic as work schedules and sickness intervened. Isabella Little wrote Harriet McIntosh reporting that she had "been sick ever since [she] left [Harriet's] house." On January 11, 1862, R. W. Little, a "cosin" Confederate soldier, wrote Harriet that he went to visit her father but missed him because he "had Just gone to the hospital." He enjoyed the box of "good cakes" the family sent. He regretted missing "christmas," where he could "eat Some of ant melindas good chicken pye." He reported the "Shoose" which "uncle elie" made "fit very well." He closed by requesting that Harriet write soon.[22]

On October 25, 1863, Bettie Little wrote Harriet McIntosh informing her that she was sick with the "Cold very bad" and encouraged her cousin to visit so they could "have some fun." On November 17 she responded to McIntosh's letter as she was making a dress for herself and then planned to visit her cousin. On February 2, 1864, Bettie Little answered Harriet's letter but had "not bin well" with "teeth achake." She was "bussy weaving and have bin for some time" and was making dresses for others. Later she invited Harriet to visit and gossiped about various "girls" who attended a party in the neighborhood, where they had "more fun." She hoped to attend "afishing partie next Saturday" and invited her friend to come. She had done a "great deal of weaving ... 30 yards in the loom Now and more to go." Bettie continued to weave a "calico dress."[23] In Dallas W. D. Glenn attended a "husking at Mrs. W. G. M.... The girls shuck the corn in absence of the men."[24]

On September 12, 1864, Elmina L. McIntosh wrote her brother-in-law, Alex, with news about neighbors and relatives. She noted that "several children died with sore throat."[25] On November 6, 1864, Bettie Little answered Harriet's letter, telling her that "William leg is improving fast his helth other wayes is good." As mentioned in her previous letter, Bettie was "weaving all the time. I have in Aweb of dresses for my Help and sis and have along web to weav for Mrs. Whitley and Aweb up geanes for Mrs. ?Naxin. When I get that all wove I am going to make me Anice dress for Christmas." She found herself "Alone this evening sis went home with Cousin Magga Bryant from church." She invited Harriet and her sister "go come Christmas," and she hoped to go to Charlotte to visit her.[26]

Violet A. Sifford reported that they had finished "sewing wheat and oats" and her mother had finished "weaving us some dresses." She invited Harriet's mother but only "until we kill hogs." "Aunt Elmina" had been "weaveing every chance" and "expect to be at it till spring." On January 22, 1865, "cousine Violet Ann" wrote Harriet that the rains had created "high waters" in the area. She hoped to "go to Charlotte this week but will not go now while the roads are so mudy.... Hannah has just finished the weaving of 2 yds of my nice black Janes cloth for to make him clothes." She planned to "have my quilt quilted some time this spring if the Yankees dont get here before I get ready." Violet Ann reported that the wet weather prevented making a garden and she "just finished making a dress for" herself.[27]

On March 20, 1865, Aunt Elmina wrote Harriet that she "and Anna have been sick for the last two weeks have dipthitara in mouth have suffered a great deal my mouth is a little better but I am very weak and feeble have not eat but verry little since my mouth has been sore.... it appears like it will have its course" even with the doctor and using "every kind of mouth wash." She reported the deaths of others and wanted to know "wheir your Pa is we heard he was at home but gone again and did not hear whear he had gone to."[28] On May 14, 1865, Bettie Little wrote Harriet that she was "still in the land of the living" but had "sufferd Agreat deal ... [and] was confine to my bed."[29]

Violet Ann did not think she "can stand the harvest this time our wheat will have to be cut in a few days. Uncle Miles will cut for us." She "looked for some of you over last Saturday we had Brothers funeral preached last Sunday at Friendship." She planned to write but did not "having no mail running." "Mr Thompson preached [the funeral], it was an excellent sermon leaving the deceased a high calling and character."[30] On July 6, 1865, Harriet McIntosh received a letter from an unsigned correspondent who "hant time to rite you.... I am weaving for Bell." She also "Went afishing yesterday and never caut but too fish and both of them got back in the River." "Isabella sends her love to you and also you fathers family."[31] For yeomen and farm laborer families, creating their own clothes, sewing for others, farming, and sickness seriously limited wartime recreational diversions.

The more affluent Phifers owned pigeons, which served as pets and as food. On November 5, 1862, William L. Phifer wished he could see them. Willie wrote his mother in December that "I do not want you to kill all of my pigeons but you can kill the best part of them, leave all the prettiest ones, give some of them away, as many as you think is right to do but don't give two many of them away for I come home." In August 1863, Edward also inquired about his pigeons.[32]

Though more affluent citizens of Lincolnton continued having parties, there was at least one exception. Minnie Gray reported to Edward Phifer that his sweetheart, Ada Conley, "was invited to a large party last night at Mrs. Stowe's and she certainly looked lovely. I did not attend the party. I have made up my mind not to go to any more soon. Oh how earnestly do I pray for this miserable war to end." Some Confederate women did their part to support the war by abstaining from parties. She participated in other entertainment. "Your mother, Mary, and myself went fished a few days ago. We spent the blessing evening at it and did not catch thing, oh! How your father laughed at us." Minnie Gray recognized that the war had changed Lincolnton's social life: "This little place is not very gay now. We have a very pleasant time walking late in the evening and especially after tea by the moonlight." She hoped to have "some card-parties" for the girls "when the weather [got] more pleasant."[33]

"Jennie" informed Edward Phifer that she had been traveling, "three weeks at home and two weeks at my Aunts" and had "not been in Lincolnton for the last four or five weeks." In addition she was involved in a "Grand Concert" but feared it would "be a failure." Ed Phifer encouraged his mother to have dinner with "Miss Jennie Adams" and "Cousin Frances."[34] While the Lincolnton social scene exhibited limitations, it was still alive and well.

The *Western Democrat* reported that the "Grand Concert" was held at the Lincolnton Female Seminary on December 23, 1863. The article described "the steps, doors, and passages, all, already filled with anxious visitants." A thorough listing of songs and participants preceded the principal's expression of thanks for the "very large assembly." The newspaper correspondent stood for the "three and a half hours" performance and complimented principal, school, and teachers.[35]

"Church [and] campmeeting"

Families found solace and companionship in religious activities during the war. Bettie Little had "bin to Church to days At Hillis Chapple ... it look like campmeeting."[36] On December 4, 1864, Violet A. Sifford of Cottage Home wrote "Cousin Hariet" wishing Harriet and "Julia were here to go with me this evening. Mr. Hanna? A Protestant preacher there. He is a very good preacher." George May, her regular preacher, has not been "around yet" as Harriet should remember him at "rocksprings." "[H]e is nothing extra," she commented, "we did have an excellent preacher, Mr. Darby, he always had large congregations and everyone seemed to love him."[37]

On January 15, 1865, "Aunt Elmina" "went to Hills Chapel today to hear our niew preacher but got disappointed as he did not come. some say we will not have any preaching this year but I hope that is a mistake." On March 3, Violet Ann Sifford remarked that "we don't have preaching any more our preacher I hear will be at Friendship 2 weeks from today his first time." On April 8, "Isa Sifford" wrote "neace" Harriet since "all gone to preaching at Salum." On May 14, Bettie Little remarked that "we had agreat meeting at Hillen Chapple some time back. Thea Was forty five Joined the church that is White pursons and a great many black persons We Will have preaching next Sunday Again."[38]

On June 3, 1865, Violet Ann wrote Harriet that "Friendship church was more than full of people our circuit preacher has thrown out that church and members with it unless they chose to move to some other church."[39]

The war disrupted regular church services. On August 31, 1862, D. H. Dellinger wrote his son that "Dr. A. J. Fox preached" a funeral at Bethphage Lutheran in western Lincoln County. "Their was a large Congregation their of women but not but a few men and a good many little boys." He also reported that Rev. Dr. A. J. Fox was going to stop regular preaching at Bethphage so that he could "practice Medicine and as he was Your instructor as well as your Pastor I want you to write him a letter" because he requested it.[40] By November 20, 1864, Rev. Fox had resumed some of his ministry. Last Wednesday "we had preaching at Bethphage [which] was fast day. Dr Fox Preached for us and as Usual preached an excellent Sermon."[41]

Jacob Froneberger observed in his diary inconsistent religious services in Dallas. On June 27, 1864, he noted that "Rev Monroe Anderson preached in Dallas church this morning." Later on September 27 he noted that "We had a preaching in the Church yesterday by mr. Singleterry. We have no regular preaching now."[42]

"the Boys had better Chop and get all the wood you Can in good Weather"

Soldiers offered advice, instructions, and delineated day-to-day operations for their children's chores and required obedience.

Senior Reservist Daniel Haynes Dellinger of western Lincoln County, stationed at the Salisbury Prison, asked his brother, George, to check on his "little boys" who were "Sawing Wheat." He suggested that "the Boys had better Chop and get all the wood you Can in good Weather and if you can do Eny thing at the StillHouse take good care of the things and Not leave No Water in the Vessels at the Still House." He encouraged his children to "take good ceare of our Stock." Later, his wife Frances wrote that "wee have got rit smart [wood] halld" and that the family "can git along on the wood"; Philip Spake helped "the boys" chop wood and made rails; and "the Boys have got the Found a tion layed at the wood pile. i think they halled 2 Days." After receiving a letter from his sons, he encouraged them to attend school and to look after mother and grandmother. He implored his children to "do right and mind your dear Mother for if I never git home anymore you had better do the way your Mother sez."[43]

The war altered family structures. After his father-in-law's death, William Morris advised his wife that "if your Mother wishes to Live with us She is Welcome." Later letters confirm that she did in fact move in. Morris required obedience: "Tell the children to Obey you & treat there Grand Mother with Kindness & Respect." Adding a note in a letter, he entreated them to be "Good Children." He expected his children to be "an ornament to Society," "above the conduct of Some in the Neighborhood." He valued discipline: "I have always thought that thre Was too Much Pride and Looseness among Some of our Neighbors With there Children." As a war prisoner, he entreated his children to "comfort" their mother and suggested the fourth chapter of Proverbs as "verry interesting" reading. He cautioned his children to be careful "in there walk & conversation.... Becoming a Member of the church alone dose Not constitute a christian."[44] Mary Ann Dellinger Rhyne also moved into her father's residence prior to her husband's death and remained

The original William G. Morris House was constructed by Morris and his wife, Louisa Costner, on land owned by Costner's father. Mrs. Morris and family resided in the two-room house as she exchanged letters during the war. It has been moved and restored and can be seen at Heritage Park at Gaston County Park in Dallas (courtesy Melany Dawn Crouse Photography).

there throughout the war. Disagreements often occurred in these war-induced extended families. Soldier Thomas Davis attempted to mediate between "[his wife] and [aunt] Sarah [who] cant agree." He closed another letter encouraging his children to attend "Sunday School."[45]

For the Morris family, separation affected family dynamics. Apparently in response to a letter from his wife, Morris reminded her that she was surrounded by "loved Ones" and had "Many things" for which to be thankful. "To be permitted to Meet around our fierside with our dear little children is a blessing higley to be appreciated." He reminded her that they should "beare our trials with patience & resignation." Two months later he began his letter: "I am allmost out of patience waiting for a letter from You." Separation also enhanced romantic thoughts, which Thomas Davis emphasized: "Margaret you have no Idy the love a man has for his wife and dear children till he is drodg of [drug off] from them." "I am glad we have that love for each other that war nor no other trubles can brake," he continued.[46]

Caleb Senter expressed similar concerns as he worried about his family and their welfare. Soon after departure to the army, he wished he was at "home, home sweet home, oh glory my home." Later he confided, "i am tired of this troublesum times i am afraid that my dear wife and Children will Suffer yet Be four i can get home.... when i think of my family per haps Starving for the wante of my laber ... [yet] i hope and trust in the lord." Senter's desperation increased as he anticipated deserting, "i Cant for get youe and the Children." Upon his return from desertion, he despaired: "if I never Shold return, i want youe to try to rais the Cildren in the way of the Lord and let us boath try to prepar to meate in Heaven whate a hapy time it wold Be."[47]

W. C. Wolfe, who resided near the Gaston and Cleveland County line, expressed his feelings for wife and family thusly: "I allways remember you and the children let us pray for one another and if we never meat on earth a may we all meat in hevan whare wars and trubale wil be knomore.... Kiss the children for me. Youre husband til death."[48]

Wolfe's friend and Cleveland neighbor, Thomas Davis, also concerned himself with his children's behavior and adherence to chores. On May 25, 1862, he instructed "Daniel I want you to ba good boy and mind your mother and help your aunt Sarah work and try to make all the corn you can." He felt guilty he could not come home to attend to his sick son Jefferson as "there is no chance to gt a furlow now." He assured his wife that she "must do the best you can and I hope that the Lord will be with you while I am absent." He implored Daniel to "be a smart boy and plow and Make lots of corn so you can have bread plenty to eat." He challenged "My Dear little Son" to "be Smart and take good cear of your hogs and Jule and make them all fat if you can ... see if you cant beet Thomas Jackson and James David making corn." He instructed, "Daniel ... write me wether you have any cane seed planted or not."[49]

"Keep the Children at School"

The research indicates that most soldiers valued education, even in the toughest of times. On January 25, 1860, student Belinda Morris informed her friend Harriet McIntosh that "Scool [was] out ... last week." To honor their teacher they held a "Candy Stew" attended by "a heat of people," where they had a "big time."[50] On September 12, 1864, Elmina L. McIntosh wrote that "the children has been going to school and Anna and Craig are going yet but Michael and Willy had to stop to pull fodder." Violet Ann wrote that Mrs. W. P. Bynum's daughter "has been at home 6 weeks but will start back to her school this week in Hillsborough. She is a very pretty girl."[51] Schooling was valued by rich and poor alike.

Middle-class soldier William Morris conveyed his concern about his children's education, as he "want[ed] the Children to Go to School Next Summer if possible." "I am anxious for them to learn all they Can." Later, he admonished, "Keep the Children at School." His wife noted that, since there was no school in the Dallas area at that time, she requested that brother Ambrose Costner keep Ella as "we want her to go all she can although I need her. Pa says I must try to keep them at school." Morris again emphasized, "[k]eep the Children at School if possible. I hope to find them all advanced in there Studyes when I arrive home." "Doo Not Neglect your books," he advised his children.[52]

On October 2, 1864, Jacob Froneberger described school in Dallas: "Mary Ward ended her school on Friday last and had a picnic dinner. Sue Pegram, Mary Lovenia and Maggie Barrett was head of their respective classes. Mary Lizzie was second in her class and Washington was third in his."[53]

In Lincolnton, "Mr. Lander's school has commended again." Some affluent Lincolnton citizens had their children tutored during the war. Minnie Gray had "two little scholars—Mamy and Nannie Michal—they come up everyday for me to hear them recite their lessons. Mamy really will write a pretty hand after awhile."[54]

The war also interrupted schooling. Frances Dellinger reported in late 1864, "the boys [are] going to schoole.... Jake to Mr. Hoke and the rest ... to Mary Leonhardt. She teaches very low—2 dollars a month in Confederate money." Two days later plans had changed: "Mister John Hoke [was] not going to have any School" and that all the children would attend Leonhardt. "Seventeen were enrolled in her school."[55] Dellinger entreated his wife, "I want the children to get to school, learning is best thing young people can have on earth with the exception of health and Christianity." He received a letter from his sons and encouraged them to attend school and to look after mother and grandmother.[56]

On August 13, 1862, illiterate Thomas Allen Davis cautioned his children "they must be smart and learn ther books and be good to each other and they mustn't qurel nor fite." Unable to come home for Christmas, sadly he encouraged: "My dear children I want to see you all very bad and I want you to be good children and mind your mother and go to school and learn your books." On April 5 he challenged his sons, "Daniel I want you and James to se if you cant be the two Smartest Boyes in the Setlement." "Sarah you and Susan must be Smart children and mind your mother," he continued. He sent a Bible with the children's names listed and "four small Bibles and a fine comb and some rings home." He encouraged his son to read "a nice book" he sent, "be a Smart boy and save all the foder and feed you can to feed your mare and hogs on through the winter." He also sent "two Splling books and two Primers" home. In 1863 he encouraged schooling "the children ... this fall."[57]

J. J. Brown summed up the value of an education when he encouraged his wife to "send Luther to school ... and Sarah Ann too for larning is worth more than Riches."[58] James Fulton valued education as he communicated with his daughter Rachel to "Tell Mary and Lizy to be smart girls and do all they can and above all to be manorly.... Tell Elizabeth I will send her something some of these times, and be a smart girl. Write me how Elenora grows."[59] Caleb Senter hoped that his son, Ephraim, was "learning to write at school."[60] Soldiers far from home communicated hopes for their children's future.

"Ladies Relief Society"

Loyal Gaston women, when not tending crops or managing children, occupied their time by supporting the Confederate cause. On April 29, 1862, *The Daily Bulletin* reported that the "Ladies Relief Society" of "Olney Church and vicinity" had labored "for our brave soldiers with busy hands, ever since they have been called to battle in defence of our rights" and publicized donations of money and clothing items to the soldiers. Having organized their Society on February 6 they elected Mrs. R. F. Holland, President; Miss Margia Bradley and Miss M. A. Torrence, Vice Presidents; Miss N. J. Holland, Secretary; Miss M. J. Wilson, Treasurer. The "Relief Society" also elected 10 Gaston women as members of the Executive Committee. As of April 16 they reported having collected money, socks, shirts, gloves, blankets, drawers, pants, and other clothing and materials for their soldiers. First on the list included money collected from men in the community, followed by money donated by women, and finally by clothing and items created by women to be given to the soldiers. Some interesting donations included "Miss M E Ratchford, 7 years old 1 pr socks knit by her own hands"; "Jinny and Harriet, servants of Capt W I Stowe 25 cts each. Susan, servant of Mrs. M. Gingles 25 cts. Adeline, servant of Miss Eliza

Wilson 1 pr socks. Siena, servant of Mrs. M C Holland one pr socks." Monetary donations ranged from $3 to 25 cents. Some contributions, like that of "Mrs. E L Stowe," included "$3 2 pr shirts 2 pr drawers 2 pr gloves." While women of the Olney Presbyterian Church in south-central Gaston County organized the "Ladies Society," they solicited items and money from persons in South Point, Dallas, and throughout the southern part of the county. Only a few donors shared the largest monetary donation of $3, as most donations were $1 or less with a significant portion being 50 or 25 cents.[61] Southern governments also became involved in caring for soldiers' families.

Gaston County's local government recognized the need to support soldiers' families on June 8, 1861, when the County Court "proceeded to lay a tax for the Support of the Families of those who have Volunteered and gone into the Army." The Court appropriated "18 pr. Ct. of the total State & County Taxes laid" to devise $2 per family per month. At this early date there were few soldiers. The County Court assigned agents to oversee these families and ordered that "J. Fronebarger Treasurer of the Military Funds" pay the families or their agents. By October the Court ordered a settlement between the agents and Jacob Froneberger with monies not to exceed "one dollars worth of provisions per head or one dollar in money per month."[62]

By September 1861 the County Court sought to consider "the propriety of providing winter clothing for the Soldiers from this County" by appointing a committee chaired by William T. Shipp. The committee determined that each soldier should receive "1 pair of Shoes, ... 1 Blanket, ... 2 Linsey Shirts, ... 1 pair of Brown Jeans pants, ... 1 pair of Linsey Drawers" at a total cost of $9. The Court appointed agents to "ascertain how much of Said Clothing can be furnished by the families of Volunteers in Stowes Company." Each agent was to settle their expenditures with Jacob Froneberger.[63]

The issue of supporting local soldiers' families became more serious as the war progressed. In December 1862, the North Carolina legislature adopted a law allowing each county government to distribute money among the poor, an early welfare system. By 1863 the war had seriously impacted families with the combined issues of inflation, mass conscription of heads of household, food and commodity shortages, and violence which often arose in securing basic necessities. The state authorized counties to fund and allocate resources to the "indigent families of souldiers." By April 1863, the Confederate government allowed North Carolina counties to purchase supplies from the 10 percent, tax-in-kind, for indigent families. Historian Paul Escott estimates that North Carolina furnished $20 million to aid the needy during the war.[64]

While no Gaston County sources for these allocations have been located, a treasure trove of documents has been located for Lincoln County, which suggests how Gaston provided for soldiers' families. Lincoln County tasked the sheriff, L. H. Lawrance, with collecting and distributing provisions to "souldiers famales." Documents from 1864 include receipts for commodities purchased like corn, wheat, and salt. For example, Lawrance paid local farmers $5 per bushel for corn. He also paid persons for "halling corn" and "halling County salt." As the salt "Agent for Lincoln Co," he also acquired and distributed this essential commodity.[65]

He settled his 1864 accounts totaling $31,965.74 by using state and county funds, including county bonds. Of that amount $27,593.28 purchased salt, corn, wheat, and other commodities, which left a $4,372.46 balance to be distributed among indigent soldiers' families. The files reveal that agents often signed for commodities or cash received by many wives or widows, while some women signed as they received relief. For example,

"Mrs. David Ramsey" received three payments of $15, $35, and $20 for "self & 5 Children."[66] One is struck not only by the serious need of these women and their families but also with how little money actually was appropriated to them.

To illustrate further, Catharine Wortman from Cleveland County wrote to Governor Vance about her "most piteous and helpless Condition." She was a "poor Widow of 65 years of age who was left of her Husband a widow in Oct 62 with 2 only sons both in the services one of which is Dead." Since she had no "means of Sustenence" she requested that Governor Vance would discharge Samuel, her only surviving son to provide for her. There is no indication whether Governor Vance was able to assist.[67] Mrs. Wortman's condition is indicative of many others.

"I was glad to hear that you had a fine son"

While scarcities and death were constant companions for the soldier and his family, new lives were being born at home. Of the Gaston soldiers studied, four experienced the birth of a child while in service. Their reaction to the event, subsequent stress of separation, and dialogue with their wives create a dynamic which varied by person and circumstance.

As the oldest and longest married, William G. Morris greeted the news of another child with some detachment after the Battle of Fredericksburg: "You can name the Baby to Suit yourself. If you prefer it you can call him William Lee." "[Y]ou can have him Babtised any time that Suits you," he continued. Later, on March 15, 1863, he asked his wife to "tell the Children I would rather they would call there Little Brother Lee than Willy as I would prefer Bill to Willy." He wished to "See little Lee crawling about on the floore" and the "red cheeks" of Luly, his daughter.[68]

Younger married men exhibited great emotion with the birth of their child, as evidenced by the birth of Franklin S. Hanna's first child. On May 2, 1863, he expressed his feelings: "I would like to go and See you and our little babe the best Sort I dreamed last night of being at home and of going to Churtch with you and carrying the little babe in my arms (but God only knowns wheather I will be permitted to pullfill my dream or not)." He suggested a name, "James Franklin but if you want any thing else write it to me for I want you to be Satisfied with the name." As Hanna weighed whether he would remain in the army, the birth complicated his decision, "I want to see you and the Babe verry bad." On September 16, 1863, Caroline Hanna, apparently unaware her husband was in the hospital, commented "I dont know how you can stay away from him." The issue of the infant's baptism also elicited Caroline's concern: "let me know if you want me to have our Babe babtized now or wit until you get home rev Moore is to be at the two days Meeting at Shilo on the first Sabbath in Oct and I would rather get hime to do it if you want it done now." She continued, "I would much rather you would be here or if you have any choice of Preachers let me know for I want you to be Satisfied about it."[69] The new baby was a factor in Hanna's desertion prior to Christmas 1863.

J. J. Brown, a thirty-year-old enlistee, responded to his wife's letter about their son's birth: "I was glad to hear that you had a fine son and you wanted me to send him a name you can call his name Jacob Jackson if you want to." "I want you to have your baby crisended," Brown suggested.[70]

Newlyweds James Wellington and Elizabeth Linebarger expected their first child.

As the delivery date approached, Lt. Linebarger applied for a fifteen-day furlough as he had "some verry important business to attend." After his furlough he informed his wife, "I have got back to the company safe." With a new baby at home, Linebarger sought another furlough. He wished to know "how the baby looks and if its pirty and if you need any thing for it." Three days later, "I am ancious to hear how you and the baby is getting a long if I only could get home to see you and son I would be glad." He complained yet four days later, "I have not received nary [a letter] from you since the 26the of December and I think it is time that I am hearing from you." He received a furlough and saw his son for the first and last time. Naming children often came after their birth. For Linebarger, he referred to his son as "Henry" on February 21 and as "Henry Brevard" on March 25. Yet, on March 25, he suggested that "you can call him Henry Alexander or Henry Brevard just which suits you best or if you want me to decide let me know in your next letter." "[K]iss the baby for me," he demanded, "write soon & let me hear from henry for I would like to see him.... I would like to see Brevard if he groes any or not and see him laff but I fear you have got him spoilt so bad that he cries all the time and never gets in a good enough humor to laff." Elizabeth wrote her husband as he lay dying in a Virginia hospital, "me and buddy is well," but her son "was very cross now but think he is cutting teeth and is spoilt too and cant set alone yet but he is too chunky."[71] At least "Willy" Linebarger saw his son once.

"But how can i Bear the thoughts of my Sweete litle Baby Being gon"

While soldiers were away, some children, family, and friends died or met unfortunate circumstances. On May 31 Caleb Senter wrote his last letter home. He responded to his wife's notification that their daughter had died. With sadness he exclaimed, "But how can i Bear the thoughts of my Sweete litle Baby Being gon. O, if I ondly Cold a been at home to sean her onst more But let us try to meet our diear Baby whear war nor death Cant parte us no more." He wanted details about how she died. He lamented and anticipated his demise, "this is a nughf to break your hart not knowing when you may hear that i am cild." To his aunt he instructed "Donte fret no moore then you Can i Cant help But feal dis tresst But i no my diear Child is at rest." He closed with: "'may the Lord bless you all and save us in his kingdom.'"[72]

The death of William G. Morris's father-in-law created additional family stress. On February 11, 1862, he learned that his father-in-law was ill and on April 11, brother-in-law Ambrose Costner notified him that Jacob Costner was dead. He informed Morris that "Fathers Will" was "awkwardly worded and rather indefinite" and that David Schenck went to Dallas "last week" and saw Costner's mother and sister. "Schenck & I differ about Randle he thought he would have to be Sold but it was clearly Fathers intention to leave him on the place. He told Mother his opinion & distressed her some but every thing has been reconciled in that direction I think. Schenck says he cannot Qualify as Executor but act as counsel." Morris had been named executor of the will. Costner suggested Morris come home "to consult" on the matter. He understood the conflict Morris experienced between "Family & country." On April 13 Morris wrote his wife, "I need a note from Schenck Stating that he could Not Except or qualify as Executor to that [Jacob Costner's] will. I also Recd a Note from Ambroce Stating the Same fact & that Schenck thought

Henery would act as Admr if appointed." While Morris was needed at home, he was needed on the battlefront. He had been elected captain. Legal ownership of Randle remained an issue. Morris contended that Randel had been given to him but also had to consider his being sold. "If they are Going to Sell randle I would as soon they would Sell him Now as to Leave him on the place this summer & then sell." He contended, "if he is sold I will Buy him.... It is Enough to Dishearten him to think he May be parted from his wife in his old Days."[73]

By April 25, 1862, no resolution to the administration of Jacob Costner's will was apparent, "If Henery Nor ambroce is willing to take Charge of the buissiness My Next Choyce is Jonas Hoffman," Morris wrote. By May 5 Morris remarked that he was "very well Satisfied with your [his wife's] Management in Regard to the Sale." Yet, Morris often reconsidered his remaining in the army, "I think some times I had better Resign & Go home.[74]

"Father W. Pegram was killed by a tree falling on him"

Other tragedies struck on the home front. Jacob Froneberger relates in his diary the precarious nature of life and death involving his father-in-law and sister. On November 28, 1861, he reported that "Father W. Pegram was killed by a tree falling on him. His death was easy and he is now at rest." He explained another accident. On October 12, 1862, "Lizzie Ormand got her hand caught in a sugar cane mill and her arm was crushed to the elbow. On the day following Dr. Slone, Miller, Price and White met there and amputated her arm while she was under the influence of chloroform. Their charge for the operation was $50 and was paid by I and Rufus Froneberger."[75]

Ormand recovered and suffered from "Billious feaver" on June 20, 1864. "[T]he feaver was controlled by medicine and now she is free from feaver but is quite weak—not able to stand alone at this time, but with proper care we apprehend no danger about her recovery soon." Sickness struck Froneberger's own family as "Mrs. Fronberger [his wife] has just recovered from a severe spell of typhoid fever. She was very sick for more than two weeks, but is now able to be up."[76]

Near the war's end, Froneberger further reported the war's devastating effect on his family. "Brother Lewis died on the 17th April [1865] at Dr. Skeltons, 28 miles this side of Richmond Va. Was buried in the Episcopalian Church yard near by Dr. Skelton's. His funeral was preached in the Church, his body was decently interred. He was at Dr. Skelton's 11 days and died of chronic diarrhea. He left no requests for his friends and it is for our comfort now that his soul is happy in Heaven" free from the trials of "this troublesome world."[77]

Teenage boys at home got themselves in trouble. E. C. Phifer informed her son, Edward, of a particularly unfortunate incident: "Frank Burton shot young Broadfoot you remember him I suppose." About 4 or 5 boys were at "Canslers pond" hunting, then throwing things, then throwing rocks. The boys pointed guns and as Broadfoot looked around a tree the gun fired. He died in "Laban Stowe's lap." Broadfoot was buried at the Episcopal Church. "Profit by there lessons my dear child," she lectured a Confederate soldier.[78]

Family life, church activities, school, and familial relationships were dramatically affected by the Civil War. As soldiers' wives and mothers, siblings, and other relatives attempted to survive, the war altered patterns of behavior, lines of authority, opportunities for pleasure activities, and attendance at church and school. The stresses of attempting to maintain normalcy are evident as children, wives, and mothers accepted added responsibilities. They coped as best they could, as North Carolina provided a welfare system for widows and their families. The scars of war and its consequences are written in the letters and diaries of contemporaries. No one was ever the same.

6

UNIONISTS AND DESERTERS

Often the history of the Civil War in the South is told with a sweeping narrative which includes consistent Confederate support and dedication to "the cause." Recent historians have examined southerners who felt disconnected with the war and the Confederacy, pointing out that North Carolina reluctantly joined the Confederacy with a large and vocal Unionist contingent. Most research has focused on dissention in the mountains and in the central part of the state, known as the Quaker Belt, whose voters overwhelmingly rejected the call for a Secessionist Convention and where violence such as the Sheldon Laurel Massacre and other atrocities created headlines.

This project began with my expecting little or no documented Unionism or violence in Gaston County. Instead the data indicate that fear and violence, serious economic shortages, threats and intimidation became commonplace, revealing Unionist sentiment in 1860 and 1861, the growth of dissent in Gaston County as the war continued, and socioeconomic and political factors which resulted in soldier desertions. Profiteering, combined with war conditions, undermined Confederate support and added to the Unionist contingent. This chapter conveys the sentiments of Unionists and how circumstances caused dissent and desertion. The following chapter chronicles violence and lawlessness which pervaded the area during the war.

Some historians have described these conditions as a "civil war within the Civil War" or as an "inner Civil War."[1] The lack of food, increase in economic uncertainty, inflated Confederate currency, and the loss of farm workers strained the loyalty of soldiers in the field and their families.

Extortion and Speculation

Profiteering from war has been observed during various conflicts. During the Civil War many well-to-do entrepreneurs remained at home "speculating" to make enormous profits, while their comrades fought for Confederate independence. In Chapter 3 W. W. Holden accused Gaston's Jasper Stowe of such behavior. These divisive issues created a chasm between the citizenry and "speculators," as newspapers and individuals were quick to notice and condemn.

On September 17, 1861, Charlotte's *North Carolina Whig* article "Extortion" stated "our State is infested with a class of individuals who, having only *self* in view, are pursuing a course, which, while it is calculated to enrich themselves, grinds to powder the humbler and poorer classes" and negatively affects all citizens. The extorters were accused of making double and quadruple the profits and were compared to President Lincoln and Secretary Seward. On November 5, the paper reported that salt was $10 a sack with expectations of it rising further and encouraged farmers not to pay such high prices since they deemed it due to extortion, further informing the public that "a gentleman" was soon to leave Charlotte to New Orleans to purchase salt and molasses. On February 11, 1862, the newspaper noted "Another Call for Volunteers" and reprinted an article from the *Goldsboro Tribune*, which condemned "Distilling Corn." The *Whig* began accepting in-kind payment, "Eggs, Butter, Lard, Chickens, in fact anything that is in the market" to pay for a subscription, and it declined in size and quality with misspelled words and in the number of advertisements as the war wore on.[2]

On April 24, 1862, another Charlotte paper titled an article "Our Enemies" to warn residents that "a few persons now doing business in Charlotte, as merchants, who have deserted the seaboard" were buying commodities like butter, poultry, bacon, eggs and were exporting them to Charleston, where they received a higher price.[3] On July 15, *The North Carolina Whig*, quoting *The Standard*, writes "The most stringent measures ought to be adopted and kept up by our State government, to prevent flour and bacon from being sent out of our state." The culprits were "Speculators ... the worst enemies of the South." Bacon cost 40 cents a pound, meal $1.75 per bushel, and flour $12 to $15 per barrel. Speculators were termed "Lincolnites, ... the scorn of all good men and patriots, and the frown of God himself."[4]

As early as 1862, David Schenck condemns in his diary that "[e]xtortion and speculation are the besetting sins of our people" and that manufacturers and merchants were charging exorbitant prices, as sellers increase their prices "to meet the enhancement of his neighbor and together the non-producer suffers all the burden—and from this latter class comes most of the soldiers." Lt. Lemuel Hoyle on furlough to Lincolnton, observed the "extortion and the great rage for speculation which now exists in the country."[5]

On November 26, 1862, newly elected Governor Zebulon B. Vance addressed the issue with a proclamation which prohibited exporting salt, bacon, pork, beef, corn, meal flour, potatoes, shoes, leather, hides, cotton cloth and yarn, and woolen cloth out of the state. He called on the military and militia to enforce the order, prohibiting quartermasters and others from selling out of state for a profit.[6]

By 1863 Governor Vance condemned Gaston County's cotton mills for making above the 75 percent profit margin dictated by the Confederate Congress.[7] The *Western Democrat* conveyed that "certain iron-masters in Gaston and Cleveland are selling their iron at thirty cents per pound, and that they have a considerable number of conscripts in the establishments." The paper suggested that the workers "would have thought it a disgrace to work in iron before the conscript law ... [that they] ought to be put in the ranks of the soldiers."[8]

By March of 1863 the extreme scarcity of flour caused women from Salisbury to riot. The *Carolina Watchman* reported "A Female Raid" in which about 40 to 50 ladies "made an attack on several of our businessmen last Wednesday, whom they regarded as speculators in the necessities of life" and secured flour, molasses, and salt. Merchants were bullied and intimidated. An attack at High Point was also reported.[9] Other examples of aggressive women raiding merchants, cotton mills, and Confederate authorities have been documented. Many of these aggressive women were Confederate soldiers' wives, who initially received sympathy, but later condemnation as the fear of a breakdown in civil authority became real. The *Western Democrat* by April opposed the "female raids" as doing "much harm."[10]

The "speculation" problem occupied much of Governor Vance's time. On April 6, 1863, he encouraged North Carolinians to farm, stop distilling liquor, and to limit the "scarcity of provisions and threatened famine" by planting food stuffs and refrain from planting tobacco and cotton.[11] Later the same month the governor followed up with a Proclamation to stop the *"speculating in the necessities of life"* reinstating for 30 days the proclamation prohibiting the exporting of commodities and food stuffs. By the next month Governor Vance announced that he had accumulated foodstuffs for the poor.[12] Newspapers commended fair-minded businessmen. L. D. Childs of Lincolnton was praised for selling his yarn at "exceedingly low prices." The *Western Democrat* and the *Carolina Watchman* reported that "Mr. Sam. L. Ewing of Gaston county has been selling to the poor in his neighborhood corn at $1 per bushel, bacon and lard at 12½ cents per pound."[13]

"Ruined for the Speculators and Farmers have becom to be Exstorioners"

On April 16, 1863, Daniel Hoffman of Dallas' Hoffman Hotel expressed his frustrations to the governor. He noted that South Carolina had instituted price controls on corn, bacon, and salt and complained that people would be "Ruined for the Speculators and Farmers have becom to be Exstorioners [extortioners]." While Hoffman could not offer

Daniel Hoffman, who built Hoffman Hotel, wrote Governor Vance summarizing some of the economic challenges the war brought. Built in 1852, as Dallas was being created, the hotel served as a prominent boarding place for politicians, persons attending court or shopping, and at the end of the war, Union soldiers. It currently houses the Gaston County Museum (courtesy Melany Dawn Crouse Photography).

specific advice, he suggested calling a special legislative session, observing that "our poor in the Neighbourhood and our poor Soldiers must sufer and suffering at this time there is." He accused farmers of charging high prices for their goods and supposed that they would increase their prices without governmental intervention. Hoffman closed his "blunt addres" by emphasizing that "thare Should be Something Done. Thare is Speculators that will Soon Demand 150 to 200 per lb for Bacon." Governor Vance received another letter dated the same day reporting that North Carolinians had ignored his proclamation, had sold food stuffs outside of the state and that the railroad had transported food to other states.[14]

By April 27, 1863, the *Carolina Watchman* reported a drop in the price of flour, attributed to Governor Vance's interventions. However, the newspaper also increased its subscription rates because of the "prices of provisions, paper and other articles."[15]

The Daily Bulletin printed a letter from Rutherford County which contended that "our enemies here at home" posed a significant threat. The writer classified these people into three categories: "speculators and extortionists," "deserters," and "Union men or black Republicans, who are harboring those deserters and encouraging them to forsake their honored posts." The writer contended that they were working in concert to rob, plunder, and create desolation "to the home of every truly Southern man." His solution was to raise 150 men to swear allegiance "to the Southern Confederacy," "to impress the speculator's trading stuffs, and arrest deserters and send them to camps."[16] Unionist and deserter families were singled out.

An example from Cleveland County illustrates. On December 15, 1863, Andrew Parker wrote Governor Vance seeking advice. Serving as a justice of the peace and operating a grist and saw mill, he told the governor that he "got orders to not grind for the women and children that their men had deserted from the army & those that ... thought to harbor them." He inquired what to do. "[T]he women & children cant help what their husband & father does & I do not know who to grind for." He feared the "Militia officers" since they were "surging a but and has shot Some men dead when they had them Surrounded & could have took them with out killing them." Parker wished to "do what is Rite if I know hit." Parker also accused the militia of capturing men, "& put them in Jail without any proof at all." Men were "kep ... in Jail for severl days and had no proof against them." Parker of Knob Creek post office in northern Cleveland County asked the governor to direct him. Governor Vance responded: "to grind for who ever takes corn to the mill." Parker's dilemma is indicative of the vigilante sentiment which further exacerbated starvation and hard times for women and children and exemplifies the social dynamics of the war. Extreme pressures on Unionist and deserter families caused them to collaborate, trade goods, and commit theft.[17] For deserters, Unionists, and their families, it became a matter of survival.

"provisions will be very high and scarce"

The scarcity of commodities and inflation made life difficult for all southerners. In his diary, Dallas merchant Jacob Froneberger observed in September 1862 that "provisions will be very high and scarce." He attributed agricultural costs and scarcities to "dry weather" but also noted that "all kinds of merchandise has sold out pretty much." Better weather in 1863 provided local farmers with "an abundance of subsistence raised for both man and beast in the Confederacy." Yet, "[p]rices for all kinds of produce is very high" with salt being both scarce and expensive. "Groceries and merchandise are out of the question and can only be bought at exhorbitant prices."[18]

As economic conditions deteriorated in 1864, Froneberger observed, "[p]rovisions are scarce and high.... Gold and silver are not known as a currency now. One dollar in gold is worth twenty-five in Confederate currency and all purchases are made with the paper currency. Consequently, prices are high." The Union blockade limited commodities and by 1864 it controlled Confederate trade. Froneberger wrote, "nothing comes in now without running the blockade and running the risk of being captured.... [M]any a valuable vessel and cargo have been captured and destroyed." Froneberger condemned the inflation and worthless Confederate money: "Most of the people refuse Confederate money only at a great depreciation, but hereafter money will not be so plenty ... a heavy tax will soon be collected." The taxes included the Confederate 10 percent tithing tax on "our produce" and the "state tax of $5 on every hundred dollars worth of property." By the end of 1864 Froneberger observed the effects on the citizens: "The war is pressing very heavily upon the welfare of every family in the Confederacy. I think all class of men and women in the Confederacy are more or less distressed and scourged by the war, and I fear the worst has not been attained."[19] Whether economic distress, worry about husbands and family, or hearing of Confederate battle losses, Gaston County citizens became more pessimistic about their future.

Dallas resident W. D. Glenn agreed in late 1864: "war, want, and desolation, are rife and rampant the gloom thickens."[20]

Other contemporary accounts agree with their observations. In 1863 Lincolnton's David Schenck commented that while the war raged, the other "enemy" on the home front involved food and raiment. He noted that blockade runners continued to get through sufficiently to provide clothes for the people, but food remained a serious problem. Much of the South had been destroyed by war and "citizens everywhere have been seized with a mania for speculation and riches, which blinds their patriotism and induces them to raise Cotton and Tobacco, when they ought not to spare an acre from breadstuffs." Currency inflation escalated, "Gold is worth 5 to 1—Bank bills 2 for 1." The Union's control of the Mississippi restricted food quantities and caused Schenck to observe: "Food or Famine!" Local and state governments formed committees to "raise contributions and fix their own prices, and alarm is considerably excited by the fact." Schenck noted that the crisis "incited to an unparalleled spirit of industry and perseverance. Large crops are pitched and there is no time lost in idleness...." He proudly planted his own garden.[21]

By late 1863, Schenck noted that "[o]ur currency is daily rapidly decreased amounting almost to utter ruin. Gold is now worth 30 for 1." The travails of war affected everyone. "Good men everywhere tremble and pray ... while the wicked grow worse and more hardened." Schenck noted that "vice, debauchery, fraud, profanity, covetousness, and every sin of the world seems to increase in alarming strides" and sought God's mercy on southern people.[22]

Schenck described many "respectable families" of Lincolnton "without meat, sugar, coffee, butter and other usual articles of food." "Negro property is looked on as almost valueless in the situation. Negro men are being sold in market for 100 gallons of Brandy." Theft had increased and "maurauders and deserters" regularly emerged from the "night to rob and plunder." "Our people," observed Schenck "are greatly demoralized—virtue, honesty and truth have almost deserted our country."[23]

The tax burden, "quintupled" according to Schenck, adding to citizen misery. Confederates at home in early 1864 survived by "wearing old clothes," "dispensing with luxuries," using molasses instead of sugar for sweetening, making hats from "Rye and wheat straw," making a coffee substitute using "Rye, Okra, Wheat, Sweet Potatoes and even Corn meal; but chiefly Rye," and by wasting nothing. Women used "old woolen rags" for dresses and "Cotton rags" were used for paper.[24]

As 1865 dawned, Schenck noted that gold had inflated to $50 or $60 for $1 and, closer to Union lines it was as high as $100 to $1. Slave values "are rapidly declining in price, in fact they can scarcely be sold at any price." Gold regularly traded in January 1865 $75 for $1.[25]

Newspapers regularly printed commodity prices, which documents the inflation described by Froneberger and Schenck. The same pattern emerges: inflation for purchased goods, devaluation of Confederate paper money, and unavailability of essential items. Even farm commodities such as corn, wheat, flour, bacon, and beef exhibited significantly inflated prices. Imported items such as coffee, calico, sugar, and salt became unattainable near the end of the war. Shoes and leather remained a scarce commodity for both home front and soldier. Based upon the research project, some of the largest rates of inflation included: coffee, 4,247 percent; calico, 5,000 percent; sugar, 900 percent; wheat 2,233 percent; corn, 1,500 percent; jeans, 2,566 percent; and flour, 1,011 percent.[26] These serious financial challenges contributed to home front discontent.

"Act of Sequestration"

Some "speculators" were actually part of the government and their activities contributed to discontent and profiteering. While David Schenck condemned "speculation" in his diary and regularly noted the difficult economic times, he failed to report his own efforts to profit from the war. Rod Steward's *David Schenck and the Contours of Confederate Identity* documents Schenck's use of his office to enrich himself. On August 30, 1861, the Confederate Congress passed the Act of Sequestration. The law authorized states to appoint receivers who would confiscate lands and property owned by northerners. The lands would be sold at auction, hoping to deal a severe blow to northern financial investors. The vague wording in the law provided the opportunity for personal financial gain, concealed proceedings with secrecy, and allowed receivers, judges, and grand juries to exercise significant unregulated power.[27]

By June 1862 David Schenck received the prestigious appointment of receiver and began conducting business in western North Carolina counties: Cleveland, Catawba, Lincoln, Gaston, Iredell, and Mecklenburg. Steward frustratingly describes attempts to document Schenck's activities, since the participants kept no minutes of their secret proceedings.[28]

Evidence of Schenck's activities has been discovered in Gaston County. On December 19, 1862, "D Schenck Receiver under the Law of Sequestration of the Confederate States" deeded about 266 acres on the waters of Hoyles Creek in Gaston County to Leonard E. Thompson for $2,202. The land had been owned by Yates and McEntire from New York, "enemies of the Confederate States." The land had been "Seized and possessed" through the "district of Cape Fear" during its June 1862 session, which authorized Schenck to auction it to the "highest bidder." R. R. Heath signed the deed as the "Judge &c," and it was proven November 21, 1863.[29]

A second transaction is dated December 1, 1862. Under similar language D. Schenck sold 170 acres on the waters of the South Fork River to Jasper Stowe. Yates and McEntire previously owned the land, and Stowe paid $815 for it. Samuel Lander swore to the witnessing signature of W. Lander since the deed was not proven until September 16, 1869.[30]

These transactions suggest that Schenck chose to sell land to fellow secessionists and political allies L. E. Thompson, a Lincolnton attorney, and Stowe, co-owner of Stowesville Cotton Mill and former state senator. William Lander, witness to the Stowe deed, served in the Confederate Congress.

Steward points out that politically and socially Schenck "had grown increasingly out of step with the majority of his fellow North Carolinians." Steward also provides convincing evidence that Schenck's financial prosperity during the war emanated from profits he received as the Receiver, all the while complaining about speculators and profiteers.[31]

Conscription, Tithing Law and Home Front Pressures

Financial distress, absent husbands, and the failing Confederate war effort created unbearable pressures at home. While governmental intervention tried to assist the citizenry, other governmental policies exacerbated them.

By early 1862 Confederate officials realized that volunteers would not provide a sufficient quantity of soldiers. In April 1862 the Confederate Congress enacted the first Confederate Conscription Act, requiring the mandatory draft of southern men between the ages of 18 and 35. The unprecedented power-grab by the Confederate national government, and the law's extensive exemptions of officials, merchants, manufacturing proprietors, and certain trades alienated southerners. But the most hated exemption was the "20 Nigger Rule," which excluded from military service plantation owners and overseers who managed more than 20 slaves. In addition, the law allowed draftees to purchase a substitute. For volunteer soldiers already serving, the law extended their service until the end of the war.[32] To many, it seemed patently unfair that wealthy, landed, slave owners were exempted from fighting a war which would financially benefit them.

Other equally disfavoring legislation, impressments, allowed Confederate officials to seize private property for military use and to impress slaves to build fortifications or otherwise labor for the government. Slave owners especially found this law troubling. The Richmond government also passed the dreaded "tithing law," which assessed each southerner 10 percent of their produce to be paid "in kind." For the soldiers' wife, that 10 percent represented survival of the family and livestock.[33]

North Carolina newspapers took sides as the new laws were discussed. By April and May of 1862 W. W. Holden's *The Standard* of Raleigh opposed conscription based on "State Rights," while Charlotte's *The Daily Bulletin* and *North Carolina Whig* supported the law as a necessary war measure.[34]

To make the draft more palatable, a $50 bounty was offered to motivate volunteering before the law took effect. Two farm laborers took advantage. On June 10, 1862, Cleveland County's Thomas Davis triumphantly announced, "I have got my bounty" to pay his debts. Gaston's Caleb Senter wrote his wife, "we are a bout to get our Bounty and then i will send you sum money." Even patriotic Confederates, like Lt. Lemuel Hoyle, found arbitrary conscription troubling, especially when it affected young relatives. Referring to his young cousin, Robert Roseman, he reflected, "so innocent, harmless, so perfectly childlike—it seems cruel to make him go."[35]

Citizens also reported conscription law abuse. On June 25, 1863, John H. Roberts of White Pine post office Gaston County, current Cherryville, wrote Governor Vance complaining that Robert Harris enlisted in the 49th Regiment as a substitute for Jacob Borders, "a stout hearty young man" of Cleveland County. Roberts reported that Borders "Got Harris drunk and then got him to agree to go for five hundred dollars." In exchange Borders promised to "do all the Harrises halling wood to have his ground plowed" and promised to travel to the battlefront to get Harris if he wanted to come home. Roberts reported that Borders had failed to comply with the agreement and bragged about the arrangement. Harris was in a hospital nearby, and Borders failed to bring him home. Roberts represented "the community" when he requested Governor Vance to "discharge Harris and send an order for Borders." Roberts further noted that Harris had two sons in the army, could not tolerate "camp life," and had "small girls." Vance responded that he had "no power to comply."[36]

Southerners with financial means often employed substitutes. On November 5, 1862, Caroline Hanna wrote her husband that "M. S. Rhyne Died yesterday was a week his Father hired a Substitute and sent and brought him home but he was Sick and had been for three or four weeks." He died at home after only three weeks and spent most of the time "deranged." Colonel Morris reported that "Jacob Rusicell [Rudisill] could not Guet his substitute in. he will have to stay. I think he will Go Crazy."[37]

On March 5, 1863, the North Carolina Adjutant General's office notified citizens of another wartime measure, prohibition of the distilling of "spirituous liquors." This action also fomented dissent as it restricted the use of corn for human and animal consumption, not alcohol.[38] Not everyone supported what ordinary citizens viewed as another infringement upon their rights. Many yeomen profited from manufacturing alcohol and doctors used it as medicine. The directive met local opposition and inadvertently caused loyal Confederates to question their government.

In early 1864, prominent Gaston County politician, James H. White approached the governor with the issue. White requested that Jacob Plonk, "a Practicing Thompsonian Doctor," who resided north of Dallas, be allowed to distill "2 or 3 runs of whiskey" for medicinal purposes. The law met with considerable opposition from all quarters. Previously, Doctor Goode of Cleveland County mailed a similar request on March 20, 1863. On April 2, 1863, Captain J. H. McIntosh of "Castina Grove Gaston County" post office reported that an "old man" refused to obey the law and threatened to get "one hundred men" to kill Captain McIntosh. Vance's response to Goode and McIntosh was to uphold the law, but his response to White has not been located. On December 1, 1863, W. O. Harrelson of Craigsville also requested permission to distill whiskey because he was "afflicted with chronic Rheumatism" for the previous sixteen months. Because of his condition he had resigned as captain of Company E, 34th Regiment, and Dr. Goode had recommended whiskey.[39]

"Most of the able-bodied men have been conscripted"

As more southern men were drafted, a shortage of white males further exacerbated conditions on the home front. Wives, often unaccustomed to farm work, discovered they were responsible for the cattle, horses, and farm produce. They were also responsible for marketing the products, managing the family's survival, and raising the children. Even elite white women with formal education found their newfound responsibilities overbearing and emotionally burdensome.[40]

On February 14, 1864, Jacob Froneberger recorded in his diary that "Most of the able-bodied men have been conscripted to that age [45] and there is almost an insecurity felt throughout the country for the want of a male population at home." By June he noted the expansion of the law to include men aged 45–50. On August 15 he noted that on "next Friday all the men at home as Blacksmiths, Shoe Makers & Co. will have to leave for the Army. It is a hard call but exempts none and there will be a great deal of trouble among their families when they leave." Froneberger maintained his exemption until December 19 when "the third class of Home Guards" was called into service.[41]

W. D. Glenn, court clerk in Dallas, observed on November 3, 1864 "today the detailed men from this co. start to the armies. They have my sympathies probably some of them have looked upon their native hills the last time and parted with all they hold most dear."[42]

Local opposition to the Tithing Law was pervasive. Senior Reservist Daniel Haynes Dellinger instructed his wife, "Shell out corn and put it on the loft Sorte of Secrete it if you can for the Corn Pressers will be round before very long and the most corn and wheat and meat you can put away the better it is for you"; kill the hog "as soon as you can."[43] "Corn Pressers" were Confederate agents enforcing the 10 percent law. War conditions, speculation, and governmental interference promoted Unionism.

Unionists

The evidence examined in this project demonstrates that from 1860 the 20 percent to 25 percent Gaston Unionist population grew as the war progressed. Confederate vigilante intimidation simply sent Unionist activities underground. Extant records have identified Unionists throughout the county with three strongholds including the Duharts Creek tax district, northwestern Gaston County in Cherryville and Rudisills Company, and areas around Dallas. Common themes for these areas include lower numbers of slaves and slave owners, political conservatism, and high numbers of yeomen and farm laborers.

After the war the federal government passed laws which allowed southerners to apply for reimbursement for property the Union military confiscated during the war. Southern Loyalist Claimants had to meet two criteria. They had to prove that they lost property or commodities. The second criterion was more problematic: claimants had to validate that they had remained loyal to the Union throughout the war and did not materially support the Confederacy. Thirty Gaston County citizens applied to the Southern Claims Commission, and the scanned files are located under Civil War records at the website www.fold3.com.[44] This project identified the socioeconomic status of these Unionists.

For the analysis, Paul Escott's parameters for North Carolina social class were used.[45]

One might expect that the majority of Unionists in Gaston County were yeomen or laborers. The data confirms that assumption. Analyses of the 1860 Gaston County census, 1860 Slave Schedule, and the 1863 tax list were made for each of the 30 persons who filed claims. They are represented in the appropriate category in the table below:

Smyre Pasour House, built in 1850 on the Dallas Square, housed Eli Pasour during the war. Pasour wrote numerous depositions in support of Unionists seeking Southern Claims. The house still stands, representing an example of a modest home of the period (courtesy Melany Dawn Crouse Photography).

	Elite	Middle Class	Yeomen	Laborer	Unidentified
Total	0	8	18	3	1
Percentage	0	26%	60%	10%	3%

Two persons actually changed their status from the 1860 census to the 1863 tax list. One moved from middle class to yeoman and one moved from yeoman to middle. Eight taxpayers owning land and slaves in 1863 accounted for 26 percent of the Unionist total. Yeomen and laborers were significantly more numerous with 21 persons comprising 70 percent of the persons examined in the study.[46] No gentry or elite submitted claims.

Further analysis indicates that all eight middle-class Unionists personally owned less than ten slaves by 1863, three of whom saw their slave numbers drop from 1860 to 1863. Their total acreage and value was 1,447 acres at $13,639 valuation, which averaged 207 acres at $1,948. Their total slave values were $24,469, which averaged $3,496 per slaveholder. Bondsmen's assessed value exceeded the land's value.

In contrast Unionist yeomen farmers owned 3,090 acres and one town lot valued at $17,965, which averaged 206 acres valued at $1,122 per taxpayer. Unionist yeomen farmers in the study appear "land poor," owning as much land as their middle-class counterparts with its value being 60 percent less. When one adds the value of slave capital, middle-class citizens held significantly greater assets.

Other sources confirm that Unionists were primarily yeomen. Peace Movement supporters attended "The Public Meeting" in Duhart's District in 1863. None of the identified attendees owned slaves and most were yeomen. Attendees included: W. B. Lay with 140 ¼ acres valued at $980; Jas M. Hanna with 264 acres valued at $1,350; J. W. Bradley with 233 acres valued at $1,600; S. H. Hoffman with 123 acres valued at $1,250; and Coleman H. Abernathy who submitted a Loyalist claim. Of those in the newspaper article only H. Jenkins was not identified and may have been a landless farm laborer. Other members of the Lay family, Jesse, and C. H., also lived in Duhart's district and were yeomen. Exceptions were Unionists, David A. Jenkins and Dr. William Sloan, who were middle-class.[47]

The Loyalist claims provide unique insights into the challenges of Unionists during the war.

"in great danger of being damaged"

Jacob F. Plonk, who resided north of Dallas and was the only Gaston County citizen awarded a Loyalist claim, stated that he was "never molested or injured more than [he] was not allowed to express [his] sentiments ... publicly ... for fear of personal injury." He stated that persons who did express their Unionist sentiments were "in great danger of being damaged." Witnesses also related that he only spoke to them in greatest confidence "as it was dangerous for such sentiments to be publicly expressed." He did report that Unionist neighbor, Rufus Bynum, was "arrested[,] hand cuffed & sent to Fort Macon" where he died in "close confinement."[48] Bynum's example served to deter Plonk.

Many unionists did not volunteer and conscripts often performed poorly as soldiers. Austin Groner, a Dallas resident, was conscripted, deserted, and never returned to duty. He became part of an underground network of Unionists and deserters near Dallas. Groner testified that Isaac Murrell, a neighbor, owned slaves but "wanted them free." Murrell "assisted deserters," feeding them, communicating and hiding them. Members of the Lay family supported many Loyalist claims through depositions.[49] Confederate James "Willy" Linebarger observed on February 14, 1864, that "we have some hard conscripts that would like to do any thing but what is write."[50]

Aaron Jenkins, who lived about one or two miles west of Dallas, claimed to have aided "deserters and conscripts from the rebel army." He bragged in his testimony that he had "six men under [his] control" and listed them. He cleverly kept his son from going to the army after he was conscripted. He "dug a hole in the ground and kept him out of the army the whole time." He also stated that he "was molested several times" without specifying his treatment.[51]

Former Gaston County resident, Michael Cloninger, resided in Wayne County, Missouri when he submitted his Loyalist claim. He stated that the rebels wanted him to "hunt deserters," but he refused and they threatened him. He stated that his son was conscripted and died in Confederate service. "[I]n the second year of the war.... Valentine Tarr" sent six men, who took Cloninger to Brevard Station "to try" him and hang him "for aiding the Negroes to rebel against the Confederacy." Five justices of the peace tried him; he contended that they tried to "scare me and make me run." Cloninger confessed that he was a "union man," and late that night they released him. He also related that "about a year before the end of the war" some Union prisoners who had escaped from a railroad car from Charlotte came to him and asked for food. He gave them meat and cornbread.

He talked with them and told them to never tell "anyone around there" that he had helped them.[52]

"eradicate such disloyalty"

Another family residing near the boundary with Gaston, Cleveland, and Lincoln Counties experienced conscription, imprisonment, and desertion. On January 20, 1863, W. O. Harrelson, home from the army, wrote Governor Vance concerning Jacob Carpenter. Harrelson informed Vance that Carpenter's two sons, Jacob M. and Peter H., had been conscripted and had deserted in July or August of 1862. He stated that neighbors believed "the sons are either directly or indirectly provided for by said Father" and in hiding. Harrelson indicated that efforts had been made to locate the brothers with no success, and he requested "the authority to go to said Carpenter's with armed force sufficient and arrest said Farther and imprison him [at the Cleveland County jail in Shelby] … at his own expense until he discloses the secret of the whereabouts of his two sons." "The old man," commented Harrelson, "has considerable possessions." Harrelson further indicated that "the family has an unfavorable reputation hanging over them from the American Revolution and are not likely to redeem it in this death struggle for a white man's Government." He name dropped Gaston's Senator James H. White and Representative Wesley Davenport, who could assist in his request.[53]

As a result of Harrelson's activism, Jacob Carpenter was imprisoned in Shelby. His sons had avoided military service "[s]ome 7 months." Instead of allowing their father to "lie there and suffer [they] come in and gave themselves up."[54] Their service records indicate that they enlisted February 26, 1863, soon after their father had been imprisoned. Both brothers were in the 12th Regiment, Company D. In April and May, Jacob Mauney Carpenter wrote his wife and uncle Daniel Carpenter that the brothers had passed as conscripts. "[T]here never has Ben a word said to us About Being absent. [N]o punishment at all." At the Battle of Chancellorsville Mauney Carpenter suffered an injury when a tree fell on him, being "[b]ruised in the face and side." Later he was wounded on Gettysburg's first day and hospitalized at Chambersburg, when a minie ball passed through his finger and it was amputated. In August 1863 he was in the hospital but listed as deserted on September 7. Apparently he rejoined his unit as he continued to fight until May 1864 when he was captured at Spotsylvania.[55]

Brother Peter Hoke Carpenter was captured on the same day at Spotsylvania, and they remained together as prisoners at Point Lookout until they were transferred to Elmira, New York. On March 3, 1865, Peter Hoke Carpenter died of typhoid fever.[56]

On June 15, 1863, another citizen complained about Jacob Carpenter. Henry Summitt reported to Governor Vance that Carpenter harbored his two sons "nearly twelve months to keep them out of the army." Summitt also complained that Carpenter refused to exchange Confederate money for wheat and corn. Instead Carpenter wanted payment in bank bonds. Summitt requested that the governor take action to "eradicate such disloyalty."[57]

Harrelson's letter to Governor Vance accused the family of suspected Toryism during the American Revolution, which accusation other Confederate supporters often leveled against Unionists. The accusation against this family is confirmed as "Jacob Carpenter Jr.," Jacob Mauney and Peter Hoke's grandfather, was listed as a suspected Tory.[58]

"extremely overbearing and intolerant"

Another glimpse of Unionism involved L. M. Hoffman's family. In *Our Kin*, Laban Miles Hoffman related stories about his father, Jonas Hoffman, and father-in-law David A. Jenkins. Writing in the 1900s and 1910s during the Jim Crow south, Hoffman described his father's sentiments: "In politics before the war, he was a Democrat, but being much attached to the Union, when the storm of 1860 came up he found himself siding with the Douglas Democrats and opposed to secession." Jonas Hoffman considered most secessionists to be "extremely overbearing and intolerant of that position." L. M. Hoffman supposed his father acknowledged the right of secession but thought "it was bad policy." His father received the "stinging shafts of abuse from neighbors" and "coolly held his own [opinion]."[59]

"After the war commenced," writes Hoffman, "[his father] was entirely loyal to the new government and rendered great service to the manless families of his neighbors who were in the army." He contended that his father "was not an advocate of slavery, but was not an abolitionist." Jonas Hoffman owned "three or four slaves and these he often took to plow the fields for the neighboring families whose male members were in the army." At least one slave had been a gift from his wife's family. Hoffman stated that his father treated his slaves in a "kind and humane" manner only whipping slave children as he would his own. He was over the age limit for Confederate service but in the last year of the war "enlisted in the Confederate Navy," in which he served at Wilmington and on the James River in Virginia. L. M. Hoffman even visited his father in Wilmington during the war.[60]

After the war Jonas Hoffman became a Republican being "against all lawlessness and spirit of intolerance and revenge." He later served as a legislator from Gaston County, supported creation of Gaston College, and supported the railroad coming through Dallas.[61]

L. M. Hoffman was either unaware or decided to omit his father's application to the United States government for a Loyalist Claim. On February 7, 1872, Jonas Hoffman contended that on April 20, 1865, some of General Stoneman's troops confiscated two mules, one saddle, and one bridle. He stated his loss at "$344." No "interrogatories" for Hoffman concerning his Union loyalty were located.[62]

Laban Miles Hoffman married the daughter of David A. Jenkins. After the Civil War Jenkins also became a Republican and in 1868 was elected State Treasurer, in which he served two terms. According to L. M. Hoffman, before the war Jenkins was "opposed to secession." Hoffman assisted his father-in-law in Raleigh and had the opportunity to work in W. W. Holden's administration during Reconstruction. Hoffman considered Holden a "quiet, kindhearted, lovable man" who endeavored to "protect all citizens at whatever cost necessary" and attempted to "suppress the Ku Klux outrages."[63] Jonas Hoffman of Duhart's district and David A. Jenkins of Tanyard District were middle-class Unionists with acreage, 5 and 12 slaves, assets in solvent debts, cash, cotton and liquor profits. Other assets included carriages, furniture and dogs.

The research project uncovered other examples of Unionism and desertion.

"to take to the woods"

North Carolina has the distinction of providing the most Confederate soldiers and conversely of having the highest number of Confederate deserters. North Carolina had double the number of desertions than any other Confederate state. Historians have grappled for explanations. They have speculated that proximity to the Virginia battlefields, a reluctance to secede, a strong Unionist yeoman population base, a strong two party system, and adherence to a "state's rights" philosophy explain the high number of desertions.[64]

Sources examined in this project reveal various reasons for desertion. One was philosophical: they opposed slavery, opposed secession, or favored remaining in the United States. Other personal reasons involved economic, health, or family conditions and pleading by wives or loved ones. Younger soldiers exhibited rash decision-making, and as the war dragged on, the Conscription Law often drafted soldiers who were not physically or emotionally fit for battle. Social class distinctions, camp life, and conservative political inclinations also explain Gaston desertions.[65]

To understand the issues facing deserters and their families, the project utilizes the soldiers' own words in letters home and to Governor Vance. Four Gaston Confederate soldiers left personal dialogue explaining their thoughts.

Caleb Senter and Franklin S. Hanna both deserted partially as a result of letters written by their wives. Senter joined to receive a bounty to pay his bills. Spring 1863 was a low time for him. Hospitalized since October 1862 with "a very hard spell of feaver," Senter returned to duty on February 9, 1863. Expectations of a furlough home had not materialized. By May he speculated about deserting: "i Can tell youe that if they dont fead Beter thear will Be a meny man run a way if they do Starte I donte know but what I will be one of them for i donte ?[intend] Stay hear for to Starve and Be kild i think that a man had just as well be kiled a tring to get home"; Senter contemplated, "it is un Sirting how long i will Stay hear thear is 18 of us that has a Strong notion of runing a way i don't think thear is much Dainger of Being hirt they have Stopt giving furlows." On May 23 Senter speculated about whether to follow the army or "to take the woods i donte know which wold be the Best i cante say what i will do yet." He continued, "But Be death eary way and if i have to Starve let me Starve in my native land."[66]

On April 5, 1863, Frances Senter wrote her husband that she was "mity sory that you are so out of hart." She expressed frustration: "the truBle an hard times you have sean is a nuf to put any Body out of hart i am out of hart too sometimes i think thay is no chance for me to live mush longer for every thing is so scase [scarce] an by that it lookes like thay is no chance for a poar woman an children to live." With no slaves, feeding children and farming proved difficult. She reported "get ing along toliBle well with our work, have got aBout three akers planted an the Big feald redy to lay off." But there was no end to bad news, as she needed money to buy "swete potatoes seed" at $2 per bushel, frost and cold weather affected her work, and the chickens had stopped laying eggs. She was lonely, scared, penniless, and nostalgic. She feared that she would never see her husband again "on earth." But in "heaven wher thay is no more war no no [sic] more truble" may become their next meeting place. Her hope was that more will go to war, "not that wash them any harm But give them a sper [scare] an then pease made an ceap [keep] them until last ons [?] is at home." Her postscript may have been the final proverbial nail in the coffin: "i want to see you so Bad." By May 22 she and Caleb received news that Frances's only brother, soldier Thomas W. Barnett, had died.[67] These conditions caused Caleb Senter to leave the Confederate army and come home.

On September 16, 1863, Caleb Senter wrote from "the woods," where he had been hiding for about three months. He vowed: "if God will, i never will go batc for i never taken eny part in this un halowed war for the founDation is not good. i cant say i am a union man for it is DeStroyed … we onst had a glories union." But Senter had also grown weary of fugitive life, and by September 23 he felt it his "duty to go Back and shear with the rest of our Boys."[68] While personal issues affected his decision, Senter's economic status and his lack of support for the "founDation" for the war motivated his desertion.

"I have Set to Eat my dinner at home on the 25 of December"

F. S. Hanna was a reluctant August 8, 1862, conscript.[69] By October he communicated his desire to leave the army and sought help with an exemption. His wife, Caroline, wrote that her father might be able to help, "But he said if you could not get Home on Furlow that he would try and go to Raleigh," she continued, "Pa said if he found out that he could get you off he would go and do all he could for you." By November Hanna was in the hospital with measles.[70]

On December 14, 1862, F. S. Hanna wrote his wife from Fairground Hospital in Wake County, N. C. Apparently after a furlough on January 25, 1863, Hanna wrote her that he had returned to duty. He entreated her to "get that Petition drawen as Soon as you can and I would like to have 20 or 25 signers to it," seeking a petition for an exemption. He "did not get to See the Governor but but [sic] they say that their has several got off in that way … do not fail to have the thing attended to and Send it to me as Soon as you can," he encouraged. By May and June Hanna's artillery unit was in Wilmington, and he had been detailed as a cook. Hanna found "it is a Strange Ideah to me that our people will trade with the Yankies and Fight them at the same time but this is a Strange war." Hanna believed "at the Start … that it was a war of Speculation and I am geting to believe it more and more every day."[71]

On August 25, 1863, Hanna expressed his lost hope in an exemption, a furlough, and the war. He opined, "I think the Confederacy is about out I do not think that the war will be over before a great while." He believed that "the men in the Army is not going to Stay verry mutch longer the most of them here is talking of leaving before long you need not be surprised if you see me Step in Some night and if I do it will be to Stay for I have [been] in the army as long as I care abot living on what Cornbread and old Bacon that the dogs would hardly eat if they could get anything else…. I think that their is as good a chance to get out of the Scrape now as any at any other thime and there is no chance to get a Furlow now they Stopt." Another motivator to come home had arrived, his first born: "I want to see you and the Babe verry bad." Understanding the incriminating evidence in the letter, he advised: "Ps you need not let every one See this letter." After his previous letter of August 25 Hanna chose to "hold on a while longer" and not come home. He pledged: "if I dont get a Furlough between this and Christmas and I Live and keep my health I have Set to Eat my dinner at home on the 25 of December Furlough or not I will take a high Cow and go or be found trying I hope that I will not have to go in that way for I do not want to have the name of a diserter So I will make it my last resort."[72]

On September 2, 1863, from Wilmington Hanna wrote his wife the last letter found in his papers. His attitude remained constant. He felt that no European allies would support the Confederacy, "advise[d new conscripts] not to come," and expressed opposition to the Tithing law—"Some have to Suffer for Something to Eat if they could stay at Home the Tithing Law as they call it is going top opperrate against the poor class of People verry hard the People ought to rise in their and put down all Sutch tyrannical Laws." He observed, "Furloughs has Started but there is one absent without leave from our Company and we will not get any until he comes in…. I hope that I may get one before long."[73]

A few days later on September 9, 1863, Confederate records list Hanna in the Hospital in Wilmington suffering from "Diarrhea." On October 2 he received a "Furlough for 30 days." Company records for September and October indicate that he was "Absent on sick furlough for 30 days Oct."[74]

Unaware that he was ill and in the hospital, Caroline Hanna wrote on September 16, 1863, to express her desire to "se you once more." She "got my obligeing Sack of Salt I am nearly out of money or Such stuff as they call money I only Paid 17 dollars of it and Father paid the balance." She offered, "you had set to come home at Christmas if lived and kept well but that is so uncertain and I dont know how I can wait that much longer to se you … may the good Lord grant that the time may Soon come I often think of you and look at our little Babe and it seems like I dont know how you can stay away from him … no one knowes what they can bear till they placed like you where they cant help theirselves." She addressed the serious issue of the baby's baptism, whether her husband should be present, and when it should occur. She sought his advice and hoped he would be home.[75]

Franklin S. Hanna in late 1863 was ill in the hospital for the second time in less than a year. He had been a reluctant warrior, a draftee; his relative, James Hanna, led the Peace Movement in the area; he failed to secure an exemption; he wanted to see his wife and newborn son; and his wife was out of money. It is not surprising that in the company returns of November and December he is listed as "Deserted Dropped from Rolls Absence without leave."[76] Hanna chose wife, son, and home over a war far removed from his own economic, social, and political values.

"the poor man was fighting that the rich man might keep his slaves"

The story of Larkin Thornburg differs from Senter and Hanna only through circumstances. As an old man, Larkin Thornburg provided a first-hand account of his journey from hiding out, conscription, soldier, and deserter. His family "lived on a rented farm" north of Dallas, and his father, Moses, and other Thornburgs in the area did not own slaves. Larkin opposed slavery and his refusal to fight in the support of the "peculiar institution" was a matter of "conscience." Thornburg was a "youth of seventeen taken away against his will."[77]

Thornburg recalled hearing his father, an uncle, and a neighbor, who "were not in favor of the war … pronounced Union men," discuss the issue, and he described the availability of Unionist newspapers, *The Standard* and *New York Sun*. These discussions left "a deep impression upon [his] mind," that the American government was "amongst the best in the world." His uncle would quote from George Washington's farewell address "for the union's preservation." He opined, "the poor man was fighting that the rich man might keep his slaves, who were … of no use to the poor man." He believed that "the idea of secession was wrong, and that an institution that fostered such cruelties and injustice as did slavery deserved to have but little said in it's favor." Reflecting during the southern Jim Crow days and the days of the ascendancy of the "lost cause," he affirmed his belief in the Union and would have "violated conscience" if he had supported the Confederacy. Commenting with Christian principles he further asserted that God must have intervened in the war to permit the "righteous cause," "North was in the right," to succeed in the war. Thornburg, claiming to be "a true American," "considered slavery as being founded upon wrong principles and that this institution was the real cause of the war." He defended his actions, his belief "in the Union and the abolition of slavery," and hoped "that all bitterness and ill feeling on account of the war should cease," restoring political and religious unity.[78]

Thornburg participated in the Battle of Cedar Creek. After the battle, he and others deserted to North Carolina. He burst into his one room cabin home and discovered his older brother, who had served and lost a leg in the war. The brother sent Larkin to the loft with guns. "Defend yourself –," his brother advised, "don't go to the war again."[79]

Senter, Hanna, and Thornburg were from farm laborer families. Senter was married with children, Hanna a newlywed, and Thornburg a seventeen-year-old forced conscript. Their stories compare in ideology, opposing slavery, the war, supporting the United States government, expressing social class distinctions, and suffering disenchantment with living conditions and the rationale for fighting. Their words convey a multiplicity of concerns—wife, children, money and food, sickness, and the loss of hope. Records of other deserters provide additional understanding.

Newton Sellers was conscripted on August 16, 1862. He resided near the line with Cleveland and Gaston.[80] On June 4, 1863, he wrote to his wife that "I never did want to goe to virginia any more but we will have to." He hoped to be home "to see you and mary margeret." "I want you to trye and Save the wheat," he advised, and to hire someone to work. "I haint got but 3 letters yet from home," he complained.[81]

After being hospitalized in Charlotte, on March 3, 1864, Newton Sellers reported to his wife that the army had marched through the rain, sleet, and snow and mud "up to the Shoo mouth." In the midst of the "Peace Movement," he predicted that "if the would leave it to a vote for North Carolina to goe back to the union it would goe five to one they is lots wount Reinlist and I don blame them." Expressing social class antagonism he speculated, "the[y] want this war to hold on. let Some of the big men trye it,"[82] referencing wealthy and powerful persons.

On April 21, 1864, Sellers wrote his wife that he was "nearly well again" after another bout of sickness. He was "So glad to hear from home and to hear that you was well and the poor little babe." He was "sad" that "Eli was conscripted but I was glad that james Vandik was conscripted but it will take all the men we can Scrap to whip the yanks and then we will not do it." He feared "lots of hard fiting this Summer but I don't crave it … dear wife I hop this war will end Soon So we can all git home to live in peace one time more." He speculated that the army would "have to fight it out this Summer" or "we will Starve out that is sertin."[83]

On April 28, 1864, Newton Sellers had fear of a "big fight hear before long" and was "gitting tired on [coffee]." He had some "eggs to eat" and was getting "tired on bred and meat."[84] Newton Sellers' desire to go home to see his young wife and family, poor battle conditions, and negative prospects for success overwhelmed him. In September and October 1864, he was listed in the official records as being "absent without leave at home."[85] Official records do not relate whether he returned to the battlefront.

Newton Sellers expressed support for the Peace Movement and recognized the futility of continuing the war. Documents reveal that no single event or circumstance motivated his return home. His desire to see his family, the fear that his wife would "kill your Self a working out,"[86] and to escape the difficulties and disenchantment of war contributed to his decision.

An interesting anecdote about desertion involves Jacob L. Workman and Jacob Kiser. On July 22, 1863, Jacob L. Workman deserted on the march from Knoxville to Martinsburg, Virginia. He had been conscripted at age 24 on August 24, 1862.[87] Jacob Kiser also deserted in Virginia on the same day. They remained out of the service until November 3 when they were captured. Kiser at age 37 had volunteered on March 15, 1862, and rejoined his unit by November 12.[88]

Workman was treated differently. On February 28, 1864, or about six months after his desertion, he wrote his wife Nancy to report that he was "in the gard house yet." Being in captivity had kept him from some serious engagements, and he told his wife not "to fret A bout me." He had sent twelve or thirteen letters to her, and he requested that she "rite to me as quick as you can." He expressed concern about the value of Confederate money and closed his letter thusly: "A close by asking you kindly to Remember me and I shall Remember you and my baby to the last [h]our I shall live I Remain your loving husband until death."[89] On March 25, 1864, Lt. H. W. Fulenwider made application for Workman's release, having been under guard four months with no charges made against him. Fulenwider noted that this was the third application he had offered for his release. Workman was eventually released and captured after the Battle of Spotsylvania on May 11, 1864, and on January 22, 1865, he died at Point Lookout, Maryland as a prisoner of war.[90]

It is unclear why Workman was treated differently than Kiser. Authorities may have valued Kiser, a volunteer, over Workman, a conscript. It underscores inconsistent treatment of service men, breeding distrust. Both joined from Lincoln County and were of German origin, and their approximate three and one-half month sojourn demonstrates the ability of soldiers to evade capture.

"Several of My old co have Deserted"

Loyal Confederate soldiers expressed anger and disgust with deserters and their sympathizers. On December 2, 1863, Colonel William G. Morris reported that "Several of My old co have Deserted." They included "O P Byrd, Caleb Hullet, Eli Rudicell," and Morris blamed Byrd for influencing them. The need for soldiers created unique methods in dealing with desertion. Morris reported a five-day trip to Camp Gragg in Virginia. Deserters, "Jacob Rudicill & O P Byrd Came through with Me they will Not Bee Punished for past offences Eli Rudicill Came as far as Charlotte with us but Gave me the Slip after Guetting in the Cars as I had No Suspicion of such thing." Morris observed, "From What George Hines told Me Dr. Wm Sloan is the cause of Eli Rudicill acting as he Dose I am Satisfied that Sloan is Dooing all he can to Encourage those men Not to Return to the armey." Later in the month he "read a Letter from Caleb Hullet a Soldier that left when the Rudicells did he says if Coln Barber will promise Not to have them Shot they will all come Back Byrd & Jacob Rudicell has Recd there Bounty and will Not be punished I am Sorry Eli Rudicell acted so foolish."[91]

Inconsistent Confederate treatment of deserters troubled Caleb Senter. After his desertion and return, "i never he[a]r eny Body Say eny thing a Boute our Diserting all the Company Seams glad that we Cum BaCk But if we had a S[t]aid at home and a Bin Caught and Brought BaCk we wold a Bin put to Deth for thear is too to Be Shot to morrow in the 47 regt." He believed his decision was good, "thanks Be to the Lord that it was his will for us to give up ... i hope the Lord will Bless me and Bring me threw this Cruel war."[92] He communicated an "awfull Site this morning i Saw a man was oute and tide to a Stake and Shot thear was 10 guns fired one him he fell over died my god my god what is to be Cum of this wicked nation ... the poar man Standing in perfect helth and yet Deth So near." Senter observed, "i never herd of one Being put to Deth that voluntearly Cum BaCk But all or nearly all that is Brought BaCk has to Sufer that and feell Deth." Later in November he reported to his wife that "all the Company is very kind to me" and advised a deserter at home, to remain there or to get "Sum Smart man to at tend to it ... if they Do CetCh him and Bring him BaCk they will put him to death." Senter also inquired about whether a fellow volunteer, Albert A. Bynum, had been "shot."[93]

While the Confederate government accepted many soldiers back into the fold, they also enacted punishments. Morris related that "there is 5 Men in the 35 Va to Bee Shot for desertion I saw 2 in the 22 N C Whiped on Bare Back yesterday for desertion," and on June 29, 1863, he reported, "Fred Hoffman has deserted."[94] James Wellington Linebarger hoped that "they will quit harboring deserters and let them come back to the army where they belong." By the end of the year, he confided to his wife that "they are som six men to be to Death next Wednesday for desertion." On February 20, 1864, Linebarger "saw one man exicuted that had bin sentenced by the court they was twelve men shot at him he looked as if he did not care and did not mind it there is more to be shot & Zimri Costner's doom is death if they evr git him if he is a bout home he would better look sharp." Linebarger was one of Costner's "witnesses." Authorities caught Costner because, on April 28, 1864, Linebarger reported that "Zimri Costner will be shot to morrow if not this evening it looks bad but it seames as there is no other way to do with the deserters he never has don any good yet in the army."[95] In a chilling description, Thomas Davis conveyed to his wife that deserters "was to be Shot and ther coffens was brought along behind them They then Sat down on the coffens and then a preacher praid for them nealing on their coffens then the coffens was removed and they got on their neas and 20 men marched up in 8 or 10 Stepes of them and all fired at them at once it maid me feal very Solem [sic] to se it." Later Davis "got out of" a firing squad and was "mity glad of it."[96]

The need for troops sent mixed messages to deserters. To entice deserters to return to duty Governor Vance, and later President Davis, communicated proclamations on a number of occasions which granted pardons if the deserter returned within a set time. Governor Vance issued a new February 2, 1863, proclamation to "deserters and runaway conscripts," which he periodically renewed, ordering them to return immediately to their units and they would face no repercussions.[97] Some soldiers, like Caleb Senter, returned to duty.

"brought on myself disgrace and contempt"

On June 16, 1863, James McLure, a Lincoln County resident, wrote Governor Vance that he had "brought on myself disgrace and contempt of my frie[n]ds ... by absenting myself from my company without leave." He described his encounter with his father:

"My old grey headed Farther met me at the gate with Joy, happy to see me." When he told his father that he was not on furlough, "the old man broke in tears and told me. I could not stay with him that I must go and Join my Regt." He threatened to arrest his son. What was McLure's excuse for deserting? He "wanted some Clothes and a pair of shoes"; he wanted to see his family once more. McLure wrote the governor in order to return to duty, but also to get a "pardon" and permission to rejoin his company without penalty. He apologized continually and promised to never desert again.[98]

McLure from Cottage Home along the eastern Lincoln and Gaston County line was conscripted July 15, 1862, as a twenty-four-year-old. By late 1863 and early 1864 he had rejoined his unit. On June 11, 1864, he was listed as sick in the hospital. On March 15, 1865, he was recorded as a "rebel deserter."[99] He journeyed from conscript to deserter, returning to his unit, and finally to deserter once again.

In 1863 Bartlett Nixon and D. F. West also wrote the governor for permission to return to their units. Nixon of Cottage Home stated that he was a conscript, had been sick, "was barefooted and almost naked." He was "broken down in body & mind." He returned to his old widowed mother, had recovered, and sought to return to duty. He promised to "spill my blood like water in defense of our right & liberties" and requested a pardon, a passport, and no punishment. West from nearby Brevard Station admitted his desertion and requested a transfer to a cavalry unit because he was "Rhumitised" and could not march well. While home West even admitted to shooting squirrels and "at the malishia [militia]." West closed by requesting "some time to fix up my Bisiness."[100] One marvels at the honesty and audacity of these young men.

J. M. W. Abernathy of Woodlawn communicated his request to the governor with many details. Arriving home in August 1863 to visit his "aged parents," he was very sick. Once recovered, his parents insisted that he return to duty. As with McLure, Abernathy's father hoped that he was on furlough when he arrived. Abernathy wanted to see his parents "all once more" and needed shoes as he "had been barefoot for a long time." From the governor he requested a pass but would go under guard to his unit if necessary.[101] All three young men gave their home addresses and requested a letter from the governor.

"over stayed the time"

Attorney L. E. Thompson, of Brevard Station wrote Vance on behalf of Robert Davis. Davis promised to return to duty if he were not punished. Thompson suggested that Davis could accompany an officer on furlough in the community.[102] Other deserters secured politicians to assist them. On April 13, 1863, state Senator James H. White wrote on behalf of Eli Rudisill, who had deserted Colonel Morris's company in January previous, or as White stated, he "over stayed the time." He and a "large majority of the Citizens of the County" enlisted White's support, as Rudisill wanted to return to his company without penalty. Typical of other such requests Vance received, he responded that he could not transfer Rudisill nor could he pardon him, but he would send a letter to accompany him back to his unit. Rudisill returned to duty by February 29, 1864, when he was counted present with the stipulation that he had forfeited two year's pay because of his desertion. Union forces near Petersburg captured him on July 28, and he served the remainder of the war in the Elmira, New York prison, where he took the Union oath of allegiance on December 16, 1864.[103]

On August 28, 1864, William T. Shipp summarized Gaston deserter problems to the governor. Even though he had resigned as captain of the Home Guard, he reported that the proclamation motivated deserter Noah Smith to surrender immediately to him because of the governor's proclamation. Shipp further reported that there had been "a revolution in our midst since the election." The "Holden men" assisted Shipp in gaining more deserters, and Shipp blamed "Dr. Wm. Sloan" as the chief Holden supporter. Shipp indicated that the "Home Guard organization and Confederate organization of State reserves have been so twisted up together" that Shipp felt very frustrated.[104] Home Guard member, Jacob Froneberger, recorded in his diary in September 1864 that "Most of the deserters in the county have come in and gone off under a late proclamation of Gov. Vance. We have two in the Dallas Company to catch yet, Dickson and Cloninger."[105]

"Galvanized Yankees"

The research project has also uncovered area southerners who fought in the Union army. While no examples of area men making the arduous trek across the Appalachian Mountains to Union lines to enlist have been discovered, some captured soldiers took another opportunity afforded them. Confederate prisoners at Point Lookout Prison in Maryland took the oath of allegiance to enlist in the United States army. If they did, they could leave behind their prison life and became known as "Galvanized Yankees."

A number of area soldiers took advantage. Marshall Ramsey, Jr., provided the author with information about John Jacob Cornwell, a Lincoln County enlistee, who joined Company G of the 57th NC Regiment after conscription. He was captured on November 7, 1863, and sent to Point Lookout. The offer to exchange a prisoner's uniform for a U.S. soldier's one occurred in early January 1864. On January 25 Cornwell, "Carriage Maker" of Cleveland County officially joined Company B of the 1st Regiment, U.S. Volunteers. Cornwell and the other recruits understood that they were to guard the western frontier. Eventually almost 600 Confederates would volunteer, of which 73 deserted, most likely to head straight home.[106]

Often enlistees joined with relatives, neighbors, and some documentation has confirmed that wives and family back home encouraged their decision. Most "Galvanized Yankees" originated in areas of North Carolina with low slaveholding totals and often strong Unionist tendencies. Cornwell's adventure took him to the Missouri River frontier into the area of the Dakotas, Montana, and Kansas. His regiment's task was to survive the unbearably cold winter, stand guard at various federal forts, and battle Sioux and other raiders on the frontier.[107]

Whether to escape horrid prison conditions, risk the opportunity to return home, or embrace original or acquired Unionist beliefs, Cornwell was not alone in his decision to enlist in the United States Army. The author compared prison records with Confederate and Union service records and confirmed that a number of local Point Lookout prisoners enlisted in the Union army. A total of 16 Lincoln County residents joined the U.S. Army. From Gaston County six persons joined and ten joined from Cleveland County.[108]

In Gaston County the prisoners included William Brown, Jacob B. Costar [Costner?], Jesse Eaker, D. Eaker, John Finger, and Nath. T. Garrento/Garnto/Gurentto, variously spelled. Some Lincoln and Cleveland enlistees may have resided in Gaston County and vice versa.[109]

For Cornwell and doubtless others, his enlistment lasted about two years. On November 27, 1865, he mustered out of the U.S. Army as a corporal and returned home to his wife and family. Cornwell spent the remainder of his life in Lincoln County.[110]

The stresses of battle and camp conditions, home front challenges, familial concerns, and unfair treatment confronted all southerners often resulting in desertion. Lt. Lemuel Hoyle noted that "a great many men" had deserted after Gettysburg. He was also disturbed that his mother's neighborhood "was becoming so infested with deserters." He believed that they would "hardly commit any acts of personal violence, but it will be well for you, and everyone else," he cautioned, "to look closely after their corn cribs and smoke houses, and etc." He believed that desertion would "eventually ruin our army."[111]

However, Lt. Hoyle's hope that violence would not erupt would remain only a hope. This project has revealed that violence and lawlessness pervaded the Gaston County area disrupting family life, economics, and the Confederate war effort.

7

Gaston Violence and Lawlessness

Historians have documented violence and lawlessness in the North Carolina Mountains and in the central North Carolina Quaker Belt. As I conducted my research, I expected to find little or no documented violence in the Gaston County area; however, the evidence indicates that violence, serious economic shortages, threats, and intimidation became commonplace. Secessionist leaders used vigilante tactics, intimidation, and terror to defuse Unionist sentiment. Many families discovered that the anticipated quick Confederate victory evaded them. As disillusionment, poverty and crime rose, the state government sought to quell "the civil war at home" with special courts that meted out harsh punishments and by creating the Home Guard, which often exacerbated the anarchy.

As the wartime southern economy faltered and sharply declined, profiteering increased, taxation increased with spiraling inflation, and conscription left women and children to struggle with managing family farms and survival. Vigilantes dragged men from their homes during the night; people spied on their neighbors; and Unionists harbored deserters. Fugitive deserters roamed about, preying on defenseless families, whose husbands and fathers had gone to war. Fear became universal.

Further, the evidence indicates that some Gaston County Unionists defied the Confederacy by harboring deserters and even joined the anti–Confederate organization, Heroes of America, and flaunted Confederate authority. Indeed, the research exposes that Gaston County also fought a "civil war at home."

"Vigilantes"

With the advent of secession, southern secessionist leaders sought to create unanimity, as they encouraged North Carolina to join their Deep South neighbors. As secessionist propagandists traveled throughout the Upper South to motivate secession,[1] local authorities sought to silence dissenting opinions.

The organization of vigilante justice is steeped in secrecy. Newspapers sporadically reported incidents. For example, after the 1860 election and on Christmas Eve, a "Public Meeting" was "held at Cansler's Store Gaston County to organize a Vigilance Committee." The participants approved resolutions to "examine any person or persons who may be suspected of evil"; to meet once a month; directed members to report to a "Justices Committee"; and allowed for "no collection of slaves be permitted to assemble at any one place during Christmas." Thirty one persons were listed as the committee and an additional 53 were assigned to "patrol." Richard Rankin motioned Alexander Rutledge as chair and John D. M. Rankin as secretary, indicating a northeastern Gaston committee.[2] Doubtless vigilante committees were organized in other sections of the county.

Vigilantism became commonplace. On March 26, 1861, the *Western Democrat* reported "Lynched," a reprint of an article from the *Salisbury Banner*, in which "a free negro named Sib Rankin" was accused of "making threats using incendiary language, and who knocked down an officer while attempting to arrest him." A "mob ... violently [took him] from town authorities," where he was "carried to the woods and hanged by the neck until it was thought he was dead." After he was "cut down... , the fellow recovered" and the "dangerous negro" departed toward Charlotte.[3] On June 11 apparently in Concord another "Mob ... violently entered the jail, breaking locks and doors ... and forcibly took out a negro whom they executed." Oscar Ford had been accused of attempted rape of Mrs. Bryant of Concord but was acquitted "against the general feeling of the community as to his guilt." The mob of 40 to 50 people with "clubs and pistols" took him to the outskirts of town, "hanged him up, fired several shots into his body and left him dead." While the paper felt him guilty, it appealed "for the sake of humanity, civilization, and domestic peace [to] deliver us from the predominance of mob law."[4]

Locally, mob violence in neighboring Cleveland County set the tone. The *North Carolina Whig* reported that on May 10, 1861, a "Mob" in Shelby hanged "Timothy Hainey, a man of a white face but a *nigger* by nature."[5] The *Western Democrat*, quoting the *Yorkville Enquirer*, indicates that "Haney" had been arrested by the "Vigilance Committee," being placed in jail for "tampering with negroes, harboring runaways and furnishing them passes." He had been released on his own recognizance when a "crowd" seized and "con-

The Gaston County Jail in Dallas was constructed as part of the creation of Dallas in 1848. It housed deserter Joseph Carpenter during his trial but was deemed not secure enough as he awaited his hanging. It is owned by the Gaston County Museum of Art and History (courtesy Melany Dawn Crouse Photography).

veyed [him] to the suburbs of the village, and hanged until dead. The names of the persons concerned in the affair are not known, and from all we can learn, no exertion will be made to identify them."[6] The newspaper suggests no investigation into the lynching and general complicity.

At least two Gaston County citizens document early vigilante intimidation. In the Fall of 1861, local vigilantes visited John Huffstetler in the northwestern portion of the county and ordered him to leave his home. At neighbor J. H. Ramsour's home, "Danl Froneberger was chairman" of the vigilante group which threatened "to try him for his life for [his] political feelings or sentiments." Huffstetler reported "three other men were brought to trial the same day for union sentiments." At the arranged vigilante trial, Huffstetler admitted to being an "Abolitionist," having stated that "the negroes ought to be freed and colonized." After the frightening ordeal, he was "released about night." He contended that John H. Roberts "of Dallas who was a militia captain" received orders to "arrest every Union man ... and hang two of them on each way Friday in each week until all were disposed of in that way." He stated that Roberts had a list which included "the Robinsons, Isaac Rhom, Alexander Bradley & others."[7]

The "Vigalance Committee" also visited Elhanan W. Robinson[8] in 1861 "for union Sentiments." Joseph Lusk, the county sheriff, gave Robinson a warrant signed by Paul Froneberger, the former sheriff. He and "15 others" attended the next day at "Deck's old field muster ground." Robinson anticipated that he might be hanged but learned from Huffstetler's example that he might "go free." James B. Oats, a neighbor, remarked that Robinson was "always very bold in expressing his Sentiments & did so publicly." Robinson became even more "stubborn" after his brush with the "Vigalance Committee," and Oats opined that Robinson would "fight for Abe Lincoln in blood knee deep."[9] The Deck and Ramsour properties are in western Gaston County near present Bessemer City. The evidence suggests that as many as 20 persons suffered intimidation there. Others most likely suffered the same violent threats throughout the county.

In 1862 *The Daily Bulletin* of Charlotte reported that the "Vigilance Committee of Charlotte Beat" informed the public that some speculators were "depreciating the Confederate Notes and North Carolina Treasury Notes, by refusing to take them and by buying up coin, gold bullion, and silver plates." The "Vigilante Committee" threatened such persons with having their names published and "take such course as they may deem necessary."[10]

Unionists, deserters, and their sympathizers feared home invasion, threats upon their lives, and death. But they also motivated Confederate fears, which caused the legislature to pass laws to control potential lawlessness.

"most diabolical outrages on record"

The Emancipation Proclamation took effect on January 1, 1863. Fears of slave insurrection and the loss of civil control caused the North Carolina legislature to pass a law which would allow the governor to convene a Court of Oyer and Terminer for capital cases of murder, burglary, and rape, especially concerning slaves or others disturbing the peace. The Court meted out capital punishments when, under normal circumstances, such punishment was not justified.[11] Governor Vance would authorize the Court as civil disorder increased after 1863.

On March 16, 1863, four Lincoln County justices of the peace petitioned Governor Vance for justice. The "most diabolical outrages on record" occurred against Hugh Lyttle, "one of the good Citizens of our County, by two of his own Slaves (Bill & Frank) by the murder of their own master in the Most brutal manner, and the Culprits now confined in the Jail of Our County." Members of Lyttle's family were "very much incensed against the negroes, so much so that there is reason to believe that they may seek an opportunity to rescue the culprits and dispose of them in the most summary manner." The justices, H. Cansler, R. H. Abernathy, C. J. Hammerskold, and B. J. Johnson, requested a judge to deal with the accused, and Governor Vance agreed for Judge Heath to hear the case.[12] While the public record of the Lyttle Murder fails to address the motivation for the killing, oral traditions pose two possible scenarios.

Hugh Lyttle often journeyed to buy and sell commodities. He did not return home one night, and the next morning family members located him in a "stable with a horse" with the imprint of a horseshoe on his head." "For some reason the cause of Hua's death was questioned," and "[t]wo teenage slaves were interrogated." They reported that "Bill and Frank took a horseshoe and nailed it to a piece of wood. When Mister Hua came home about 10 o'clock, they hit Mister Hua on the head when he put his horse in the stable." The motive was robbery and the hope that the two slaves could escape to the north.[13]

The second story indicated that Hugh was "mean to his slaves." As he prepared for his trading trip, he instructed Bill and Frank to "fell a tree growing on a hillside ... [by] making the tree fall, on the uphill side." The slaves felled the tree but it fell downhill. Fearing Lyttle's "wrath and his mistreatment and punishment ... they decided to kill Hugh before he had an opportunity to beat them for not following his instructions." While it appeared that a horse kicked Lyttle, the investigation revealed that he had traded his horse that day for a mule. The horseshoe, obviously larger than the mule shoe, provided the proof of murder instead of an "accident."[14]

Awaiting trial on March 31, "Bill and Frank [e]scaped from Lincoln county Jail," and authorities offered a "$100 Reward" for their capture. The April 7 newspaper account indicates that they "had made a full confession of the murder, and stated that they had no cause for it or any particular object in view; they were merely instigated by the devil to commit the horrid crime." Frank was described as "about 23 years old, dark complected, ordinary size. Bill is about 20 years old, about 6 feet high, stout and very black." By April they had been "Arrested ... about 4 miles" from Lincolnton and would stand trial.[15] Such publicity certainly inculcated fear and inflamed emotions.

Court was held in a "Special Term" on April 20, 1863, with the purpose of prosecuting "Bill and Frank" under the indictment of murder. They pled "not guilty," and W. P. Bynum of eastern Lincoln County prosecuted the case. The Court ordered the Sheriff to summon "45 Freeholders who also shall be slave owners" to form a jury. Twelve jurors were selected, which included prominent Lincoln County slaveholders.[16] Jury selection customarily did not preclude slave owners only.

Court documents reveal that the jury found the "prisoners at the bar Guilty of the Felony of Murder as charged." The following day on "Wednesday Morning at 10 o'clock," the Court ordered Bill and Frank to the bar for what "they have to say why the sentence of Death should not be passed." They made "no reply." They were ordered to "the prison whence they came," and on Friday, May 22 they were to be taken "to a place of public execution in the County of Lincoln." The *Western Democrat* informed the public of the judicial decision and the execution date. Between 10:00 and 2:00 they were to be "hanged by the neck until they be dead." The Court further ordered Isaac Lowe, administrator of Hugh Lyttle, to pay costs of $10 each for court costs to the state of North Carolina.[17]

The 32 days between judgment and execution suggests urgency. As all jurors were slave owners and since slaves could not testify in court against whites, the judicial decision was a foregone conclusion. The execution of Bill and Frank became a social event with spectators and picnics. "Gallows Woods" identified the location of "The old hanging tree," which became a landmark in local deeds.[18] The incident shook the area's peace and social order.

"Burglary, with an intent to kill"

Another criminal incident had closer ties to Gaston County. Two deserter relatives, William Cody and Joseph Carpenter, burglarized the home of a prominent Lincoln County citizen and justice of the peace. On the last day of July 1863 both men forcibly entered the home of Peter "Seapock" and his wife, both of whom were about eighty years old. Also present in the home was a "servant girl." Later when discovered, Cody had a women's dress, some sugar, and a razor and strap on his person with leather and other items deposited in some brush.[19]

In Fall Term 1863 Cody pled "not guilty" and was placed under the "custody of the Sheriff of Lincoln County."[20] On February 1, 1864, William Cody appeared at a "Special Term" of a "Special Court of Oyer and Terminer" in Lincoln County Court. The special state law apparently was extended to whites, who were deserters. The Court listed both Cody and Joseph Carpenter "who are charged with Burglary," and W. P. Bynum once again served as solicitor with jurors selected. On February 11, Cody was tried and found "Guilty." His attorney "moved an arrest of jugt. which was refused by the Court." On February 12, 1864, the Court sentenced him to "public execution … between the hours of 12 A. M. & 2 P. M. and there be hanged by the neck until dead." Cody appealed his conviction to the state Supreme Court arguing that he had been convicted of breaking and entering, not larceny. In other words, his attorney contended that Cody had been tried for the wrong offense. The Lincoln Court noted that Cody was "insolvant" and would be allowed "to appeal without security." By June the state Supreme Court held that the Lincoln County court had not erred in its indictment or trial.[21]

There was more drama. On April 25, 1864, Lincoln County Jailer, John P. Anthony, reported that both Cody, who was appealing his death sentence, and his yet untried accomplice, Joseph Carpenter, had escaped from the Lincoln County jail. A newspaper described the crime as "one of the most diabolical offences, to wit Burglary, with an intent to kill" and $400 was offered as a reward for their capture. They were recaptured.[22]

It is unclear why Carpenter was tried at a later time, but in the Fall Term of 1864 Lincoln County Court he was indicted for "Burglary." Aware of Cody's sentence, Carpenter requested that his trial be moved from Lincoln to his home county of Gaston because "the prosecuter peter Sepach is an old and influential citizen of this county and his numerous friends and connections have been exerting their influence to prejudice the public mind of this county against this affiont and have so far succeeded that he cannot have a fair and impartial trial in this county." His request was granted, and the trial was scheduled in Gaston County Courthouse for the fourth Monday in September.[23]

On November 15th the trial commenced, it proceeded quickly, and Joseph Carpenter was found guilty. Carpenter appealed his conviction and requested a new trial which was denied. State Solicitor W. P. Bynum ordered Carpenter remanded to the Gaston Jail in Dallas and "to be hanged by the neck until he be dead." He subsequently ordered that Carpenter be transferred to the Lincoln County jail for safe keeping and then transferred on December 15 to the Gaston jail for execution.[24]

Court clerk W. D. Glenn witnessed the trial which he characterized as a "day of Humiliation & prayer." "Judge Osborne sentenced Jos. Carpenter, who was yesterday convicted of Burglary felony to death by hanging. The prisoner heard his sentence with stolid indifference apparently and was locked up in Jail."[25]

The *Western Democrat* reported that the Superior Court tried "Joseph Carpenter for breaking into a dwelling house, knocking down the tenant and stealing leather, &c. He was convicted and sented [sentenced] to be hanged on the 16th of Dec. Carpenter is a deserter from the army."[26]

On December 3, 1864, W. D. Glenn "helped to erect a gallows to hang Joseph Carpenter on." Jacob Froneberger recorded in his diary that on the Friday prior to December 18 "Joseph Carpenter was hung here." He recorded a "very large collection of people" at the execution but that the day proceeded "without disturbance." Glenn recorded the "execution of J. Carpenter" also with a "great collection of people." Carpenter "appeared to be very pentent and expressed himself hopefully warned the bystanders against disobedience to their parents good advice. At about one oclock he was launched to eternity. a Sad Spectacle to witness. A terrible warning to evil doers."[27] L. C. Payseur also witnessed Carpenter's hanging, recalling that Carpenter, "the poor man," stated from the gallows that "he had never committed a worse crime than stealing a small quantity of leather." Payseur further recalled that Carpenter admitted to desertion and that he "would do so again if taken back."[28]

It had been assumed that William Cody was executed after the state Supreme Court ruling, even though his case was carried in the Lincoln County docket through 1867.[29] Cass Payseur's recollections suggest that Cody may have in fact escaped his death sentence. In 1914 Payseur recalled that "Bill Cody" and Carpenter had deserted and had been recaptured, Carpenter "near High Shoals." Payseur speculated that he had "heard said" that Cody was in fact "Capt. Bill Cody," of Buffalo Bill fame, which he doubted.[30] Yet, his comment and the public record suggest that Cody escaped. It is plausible that Palmer's forces, which occupied Lincolnton in 1865, could have released Cody from jail, which was done in other locations. Carpenter and Cody had challenged Confederate authority through their military desertion and unrepentant attitude.

They were brothers-in-law. By 1860 William Cody, farm laborer, had married Easter Carpenter, daughter of Joseph and Nancy Carpenter, and resided at the Old Furnace post office in northwestern Gaston County. On October 6, 1861, he volunteered for service in Dallas and joined Company H of the 37th NC Regiment. Apparently he deserted prior to October 13, 1862, as the Adjutant General instructed Colonel M. H. Hand to arrest him. On May 3, 1863, he deserted again "in the face of the enemy" at the Battle of Chancellorsville. Another record indicated that he had deserted on May 16 at Gordonsville. The company roll call for July and August of 1863 provided this snippet: "Deserted and arrested and put in Lincolnton jail." Carpenter, a farm laborer, volunteered in Lincolnton on May 23, 1861, into Company B, 23rd NC Regiment. In July of 1862 he was listed as absent and sick, and in October and November of 1862 he was listed as "absent without leave." Apparently returning to duty, his service record indicates that he was severely wounded at the Battle of Seven Pines and "Deserted May 1863," after which time, Cody and Carpenter found each other, traveling to North Carolina.[31]

Apparently the landless, young kinsmen joined the army to make money, believing as most southerners that the war would be over soon. Family members had been in Court for debt and other issues. In Fall 1859, Cody was tried for "Larceny," found not guilty, and re-tried for "Receiving stolen goods."[32] Desperate deserters, burglarizing for personal gain or for others, chose the wrong house, a prominent Lincoln County citizen.

"evidence of counter revolution and civil war at home"

Gaston area residents read newspaper accounts of the disintegrating law and order during volatile 1863, including a rash of fires. "The barn of W. T. Shipp, Esq., … was destroyed by fire week before last. It was no doubt the work of an incendiary, as Mr. Shipp's dwelling house was also set on fire at the same time, but discovered in time to prevent the spread of the flames." Shipp was a prominent militia officer in eastern Gaston County. In the same newspaper "a negro woman … was suspected" of attempting to burn the "dwelling occupied by Mr. Jas. C. Moore" of Charlotte. Also in March the newspaper related two special court proceedings against slaves for two separate murders in the Hillsboro area.[33]

Challenges to Confederate control of the home front continued. In August 1863 Lincolnton's David Schenck noted "evidence of counter revolution and civil war at home," which caused the local militia under Lt. Col. Caleb Ramsour to "attack and capture a formidable band of deserters who are collected around the 'little-mountain' some twelve miles east of this place." Schenck believed that desertion continued because of no punishment. Deserters were caught and sent back to the army, who then "turned loose to return at first opportunity." He hoped that "providential interference" may provide success.[34]

But violence continued. On September 24, 1863, Louisa Morris, wife of Colonel William G. Morris, communicated to her brother, Ambrose Costner, that "there is a good deal of excitement in the neighborhood with the deserters and conscripts. O that God would cause them all to see and know their duty and enable them to fullfill it and grant us a speedy peace. Joseph Rhyne had some leather stolen this week."[35] The summer and fall of 1863 was a violent, uncertain one for the Gaston County area. On November 24, 1863, the *Western Democrat* informed its readers that "Deserters and Tories" had been "annoying the people in a portion of Gaston County—stealing from and threatening loyal men and alarming females. We learn that these outlaws have banded together and go about doing pretty much as they please." The Home Guard had been searching for them and expected to be "pretty busy this winter."[36]

By Christmas Day two instances of violence were reported in western Gaston County. Two "deserters" attacked "Elick Dicky." When he refused to tell them where his money was located, they beat him and eventually located about $900 in paper and some gold. Two days later a "gang of thirteen" attacked "Mr. Jackson McGill" after pretending to be a party hunting deserters. They made off with $4,000 of his money.[37] In late 1863 the *Western Democrat* printed lists of deserters from the 59th Cavalry NC Regiment which included from Gaston County: "James Browning, A S Craig, J H Hoffman, J T Lay, A T Lay, Alex McDaniel, E B McDaniel, M R Sparks, J P Stone, J H Smith," and "absent without leave" Alex Craig. In September citizens learned that about 160 deserters were marching in Wilkes County. As 1864 emerged, "Another Robbery" was reported in Union County allegedly perpetrated by deserters.[38]

The area's citizens also learned of violence in other areas of North Carolina. D. F. Ramsaur from the mountains of Murphy, North Carolina wrote an unidentified person in Lincoln County describing that the community had been "visited the Second time buy the Bushwackers Sunday morning." He stated that "125 of the Bushwackers ... came in town ... searched oure Houses abused the females made them coock for them." They even chased him with a "sharp Stick" but he escaped. They threatened to "burn the town down," and Ramsaur stated that as soon as he gathered his crops he would leave. He might travel to Lincolnton or to South Carolina. guerrilla warfare continued as he described "250 of cavely here & they are a fighting have taken some prisoners and Kiled some."[39]

The *Western Democrat* reported "seven or eight deserters ... from Randolph," who were "lawless creatures ... a perfect terror to peaceable citizens and ... the militia officers." Another article, "Runaways," described "runaway negroes and deserters" who were "committing depredations and have become a terror to the neighborhood." Even though the militia and Home Guard were dispatched to arrest them, the paper warned citizens to "prepare himself with gun and a few rounds of ammunition."[40] The paper printed the North Carolina legislature's "An Act to Punish Aiders and Abettors of Deserters" and informed the public that "Militia Officers," who were "exempted from conscription," neglected their duty "in arresting deserters and inforcing the conscript and other laws ... in some sections," which allowed some conscripted to "go clear and evade the service." Violence and deserters in the foothills "in Yadkin, Surry and Wilkes counties" and the "Tory Raid" of the town of Murphy excited readers.[41]

The *Western Democrat* communicated violence in March 1864 in Macon County, in Randolph County, and in April in Yancey County. "Several yankee prisoners have recently made their escape from the trains between Weldon, N. C. and Columbia, S. C.," and "11 Yankee prisoners escaped" in Charlotte. Citizens should "Look Out" for the "set of villainous Yankees prowling through our country." On June 28 "5 Yankees or deserters were seen in the vicinity of Shelby," were "said to be armed," and the Home Guard "went out in pursuit of them" but failed. Alarming the public, "such characters are scattered all over the country committing depredations on smoke houses, poultry yards, &c."[42]

Rumors added to the tense atmosphere. P. L. Boyd's inquired in a letter to "Mis S. Reinhardt," "I hear that they had hung Pride Bradshaw for harboring Josh Marcus Rhyne's negro man and we would like to hear all about that." Pride Bradshaw resided at Vestal's Ford post office, Gaston County in 1860, a farm laborer, with wife Sarah. No Court proceedings against Bradshaw have been discovered and, in fact, Bradshaw survived the rumored incident and resided in Gaston County in 1870 and Lincoln in 1880.[43]

During the summer and fall of 1864, the *Western Democrat* notified the public of "Another Tory Raid" in Haywood County, "Deserters-Murder" in Alexander, the Home Guard ordered to Wilkes, "Deserters in Yadkin," "Murder in Davie," when a Home Guard was shot, and "Tories and Deserters Captured" in Yadkin and Wilkes. The *Shelby Eagle* reported that "Boo Revels, the notorious deserter, who has been ranging over this section of the country for over a year, was captured ... at his house in the county [Cleveland]. He was brought to Shelby and placed in jail, from where he was sent to the army under guard." In August "More trouble in Wilkes" and "Outrages of Deserters and Tories" in central North Carolina made news. Even the "Editors and all printers" at the newspaper were ordered to the Home Guard, which precipitated "Suspension" of the paper. Another "Raid into Mitchell County" of Tories was noted, and in October "The Home Guard" for Gaston, Lincoln, and Cleveland Counties was called to Goldsboro. In the same paper "Homicide in Cabarrus" described the killing of a furloughed soldier by a militia lieutenant. On November 1 the paper reported that Judge Heath sentenced a deserter to death for murder, and the month included "Outrages by Deserters," "Escaped From Jail" in Statesville of one murderer and two horse thieves, and "A Fight in Wilkes."[44] News and personal experience sent a clear message that the legal authority had lost control not only in the mountain and central counties but in the Gaston area.

"Peace Warrant"

Another example of these disruptions involved Dr. B. F. Goode, who notified Governor Vance that G. W. Hull had been exempt from the draft because he was a justice of the peace and requested that Hull be conscripted. Instead of promoting peace, Goode contended that Hull "violated the law" by consuming "Spirits on the Sabbath" and "has maid sevrel attempt to murder some of the sitazens." Goode related an incident in which Hull "shot a Rifel Ball into G. M. Wacaser [Wacaster]" and that his own family was afraid of him. Goode closed his letter by stating that Hull was an "Eniamy to his on our Government" and should be conscripted into the military.[45]

Goode succeeded in getting some resolution as Hull was the defendant in several court cases. In Lincoln County's Fall 1864 Term, the state prosecuted him in "State vs. G. W. Hull Peace Warrant" in which he was fined only one penny and court costs. In two subsequent cases, Hull was charged with "A & B" (assault and battery) against Dr. Goode and W^m. Parham, respectively. In the Goode case, Hull was fined $2,000, of which Goode's attorney received $1,500. In the Parham case, Hull was fined $200 and ordered to keep the peace "towards W^m. Parham and all good citizens of the state of N. C." Hull had prominent supporters of financial means, such as D. F. Beam, A. B. Homesley, Peter Baxter, and J. A. Roberts, all of whom stood his bond at one point or another.[46] The war divided the citizenry.

Lincoln and Gaston County and surrounding areas remained on the verge of anarchy. The *Western Democrat* reported on December 27, 1864, that the Home Guard was once again dispatched to Goldsboro. On January 24, 1865, "Deserter Killed" revealed that "Joe Wright a deserter" had been killed in Cleveland County, and five others were captured and sent back to the army.[47] In the Lincoln County records for March 4, 1865, the governor instituted yet another "Court of Oyer and Terminer." Vance had signed the order on February 9. Judge Robert R. Heath was to lead the proceedings, but only twenty four persons were summoned for jury duty. The war would interfere: "in consequence of the judge being delayed on the Rail Road and there being no case ready for trial at this time it is considered by our Judge that a certificate issue to our Said Solicitor for his attendance at this term." On the next page is the curious entry: "It is further considered that the said Court of Oyer and Terminer be and it is hereby closed How are you Rebellion." It is unclear what case was to be tried as the justice system also became a victim of disruptions and uncertainty.[48]

Many Unionists resisted the Confederate government, actively supporting deserters and Union prisoners, and after the war applied for Southern Loyalist Claims.

Drucilla O'Brian lived near Dallas and contended in her Loyalist claim that she was "threatened and badly injured on account of our union Sentiments." She stated that her son, John, was murdered by the rebels because of his Unionist beliefs and "because he would not fight for the rebel cause." Further she stated that she did "everything [she] could to aid the union cause." The captain of the Home Guard told her that he had orders to hang her. In her Loyalist application she admitted to "harboring deserters" and to using her influence "to prevent conscripts from going to the rebel army." Near the end of the war her house and outbuildings were "plundered often" by rebels. Two deponents, Andrew Long and Austin Groner, supported her claims of Union support.[49] O'Brian also aided John Dixon, a deserter. He lived with her in the 1860 census, and on January 13, 1865, W. D. Glenn noted that "Jno. Dickson, a deserter, was shot and Killed. a bad came to a bad end."[50]

Nancy S. Robinson also lived near Dallas and claimed that her house was often broken into as rebels looked for deserters. She admitted "washing, cooking and aiding in any way ... deserters from the rebel army." She hid deserters, and the Home Guard threatened to fine her $6,000 and imprison her for twelve months. She related that John Dickson, for whom she cared "for several months," was "killed near my house by a rebel officer." She contended that her three sons were conscripted and that all three deserted for about two years "and came home." Deponent, J. J. Lawing, testified that Robinson was commonly known as a "deserter harborer" and that her sons deserted. As a member of the Senior Reserves, he recalled making "frequent raids on Mrs. Robinson's house," at which times she would "abuse" the rebels and its government "in strong language." Austin Groner, her son-in-law, testified that Robinson supported the Union cause and would "express her Sentiments when & where and to whom She pleased—was independent and entirely fearless, spoke her mind freely." Groner admitted that he had hidden at her house as a deserter with her sons and John Dickson.[51]

The actions of Drucilla O'Brian and Nancy S. Robinson compare similarly with other more notorious Unionist women in the Quaker Belt and the mountains during the war. Home Guard abuse of these Gaston females is consistent with other incidents of abuse. Many women, who defied Confederate authority, also organized opposition to the war and support for deserters.[52] Confederates passed laws to quash support for deserters.

"To Punish Aiders and Abettors of Deserters"

The state legislature approved "An Act To Punish Aiders and Abettors of Deserters," and Lincoln and Gaston Counties prosecuted the crime. In Gaston County during the Spring Docket 1864, the state prosecuted "A. Robison [for] Harboring Deserters." Witnesses for the state included Francis and Mary Hovis, but they failed to appear and were each fined $80. Again during the Fall term the state prosecuted "Green Massey [for] Harboring."[53]

In the same year, Lincoln County prosecuted "Susannah Hobbs & Alfred Hobbs" for Harboring. The indictment was nol processed, even though the state Adjutant General had ordered Lincoln County Major W. H. Alexander to indict Hobbs.[54]

More extensive documentation exists in a similar case. As early as February 2, 1864, R. H. Abernathy filed a complaint against "Christy Hope & Wife, Leanadas Sherell & wife" through testimony of "Capt. W. Adams & J. Broomhed," accusing them of "harbouring deserters, contrary to law." During the Spring Term of Court, Solicitor W. P. Bynum specified that the accused "with force & arms in said county, knowingly did aid, assist, harbor & maintain one Thomas Hope, the said Thomas, then & there being a deserter from the military service of the Confederate States." Subpoenas were sent to Cleveland County for Christian and Prudence Hope and to Lincoln County for Mary Sherrill. On February 2, B. J. Johnson found Hope and wife and Mary Sherrill guilty and "Leonodas Sherrill not guilty." The cases were carried in the Lincoln Court records through April 1865 when the Hopes were "Not to be found" in Cleveland County. On March 19, 1866, charges against Christian Hope were finally dropped because the sheriff was "informed that Christian Hope is dead." In addition during the Fall Sessions of 1864, "A. Costner, Foreman" of the jury instituted proceedings against Mahala Holbrook "for harboring Allison Holbrook a deserter."[55] "Christy Hope" resided in Gaston County in 1860, listed as a "Blk Smith" with no land, with wife Prudence and two possible children, neither of whom was listed as Thomas.[56] Lt. Willie Linebarger expressed the opinion of many soldiers who hoped that "maby they will quit harboring deserters and let them come back to the army where they belong" and speculated that "trying to do better and professing religion" would motivate their change of heart.[57] Some Unionists formally organized and collaborated with one another.

"Heroes of America"

Organized Unionist groups like "Heroes of America"[58] exerted statewide influence. James H. Marsh, an English immigrant, and his Massachusetts born wife resided near present day Laboratory (then known as Hokeville) on the South Fork River about 1–2 miles north of the Gaston County line. Marsh assisted the escape of Union prisoners of war, who witnessed a "Loyal League" meeting of about forty residents. They received food, clothing, a forged permission document, and shelter. The interchange of slave cooperation with Union sympathizers suggests a well coordinated organization. Thomas H. White, escaped Union soldier, confirmed that Marsh belonged to the Heroes of America and the Union League. Most likely Gaston County citizens were also involved in these Unionist organizations. Marsh identified at least two Gaston County citizens as prominent Unionist supporters: "Dr. Wm. Sloan" and "Hon. D. A. Jenkins."[59]

Members of the Heroes of America were "united in their desire to restore the Union." They initiated "espionage, in promoting the desertion of soldiers from the army, and above all, in aiding Unionists and escaped Federal prisoners...."[60]

To manage the now common "Civil War within the Civil War," Governor Vance convened special courts, as previously observed, and laws "To Punish Aiders and Abetters of Deserters" and "Guard for Home Defense," which increased the governor's power. The second law abolished the militia and instituted the Home Guard, specifically to locate deserters and keep the peace. These actions met with mixed success, as "in some sections" militia and Home Guard "actually helped to embarrass the authorities and injure the cause by taking part with the grumblers and disaffected."[61] In other cases they often resorted to vigilante justice with atrocities like Shelton Laurel and resulted in a growing distrust of state and local government.[62]

Few official Gaston County documents detail the activities of the local militia and Home Guard, who were "exempted from conscription for the purpose of aiding the authorities at home in arresting deserters and inforcing the conscript and other laws." Yet, newspapers reported that "in some sections," the militia neglected their duties by allowing some conscripts to "go clear and evade the service." Locally, the process required militia and Home Guard Colonel M. H. Hand of Stowesville to instruct captains throughout the county to execute various state and local orders. For example he ordered all conscripts to "call on Lieut. J. Fronebarger of Dallas for order of transportation." By late 1864 Hand ordered Gaston's Home Guard to Goldsboro.[63]

The documented listing of Gaston's militia includes only 1861–62 and is more confusing than Lincoln, Cleveland, and Catawba records. On December 23, 1861, Moses Henry Hand of Stowesville was commissioned a Colonel in the 87th Regiment of the County militia and maintained that position in the Home Guard. Many original commissioned officers in the militia volunteered for military service with their names crossed off the list. A captain headed each militia company. On March 22, 1862, William Sloan of Dallas and William J. Torrance were added as surgeons, James Rufus Hand as adjutant, Marion D. Friday as assistant quartermaster, and Elisha S. Barrett as assistant commissary. On May 7 others added included Captains Eli Mendenhall, Emanuel R. Rudisell, Thomas R. Brandon, William T. Shipp, John M. Roberts, Andrew R. Henderson, and Robert C. G. Love. Others listed in 1862 include William S. Cannon, Washington F. Massey, Albert Bradley, William Arrowood, Jonas Cloninger, Samuel C. Johnston, Robert F. Lineberger, John Smith, Eli Bradley, Green O. McKee, John J. McGinnis, Thomas F. Blakely, Robert A. Falls, Leander Smith, Marquis L. Carpenter, and John Farrow. Some are listed with commissions or with dittoed commissions.[64] There is some evidence that the Lincoln County Home Guard exercised jurisdiction over Gaston County: On October 29, 1864, Major L. W. Stowe of Stowesville was required to resubmit information to a Lincoln County unit.[65] A major benefit of membership in the militia or Home Guard was exemption from the Confederate draft, but they also had many responsibilities.

They rounded up conscripts, chased and captured deserters, enforced state laws, and performed other duties. Adjutant General correspondence and the Mendenhall Papers, originally in private hands but currently held at the Lincoln County Historical Association, provide insightful documentation on the militia and Home Guard. The Mendenhall Papers are letters and notes primarily from Colonel Hand to Captain Eli Mendenhall and illustrate Gaston County militia/Home Guard activities. Hand ordered Mendenhall and other captains to initiate actions against conscripts and deserters, to secure clothing and matériel for the soldiers, to regulate Free Negroes and slaves, and to address issues relating to exemptions and detailed personnel.

Passage of the Confederate Conscription Law required the militia and later the Home Guard to locate conscripts and send them to the army. Beginning on September 3, 1862, Colonel Hand notified Captain Mendenhall to "have all conscripts from 18 to 35 that was enrolled and not exempt and all deserters" in his "company beat" to report to Dallas.[66] As the law extended to include persons aged 40–50, and 17–18, Hand ordered Captain Mendenhall to make a list of persons and to ensure they "enrolled" at Dallas.[67]

"use all diligence to arrest all deserters"

As the demand for more soldiers intensified, Hand's orders to Mendenhall became more arbitrary and comprehensive. Mendenhall received orders to provide "age & occupation of each one & whether married or single & report in person to" Hand. Militia officers who had resigned found themselves eligible for the draft as did persons who had purchased substitutes. On May 18, 1864, Home Guard William R. Scott wrote "Capt. A. L. Henderson" and Mendenhall to "notify all your men between 17 & 18 & those who have become 18 since the last involvement to have them report to" Salisbury. By August 13, Scott ordered that exempt detailed persons such as "Black Smith, Shoe makers, Tanners, Millers, Factory hands principles of Substitutes & all engaged in Iron Works &c" could no longer wait for "an anseer from their petitions, but must go" immediately to Camp Holmes.[68] The Confederate government also drafted the "Junior Reserves" and "Senior Reserves" to secure more soldiers.

Even though the newly established Home Guard was critical to securing the peace on the home front, the state provided no arms. On May 22, 1863, Hand ordered Mendenhall to "use all diligence to arrest all deserters and ... order out as many men of the militia as needed for that purpose." On December 1 Hand ordered Mendenhall to "arrest & send to camp with out delay all Deserters conscripts or persons absent," to "look into all furloughs," and listed 20 alleged deserters from Co H, 37th Regt to be detained.[69] There was often confusion over draftees, deserters, and detailed personnel. In Lincoln County the Adjutant General had instructed Col. Philip Plonk to arrest four deserters. But on February 9, 1863, the order changed because the four were actually not deserters, as they fell under the new conscription group to age 40. Plonk was to "see that they are enrolled as Conscripts." Often the Home Guard and militia created problems. Loyal Confederate W. O. Harrelson informed Governor Vance that many citizens "looked upon [them] as a nuisance in the community," which could be detrimental to Vance's reelection.[70]

The difficulties of the Home Guard spilled over in a December 15, 1863, letter from W. T. Shipp to Governor Vance. He wrote of "William Lay" who had been in Capt Brice's

Larkin Thornburg, estimated by family to be about 17 or 18 in this undated picture. He hid from Confederate authorities to avoid conscription, was captured and forced into the army, and deserted after his first battle. His brother, missing a leg from service, ordered Larkin to remain at home, which he did (courtesy Gaston County Museum of Art and History).

cavalry, had deserted, was either arrested or went back to his unit. During the summer of 1863 he had received work on detail, some government contract or work, but had not yet returned to his unit from his detail work. Shipp considered him "now a deserter." He considered Lay "a pretty hard case" but the example illustrates the conflict between deserters, sometime deserters, and the Home Guard in Gaston County.[71]

On September 6, 1864, Colonel Hand instructed Mendenhall to "furnish said deserters with an attested statement Setting forth ... the time and place of surrender" to "officers of Militia and home guards." Hand also mandated a "written report," "stating the number of days and nights they have been out, the number of deserters apprehended and the number voluntarily surrenders and the names of such officers as may have failed to do their duty." The "names of deserters arrested" was also to be sent. On September 24 Hand reminded Mendenhall to offer "no temporary furloughs to Deserters."[72]

The story of Larkin Thornburg illustrates the personal aspect of desertion and Home Guard interaction. Thornburg wrote that he and Jacob Cloninger hid to avoid conscription until learning about President Davis's offer of full pardon, furlough, and amnesty. Emerging from "the woods" in order to alleviate "the cruel persecutions and threats of the militia" placed upon "our home folks," they surrendered to "M. D. Friday, a militia officer." Friday accompanied them toward the enrolling officer in Dallas, when Thornburg persuaded Friday to allow him to visit his parent's home, which was on the way. They discovered that William R. Scott, "the enrolling officer," and "a militia officer by the name of Bordly [probably Bradley]" were at the Thornburg residence. Scott "drew his gun on Cloninger and myself and commanded the other men to tie us together," intending to send them to war "in chains." To avoid being "tied like a brute," the two "rushed furiously upon [Scott]," attempting to escape. They failed. "Scott pointed the muzzle of his gun directly in my face," Thornburg recalled, "and dare me to open my mouth, saying that if I did so he would immediately blow out my brains." Tied to Scott's horse, Thornburg walked to Dallas, where he was placed in "the County prison for the night." The next day they rode to "Stanley Creek" and were placed on the train for Raleigh.[73] Draft and desertion pitted Gaston County residents against one other.

Commodities and materials were scarce on the home front and in the military. On October 23, 1862, Colonel Hand relayed the Governor's Order "to canvass your Co Beat as agent for the State to ask donations of shoes wollen or thick cotton Socks Blankets Shirts drawers & pants for our suffering soldiers in the Army & if they wont give them you are authorized to give a fair price for them & keep a strickt amount of what you get from each one & report to me." As a postscript Hand ordered, "take nothing by force." On March 23, 1863, Hand ordered Mendenhall to enforce the anti-liquor law "conseirning Distiliries." On July 16 Mendenhall had orders to secure conscripts who were ordered to bring "one good pair of shoes, two shirts two pr socks and one Blanket and 3 days rations."[74]

Mendenhall had other duties associated with maintaining the status quo. On October 22, 1863, Colonel Hand ordered him to "have all free Negroes or free people of Colour that are Males in your beat between the ages of 18 & 45 years of age at Brevards station ... to take the train to go to Wilmington to work on the fortifications at that place." Free Blacks had no choice in the matter. On December 1 Hand reminded Mendenhall that "all free Negroes" who were "busily employed ... working for the state for indigent families or for soldiers families are Exempt from the last order."[75]

The Confederate requirement that slaves work on military fortifications solicited opposition from slave owners. On November 12, 1864, Captain A. L. Henderson, acting for Lt. Scott, requested Mendenhall to furnish "a list of slave owners in your militia beat with the number of male slaves owned by each between the age of 12 & 50 years at once." Two days earlier, the Adjutant General confirmed that if slaveholders refused to adhere to the orders, Hand should "take them using Military Force if necessary." In Lincoln County, in response to an apparent complaint by C. C. Henderson, the Adjutant General confirmed that slaves were required to work for two months on the Wilmington fortifications and that the militia would give credit to owners for their previous slave labor.[76] The state Adjutant General recommended to Colonel C. H. Ramseur, Plonk's Lincoln County replacement, "that it is not advisable" to remove slaves from working on railroads to work on Wilmington fortifications but that no slaves were exempt from work.[77]

Extant documentation concerning detailed persons and exemptions remains limited. Detailed citizens were exempt from the draft because they worked in an essential trade, and specific other exemptions were outlined in legislation. The militia and Home Guard were assigned to monitor these two groups. The issues were confusing. On July 16, 1863, Hand communicated additional exemptions to Capt. Mendenhall: "Justices of the Peace County trustees Coroners Registers tax Collectors and? Deputy sheriff where there is no tax Collector Constable.... Deputy Clerk for each Court ... one Commissioner for distributing money and provisions among soldiers families.... Militia officers counselors of State.... Board of Internal Improvements the ?Silivery board and employees of the state government."[78] New laws changed exemptions.

Some detailed trades and exempt positions were classified at one time and not another. On November 26, 1862, the Adjutant General contacted Lincoln County militia Colonel Philip Plonk to arrest three shoemakers as conscripts, who were working for C. C. Henderson, a prominent Lincolnton merchant. On December 5 the order was rescinded. The Adjutant General refused to exempt Lincoln County's O. B. Jenks from the Home Guard. Earlier on January 8, 1864, the Adjutant General confirmed the exemption for Gaston's W. W. McGinnis for being a doctor having practiced medicine for five years and also approved an exemption for Gaston's Benaga Black, who was postmaster at White Pine. Apparently the Adjutant General's office was inundated with exemption requests. Woodlawn's James A. Abernathy sought an exemption from the draft because of a physical infirmity, and the office responded that Abernathy must report to the county enrolling officer, who would decide whether he was fit for duty.[79]

Colonel Hand also maintained accurate lists of officers, enforced the governor's proclamation conscripting male cotton mill employees, investigated 2nd Lt. Freno Massey, who was accused of aiding deserters, sorted through persons to be conscripted, and enforced the prohibition of "distilling grain."[80]

The Gaston County data suggests that the Civil War period was a time of unrest, deprivation, conflict, uncertainty, and fear. A core group of Unionists increased as the war persisted, and the line between Confederate soldier and deserter blurred with circumstances. The government's desire for more soldiers pitted citizens against one another and exacerbated social, economic, and political differences. Violence, theft, fear, and vigilante activities dominated. Lawlessness and the loss of order caused governmental responses which often created more animosity. No one was immune—loyal Confederates, Unionists, deserters, families of soldiers, Home Guard and militia—as all viewed the loss of order with fear and trepidation. Gaston County may have experienced less violence, intimidation, persecution, and unlawful activities then some North Carolina locales like

Shelton Laurel and the Quaker Belt. Yet, the frequency and seriousness of the documented incidents certainly dispels the myth that Gaston County experienced a calm and unified war time atmosphere, free from crime and disruptions.

Politically, the fervor for secession and oppositional loyalty to the Union created unique political dynamics in North Carolina and Gaston County. From 1860 throughout the war, tensions tightened, attitudes changed, and the way people viewed their government shifted in Gaston County. The people's unique socioeconomic conditions, the stresses of war, and the political manifestations of these conflicts caused citizens to alter their political allegiances.

8

CHANGING POLITICS DURING THE CIVIL WAR

Previous chapters in this book have disproven the traditional viewpoint that Gaston County citizens uniformly supported secession and the Confederate war effort. It is not surprising that a thorough examination of politics during the period paints a different portrait of political opinions and their evolution. Politics was critically important as it created Gaston County, an offshoot from Lincoln. Local politicians, James H. White, Richard Rankin, and Larkin Stowe, maneuvered a bill through the General Assembly to create the new county and to adjust the boundary between old Lincoln County and Catawba. Approved on December 5, 1846, Gaston County was born.[1]

Contrary to other southern states, North Carolina maintained a dynamic two-party system from the 1830s into the 1850s. Vehement political battles between Whigs and Democrats often shifted power in the legislature and governor's mansion. Old Lincoln County had been a major political player in state politics as a bastion of the Whig Party with Andrew Hoyl and William Joseph Wilson being strong proponents of Whig political thought with their neighbors the Grahams, Morrisons, and Hokes. North Carolina Whigs suffered because of negative national Whig opposition to the Mexican War; yet, in the late 1850s the state experienced a rebirth of conservative, Whiggish ideas and political ideology within the American Party. While volatile issues seized the national mood during the 1850s—whether to extend or limit slavery in the territories, opposition to the Fugitive Slave Law, and the southern desire to add slave states, whether in the west or in Central America—unique North Carolina issues preserved competitive politics in the state. These issues arose from North Carolina's demographics which played a major role in the history of Gaston County.[2]

90 percent of county officials owned slaves

Prominent historian Paul D. Escott summarized North Carolina's social and economic class distinctions, asserting that state economic, political, and social power rested with the slaveholding gentry and middle class.[3]

Of Gaston's eleven tax districts, seven were assessed with over 65 percent yeomen. Yet, despite its significant numbers of yeomen and landless whites, this project's analysis of the social class of governmental leaders found that the gentry and middle class dominated Gaston's political landscape by managing local government and promoting their own agenda. The governor appointed members of the County Court of Pleas and Quarter Sessions for life and those officials controlled the county, acting judicially and administratively. Gaston County began operation in 1847 with 14 justices listed at the first session, only three of whom did not own slaves in the 1850 census. From its creation in 1847 to 1860, most of the county's first elected and appointed officials were slaveholders: sheriff, House of Commons representatives, state senators, county trustees, treasurers, surveyors, solicitors, processioners, coroners, register of deeds, clerks of superior court, and rangers. The five members of the "Special Court" were slaveholders, as were two out of the three sureties for the Register of Deeds; four out of six sureties for treasurer; all three bondsmen for the coroner; six of the seven Wardens of the Poor, and five of the six constables also owned slaves.[4] The Patrol Committee tasked with regulating slave movement, not surprisingly included 24 slaveholders.[5]

Of the 82 persons elected or appointed to office in 1847, all but eight owned slaves. During the period examined, slave owners controlled at least 90 percent of the elective and appointive positions in government. Many persons held multiple offices; some simply exchanged offices with one another; and usually slaveholders were replaced with other slaveholders. For example, every sheriff during these years owned slaves. Court officials also exerted control of ancillary activities and governmental contracts. Thus, slaveholders dominated as individuals or on committees in tasks such as running the boundary line with Lincoln County, managing construction of the courthouse and jail, "taking charge of the courthouse square," managing streets in Dallas, laying off town lots, and having the responsibility "to sell the old courthouse."[6] Some examples illustrate.

One of the most influential Gaston County leaders was former Lincoln County leader James Hillhouse White, who resided near the center of the new county on Long Creek a few miles west of Dallas. As early as 1842 when he was a member of the House of Commons, he had led efforts to divide Lincoln County, which resulted first in the creation of Catawba, then Cleveland, and in 1846, Gaston County.[7] Middle class James H. White, a Jacksonian Democrat, belonged to a new political generation.

White's rise is remarkable because

James Hillhouse White (1802–1883), born in Ireland, a prominent Democratic politician who participated in the creation of Gaston County, Dallas, and southern secession. He supported the war effort and Governor Vance, serving in the state House of Commons and Senate (courtesy Gaston County Museum of Art and History)

he and his family had arrived from Ireland in 1818.[8] In 1850 the 45-year-old headed a household with his mother, wife, and seven apparent children. He was listed with 16 slaves, a grist mill and saw mill with a value of $1,000 which produced both grain and lumber, and an active farm worth about $2,000, of which he worked about 250 acres of land. He owned four horses, ten milk cows, 17 beef, and 40 hogs for a total value of $720. He raised wheat, corn, oats, and produced one ginned bale of cotton.[9]

By 1860 he owned only four slaves, and his milling operation was not listed in the Industry Schedule. He was listed as a "Farmer" with $5,400 household value and $7,579 real estate value. His son, John B., was listed in the household as a "Miller," and son Thaddeus next door as a "Lawyer" with no land. Son, Henry F., was listed in Dallas living with Jacob F. Pegram as a "Student of Medicine" in Pegram's Boarding House.[10]

The 1863 tax list assessed White with 515 acres valued at $7,675, which included the "Mill tract," and four slaves. He also was taxed for $1,785 cash, a carriage worth $60, and furniture worth $100. He also assumed taxes for "Gd Shtley?" for $1,000 in cash, "?for H. F.?," a silver watch, and one white poll for "T. S." While the value of his mill and farm dropped, the evidence suggests an older White transitioned from mill operator and farmer to a governmental employee. On October 10, 1863, White contacted the governor to resign from the North Carolina Senate as he had been appointed the county tax collector, which most likely paid a higher salary without expenses.[11]

Another prominent local politician, A. W. Davenport of Woodlawn district in eastern Gaston County owned 20 slaves, 500 acres valued at $4,000, and was assessed for $150 cash, $200 solvent debts, and furniture worth $100 in 1863. During the war he was elected to the House of Commons. Listed as a farmer in the 1850 census, he farmed 150 acres of improved land at a value of $1,600, owned six horses, seven milk cows, 18 beef, 42 sheep, and 45 hogs. He grew wheat, corn, oats, and six ginned cotton bales. His slave totals included eighteen in 1850, fifteen in 1860, and 20 in 1863.[12] Davenport belonged to the county gentry.

Other Civil War period gentry who held political positions included Dr. S. X. Johnston, William T. Shipp, Abram Scott, John D. McLean, and J. D. Rankin. The tax list assessed them for gold and silver items, cash, solvent debts, furniture, "pleasure vehicles," bonds, pianos, and dogs. Middle-class leaders, Moses H. Hand, Dr. William Sloan, Richard Rankin, and David A. Jenkins also possessed valuable land, slaves, gold and silver items, carriages, furniture, cash, and solvent debts.

In 1847 three prominent non-slaveholders were exceptions: entry taker, James M. Hanna, and Alexander Weer and Frederick Carpenter, who were justices of the peace.

The tax list and census illustrate the gap between Gaston's governing social classes. In 1863, Hanna was assessed $1,350 for 262 acres, and $25 for furniture. In 1850 listed as a "Farmer" worth $700 in real property, he headed a large household with an apparent wife and 12 children, and owned 80 "improved" acres, four horses, three milk cows, seven beef, 12 sheep, and 25 hogs. He raised wheat, corn, oats, and two ginned cotton bales. In 1860 "Farmer" Hanna was enumerated with $900 realty and $1,243 personal property. Alexander Weer had died by 1863 but his tax assessment included 207 acres valued at $630. In 1850 "Alex Wier" was enumerated as a "Farmer & Mchs" with $605 land value, 50 acres of "improved land," three horses, two milk cows, nine beef, 16 sheep, and 30 hogs. He raised wheat and corn. In 1860 he was listed as "Alexander Wear," "Farmer," with $2,050 in real and $2,471 in personal property. "Frederick Carpenter Sen" in 1863 was assessed for 396 acres valued at $3,200, $1,730 in cash , and as guardian for neighbors' assets. His 1850 assets included 125 "improved" acres, four horses, six milk cows, two beef, 18 sheep, 14 hogs, and he raised wheat and corn. His fourteen children and hired farm workers furnished labor for his farming operations.[13]

The research and the examples clearly demonstrate that, while non-slaveholders had a numerical majority in Gaston County, owners of bondsmen dominated local politics and the economy.

"several bloody fights & a great deal of violent quarreling"

David Schenck chronicled a unique glimpse of Gaston County politics in his diary on August 5, 1858, when he recorded the results of the Gaston County Sheriff's election with his usual judgmental candor and cynicism. Joseph Lusk defeated Paul Froneberger by four votes, which he termed "a bad choice. my old friend the Shff is beaten, which I greatly regret. he has been a 'right arm' to me." The young lawyer observed that "[R]agan, and Derr beats McKee, the nominee for Commoner By 42 votes. neither are fit to represent a respectable community." He continued, "McKee was as ignorant as an ass, coarse in manners & vulgar in morals. Ragan is better informed but a drunkard. Both are Illiterate." Schenck delivered a "political speech" in favor of Judge Ellis for governor, and Ellis received 310 votes at Dallas, "the largest Dem. vote ever given…. There was considerable excitement during the day, several bloody fights & a great deal of violent quarreling."[14] Local democracy was often personal, violent, confrontational, and often laced with alcohol. Two issues excited the state in the late 1850s.

One issue involved "free suffrage," the direct election of state senators. The 1835 North Carolina Constitution retained much of the state's earlier policies which kept political power within the wealthy class, including required ownership of 50 acres to vote for state senator. By 1857, disenfranchised citizens in the piedmont, mountains, and the yeomen class clamored for changes, and a state constitutional amendment was approved allowing all white males over 21 to vote in the senatorial election.[15]

Within this political climate, a second polarizing issue emerged—whether to tax slave property ad valorem, according to their actual economic value. Historically, the state raised funds by taxing land at its assessed value and taxing a head or poll tax on white and black males between the ages of 21 and 45. Conservative politicians advocated replacing the poll tax on slaves with a tax assessing their economic value. The ad valorem taxation issue erupted into North Carolina politics in 1858–59, as Conservatives successfully challenged Democratic leadership.[16] The state Secessionist Convention in 1861 defused the divisive ad valorem tax issue by approving it. Democratic and secessionist leaders believed it was a helpful concession to achieve unification for the anticipated war. The issue, a victory for small farmers, meant that slaveholders' taxes would increase.[17] The 1860 presidential election further divided North Carolinians. David Schenck voiced the radical, secessionist position.

"Black Republicanism"

Prior to the election David Schenck analyzed the candidates in his diary: John C. Breckenridge represented the "Southern and Constitutional wing of the Democracy";

Stephen A. Douglas the "Northern wing of the Democracy and the dangerous dogma of 'Squatter Sovereignty' or the power of a Teritorial legislature to abolish slavery"; John Bell "The old gentlemens party, having for their platform the 'Constitution, Union & Enforcement of the Laws'—a show of glittering generalities, hiding much sin and old fogyism—it is the Whig party by the latest name...." Schenck characterized these candidates as being of the "conservative elements of the country, opposed to the fanatical Abolitionists of the North led by 'Lincoln & Hamlin' who recognize no guide or restriction on the subject of Slavery not even the constitution and profess a 'Higher law' as a sole test of duty." He predicted that Lincoln would win the election because "the conservative elements being thus divided and weakened." The result Schenck observed: "a Dissolution of the Union is in my opinion inevitable—it is almost a fixed fact." He suggested that Douglas had forsaken the South "to gain Northern influence" and that Breckenridge represented "the party who claim their strict constitutional rights, as especially defined in the Dredd Scott case ... and will yield nothing to the Black Republican party even if the consequence is Disunion." "To this party I belong," wrote Schenck, "it will carry the South." He supported these positions "not as a politician or aspirant for office, but with pure and conscientious motives—to preserve our constitutional rights and thereby save the Union, or if denied this, to choose Secession in preference to disgrace."[18] Schenck and supporters favored the Dred Scott case since it held that no federal governmental body could prohibit slavery anywhere, repudiating the Republican position, that the extension of slavery could be regulated by Congress.

Since most citizens of Gaston County were Democrats, Schenck presumed that the presidential contest would be between Breckinridge and Douglas. Schenck observed that Dr. William Sloan of Dallas was an influential Douglas supporter and had gained "some power" in Gaston.[19]

On October 27, 1860, Schenck attended a "mass meeting at Charlotte," where "Ex Senator Brown, Gov Bragg, Hon A. W. Scales, Thos Ruffin, D M Barringer and others" made "able and effective" speeches. "The doctrine of protection to slave property in the territories was forcily argued by Gov Bragg. The sovereignty of the states and States Rights and Secession &c. were presented by Bedford Brown." On October 29, 1860, Schenck and L. E. Thompson "both advocated Breckenridge and Lane in this place [Dallas]."[20]

During the 1860 presidential campaign, Schenck delivered no less than nine speeches at the Gaston Courthouse. The day before the presidential election he made a strong speech there which was well attended. He stated that secession would be the only solution if Lincoln got elected and believed that Lincoln and his party had made "war on our property." Their objective was "Equality of the negro and the white man." Schenck perceived that his speech "fell on good ground and ... [would] bring forth abundant fruit." On November 6 he returned to Dallas to cast his ballot for Breckinridge. He proudly proclaimed that Gaston had gone for his candidate with 826 votes to 131 for Bell and 56 for Douglas.[21]

The *Western Democrat* reported the results by polling place with a resounding "Hurrah for Gaston." The results surprised the paper as Gaston was "one of the counties which was said to be equally divided.... We congratulate the true democracy of Gaston." The results were:

Poll	Breckinridge	Bell	Douglas
Dallas	286	28	21
Blacks	132	6	0
Mauneys	41	7	0
Decks	34	10	0
Fergusons	70	4	4
Sandifers	97	11	12
Stowes	75	23	18
Canslers	72	28	1
Rhynes	19	14	0
	826 [82%]	131 [13%]	56 [5%][22]

The data demonstrate that public opinion was divided throughout the county. Bell polled a higher percentage in Stowes, Canslers, Rhynes, and Decks precincts than his overall 13 percent county percentage. But otherwise, the county clearly supported Schenck's secessionist candidate, Breckinridge.

"Free negro equality or resistance is the issue"

Schenck supported "constitutional rights" and secession and delineated the issues—southern defense of the right to hold slaves, support for the Dred Scott case which would allow slavery throughout the United States, and the perception that the "Black Republican party" supported racial equality. With resignation, "sadness," and "alarm," Schenck recorded in his diary that Lincoln had won the election and that citizens now discussed the probability of war.[23] While Schenck perceived that North Carolina voters opposed secession, for him and other like-minded North Carolinians the issue was simple: "Free negro equality or resistance is the issue." For Schenck remaining in the Union meant placing a "yoke" on southerners.[24]

After the 1860 election, Deep Southern states—South Carolina, Mississippi, Alabama, Georgia, Florida, Louisiana, and Texas—seceded from the Union. Schenck applauded secession and characterized local political differences with "personal animosity daily" in Gaston and Lincoln. He intimated that "[e]very one not for us is against us and is counted an enemy, a 'submissionist,' equal to a Tory."[25] Schenck and other secessionists identified themselves with Patriots of the American Revolution and their political opponents as Tories, symbolically Loyalists during the Revolution. For secessionists there could be no moderation.

Not all southerners endorsed secession as the logical consequence of Lincoln's election. Conservatives, primarily Whig and Unionist Democrats, believed that the best way to preserve slavery was to remain in the Union. These political thinkers understood that abolishing slavery required a constitutional amendment, which conversely required a number of slave states' approval. They feared that, if the southern states seceded, southern control over slavery would end. Remaining in the Union ensured southern influence to preserve the "peculiar institution." Nationally and state-wide, secession was strongest in areas with the most slaves.[26]

On the other hand, secessionists inside and outside North Carolina sought a complete political break. Seceded states of the Deep South sent delegates to facilitate Upper South secession.[27] Locally, securing adherents to their cause involved political coordination and silencing opposition. Secessionist leaders scheduled local meetings to garner public support.

"the negro must be equal to the white man in government"

On December 1, 1860, within weeks of Lincoln's election, "a large and respectable meeting" of Gaston County residents met at the courthouse in Dallas. It was attended by citizens from all sections of the county, "irrespective of party." On James Quinn Esq.'s motion the group elected Richard Rankin as chair and both William M. Ferguson and James W. Reid as secretaries. The young lawyer, David Schenck, "explained the reason for the meeting," and he and Col. M. H. Hand served on a subcommittee for resolutions. They observed that "a Black Republican has been elected president ... by an entirely sectional vote, whose principles, as announced, are that a war of extermination must be made on our institutions, and that the negro must be equal to the white man in the government." Their first resolution supported Governor Ellis and his call for a convention "to devise the best means for our safety." The second resolution contended that the citizens "would not submit to tyranny of 'higher law' principles" and would "fall back on her constitutional rights last protection." Speakers included James Quinn Esq. who supported secession, and J. G. Lewis Esq. who "depicted the enormity of allowing negroes equality in the south in forcible language, and appealed to the people to be zealous of their rights as free white men, and if necessary to unsheathe the sword in their defence." William McKee, a voice of moderation, thought a convention was "premature" but would support secession if his state sought it. Colonel Rankin supported the resolutions in a "firm and bold speech" which challenged the people to be ready "to take action for the safety and welfare" of the county. The resolutions were unanimously approved and ordered to be printed in Charlotte newspapers.[28] The resolutions mirror Schenck's diary verbiage.

A similar meeting held in Lincolnton on the same day was attended by a "large and respectable number of citizens." General Daniel Seagle nominated C. C. Henderson as chairman and A. Costner and V. A. McBee were elected secretaries. The Lincoln County resolutions, as reported in the newspapers, were less inflammatory. The "unhappy condition of the country" was blamed on "Abolitionists of the North." While acknowledging Lincoln's election on a "purely sectional" basis, the Lincoln County resolutions defined the situation as placing the south "at the mercy of a dominant and fanatical majority," whose views "would destroy all the future hopes of the South, and inevitable bring upon us ruin and disgrace." They resolved support for Governor Ellis and called on the legislature to do so as well. They further resolved to support independence if all other means failed to end the impasse and pledged their "lives" to that end. V. A. McBee, John Coulter, and Henry Cansler spoke in favor of the resolutions, which were "unanimously adopted."[29]

On December 11, 1860, a "Meeting in Cleaveland County" met at the courthouse in Shelby with C. C. Durham, Esq, chairman, and Dr. T. Williams, J. W. Toney, and Jno. T. Miller, secretaries. The group was concerned that Lincoln had been elected president "by a purely sectional party whose principles are hostile to the entire interests of the South—a party that declares theirs is a higher law than the Constitution." It approved resolutions demanding "our independence," calling a convention, and endorsing Governor Ellis's leadership. They considered the Constitution "a compact for the benefit of all States" and no longer binding, supported the right to secede, promised "to resist" any attempt to coerce seceded states back into the Union, and to print the resolutions and share with legislators.[30]

On the same day, another meeting held at White Plains in Cleveland County near present Kings Mountain also supported secession. Dr. J. W. Tracy addressed the group: He contended that the issue involved southern "rights and liberties, those rights bought by the blood of our fathers and guaranteed to us by the Constitution." He asserted that "fanatics," whom he characterized as "black Republican rule," threatened those rights to the point that he was willing to "go with you to victory or death in defence of Southern rights." He informed the group that he was "ready to sacrifice my life, my fortune, my all in defence of all the rights of the Southern soul." He contended that southern liberty was being threatened by "a set of black hearted Abolitionists." E. Dixon and William Falls echoed Dr. Tracy's sentiments and all hoped that North Carolina would soon secede. Dixon even proposed that counties within North Carolina should secede and join South Carolina and the Confederacy. Attendees resolved to leave the Union, endorsed the "Right of Secession" with their "lives, ... fortunes, ... and sacred honor, and agreed to have their meeting minutes published in local newspapers. Dixon also suggested forming "a Volunteer Company" and 26 of the "most respectable young men of the county signed their names to defend Southern rights, at a moments warning."[31]

On December 25, 1860, another "Public Meeting in Lincoln," attended by the "citizens of Lincoln and Gaston counties," met at Rock Hill School House in eastern Lincoln County. The group elected Dr. S. X. Johnston of Gaston as chair and Jas. Kincaid as secretary. Johnston stated the meeting's objective and "advocated the necessity of prompt and energetic action." The meeting resolved that Lincoln, a "Black Republican" had been elected along a "sectional vote," and southerners feared his administration since they believed it would "degrade us ... and deprive us of the dearest rights of freemen." They favored calling a secessionist convention and would "prefer to leave the Union with our sister States of the South."[32]

Not all meetings supported immediate secession. On January 12, 1861, "a very large and respectable portion of the citizens of Gaston County" voiced another viewpoint at the courthouse in Dallas. "James Hannah Esq." who organized the meeting was elected chairman, and Dr. W. W. Noland was elected secretary. The meeting's objectives were to "preserve our rights and, if possible, do so in the Union" and to "exhaust all constitutional and peaceful means to obtain our just rights, and let disruption be our last resort." Dr. William Sloan spoke "with calmness and reason" respecting "opinions of those who might differ with him." While the crisis evolved because of the "election of a Black Republican," Sloan argued that "[t]he way to meet the crisis was to defend our rights in the Union and not out of the Union—make our just demands in a proper way; after all constitutional means were exhausted and all hope of justice had failed, then let us with unity of action go out together." He viewed secession as "too hasty" and that "[s]ecession was what the abolitionist most desired, as being the most effectual way to exterminate slavery." Dr. Sloan predicted that "[a] divided action would bring about anarchy and civil war. After many years of civil war the people would become exhausted, would enquire the cause of this war, which brought so much distress and suffering. Then wives and children," Sloan continued, "would be crying for bread—this would be an appeal to the brain through the stomach. Men would turn upon the slave and exterminate him." Following Dr. Sloan's address, the meeting adopted resolutions by "wisdom, moderation and experience, to prevent the dismemberment of the republic, and avert the calamities which are sure to follow dissolution." Their resolutions regarded secession "as the greatest calamity," proposed that "rights, interests and institutions can best be preserved and protected under the Constitution and in the Union," allowed that the North "shall furnish better guarentees for good faith in the future; shall repeal all laws which deny just rights to the South" within a "reasonable time," suggested that North Carolina should not "follow the reckless extravagance and misdirections of others," pledged that they were "sincerely and devotedly attached to the Union, and that we would oppose any action having for its object dissolution of the same," and sent their resolutions to legislators. Alexander Weer, D. A. Jenkins, Wm. McKee, Dr. J. S. Maxwell, and David Wells served on the resolution committee. The resolutions passed unanimously, sending copies to *The Standard* and *Western Democrat* for publication. Alexander Weer conveyed "an able and patriotic speech—appealing to his fellow-citizens to preserve the government of their fathers as long as there was any hope."[33] The Unionist meeting advocated moderation and emphasized reason.

The predictions of Dr. Sloan were rather prophetic: "anarchy and civil war," "distress and suffering," and "crying for bread." As previously exposed, Gaston County experienced all these wartime difficulties on the home front. The differences between the emotionalism of the secessionist meetings and moderation of the Unionist meeting are striking.

Political meetings continued. In January 1861, the *Western Democrat* reported a Lincolnton meeting where William Lander addressed a large assembly for two hours. Lander did not endorse immediate secession but appealed "for a united South for the sake of the rights of the South—union of southern people for the purpose of maintaining their rights and resisting the aggressiveness of the abolition party, would do more to prevent war." Attorney L. E. Thompson offered "a few remarks ... in favor of the cause of the South." The newspaper "found the people mostly for preserving the Union if we could get our rights in it and have peace, but if this cannot be done and the Republican party does not yield, they are for resisting Lincoln and all his friends, and ready to fight if necessary."[34]

Later on January 30, 1861, another meeting was held in eastern Gaston County at Castenia Grove near present Lucia. Attendees included persons from both Gaston and Lincoln County; they elected Gaston citizens, Dr. William B. McLean and Dr. S. X. Johnston, as chairman and secretary. "L. E. Thompson, Esq., of Lincolnton" communicated a two-hour speech. Attendees unanimously endorsed the governor's proposed secession convention and resolved "that our welfare and safety, under existing conditions, can only be found in a Union of Southern States." Interestingly beside this article in the newspaper is one about "Hon. J. J. Crittendon" and his attempt at national compromise. Yet, the Crittendon article lamented that "the overthrow of slavery" seemed to be the only intent of the current government of Lincoln and the Republican Party.[35]

Accounts of the secessionist meetings and Unionist meetings indicate one commonality—all embraced preserving slavery. Each sought to protect it, one by leaving the Union, while Unionists would remain. A Mecklenburg County meeting at Berryhill's School summarized this belief system: In response to "a hostile feeling to the institution of slavery," meeting attendees held "themselves ready to shoulder arms in defence of that institution, believing our personal security and our rights of property involved in the issue," as they felt they were on the "verge of anarchy, ... destruction of our property as property."[36]

While citizens attended local meetings and secessionists advocated for immediate action, Governor Ellis's call for a Secessionist Convention met with only lukewarm support in the legislature. Most North Carolinians, agreeing with Dr. Sloan, felt that Lincoln's election was not a "sufficient cause" to secede, and the legislature delayed the call for the convention. Finally on January 29, 1861, the legislature approved a referendum in which North Carolinians would decide two issues. One would be for or against a convention; the other to elect representatives to attend the convention.[37]

At a "Public Meeting in Dallas," Gaston County nominated Dr. Sidney X. Johnston for the Secession Convention. When the election was held, Johnston polled 861 votes and J. S. Maxwell, attendee at the Unionist meeting, polled 177 votes, even though he was not a candidate. Johnston received almost 83 percent of the vote.[38]

"never to bow to the yoke of Black republicanism"

Statewide North Carolina rejected calling a convention by a margin of about 1,000 votes. Schenck observed "the centre counties of Guildford, Iredell, Randolp, and the mountain counties in which many abolition sympathizers and Whigs live, have gone almost unanimously for submission." Counties closer to South Carolina, he maintained "with one exception have declared for secession." Locally Schenck and fellow secessionists had campaigned effectively. Lincoln County voted for Lander and "[s]ecession with no opposition and polled 686 votes. The Convention polled 708 to 86—Gaston too was almost unanimous 856 to 167, Catawba about the same, indicating their determination never to bow to the yoke of Black Republicanism." Lincolnton voted 334 to 1 with intense feelings in town. In his diary Schenck once again denounced Unionists as "the tories of 76."[39]

Support for the convention often meant support for secession. An analysis of the election results in Gaston and surrounding counties indicate a profound support for the convention and, as Schenck hoped, for secession. Gaston voters supported the convention by almost 84 percent. Lincoln County cast 794 votes with an 89 percent majority for convention. Cleveland County supported convention by about 92 percent with 1,387 votes cast. In Catawba County of the 1,076 votes cast, 85 percent supported convention. Farther to the west in Rutherford County a total of 1,278 votes included a majority of about 76 percent for convention. East of the Catawba River, Mecklenburg County cast 1,700 votes, of which 85 percent favored convention. Rowan County on the other hand cast a total of 2,032 votes, of which only 43 percent favored the convention.[40] Gaston, Polk, Rutherford, Burke, Cleveland, Catawba, Lincoln, Mecklenburg, Cabarrus, and Union Counties also elected secessionist delegates.[41]

In the immediate area only Rutherford in the foothills and Rowan in the central portion of the state polled a lower percentage than Gaston in favor of convention. Gaston's 84 percent for convention mirrored the 1860 presidential election totals of 82 percent for Breckenridge, the secessionist candidate. Even with such a solid majority, about 20 percent of the Gaston voting population entered the forthcoming conflict with apparent trepidation or outright opposition.

The *Western Democrat* offered that the conventions' defeat and the election of a majority of Unionists were because "the people did not understand the issue." Despite its stinging state-wide defeat, convention supporters did not falter. They proposed a convention in Goldsboro to create a State's Rights Party. On March 18, 1861, Lincoln County citizens elected convention delegates. S. E. Alexander was elected chair of the meeting, and William H. Michel and J. C. Jenkins served as secretaries. They elected two attorneys to represent them: James T. Alexander and the young David Schenck.[42] Schenck was elected even though he resided in Gaston County. No Gaston returns have been located and it is possible that the Lincoln meeting actually served both counties.

The *North Carolina Whig* reported on March 19 that at a State's Rights Party meeting in Mecklenburg County, E. S. Barrett of Gaston attended among representatives of seven counties. Meeting resolutions included the call for another convention to vote on secession.[43] The *Western Democrat* reported other prominent attendees from Gaston: A. W. Davenport, Richard Rankin, Dr. S. X. Johnston, who was elected vice president, and Valentine Derr. David Schenck, who with A. T. Alexander represented Lincoln County, addressed the group with "one of the most eloquent and masterly efforts" with a recollection of American sacrifice at the Battle of Kings Mountain and to entreat the hearers that they "came here for action not words." James H. White and J. G. Lewis of Gaston were on the Resolutions Committee which supported "immediate connexion" with the Confederacy, a Convention of Border States, and a North Carolina Convention. Additional meetings were held in Charlotte and Monroe prior to the Goldsboro meeting.[44] All Gaston attendees owned slaves.

On March 22–23, 1861, Schenck attended the "Goldsboro Convention," where the "Southern Rights party" laid the foundation among "Whigs, Democrats and Douglas men." He addressed the Convention, as the primary purpose of the State's Rights Party was to facilitate secession.[45] Secessionists planned a follow-up Convention in Charlotte with preliminary meetings in various locations such as Shelby.[46]

On April 18 secessionists created the "Lincoln County Southern Rights Association." Leaders included David Schenck, William Lander, L. E. Thompson, and future soldier "Lem Hoyle," who served as secretary. The revolutionary organization appears modeled after the Revolutionary Committees of Correspondence with officers, a "Committee of Correspondence," and a "Committee of Arrangements."[47]

"bonfires, illuminations and firing of cannon"

Schenck happily reported in his diary that South Carolina's attack on Fort Sumter and its surrender "aroused North Carolina from the mountains to the coast and the event was celebrated by bonfires, illuminations and firing of cannon. In Lincolnton the whole town was illuminated, cannon fired, speeches made, tar and boxes burnt for bonfires &c."[48]

On April 15, 1861, the *North Carolina Whig* characterized the Lincolnton celebration with bonfires made from "tar barrels and other demonstrations of joy." Despite torrents of rain "the assemblage was large." Men, women, and the Lincolnton Brass Band attended and made merriment. The Band played "Dixie Land." The group met at the courthouse where A. W. Abernathy Esq. was named chair and secretaries included B. H. Sumner and J. Stowe Esq. General W. J. Hoke motioned to accept resolutions offering congratulations to South Carolina for the firing on Fort Sumter, unanimously approving secession of North Carolina, and printing the proceedings in newspapers.[49]

Local citizens chose delegates to the Secessionist Convention. Gaston again chose Dr. S. X. Johnston and Lincoln, Wm. Lander Esq.[50]

War fever proliferated. Schenck noted "the enthusiasm spreads until all labor is ceasing and men think only of volunteering and enlisting." He recorded in his diary that soldiers drill everywhere. On May 20, 1861, the North Carolina Secessionist Convention unanimously voted to secede from the Union. Schenck boasted that "North Carolina will never recede from this step until the last man is dead and the last dollar spent." Schenck noted a lack of partisanship, another "era [of] good feeling" among former Democrats and Whigs. While new issues will divide the government, Schenck noted "slavery will ever unite us a people or Confederacy."[51] He astutely stated the South's basis for unification.

As secessionists held political rallies to foster support, they, as discussed in Chapters 6 and 7, utilized vigilante tactics to suppress minority opinions and to intimidate Unionists or dissenters, thereby ending the open dialogue of 1860 and early 1861. Documentation of the meetings and of vigilante activities suggests a coordinated effort to move public opinion toward secession and Confederate support.

Wartime party politics in North Carolina altered traditional behavioral patterns. While Schenck felt a spirit of accomplishment with the founding of the Confederate States of America, his prediction that the State's Rights Party would become dominant proved to be false. After the convention closed in April of 1862, the state prepared for its first Confederate election. Two parties emerged. For governor the State's Rights or Confederate Party nominated William Johnston of Charlotte. He had been a life-long Whig, had operated Lincoln County iron furnaces, served as a colonel in the Commissary Department in Charlotte and President of the Charlotte and South Carolina Railroad. The Conservative Party nominated former Whig, Zebulon B. Vance, a Bell presidential supporter who had initially favored remaining in the Union. He volunteered after the firing on Ft. Sumter and was serving in the Confederate army. Neither candidate actively campaigned; instead newspapers and supporters carried their messages.[52]

W. W. Holden's highly influential Raleigh newspaper *The Standard* supported Vance. On July 1, 1862, the *North Carolina Whig* assailed *The Standard* for opposing local gubernatorial candidate Johnston and for advocating "a change [in North Carolina government], embracing more economy, vigor, and vitality in the conduct of public affairs." The paper also opposed Vance's candidacy and his embrace of "Conservatism."[53] On July 15, 1862, *The North Carolina Whig* compared Vance and Johnston and deemed Johnston a lawyer, financier, administrator, and intellectual, with abilities superior to Vance. It determined Johnston, "the man for the place and the times."[54]

Schenck also supported William Johnston, whom he regarded as an original friend of secession, "who would yield to no compromise." He noted Democrat W. W. Holden's support for Vance and characterized Holden as "a real traitor at heart. He is an unscrupulous politician who loves himself far more than his country."[55] North Carolina's gubernatorial election occurred in August 1862. Charlotte's *The Daily Bulletin* reported local election results from Gaston County, which provided Mecklenburg's William Johnston with 417 votes to Vance's 372. Mecklenburg on the other hand supported Johnston 1,241 to 421.[56]

Vance won the election. Assuming Johnston's Lincoln and Mecklenburg connections and that his brother, Sidney X. Johnston resided in Gaston, he should have strongly carried Gaston and Lincoln County. While he got a majority of Gaston's vote, it was not overwhelming—53 percent. Conservatives won a majority of the seats in the legislature. A comparison with other counties is helpful:

	Vance	Johnston	% for Johnston
Gaston	379	427	53%
Mecklenburg	425	1,335	76%
Lincoln	605	367	38%
Cleveland	523	575	52%
Catawba	605	555	48%
Rutherford	1,147	257	18%[57]

In the same election Gaston's James H. White won the Senate seat for Gaston, Lincoln, and Catawba Counties with 50.7 percent of the votes cast in the governor's race. No breakdown of the votes or opponents has been located. White likely received significant support from Lincoln and Catawba, because of his past service. A. W. Davenport of eastern Gaston won the right to represent Gaston in the House of Commons.[58] Both were secessionists.

Governor Vance soon provided reassurances that he would support the war effort. In his inaugural address, he contended that the war was fought for "our liberties and independence." He appealed for support because the Union planned "to arm brigades of African slaves against us, in whose hands our mothers and sister would find murder indeed a message of relief."[59] Schenck was pleased that Vance expressed support "for an uncompromising prosecution of the war until our total separation and independence from the North is accomplished."[60]

After the 1862 elections the Conservative Party, led by Governor Vance, instituted its brand of politics in the state. Vance and king-maker, W. W. Holden, supported the war effort but also found many Confederate laws troublesome. Conscription, revocation of the writ of habeas corpus, the Tithing tax law, impressments, and other measures exposed the preeminence of the Confederate government over state government. These issues, Confederate battle failures, plus the debilitating conditions on the home front eventually facilitated dissent. Vance supported state rule and personal individual freedoms above Confederate authority, minimizing some of the most objectionable Confederate policies.[61]

"Peace convention"

By 1863 these pressures resulted in many North Carolinians expressing dismay at the continuing conflict. Holden led public opinion, calling for a "peace convention" to negotiate the cessation of hostilities. Many counties offered supporting resolutions for the "peace convention" and selected delegates with about 100 peace meetings being held statewide[62] including Moore, Buncombe, Iredell, and Gaston Counties.

Accounts of these meetings in the August 5, 1863, issue of *The Standard* were very similar suggesting a coordinated effort, having observed the earlier successful secessionist meetings and activities. The Moore County article specified that President Jefferson Davis had requested 7,000 more men and contended that North Carolina should not send any more men until other states had fulfilled their quotas. The article also encouraged more county meetings to express North Carolinian outrage at their treatment by the Confederate government. The Buncombe County article contended that North Carolinians "never have, and never will surrender our sovereignty to any human power" and pledged to support no person running for Congress unless they commit to repealing the "tithing law." The Iredell article endorsed a State Convention to deal with the issues.[63] Moore, Buncombe, and Iredell's Unionist sentiments were consistent with their presidential votes and secessionist convention votes. These counties supported state's rights against the Confederate government.

The Sampson County meeting report differed. While they also endorsed their governor, they communicated unqualified support for President Davis. In addition they "repudiate the moral treason (to say the least) taught by the Standard, and shadowed forth in its editorials and correspondence." They challenged editor Holden to confirm whether he was a "friend or an enemy to the cause of our country" and suggested that he sought reunion and reconstruction with the North. They questioned his usage of the term "conservative" to describe his followers' beliefs and suggested it meant, "submission to the Lincoln usurpation."[64] Political agitation continued.

Gaston also held a peace meeting. On July 25, 1863, W. B. Lay and others held a "Public Meeting" in Duhart's district in Gaston County in support of Holden's platform. Others attending included: J. M. Hanna the chair, J. W. Bradley, H. Jenkins, C. H. Abernathy, S. H. Hoffman, and Lay, who was appointed the group's secretary. Because North Carolina had more soldiers enlisted in the Confederate military and her soldiers were not led by North Carolinian officers, attendees unanimously resolved that citizens were "threatened." They also resolved to instruct their Confederate representative to "procure an armistice" through "negotiation or otherwise." They accused the Confederate Congress of ignoring the states and praised Governor Vance and Judge Pearson "and others" for their efforts to support North Carolina and its citizens. They further supported W. W. Holden, as "a faithful sentinel placed on the political watchtower, whom the people will sustain...." The group opposed Confederacy President Jefferson Davis's call for more troops at least "until after the crops are gathered" and went on record opposing the appointment of a Virginian as the "principal Tithingman for North Carolina," asserting that a North Carolinian was more appropriate. They petitioned for his removal from office and supported the printing of the meeting's minutes in the North Carolina *Standard* and the Fayetteville *Observer*. J. M. Hanna, "Chm'n."[65]

Other Gaston County citizens opposed the "peace convention." The *Western Democrat* reported that on August 11, 1863, Daniel F. Ragan chaired a meeting in response to the peace meeting, which "misrepresent[ed] the public sentiment of that patriotic county," with Capt. John H. Roberts and Samuel Jarrett Esq. serving as secretaries. L. E. Thompson spoke eloquently "denouncing as treasonable the recent miserable attempt by a few disloyal persons to palm off on the public a set of disloyal resolutions." He warned citizens that adhering to that sentiment would "meet the fate and penalty it deserved." He proposed resolutions "because of the temporary reverses of our arms and the increasing cruelty of our enemies" and because "a few persons have lately met in one part of our county, and passed resolutions misrepresenting a very large majority of people." The meeting's resolutions conveyed the "unshaken confidence in the righteousness and justice of the cause" and expressed support for obedience to laws and sacrifices necessary to "acquire that independence and liberty we are contending." They "abhor[ed] the treachery and baseness ... to submit to the infamous rules of the Federal Government" and sought peace "based on entire independence," applauding the "integrity, patriotism and fidelity" of President Davis and Governor Vance.[66]

An adjoining article, "PRESENTMENT OF THE GRAND JURY OF GASTON COUNTY," repudiated the peace meeting resolutions as "an erroneous impression [of] the true sentiments of the people of Gaston county," opposing the "disaffection" between the people and the government. The Grand Jury expressed confidence in Vance and Davis and accused "those persons" of having "sinister and disloyal purpose, or have been led astray by the misrepresentation of artful and designing men." They opined that "a large majority of the people in Gaston county are loyal to our Government and the war," affirming their belief in peace only through "separation." Fifteen citizens signed.[67]

"peace or tory meeting"

The efforts of loyal Confederates paid dividends. The *Western Democrat* reported that a "peace or tory meeting" was scheduled for Saturday October 19 in Cherryville. "[A] large number of persons assembled but no one could be found who was willing to engage in such a meeting." Those present instead "organized a meeting friendly to the Confederate cause and passed resolutions" supportive of no peace without "complete independence." The article encouraged the "true men of each county" to attend peace meetings to "point out the danger of following the teachings of a few bad men," suggesting that previous peace supporters were "now quite sick of such affairs," as such "meetings only encouraged toryism and deserters." It asserted that "such meetings caused the Government to order out the militia and home guard to preserve order and arrest deserters" and applauded that "people *en masse* … are turning out to catch deserters who are prowling about robbing and committing depredations on property." The article expressed determination to "rid their sections of the few disloyal persons … producing the trouble."[68]

David Schenck blamed W. W. Holden, the "infamous traitor," for "advocating reconstruction and submission, and secretly conniving at the basest treason—encourages desertion and continually disparages our cause." He noted that meetings "are being held in every disloyal part of the state denouncing the Tithing Bill and advocating resistance to the Conscript law…. [T]reason is blighting every prospect and destroying every hope." It will only be "a matter of time when our enemies will be upon us and we will feel the full extent of his hate and power" Schenck predicted and prepared his family for "flight or destruction." Schenck was also aware of the happenings in Raleigh—destruction of Holden's office and type and a reciprocal attack on the *State Journal* offices. "Such are the first acts which I have too much reason to fear will end in bloody drama," Schenck wrote. He applauded Lincoln County's General Robert F. Hoke, whose job was to "suppress the disloyal and dangerous elements" in the state.[69]

Newspapers and citizens commented on the peace movement. The *Carolina Watchman* opposed the prospects of peace without total Confederate victory, would accept peace only if it were pursued by the Union, and only with "*independence* of the south." Conjuring up the image of "slaves to Abe Lincoln," it suggested that North Carolina would become a "Benedict Arnold" and that peace advocates were "betrayers of our country's honor." It also condemned the "treasonable" publications of the *Standard*.[70] Locally, Colonel William Morris opined that Unionist Dr. William Sloan of Dallas influenced dissention: "I am Satisfied that Sloan is doing all he can to encourage those men Not to Return to the armey." Governor Vance sought to manage rampant desertion and lawlessness through issuing a proclamation allowing pardons for deserters' return to service and by soliciting General Hoke to march through the Piedmont to disrupt Unionist and deserter activities.[71]

The peace movement impacted Confederates nationally, and many North Carolina military units commented. A "Convention of North Carolina Troops" from Orange Courthouse in Virginia, representing a "large majority of the troops from North Carolina," repudiated the Movement by offering "unqualified condemnation" of the *Standard*. Their resolutions supported freedom of the press, suppression of the *Standard*, and support for Governor Vance. Another military petition from "Camp at Hamilton's Crossings, Va" supported the above resolutions, and a "Public Meeting in Rowan County" concurred.[72] Local soldier, Lemuel J. Hoyle, attended the "Convention of N. C. Troops" as an appointed delegate that opposed peace.[73]

"destroying type, fixtures, &c"

The resolutions adopted by the "North Carolina Troops" sent a message to "peace" opponents. In September a brigade of Georgia troops passed through Raleigh. As if following instructions from their North Carolina brethren, they attacked the office of *The Standard* "destroying type, fixtures, &c." Shortly afterward, Governor Vance appeared at the scene to denounce their actions.[74]

The next morning another mob attacked the "State Journal Office," a rival Raleigh newspaper, and demolished it as well. The *Carolina Watchman* reported that Governor Vance issued a proclamation which withdrew support for meetings dealing with taxes, conscription, or other oppositional Confederate issues.[75] The Raleigh *Progress* suggested that the soldiers' resolutions had contributed to the mob violence and recriminations in Raleigh. The newspaper posed that the military resolutions misrepresented "their friends at home," and that the "bitterness and recrimination should cease, and that we should have peace and harmony among ourselves that we may the[n] better contend with the common enemy."[76]

Some Gaston soldiers supported the peace movement. Newton Sellers predicted that "if the[y] would leave it to a vote for North Carolina to goe back to the union it would goe five to one they is lots wount Reinlit and I don blame them."[77]

In the midst of Confederate losses at Gettysburg and Vicksburg, the peace initiatives, increased desertion, and a war of words in the press, the state held legislative and congressional elections in August and September of 1863. William Lander of Lincoln County announced his reelection plans to the 8th Congressional district which included Gaston, Lincoln, Rowan, Cabarrus, Union, Mecklenburg, Catawba, and Cleveland Counties. If Lander thought that he would run unopposed as he had done in his previous election, he was mistaken. By October James G. Ramsey of Rowan County and J. F. Stansill both announced their candidacies. Ramsey chose to run only after Lincoln County Judge W. P. Bynum turned down the opportunity. By November the verdict was in. Ramsey defeated Lander.[78]

Dr. Ramsey's challenge of Lander exemplified the choice between Confederate and Conservative candidates. Lander, an original secessionist, had supported the conscription law, opposed conscription exemptions, and advertised his support to increase military pay. Charlotte's *Daily Bulletin* considered Lander's loss an election upset and reported that Gaston County supported Ramsey 290 to 258, and Lincoln County turned its back on its favorite son, 256 to 251. Edward Phifer of Lincoln County provided insight into soldier participation in the Lander-Ramsey election. He noted that the company "voted for Ramsey—40 to 3—large majority for Ramsey. I would rather had Lander elected." He noted that the men thought more of his father, "Pa," and "they wanted to run him every man would vote for him."[79] The upset exemplifies southern voter unrest with the war and its unintended consequences upon civilians. The newspaper blamed Holden for the upset, which precipitated a war of words. Holden responded to a *Daily Bulletin* article entitled "Scum of Society." "Go to Mexico," he wrote, "Mr. *Bulletin* where you can enjoy military despotism, forced loans, and mob rule to your heart's content." *The Bulletin* responded that it was proud to live in western North Carolina and Charlotte and would remain unless "invaded and overrun by Holden's Yankee friends." "We thank God we are proud although poor," *The Bulletin* continued and declared Holden, a "degraded wretch," and accused him of accumulating wealth "by hiring himself to party."[80] North Carolina was fighting a public civil war.

The statewide 1863 congressional elections produced a major victory for Conservative candidates. They won nine of ten congressional seats and continued to dominate the state legislature. The only Confederate legislative secessionist holdout was Robert R. Bridgers of Edgecombe County, who held a Gaston County connection as an investor at the High Shoals Iron Works.[81]

At this juncture Vance and Holden held similar views, excepting peace negotiations. Within the Conservative Party, they had allied Union Whigs and Union Democrats with state's rights North Carolinians, who became daily more dissatisfied with the war and its consequences. Historian Marc Kruman's research summarized that Conservatives "defined liberty as freedom from an arbitrary government," and they viewed the Richmond government as more likely to "rob the people of their liberties … [creating] a 'central military despotism.'"[82] The year 1864 would bring gubernatorial elections and many North Carolinians expected Vance to run for reelection.

"the most popular man in the state"

Vance supporters like Lincoln County's J. C. Whitson, requesting business favors, heaped praise upon the governor. He encouraged Vance to blast W. W. Holden, "that consummate scoundrel and traitor," and flattered Vance as, "the most popular man in the state … throughout the Confederacy."[83]

As the 1864 gubernatorial race approached, secessionist Schenck was disgusted by Holden and wrote that "a few old Unionists, who have lost all respect and political influence are anxious for any change, even to submission that they may regain strength and destroy Southern leaders." Schenck opined that the "best element of our population" was in the army. "[Unionist] rank and file of the faction are the lowest population of the country—contemptible either by their ignorance, or generally by their vicious character, such men as never dared speak in time of peace," and were led "by a few bad men who are desperate." Schenck was "grieved" that Gaston County was "so much disaffected" and being led by "one Wm. Sloane, a man of bad moral character, but whose profession as a physician gives him some standing." Schenck took note of the governor's race between Governor Vance and W. W. Holden, equating Vance with "all patriots of the state" and Holden, "a tory to the Confederacy." Schenck speculated that Vance supported "prosecuting the war vigorously to the last unless we could obtain independence on honorable terms," while Holden supported calling a convention to consider peace with the Union.[84]

As Schenck observed, Gaston County remained politically divided. On Saturday, January 30, 1864, peace advocates scheduled a "public meeting" in Dallas. The *Western Democrat* reported that "the good people of Gaston do not want civil war brought to their own doors by party agitation" and that about two-thirds of the crowd did not support the meeting. Two resolutions, which the paper supposed had been pre-arranged, were considered. The paper reported that both failed the vote but were considered approved by the chair. The second resolution favored a "Peace Convention." At this point the paper stated that "six or eight soldiers" who were present "interfered and said the meeting should not go on." The chair summarily adjourned the meeting and the "scheme did not succeed this time in Gaston." The article afforded that the leaders of the meeting "were not present" and accused an advocate of being "an openly.... Union man." The article author, "Z," contended that "Gaston county has done her share nobly in this war, and her true citizens have determined that she shall not be disgraced by a few disloyal, factious spirits."[85]

On February 22, 1864, Governor Vance publicly broke with Holden in a speech at Wilkesboro, a Unionist area, announcing his reelection plans. His campaign strategy was to challenge the Richmond government but to remain faithful to the cause, oppose a separate peace, and support the Confederate military. Vance sought to isolate Holden by opposing separate peace negotiations and a "Peace Convention." Since the secessionist, "States Rights Party," had no candidate, he reasoned that they would back him and cast Holden as an apologist.[86]

Governor Vance held a number of electoral advantages. He was a skilled stump speaker, often speaking off the cuff and engaging his audience. His mastery of public speaking, his humble mountain social and economic background, and his astute political acumen resulted in a superb campaign.

Prior to Vance's break with Holden, Gaston's James H. White encouraged Vance. After reading *The Standard* White had words for Holden. The newspaper, White contended, "seems to be anxious to get something to complain of[.] my Old Friend Holden of late seems to be putting every obstacle he can in the way of the Southern cause. I am sorry that he has so far forgot his former teaching & practice[.] there is not an un sound man in this county who reads or pays any regard to the public prints but takes or is taught from the Standard." White opposed what he called "the Idea of reconstruction of submitting to Yankee Rule" as supported by Holden. He encouraged the governor to make his position on the matter "more certain ... for the true southern men here are your friends although many of them ?? did not support you in the last election but the[y] are with you now." White believed that Vance opposed reconstruction and that Vance's response to Union-appointed Governor Stanley "satisfied me." He closed by "hoping for the Success of the Confederacy and yours together."[87] White's January advice may have influenced Vance's February Wilkesboro speech, as others were also advocating a political split.[88]

Vance received constant correspondence, requests for favors, and opinions. On February 29, 1864, K. J. Kenedy of Old Furnace, near Bessemer City, "a private citizen," communicated reservations concerning the Confederate Conscription law adding men from ages 17 through 50. Kenedy noted that "a large portion [of the countryside] is already grown up in broom sage" and that "starvation" would be the eventual result without farmers. He also opposed suspending the writ of habeas corpus. He contended that "no man is safe from the power of one individual[;] he could at pleasure seize any citizen with or without excuse throw him into prison and permit him to languish there without relief." He feared that "mere suspicion" would cause arrest and would be "the first step of a tyrant and the death blow to civil liberty." Kenedy expressed himself to be "a strong advocate of your election and administration" and closed his letter that "a large majority of the people of this county" shared his views.[89] Kenedy represented many North Carolinians, hoping for a Confederate victory but opposing its home front costs.

Former soldier W. O. Harrelson of the Cherryville area cautioned Governor Vance that retaining the militia at home may cost him the election, "[t]hey are looked upon as a nuisance in the community." Harrelson strongly supported Vance and believed that if Holden were elected that "we are a ruined people in North Carolina and it would prove a death blow to the Confederacy." He also advised Vance to visit the western part of the state, and, while he had no "acquaintance" with him, he hoped to see him on his visit.[90]

Loyal Confederates sought Vance campaign visits. During the May Term 1864 Lincoln County Grand Jury solicited his attendance because of "powerful efforts now being made by a magnificent foe to subjugate us, despoil us of our property and bring us under his *dark* and despotic rule, aided by mercenary hirelings from Europe and stolen negroes (his beloved troops of African descent,)." His visit would "discourage as far as possible that spirit of disloyalty which unhappily exists in our midst" to facilitate the "struggle for Southern Independence."[91]

Vance scheduled his extensive campaign appearances to include Dallas on Friday, June 10, Lincolnton, June 11, Shelby, June 13, after which he would continue westward.[92]

"Governor Vance is to address the citizens of Gaston and Dallas on next Friday"

James H. White signed a petition to encourage Governor Vance to visit Dallas as the election approached. The April 30 petition may have been written by White as he prominently signed it with 15 other Gaston County citizens.[93] On June 6 Jacob Froneberger noted in his diary that "Governor Vance is to address the citizens of Gaston and Dallas on next Friday."[94] While no eyewitness account of his address has been located, Froneberger, White, and others likely attended.

An eyewitness account of Vance's Lincolnton speech affirmed his speechmaking abilities. On June 12, 1864, Minnie Gray wrote Edward Phifer. She reported hearing "Gov. Vance speak day before yesterday. I was very much pleased with his speech. He is remarkably fond of telling little anecdotes to illustrate what he say."[95]

It is not known whether W. O. Harrelson attended Vance's Shelby appearance. The governor rode the train to Cherryville where J. L. Miller transported him in his carriage to Shelby for the speech. W. C. Lee, a soldier on furlough, stated that everyone "fell in love with [him]." Clearly Vance's oratory captivated and inspired North Carolinians during these tough times. Interestingly Lee, a survivor of Gettysburg, also requested permission to remain at home until his wheat crop was mature and harvested.[96]

Vance also campaigned among soldiers in the field. On July 31, 1864, J. C. Anthony from Wilmington wrote his uncle R. W. Carson describing the soldier's votes: "the soldiers voted last week Vance got 2120 vots and Holden 279 that is the vote of the soldiers in and around here." "I think," Anthony predicted, "Vance will be elected easily." Anthony stated that Vance "came down last night," speculating that he checked on the *Advance*, a state-owned boat. Anthony also sought to learn "how the people votes at our election ground if Holden gets many votes."[97]

Upon hearing Vance's speech to the army, Caleb Senter offered a different perspective. He told his wife that "govendor Vanc was round Speeking to the men ... he spoke hear yester[day] and the grater part of the men was displeasd with his speaCh he is for hanging on as long as thear is a man or a dollar he said the best thing we Cold Do wold be to drive the yankeys BaCk and go rite over into pencilvania." Senter opined, "that won't do" and if they go this summer, "more than one half of the men [will] stay with the yankeys They all say that that they are wiling to go but they Swear they wonte cum baCk if thear is eny choice." "i wante all the men thear to do all they can for Holden for Vanc wonte do," Senter continued, "he is a rite turn Cote i Donte think we will have eny peas soon if Vanc cold have his way he said in his speach that if the yankeys over run the South that they would hang all the men from the Cornel up drot his pitchure they need hanging for Creating Such a hard war i cante help but write a litle a Bout the trifling SCoundle." Vance made Senter mad "when he said in his Speach that if we dident whip the yankes this Spring, he wold cum out and whip us and if we did, he wold treat to a Botle of Whisky."[98] Senter was not convinced.

August 1864 brought frustrating military news for the South. Politically, Schenck commented that "[o]n the whole victory is with us." While the "Peace party" gained strength and boldness, "public opinion once more inclines to the opinion that this year will end the war." Schenck happily reported in his diary that Vance had beaten Holden; "the voice of the people is for 'war to independence and no compromise.'"[99]

Vance succeeded in isolating Holden; he won 77.2 percent of the civilian vote and out-polled Holden 13,176 to 1,824 with the soldiers.[100] The 1864 governor's election results expose some interesting data. The area breakdown follows:

	Vance	Holden	% for Vance
Gaston	612	269	69%
Lincoln	566	104	84%
Cleveland	1127	137	89%
Catawba	897	42	96%
Mecklenburg	1708	113	94%
Rutherford	799	379	68%

To further illustrate the election dynamics, a comparison of Vance's vote percentages from 1862 and 1864 suggests that with the exception of Rutherford and Gaston his increases were significant.

County	Vance's % of votes in 1862	Vance's % of votes in 1864	Increase or Decrease
Gaston	47	69	↑
Meck'berg	24	94	↑
Lincoln	62	84	↑
Cleveland	48	89	↑
Catawba	52	96	↑
Rutherford	82	68	↑

Rutherford County, which possessed a significant mountain Unionist population, gave fewer total votes to Vance than Gaston County. While Vance's totals increased in Gaston, the increase was significantly lower than in surrounding counties. The departure of secessionist fervor, the length of the conflict, and a growing peace and Unionist contingent added to Holden's appeal in Gaston.[101]

Gaston citizens elected secessionist and former militia captain, W. T. Shipp, to the House of Commons with 410 votes to Mason's 203. In Lincoln County Ambrose Costner won re-election, and M. L. McCorkle was elected senator without opposition.[102] The split vote in Gaston suggests that the unanimity of 1861 had eroded.

In November, Gaston Court Clerk W. D. Glenn commented in his diary about the radical proposal of President Jefferson Davis to allow slaves to fight in the Confederate army in exchange for their freedom. While in Raleigh visiting Senator Shipp, Glenn observed speeches by John Pool, R. B. Dick, and J. B. Odom, a "very good looking body of elderly men." Glenn felt that the North Carolina legislators took "extreme State's rights views of the question," as they conveyed a "vein of opposition to all measures proposed by" President Davis. Unfortunately Glenn did not specifically write about their comments on this most interesting and divisive issue.[103] But war came to Gaston.

As Sherman entered North Carolina and Jefferson Davis and his cabinet fled into the state, Gaston County responded to the Governor Vance's March 1865 proclamation to provide supplies to the army. At a March 18, 1865, meeting in Gaston County, John H. Roberts served as chairman and W. D. Glenn as secretary. They recognized their "plain duty as patriots and good citizens" to "contribute to the utmost of our ability" to the Confederate government and General Lee. They appointed leading citizens to collect "subscriptions of supplies from our citizens on the west side of the South Fork" and to deliver them to the nearest government commissary.[104] Loyal Gaston supporters remained loyal to the end.

Understanding politics in North Carolina during this period is challenging. In 1860–61 secessionist politicians had persuaded Gaston County citizens that the war defended their way of life, slavery, and confronted northern abolitionist challenges. But the war did not end quickly or easily, as the secessionists had proposed. The 1863 elections provided Conservatives control of the legislature and Congressional delegation. Yet, their titular leader, Holden, lost the gubernatorial race the next year. After his reelection Vance expressed his perception of politics and his reading of the people. He stated his disgust with the lack of southern guerrilla warfare and resistance as Sherman marched through Georgia and Grant through Virginia: "I have always believed that the great popular heart is not now & never has been in this war! It was a revolution of the politicians not the people; was found at first by natural enthusiasm of your young men; and has been kept going by state & sectional pride assisted by that bitterness of feeling produced by the cruelties & brutalities of the enemy."[105] Vance, once a Unionist, then a soldier, and then a successful governor, had used those same political strategies as he defeated Holden. His insightful expressions of frustration paralleled rising sentiments against the political status quo.

Vance's suggestion that politicians had managed to control the state's voters was tested as the war ended. While erosion of Gaston's voters' support for the status quo is evident in previous election results, in 1865 after the war concluded, Gaston citizens elected David A. Jenkins, the future North Carolina Republican Treasurer, to the state House of Commons. He ran against war hero Colonel William G. Morris. In the same election John F. Hoke won the House seat for Lincoln County in a very close three-way candidate vote: 289 to 247 to 61. The State senatorial race posed W. P. Bynum, wartime solicitor from Lincoln County, against Ambrose Costner, a veteran legislator who had been born in Gaston County. Gaston gave Bynum 418 votes to 201 for Costner. Bynum won the election 850 to 682.[106] The defeat of brothers-in-law, Morris and Costner, indicates a tilt in both counties to Conservative candidates, Bynum, Hoke, and Jenkins.

The race for Congress pitted two Conservatives, Dr. Ramsey of Rowan County and Dr. Sloan of Gaston County. The *Daily Carolina Times* referenced Sloan as "a consistent Union man, both before and during the war—never sympathized with what he was please to call the rebellion—said he could conscientiously take the oath [to the United States]."[107]

The governor's race also exemplifies Gaston's political shift away from traditional Confederate candidates. W. W. Holden, who President Andrew Johnson had appointed provisional governor to relieve Vance, ran against Jonathan Worth, who had served as state treasurer during the war. Both were Conservatives but Worth represented the state Confederate establishment. Election results are very interesting:

	Holden	Worth	% for Holden
Gaston	416	163	72%
Lincoln	295	309	49%
Cleveland	302	368	45%
Catawba	316	715	31%[108]

Gaston County overwhelmingly supported Holden.

The Gaston County election results from 1860 through 1865 delineate a 180 degree journey for the electorate, demonstrating a gradual shift in opinion and political alignment. In 1860 and 1861 the county overwhelmingly supported secession. By charting Gaston's vote totals from 1860 through 1865, election results favoring secession and the Confederate government declined: 82 percent and 84 percent in 1860 and 1861; 53 percent in 1862; 51 percent in 1863; 69 percent in 1864; and only 28 percent in 1865. By 1865 Gaston County turned its back on Confederate veteran William G. Morris, and his brother in law, Ambrose Costner, war-time office holder, and reversed itself by supporting W. W. Holden for governor. While other factors impacted these election results, the trend away from radical Confederate rhetoric and toward more conservative positions is apparent. The political winds of change emanated from the people. While much of the South in 1865 elected Confederate generals, soldiers, and unrepentant secessionists, Gaston voters supported Holden, Jenkins, and Bynum, three moderate, conservative leaders, two without combat experience. Neighboring counties exposed less dramatic voting shifts. The county's reversal came before the rest of the South was forced to face Reconstruction and the African American vote. The election results also expose an unexplained decline in voting from 1,023 votes in 1861, to 980 in 1864, to 579 in 1865.

The 1865 election results appear more consistent with the demographics of the county. The county's voting results seem to confirm Governor Vance's observations that politicians supported the war to the exclusion of the citizenry. The political struggles within the county, mostly ignored by previous historians, are another unexpected consequence of the project. The consistency of Schenck and Sloan, to preserve slavery and the southern way of life from completely different political objectives, leads us to examine the institution of slavery.

The next chapter will examine slaves, Free Blacks, and how they lived. Local sources document that slavery remained the major factor in secession, political and economic success. How slaves perceived the conflict, lived through it, and impacted their county is examined in detail.

9

THE AFRICAN AMERICAN DURING THE WAR

Many southern historians have treated slavery and African Americans as the proverbial elephant in the room, influencing events and people's lives but with sparse documentation, insight, and often their existence and impact have been ignored. It is very common to read a local, regional or even state history with scant mention of slavery. This chapter describes African Americans—slave and free—how they interacted, lived, viewed their circumstances, and impacted Gaston County and its residents. The project's unique assimilation of white observations, newspaper accounts, slave recollections, census

According to family tradition, Randal Costner, slave of William G. and Louisa Morris, made this small hatchet for Lee Morris, their son. Lee was born in 1862 and his parents discussed what to name him in their letters (courtesy Melany Dawn Crouse Photography).

records, and the 1863 tax list offers new insights into slavery and its central role in southern society.

By 1863 all European countries had abolished both slavery and the trade in human cargo. In the western hemisphere the only countries allowing slavery were Cuba, Brazil, the United States, and the Confederacy. From colonial days, slavery had been an essential social, economic, and political institution in the southern states, including North Carolina.

Beginning with a statistical analysis of slavery in Gaston County and followed by sources personalizing blacks and their experiences, a contemporary, multifaceted portrait of the African American has emerged: Randal Costner and Tom Stow were trusted slaves and allowed more discretion, mobility and responsibilities; former slave Wesley Mauney conveyed a child's pain over being taken from his mother; and Gabriel Revels concealed his race and passed for white. Their stories represent others.

Slavery in Gaston County

Summarizing the African American experience in Gaston with raw data does not minimize the inhumanity of the slave system, as the data confirm the extent of the slave culture.

The 1850 Gaston County census reports that Gaston had 8,073 residents, of which 2,112 were slaves or 26 percent of the total population, and twenty-six persons were listed as Free Blacks. There were 333 slave owners, which was about 4 percent of the population but 31 percent of the households. Extant 1850 county tax lists indicate that 859 slaves were taxed as black polls, male slaves between the ages of 21 and 45. The Gaston slave population in 1850 was 60 percent female, children, or males under 21 or over 45. The 1850 tax lists also indicate the 859 black polls outnumbered the county's 645 white polls. Seven tax districts held a majority of black polls.[1]

By 1860 the county population increased about 1,200 persons with 9,307 whites and 2,192 slaves, who comprised about 19 percent of the total population, a slight percentage decline from 1850. The census includes 364 slave owners, an increase of 31, with only one person owning more than forty slaves.[2] Consistent with the previous census, slave owners made up only about 3.2 percent of the total population and 28.6 percent of the householders, a decline of about 3 percent. While the number of slaves and slaveholders increased during this ten year period, whites were increasing at a higher percentage. Gaston County ranked 58 out of 87 North Carolina counties in 1860 slave population. While exceeding all bordering counties except Mecklenburg for numbers of slaves, Gaston certainly could not be described as a major slaveholding area, since it averaged only seven slaves per slaveholder.[3]

A comparison of the 1860 census and 1863 tax list indicates that there was a dramatic increase of 30 slaveholders in just three years from 364 to 394.[4] During the same three years, slave totals grew by 554 slaves. This dramatic growth was partially due to the influx of the Edgecombe County investors at both High Shoals and the Crowders Mountain iron manufacturing operations, accounting for 323 slaves, or 58 percent of the total increase. The Edgecombe investor's influx of bondservants does not account for the total increase, as 42 percent increased from other sources.

Further analysis reveals that as slave ownership increased in Gaston County during the Civil War, it also became more concentrated. The number of persons owning only one slave remained stagnant between those three years—89 to 91. In 1860, 59 percent of the slaveholders owned less than five slaves, while in 1863, 56 percent owned less than five. Conversely, the number of persons owning more than 20 slaves more than doubled from 11 in 1860 to 27 in 1863, of which only five included the Edgecombe investors. The number owning more than 40 went from 1 in 1860 to 6 in 1863. The data suggests that Civil War factors precipitated not only an increase in slaves and slave owners in Gaston County but concentrated slave ownership into fewer hands.

One way to measure the economic impact of slavery is to compare the assessed value of slaves in the 1863 tax list to the assessed value of the slave owner's land. The following chart demonstrates that slave economic values exceeded land values in every militia company. The data differentiates the number of slaveholders with more assessed value in slaves, more value in land, and the total.

Assessed Tax Values from the 1863 Tax List[5]

	Slave owners with more Slave Value		Slave owners with more Land Value		Total
Cherryville	13		5		18
Crowders Mtn	32		8		40
Dallas	26		11		37
Duharts	18		4		22
High Shoals	26		5		31
River Bend	35		4		39
Roberts	28		10		38
Rudisill	13		7		20
South Point	48		16		64
Tanyard	35		7		42
Woodlawn	36		7		43
Total	310	79%	84	21%	394

Fully 79 percent of Gaston County slave owners held more economic value in their slaves than in their land, documenting that slave ownership provided the best means for southern economic prosperity.

Concurrently, an analysis of the county as a whole further validates that assessed slave valuation was higher than real estate. The total Gaston County land value in 1863, which included slave and non-slaveholders land, was $1,626,087, and the total slave value was $1,910,846. Slave assessments exceeded total land assessments by $284,759 or about 15 percent. Slavery provided southerners with huge capital assets, economic prowess, and social mobility.

Slave owners, whose assessed real estate value exceeded their slave assessed value, fall into two categories. The 63 slave owners with only one or two slaves constituted the largest category. The remainder included highly valued manufacturing operations like J. & E. B. Stowe of Stowesville Cotton Factory, L & Co Linebarger of Woodlawn cotton mill, and T. R. Tate who owned Mountain Island Cotton and Woolen Factory.

The data clearly demonstrate that slave ownership was singularly and collectively more economically valuable than land. Slave owners in Gaston County and across the South understood this fact. It is not surprising then that the county officials and most prominent business leaders owned slaves.

An examination of Gaston County's political leaders, as demonstrated in Chapter 8, indicates that they were overwhelmingly slaveholders. Only a few court officials did not own slaves, and most hailed from areas in the county where few slaveholders lived.[6]

Slaves provided economic value to their owners and facilitated political success. Their labor contributed to the creation of Dallas, as the slave labor force of Abraham Mauney and others made and laid the brick for the jail, courthouse, Hoffman Hotel, and Rhyne Store. The quality of their workmanship is obvious as all four survive (2015). Slaves most likely also performed other town building duties like cutting trees, constructing other buildings, building roads, loading and transporting goods. They composed a significant portion of the town's population and skilled labor force.[7]

Slave labor also contributed significantly to the success of the county's iron and gold manufacturing operations. They performed various tasks such as mining, cutting trees, making charcoal, loading and transporting materials. They also held critical skilled positions such as molder, hammerman, furnace operator, often utilizing African iron processing skills. For iron and gold operations, slave labor was critical for economic success: High Shoals had 244; the Garrett Brothers had 93 and Kings Mountain Gold Mining had 22 slaves.[8]

All three county cotton mills utilized significant slave labor—Tate's Mountain Island woolen and cotton operation with 63 slaves; Stowesville had about 20 slaves; and Lineberger's Woodlawn Mill about 35 slaves. Slaves picked and hauled the cotton and performed various tasks around the mill. Some researchers have speculated that they even operated mill machinery.[9]

The wealthy, middle class, and local governmental employees benefited from slave ownership. But slave ownership varied in Gaston County based upon geography.

Geographic Distribution of Slaves

The 1863 tax list indicates that slave ownership and therefore economic wealth was not evenly distributed throughout the county.[10]

Two militia companies located in the northwest, Cherryville and Rudisill, evidenced few slaves with only 39 slave owners in both companies. When compared to other companies, both rank last in the number of slaves, slave owners, amount of acreage, real estate value, state and local taxes paid, and slave valuation.

In contrast eastern Gaston County along the Catawba River exhibited the greatest concentration of slaves and slave owners. South Point, Woodlawn, and River Bend Companies ranked in the top four companies for the number of slaves, slave owners, and slave assessed value. South Point and River Bend ranked first and second in total state taxes paid.

High Shoals Company, along the north-central border with Lincoln County, held significant contrasts. Six taxables owned more than 20 slaves, while 68 percent of the taxpayers owned no slaves, thus creating a wide disparity of wealth. The concentration of wealth around High Shoals Iron Manufacturing and a few farmers with inherited wealth validated that it had the highest numbers in: slaves, slave value per owner and assessed tax slave value. The diverse population of the town of Dallas and its neighboring rural areas ranks it first in the average slave value per slave owner. Slave ownership increased as one traveled from west to east.

The tax list also illustrates that slave populations were concentrated among families.

For example, the Friday family was a prominent farming family in both the Dallas and High Shoals districts. In Dallas all three Friday taxpayers owned land and slaves; in High Shoals six family members owned land or slaves or both, meaning that the nine family members averaged owning almost 8 slaves with the highest numbers being 23 and 21. In River Bend Company nine persons named Abernathy were taxed with five owning land and slaves, two owning only land, and two women owning only slaves, averaging 5.9 slaves per owner.

In South Point district five out of six members of the Armstrong family owned slaves. All five members of the Beattie family owned slaves from 13 to 1; four out of five members of the Hand family also owned bondsmen, ranging from 18 to 1. Two of four members of the Leeper family owned slaves from 13 to 2; three of the four Neagles also owned slaves; and all four Ratchfords owned them, ranging from 15 to 1.

In Woodlawn Company seven of the nine Rankins owned slaves, ranging from 28 to 1. Members of the prodigious Rhyne family are found throughout the county. Three of the four Woodlawn Rhynes owned slaves, 16, 12, and 7. Ten members of the Rhyne family resided in Dallas Company, of which four owned slaves. Of the 21 Rhyne taxpayers listed, ten owned slaves.

Conversely some families owned few slaves. The Carpenter, Kiser, Hanna, and Robinson families serve as examples. Of the 22 Carpenters residing in the Cherryville and Rudisill Companies, only three owned slaves. Five Kisers resided in Rudisill and thirteen in Roberts. Two in Roberts Company owned one slave each. Of the 40 taxpayers of both families, only 13 percent owned slaves. The three Hanna family members in Duhart also owned no slaves. Of the seven Robinsons in Tan Yard district, two owned slaves, only one each. Yet, in Rudisill's Company in northwest Gaston all five members of the Rudisill family owned bondsmen, and one out of two in Cherryville owned them. While geography played a role in the propensity for slave ownership, the data clearly demonstrates that slaveholding was concentrated among families.

While family transfers, geography, and occupational issues affected slave ownership, other factors were also present. At least two anecdotal traditions in the Carpenter family illustrate. Frederick Carpenter of Rudisills Company, refused to own slaves even though his father and grandfather were slave owners. Carpenter owned 396 acres—worth $3,200 and was fortunate that his eight sons, four of whom served in the Confederate army, could work most effectively on it. He became one of the county's few non-slaveholding justices of the peace.[11]

Carpenter's cousin found the southern slave life style disturbing. Around 1856 Daniel Carpenter left his North Carolina home and moved to Arkansas and later to Missouri, where his sons joined the Union army. The family's opposition to slavery and the slave culture contributed to their move. Daniel's brother, Andrew, lived in River Bend Company in 1863 with 16 slaves and 7,124 acres of land; Daniel's father and other relatives also owned slaves. Family tradition indicates that Christian and anti-slavery values motivated Daniel and that he "voted for Abe Lincoln before he left Arkansas ... only two votes cast at the Box for the Republican Party ... [with Carpenter being] one of them."[12] Other Gaston County citizens found slavery disturbing.

John Huffstetler of northwest Gaston considered himself an "abolitionist."[13] Larkin Thornburg, living north of Dallas, wrote that "the institution of slavery was an actual hinderance to the poor man's rising in social standing and advancing in wealth." He repeated stories of "injustice and cruelty, ... whipped until the blood flowed, ... children ... sold from their mother's arms ... husbands and wives had been seperated forever, and families completely broken up." Thornburg commented on the rationale for these actions: "to satisfy the cruel master's desire for gain or perhaps to pay his debts made by fast living and heedless dissipation."[14]

There is no evidence that Gaston County yeomen and farm laborers supported racial equality, as racism permeated American and Gaston County perceptions of African Americans.[15] For Gaston County citizens seeking economic prosperity and political power, slavery was the common denominator. Sources also expose how slaves lived.

"Tell randle that I am under obligations to him"

Contemporary sources describing slave life during the Civil War include white observations, an analysis of the tax list and censuses, and voices of the former slaves. Civil War soldiers—William G. Morris, Lemuel Hoyle, Leonidas Torrence, David Eddleman, and the Phifer brothers of Lincolnton owned slaves. Much may be learned and surmised from their letters.[16]

William G. Morris received Randall from his father-in-law. Through letters to his wife, Morris authorized Randall to make farming decisions. A postscript on almost all of his letters included, "Give Randle, Sarah & Harriet Howdy for Me"; Sarah and Harriet were also slaves of his father-in-law. Morris communicated directly to Randall in his letters: "Tell randle that I am under obligations to him"; "you can Give him & Sarah Tenn Dollars Each to by there Tobacco or any thing they May Kneed"; "Tell randle I will Depend on his Judgement to pitch & Make me the Next crop." For Morris, Randle's services were indispensible, "Randle you May think that you have a hard time of it but if you were Ever to bee Sold I will Buy you if it is your request." He also instructed his wife to depend upon Randle's judgment about hiring other workers. Morris expressed more than ownership, "Give My Love to Randle & Harriet & Sarah; tell them to Doo the best they can till I come home." Randle also received the opportunity to travel alone, visiting Morris's brother-in-law, Ambrose Costner in upper Lincoln County and with Morris to rejoin his Confederate company.[17] The specificity, with which Morris addresses Randall and the confidence he imbibes, exemplifies a personal relationship and exposes the critical role slaves played in these tough economic times.

Yet, in December 1864 even "Randle" seemed to cause problems. Ambrose Costner made a curious statement to his sister, Mrs. Morris: "What has gotten into Randle. Cheer up and look on the bright Side as much as you can."[18] It is very possible that the collapse of the Confederacy, communication of slave emancipation, and the proximity of the Union army caused the loyal Randle to seek his freedom or to act more rebelliously.

The Morris relationship with Randle contrasted with others. Lemuel Hoyle, whose family also owned slaves, wrote many letters. Some of his letters have the postscript, "Tell the darkies 'howdy' for me." Hoyle's references to the slaves were sporadic, and he almost never referred to the slaves by name. On only three occasions out of about 85 letters does one find: "Tell Dave and Jane, 'Howdy,' for me."[19] The detachment contrasts with the closeness of the Morris communications. Leonidas Torrence's father also owned slaves. Yet, Leonidas never addressed them in his letters home, while often mentioning relatives and neighbors. The letters of W. L. and Edward Phifer were the only war letters examined of members of the gentry. Of the 106 letters examined, there are no instances of dialogue with or concerning the 63 Phifer family slaves, while the Phifer brothers often discussed relatives, friends, and other soldiers.[20]

The relationship between the Morris family and Randall, Sarah, and Harriet continued after the war. In the 1870 Gaston County census "Randolph Costner," listed as age 50 with Sarah age 50 and four persons age 22 through 16, appears three houses away from Colonel Morris. "Harriet Friday," apparent wife of Charlie Friday with Ruben, John and Sarah E., conforms to the slaves listed in the tax list of deceased Jacob Costner, Morris' father-in-law.[21] Efforts to locate Dave and Jane near the home of Lemuel Hoyle were not successful. William W. Torrence, Leonidas's father, owned Margaret age 17 in the tax list. In the 1870 census she appears next door to W. W. Torrence as "Margaret Torance" age 30, black, with apparent children aged 1 to 6.[22] Slavery was an economic system but could impact white-black personal relationships.

The evidence indicates that aspiring middle-class southerners, even with small numbers of slaves, remained attached to the slave system. In October 1858 aspiring young lawyer David Schenck purchased "a negro girl & child last week 'Harriet' formerly belonging to Jas. T. Alexander," and he proudly proclaimed in his diary, "so I am a slave owner." Schenck, ever aware of social distinctions, recognized that as a slave owner, he had increased his stature. During the war he proudly added "Charles, my negro boy" and later Nancy.[23] Schenck, Morris, Hoyle, Torrence, Eddleman, and other contemporaries understood the opportunities slave ownership provided. Morris also expressed interest in buying a slave during the war. He notified his brother "that he might buy a young Negro for Me" of about 12–14 years old for $1,000 or $1,200. David Eddleman, whose one letter was examined, owned four slaves in 1860 and added two more by the 1863 tax list. His slave valuation exceeded his land by $1,616. Schenck, Morris, and Eddleman expected to win the war and for slavery to continue.[24]

Early in the war Lincoln County businessman, B. F. Withers, "purchased the negro man Hiram (whose wife I own) for $1,000 & an negro boy eighteen years old for whom I paid nine hundred dollars—the boy I think decidedly the best purchase as he is an excellent boy and ten years the youngest."[25] For mid-range white slave owners, slavery made economic sense.

"Negroes are Hireing here for one thousand dollars a year and as High as Eleven Hundred"

Contemporary newspapers document the value and necessity of slave labor through 1865. On August 12, 1861, J. D. Holland offered a $300 reward for the capture of the slave, Tom, who was charged with Grand Larceny and was property of Leroy Stowe. L. E. Thompson, Lincolnton attorney, offered "A Hatter For Sale," a thirty-five-year-old "BOY." On August 29, 1863, "J A Cob," a twenty-year-old male slave, escaped from A. R. Homesley's woolen mill in Cleveland County and appeared headed to Virginia.[26] On March 4, 1864, Samuel R. Oates of Lincolnton sought to hire "50 able bodied NEGRO MEN." In the same newspaper was a "Notice" for a runaway slave girl named Sarah, who was about thirty years old, about 5'2", stuttered, and had several front teeth broken. L. M. Summit of Dallas offered a $500 reward for her return. Another notice in 1865 offered thirty slaves for sale. As late as March 1865, A. R. Henderson who lived near the Catawba River offered a $100 reward for the return of a "Young boy." While David Schenck observed in 1865 in his diary that slave values "are rapidly declining in price," other accounts validate their increasing value and attempts to recover runaways.[27]

Hiring of slaves was profitable and convenient to both slave owner and persons hiring. The tax list and other documents confirm examples of slave hiring in Gaston County, some of which involve manufacturing. "High Shoals Iron Co." owned two slaves, and hired four "For Cook of VA," four "for Dr Wallace of NC," three more "for Garlond NC," and one for "Widow Styren NC." The Stowesville Cotton Mill also utilized hired slaves. In addition to the twelve slaves they owned, "J & E B Stowe for Dr. Taylor" included three more, "for Dr. Hines" three, and "for Dr. Arendell" two.

William L. Kennedy hired out his slaves to the High Shoals Company, and B. B. Barron spent much time managing the Kennedy slaves, which included locating them in jail, discovering one's death while working on fortifications in Wilmington, and providing travel passes, food, shelter, and the necessities. By 1864 runaways were a major concern, and doubts of their recovery were voiced; yet more slaves were needed with specialized skills, like a blacksmith.[28]

On January 9, 1865, Harriet Spake of Gaston County wrote her soldier husband about conditions at home which confirmed that slavery remained a viable economic option. Since most slaves were hired at the beginning of each year, the hiring process had begun. Spake reported that "Negroes are Hireing here for one thousand dollars a year and as High as Eleven Hundred" Confederate money, which she characterized as "worthless ... not worth the ink and paper to rite it on."[29]

As 1865 dawned, eastern Gaston County "Agent" S. X. Johnston advertised "The Negroes of Misses Mary and Martha Johnston, who are not hired privately, will be put up at Castania Grove ... to the highest bidder, on January 2d. 1865 for the ensuing year."[30] Slave hiring perpetuated the slave culture by allowing yeomen slave labor, one year at a time. The opinions of Spake, Summitt, Henderson, Johnston, and local newspapers were consistent as Gaston County slave owners expected to retain their slave property despite Confederate defeats, armies on the run, Confederate and North Carolina governments in flight, and the loss of law and order in the South.

As disturbing as it appears, white southerners established monetary values to their human chattel property. Gaston County tax assessors adhered to the 1863 law determining slave values in an arbitrary fashion with little consistency. For example, they assigned the highest values to males aged 18–30 of $900 to $1,700. Younger males of 10–17 were assessed at $650-$1,400. The assessed value of older male slaves varied significantly from $0 to $1,300 with diminished values for aged slaves, unless the list delineated a trade such as "shoemaker," "BSmith," or "Carpenter."

Tax assessors generally listed females with less overall value. Those aged 13–25 were valued $800-$1,400 with higher values from adolescence into the early 20s. Younger and older females varied greatly in price with infants and elderly having the least value. Most females lost assessed value as they approached age 40, being past child-bearing years.

All slave values were affected by infirmities. Descriptions such as "Rapted," "not s[oun]d," "Deficent," "Diseased," "1 arm," "Sickly," "D & Dumb," "idiot," "B. Leg," "sore leg," "hand off," "not hearty," "lame arm," "Burnt hand," "Deform," "lunat," "Pains," "lame," "cripple," "simple," "Fits" accompanied a lower assessment.

As abhorrent as this examination has been, it historically defines white perceptions of slave property. The project also documents Confederate inflation from the 1863 value of $900-$1,700 for a prime male to $5,000 by 1864. By 1865 the advertised price for slave hires of $1,000-$1,100 equaled their purchase value two years earlier. The data also documents that southerners held slave property in high regard as the war ended with purchases, hiring, and investments. Individual slaves displayed their own opinions about the "peculiar institution."

"Ole Missus ... never allowed the Massa to buy or sell any slaves"

The graves of Wesley Mauney and wife Naomi are at Ebenezer Baptist Church Cemetery on Highway 216 in Cleveland County. Mauney, born into slavery in northwestern Gaston County, was separated from his parents and returned to them after emancipation. His life demonstrates the perseverance of Gaston County slaves (courtesy Melany Dawn Crouse Photography).

Autobiographical interviews and a memoir personalize the African American experience. Two sources are interviews conducted through the Works Progress Administration (WPA) during the Great Depression. Since no interviews for persons residing in Gaston or surrounding area have been found, two interviews of nearby locations were examined: W. L. Bost of Catawba County and Sarah Gudger of McDowell County. Wesley Mauney, a Gaston County resident, dictated the "PenPicture," a memoir of his life. These three people provide an insightful portrait of their personal recollections and experiences.[31]

W. L. Bost provided a vivid picture of slave life of nearby Catawba County from his interview residence of Asheville. Bost related that his master, Jonas Bost, owned a hotel in Newton and two plantations. He employed "the women folk" to work in the hotel. Both W. L. Bost's mother and grandmother were owned by Jonas Bost, and "Ole Missus ... never allowed the Massa to buy or sell any slaves." Bost contended that "We niggers lived better than the niggers on the other plantations." His masters provided them with "plenty to eat ... no fancy rashions. Jes corn bread, milk, fat meat, and 'lasses but the Lord knows that was lots more than other pore niggers got. Some of them had such bad masters."[32]

Sarah Gudger recalled her first master with fondness and "Missus" as elderly. She characterized their son, William Hemphill, as free with the "lashins," requiring "wok all de time f'om mawnin' till late at night," and working in "any kine ob weathah." Gudger stated that she never slept in a bed until after emancipation, instead sleeping on "an ole pile o' rags in de conah," and suffered from lack of food, "All cold 'n' hungry."[33]

Bost recalled slave traders and slave auctions. When the "speculators" came, the slaves to be sold "always stay at our place. The poor critters nearly froze to death. They always come 'long on the last of December so that the niggers would be ready for sale on the first day of January." Bost continued, "Many the time I see four or five of them chained together. They never had enough clothes on to keep a cat warm." Women wore "a thin dress and a petticoat and one underwear." He recalled seeing "ice balls hangin' on to the bottom of their dresses," and they never wore shoes. The "speculators" rode horses and the slaves walked; they looked "like droves of turkesy runnin' along in front of them horses." During the night he would hear them "mornin' and prayin.' I didn't know the Lord would let people live who were so cruel." Bost also recalled the slave sales: "they put 'em on the block to seel 'em. The ones 'tween 18 and 30 always bring the most money." The auctioneer would "cry 'em." He referred to a young man as "a big black buck Negro. He's stout as a mule. Good for any kin' o'work an' he never gives any trouble." He auctioned the female slave differently: "Here's a young nigger wench, how much am I offered for her? The pore thing stand on the block a shiverin' an' a shakin' nearly froze to death." Bost reflected upon selling wives away from husbands: "the pore mothers beg the speculators to sell'em with their husbands, but the speculator would only take what he want. So maybe the pore thing never see her husban' agin."[34]

Gudger confirmed Bost's recollections of the slave sellers. She described how they would watch slaves in the fields prior to purchasing them. If the "Speculator" purchased, and a slave was reluctant to go, they were placed in "han'cuffs," "he thrash 'em," and "tie'em hind de waggin an mek 'em run till dey fall." She described how "de ole nigga mammy" would cry losing a son, husband, relative or friend.[35]

Wesley Mauney, a slave of Abraham Mauney, resided in Rudisill's Company in northwestern Gaston County. "Abe Sen Mauney" was listed in the 1863 tax list with 384 acres valued at $2,700 and with only one slave valued at $877, whose name was not listed. Mauney, aged 72 in the 1860 census, had experienced exceptional economic success, owning as many as 20 slaves in 1850, and won the bid to construct the courthouse, jail, and Hoffman Hotel in the Dallas.[36]

Entitled "A PenPicture of Wesley Mauney—an Ex-Slave," Mauney repeated his life story to "J. W. Roberts D. D." of Shelby, North Carolina, who transcribed it. Mauney stated that he was "borne a slave of Col. Abe Mauney in the year 1849 in Gaston County N. C." When he was a little child, six years old, he was given "to the daughter of Abraham Mauney who had married a Little, and carried to Limestone Springs near what is now Gaffney, S. C." He remained with the Little family until emancipation in 1865, then "came back to his parents, Samuel and Priscilla Mauney, and helped to cear [care] for them until they died."[37]

"I were a slave and the best they would do was not good"

Wesley Mauney recalled that he "stayed ten years or until [he] were set free." As a young child Mauney reported little about slavery in specific descriptive terms but opined thusly: "Its not worth while of me trying to tell you about those days, because I were a slave and the best they would do was not good." His feelings of separation from his mother and family held strong emotions as an eighty-four-year-old man: "Think if you please of a child taken and kept from mother, no matter how good, and you can guess at the good."[38] Mauney was not alone in being separated from loved ones.

Owning slaves was a financial arrangement for whites but emotionally traumatic for blacks. Buying and selling sometimes separated families. For example, on July 17, 1860, Ann Gamble "for the consideration of Too hundred dollars" sold "a negro boy named George about 6 or 7 years old … unto my son Andrew Jackson Gamble."[39] The decision obviously deprived young George from living with his mother, disrupting the home environment. As previously observed, David Schenck purchased a young boy from Richmond away from his family.

John Gamble sought to purchase a "negro girl & child of Col H Fulenwider." John Webster noted that Gamble should "meet the Col at the furnace on Monday night" to facilitate the purchase.[40] It is unclear whether this slave "girl" had other children, a husband, or other family.

Wesley Mauney resided over 50 miles away from his parents in the Northern Division of Spartanburg County in 1860 at Limestone Springs post office. He was most likely the black male listed as age 8 in the census, one of eight slaves. Thomas Little was enumerated as a "Mechanick" and born in Scotland, and the family included six apparent children born in South and North Carolina and a white Farm Laborer, Sidney A. Shuford, also born in North Carolina.[41] Mauney did not relate seeing his parents after his departure to South Carolina until emancipation.

Sarah Gudger also related a sad story of separation "when may ole mammy die." A white man one day told her "'did yo' know yo' mammy daid?'" Sarah wanted to "see may mothah afoah dey puts huh away." She asked "t' Ole Missie" to go see her mother. Her response, "'Git on outen heah, an' git back t' yo wok afoah I wallup yo good.'" While Sarah never got to see her mother, she related that soon afterward "Ole Missie" got very sick and also died.[42]

W. L. Bost offered that slaves were "never 'lowed to learn anything" and only heard reading from the Bible. Bost recalled "one nigger boy in Newton who was terrible smart. He learn to read an' write. He take other colored children out in the fields and teach 'em about the bibl, but they forgit it 'fore the nex' Sunday.'"[43] Sarah Gudger stated that there were "ve'y few skules" but that her first "Missus" read from the Bible to the slaves.[44]

There is evidence that at least two blacks unlawfully attended school. An early Lincoln school record from northwestern Gaston County included "Abraham Mauney colers 2."[45] Wesley Mauney, apparently illiterate, expressed strong support for education and may have known the slaves who attended the school, but this arrangement was clearly exceptional.

Bost recalled that "Us niggers never have chance to go to Sunday School and church. The white folks feared for niggers to get any religion and education, but I reckon somethin' inside jes told us about God and that there was a better place hereafter." He recalled that they "would sneak off and have prayer meetin." If the "pattyrollers" caught them, they would "beat us good but that tidn't keep us from tryin." He recalled the words of a song his mother sang "an' pray to the Lord to deliver us out o' slavery. She always say she thankful she was never sold from her children, and that our Massa not so mean as some of the others."[46]

Some whites allowed slaves to attend church but under controlled conditions. For example, slaves worshiped in balconies at St. Paul's Lutheran and Salem Lutheran and Reformed Churches. Yet, the balconies were constructed to minimize white-slave contact. Whites and blacks entered the church through separate doors and never sat together in worship. A similar arrangement occurred at Machpelah Presbyterian Church.[47]

While Wesley Mauney failed to mention church or educational opportunities during his childhood, he and his father supported both after emancipation. He stated that "like so many men coming up out of slavery, [his father Sam] wanted a place for a school where the children could be taught to read, write and work arithmetic." Wesley Mauney described numerous efforts on his and his father's part to construct schools and churches after the war and subsequent efforts by the Ku Klux Klan to disrupt their efforts or burn the buildings. J. W. Roberts, who transcribed Mauney's oral memoir, stated that Mauney built "Two Baptist churches and two Methodist churches ... and four or five schools." Mauney described himself as "unlettered and unlearned."[48] While the Reconstruction period of which Wesley speaks is of great interest, it does not adhere to the scope of this project.

W. L. Bost emphasized the role of fear and brutality within slavery. He related that the "Patrol Committee" or in his words, "the paddyrollers" kept "close watch on the pore niggers so they have no chance to do anything or go anywhere." They required a "pass from his master" to "let the niggers go anywhere." If a slave was not "in your proper place, ... they would lash you til' you was black and blue. The women got 15 lashes and the men 30. That is for jes bein' out without a pass." For worse offenses, slaves were placed in jail and "put on the whippin' post. They was two holes cut for the arms stretch up in the air and a block to put your feet in, then they whip you with cowhide whip. An' the clothes shore never get any of them licks." He recalled an instance when a "stubborn Negro" was whipped until he died. He "didn't do as much work as his Massa though he outh to."

They took "him to the whippin' post, and then they strip his clothes off and then the man stan' off and cut him with the whip. His back was cut all to pieces. The cuts about half inch apart. Then after they whip him they tie him down and put salt on him. Then after he lied in the sun awhile they whip him agin. But when they finish him he was dead."[49]

Bost also discussed "the driver, he was the man who did most of the whippin,' use to whip some of the niggers. He would tie their hands together and then put their hands down over their knees, then take stick and stick it 'tween they hands and knees. Then when he take hold of them and bet 'em first on one side then on the other."[50] Bost recalled that these images served as a deterrent to escape or disobedience.

"a prodical son coming home"

As a youngster, Bost remembered little about the war itself. He recalled that in Newton there was "Jes a skirmish or two." "Most of the people get everything jes ready to run when the Yankee sojers come through town. This was toward the las' of the war." He communicated the duplicity of the situation: "Cose the niggers knew what all the fightin' was about, but they didn't dare say anything. The man who owned the slaves was too mad as it was, and if the niggers say anything they get shot right then and thar." Bost also recalled a neighbor named Solomon Hall. He "was a good man.... He freed all of his slaves about two years 'fore 'mancipation and gave each of them so much money when he died, that is he put that in his will. But when he die his sons and daughters never give anything to the pore Negroes."[51]

The war was perplexing to Sarah Gudger and "Us da'kies [who] didn't know whut it wa all all [sic] bout." Emancipation came suddenly, "Marse William" one day announced, "Did yo'all know yo'alls free. Yo free now." Gudger remained with the "white folks 'bout twelve months." She then went to stay with her "pappy" until he died.[52]

Sixteen year-old Wesley Mauney viewed emancipation with great emotion. He was "a prodical son coming home" to both parents. Notably, Mauney did not speak of having any relationship with the Little family but went to great lengths complimenting his father, Sam Mauney. The "PenPicture" describes Sam as being "a real mechanic. He was a blacksmith, carpenter and wheelwright and able to do anything needed on the plantation." Mauney stated that his mother, Priscilla Roberts, was a daughter of Silvy Fulenwider Roberts and one of seven sisters. Priscilla "had 11 children, 5 boys and 6 girls" of which Wesley was the second oldest. His father Sam helped build the county buildings in Dallas.[53]

Wesley Mauney emerges from his autobiography as a determined, hard working, self-made, illiterate, Godly, and family-centric man. The slave system which demeaned and limited persons of African descent could not control nor limit Wesley Mauney. Eventually he owned 677 acres of land and managed work crews of up to "100 hands."[54] Yet, he never recovered from the family separation and could find no words to describe slavery. He married Naomi Wellman, whose heritage included a white grandfather, and they raised a large and successful family.[55]

In his narrative W. L. Bost discussed interracial relations. "Plenty of the colored women," he recalled, "have children by the white men. She know better than to not do what he say. Didn't have much of that until the men from South Carolina come here and settle and bring slaves." Bost found it astounding that they would "take them very same children what have they own blood and make slaves out of them." The "Missus" seldom discovered the relationships but when she did "she raise revolution."[56]

Bost personally knew about the racial mixing. In 1860 Jonas Bost was listed with 13 slaves. W. L. was most likely listed as either age 13 or 9 in the census and as "Black." However Jonas Bost's four youngest slaves were listed as "Mulatto."[57]

Bost delved further into the issue of race. After the war he and his wife adopted a "small" boy. The boy was "part white" and "never did like to 'sociate with colored people." He recalled one situation when "he was a small child I took him to town and the conductor made me put him in the front of the street car cause he thought I was just caring for him and he was a white boy." Bost related that, they "sent him to school until he finished," after which he joined the navy; "he ain't spoke to a colored girl since he has been there," and Bost "took his insurance policy [on his adopted son] and cashed it.... I didn't want nothin' to do with him, if he deny his own color."[58]

Wesley Mauney offered his ancestry in simple terms. He stated that his father was Sam Mauney. Dewey Maceo Mauney, Wesley's son, indicated that Wesley's grandfather was a white man, "the old slave owner's son."[59]

Rudolph Young, local African American researcher, compiled data entitled "Mauney." In it he states that Sam Mauney "was a former slave of Abram Mauney and had helped to build the Gaston County courthouse and jail in 1848. His work at the iron works [at High Shoals] included the making of charcoal." Young continues, "Sam was a stepfather of Wesley Mauney who is a direct ancestor of Congressman Mel Watts." Young contends that Wesley was the son of Abraham Mauney.[60]

However, Wesley Mauney and his son recognized Sam Mauney as Wes's father; they also knew that Sam was the grandson of Abraham Mauney. To further substantiate the issue, Wesley never appeared as a mulatto in census records, only as black.[61]

"the mistress of her master"

Historical documentation concerning the Thomas Jefferson-Sally Hemings relationship and the revelation that South Carolina's deceased Senator Strom Thurmond had a twentieth century interracial relationship has brought the issue of racial mixing to the forefront. Rudolph Young's writings also document the practice. Escaped Union soldiers learned of white-slave relationships: a young mulatto visited them, "She was the wife of a slave; but her companions told us that she had been compelled to become the mistress of her master. She spoke of him with intense loathing."[62]

To document the extent of the mulatto population in Gaston County, I analyzed census data by counting the number of mulattoes beginning with the Slave Schedules of 1850 and 1860 through the federal 1870 and 1880 censuses. "Mulatto" was a separate category in the census used at the census-takers' discretion. The Gaston County 1850 Slave Schedule lists 71 mulattoes, and in 1860 the number had risen to 98.[63] The data from the 1870 census reveals a total of 97 mulattoes.[64] The breakdown by township may be found in the chart below. The 1870 data suggests that mulattoes are more prevalent in areas of lower slave populations.

The research project was expanded to the 1880 census to test whether under-reporting may have occurred in 1870. The total mulattoes listed in 1880 included the significantly higher number of 469 persons, which was an increase of 372 or 384 percent.[65] A breakdown of the statistics by township also varies significantly with the 1870 figures, followed by the percentage of increase or decrease:

	1870 Census	1880 Census	% increase/decrease
Cherryville	28	30	7%
Crowders Mtn.	32	18	-44%
Gastonia		10	
South Point	11	151	1,272%
River Bend	3	157	5,133%
Dallas	23		
West Dallas		29	
East Dallas		74	348%
Total	97	469	384%

The data confirms that racial mixing occurred and supports contemporary sources.

The research also documents that slave family life suffered because of inter-racial relationships; white slave owners' ability to divide slave families through purchase, to separate children from their parents at will, to prohibit slave marriage, and to limit the slave's religious activities, created a hostile family environment. But other interpersonal variations have been documented.

Jonas Derr is one example. As a white Lincoln County "iron monger" who owned 29 slaves in 1860 and had Gaston County relatives, he never married a white woman but had children with slaves. He headed a household in the 1860 Lincoln County census as a 29-year-old worth $29,500 real estate and $25,675 personal property with an assortment of others in his household, including two white "Moulders" and one white "Millwright." Also present were three Free Negroes, members of the Demps family, of which the two males assumed occupations of "Wagoner" and "Hammerman." The female held no listed occupation. All three were listed as Black, even though their kinsmen in the 1860 Gaston census were listed as mulatto.[66]

Rudolph Young describes Jonas Derr's interracial relationships. He had "at least three daughters" with slave women. Derr thought so highly of the mothers of his children that he willed 184 acres to "Frances Derr, Jane Derr, and Manirva king." Young continues that Jonas Derr requested "to not let his name die out," and Frances and husband Amos Johnson named a daughter Derr Johnson. Young relates a story involving Jonas Derr's opposition to his daughter Frances marrying Amos Johnson, as he resented this "Johnson Negro" wooing his mixed-race daughter. Another twist to the story involves an apparent debt Derr owed to Amos Johnson's master, which landed the "Johnson Negro" in the middle of a financial dispute.[67]

Documentation does not resolve the exact relationship Jonas Derr held with the African American women. Was there romance? Was it exploitive? Derr's will directs that 184 acres be "equally divided among" the three women, "being the place upon which Adolphus King now lives." Interestingly, Derr devised the land to the three women and "their heirs in fee simple ... during her natural live [sic] & at her death [Manirva King] the sum shall go to my heir at law living at the time of my death & in fee simple." Jonas Derr also devised $10 to Jane Derr and gave Charley King 60 acres. Derr further devised money, land, and interest in land to others including his Gaston County brother, "A. J. Derr" and his sister, Sarah Boger's, family.[68] "Manerva King" headed a household in 1870 Lincoln County, Union Township, two pages from Jonas W. Derr, with "Charles King," who was listed as a mulatto, age 15.[69] Derr felt some responsibility and possibly love for the children of these women.

Another example of a divergent relationship involves the ancestry of Rachel K. Eickemeyer, who shared her "The Descendants of Pinkney and Harriet Mauney of Lincoln County, North Carolina," which postulates that Pinkney Mauney was a white man who lived with a slave as man and wife.[70]

She persuasively documents the ancestry of Pinkney Mauney and contends that he purposely misled others about his racial identity. In 1870 he is listed as mulatto and married to Harriet, who is listed as black. Eickemeyer relies on a number of independent oral traditions which relate that Pinkney was indeed a white man married de facto to a slave. She reasons that, since such a marriage was illegal, her ancestor pretended to be of African descent.[71]

Rudolph Young, one of Mrs. Eickemeyer's sources, disputes her conclusions, contending that Pinkney Mauney was a son of Colonel Abraham Mauney and slave, Adelphia, and therefore a half-brother to Wesley Mauney.[72] The traditions and lineage of Pinkney Mauney illustrate the complexity of discovering African American history and genealogy. White men of the 1850s and 1860s could and did hold consensual romantic relationships with women of color. While social mores objected, love may have triumphed. Bonnie Mauney Summers told the author the story from the antebellum period of a Gaston County white man, Joseph Carpenter, who "ran off with a mulatto." Victoria E. Bynum in her book, *The Long Shadow of the Civil War Southern Dissent and its Legacies*,[73] documents interracial relationships throughout the south and their social and political implications.

Another insight into Gaston County slavery begins with a brief comment by Minnie Stowe Puett in her 1939 book, *History of Gaston County*. While commenting about her ancestor Jasper Stowe and the Stowesville Cotton Mill, she recalled the wagoner, "[o]ld 'Uncle Tom,' a family slave noted for two things, his devotion to the family and his big feet. He would take the yarns and cloth to Woodlawn, cracking his whip over two big mules, and bring back the mail. The factory was then a post office known as Stowesville."[74]

The brief entry details a very important task performed by slaves; loading, unloading, and carrying freight was critical for the success of the mill. The physical characteristic and Tom's dedication to the white Stowe family were recollections of note. Learning more about Tom Stowe led me to explore census and the tax list.

In the 1860 Gaston County Slave Schedule, he may be the thirty-four-year-old Black male belonging to Edwin B. Stowe, brother Jasper's partner and Tom's brother may be the thirty-year-old Black male. In the 1863 tax list Tom was listed as a slave of J & E B Stowe Company, aged 35, valued at $1,055. His brother, Jordan, was listed as 33, "(Sickly)," and valued at $211. In 1870 "Thomas Stowe," age 47 and a Farmer, headed a household with wife Vena and 8 apparent children. All were listed as "Black." Yet in 1880, "Thomas Stowe," age 55, Farmer and mulatto, headed a household with wife Vina, a daughter, a son, a grand-daughter and grandson, all listed as black. Also in the household was "Bro" Jordan, also a mulatto, aged 52. Stowe and family resided in the South Point area.[75]

Truly Tom Stowe was a valued member of the white Stowe family. After the war, he is listed for a number of years as an employee of the Cotton Mill, receiving "wages" of $15 per month, selling farm commodities to the company, and purchasing considerable merchandise from the Company Store.[76] Unfortunately I have not located Tom Stowe's account of why he continued to work at the Mill, his racial make-up, or his opinion of his slave and free condition.

Life in the South and in Gaston County was complex. Understanding how African Americans responded to the war requires further documentation.

"hoe cake, white bread, and a little butter"

A few sources suggest black collaboration with their Union liberators. On July 7, 1864, *The Bulletin* notified the public that five "Yankee prisoners" had escaped in Mecklenburg County and were headed toward Beaty's Ford Road.[77] These five "Yankee prisoners" crossed the Catawba River near present Mt. Holly where they encountered slaves living on the "plantation of a Mr. Broadway." The tax list records "Wm. Broadaway" residing in River Bend Company with eight slaves ranging in age from 36 to 5. The slaves informed the Yankee soldiers that their master was on his way to the bridge with his gun to guard against their crossing. They provided the soldiers with "hoe cake, white bread, and a little butter." They also furnished them with a "new shirt," and a helpful slave stated that his master was "'berry hard on us.'" An unnamed slave accompanied the soldiers for five miles in the dark and provided further directions using the stars and road directions. Following these directions the Union soldiers reached the railroad tracks which they followed until they were "about six miles east of Lincolnton." In the Lincolnton area, slaves on the "Kensler plantation" invited them into their homes, gave them "corn pone and bacon," concealed them in the woods, and solicited John H. Marsh. Marsh guided them to his residence to prepare for the journey to Union lines. Marsh collaborated with a "Mr. Ballard," and Mrs. Marsh cooked them a "scruptuous" meal. The account indicates that Marsh "manufactured liquor for the Confederates" at "Oakville or (Confederate Laboratory)," the soldiers' understanding of Hokeville. Later that night the soldiers were taken to "an old grist mill" where they met "several members of the 'Loyal League,' whose total membership consisted of about 40 persons." They hid in Marsh's barn and were fed with a basket hoisted to them. They remained in the area for a few days and also hid "in the barn of a Mr. Wizewell." They were furnished a knife, Confederate money, and fraudulent rebel prisoner furlough papers, allowing them to pass through Confederate lines into Tennessee. Marsh even forged the signature of "Wm. J. Hoke, Colonel Commanding Post" and provided one of the men with a "Rebel jacket," giving them directions toward the Blue Ridge with a slave guide.[78]

Also in 1864, a similar incident occurred in the Salisbury-Statesville area, when Union prisoners escaped from the Salisbury prison. Both incidents confirm slave collaboration with white Unionists assisting their Union liberators. Despite the risks, slaves willingly concealed the escaped Union prisoners—"every black face was a friendly face." A Union soldier described blacks as "always ready to help anyone opposed to the Rebels. Union refugees, Confederate deserters, escaped prisoners—all received from them the same prompt and invariable kindness." There is no evidence in either incident that the slaves attempted to escape with the soldiers.[79] Instead they remained in their log cabins waiting for the eventual end of the war and their hoped for emancipation. While some area slaves did escape, the majority remained until emancipation.

Not all slaves aided the Union. The project documented one instance of slave participation in the Confederate cause. Robert Newton Wilson was originally a member of the local militia. He joined the army on May 27, 1862, under Captain C. Q. Petty of Gaston County in Company H, 49th Regiment. Sixty-seven years later, on July 1, 1929, 86-year-old "Jerry Wilson, (Co)" applied for a Confederate pension because he served "as a servant of Col. R. N. Wilson." Being a servant, it is unclear whether Jerry willingly served, and it is unclear whether he received the pension as only his application has been located.[80] In 1863 Jerry, age twenty-one, was assessed in Tanyard District under Robert Wilson.

"rude almost to squalor"

Neither W. L. Bost nor Wesley Mauney specifically described their home life. Mauney compared the current landscape with that of his memory: "At that time the county that now has so many attractive homes, beautiful farmes, and lovely highways, was but a little more then a dense wilderness infested with wild beasts and dangerous reptiles. There were miles between plantations and homes and it was a treat to see one from another plantation."[81] Other sources provide descriptions of slave homes.

Escaped Union soldiers described slave quarters as a one room log cabin, "rude almost to squalor," which was dark with many persons living there. "There was a soft bed with white sheets ... chairs, a table, plates, knives, and forks."[82] The picture is clear—no privacy, little room, and intermingling of sexes and ages and families. Yet, the inhabitants created a warm inviting environment.

The Gaston County 1860 Slave Schedule provides a cursory portrait of slave homes. A sample of the documentation may be examined: On one census page, for example, twelve small slaveholders actually listed no slave homes on the census, which suggests that they lived in the slave owner's home or another outbuilding like a barn or in a cellar. Samples from the same census page include four slaves living in two slave houses; two in one home; four in one house; five in one home; two in one home. In another instance seven slaves lived in one home, females aged 56, 26 and 24 lived with four children aged seven through a nine-month-old infant. Other examples include eight slaves residing in one home; five in one home; four in one home. In another example ten slaves lived in one residence; eleven in one home; and twelve lived in two slave homes. Another slaveholder placed sixteen slaves in two homes.[83] How did larger slave owners provide housing?

B. F. Briggs, the ironmaster at Crowders Mountain, had 18 slaves listed in five houses. Lawson Wilson owned 22 slaves housed in only three residences. Dr. John D. McLean domiciled 32 slaves in six slave homes. Milton H. Gullick housed 21 slaves in three residences; Abram Scott housed 21 in 3 homes; and Caleb W. Hoyle domiciled 29 slaves in 5 houses.[84] According to the data, Gaston's largest slave owners housed their bondservants on average from 5 to 8 persons per residence. The data suggests that as slave numbers increased they resided in more cramped quarters. The mixture of genders, familial relationships, and ages created a hodgepodge living arrangement.

While one may argue that yeomen and farm laborers often had similar density in their residences, a primary difference was that most whites resided in nuclear or extended families of relatives, while the slave homes held persons of much more diverse familial relationships.

The influx of the Edgecombe County slave owners also presented housing problems. In 1863 the 301 slaves of Bridgers, Barron, Powell, and High Shoals had to be housed at the High Shoals Foundry or nearby. It is unclear how such a large number of slaves were housed in 1863, as no bond residences were described for High Shoals in the 1860 census. By 1863 the Garrett Brothers had moved their 93 slaves to the Briggs iron and gold operation. It is not known whether the Edgecombe investors built additional housing, forced slaves to reside outside, or to reside in barns or other buildings. The samples examined suggest that slave quarters were crowded and sparse in accommodations.

Slave families

Bost, Mauney, and Gudger provided few descriptions of slave family structure. Would the tax list provide clues of nuclear family groupings and how would these clues appear? North Carolina and other southern states prohibited slave marriage; therefore, the author defined a slave family within the tax list as an adult female and a number of children in order of birth. When a similarly aged male is also listed, the possibility of a nuclear slave family, owned by the same person, is surmised. Random adults and children suggest no effort on the part of the tax agent to record family groups and were not considered in the analysis. While the data is inconclusive, analysis suggests some family groupings.

Out of a total slave population of 2,746, the author identified 60 slave families from the 1863 tax list, of which 55 were headed by females. Of the total, nine mothers gave birth under the age of 17 with the youngest being 15. The data suggests that females headed over 90 percent of the slave families. It further suggests that only 15 percent of the slave mothers gave birth before age 17. The analysis could not account for husbands domiciled on another farm. Yet, such a marital relationship fostered two-residences only with occasional visits and children residing with the mother.

Mauney described his family with the same owner possessing both parents. Gudger knew her mother and father and where they lived. Bost spoke of his mother and grandmother being owned by Jonas Bost. It is very likely that many slave families were divided by separate ownership. The research suggests that slave families were predominately headed by females with many variations.

The author used the 1860 Gaston County Mortality Schedule as a case study to shed additional light on marriage and family. In the one year documented by the Mortality Schedule, 92 persons died, of which 17 were black males and 16, black females. Of the 33 African American deaths, 29 were listed as slaves. Seventeen were listed as adults and sixteen as children. The data reveals that 35 percent of the deaths involved African Americans, even though they represented 23.6 percent of the population. Half of the black deaths involved children compared to 47 percent white infant mortality. Of the seventeen adult slaves, four were listed as "married" or about 24 percent. Of the four Free Blacks, two were adults and one was married; two were children and all Free Blacks were listed as "mulatto."[85]

The incompletely recorded 1850 Gaston Mortality Schedule enumerates only 35 persons. About 11 slaves were surmised (persons listed with no last name). Slave deaths represented about 31 percent of the total, of which about 45 percent were children. Only six white children or about 25 percent of the total are listed as deceased. While the 1850 data is incomplete, it supports the 1860 data.[86]

Both sources confirm that African American deaths exceeded their percentage in the total population; they were more likely to die than their white counterparts. Black infant mortality reached 50 percent, which is slightly above white infant mortality. Finally, only 25 percent of blacks were listed as married. Anecdotal information suggests that whites allowed non-legal slave "marriage," as mentioned by William G. Morris, but clearly at a low percentage. The slaveholder could break up a non-legal marriage at any time. Crowded housing, harsh working conditions, and poor nutrition negatively affected lives of African Americans.

"Free Negroes"

During the Civil War, Confederates believed that Free Blacks posed a threat to the war effort and were disruptive to society as a whole. The North Carolina legislature passed laws, allowing them to become slaves, further limiting their movement, and providing strict parameters to their societal and economic activities.[87]

African Americans received free status through three methods: Their owner may legally manumit them; some owners allowed slaves to be "hired out," allowing them sufficient funds to purchase their freedom; and the third method involved their parentage. The slave or free status of the mother determined the child's status. If a white woman birthed a mixed race child with a man of African descent, the child was born free. North Carolina and other southern states regulated the rights of these children. The normal legal process involved all unmarried women to be charged with "Bastardy," unless they provided the name of the father. The father then became legally responsible for the welfare of his child. If there was no financial support for these children, the local Court of Pleas and Quarter Sessions apprenticed them to white males. The Gaston County Court apprenticed a number of mixed race children from 1847 to 1860.[88]

In 1860 the Gaston census documents 111 Free Blacks: 52 "Colored Males" and 59 "Colored Females." The 1850 census only lists 26.[89] A few examples bring them to life.

Gabriel Revels resided in the 1860 census at Crowders Creek post office. He was listed as white, born in Sampson County, NC, with a probable wife named Ann and five possible children from age 24 through 14. Gaston researcher Rudolph Young reported that Gabriel Revels was the brother of Hiram Rhodes Revels, the Reconstruction U.S. Senator from Mississippi. Originally from the Sampson, Cumberland, and Robeson County areas of eastern North Carolina, brothers Hiram, Absalom, and Elias settled in Lincolnton. In 1850 Gabriel resided in Rutherford County, where he and his wife, Ann, and entire family were listed as "mulatto." Later he moved to Gaston where he labored as a shoemaker. Young observed: "After the Civil War, his family passed for white"; he "was exempted from conscription" because of his occupation. The research has determined that by 1860 Revels had already chosen to pass for white, most likely benefitting from his skin color and his move from Rutherford County. Young's sources indicate that the Revels family had been free for many years. Gabriel Revels also appears in the 1860 Gaston County Industry Schedule as making "Shoes & Boots" with $120 invested in 600 pounds of "Leather." He worked by himself and produced "275 Pr. Shoes" valued at $325 and "60 Pr. Boots" valued at $175. Interestingly, he was the only shoemaker listed in the Gaston Industry Schedule.[90] Listed in 1863 in the Crowders Mountain Company, he was one of only a very few Free Blacks listed on the tax list and was taxed for 217 acres with approximate $350 valuation. He made the transition from Free Black to white shoemaker and was exempted from conscription.

Jonas Rankin was another Free Black, who was taxed in 1863 as "Jonas, Free" in Woodlawn Company for 50 acres valued at $150. He was listed in the 1860 Gaston census, Dallas post office, as a mulatto "Rail Road hand" with a possible wife and five possible children aged 11 through 1. Rudolph Young noted that Rankin "worked on the Kings Mountain railroad." In an 1859 petition to build a Gaston County road, the route description includes "by the way of free Jonas."[91] While his status in the community allowed his residence to mark the road, he was restricted from signing the petition.

Most Free Blacks in Gaston County were not listed on the tax list. Jerry Brooks was listed in the 1860 federal census as a farmer and by the name "Leroy Brooks." Rudolph Young claims that his mother was named Sarah Clem, residing in Cleveland County in 1860. Brooks was listed as Black on the census, while his wife, Eliza Clark, was listed as mulatto and their children listed as mulatto. According to Young, Eliza Clark Brooks was the daughter of Dorcas Clark, who was listed as a mulatto nearby. Young contends that Brooks accumulated over 1,000 acres of land in Crowders Mountain area and that Sarah

Clem was originally Sarah Brooks, the daughter of a white Maryland woman and a slave. Young states that the Clark family was a free family from South Carolina. Young also documents attempts made to re-enslave a member of the Brooks family.[92] Interestingly, Brooks and Revels are listed near one another in the Crowders Mountain mining area where many free African Americans lived.

An analysis of the 1860 Gaston census demonstrates that Free Blacks had some commonalities. Of the 111 listed, 73 percent were mulatto; 74 were children; 23 were specifically listed as "Bound"; 13 females headed households or appeared as a parent to children without a male present; 8 were listed as apparent husband and wife or with a white male.

The data indicates that nuclear family structure was more prevalent among Free Blacks, 40 percent, than among slaves, 25 percent. The census listed occupations for about 27 adults, including domestic, farmer, farm laborer, shoemaker, miner, cook, "Rail Road Hand," "Wood Chopper," "Apprentice," blacksmith, and "Wagoner." Possessing a trade created advantages not often available to slaves.

Having a trade and residing in a more cosmopolitan community like Dallas, Brevard Station, Woodlawn, or near mining and iron works, free African Americans could accumulate property and ply their trades for wages. Rudolph Young specified the Revels family as being barbers, shoemakers, blacksmiths, and other tradesmen.[93] Such trades lent themselves to urban or, in the case of antebellum North Carolina, town settings. The small town of Dallas became a haven for a number of Free Blacks during the period. In the 1860 census sixteen were listed, some as bound servants. Mansfield Chambers, born in Rutherford County, was listed as head of a household and "Wagoner" with an apparent wife. James Rabb, a mulatto boy of ten, was listed as bound to Daniel Hoffman of the Hoffman Hotel and Festus Crow, mulatto "Rail Road Hand," was also in his household. Ed. H. Bissel, a white "Miner" from Hartford, Conn was listed with Emily Cooper a "Mulatto Cook," born in Mecklenburg County with six mulatto children. All but one of the sixteen Free Negroes listed in the Dallas town census were mulattos: Robert Prince, a "Blacksmith" aged 22, was listed in the household of Catharine Rhome, a white "Seamstress."[94]

Free Blacks accumulated some wealth in Gaston County. On May 22, 1860, the County Court appointed administrator William R. McLain, a white slave owner from South Point district, to manage the sale of the property of "Lee Hunter a Coloured man Deceased," who had died intestate. The amount of the sale was $96.40. Sold items included four hogs, one book, "Deceased Clothing," "1 Bed & Furniture," "1 Bureau & Contents," another "Bed & Steds," two "Rasors" and a "Soap Box Brush Strap," "1 Desk," "1 Cupboard," assortments of "Gugs," "Crockery," "Buckets" and "pitchers." Also sold was a "Hoop Box," "Coffee Pot Shears," "1 Churn," "Dogiron & hooks," "1 Clock," "1 Watch," a cow and a calf, "1 Trunck," a number of axes, iron material, "1 Matock," a saddle, "Hoes," baskets, barrels and chairs. The administrator, William R. McLean, also sold "1 Seine," "1 Keg," "Scythe & Cradle," "1 Plow" and "Plow Singletree," "1 Trukel Waggon," "1 Slede," and "1 Horse and Geer."[95]

Hunter's property included items useful to a yeoman or farm laborer. A cow provided milk for the family; a horse allowed transportation and farming. He owned two beds and other items for everyday activity. But Hunter owned a clock, watch, and furniture, which could be found in middle class and yeoman homes. Possession of a book suggests that he or someone in the family could read.

The estate's administrator McLain reported the total proceeds of the estate sale and interest as $106.04. M. H. Hand and D. F. Ragan, committee members, reported that vouchers against the estate totaled $95.86 and commissions included $9.70 which left a balance of 48 cents to the family.[96] No vouchers were found in the estate file.

In 1850 Lee Hunter is listed in western Mecklenburg County, Steel Creek District. He was age 30, mulatto, a farm laborer, and had an apparent wife named Jane who is listed as black and 35 years old. Possible children included Rush, Jane and Eliza. Hunter was not found in the 1860 Gaston census and presumably died before it was taken.[97]

In 1860, Jane Hunter, 55, headed a household at Stowesville post office with nine youngsters aged 18–2, including Rush and Eliza, who were in Lee Hunter's 1850 household and a female, Sylvia aged 60. All were listed as "black." The late Lee Hunter's estate administrator, "William R. McLean" (McLain), headed a household only two houses away.[98] As a Free Black, Lee Hunter migrated in search of work and accumulated personal property.

An indication of public opinion about Free Blacks is apparent from an 1860 Gaston County murder trial. Attorneys, David Schenck and L. E. Thompson, defended William Murrell, on trial for murdering a Free Black named "Make" after a scuffle. With a spirited defense the Gaston Court jury found him guilty of manslaughter, "felonious Slaying only," and sentenced him to be branded "with the letter M" and to serve twelve months in jail in Charlotte since the Gaston jail was not secure. Schenck opined that while "public opinion ran against Murril," the verdict proved that "juries will not hang white man for killing free negroes." By Spring 1861 Murrell returned from imprisonment, "was permitted to take the Oath of insolvency & was thereupon Discharged."[99] "Make" was actually "Macon Rankin," a married mulatto "Wagoner," who the Mortality Schedule listed as "Shot Intentionally."[100]

The research project encountered no Free Blacks in Gaston County with slaves.

Understanding the centrality African American slaves played in the Civil War may be summarized in the statements of Governor Zebulon B. Vance after the war. Originally a Unionist and Bell supporter for president, Vance moved from Unionist to Confederate soldier to nationalist governor. His rationale was "that war and defeat were equivalent to not only the abolition of slavery, but to the subjugation—and all that carried with it—of our country." He chose to support the Confederate cause since "the great desire of the North was to abolish Slavery and to humiliate the Slaveholders whom they had been taught to hate." He went "with my state and to fight—not for secession—not for the Confederate States [as] an object desirable in itself—but to avert the consequences—the abolition of slavery."[101] The Confederate Congress' reluctance to employ slave soldiers, and President Lincoln's rebuff of Vice President Alexander Stephens' 1865 peace proposal, in part because the Confederacy insisted upon maintaining slavery as a condition for peace, further documents the centrality of slavery.

The evidence of the Gaston County research affirms that slavery was the most significant financial, social, and political aspect of southern life. White slave owners controlled the local government, accumulated property and possessions, and passed their slaves to family members. Slavery acted as the primary means for social mobility. Slaves suffered from bondage, limited resources, cramped homes, fragmented and sometimes tormented family life, consistent patterns of fear, and a lack of control over their lives. The slave culture inculcated permanent white ascendency and black dependency. Everyone knew their place. Only a few variations and outright opposition have been observed. White Gaston County citizens, slaves, Free Blacks, politicians, and economic leaders represented the culture and social mores of the time.

The most unexpected discovery was that the Civil War acted as a catalyst in Gaston County to increase the slave population, the number of slave owners, and the accumulation of slaves into fewer hands. Gaston citizens would have agreed with Governor Vance's statements above. Gaston County found the "peculiar institution" politically, economically, and socially essential.

The examination of the 1863 Gaston County tax list in this book provides insights into the citizen's life.

Concluding Thoughts

This historical journey has taken us to unanticipated places. The entirety of the project exposes a number of significant conclusions that our citizens conveyed to us in their writings and actions.

They initially supported secession and many volunteered to support the Confederacy. Many men fought bravely to defend the southern way of life, some giving their lives. Soldiers focused upon combat but were distracted with home front problems, communicating often with loved ones. They went into battle for various reasons—southern independence, to support the southern life style, for adventure, to pay bills, and some were conscripted, forced into battle. The irony is that when southerners seceded they actually facilitated the destruction of their way of life. This project has discovered that, hidden in various texts and society's consciousness, is the other political solution to the slavery issue for southerners: remain in the Union. Without slave states' support no constitutional amendment to end slavery could pass. William Sloan's able defense of Unionism postulated that by staying in the Union the South could prevent the abolition of slavery and protect the southern life style. He, secessionists like David Schenck, and others possessed the same goals but sought them in different ways. When war commenced at Fort Sumter, hope for moderation ceased.

The second major insight involved the issue of state's rights, as the war actually produced some interesting ironies. The Richmond government superseded state authority in a number of ways—conscription, impressments of slaves and goods, high taxation, the tax-in-kind, revocation of the writ of habeas corpus, price controls, and limits of corporate profits. All of these Confederate governmental mandates exceeded many citizens' concept of representative government. The Confederacy instituted the draft one full year before the United States, imposed higher and more onerous taxes, and failed to support a sustainable infrastructure in which to wage war. Thus the Confederate economy collapsed with crippling inflation and devolved into a barter economy as the war ended: Confederate money was viewed as worthless. When the rebellious ladies of Salisbury and other towns took the law into their own hands securing flour and food necessities, they struck at the core of the Confederacy. Their violence in support of their families repudiated the cause. When Confederate soldier Daniel Haynes Dellinger instructed his wife to hide their food stuffs to avoid the tax-in-kind, he did, as many did: he defended his property rights and provided for his family's survival. It is certainly ironic that the war supposedly fought to support state's rights evolved into a major Confederate government power grab and that, even loyal Confederates such as Jasper Stowe, failed to follow the strict demands of the law. Persons living during the times observed, protested, and violated these governmental usurpations.

The research also reveals that Gaston County actually fought a civil war at home. I have heard many historians speak of how the Civil War involved "brother against brother." I never understood such an analogy in Gaston County or even in North Carolina. As a researcher of colonial and Revolutionary War history, I clearly understand how Tories fought Whigs, Loyalists fought Patriots, neighbors fought neighbors. This was a true civil war. I never understood that within Gaston County some citizens, Unionists, battled economically, politically, and physically with loyal Confederates. I never understood that at the beginning and during the war vigilantes lynched, intimidated, arrested, and physically abused neighbors who did not support secession or the Confederate cause, even mistreating women. The militia and Home Guard had a difficult task, but they often conducted their affairs with wanton violence. Neighbors spied on each other; some were refused food and shelter; and many broke the law. The documentation shows that Gaston citizens fought one other as the war progressed into anarchy at home.

Slavery remains an emotional issue. As I began the project, I believed that Gaston County held few slaves or plantations, and that slavery held little impact. My first discoveries seemed to confirm these beliefs—70 percent of its citizens owned no slaves, there were few plantations, and Gaston County ranked in the lower half (58 out of 87) in slave ownership in the state. In fact, the county's upper class elite numbered only about 2 percent of the county citizens, well below the state average. A more extensive analysis of the data and contemporary accounts contradict these earlier assertions. I discovered that 90 percent of all officeholders, county contractors, and other leaders owned slaves; that almost 80 percent of all slaveholders actually held more tax value in their slaves than in their real estate; and that slave assessed value exceeded land value by almost 15 percent in the county as a whole. When I functioned in the comments and actions of Schenk, Morris, and others, it is clear that they realized the social, economic, and political ramifications of slave ownership, as many wanted to add slaves during the war, sought to rent them, and recover runaways. For people living in Gaston County their southern life style revolved around the ownership of bondsmen and women. These astonishing facts, the inherent racism of the times, and the expectation that slavery would survive the war bound white citizens together, as Schenck insightfully noted in his diary. What was even more amazing in Gaston County is that during the war the number of slaves and slave owners dramatically increased, while ownership became more concentrated into fewer hands. The war effort seemed to promote the institution.

The project also exposed that Gaston County residents held many varying views about slavery, the war, politics, secession, and soldiering, debunking the illusion that there was a unified front supporting secession and the Confederacy. Many soldiers were drafted into service, deserted, and some families supported the United States in the conflict. Heavy taxation, men away from home, monetary inflation, and scarcity of goods and services produced economic hardships on all citizens. Some responded with outright opposition, others quietly supported the government, while others survived the best they could. Women—wives, mothers, aunts, and sisters—preserved the family, the farm, and the hopes and dreams of all. Their strong devotion to family and survival was critical to their soldiering men. Each reacted to wartime factors in unique and revealing ways.

While some consistencies within groups of people, soldiers, wives, and families have been observed, the research also conveys that people during these difficult times responded to challenges and opportunities as individuals. Loyal Confederate Lemuel Hoyle strongly opposed the draft enlistment of his young cousin, and Colonel William G. Morris grappled with whether to remain in the army or come home. Conversely, Caleb Senter expressed opposition to the war, slavery, and the trying times on the home front. Yet, he returned to duty after his time "in the woods." Wives and mothers could support the Confederate cause while hiding commodities from the dreaded tax-in-kind. Faced with such difficult choices and conflicting views, it is revealing that people reacted differently, sometimes instinctively, and often inconsistently. Their primary tasks involved survival, the raising of their families, and creating a future.

Gaston County's portrait of the Civil War contradicted many previous perceptions. Through their words and actions the county's citizens demonstrated bravery, resilience, dedication to their beliefs, and a pervading concept of what government should be. Hopefully, the book has provided some insight and added understanding of the trials, conflicts, bravery, and values which Gaston County citizens exemplified. They speak to us in their own words and deeds. We can learn much from them and about our past.

APPENDIX: GASTON COUNTY TAX LIST OF 1863

The Map Key

Creating a map of 1863 Gaston County became a goal of the project. Few historical maps exist for the county. Initial rationale for the map was to delineate the eleven militia companies in the tax list, to locate Dallas, the cotton mills and iron works, the Catawba and South Fork Rivers, and the railroad paths through the county. I then added some historical sites prominently mentioned in the book.

I researched various maps including Hugh E. White's map of 1931, a map printed by the North Carolina State Highway Commission in 1970, maps on the sleeves of Cope and Wellman's *The County of Gaston*, "Historical Sites of Gaston County" created for the National Bicentennial Celebration in 1976, maps drawn by Garland P. Stout on March 23, 2013, historical maps located at: http://alabamamaps.ua.edu/historicalmaps/us_states/northcarolina/index2_1851-1885.htm, and the GIS mapping system for Gaston County located at: http://gis.gastongov.com/GastonGIS/Default.aspx. Using these maps, I created the county as it may have looked in 1863.

The most difficult aspect of the project involved transposing the eleven militia companies onto the map as no boundaries existed for them in contemporary documents. I used waterways and physical descriptions on the tax list and persons listed on the tax list in comparison with the 1850 and 1860 census listings. I assumed that tax militia companies adhered to specific geographic boundaries in some consistent pattern. By painstakingly comparing the tax lists, maps, censuses, and other historical documentation, I propose boundaries for the tax lists based upon the outline map of Garland P. Stout.

Understanding the process includes the delineation of waterways and physical characteristics within each militia company:

Blacks/Cherryville Company—Lick Fork, Indian Creek, Muddy Fork, Beaverdam Creek, Poplar Branch, Cam Branch, Buffalo Creek, Mill Creek (Black was the militia captain's surname)
Crowders Mountain—Crowders Creek, Crowders Mountain, Kings Mountain
Dallas—Olney Branch, Kettle Shoal, Big Long Creek, Little Long Creek, South Fork River, Catawba Creek, Ridge, Dallas, Tanyard, Crowders Creek

Duharts—Long Creek, Duharts Creek, Crowders Creek, South Fork River, Catawba Creek, Ridge

High Shoals—Hoyles Creek, South Fork River, Brevards Creek, Long Creek, Duharts Creek, Catawba Creek, Railroad, Ridge, High Shoal, Vestals Ford

River Bend—Stanley Creek, Leepers Creek, Dutchmans Creek, Lippards Creek, Plank Road, Catawba River, Riverbend, Ridge, South Fork River, Tools Ford, Killians Creek

Roberts—Crowders Creek, Long Creek, Beaverdam Creek

Rudisill—Indian Creek, Pine Fork, Pine Mountain, Beaverdam Creek, Mountain Branch, Pine Land

South Point—South Fork River, Catawba River, Catawba Creek, Mill Creek

Tanyard—Catawba Creek, Mill Creek, Crowders Creek

Woodlawn—Catawba River, South Fork River, Stanley Creek, Taylors Creek, Dutchmans Creek, Fites Creek, Hoyles Creek, Ridge land, Olives Ford

It is probable that references within each district may not be universal. For example, when a reference is made to "Ridge," this geographic distinction may refer only to a Ridge within that area and not to a county-wide ridge.

I believe that most militia boundaries are reasonably accurate, as a few physical characteristics separated some of the companies. Some examples: Rudisill and Roberts Company bounded one another along a ridgeline between the Long Creek and the Beaverdam watersheds, approximate present Dallas-Cherryville Highway, Highway 279; Roberts' and Rudisill's eastern boundary was the Pasour Mountain ridge; Tanyard included most of the Catawba Creek watershed; High Shoals' western boundary was the South Fork River and it included the Hoyles Creek watershed on the east; the Dallas-Duharts boundary was Long Creek; Duharts was where present-day Gastonia, Eastridge Mall, Caromont Hospital, Franklin Square, and Gaston Mall are located and included the Duharts watershed to the South Fork River; South Point included land on both sides of the South Fork River in the extreme southeastern portion of the county, including present Belmont. I propose that the boundary between South Point and Woodlawn was a ridge between Fites Creek and water flowing into the South Fork and Catawba Rivers. The delineation of the River Bend district remains more speculative as a clear boundary with Woodlawn and High Shoals is uncertain. Also, the western and southern boundaries of Crowders Mountain Company were clearly the Cleveland County and South Carolina lines, but its northern boundary with Roberts, Duharts, and eastern boundary with Tanyard remains unclear.

Gaston County of 1863 had a different western boundary than the present day. In the 1900s Kings Mountain seceded from Gaston County and joined Cleveland in at least two acts of the General Assembly, creating the present jagged lines. Historical maps vary concerning the boundary with Cleveland. I accepted the border as created by Garland P. Stout since his depiction adhered consistently with historical maps and was more esthetically drawn.

KEY

Railroads are delineated as crossties.

The Catawba and South Fork River are identified with curvy lines with their names.

A   High Shoals Iron Works
B   Briggs Iron Works which was acquired by the Garrett Brothers
C   Mountain Island Cotton and Woolen Mill

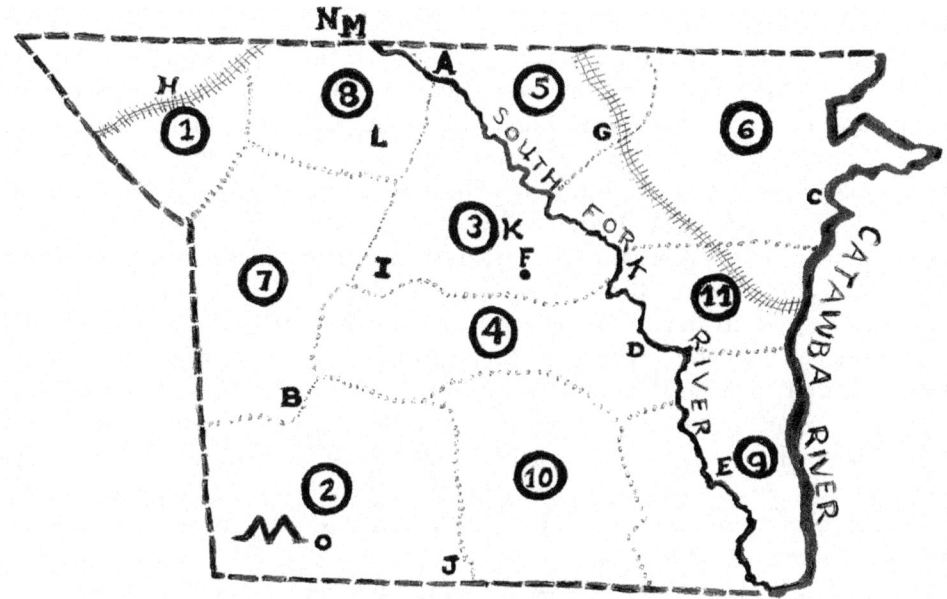

Gaston County (Brenda Beard-Bostian).

D   Woodlawn Cotton Mill (Linebarger's Mill)
E   Stowesville Cotton Mill (J & EB Stowe Mill)
F   Dallas
G   Brevard Station Depot
H   Cherryville Depot
I   James Hillhouse White home and grist mill
J   William Joseph Wilson home, later owned by Lawson Wilson
K   Homesite of William G. and Louisa Costner Morris
L   Abraham Mauney homesite, home of young slave, Wesley Mauney
M   Long Shoals in Lincoln County
N   Hokeville and the Confederate Laboratory in Lincoln County
O   Crowders and Kings Mountain

Tax List Militia Companies:

1	Cherryville	7	Roberts
2	Crowders Mountain	8	Rudisills
3	Dallas	9	South Point
4	Duharts	10	Tan Yard
5	High Shoals	11	Woodlawn
6	River Bend		

I located the tax list at the North Carolina Archives, Gaston County Collection, Tax Lists, 1847–1860; 1863–1868, CR040.701.2. One may access the law at http://digital.ncdcr.gov/cdm/ref/collection/p249901coll22/id/177014.

Passed on February 11, 1863, the Confederate North Carolina General Assembly approved the sweeping "Revenue" law, which increased taxes on farmers, persons of modest means to significant increases on luxury items held by the richest North Carolinians. A portion of taxholder possessions were taxed at the increased ad valorem rate of ⅖ of 1 percent of the assessment. Land, the major source of previous tax revenue, was taxed at this rate with slaves being taxed at this rate based upon their valuation. Ad valorem taxation of slaves was an additional tax, as previous tax laws did not tax enslaved females, children, and males younger than 21 and older than 45. The ad valorem tax rate also included taxes on persons who held cash on hand and solvent debts, manufacturing, state or county bonds, furniture worth more than $200, horses, mules, cattle, hogs, cotton and tobacco. Town lots and toll bridges were also assessed at the new rate. Luxury items such as carriages worth more than $50, gold or silver plated jewelry, watches, or canes were assessed at 1 percent of their value. Taxes were added to professionals, profits from manufacturing and dividends. The complex law provided for a three person valuation board for each militia company and authorized the sheriff and clerk of court to implement the tax law after each taxable had their property appropriately assessed. An appeals process was outlined. Passage of this monumental tax bill which significantly increased taxes on all North Carolinians was a major undertaking, as it shifted the tax burden to wealthy slaveowners, even if there was little consistency in slave valuations. In the surrounding area no complete tax lists have been located with only three Cleveland County companies having partial returns.

The 1863 tax list is divided into two sections. The first section found below involves land and slaves; the second which follows includes other taxable property as defined by the state law. The transcriptions were made as exactly as possible. I made some alterations to create consistency. For example, the original sometimes had last name first and other times it was last; there was also a lack of consistency with the ordering of slave names and ages; and slave values were written variously throughout the original. The following format begins with the taxable, last name first; acreage; valuation and land location. If the taxable has more than one tract, it is listed below the taxable. Some entries are dittoed while others are not. I adhered to the original. Beside each taxable are slaves, age, and valuation. At the end of the slave listings are the taxable's slave totals following "No" and the total slave valuation. Land and slave values are in Confederate dollars. Where possible I have footnoted probable census listings referencing *The 1860 Census of Gaston Co., North Carolina*, by Gladden and Bell by page number with the house number and post office to allow for a perusal of the original. If I was fairly certain of the census identification, I wrote "See"; if I was uncertain I wrote "Possibly." I also footnoted locations of residences if they currently exist, idenfication of waterways or physical characteristics, and other pertinent information. When I was unable to transcribe accurately, I placed a question mark ? with the entry. Occasionally the list left some data blank, and I also left it blank. Edits are surrounded by brackets.]

[On the first page:] W. P. Bynum's Book

[W. P. Bynum resided in eastern Lincoln County, served as a soldier, and came home to become the prosecutor for the area.]

Assessment of Land and Slaves [for] Blacks Com[pany] 1863

[After the first page all entries were listed as Cherryville Company or Cherryville Dist]

Taxable	Acres	Value	Location	Slave	Age	Value
Aderholdt D.[1]	404	1600	Lick Fork[2]	Jake	36	$619
Aderholdt M.[3]	118¾	1200	Indian Creek[4]	Martha	26	841
Black, Eph Senr[5]	504	2000	Muddy Fork[6]	Bill	14	817

Taxable	Acres	Value	Location	Slave	Age	Value
" "	75	400	" "	Alex	13	742
" " N Dellinger tr	34	150	Ind Crk	Ben	9	446
" " admr M Evans	67	200	Lick Fork	Harriet	7	569
				Adaline	4	279
				Julian	9/12	93
				No 8		4406

[the slaves were listed without differentiation of who was the owner; assumed to be D. Aderholdt.]

Taxable	Acres	Value	Location	Slave	Age	Value
Black, E. Widow	100	600	Beaverdam[7]	Wallace	21	1165
				Edwin	15	891
				Barbara	19	841
				Milly	70	000
				No 4		2895
Black, S?. or ?L.	281½	1000	Beaverdam			
	107	555	" " [bracketed with preceding entry]			
Black, E. Junior	105	525	Lick Fork			
Black, B.[8]	116½	600	Beaverdam	Caty	16	841
	61	360	" "			
Black, Saml Senr[9]	212	800	Beaverdam	Nelly	60	[blank]
	185	1200	Poplar Branch	Martin	45	817
	25	75		Boss	33	1163
	25	75		Eph	30	1117
				Jack	27	742
				Matilda	40	594
				Isaac	14	1040
				Elis.	8	668
				Saryan	4	371
				?Misssouri	20	841
				Leander	8/12	93
				No 11		7446
Black Thomas[10]	157	625	Lick Fork	Clay	?17?	742
	60	255	Ind. Crk			
" " as Gd E. Anthony	84	500	Lick Fork			
Brown, James[11]	138¾	600	Lick Fork			
Brown, R. H.	80	1000	Indian Cr.			
Beam, J. F. & D.	140	900	Indian Cr			
Barber, Barbara	78¾	300	Poplar Branch			
Beam, J. T.	107	600	Beaverdam			
Barnhill, Mary[12]	30	50	Cam Branch			
Black, S. Junr	126	600	Cam Branch			
" " as Gd. Of M. Stroups Heirs	4½	15	Cam Branch			
	157	600				
" "	143¾	500				
	111	300				
	90	450				
	22	60	[all bracketed together]			

Assessment of Land and Slaves for 1863 Cherryville Comp[any]

Taxable	Acres	Value	Location	Slave	Age	Value
Black, Janie	145½	586	Muddy Fork			
Beam, Ann	125	625	Beaverdam			
Brown, Mary	42½	126	Buffalo			
Beam, Michael[13]	70	350	Beaverdam	Lawson	40	1058
	153	650	" "	Dave	30	1058
	151½	1350	" "	No 2		2116
Collins, J. M.	40½	160	Ind. Cr.			
Carpenter, James	722	2500	B D[14]			
Cannon, Wm	44	135	B D			
Carpenter, B. M.[15]	56	224	B D			
Carpenter, Wm[16]	34	105				
Carpenter, Joshua	120	750				
Crouse, D.	69	200				
Craft, J. P.	398	1990	Buffalo	Sam	29	1163
Craft, M. J.	133	540	Muddy Fork			
Cannon, E.	100	600	Muddy Fork			

Taxable	Acres	Value	Location	Slave	Age	Value
Critz, H. J.	100	300	Muddy Fork			
Dellinger, Polly	42½	125	Muddy Fork			
Dellinger, Peter[17]	211¾	1050	Lick Fork	Clementine	20	891
Dellinger, George as Ex. Of Peter Dellinger Decd	105	500	Muddy Fork			
Dellinger, C.	121	600	Lick Fork			
Dellinger, A.	118	200	Lick Fork			
Dellinger, ?S.	40	160				
Eaker, S. C.	370½	3000	Indian Cr	Mack	16	841
				Suff	9	694
					[total]	1535
Eaker, C.[18]	50	500	Cam Branch			
" "	115	500	Lick Fork			
Eaker, David[19]	100	300	Muddy Fork			
Glassoock?, S. S.[20]	40	250	?Muddy Fork			
Farris, R. B. W.[21]	110	3?00	Muddy Fork			
Farries?, S.	127	500	Poplar Branch	?Farrier?		
Homesley Heirs	233	400	B D			
Hallman, Jack ? Jacob	103	475		Andy	24	1117
Harrelson, Wm[22]	264½	1050	Muddy Fork			
" "	11	35	Lick Fork			
Harrelson, W. O.	74¾	370	M. F.			
Homesly, A. B.[23]	170	500	M. F.			
Hoyle, J.[24]	100	600	Ind Cr.			
	35	200	" "			
Hovis, George[25]	163	700	Ind. Cr	Adaline	38	668
				Mike	20	1117
				Calvin	14	768
				Wills?	4	371
				Labe	10	690
				Frank	2	223
				No 6		3837
Harrelson, J. F.	132½	700	Ind Cr			
Lany, Barbara	50	200	M. F.			
Lowrance, L. H.	136	550	Mill Cr			
	124	550	Mill Cr			
Lusk, Joseph[26]	116	500	Beaverdam			
Lacky, James as Ad. Of M. Sellers	145	700	Beaverdam			
Kendrick. S. L.	80	400	M. F.			
McGinnas, J. J.	266	1300	Lick Fork	Frank	39	742
				Fanny	27	817
				Harriet	9	643
				Ann	2	174
				Aly	7/12	93
				No 5		2469
Mauney, D.	281	1200	M. F.			
	75	250	Ind Cr.			
Morrison, B.	117½	330	Lick fork			
McGinnis, W. W.[27]	177	700	Lick Fork			
" "	100	600	?Ilers Cr			
Morrison, J.	4½	15	Lick F			
Neill, James	75	225	Poplar Branch			
Putman, L.	100	400	Lick Fork			
Putman, H.	46	225	Lick Fork			
Plonk, D.[28]	150	550	B D	Harriet	8	668
				No 1		668
Reynolas, W.	2	8	C. B.			
Reynolas, B.	60	175	C. B.			
Rudisill, J.	67	250	B. D.			
Rudsall, J. M.	317½	1050	C. B.	Caroline	38	594
				?Inv.	18	1058
				Ruff	16	1058
				Milt	5	472
				Pink	10	594
				Abe	12	694
				No 6		4470

Taxable	Acres	Value	Location	Slave	Age	Value
Roberts, E. H. as Adm Of M. M. Roberts	350	1050	Ind Cr	Lawson	50	223
	1	4		Peg	20	804
	50	300		Ann	18	866
	100	200	C. B.	Adam	16	965
				Mark	4	337
				Bill	1	140
				No 6		3335
Rutledge, E. J.	15	30	Poplar Branch			
Stroup, A. W.[29]	57	200?	Muddy F.			
Stroup, J. C.[30]	181	800	Muddy F.			
Stroup, C.[31]	323	2000	Muddy F.	Jake	36	1117
" "	44	150	Muddy F.			
" "	14	100	Lick Fork			
Stroup, B.	210	840	B Dam			
Smith, H.	143	175	M. F.			
Spake, Chris	138	600	?Ind Cr			
Spake, S.[32]	38	200	M. F.			
Summerow, H.	114¾	466	Ind Cr			
Smith, J. R.	150	600	BD			
Shull, A.	100	400	I C			
Sellars, Wm	70	200	P. Branch	Bill	[No age]	891
Summit, H.[33]	236	1800	M. F.	Andrew	53	464
				Hetty	42	464
				Jess	14	1039
				Tom	13	866
				Bob	13	866
				May	11	643
				George	6	569
				Harriet	6	371
				Jane	6	285
				Lawson	17	1117
				No 10		6884
Smith, D.	17½	200	B. D.	Dice	17	186
" " for C. Roberts	23	100				
" " for J. Roberts	26	100	C. B.			
" " for Wm Ensly	21	100	C B			
Saylor, E.	33⅓	200	C B			
Whitworth, ?Nyoma	89	400	?Iles cr			
White, Barbara	88	400				
Warlick, P. H.	66	350	Lick Fork			
Warlick, Lydia	259¾	800	Lck For			
Warlick, S.	109	450	B. D.			
Wacaster, Levi[34]	60	240	Muddy F.			

Assessment of Land and Slaves for 1863=Crowders Mountain Dist[rict]

Taxable	Acres	Value	Location	Slave	Age	Value
Adams, John H.[35]	275	2800	Cr Cr	Lewis	44	787½
				Jane	33	875
				Anthony	33 Def	525
				Joe	30	1050
				Eli	18 Deficent	700
				Frank	17	1312½
				Mary	14	1137½
				Cinda	13	962½
				Nancy	12	875
				Molly	10	787½
				Sam.	6	525
				Josiah	4	350
				Stephen	1½	131¼
				No 13		10,018
Anthony, Jas. C.	144	432	Creek	Harriet	25	1095¾
				Haley	5	393¼
				Walker	1½	131¼
				No 3		1618
Adams, Margaret[36]	200	1200	Crowders Cr[37]	S?elly	45	612½

Taxable	Acres	Value	Location	Slave	Age	Value
				Rebecca	22	1181¼
				Fite Diseased	20	1137½
				Mariah	18	1225
				Harriet	17	1225
				Milly	10	787½
				Harry	26	1225
				Charles	22	1312½
				Cinda	14	1225
				George Ins	10	[no value]
				Sarah	3	218¾
				No 11		10,150
Beattie, Francis[38]	154	1200	Crowders Crk			
Beattie, Frances V. Tr.	130	160	" " ?Mt?			
Beattie, Wm[39]	102	500	" " ?Mt?			
Beattie, James O.	107	500	Crowders			
Bell, Rachel R.[40]	54	350	Crowders Cr			
Bell, Robt. H.[41]	79	550	Crowders Cr			
Boyce, E. E.[42]	346	2000	Crowders Cr	Caleb	36	918¾
				Mahala not Sd	29	437½
				Sarah	15	1050
				Mathew	13	962½
				Miles	11	787½
				Jane	7	525½
				Catharine	70	21?¾
				No 7		4703
Blackwood, Joseph[43]	71	350	Cr. Creek			
Blackwood, Ann	73	350	" "			
Blackwood, Jane	71	350	" "			
Blackwood, Nancy[44]	73	350	" "			
Boyd, Robt. M.[45]	408	2500	Cr Creek	Harriet	44	656¼
				Alex	24	1268¾
				Dave	23	1312½
				Pink	18	1312½
				Jenny	20	1181¼
				Neal	16	1225
				Morris	11	875
				Sam	9	875
				Caroline	5	437½
				No 9		9143
Bell, Eli[46]	119	200				
Crawford, James	399	2400	Crowders Crk	Isaac	57	175
" " Mt tr	90	90		Linda	49	175
				Lawson	26	1225
				Mariah	27	1006¼
				Margaret	17	1225
				Rachel	15	1225
				Jane	13	1006¼
				Hannah	13	1006¼
				Major	10	787½
				Chambers	7	612½
				Roswell	5	437½
				Pink	5	393¾
				No 12		9275
Crawford, Jas. L.[47]	189	1500	Crowders Creek	Daniel	36	875
Crawford , Jno. O Gard				Edney	17	1312½
				No 2		2187
Heirs of T. O.				Lucinda	37	612½
				Ben	4	393¾
				Mary	3	262½
				Anderson	1	87½
				No 4		1356
Crawford, Wm. N.	120	150	Crowders Crk			
Carroll, W. D.	39	350	Crowders Crk	Philis	17	1181
				No 1		1181
Carroll, Mary	106	150	Crowders Cr			
Carson, Jas. W.	126	700	Crowders Cr			
Carson, Robt.[48]	60	800				

Taxable	Acres	Value	Location	Slave	Age	Value
	14	50				
Carson, Jas. M. Esq	56	250	Crowders Crk [next 3 are bracketed together]			
" " Oates	113	1000				
" " Montgomery ?trat	29	200				
" " Exr T. O.	77	1300				
" " Adams tract	87	250				
Carson, Martha A.	200	1300		Harriet	?8??9	700
				No 1		700
Carson, Martha as Gd Of her child				Rufus	12	1093¾
				No 1		1093
Carson, Rachel J.	680	3000	Crowders Crk	Carry	42	875
				Nancy	35	787½
				Viney	31	918¾
				Calvin?	16	1050
				Margaret	14	1137½
				Melinda	13	962½
				Giles	10	744?¾
				Sarah	10	393¾
				Patsey	7	568¾
				Ann	7	612½
				Elvira?	4	350
				Hannah	4	350
				Jim	2	153
				Joe	1½	153
				No 14		9057
Carson, Isabella[49]	130	350				
" " Stiles tr	145	350				
" " Montgomery ?tr	90	300				
Cobb, M. D.	85	927	Cr Crk	Ezra	80	87½
				Molly	12	875
				Abram	9	700
				Philis	24	1070
				Anderson	2	175
				Betsey	18	1225
				Billy	1	87½
				No 7		4200
Dickey, And. J.[50]	270	1650		Jack	73	131
				Ann	13	1181
				No 2		1312
Dickey, And J. ?Flyo	50	200	[Preceding and next two tracts bracketed]			
" " Mill tr	116	1100				
" " ?gt. Jas.						
" " Hoyle tr	54	500				
" " Floyd "	151	200				
" " W. Patterson tr	100	700				
J. Peterson	150	1050				
Ferguson, Jas. Senr	233	2600	Cr Crk	No 2 [no slaves listed]		1014
Falls, Robt. A.	126	350	Cr Crk			
" " Ola tr	100	1050				
Falls, Rebecca[51]	99	1350				
Falls, Wm.[52]	337	2200	?Intent?	Jchech??	9	787
				No 1		787
Falls, Wm. Agt J. M?iane				Keeve	9	787
				No 1		787
Ferguson, Wm. M.	482	2400				
Ferguson, Wm. Tr Thos. F.	111	1200				
Ferguson, Elis. J.	89	800				
Ferguson, Jas. Jur[53]	108	150				
" "	100	300	[Bracked with preceding entry]			
Ferguson, Thos. Senr[54]	201	800				
" " ola tr	220	1500				
Ferguson, Milton	41	200				
Ferguson, Thos. W. Jr.	100	800				
Forbes, John H.[55]	195	500				

Taxable	Acres	Value	Location	Slave	Age	Value
Froneberger, Lewis	220	1500				
Foy, James[56]	39½	120	Cr Mt.			
Falls, Jno. R.	533	7000	Cr Creek	York	55	525½
" " Bell tr	105	1000	" "	Tom	62	262½
				Adaline	46	612½
				Philis ?1 arm?	45	262½
				Margaret	26	1137½
				Eli	22	1312½
				Calvin	19	1312½
				Lepsey	17	1137½
				Walker	15	1093¾
				Ann	15?	1137½
				No 11		8794
Ford, J. W.	933	1600		Jeff	60	175
				Phebe	34	875
				Nelly	32	787½
				Lepsey	12	962½
				Lewis	10	962½
				Henry	8	700
				Hannah	7	568¾
				Mariah	7	568¾
				Gilbert	4	371¾
				Alex	2	171
				No 10		6146
Gamble, Robt. F.[57]	87	550	C. C.	Lea	19	1225
				Jacob	2	175
				No	2	1400
Gamble, A. J. by Robt.	93	800	C. C.	Nelly	40	656
				Gev.	9	787
				No 2		1443
Henry, Thos. C.	140	650				
Hill, Alex M.	132	1200				
Hays, Marys Est.	79	100				
Holland, ?Pns. R.	180	1660		Frank	53	350
McIlwain	107	400		Alse? [Alex]	43	262½
				Dinah	27	962½
				?Rariah?	16	1050
				Alex	11	875
				George deaf	9	262½
				Caroline	7	568¾
				Grace	5	350
				Sam	3	262½
				Sandy	2/12	43¾
				Harriet	6/12	525½
				Susan	3/12	43¾
				Miles	1	109¾
				No 12		5657
Henderson, Wm.	71	500	Crowders Crk			
Hill, ?G. S.	126	1600	" "	Dine	around 25	525½
" "	3½	25		Bill	23	1268¾
				Richard	15	1225
				Rhine	9	612½
				Rufus	7	612½
				Sam	4	393¾
				Joe	2	196¾
				John	4/12	43¾
				Vice	62	131¼
				No 9		5009
Holland, W. R. Guard.				Cephas	16	1312½
				Tom	12	1006
				Fed	9	787½
				No 3		3106
Lowrance, M. C.[58]	83	350	C. Crk			
Love, Eliza E.	124	1000		Tildah	18	525½
" " Mt tr	191	191		Alfred	16	1137½
				No 2		1663

Taxable	Acres	Value	Location	Slave	Age	Value
Love, May				Beny	15	1050
				No 1		1050
Love, Naomi E.[59]	93	1000		George	43	875
" " Mt tr.	65	65		Amanda	14	1137
				Abram	9	787½
				No 3		2799
Love, Jennet	171	800		Roxanna	7	612½
				Margaret	1	109¼
				No 2		721
Love, Sarah				Mingo	12	1006
				No 1		1006
Love, May M. A.	200	1500		Moses	25	1268
				No 1		1268
Love, Isabella S.	386	2500				
Love, Mary (widow)				Hany	13	918
				No 1		918
McGrady, Jno.[60]	50	300				
McGrady, Wm.[61]	91	300				
McNair, Enock[62]	141	1200		Amzi	25	1225
				No 1		1225
McLurd, Jas. H.	403	4400				
Mendenhall, Eli[63]	136	1200				
" " for J. H.				Priscilla	37	525½
				Andy	21	1312½
				George	2	175
				No 3		2013
McAlister, G. W.[64]	94	800				
Oates, Wm.[65]	84	400		Laura	?13	1137½
	83	250		No 1		1137
Obrian, Drucilla	40	40				
Patterson, Wm.	75	200				
Packard, Wm.	50	150	Kings Mt.[66]			
Petty, C. ?Q.[67]	311	3000	Cr Crk	Lewis	21	1312½
				Anne	25	1050
				Rachel	21	1137½
				Hister	5	437½
				Martha	5	437½
				Jno.	1	87½
				Ben	2	196
				Haley	3/12	43¾
				No 8		4703
Pearson, Wm.[68]	106	500				
Revels, Gabl[69]	217	350?				
" " Barber tr	160	450				
Service, Saml T.[70]	60	450				
" " old tr	145	950				
Sammons, R. L.	70	770				
Wilson, L. & E. B.	678	698		Charlotte	50	131¼
" " Lawson[71]	445	7000		Grace	51	175
				Charles	38	875
				George B. S.	31	1312½
				Sandy	41	787½
				Christy	27	612½
				Dare	27	700
				Cinda	29	700
				Harriet	13	875
				Minor	10	744¾
				Leander	9	350
				Sophia	8	568¾
				Flora	6	437½
				George	3	262½
				Fite or Tite	14	90
				Margaret	10	700
				Martha	8	568¾
				Miles	6	?4814
				Laura	5	437¼
				Jim	4	350

Taxable	Acres	Value	Location	Slave	Age	Value
				Patsey	13	1181¼
				Gracy	11	831¼
				No 22		13,191
Wilson, Edwin	93	800	Cr Crk			
Wilson, E. B.[72]	500	3200		Fan	50	175
" " Mt tr	176	176		Bettie Defic	43	350
				Fite	35	875
				Emeline	17	1225
				Cyrus	16	1137½
				Petre	15	875
				Rinah	13	962½
				Lawson	8	700
				Charlotte	3/12	43¾
				No 9		6343
Wilson, Saml M.	100	200		Lawson	10	787
				No 1		787
Whitesides, Edwd[73]	196½	3000		Peter	5	481
				No 1		481
Whitesides, Edwd as Gud ?S. Ml	154	700				
Whitesides, Mary[74]	70	500				
Wier, W. O. Admr	178	1200				
Of A. Wier Esqr. Gill tr	207	630				
" " Entry	16 2/3?	17				
Wilson, Wm.[75]	215	1200				
Wilson, Saml.[76]	165	500				
Torrence, W. W.[77]	217	2300		Margaret	17	962½
				Gilly	9	912½
				Du?ffy	6	525½
				Columbus	3	131¼
				Grace	2	153
				Charles	1	87½

Assessment of Land and Slaves for 1863 Dallas Com[pany]

Taxable	Acres	Value	Location	Slave	Age	Value
Brown, J. L.	73	400	Olney Br.			
Black, Saml Esqr	3	15	Kettle Shoal[78]			
Bell, John[79]	230	1700				
?Barrett, E. S. for						
M. L. Phifer	158	1600				
For						
J. Phifer				Ezra	50	
				Tilda	16	
				No 2		[no value given]
Costner, Joseph	90	550	Kettle Shoal			
Costner, Vs Heirs	280	1225				
" "	51	325				
" "	213	950				
Costner, Henry	307½	2475		Delph	55	371
				Rine? Or Rene	21	928
				?Fredaline	3	132
				No 3		1431
" " as Admr Of Jacob	301	1800		Harriet not snd	40	461
				Kate	10	649
				Reuben	6	461
				John	4	278
				Sallay	½	98
				No 5		1947
" " for Ambrose	275	2550				
Cloninger, David[80]	65	325	Olney Br			
Cloninger, Jonas[81]	109	550	Olney Br			
Clemmer, Levi	96	800	B. L. Crk[82]			
Clemmer, L. L.	140	875	B. L. Crk	Hillory	22	1578
				No 1		1578

Taxable	Acres	Value	Location	Slave	Age	Value
Clemmer, Arabella[83]	88	400	B. L. Crk			
Clemmer, Adam[84]	371	2850	Little L. C.[85]			
Clemmer, Georges Est.[86]	209	1850		Hannah	44	928
				Ann	21	1392½
				Jim	19	1484¾
				Lid not sd	17	649¾
				Nance	14	1021
				Jane	14	1021
				Rhoda	11	742½
				Abe	9	742½
				Chila	¼	92¾
				No 9		8071
Costner, J. P.[87]	218	1200	K. Shoals	Silvy	39	742½
	75	450	K. Shoals	Mose not sd	16	464¼
	62	375	S. Fork	Bill	5	371
				Barbara	2	278
				Roy	80	
				No 5		[no value]
Lineburger, Jno.	227	1500	S. Fork			
Lineburger, J. W.	169	1150	S. Fork			
Lineburger, Margaret	130	800	S. Fork	Ann	46	649¾
				Mary not sound	40	46½
				?Sefe	30	1484¾
				Isaac	19	1578½
				Marcus	16	1298½
				Gustus N. S.	14	742½
				Adaline	14	928¼
				Sidney	10	557
				Kate	6	464
				Alburtus	3	223
				No 10		7979
Lineburger, Michael[88]	166	1100	S. Fork			
Lineburger, L. J.	79	575	S. Fork			
Lineburger, F. L. Hoffman	71	550				
Lineburger, Caleb[89]	130	1225	B. S. Crk			
Lineburger, Jonas[90]	98	1000	B. S. Crk			
Friday, David[91]	388	2750	K. Shoals	Lawson	16	1392½
				Sarah	13	742½
				No 2		2134
Friday, M. D.	?316	1350	K. Shoals	Monroe	24	1671
" " as Adm						
" " Jno Friday	321	2550		Bill	56	557
				Alfred	23	1392
				Pink	20	1578
				Ann	22	1206¾
				Elmina	22	1114
				Frances	3	278½
				No 6		6125
Friday, M. D. for M. Link	180	1100	K. S.[92]			
Friday, Elisabeth[93]				Caleb	42	928
				Clem	34	1114
				Abe	70	159
				No 3		2181
Featherstone, James B.[94]	130	725	L. L. Crk			
Flowers, Green[95]	136	600	L. L. Crk			
Froneburger, Ambrose[96]	217	1475	L. L. Crk			
Fraley, Stephen[97]	89	300	L. L. Crk			
Ford, Amzi[98]	?3=48	450	Dallas	[Probably town lot]		
	=10	100		[Probably town lot]		
	5	25	Catawba Crk[99]	[all three were bracketed together]		
Fronebarger, Jac. Jr.	192	2325	Ridge	Fite	60	371
				Charles	28	1578
				Elmina	19	1392½
				Ann	11	835
				Bob	2	139

Taxable	Acres	Value	Location	Slave	Age	Value
				Charlotte	¼	92
				No 6		4407
" " ?G a W. F. Holland				Caroline	33	1206¾
				Caharine	13	928
				Laben	10	835½
				John	8	640¾
				Susan	4	278½
				No 5		3887
Gladden, Jno. J.[100]	170	950	Ridge	Ruben	21	1578
				Nathan	18	1485
				Lewis	16	1299¾
				Cloa	13	1121
				May	45	464
				No 5		[no value given]
Hovis, Absalom	500	2625	Dallas			
	167	700	S. Fork			
Holland, J. D. for E. B.	30	1300	Dallas			
Holland, Julius[101]	129	1325	Little L. Crk			
" "	1-50	25	Dallas	[Probably town lot]		
" "	1	50	Dallas	[Probably town lot]		
Hoffman, Daniel	428	4175	Mill tract	Ginney	90	
	270	2500	Tuckasge	Ione	60	185
	4-8[102]	200	Tan Yd	Ike	46	1114
				Jim	45	464
				Viney	52	742
				Jane	42	742
				Cephus	24	1485
				Betty not Sound	10	464
				Amos	6	464
				?Flory	5	371
				Charlotte	2	139
				No 11		6170
Hoyle, C. W.[103]	850	9000	S. Fork	Dan	71	46½
				Betty	76	46¼
				Matt	50	649¼
				Caroline	41	742½
				Ben	25	1671
				Cansada	18	1392½
				Elmina	16	1392½
				Elvira	14	1297½
				Frances	11	898½
				Linda	32	1206¾
				Cate	17	1392½
				Laban	15	1297¾
				Violet	10	742¾
				Jane	12	928¼
				Jim	9	649¾
				Adaline	7	557¼
				Bob	5	371¼
				Ann Sickly	29	92¾
				Tom	9	649¾
				Mag	7	557
				Joe	5	371¼
				Hoyl	4	278½
				Charles	2	139¼
				Jeff	5/12	92¾
				Nelson D & Dumb	39	371¼
				Rufus	37	1392½
				Alace	55	1392½
				Bill	27	1206¾
				Saml Def Dumb	19	371¼
				John	23	1392½
				Sarah	21	1298½
				No 31		24,875
Holland, Robert[104]	343	1800	B. Crk	Lucy	10	
" "	183	1450	Dallas	George	24	1494

Taxable	Acres	Value	Location	Slave	Age	Value
" " for ABR	20	1600	Mill tract	No 2		1494
Hoffman, David	230	1550	LL Crk			
Jenkins, Eli	47	300	Ridge			
Jenkins, Harrison[105]	140	500	Ridge			
Jenkins, Catharine	79	400				
Jenkins, Aaron	150	825				
Jenkins, Joseph[106]	121	1000				
Jenkins, Berryman	54	375	Ridge			
Jarrett, Saml.[107]	85	650	B L Crk	Cyrus	26	1392
				No 1		1392
Jenkins, Wm.	426	4875	B. L. Crk	?Lize	55	557
				Philis	49	185½
				Jake	18	1578½
				John not sd.	18	640
				Florence	18	1392½
				Delph	14	1021
				Cephus	15	1398½
				Kate	10	835
				Lee	¼	92¾
				No 9		7602
Jenkins, Smith[108]	161	800				
	155	800	[both are bracketed]			
Kahnniler, K.	11¼	600	Tanyard			
Long, Andrew	160	1450				
McAlister, H. C.	121	725				
Obrian, (Widow)[109]	246	1175	Olney Br			
" "	40	75	Crowders Ck			
Pasour, Hannah[110]	69	175	Ridge	Ike	46	649
" "	53	150		No 1		649
" "	11	25	[bracketed together]			
Pasour, Saml.[111]	284	900				
Pasour, Jacob[112]	2½	200	Dallas			
Pasour, Manassah	220	1000	Kettle Shl	Lydia Bld	60	[no value]
	161	750		Caroline	16	1392½
	88	150		Martin	17	1568½
	105	325		Joe	14	1205¾
				Margaret	12	928¼
				No 5		5103
Pasour, George[113]	117	375	Kettle Shl	Lucy	70	
Peterson, J. R.[114]	109	925	S. F.			
Pasour, Levi	136	350	Olney Br			
Rhyne Jos. K.[115]	147	1200	Olney Br			
Rhyne, Jacob K.	175	1250				
Robison, Nancy[116]	180	1350	B L Crk			
Rhyne, A. A.[117]	137	1225		Philip	55	599½
				Martina	21	1392½
				Caroline	10	742½
				Luckey	2	139½
				No 4		2872
Rhyne, Dorcus[118]	280	2575	B. L. Crk	Ann	70	
				Jim	37	1205¼
				Mary	32	1114
				?Critty	40	1021
				Cephe (idiot)	15	278½
				Wade	11	835½
				Boo	6	599½
				Laban	4	371¼
				No 8		5423
Rhyne, J. J. Est[119]	564	5150				
Rhyne, Jacob M.[120]	1108	7150		Sarah not sd	50	371¼
				Amzi	28	1578½
				?Linzy	20	1021
				Elzy	14	1299½
				John	16	1299½
				Elisabeth	12	928¼
				No 6		6496
Morris, W. G.[121]	301½	1800		Ron	55	557

Appendix

Taxable	Acres	Value	Location	Slave	Age	Value
				Sarah	40	461
				No 2		1081
Rhyne, Christy[122]	741	5725	Big L Crk	Gill	50	46¼
				Lize	50	46¼
				Miles	21	1583¾
				Sarah	13	1206¾
				No 4		2881
Rhyne, Moses H.	40	100	Mitchem			
	33	275	Costner			
	4½	175	Meadow			
Roberts, John H.				Milly	28	1398½
				Mary	17	1299½
				Tom	11	928¼
				Bill	9	742¼
				Pink	6	464¼
				Kitty	5	371¼
				Morris	1½	98¼
				Sam	2	139¼
				No 8		5439
Rhyne, Jacob H.[123]	140	100	from South Point			
Rhyne, Esli	162	1450	S Fork			
Sloan, Wm.[124]	416	2200	Kettle Shoal	Lucy	42	928¼
	334	1325	Mauneys	Adam	40	1671
				Jenny	22	1485¼
				Cass or Cap	16	1299
				Violet	11	835½
				Henry	9	742½
				Emeline	7	464
				Dilsey	18	1299½
				No 8		8723
Setzer, Henry[125]	340	3000	South fork	Jim	40	1021
	390	2750	Mill tract	Cain	35	1398½
				Harriet	20	1299½
				No 3		3718
Smith, Eli[126]	115	825	B. L. Crk			
Smith, Andrew[127]	135	775	Dallas			
	1¼	150	[bracketed]			
Stowe, LeRoy	279	1200	L L Crk	Luckey	40	835½
	70	400	S fork	James	32	1856
	5	25	S fork	Laura	30	1398½
				Joe	22	1671
				John	20	1583¼
				George	15	1266¾
				Burt	14	1021
				Albertine	11	833½
				Boliver	9	742½
				Green	7	557
				Susan	7	464
				Emma	5	371¼
				Bill	3	185½
				Infant	1/12	98¾
				No 14		12,880
Summit, Lawson[128]	1	25		Magdaline	70	46½
				Sarah	30	1299½
				Sylv?	10	835½
				Candace	10	835½
				No 4	Q	3015
Wells, David	273	2200	B L Crk			
Withers, Susanah	33	275	S fork			
" " for sons	2	800	Dallas			
White, Jas. H.[129]	303	2675	L Crk	Milly	60	185½
	25	3800	Mill tract	Albert	26	1583¾
	187	1200	Shetly tract	Andy	23	1485?¾
				Sarah	21	1299½
				No 4		4552
White & Young By J. H. White	1000	1500	Ridge			

Taxable	Acres	Value	Location	Slave	Age	Value
Withers, C. C.	118	850	Big Long Crk			
" " M R						
Withers Admr	103	650	Big Long Crk			
Abernathy, Sterling	60	325	Olney Br			
Deck, Jonas[130]	336	2000	B. L. Crk			
" " for C. Costner	47	300	S. Fork			
Cross, Tabitha[131]	22	100	Kettle Shoal			

Town Property[132]

Taxable	Acres	Value	Location	Slave	Age	Value
Pegram, J. F.[133]	15–1[134]	3000		Vina	60	185½
	78–1	25		Esther	32	1114
	79–1	25		Rilty	30	1206¾
				George	8	649¾
				John	6	464
				Pink	½	99¾
				Sally	9	649¾
				Amanda	7	510½
				Alice	9	649¾
				Kate	3	185½
				Margaret	½	99¾
				No 11		5809
Pegram, J. F. as Exr of W. P.				Anthony (nsd)	44	185¾
				Amzi	24	1671
				John	15	1299¾
				Eliza	32	1206¾
				Amanda	28	1299¾
				Fanny	11	835¼
				Vena	9	649¾
				Jenny	7	510¾
				Cloe	7	510¾
				Milton	5	371¾
				George	2½	185¾
				Ned	2½	185¾
				Wallace idiot		worthless
				No 13		8905
Ward, Mary				Martha	20	1398½
				Milly	3	185½
				Leah	1½	139¼
				No 3		1722
Stowe, F. M.				Lila	23	1398½
				Ann	18	1299½
				Juda	12	928¼
				Charles	2	139¼
				No 4		3764
Gantt, Mary by J. W. Fite				Mera	35	1206¾
				Mack	20	1398½
				Frone	17	1392½
				Hida	1	92¾
				Mary	½	92¾
Hoyle & Co[135] by J. F. Pegram	49–1	150				
Smith, D. B.	38–1	250				
" "	40–1	600				
Rudisill, Jno.	1–59	700		S. W. Love Gd.	2	175 [ambiguous][136]
" "	1–57	300		" "	61	75 [ambiguous]
" "	1–20	300	Oates & Pegram			
				B A Wier	39	100 [ambiguous]
Pasour, S. P.[137]	32	200		Pasour, Eli	8	600[138]
" "	33	400		Rudisell, Jno.	7	175
Groner, Austin[139]	18	500		Rankin, Rich	25	50
Rhyne, M. H.	17	1400		Rankin, J. D.	3	200
Lewis, J. G.[140]	66	400		Wier, Alex	91	25

Taxable	Acres	Value	Location	Slave	Age	Value
" " for						
P. Froneberger Est	41	125		Bradley, Elis.	23	150
	42	125		" "	24	75
Fronebarger, Jacob[141]	16	3000		Dellinger, ?Alj.	82	50
" "	50	50		Friday, J. N.	31	400
" "	67	500		Beattie, Franas	29	50
" "	86	25		" "	30	75
" "	87	25		Rhodes, Caleb	14	500
" "	88	200		Rutledge, Wm.	59	50
" "	89	75		Mason, L. A. ?for?		
" "	64	50		Latta	4	600
" "	58	50	The Following lots unsold 92, 93, 94, 95, 96, 97, $25 each			
Rhyne, Catharine	68	300				
Morris, May[142]	21	500				
	22	100				
Hoffman, Daniel[143]	5	4000[144]				
	19	600				
	83	50				
	84	50				
	85	50				
Jarrett, Saml.	62	400				
Long, Andrew[145]	47	300				
Clemmer, George	10	1800				
All the following were not qualified to viz:						
Beam, J.	9	200				
Holland, W. M.	6	600				
Holland, Jane	46	300				
Mauney	34	150				

Assessment of Land and Slaves
for 1863=Duharts Creek Dist[rict]

Taxable	Acres	Value	Location	Slave	Age	Value
Allen, Nancy L.	129	650	Long Crk			
Armstrong, Mathew[146]	282	1400	Duharts Crk[147]			
" "	28	125	Southfork			
" " J. Martin trct	76	325				
Abernathy, C. H.	250	1500				
Anders, E. M.[148]	64	375	Duharts Crk			
Bradley, Caleb	173	1200	Crowders Crk			
Bradley, A. S.[149]	590	4800	Long Crk			
Bradley, J. W.[150]	233	1600	Long Crk			
Bradley, Eli H.[151]	50	350	Cr Crk			
" " Dilling tr	185½	1000	Cr Crk			
Cox, Eli	237	1000	Duharts Crk			
Cherry, John[152]	143	575	Southfork			
Clemmer, John Ad.	168	1100	Southfork			
" " Linebarger tr	121	300	Southfork			
Davis, O. W.[153]	21	1215	Catawba Crk			
" "	168	900	Catawba Crk			
" " Ex	129	775	Catawba Crk			
" " Mt. tr.	150	800	Southfork			
Davis, John W.	70	350	Catawba Cr			
Dickson, Wm. S.[154]	60	600	Catawba Cr			
Dickson, John T.	247	950	Catawba Cr			
Dickson, Alex	100	850	Catawba Cr			
Floyd, H. H.	105	525	Catawba Cr			
" "	35	100	Ridge			
Floyd, John	234	2300	Duh crk			
Ford, Jas. M.[155]	136	475	Duh Crk			
Ford, Jas. H.	150	675	Duh Crk			
Gaston, Rachel	114	375				
Gaston, Adaline	76	350				
Gaston, Pinckney Erx	230	925				
Gaston, Sarah[156]				Manuel	20	1058
				No 1		1058
Gordon, John[157]	513	1700	Duharts Crk	Thomas	48	411
				James	45	411

Gaston County Tax List of 1863

Taxable	Acres	Value	Location	Slave	Age	Value
				Adaline	40	176
				Franklin	14	1058
				Rufus	12	940
				Moses	10	823
				No 6		3819
Grissom,	108	425	Duharts Crk			
Gingles, Mary	61	300	Duharts Crk			
Hanna, Jas. M.[158]	106	550	Catawba Crk			
" " Dameron tr	158	800	Catawba Crk			
Hanna, Saml. B.[159]	73	500	Catawba Crk			
Hanna, Thos. M.[160]	100	500	Catawba Crk			
Holland, M. L.[161]	122½	750	Catawba Crk			
Holland, W. R.[162]	1048	10,000	Catawba Crk	Green	40	1058
				Anise?	35	1058
				Ann	27	882
				James	20	1058
				Louisa	11	764
				Andy	7	529
				Isabel	5	411
				Minerva	3	294
				No 8		6054
Holland, Mary C.[163]				Aggy	60	
				Salina	50	235
				Ned	31	1175
				Thos.	21	1058
				Harriet	16	999
				No 5		3467
Houser, Abram[164]	136	700	S. F.			
Holland, Nancy J.				Prince	37	1127
				Amanda	25	999
				Miraim	12	823
				Rose	?3/12	294
				John	1	147
				No 5		3390
Holland, M. M.				Eli	27	1058
				Minerva	24	999
				Missouri	23	999
				Violet	13	882
				Lizzie	2	206
				No 5		4144
						[written in pencil]
Hand, Uriah[165]	70	300	Cat Crk			
Hoffman, John	85¼	385	Long Crk	Ezekiel	37	882
				Fanny	23	999
				Mary	6	670
				Cephas	7½	103
				No 4		2654
Hoffman, Jacob	200	1900	D. Crk			
Hoffman, Miles[166]	333	1500	S. Fork			
Hoffman, Jonas[167]	140	1400	D. Crk	Ann	63	
" " Linebarger tract	99	500		Joe	32	1058
				Minty	25	999
				Charles	4½	382
				Cephus	1½	200
				No 5		2645
Hoffman, Solomon[168]	123	1250	S. F.			
Helton, Milton	121	1000				
Jenkins, Jonas	63¾	325	Long Crk			
	16	50	Long Crk			
Jenkins, Daniel	75	325	Long Crk			
Leeper, Mary	99	500	D C			
Love, R. C. G.[169]	178	1050	C. C.	Peter	16	1058
				Joseph	11	764
				No 2		1822
Linebarger, Cath	213	1075	Long Crk			
Linebarger, Peter	50	400	D C			
Linebarger, C. J.[170]	161	4000	D. Crk	Jane	65	

Taxable	Acres	Value	Location	Slave	Age	Value
				David	50	588
				Ben	33	1058
				Ann	33	647
				Joe	26	1058
				Adeline	16	999
				Henry	12	852
				Elisabeth	11	764
				Ephraim	8	588
				Ambrose	4	351
				Ezekiel	2	235
				Roxan	2	89
				No 12		7229
Linebarger, J. L.[171]	528	3500	S. F.	Comfort	80	
				Batey	47	588
				James	40	647
				Berry	20	1058
				Jinney	45	411
				Dilcey	27	812
				Sarah	25	940
				Jane	20	999
				Caroline	6	690
				Lize	5	411
				James	2	235
				Sophia	10/12	117
				Andy	2	235
				Laura	4	351
				Jessey	7	529
				No 15		8023
Linebarger, L. & Co[172]	665	50,000	S. Fork	Mike	23	882
				Saml.	20	1058
				William	18	1058
				Laban	16	1058
				Joseph	15?	882
				Andy	31	1175
				Nancy	23	999
				Infant	1 8/12	206
				No 8		7318
Lay, W. B.[173]	50¼	350				
" "	90	630				
Lay, Jesse[174]	75	350				
Lay, C. H.[175]	129¾	850				
Mason, L. A.	438	4000	Long Crk	Eliza	40	529
				Alice	24	999
				Giles		1058
				Eliza	18	999
				Jacob	17	1058
				Louisa	14	940
				Thornton	12	823
				Caser	12	823
				Dick	12	823
				George	8	588
				Cylva	10	702
				Clara	8	670
				No 12		10,012
Morrow, S. L.	168	1250	Cr Crk	Julia	40	294
				Mary	20	999
				Oliver	8	329
				Peter	?2½	206
				No 4		2028
McCready	50	400	Cr Crk			
Murrell, Isaac[176]	245	800	Long Crk	Minerva	31	676
" "	239	800	Long Crk	Perlina	28	882
				Pinckney	22	1058
				Jane	12	823
				Aggy	10	702
				Melissa	11	764
				Joseph	7	529

Taxable	Acres	Value	Location	Slave	Age	Value
				Beauregard	6	670
				Nancy	5	411
				John	3	294
				Charlotte	?½	89
				No 11		6898
McKee, Jemima				Emeline	20	117
				Dallas	17	1058
				No 2		1175
Noland, M. L.	111	800	Long Crk			
Perkins, Isaac[177]	104½	325	Long Crk			
Plonk, Jacob McAl	70	2210	Long Crk			
" " Hazlitt tr	250	750	Long Crk			
" " Spencer Mt	140½	70	Long Crk			
Quinn, J. R.[178]	264½	1500	Catawba Cr	Patsey	43	411
				Rachel	11	764
				Jane	7	529
				Margaret	4	351
				No 4		2055
Rhyne, Jonathan[179]	423	2200	L. Crk			
" " Adm	215	800				
Rhyne, Jacob H.[180]	747	7500				
" " Wheeler tr	509	2500	Cr Crk	Porter	46	411
				Eliza	17½	999
				Alice	14	940
				Amanda	14	823
				Jane	3	394
				Ned	⅓?	89
				No 6		3556
Rhyne, Daniel[181]	368	1400	Duharts Crk	Mindra?	30	588
				Jefferson	25	1058
				Margaret	3	206
				Elisabeth	1	117
				No 4		1969
Rhyne, Jacob A.[182]	136	550	Duharts Cr			
Rhyne, Emanuel[183]	153	775	Long Crk			
Ratchford	233	1150	Catawba			
Rankin, Rebecca	57	275	D Crk			
Reed, Eliza	98	400	D Crk			
Sarvice, Saml.	60	350	Crow Crk			
Stowe, E. A.	61	225	D. Crk	Jacob	65	117
				No 1		117
Smith, J. D.	253	1250	D. Crk			
McArver tr	140	1100	D. Crk			
Suggs, Mary S.[184]	70	300	D Crk			
Stroup, Rebecca	233	700	D Crk			
Stroup, Rufus[185]	67	200				
Stroup, Wesley	184	650				
Shannon, Hugh	245	1250				
Shannon, James	201	1250				
Stowe, Logan	83	550				
Stowe, J. R. Est.	155	900				
Stowe, Delphia	77	465				
Selvy, Wm.[186]	96	575				
Spencer, Wm.[187]	10	50	Catawba Cr			
Stowe, Jasper			South Fork			
Titman, A. B.	448	2700	D. Crk	Sophia	69	[no value]
" " Admr	161	485		Granville	30	1058
				Rhoda	28	764
				Jacob	10	702
				Miles	8	529
				Wilburn	4	351
				Mary	2	235
				No 7		3639
Titman, Anthony	200	1900	South Fork			
Whitesides, Wm.[188]	148½	1150	Crowders Cr			
Whitesides, Edward	113	600	Crowders Cr			
Wilson, Thomas	317	1900	Long Crk	Philis	24	940

Appendix

Taxable	Acres	Value	Location	Slave	Age	Value
				No 1		940
Wilson, Robert	500	2500	Crowders Cr			
Williams, C. H.	163	1100	Duharts Cr			

Assessment of Land and Slaves for 1863 High Shoals Dist[rict]

Taxable	Acres	Value	Location	Slave	Age	Value
Aydlotte, Susan[189]				Grace	36	648
				Trifena	8	567
				Tom	16	1134
				Jane	9	648
				No 4		2997
Arents, Jonas heirs	46	375	Hoyles Crk			
Bynum, Martha	165	500	Hoyles Crk			
Black, Vincent[190]	132	1200	Southfork			
Beattie, Rufus	61	300	Brevards St[191]			
Barron, B. B.				Wash	6	526
				Isaac	40	810
				Infant		81
				West	3	243
				Lewis	9	648
				Sidney	10	688
				Hin?on	35	1053
				Henry	9	648
				Mark	18	1215
				Willis	30	1174
				Dick	18	1174
				May	19	972
				Manda	11	648
				Love	2	162
				Temp	10	648
				Martha	32	648
				Lucy	1	81
				Edy	36	162
				Dilsey	65	81
				Jane	1	81
				Isam	6	526
				John	22	1215
				Bill	40	810
				Turner?	38	972
				Monroe	40	810
				Jack	8	608
				Eph.	21	810
				Infant		81
				Hillyard	20	1215
				Bill		81
				Olive	45	405
				Morning	32	648
				?Cab or Cub	9	608
				Fanny	36	567
				Milly	7	486
				Peggy	7	486
				Mary	6	486
				Louisa	13	810
				May	30	810
				Mary	21	972
				Bat	14	972
				Ellice	40	810
				Bill	9	648
				Dan	11	648
				Henry	12	932
				Janie	4	364
				Alfred	25	1215
				Susan	22	1215
				Tom	33	1215
				?Bretis	20	1215
				Mariah	38	486

Taxable	Acres	Value	Location	Slave	Age	Value
				Ninif?	14	810
				Miram	5	324
				Emaline	13	810
				Violet	5	324
				Ester	3	202
				Dinah	2	201
				Betty?	8	486
				Ann	18	972
				Leah	19	972
				No 61		38,569
Bridges, R. R.[192]				Danse	35	1053
				Ben	22	1215
				George	21	1620
				Charles	21	1215
				Joe	53	405
				Dick	37	810
				Jenny	30	1175
				Nash	21	1215
				Ashley	18	1215
				Aaron	48	567
				Fields	14	932
				Keener	14	931
				George	9	648
				Wash	10	648
				Robt	6	486
				Dan	45	729
				Suck	13	810
				Isabel	4	324
				Pamela	26	324
				Rachel	33	648
				Hasley	33	648
				Clarrisa	11	648
				Jane	4	324
				Caroline	14	810
				Lizzie	25	972
				Betsey	36	324
				Betsey	2	182
				Lewis	36	486
				Harrison	33	1053
				John	23	1215
				Allen	21	1215
				Rasbourn	45	729
				Jerry	35	1053
				Joe	20	1215
				Wm	18	1215
				Herbert	32	648
				Frank	21	1215
				Cane	13	931
				Wm	5	365
				Grier	6	486
				Henry	8	427
				Eph	1	81
				Anna	8	527
				Lucy	12	810
				Hannah	28	810
				Lucy	26	891
				Jane	17	972
				Miriam	12	810
				Nancy	4	324
				Fanny	2	163
				Harretta	3	103
				Martha	25	972
				Chole	12	810
				Nathan	25	1215
				?Fisher	21	1215
				?Fenton	21	1215
				Philis or Lilus	22	1215

Appendix

Taxable	Acres	Value	Location	Slave	Age	Value
				Wash	50	567
				Riddick	35	1053
				Hines	22	1215
				David	20	1215
				Liberty	30	?427
				Charles	15	931
				Bob	14	932
				Frank	1	81
				Sam	4	365
				Isaac	8	427
				Isaac	4	324
				Leroy?	30	810
				Betty	25	972
				Eliza	18	972
				Junea	53	162
				Sally	15	832
				Elvey	35	648
				Charinsa?	30	810
				Charty	35	648
				Ninerva	32	648
				Alice	8	486
				Allen	6	486
				[no totals given	79	60,275]
Bridges, Jno. L.[193]				Jim	45	729
				Dan	20	1215
				Sam	2	162
				Lawrence	25	1215
				Cornelius	4	324
				Louis	28	1174
				Austin	27	1174
				Owen	5	972
				Arther	32	1094
				Green	17	1134
				Frank	22	1215
				Vergo	4	324
				Reuben	5	405
				Boon	34	1053
				Wash	3	243
				Ellis	6	486
				Tom	13	823
				Milley	11	648
				Lula	26	648
				Susan	18	972
				Mel?vina	7	486
				Rose	28	810
				Hisber?	2	162
				Leah	8	486
				Infant		81
				Emily	20	972
				Betsey	1	81
				Nerla	3	486
				Nina	6	486
				?Judy	41	446
				Ned	53	324
				Joe	22	1215
				Ron	6	486
				Henry	26	1174
				?Took	20	1215
				George	24	1215
				Stewart	20	1215
				Charles	38	810
				Calvin	6	486
				Ben	25	608
				Hill?	17	1134
				Silas	23	1215
				Bill	3	254
				Aaron	8	567

Taxable	Acres	Value	Location	Slave	Age	Value
				Frank	10	689
				?Ireal	20	1215
				Isam	35	1053
				Fanny	7	508
				Milly	9	508
				Patsey	14	810
				Betty	5	324
				Ann	8	486
				Infant		81
				Becca	18	972
				Jane	26 months	
				Snowrance	17	972
				Hannah	42	405
				Hannah	55	283
				Sarah	30	810
				Charlotte	?53	648
				Fed	24	1215
				Martin	4	365
				Cicero	23	1215
				Amos	14	972
				Peel	24	1215
				George	20	1215
				Nan	6	486
				Polly	24	972
				Clara	24	162
				Ruth	11	648
				Amos	4	324
				George	17	1174
				John	6	486
				Harris	20	1215
				Edward	22	1215
				Dan	15	832
				Steve	34	1053
				Infant		81
				Grand	4	324
				Levi	8	567
				Nathan	22	1215
				Siller	40	486
				Fanny	11	648
				Pheby	38	?526
				Tilda	12	729
				Caroline	2	162
				Silvey	4	526
				Pheby	38	526
				Edd	2	162
				Betsey	42	405
				No 90		63,115
Cloninger, Mike[194]	116	750	Railroad			
Cloninger, Elis R. (wid)	180	1100	Hoyles Crk[195]	Roxann	28	810
				Eph. Refuegee		1215
				No 2		2228
" "	49	500	Hoyles Crk	Fanny	2	202
Cloninger, Moses	142	700	Hoyles Crk	Boy Refuge	13	1050?
" "	72	450	" "	No 1		1050
" "	50	525	" " [three bracketed together]			
Cloninger, Fanny	81	200				
Derr, Jno. H.[196]	60	150	Hoyles Crk	[ditto marks written over ~~Tuckasege~~]		
Dellinger, Alfred	53	200				
Friday, Ephraim[197]	483	3750	S. Fork	Tiny	54	527
				Sarah	40	162
				Ben	37	810
				Margaret	26	792
				Adam	24	1458
				Eliza	22	972
				?Grief?	19	1215
				Sidney	17	1134
				Joseph	14	932

Taxable	Acres	Value	Location	Slave	Age	Value
				Delphia	13	769
				George	11	689
				John	10	648
				Wade	8	527
				Sam	6	486
				Andy	4	243
				Albert	3	162
				Martin	10	81
				Marshal	7	81
				Elitha	52	162
				Harriet	11	648
				Cephas	15	932
				No 21		13,432?
Friday, Jno. N.[198]	624	5000	Hoyles Crk	Mary	29	729
				Judy	34	324
				Barbara	22	972
				Jim	18	1215
				Mary	14	972
				Mariah	10	648
				Arther	3	243
				Infant		81
				Sally	52	162
				Henry	42	891
				Charles 3	1	1134
				Cephas	17	1174
				Dorcus	12	972
				Tom	7	527
				James	3	243
				Infant		81
				Walt?	44	810
				Joe	34	1215
				Elmina	28	810
				Betsey	15	972
				Frances	10	648
				Clem	6	486
				Angeline	2	162
				No 23		15,671
Friday, Polly[199]				Adam	70	81
				Rufus	46	324
				No 2		405
Friday, Elizabeth[200]	92	900	Hoyles Crk	Sarah	11	648
" "	5	150	" "	Jilius	14	932
				Augustus	8	527
				No 3		2107
Friday, Michael[201]	435	6000	Southfork	Jeff	33	1053
				Jack	30	1175
				Mary	28	810
				July	12	810
				Nancy	7	486
				Addeph	3	243
				Luther	2	162
				Saml	70	243
				Dolly	72	81
				No 9		5163
Friday, Jacob W.[202]	101	900	Hoyles Crk	Tom	51	405
	7	225	" "	Milton	30	1175
				Susan	34	324
				Eli	12	811
				No 4		2715
Gregory, S. B.		111	550	Hoyles Crk	Henry	18	1215
				Musk	18	1215
				No 2		2420
						Refugees
High Shoal Iron Co.[203]	14,750	90,000	S. Fork	Edow	42	1215
			Long Crk	Willie m	21	1408
For Cook of VA				Wm m	28	1620
				French	20	1215

Taxable	Acres	Value	Location	Slave	Age	Value
				Abraham	30	1175
				Sip	40	810
				No 6		7493
						Refugees
" " for Dr Wallace of NC				Tim	32	1053
				Ann	20	1215
				Ann	19	972
				?Gragel	19	972
				No 4		4212
" " for Garlond NC				Man	40	810
				Woman	25	972
				Infant		81
				No 3		1863
" " Widow Styren NC				Man	25	1215
				No 1		1215
Hovis, Adam	186	1150	Hoyle Crk			
Hovis, Philip	236	1000	R. Road[204]			
Hovis, Jacob[205]	35	200	H C			
Kistler, Lawson	30	150	H C			
Linebarger, J. D.	124	1250	H C			
Linebarger, Eli	46	375	H C			
Moore, Mary				Emanuel	47	561
				Easter	38	162
				Jasper	14	891
				Houston	81	[no value given]
				Rufus	45	729
				Rebecca	16	972
				Henry	4	324
				[no statistics given]		
Moore, Margaret				Abram	44	729
				No 1		729
Moore, John C.	343	1800	Hoyle Crk	Mariah	7	486
" "	54	300	Rail Road	No 1		486
Moore, Ann	54	300	Rail Road			
Morris, Stephen	250	1500	Hoyle Crk			
McGinnis, J. A.	207	1100	Hoyle Crk	Eliza	25	952
	46	200	" "	Mary	6	486
				France	4	324
				Mike	2	162
				Infant		81
				No 5		1985
" " Trustee of Mary Smith	50	150	Hoyle Crk	Caroline	38	486
				Isaac	28	1175
				Stewart	23	1134
				Mary	14	810
				Elvey	13	729
				No 5		4434
Nantz, Lawson[206]	25	100	Ridge			
Oglisby, Saml.	82	400	Hoyl Crk			
Plonk, J. F.[207]	182	1900	Hoyl Crk			
" "	44	150	Hoyl Crk			
" "	7	225	High Shoal			
Pasour, G. I.[208]	59	475	Vestals Ford[209]			
Powell, J. W. Est.				Henry	40	648
				Mose	40	810
				Toney	27	810
				Harry	28	1175
				Charles	18	1215
				John	15	972
				Henry	27	1175
				Jesse	6	486
				?Sack	12	832
				Holly	22	1215
				Wm	30	1134
				Lucy	7	486
				Caroline	3	103
				Judy	32	648

220   Appendix

Taxable	Acres	Value	Location	Slave	Age	Value
				Ann	5	324
				Caroline	1	81
				Caroline	33	162
				Lucy	38	486
				Milly	4	324
				Milly	4	324
				Phillip	40	729
				Jack	40	810
				Edmond	28	1175
				Carry	16	1153
				Harry	16	1134
				Dick	14	832
				Lewis	10	648
				Dennis	8	567
				Mice	4	324
				Madison	16	1134
				Osca	9	648
				Mack	9	648
				Laura	5	324
				Infant		81
				Eliza	22	972
				Wince	20	648
				Winner?	20	972
				Laney	11	648
				Betty	34	648
				Henry	60	122
				Elijah	40	810
				Carry	30	1134
				Spree	24	1215
				Henry	18	1215
				Dick	30	1134
				Bill	12	832
				Dudley	6	486
				Norol	2	162
				Smith	18	1215
				Eurre?	3	243
				Jane	34	162
				Dice	30	810
				Easter	32	163
				Lavinia	1	81
				George	6	486
				Louisa	16	972
				Manda	32	642
				Titus	6	486
				No 57		39,456
Rutledge, Robt	357	5000	Hoyl Crk	Amanda	17	972
" "	56	375	Rail Road	Grief or Gruf	20	325
				No 2		1297
Rutledge, James	58	325	Rail Road			
Rhodes, Melchi[210]	420	3000	Hoyl Crk			
Rhodes, M & C	1	1000	S Fork			
Rhodes, Caleb[211]	416	5000	S. Fork	Clim	34	1053
				Manda	30	648
				Edward	10	648
				Mat	6	486
				Bill	2	162
				Isaac	28	1175
				Jim	11	891
				Nercis	7	486
				Texann	4	324
				No 9		5873
Rutledge, A. R. Agt W. C. & R. Rho.	100	2500	Brevards D[212]			
Rhyne, Solomon[213]	200	2000	S. Fork	Willy	20	972
	130	1300	H Crk	Cephas	14	832
				Child	2	162
				Margaret	17	972

Taxable	Acres	Value	Location	Slave	Age	Value
				Julian	10	648
				No 5		3586
" " heirs	301	1200	S. Fork			
Robison, Thomas	48	150	Ridge			
Richards, Wm.	5	200	Brevards Depot			
Smith, Mary	46	275	R. R.			
Smith, David	113	300	W. H?. Crk			
Summey, Elisabeth	214	1500	Sheep hollow	Levi	35	1053
" "	162	1300	S. Fork	No 1		1053
Stroup, Caroline	40	125	W. H. Crk			
Stroup, Bartlette[214]	147	600	" "			
" "	60	300	" "			
Stroup, Benjamin	103	400	" "			
Stroup, Jane	116	300	" "			
Stroup, Hosea[215]	122	750	" "			
Stroup, John D.	68	450		Amy	45	162
				Silvanus	6	486
				Jim	3	243
				Violet	18	972
				Perry	4	324
				No 5		2187
Stroup, Nancy (wid.)[216]	263	1300				
Stroup, Israel R.	394	2300				
Stroup, Solomon[217]	184	1200				
Stroup, Wesley	62	200				
Stroup, Nancy Exr	111	555				
Sifford, D. M.	162	725	S. F.			
Setzer, Henry Exr						
Setzer, Alex Dec.	450	1300				
Setzer, Henry	7	50	Hoyl Crk			
Thompson, F. W.[218]	205	1500	Hoyl Crk			
Thompson, L. E.	270	2500	Hoyl Crk	Mahala	38	486
				Monroe	19	1215
				Bill	17	1175
				Laura	16	972
				Fanny	13	810
				Alice	7	527
				Frank	11	648
				Lucy	6	486
				Fayette	3	253
				Margaret	32	648
				Adaline	10	648
				Draper	8	486
				Harriet	3	203
				Buster	½	122
				Saylor	16	1134
				Manda	½	81
				No 16		9894
Williford, E. by				Male	6	486
B. B. Barron				Female	4	246
				No 2		729

Assessment of Land and Slaves for 1863=River Bend Dist.

Taxable	Acres	Value	Location	Slave	Age	Value
Abernathy, Jas.[219]	242	1450	Stanly Crk[220]	Milly	37	780
				Nance	19	1040
				Ann	18	1040
				Amanda	11	624
				Joseph	5	364
				Mila	3	260
				Wallace	1	104
				Martin Rupted	4	260
				Sam	2	208
				No 9		4680
Abernathy, M. Luther[221]	199	1825	Leepers Crk[222]	Margaret	23	936
				Mary	20	936

Taxable	Acres	Value	Location	Slave	Age	Value
				Ann	3	260
				No 3		2132
Abernathy, D. M.[223]	125	1100	Ridge Lippard Cr	Hartwell	40	1040
	21	125	Dutchmans[224]	Elisabeth	37	832
				Monroe	13	832
				Harriet	12	624
				Olly	11	624
				Theodore	7	520
				Litha	5	416
				No 7		4888
Abernathy, John P.[225]	129	1300	Lippards Cr	Sela	33	624
				Jane	30	728
				Salina	21	936
				Roxana	10	624
				Gus	1	104
				Isabella	6	312
				Mary	4	312
				Alice	2	208
				Lawson	42	832
				No 9		4680
Abernathy, Milton S.	22 ¼	450	Lippards Cr			
	40	250				
Abernathy, Miles L.[226]	180	700	Stanleys Crk			
Abernathy, Barbar[227]	193	1750		Mingo	55	624
				Laura	36	780
				Mary	9	468
				Jenny	3	312
				Harriet	2	210
				No 5		2394
Abernathy, Miss Ann				Linda	21	936
				Frank	18	1144
				Bill	16	1144
				Liz	1	104
				No 4		3328
Abernathy, Miss Bettie				George	19	1144
				Martha	15	1040
				Sue	11	728
				Joe	10	624
				No 4		3536
Armstrong, M. R.	116 ½	800	Plank Road[228]			
Broadaway, Wm.[229]	292	2000	Plank Road	Peter	36	1144
" "	215	2000	D. Crk	Edmund	31	1144
				Lizzie	30	936
				Jane	13	832
				Alice	10	624
				Margaret	8	468
				Mary	8	468
				Cephus	5	312
				No 8		5928
Burke, Munroe[230]	106	400	Stanly Crk			
Bessell, E. H.	95	650	Cat River			
Black, J. F.[231]	195	800	Plank Road			
Black, Jas. L.	78	700	D. Crk			
Cansler, R. T.	151	1800		Dudley	21	1144
				Charley	10	780
				Lawson	5	416
				John	3	312
				Lucin?	1	104
				No 5		2756
Cansler, Peter[232]	204	1500	Plank Road	Doll	25	728
" "	212	2125	Riverbend[233]	Pink	12	1040
				Clay	10	?888
				Bob	12	1040
				Nat	10	832
				No 5		4472
Connell, David[234]	143	650	Ridge			
Connell, James	163	560	Dutchmans Cr			

Taxable	Acres	Value	Location	Slave	Age	Value
" "	41	175	" "			
" "	4	25	" "			
Connell, Martha	37½	175				
Connell, Mary E.	37½	175				
Cox, Patrick	145	1150		Prince	57	312
				No 1		312
Cannon, Wm. F.[235]	395	3950		Doll	36	832
" "	115	700		Jane	15	936
				No 2		1768
Cannon, W. Sidney[236]	148	800		Viney	22	936
				Tayler	13	832
				Marshal	4	312
				Tom	3	260
				Linda or Sinda	½	104
				No 5		2444
Cannon, David E.				Walter	3	260
				No 1		260
Carpenter, And.[237]	7124	5000	Lippards Cr	Ike	25	1144
				Dan	18	1144
				Bob (Unsound)	16	936
				Jim	16	1040
				?Loge	15	1144
				?Lop	11	624
				Alfred	5	364
				Joe	3	260
				Winn B. Leg	55	312
				Mill	42	624
				Mott or Moll	23	936
				Call	17	936
				Harriet	14	936
				Bet (Diseased)	5	260
				Suse	2	260
				Bob (unsound)		936
				No 16		11,859
Clanton, Isaac[238]	163	800	Stanlys Cr			
Clanton, Lawson[239]	100	500	Stanlys Cr			
Cloninger, Wm	100	400	Stanly Cr			
Cloninger, David R.	96	350	Stanly Cr			
Derr, V.[240]	341	1700		Henry	4	260
	104	400		Harry	1	104
				Nance	61	104
				Anny	51?	104
				Harriet	41	624
				Charlotte	37	676
				Mary	9	520
				Junius	31	1040
				Neales	22	1144
				Moses	21	1144
				Cephas	20	1144
				James	18	1144
				Green	17	1144
				Marshal	14	1040
				Wm.	9	520
				No 15		11,232
Derr, John H.[241]	172	650	Stanlys Cr	Frank	1	104
				Vina	3	260
				Girl	1/12	15
				Isabella	22	884
				Sofe	22	884
				Wm.	3	312
				No 6		2994
Derr, And. J.[242]	220	2400		Sallie	34	728
				Elvy sore leg	31	520
				Julia	19	936
				Mary	20	936
				Mariah	12	728
				Emma	10	520

Taxable	Acres	Value	Location	Slave	Age	Value
				Amanda	4	416
				Willie	1	104
				Herbert Shoemaker	50	1040
				Turners hand off	28	728
				Jim	19	1144
				Monroe	14	1144
				Oliver	10	832
				Morrison	8	572
				Wm.	5	364
				Quince	1	104
				No 16		10,816
Eddleman, Dicey[243]				Dan	42	1040
				No 1		1040
Eddleman, David F.[244]	142½	1400	Forks Crk	Alice	2	212
				Amzi	¼	100
				Mary	23	936
				James	12	780
				Milly	10	676
				Cern	4	312
				No 6		3016
Edwards, Wm.[245]	150	500	Ridge			
" "	30	250	D Crk			
Edwards, Lewis[246]	40	200	Plank Road	Perry	7	624
				No 1		624
Farrar, Margaret[247]	125	650		George	7	520
				Ida	7	416
				Aaron	47	780
				Juno	51	520
				Hannah	35	676
				Harriet	19	832
				Clay	15	1040
				No 7		4784
Farrar, Nathanuel P.				Grief?	28	624
				No 1		624
Farrar, John	191	2000	Duch Crk			
Henderson, A. R.[248]	455	4550	River Bend	Margaret	26	1040
				Jinny	16	936
				Nancy	14	936
				Violet	4	416
				Ellenr	½	104
				Henry	36	1144
				Dick	15	11?44
				Daniel	7	624
				Charles	2	312
				Peggy	53	520
				Cherry	45	832
				No 11		8008
Henderson, Jas. A.[249]	193	2500	River Bend	Jess	39	1144
	168	1500	River Bend	Ben	37	1040
	95	450	River Bend	Billy	17	1144
	70	350	River Bend	Jim	15	1040
	222	2000	River Bend	Alice	4	312
				Martha	2	260
				Sally	64	50
				Leah	43	520
				Ann	20	940
				No 9		6450
Henkle, Osborne[250]	254¾	2000	Plank Road	Lackey	8	624
				William	3	416
				Alice	¾	104
				Jess.	44	1040
				Elmina	39	936
				Romulus	25	1144
				Lewis	16	1144
				Sidney	15	1144
				Leanorah	11	728

Gaston County Tax List of 1863

Taxable	Acres	Value	Location	Slave	Age	Value
				No 9		7280
Henkle, Hannah[251]	85	350	Ridge Land			
Handsell, John P.[252]	31	150	Sl Crk			
Hart, Isabella[253]	27½	50	Ridge			
Holland, Sallie				Amanda	13	884
				Ann	4	312
				No 2		1166
Huthison, C. L.[254]	225	1000	S. Crk			
Johnson, Dr. S. H.[255]	1763	12,300		Lizzie	32	832
				Judy	12¼	634
				Alice	11	624
				Albert	9	520
				Rose	6	416
				Edmund	[blank]	1248
				Martha	26	936
				Jim	25	1144
				Bob	45	832
				Manuel	37	1144
				Caroline	18	936
				Esther	2½	260
				Isaac	19½	1144
				Margaret	12	676
				Malvina	10	520
				Marria	21½	936
				Dana	6	416
				Ann	3½	364
				Jink	42	1040
				Coleman	44	1040
				Eliza	16	936
				Andy	66	364
				Henry	22	1144
				Monroe	20	1144
				Alexander	18	1144
				Alf	17	1144
				Franky	45	676
				Tom	33	1040
				Rhoda	17	936
				Ozier	14	1040
				Hannah	19	936
				Frank	2½	260
				Mary	1	104
				Clara	29	936
				Lee	13½	1040
				Mary	11	624
				No 36		29,120
Johnston, John R.[256]	680	8000		Albert	35	1040
				Willis	35	1040
				Elias	41	936
				Minda	50	520
				Joe	60	312
				Priscilla	66	104
				Rufus	1	104
				Mary	6	312
				Miles	10	832
				Rachel	13	936
				Emeline	15	936
				Henry	15	1144
				High	19	1144
				Sid	24	1144
				Viney	29	936
				No 15		11,440
Johnston, J. F.	377½	3700	Fork Crk			
" "	2000	6000	Coaling ground[257]			
Jenkins, Saml.[258]	58	350				
Jenkins, Sarah	34	175				
(Garvins or Harvins wife)						
Lineberger, Eli	209	2000	River Bend	Marian	6½	520

Taxable	Acres	Value	Location	Slave	Age	Value
" " D & Co	213	600	S Fork	Sarah	4½	312
				Frances	2½	208
				Mack	½?	104
				Kizer or Kiza	31½	728
				Joe	24½	1144
				Elvira	16½	936
				Bill	15	1144
				Mag	13	936
				Fayette	11	832
				Ann	8½	728
				No 11		7592
Moore, J. W.[259]	500	5000	Tools Ford	Prudy	20	936
				July	19	936
				Hannah	16	936
				Franky	17	936
				Violet	17	936
				Silvia	15	936
				Sue	14	520
				Mary	14	520
				Grace	9	520
				Delia	8	416
				Liz	6	312
				Helen	5	312
				Laura	3	260
				Jane	1	104
				Sarah	1	104
				Nora	½	104
				Jerry	52	624
				Jimbo	23	1144
				John	21	1144
				George	19	1144
				Trial	18	1144
				Charles	17	1144
				William	12	832
				Abram	11	832
				Humphrey	10	832
				Chaudins	9	520
				Tom not hearty	7	312
				Henry	8	520
				Simon	3	312
				Amy	39	624
				Cornelia	38	520
				Sallie	38	520
				Jane	23	832
				No 33		21,788
Mulligan, James[260]	140	800	D Crk			
McGee, Elizabeth[261]	120	900	D Crk			
McCall, Jane[262]	12¾	75		Judy	58	416
				No 1		416
McIntosh, Isaac L.[263]	15	75				
McIntosh, Wm.[264]	76	380	Plank Road			
	106	400	Ridge			
McDowell, Robt. ?J.[265]	1334	13,000	Killians Ck[266]	Augustus	8	624
				Charles	5	520
				Ned	2	312
				Green	1	104
				Albert	1	104
				Cooly	54	416
				Betzy	23	1040
				Caroline	19	1040
				Rose	3	260
				Jake	58	624
				Henry	55	728
				Ephraim	57	676
				Prince	45	1040
				Abram	43	1040
				Henderson	38	1144

Taxable	Acres	Value	Location	Slave	Age	Value
				Daniel	32	1144
				Henry	30	1248
				Isaac	21	1144
				George	17	1144
				West	17	1144
				Richie	14	1040
				James	7	624
				No 22		17,160
Pryer, Wiley[267]	71½	300				
Rutledge, James	348¾	3500	D Crk	Adeline	21	936
" "	65	250		Polly	11	520
				Laura	9	416
				Go	1	104
				Dick	43	1040
				Miles	30	1144
				Daniel	11	832
				Patsey	50	520
				Jane	22	936
				No 9		6448
Rhyne, Michael[268]	690	3500	Stanly Crk			
Ransom, Ellen	30	100	Free or Tree Port			
Smith, M. A.[269]	225	2250	Leppards	Ellen	12	780
				Austin	4	364
				Laura	1	104
				Betty	48	676
				Henry	17	1144
				Adam	15	1144
				No 6		4212
Sadler, Henry[270]	303?	2700		Sophia	11	520
				Lovinia	9	468
				Leah	7	312
				Hubbard	28	1040
				William	15	1040
				Lawson	5	260
				Jane	13	728
				No 7		4368
Summerow, David	193	1750	Dutchman	John	9	520
Adm. W. P. Eddleman				Bartlett	3	260
				Priscilla	37	780
				Lucinda	13	936
				No 4		2496
Sadler, Elisabeth	30	300	Dutchman			
Stroup, Caleb[271]	95	400	Stanly Crk			
Sample, Wm. A.	145	1600	River Bend			
Tate, Thos. R.[272]	1245	150,000		Cap	16	1144
				Rose	14	1040
				Jasper	10	832
				Frank	15	1144
				Lewis	¾	104
				Charles	1½	104
				Sam	6	312
				Emeline	30	832
				Diza	53	624
				Delphina	25	936
				Jemima	17	936
				Harriet	22	936
				Sophia	3	260
				Margaret	2	208
				Jane	45	728
				Cricy	8	416
				Lizzy	7	364
				Tavis sickly	45	208
				Catharine	14	832
				Clarky	39	624
				Margaret	13	624
				Jane	5	312
				Milly	3	260

Taxable	Acres	Value	Location	Slave	Age	Value
				Charlotte	26	832
				Tom	55	728
				Cooper	70	52
				Lafayette	12	832
				Stephen	14	1040
				Levi	12	832
				Kit	18	1144
				Lewis	30	1040
				George	40	936
				Wesley B Smith	50	1248
				Willis	18	1144
				Lolan B Smith	56	1144
				Henry	35	1560
				Jim	11	832
				Brad	40	1040
				Calvin	33	1144
				Isom Rupted	33	936
				Milton	31	1144
				Abram	29	1144
				Bill Painter	27	1560
				John	8	520
				George	4	312
				Bob	18	1144
				Elie	21	1144
				Dave	10	832
				Dan (sickly)	50	520
				Jim	16	1144
				Mack	15	1144
				Jerry	11	832
				John	10	624
				Daniel	4	312
				Horace	¾	104
				Lydia	47	624
				Charlotte	29	832
				Fanny	21	936
				Georgiana	17	936
				Matty	15	530
				Anny	8	416
				Cornelia	6	312
				Laura	3	260
				No 63		47,590
Underwood, Henry[273]	29½	2650				
Underwood, Emma				Negro	12	832
Underwood, Jacob[274]	123	750				
Willis, S. S.[275]	248	3000				

Assessment of Land and Slaves for 1863=Roberts Com. Dist.

Taxable	Acres	Value	Location	Slave	Age	Value
Adams, Margaret (wid)[276]	137	300	C. Crk[277]			
Adams, Saml.	53	133	C. Crk			
Abernathy, Starling G.	66	200	C. Crk			
Arrowood, Wm.	238	1500	L. Crk[278]	Molly	11	787
				No 1		787
Arrowood, Wm.[279] Mt tr.	185	450				
" " Love tr.	68	204				
Arrowood, Margaret, (wid)	120	725		George	36	831
				Harriet	60	131
				No 2		962
Arrowood, B. F.	141	400		Lewis	35	1312
" " Blackwood tr.	126	650		Sarah	28	1050
" " Underwd tr.	82	120		Jenny	13	962
" " Rhom	1	8		George	8	612
				Lottie	5	350
				Patsey (unsound)	5	87

Gaston County Tax List of 1863

Taxable	Acres	Value	Location	Slave	Age	Value
				Titus	3	262
				No 7		4635
Blackwood, Gideon[280]	560	2200	C. C.	Violet	55	175
				Leander	33	1312
				George	28	1312
				Peter	26	1312
				Hannah	24	1050
				Kate	22	875
				Charles	17	1225
				Jake	15	1137
				Ellen	13	962
				Titus	9	656
				Sidney	8	612
				Manda	6	437
				Isabella	2	175
				Nancy	6	437
				Mariah	4	306
				Infant		87
				No 16		12,070
Best, Saml.[281]	305	2675	L. Crk	Dicey	42	437
" " Blkwood tr.	109	800		Evaline	25	1050
" " Love tr	243	500		Harriet	23	1050
" " Fronbgr	25	100		Isaac	24	1312
				Albert	12	962
				Wade	10	787
				Linda	7	481
				John	6	481
				Hannah	6	437
				Joe	4	350
				Louisa	2	175
				Lizzie	2	175
				Fanny	3	262
				Margaret	1	131
				No 14		8090
Best, Michael[282]	141	1100	L. Crk	Jimmy	20	1050
				No 1		1050
Best, A. J.[283]	165	900		Alsey	17	1050
				No 1		1050
Boggs, Joseph G.	222	800	C. C.	Martha	13	962
				No 1		962
Black, Saml. Esq?	46	100	B. D.[284]			
" " Gd J. Kisers heirs	102	250	B. D.			
Carpenter, Levi. B.[285]	82	300				
Clemmer, L. J.[286]	59	300	C. C.			
Clark, Wm.[287]	100	300	L Crk			
Clark, Adam[288]	30	120	L. Crk			
Clark, J. W.[289]	43	129	L. Crk			
Deck, Peter[290]	369	1500				
Deck, & Fules Heirs	185	450				
Dameron, George	52	150				
Dickey, Alexander[291]	468	1600	C. C.			
" " Mt tr	129	130	C. C.			
" " for Jas.	300	600	C. C.			
Coaling Gr	136	272	C. C.			
Sims tr	100	100	C. C.			
Entry	90	100	C. C.			
Gold mine	50	100	L. Crk.			
Eaker, Catherine[292]	61	150	L. Crk.			
" "	30	45	L. Crk.			
Eaker, Hiram[293]	55	100	L. Crk.			
Fronebarger, Marg. Est	61	150	L. Crk.			
Fronebarger, John Sen.[294]	410	1600				
Fronebarger, J. Junior	17	25				
Fronebarger, Elizabeth[295]	250	1000				
Fronebarger, Jacob Senr.[296]	238	1300		Jimmy	56	175
				Lottie	35	787

Taxable	Acres	Value	Location	Slave	Age	Value
				Jim	32	1400
				Ann	22	1050
				Mariah	20	1050
				Joe	18	1312
				Peter	16	1137
				Willy	13	962
				Mary	12	875
				John	20	1312
				Hannah	17	1050
				Sarah	15	962
				Sidney	14	1050
				Lise	11	787
				Wesley	7	525
				Nancy	4	306
				Martha	3	262
				Bob	1	131
				Anny	19	1050
				Caroline J.		87
				Easter		87
				No 21		16,358
Fulton, Jerome B.				Sophie	14	962
				No 1		962
Ferguson, James Sr	338	1200		Harry unsound	55	175
				No 1		175
Ferguson, James[297]	172½	1700	L Crk			
" " Wm.	270	1000	C C			
Falls, Robt. Esq.	200	500				
Ford, Hiram[298]	200	600	C C			
" "	50	100	C C			
Gamble, Joseph[299]	628	3000		Walker	22	1312
				Alfred	18	1312
				Anderson	16	1225
				Adeline	14	962
				Saml	12	962
				Washington	8	612
				No 6		6385
Gant, A. J.	102	300				
Garrett, Brothers F tr[300]	400	1800	Crowders Crk	Adai	2	175
" " Whitstine ?? tr	200	800	" "	Ann	4	306
" " K. M. S tr[301]	6200	6000	" "	Lucy	10	745
" " C. M. tr[302]	1100	550	" "	Mima	7	525
" " Carroll tr.	400	800	" "	Winny	5	393
" " Mauney	430	1070	" "	Sarah	1	131
" " Blkwd	300	600	" "	Louise	5	393
" " Oates tr	1100	25,000	" "	Martha	1	131
" " Yellow Ridge[303]	75	5000	" "	Elizabeth	1	131
" " Stone tr	20	900	" "	Carolina	1	131
" " Saw mill	117	250	" "	Martha	1	131
				Beula	3	262
				Adaline	2	175
				Fanny	2	175
				Margaret	3	262
				Sabra	2	175
				Amma	14	962
				Della	14	962
				Dick	16	1225
				Hardy	2	175
				Tony	12	962
				Aleann	3	262
				Jane	1	131
				Reuben	52	350
				Harry	52	350
				James	54	306
				Nat	36	1250
				Allen	35	1250
				John	36	1250
				Lewis	32	1312

Gaston County Tax List of 1863

Taxable	Acres	Value	Location	Slave	Age	Value
				Willis	32	1312
				John	26	1312
				Isaac	30	1312
				Oliver	22	1400
				Jake	26	1312
				General	20	1400
				?Engal	20	1400
				Willis	21	1400
				Willis	18	1312
				Red	18	1312
				Haywood	18	1312
				John	15	1225
				Reegal?	12	962
				George	16	1225
				George	25	1312
				?Glosea	12	962
				Dorsey	10	787
				Robert	12	962
				Certen?	13	962
				George	11	831
				Benjamin	11	831
				?Miliard	8	612
				Isaac	6	457
				Moses	5	457
				General	2	175
				Abraham	9	700
				Jacob	12	962
				Alicia	47	437
				Leah	33	787
				Fanny	23	?1050
				Lucy	26	1050
				Emily	22	1050
				Matilda	21	1050
				Martha	25	1050
				Cherry	25	1050
				Mary	25	1050
				Delphia	20	1050
				Bytha	30	875
				Susan	30	875
				Frances	28	918
				Liza	30	1050
				Anna	49	350
				Lucy	47	656
				Briney	45	525
				Grace	25	1050
				Hannah	30	875
				Mary	21	1050
				Niney	17	1050
				Delia	19	1050
				Mariah	13	962
				Sinda or Linda	10	743
				Alice	11	787
				Mary Jane	8	612
				Malvina	9	656
				Sillar	8	612
				Cherry	6	437
				Marah	10	743
				Edith	10	740
				Adaline	15	1050
				Hagia?	14	962
				Ann	12	962
				Caroline	9	700
				No 93		64,221
Herron, John	120	360	L. C.			
" " Blkwood tr	39	250				
Hager, George	33	100	C. C.			
Hager, John	500	2500	L. C.			

Taxable	Acres	Value	Location	Slave	Age	Value
Hager, Wm	118	850		Bill	49	787
				Lucy	11	831
				No 2		1518
Hager, Wm	10	20				
" "	116	232				
Holland, Franklin				Ned	14	875
				No 1		875
Holland, Julius	251	1100	L. C.	Fanny lame arm	30	612
				Jim	8	612
				Sarah	8	437
				George	4	350
				Nancy	2	175
				No 5		2186
Hovis, Jacob D.[304]	234	800	Long Creek			
Huffstetler, John[305]	226	700				
"H. B." home tr	81	800				
" " Wilson tr	70	500				
" " Hullet tr	150	400				
" " Wier tr	102	200				
" " as Adm Charity	200	400		Ellen	20	1050
				Bob	?15	1137
				Fanny	9	612
				Rufe	5	437
				Liner?	4	306
				Jim	3	262
				Jake	2	175
				Infant	1/12	87
				No 8		4066
Huffstetler, ?Walter?	50	100	C. C.			
Johnston, Dicy	278	800	C. C.	No 1		000 [unnamed]
Kennedy, J. R.	100	200				
Kiser, George[306]	168	504	L. Crk			
Kiser, Mary M.	250	1000	L. Crk			
Kiser, Jacob	29½	150	L. Crk	Harry	27	1312
" "	10	30	L. Crk	No 1		1312
Kiser, Zimri	56	300	L. Crk	Jane	7	525
				No 1		525
Kiser, Joseph	60	240				
Kiser, Fanny (wid)[307]	51	150	P. B.			
Long, Joseph[308]	88	200	L. Crk			
Long, L. H.?[309]	193	675	L. Crk			
Love, Mary	170	510	C C			
Mauney, Abe Sen	10	22	L. Cr			
Mauney, Michael[310]	287	1000				
" "	139	345				
" " Entry	60	180				
Mauney, John	52	250				
" "	39	125				
" "	11	33				
Mauney, Wiley	96	500				
Mauney, Susannah[311]	62	200				
Mauney, Caleb[312]	75	300				
Mauney, Barbara	75	150				
Mauney, Lawson				Stewart	60	262
				Fanny	34	787
				Stewart	12	962
				Rener	15	1050
				George	10	787
				Jim	5	437
				Manda	3	262
				No 8		4547
McKee, James[313]	125	400	L C			
McNair, James	158	1100	Crowders Crk	Benen	36	787
" "	106	212	L. Crk	Jake	124	1050
				Lewis	3	262
				No 3		2099

Taxable	Acres	Value	Location	Slave	Age	Value
McGill, Thos. P.[314]	644	2254	L. Crk	Zenith	42	525
" " Entry	83	120	L. Crk	Toney	26	1312
" "	35	70	L. Crk	Milly	22	1050
				Violet	30	1050
				Alice	3	262
				Child	½	87
				No 6		4286
" " Wifes				Giles	50	612
				Lewis	33	1312
				Rachel	7	525
				Ben	5	437
				No 4		2886
McGill, Alex D.[315]	312	1800	L. Crk	Minder?	14	1000
				No 1		1000
McGill, Tos. J.[316]	307	1600	L. Crk	Frank	11	831
				Harriet	7	481
				No 2		1312
McGill, John	230	1400	L. Crk			
Neill, Sarah (W.)[317]	99	297	L. Crk			
Neill, John W.	48	36				
Oates, Thos. M.[318]	115	575	C. C.			
Oates, James B.[319]	152	575	C. C.	Sam	41	875
				No 1		875
Oates, John R.[320]	187	1100	C. C.			
Ormond, T. S.	501	1250				
" "	60	40	CR			
Ormond, John J.[321]	1000	1200	L. Cr	Betsey	15	962
" " Chestnut R	32	24		No 1		962
" " OreB[322]	15	60				
" Bery. M.	110	500		Eli	13	962
" " Ch. R.[323]	32	24		No 1		962
" " OreB	15	60				
Ormond, Robt D.	80	800				
" " Ch R	32	24				
" " OreB	15	60				
Pasour, Susan (Wid)	127	325				
" "	1	5	B D			
Parker, Hester	43	100	C. C.			
Prier, Jno. J.	293	1000	L. Cr	Julia	26	1050
				George	6	481
				Doctor	3	262
				Lucinda	1	131
				No 4		1924
Roberts, Jno. M.[324]	365	1500	L. Crk	Arter sickly	48	525
				Sarvel?	15	1137
				York	13	962
				No 3		2624
Rhom, David[325]	125	250	L. Crk	Jinny	80	[blank]
				No 1		000
Rudisill, Mary (wd)	45	393		Bob	45 Not sd	393
Sellars, Abram[326]	120	240				
Stroup, Moses[327]	455	1820		Rose	12	875
				No 1		875
Service, Jos. W.	51	150	C C			
Thornburg, Joseph[328]	308	1200	L Crk			
Thomas, Saml[329]	205	700	CC			
Torrence, Saml A.[330]	16	1000	L Crk	Falls	9	700
" " Wiles tr	144	500	L Crk	James	7	568
" " Picky	52	100	L Crk	Jane	6	437
				Maria	3	262
				Charles	4	350
				No 5		2317
" " as Adm	679	4500	L Crk	Thomas	47	612
	49	50		Mary	47	437
	125	185		Fanny	18	1050
				?Cloah	16	1050
				Lottie	14	962

Taxable	Acres	Value	Location	Slave	Age	Value
				Henry	13	?875
				Milly	?10	700
				Patty	8	612
				Sam	7	568
				Miles	4	350
				Jeffrey	4	350
				Lucy	1	131
				Magg	1	131
				No 13		7828
Vandyke, Jas. A.³³¹	49½	300	B. D.			
White, Mary C.³³² h. t.	142	1562	L. Crk			
" " Kiser tr	176½	1056				
White, Mary³³³	588	2600		Moses	52	306
				No 1		306
Wilson, Lawson for K M Gold M Co.³³⁴	482	5000				
White, Jas F.³³⁵	182	1000		Polly	20	1050
" "	18	30		Child	½	87
				No 2		1137
Whitesides, Major³³⁶	174	1740				
" " entry	12	12				
Whitesides, Mary (wid)³³⁷	300	1200	C. C.			
Whiteworth, F. R.³³⁸	181	2500	C. C.	?Talby	63	87
				Ester	30	700
				Ben	37	787
				Stiles	27	1312
				Caroline	25	1050
				Stanford	24	1487
				George	19	1400
				Ellen	15	1050
				Betsey	13	962
				Mary	11	787
				Frank	10	787
				Lucinda	6	487
				Tom	3	262
				Columbus	3	262
				[blank]	1	131
				No 15		11500
Kiser, Noah³³⁹	23	75	[following two bracketed together with this line]			
" "	18	75				
" "	28	75				
Kiser, Margaret	48	75				
Kiser, Elizabeth	19	75				
Kiser, Barbara	18	75				
Kiser, ?James	37	75				
Kiser, Jane	16	75				
Kiser, Philip	18	75				
Lewis, Jno. G. Ad PF	397½	1600				
" " Trustee D. Frone	150	700				

Assessment of Land and Slaves for 1863=Rudisills Com[pany] Dist[rict]

Taxable	Acres	Value	Location	Slave	Age	Value
Aderholdt, David³⁴⁰	373	2700		Ann	12	877½
				No 1		877½
Alexander, Noah³⁴¹	187	800		Peggy	60	87½
				No 1		87½
Aderholdt, Emuel³⁴²	160	2000		Winny	60	87¼
" " PF?	80¾	400	S Fork	Harriet	27	702
Pine Fork				Julia	9	801
				Frank	7	614¼
				Henry	6	526¼
				Rose	4	351
				Martha	1	174
				No 7		3255
Baker, Eli	96½	750				

Taxable	Acres	Value	Location	Slave	Age	Value
Black, Alfred	17	190	Ind Cr			
Black, Saml Sen	5½	16½	Pine Mt.			
Black, Saml Jr	5	75	M. B.[343]			
Beam, Peter[344]	314	1850		Ned	46	614¼
	5¾	85	M. B.	Biney	51	263
	113	575	B. Dam	Margaret	13	877
	151½	1350	B. Dam	Sarah	11	794¾
				Lizzie	10	779
				Rena	8	702
				No 6		4029
Baker, Allen[345]	80	350	B. D.[346]			
Baker, Edward[347]	188½	940	B. D.			
Crouse, Rufus[348]	167	1500	B. D.	Sarah	45	357
				Vine	27	977
				Frank	4	350
				Julia	2	218
				No 4		1903
Carpenter, A. G.	230	700		Clara	62	81
				No 1		81
Costner, Manda	6	18	Mt. Br			
Carpenter, Frederick Jr[349].	154	462	B. D			
Carpenter, John	75	375	B. D.			
Carpenter, Alfred	100	450				
Carpenter, Wm.	70	500				
Carpenter, Saml	256	1000				
Carpenter, B. M.[350]	97	500				
Carpenter, Fred Sen[351]	396	3200				
Carpenter, Ann[352]	160	1100				
Carpenter, Henry	177	800		Frances	11	826
				No 1		826
Carpenter, Emanuel[353]	135	550				
Carpenter, Abel	55	110				
Carpenter, Danil[354]	10	50				
Carpenter, Joseph[355]	520	4000	Ind Cr			
" "	50	150				
Carpenter, George[356]	226	1300	B. D.			
Carpenter, Wm	167	1400	B. D.			
Carpenter, Marcus	86½	500	B. D.			
" " for W. Reinhardt				Rufus	17	1222½
				No 1		1222½
Carpenter, J. L.	198	693				
Smith, Land	83			?Nay	13	967
				Allen	9	7?15¾
				No 2		1705
Crouse, David	114	798				
Cathey, Francis	300	1500		Jim [no summary]	68	175
Eaker, Christian[357]	432	2900	B. Dam	Jess.	43	702
	41	82	Pine Land	Dan.	40	877
				Julia	30	789
				Emma	21	1070¼
				Reuben	15	1044
				Elmina	10	787¼
				Ben	10	787
				No 7		6060
Eaker, Jesse[358]	80	400				
" "	30	150				
Eaker, Jacob[359]	104	416				
Evans, Edward	150	480				
Eaker, Mary (wid)	100	400				
Gardner, Andrew	84	336	B D			
Hines, Daniel[360]	420	2400		March	11	833
" " Jo. S. Carpenter for JS. C	130	900		No 1		833
Kiser, Phillip[361]	155	750	B D			
" "	93	495	B D			

Taxable	Acres	Value	Location	Slave	Age	Value
" "	44¼	200				
Kiser, Susan[362]	175	1400				
Kiser, Jacob[363]	233	696	Mt. Br			
Kiser, Levi[364]	192	1750	Pine Land			
	51	150				
Mauney, Abe Sen[365]	184	920		No 1		877
				[no name]		
Mauney, Abe Jr.[366]	384	2700		Wallace	28	1048
				Mahala	23?	1096
				No 2		2144
Mauney, Barbara				Pink	32	877
				No 1		877
Mauney, Max	120	850	Ind Crk			
" "	80	480				
Mauney, Lawson	50	600	Ind Crk			
McLurd, John[367]	200	1000	B D			
McBee, Jno?[368]	69	200	B D			
Mauney, Lavina	144	1150	Ind Cr			
Rudisell, Wiley[369]	335	2400		Charlotte	21	526½
" "	60	180		Henry	17	1135
"for SCarpenters Hrs	50	150	Mt. Br	Lee	13	877
				Pink	10	787
				Adaline	8	702
				Lauson	5/12	125
				No 6		4154
Rudisell, Jonas[370]	228	1100		Mary	43	438¾
	21¾	200		Noah	33	877
				Lyn	26	1096
				Solomon	9	745
				Laban	7	614
				Frances	7	614
				Dan	4	551
				Adolph	2	219
				No 8		4954
Rudisell, E. A.	177	1800		Dan	26	1096
	126	700		Ann	25	1080
	1?	165		Elmina	20	877
	14	112		Em	8	702
				Can	5	498¾
				Saml	2	219
				No 6		4488
Rudisill, Mary	196	1000		Lauson	22	1155
				Jacob	21	1222
				Hannah	20	1048
				Rufus	13	877
				Shamm?	36	877
				David	48	702
				Barbara	2	219
				No 7		6100
Rudisill, Eli[371]	186	900		Martha	25	1096
				Jacob	2	219
				Jane	6	526
				No 3		1861
Summey, John[372]	129¾	750				
Shuford, Cynthia[373]	262½	1300		Rachel	36	658
				John	31	658
				Silas	53	351
				Munroe	26	1155
				Lawson	17	1155
				Kissy	11	833
				Martha	7	614
				Wallace	5	458
				Jim	1½	219
				No 9		6061
Smith, Robt	57	300				
Pasour, John[374]	118	600				
" "	67	300				

Taxable	Acres	Value	Location	Slave	Age	Value
Pasour, Saml[375]	78	275				
Vickers, John[376]	497	1500	B D			
Williams, Jacob[377]	81	324				
Kiser, John	42	168				
" "	115	700				
Senter, Jones[378]	126	378				

Assessment of Land and Slaves for 1863=South Point Dist[rict]

Taxable	Acres	Value	Location	Slave	Age	Value
Armstrong, Jno. L.	120	732	South Fork	Peter ?Rapted	48	422
				Sarah	23	1055
				Tom	21	1055
				Amanda	10	676
				Zenas	1	105
				No 5		3313
Armstrong, Arthur[379]	103	732	South Fork	Ned	29	1110
				Abram	32	1055
				Wilburn	16	1055
				Annie sickly	39	740
				Catharine	5	356
				Joseph	3	232
				Martha	2	168
				No 7		4716
Armstrong, Elizabeth				Granville	33	1055
				Esther	20	1055
				George	18	1055
				Rachel	3	232
				Abram	74	000
				Dinah	52	211
				No 6		3608
Armstrong, John W.	444	3100				
Armstrong, Matthew Jr.[380]	110	550		Mariah	23	1055
				Anny	8/12	79
				No 2		1134
Beattie, Robt. A.	146	800		Rachel	73	000
				Sherill	48	475
				Vina	42	634
				Cyrus	34	1055
				No 4		2164
Beattie, Rufus, J.[381]	142	568	C. River	Simon	23	1162
				Baily?	20	1162
				Grace	11	740
				Luce	20	1055
				Martha	2	169
				Eliza	??	74
				No 6		4288
Beattie, Saml.[382]	769	6152		Jacob	63	105
				Eliza	50	370
				Fan	32	950
				Ann	28	1055
				Jane	25	1055
				Frank	11	740
				Bart	8	530
				Bytha	6	422
				George	7	476
				Ephraim	7	476
				Lee	4	295
				Joana	2	169
				Elan	1	105
				No 13		6748
Beattie, Smith[383]	344	1500		Jasper	31	1055
				No 1		1055
Beattie, Jonathan[384]	129	387	Catawba Crk	Albert	42	952
				No 1		952
Beattie, John[385]				Wesley	25	1160

Taxable	Acres	Value	Location	Slave	Age	Value
				Peter	13	801
				No 2		1961
Berry, W. R.				Wiley	12	801
				No 1		801
Brandon, Rachel	180	1080	Mill Crk	Mary	57	126
				Abe	37	1012
				Wallace	2	168
				Green	22	1160
				Vina	18	1055
				Caroline Burnt hand	15	844
				No 6		4365
Craig, Saml W.[386]	264	2904		Caroline	41	780
				Limbrick	40	801
				Amanda	27	1055
				Lucinda	15	991
				Zenas	9	611
				Sarah	8	548
				Hannah	5	358
				Alice	3	232
				Charly	4	295
				Ida	4/12	74
				No	10	5745
Dameron, John[387]	194	1358		Dorcus	15	1055
				No 1		1055
Bradley, Albert[388]	76	300				
Caldwell, Saml[389]	515	2775	South fork	Tom	75	[blank]
	4	20	Chittem Land	Silvia	80	[blank]
				Violet	22	1055
				Mary	20	1055
				Nancy	16	1055
				George	13	865
				Jasper	8/12	94
				No 7		4104
Ewing, Saml.[390]	566	5000		Delila	60	105
				Jacob	31	1131
				Jack	26	1160
				No 3		2372
Ewing, Hugh Sen.[391]	94	450				
Ewing, Hugh Junr	94	450		No 1		?
						[no name given]
Finley, Robt. W.[392]	115	700	C. C.			
Finley, Wm. G.	?38	200				
Finley, ?S. S.?				Samson	32	949
				No 1		949
Finley, Jane				Eliza	45	633
				Luce	13	865
				Mary	9	611
				Roxanna	8	548
				Sarah	6	422
				Miles	4	295
				Amanda	2	168
				No 7		3542
Fite, Solomon[393]	216	648	S. F.			
Groner, H. L.[394]	241	1000	S. F.			
Glenn, Robt. Est.	192	960	Mill Crk	Jack	65	105
				Celia	38	844
				Wiley	34	1055
				Eliza	19	1055
				Sam	7	485
				Bruce	4	295
				Neill	2	168
				Lawson	6/12	74
				No 8		4081
Gingles, Margaret[395]	187	700	C. R.	No 1		000
						[no name given]
Gullick, Milton M.[396]	324	2916	C. C.	Jane	41	780

Taxable	Acres	Value	Location	Slave	Age	Value
" " J. N. Decd.	166	500		Andy	39	822
				Anne	31	1002
				Clara	29	1055
				Sarah	25	1055
				Harriet	21	1055
				Tom	18	1055
				Able	16	1055
				Sam	14	928
				Jonah	12	822
				Silva	13	865
				Martha	9	611
				Bob	9	611
				Neal	8	549
				Jinny	4	295
				Ann	5	358
				Edd	3	232
				West	3	232
				Caroline	2	168
				Hannah	1	105
				Infant	3/12	74
				No 21		13,729
Hanks, Wm.[397]	360	3600		Milly	65	52
				Lark	32	1162
				Adaline	24	1055
				Elmina ?lunat	20	896
				Roxana	3	230
				Margaret	2	150
				Anne	8/12	80
				No 7		3635
Hanks, G. W.[398]				Isom	65	80
				Harriet	35	950
				Sucky	12	738
				Mag.	4	295
				Anne ?Deform	2	80
				No 5		2143
Henry, Robt.[399]	212	1696		Mary	46	549
				Constantine	7	485
				No 2		1034
Hammel, Alex[400]	136	800				
Hand, M. H.	70	1400	Catawba River	?Senah	57	105
				Jinna	43	611
				Marg.	24	1055
				Lez.	24	1055
				John	22	1162
				Frank	20	1162
				Tom	18	1162
				Rob	16	1092
				Martha	15	991
				Julius	14	928
				Caroline	12	811
				Jasper	9	611
				Isaac	5	350
				Rhett	3	?232
				Infant	4/12	80
				Sepp	12	801
				Sue	5	558
				Jane	2	168
				No 18		12,732
Hand, M. H. As Exr. M Leeper	247	2200	C. River	Green	27	1162
				Lena	70	000
				Sip or Lip	24	1055
				Silva	25	1055
				John	3	168
				Infant	½	80
				No 6		3520
Hand, J. R.	815	4890	S. Fork	Abby sickly	55	158
				Dinah	44	590

Taxable	Acres	Value	Location	Slave	Age	Value
				Joe	31	1107
				George	28	1162
				Syler	20	1055
				Isabella	21	168
				Jane	13	865
				Sarah	9	611
				Dilsa	3	232
				No 9		5948
Hand, Jane[401]	87	250				
Harrison, John[402]	294	900				
Hand, ?M. H. for M Neagle				Elmina	9	611
				No 1		611
Hall, J. D.[403]	553	4424	Southfork	Tom	68	105
				Smart Shoemaker	32	1688
				Isaac shoemaker	29	1688
				Big Sam	31	1107
				Little Sam Carpenter[404]	31	1688
				Elick	14	928
				Wash	10	675
				Marshall	7	485
				Longstreet	2/12	74
				Andy	5	358
				Caroline	26	1055
				Susan	26	1055
				Mary ann	20	1055
				Emeline	18	1055
				Lucy	8	549
				Etta	6	422
				Sally	6	422
				No 17		14,409
Kirkland by Hall	119	1110	C River			
Johnston, Wm. H.[405]	335	1675				
?Mannen tr.	97	400	C. Crk	Ells	70	105
				Nancy	64	000
				?Silva	60	000
				Jim	46	569
				Moses	43	633
				Mary sickly	36	464
				Louisa	23	1055
				Taylor	15	997
				Edward	15	997
				Emeline	15	997
				Neal	6	422
				Eliza	3	232
				Henrietta	36	952
				No 13		7423
Leeper, James[406]	200	1400				
Leeper, Andrew	159	1570		Charles	15	997
				Harriet	16	1055
				No 2		2052
Leeper, James for Jno Armstrong	145	700	S Fork			
Leeper, Naomi[407]	187	1125		Simon	45	527
				Stanhope	27	?1109
				Minerva	25	1055
				Bonapart	22	1055
				Margaret	19	1055
				Bruce	17	1055
				Jasper	13	865
				Lawson	12	790
				William	4	295
				Monroe sickly	4	211
				Adaline	3	232
				Esther	2	168
				Susan	45	526

Taxable	Acres	Value	Location	Slave	Age	Value
				No 13		8943
Lonergan, Edward[408]	300	2500	C River	Paul	46	633
				Jane	35	949
				Jim	1	105
				Stephen	3	132
				No 4		1819
Lonergan, James Est.	450	4000	S Fork			
Lewis, James	153	400				
Lineberger, Manassa[409]	133	1066	S Fork			
McLure, Bermudas?	100	300	S Fork			
McLane, W. R.[410]	155	800		Giles	46	738
" ", chittim tr	5	25				
McLane, Robt. G.	550	3850	C. C.	Julius	41	738
				Solomon	37	1012
				Augustus	20	1055
				Dinah Pains	4	526
				Ann	17	1055
				Mary	14	928
				Oscar	11	738
				No 7		6152
McLane, Margarets Est.	240	2400	S. F.			
Martin, Elisabeth[411]	171	684	C Crk			
McLean, John D.[412]	656	5240	C C & R[413]	Dick BT	49	844
L McLean tr	65	450	C R	John Dick	6	422
Glenn tr	60	240		Sidney	50	378
Jos McLean tr	176	1122	C. C.	Silva	66	[blank]
				Sarah	44	590
				Anthony	29	1055
				Green	19	1055
				Neal	16	1055
				Mils?	29	1055
				?Myma	33	948
				Tom	17	1055
				John A.	14	928
				Malinda	11	738
				Emma	13	866
				Elvira J.	9	610
				Abba	9	610
				Isabella	8	548
				George	8	542
				Cyrus	7	485
				Harriet	6	422
				Kate	5	358
				Starling	4	295
				Humphrey	3	232
				Lize	3	233
				Julius	2	168
				Dave	2	168
				Andy	9/12	80
				Mage	30	949
				Joe	5	358
				Caroline	30	949
				Ann	30	1055
				Louiza	20	1055
				Nancy	40	800
				Charlotte	15	991
				Little Ann	18	1055
				Henry	20	1055
				Amzi	21	1055
				Sam	11	738
				No 38		25,799
McKee, Jas. L.	90	300				
McKee, Wm.[414]	656	2296	S Fork	Anne	60	105
" " Fite tr	20	70		Hanna	27	1055
				Hogan	25	1055
				?Landa	23	1055
				Harriet	19	1055

Taxable	Acres	Value	Location	Slave	Age	Value
				Martha	16	1055
				No 6		5380
Melton [or] Mellon, G. W.	144	800	Mill Crk	Starling Sickly	39	800
				Mariah	33	1010
				Eliza	17	1055
				Margaret	13	866
				Nancy	9	610
				Andy	7	485
				Jim	5	317
				Dave	2	232
				No 8		5175
Neagle, Andrew[415]	377	3000	C River	Noah	20	1055
				Phillis	31	948
				Scott	14	928
				George	12	738
				Eliza	5	317
				Rob	4	295
				Miles	½	80
				No	7	4361
Neagle, John E.	57	350		Jim	2	168
				Isabella	30	948
				Frank	35	1055
				Ephraim	17	1055
				Mary	15	990
				Andy	10	675
				Mag?	8	528
				Livingston	6	422
				Durett?	4	295
				Camella	3	232
				Infant	?	63
				Martha	20	1055
				No 12		7486
Neagle, Jno. P.	135	1110				
Neagle, James B.	214	1700	C River	Dorcus	34	1000
Lattimore	75	560	C River	Susan	32	1026
				Charles	16	1055
				Henny	14	928
				Rufus	12	738
				Esau	9	610
				John	6	422
				Margaret	4	295
				Infant	2/12	80
				No 9		6155
Neely, John	272	1400		Bill	67	105
				Mariah	64	000
				Sipp	40	800
				Ancell	36	1055
				Nancy	30	1027
				John	15	990
				Andy	13	865
				Mary	9	610
				Martha	4	295
				Margaret	2	168
				No 10		5915
Ratchford, Joseph[416]	162	1782	S Fork	Adaline sickly	44	422
Brimm tr	295	1475	C C	Phillis	42	762
				Larkin	22	1055
				Eliza	12	800
				Jane	16	1055
				Paris	11	738
				David	9	610
				Lucy	9	610
				Laura	6	422
				Andy	2	168
				Alice	2	168
				Mary	2	168

Taxable	Acres	Value	Location	Slave	Age	Value
				Green	9/12	90
				Henry	18	1055
				Violet	14	844
				No 15		8965
Ratchford, Robt C.	341	1705		George deaf	14	548
				Jasper	6	548
				No 2		1196
Ratchford, Nancy[417]	125	1000		Frank	40	633
				No 1		633
Ratchford, John[418]	200	2000	S. Fork	Jim	74	[blank]
				Hannah	64	80
				Harriett	28	1055
				Russell	27	1160
				Andy	12	800
				Isaac	10	680
				Lize	8	448
				Nancy	6	422
				Mary	5	358
				No 9		5003
Reed, Wm.[419]	241	2410		Charity	58	105
				Harriet lame	40	732
				Phillis Pains	38	633
				Jacob	36	1055
				Martha	17	1055
				John	15	990
				Adaline	17	1055
				Jonas	15	990
				Ann	13	865
				Selina	10	675
				Wade	6	422
				Eliza	12	800
				Lucy	9	610
				Hannah	5	358
				Bob	9	610
				Sam	2	168
				No 16		11,129
Rumpheldt, H. W.	184	2760	Cataba R Gold mine			
Reed, James W.[420]	166	1600		Abe (cripple)	32	844
				Sarah	16	1055
				George		548
				No 3		2447
Rankin, Wm. R.	225	1350	S Fork	Jordan	55	263
" " Ola tr	150	800	C R	Mary	28	1055
				Russell	7	485
				No 3		1803
" " as Admin J. P. S.				Neal	25	1055
				Isaac	12	738
				No 2		1793
Smith, Judith[421]	314	1400				
Smith, Sarah	71	310		Sam	4	295
				No 1		295
Stowe, Wm. A.	553	2800		Lebo	60	80
				Rinda	28	570
				Anne	70	000
				No 3		650
Stowe, Leroy W.	309	1800		Ben simple	12	422
				No 1		422
Stowe, J & E. B.[422]	745	50,000	Cotton Factory & C[423] South Fork	Granny	70	000
				Tom	35	1055
				Jordan (Sickly)	33	211
				Dallas	25	1160
				Henry (B.Smith)	33	2110
				Jack	22	1055
				Alfred Workm	25	1577
				Peter	65	80
				Jane	15	991
				Eliza (Deformed)	12	211

Taxable	Acres	Value	Location	Slave	Age	Value
				Novel Potter	55	316
				Anne	60	000
				No 12		8766
Stowe, J & E. B. for Dr. Taylor				Mathew	25	1055
				Ceaser	25	1055
				Jim	21	1055
				No 3		3165
Stowe, J & E. B. for Dr. Hines				George	25	1055
				Hilliard	25	1055
				Nancy	22	1055
				No 3		3165
Stowe, J & E. B. for Dr. Arendell				Henry	18	1055
				Caser	13	865
				No 2		1920
Stowe, Laura				Silva	28	1055
				Ben	5	316
				Cloda	3	211
				Dick	2/12	64
				Sarah	28	1055
				Nerve	8	527
				Amos	3	232
				No 7		3460
Stowe, M. G.				Martha cripple	13	211
				Hetta	10	633
				No 2		844
Stowe, Eliza				Luce	55	263
				Marth	16	1055
				No 2		1318
Stowe, C. Theodore	127	700				
Stowe, Leroy[424]	66	264				
Stowe, Wm. J. Bottom	39	790				
" " Miller tr	179	895				
Thomson, E. D.?	53	530				
Wright, J. M.[425]	342	2000		Vina	35	896
				George	27	1160
				Harriet	13	865
				Mary	12	800
				Albert	9	611
				Hetta	7	485
				Jack	5	358
				Henry	4	295
				Silva	2	168
				Infant	?	74
				No 10		5712
Wright, Saml's Est.	76	228				
Wells, B. F.[426]	371	3710	C River Gold mine	Ann	46	548
				John	31	1055
				Sarah	29	1055
				George	29	1160
				Minta	28	1055
				Adaline	24	1055
				Martha	16	1055
				Dinah	15	991
				Joseph	13	865
				Jim	12	696
				Roxana	12	800
				Leah	4	295
				Esther	2	168
				Henry	1	105
				Sam	11	758
				Rose	1	105
				No 16		11,746
Wallace, D. G.	76	650				
Wagstaff, John	70	250				

Taxable	Acres	Value	Location	Slave	Age	Value
Yarbro, Wm.[427]	154	870				
Sandifer, Phillip	276	1000				

Assessment of Land and Slaves for 1863 Tan Yard Dist[rict]

Taxable	Acres	Value	Location	Slave	Age	Value
Adams, Wm.	25	150	Crowders Crk			
Armstrong, John[428]	104	400	C. C.			
Berry, E. M.	276	1200	Mill Creek			
Berry, E. Milton[429]	55	300	C. C.[430]			
Brison, Geo. R.[431]	155	600	Mill Creek			
Brison, Jane A.[432]	52	250	C. Crk			
Brison, Wm's children[433]	53	250	C Crk			
Brandon, Thos. L.[434]	150	600		Candace	39	615
				Deb	60	[blank]
				No 2		615
Baird, Robt.	192½	1000				
Baird, Jas C.s Est.[435]	305	900		Abe (unsound)	35	718
				Wilson	31	923
				No 2		1641
Baird, S. F. D.	92	450				
Beattie, Wm.[436]	176	700				
Brown, Elisabeth	64	200	Mill Crk			
Cook, Demsey	131	500	C. C.			
Craig, R. H.	271	1050	C. C.	Jennie	42	513
				Alfred	3	307
				Jane	3/12	51
				No 3		1072
Craig, Thos. N.	73	350	C. C.			
Craig, John H.	277	1200		Annie	21	1129
" " Clark tr	120	500		Lewis	13	1129
				Ben	9	769
				Frances	2	153
				Rufus	25	718
				No 5		3900
Craig, William[437]	234	1000		Jane	21	715
				Prince	7	715
				Ann	1/12	102
				No 3		1534
Clark, R. F.	150	900	Mill Crk			
Combest, William[438]	80	250	C C			
Combest, Sarah J.	40	125				
Clemmer, J. L.[439]	129	500				
Clinton, Martha[440]	108	350	C C	Fed	25	1334
				Eliza	6	461
				No 2		1790
Choate, A. D.	243	850	C. C.			
Detter, Andrew[441]	310	2600	Crowders Crk	Chloe	43	565
				Jake	15	1026
				Myles	3	307
				Lee blind	2	[blank]
				No 4		1898
Dixon, A. S.[442]	65	500	Catawba Cr			
Falls, A. J.	300	2000		Cinda	18	1231
				Child	?3/12	51
				No 2		1282
Falls, Sarah	50	250		Harry	43	1026
				Darky	40	615
				Jennie	26	1026
				Peter	21	1334
				Ann	8	615
				Harriet	1	102
				No 6		4721
Falls, Sarah L.	287	1400		Letty	27	725
				Milly	27	821
				Newton	13	923
				Harriet	5	359

246   Appendix

Taxable	Acres	Value	Location	Slave	Age	Value
				Jane	3	359
				Harry Def eye	1	102
				No 6		3289
Faires, E. M.[443]	250	1600		Ben	15	564
				Jinny	44	410
				Kisiah	18	821
				Rachel	15	1129
				Samson	2	102
				Millie	70	000
				No 6		3027
Featherston, C. A.[444]	100	600		Maria	51	309
				Reuben	36	1282
				Wyatt Pains	35	821
				Mariah Jane	35	715
				Henry	23	1539
				Mary	14	923
				Fanny	13	715
				Bob	6	410
				George	4	307
				No 9		7025
Ford, Isom[445]	132	600	C Crk			
" "	39	100				
Ford, Amzi	5	25				
Ford, Wm.	3	50				
Ford, Mary Ann				Deb	10	1026
				No 1		1026
Fewell, John[446]	71½	250				
Fewell, Jas. S.[447]	71½	250				
Floyd, J. L.	140	600				
Friday, Ephraim	106	400				
Glenn, J. F.'s Est.[448]	121	600				
Glenn, J. F. Sen	123	900	Mill Crk			
Glenn, E. B.'s Est.	295	1200	Cr Crk			
Gaston, Robt. Esq[449]	100	100				
Gingles, Ruth[450]	50	300	C C			
Gingles, Dorcus[451]	330	1700	C C			
Gingles, Charlotte?	31	250	C C			
Goble, Absolom	87	350				
Glenn, Mary L.				Rhoda	25	1026
				Mary	9	615
				Jane	5	410
				Sam	4	?256
				Julius	1	153
				No 5		2460
Grier, Thomas				Violet unsound	12	821
				Manuel	10	821
				No 2		1642
Herdman, Rosanna[452]	64	250				
Henderson, W. A.[453]	171	500	Cr Crk			
Hill, Wm. R.[454]	153	900				
Hill, Sarah	107	400		?Flora	25	1026
				Minor	7	564
				Mary	6	307
				Green	2	205
				No 4		[none given]
Horsely, Richard[455]	77	300				
Horsley, Resin	319	1600		Jane	33	615
				Abe	1	153
				No 2		769
Huffstetler, J. W.	184	500	Cr Crk			
Huffstetler, C. A.[456]	127	700				
Holland, Melissa M.	260	1000				
Holland, Nancy J.	250	1000				
" " Wm. M.[457]	223	1500		Hannah	34	923
" " Wm. M. Ford tr	16	80		Elisabeth	23	1026
				Sarah	17	923
				Harriet	12	1026

Taxable	Acres	Value	Location	Slave	Age	Value
				Joe	10	718
				Morris	8	718
				George	5	410
				Lee	4	307
				Sam	2	205
				No 9		6260
Hoffman, Levi[458]	223	1600		Joe	51	513
Hoffman Daniel or	140	600		Hannah	41	564
W Milling Lvw Henry				Caroline	6	461
				Jim	4	307
				Nancy	1	102
				No 5		2050
Holland, Wm. R.[459] as Gard. J. Q. Holland				Margaret	37	615
				Alfred	9	615
				Sylvanus	5	461
				Amanda	3	307
				No 4		2001
Holland, Mary[460]				Lett	60	102
				No 1		102
Hope, James	30	100				
Henry, Wallace	140	600				
Jenkins, D. A.[461]	250	2000	Cr Crk	Charles	34	1231
				King	32	1334
				Lee	11	1026
				Pink	10	923
				Monroe	9	573
				Andy	7	615
				George	3	205
				Ned	3	205
				Cina	35	718
				Jude	13	1129
				Rachel	11	1026
				Margaret	9	821?
				No 12		9850
Johnston, Marg. Est	79	300	Cr Crk			
Johnston, Susan's Est	262	1100	Cr Crk			
Kincaid, J. R.[462]	102	800	Mill Crk			
Kendrick, M. L's Est	84	700	Catawba Crk			
Kendrick, Ellen[463]				George	14	1231
				No 1		1231
				[off line]		
Kendrick, J. W.	104	600	Catawba Crk			
Linebarger, Jacob[464]	312	2000	Cr Crk	Jim	50	307
				Jinnie	30	718
				LeRoy	17	1077
				Hall	11	821
				Andy	12	923
				Jane	10	718
				Lizzie	8	615
				Sarah	6	513
				Margaret	4	410
				Mary	1	102
				Turner	3	205
				Catharine	17	1385
				Chila	2/12	50
				No 13		7952
Linebarger, Ephraims Est	100	500				
Lewis, J. J.[465]	71	350	C C Mill Crk	Pink	21	1539
				No 1		1539
Lewis, Anns Est.[466]	129	500				
Lockhart, Wm.[467]	110	500				
Love, A. J.[468]	54	500	Cr Crk	No 2		000 [no names]
Moore, Walters Est.	174	700				
Mendenhall, Nathan	200	1200				
Mendenhall, John J.	176	1500				

Taxable	Acres	Value	Location	Slave	Age	Value
Mendenhall, Margaret				Betsey	53	256
				No 1		256
McCullough, J. F.	220	600	Catawba Cr			
McCullough, Vincent[469]	93	275				
Massey, W. F.[470]	140	1000	Crow Cr			
McDaniel, Elisha[471]	81	400	Catawba Crk			
McAlister, Jane	57½	250				
Nolen, Wm. M.[472]	234	900				
Neagle, Dr J. L.	73	350				
Neagle, Ann R.	95	500				
ODaniel, Joseph Est.[473]	140	500				
Pursley, S. M.[474]	50	250	C C			
Pursley, David	52	250				
Pettus, Jas. T.[475]	150	1000	Mill Crk	Esther	30	923
				Harriet	11	872
				Violet	8	513
				Hannah	7	461
				Robert	1	102
				No 5		2873
Quinn, Jas. Esq[476]	250	1500	C Crk	?Luff	?50	307
				Sylvy	30	821
				Harriet	28	923
				Haley	22	1026
				Mollie	10	975
				Ellen	3	205
				George	30	1231
				Warren	27	1436
				Walker	12	923
				Caid?	8	615
				Lark	7	615
				Thos.	7	615
				Marion	9/12	102
				No 13		9802
Quinn, Thos. F.	96	600		Andy	13	923
				No 1		923
Ratchford, J. F.	150	750	C. C.			
Ratchford, Cath's Est.	140	1000	Cr. Crk			
Ragan, D. F.[477]	116	500	Catawba Crk			
Ragan, Jaspers Est.	62	200				
Robison, S. C.	579	2500	Crow Crk	George	47	769
				No 1		769
Robison, Zimri[478]	288	900	Catawba			
Robison, Elam[479]	177	700				
Robison, Mary A.	96	400				
Robison, James Est.	88	400				
Robison, Harriet	96	400	Catawba			
Robison, Eli J.[480]	352	2000		Morris	28	1334
				No 1		1334
Riddle, J. R. F.[481]	196?	1000		Chambers	25	1539
				No 1		1539
Riddle, J. M. A. C. 's Est.	200	1000				
Riddle, Jane M.	[nothing further listed]					
Stowe, Wm. J.	140	1100	Crowders Crk	Ephraim	26	1436
" " J. Holland tr	122	400		Teder	19	1436
" " ½ W Ford Tr	81½	600		Anderson	16	1539
" " South Point	39	[blank]		Monroe	18	1436
" " Mellen tr	179	[blank]		Jennie	48	410
" " A Bottom tr	49	500		Harriet	26	1026
" " Warren tr	98?	400		Margaret	12	1129
" " part of m. tr	60	250		Robt.	6	615
" " Gaston tr	112	600		Frances	4	359
" " Entry	5	25		Violet	2	205
				Charley	1	102
				Vina	67	[blank]
				No 12		8699
Stowe, Elisabeth[482]				Zimri	50	513
				Lizzie	45	564

Taxable	Acres	Value	Location	Slave	Age	Value
				No 2		1078
Stowe, Nancy	132	650	Catawba Crk			
Stowe, Abram (Miller)	270	1400				
Stowe, Johns Est.	75	300				
Stowe, Theo. B.	40	200				
Stowe, J. F.	262	2000		Charlotte	34	821
				Anthony	20	1334
				Susan	18	1129
				Roberts (Fits)	29	000
				Louisa	9	718
				LeRoy	9	667
				Amzi	7	461
				Thomas	5	461
				No 8		5693
Stowe, LeRoy	157	600	Catawba Crk			
Stroup, Maxwell	289	1400				
Smith, John W.	100	500		Leanoh	40	256
				No 1		256
Smith, Elijah	140	500				
Stowe, Catherine				Gilbert	16	1026
				Sarah	21	923
				No 2		1950
Torrence, John C. H Tr[483]	321	1500	Cr crk			
Torrence, John C. Hill tr.	207	1600	Cr Crk			
Torrence, Robert	241	1000				
Torrence, Harrison A.	137	600				
Torrence, William	270	1000				
Torrence, Mary[484]	370	1400		George	35	1231
				Phillis	28	1026
				Elmina	22	1129
				Wylie	11	923
				Adam	8	615
				Jim	6	410
				Ann	3	205
				No 7		5542
Wilson, Robt.	545	4450	Cr Crk	Margaret	54	256
Beard tr	315	2000		Off	42	564
				Jim	37	1026
				Lyle	36	615
				Hannah	32	718
				Minor	23	1436
				Jerry	21	1231
				Ann (Deaf)	16	307
				Alfred	14	1231
				Harriet	10	1026
				Sam	4	205
				Louisa	2	153
				Tom	1	102
				No 13		8878
Wilson, Edwin	2½	25	Catawba Cr			
Wallace, Tho.[485]	100	500				
Wilson, Robt. W.	178	1600	Mill Crk	Davis (Rept)	13	821
Culb Tr	140	650	Mill Crk	Nelly	48	513
				Randolph	11	718
				Peter	61	256
				West	25	1436
				Jane	35	769
				John	21	1539
				Bill	18	1026
				Arther	13	1026
				Warren	11	718
				Hamp	11	718
				Harriet	8	718
				Newt.	6	359
				Leander	4	256
				Ann	16	1334

Taxable	Acres	Value	Location	Slave	Age	Value
				Hettie	8	615
				Martha	1	102
				Sallie	9	718
				Tom	11	821
				Jim	13	821
				No 20		15,290
Warren, W. G.[486]	126	500	Catawba Crk	Sampson	21	821
				Amy	36	615
				Sallie	25	1129
				Lewis	8	615
				Henry	8	564
				Rose	3	205
				Margaret	1/12	51
				No 7		4003
Walker, D. M.	74	750	Cro Crk			

In footing up the amt of the assessment of Slaves the cents were counted, which are left out in this record; the total therefore, is sometimes larger than the Several amts. will make as they Stand. [in the original]

Assessment of Land and Slaves for 1863 Woodlawn Com[pany]

Taxable	Acres	Value	Location	Slave	Age	Value
Alexander, Nancy	151	900	C River	Mary	18	1035
				Julia	2	230
				Tom	1	115
				No 3		1380
Abernathy, G & Co.	374	2700	S. Fork			
Abernathy, C. W. for OW & Co	108	600	R. R.	Ben	47	575
				Elam	27	1150
				Dallas	17	1035
				No 3		2700
Abernathy, M.[487]				Cinda	50	345
				No 1		345
Brevard, R. A.	127	700				
Blufort, Wm.[488]	88	300	S. Fork			
" " Entry	85	170	S. Fork			
Clemmer, A.	176	600	Tayler Crk			
Clemmer, John[489]	158	800	D. C.			
Clemmer, Jones?	158	800				
Cannon, J. F.[490]	319	2200	Stanley crk			
Cannon, J. A.	135	900	S Fork			
Davidson J. S.	1079	7500	Taylors Cr	Henry	46	575
				Dick	40	575
				Wilbert	40	575
				Austin	31	805
				Lawson	18	1150
				Peter	16	1035
				Lambert	14	1035
				Albert	12	1035
				Wm.	13	1035
				?Tish	3	230
				Tom	6	460
				Bob	4	460
				Green	5	460
				Fanny	50	575
				Evaline	37	805
				Rhody	33	805
				Amy	21	1035
				Harriet	19	1035
				Catharine	11	690
				Sill	17	1035
				Amanda	6	460
				Margaret	9	690
				Elisabeth	5	460
				Mary	1	115
				Polly	2	230

Taxable	Acres	Value	Location	Slave	Age	Value
				Jeff	1	115
				No 26		17,480
Davenport, A. W.[491]	500	4000	D. C.	Frank	35	1150
				Joab	27	1150
				Will	26	1265
				Bob	19	1150
				Jim	17	805
				Green	12	1035
				Andy	6	460
				Tom	4	460
				Pink	1	115
				Hannah	54	230
				Vine	45	575
				Harriet	28	1035
				Jude	21	1035
				Jane	20	1035
				Amanda	14	1035
				Adaline	15	1035
				Lizzie	5	460
				Kate	4	460
				Sallie	3	230
				Vene	1	115
				No 20		14,835
Davenport, Wm.[492]	250	2000	D. Crk			
Ewing, S. R.[493]	68	500	S Fork			
Dunn, Wm.[494]	106	500				
Fite, G. S.[495]	79	800	C. River	Sam	7	460
				Joe	5	460
				Isaac	4	460
				Dinah	24	1035
				Martha	17	1035
				Drucilla	1	115
				Sarah	1	115
				No 7		?3680
Fite, W. J.[496]	238	1200	C. River	Lewis	25	1035
				Catharine	16	1035
				No 2		2070
Fite, Henry	215	500	Fites Crk[497]	George	23	1150
				Frank	2	230
				Jane	38	805
				Mary	20	1035
				Mag.	4	460
				Lizzie	1	115
				No 6		3795
Grier, Ann[498]	344	900	Hoyle Crk	Ben	48	575
				No 1		575
Gaston, Robt.[499]	76	400	Taylors Crk[500]			
Hand, Jack[501]	116	300				
Hoffman, Caleb[502]	618	2700				
Hoffman, May[503]				Bill	48	575
				No 1		575
Hoover, Jacob[504]	206	600	Dr. Crk			
Hoover, John	101	500				
Hanks, E.	216	1000	S. Fork	Alberry	22	1150
				Joe	11	690
				Miles	10	230
				Tom	8	690
				Laben	1	115
				John	1	115
				Miller	35	805
				Ann Deficit	30	345
				Betsey	23	1035
				?Mile	21	1035
				Sue	9	690
				Susannah	6	460
				Harriet	1	115
				Baby	1	115

Taxable	Acres	Value	Location	Slave	Age	Value
				No 14		7590
Hunter, C. L.	520	3000	Taylers Crk	Manuel	46	460
				Zenas	23	1150
				Marces	17	1035
				James	14	1035
				Joe	14	1035
				Morris	3	230
				Webb	2	230
				Tait	1	115
				Robert	1	115
				Rufus	13	1035
				Mary	20	1035
				Adaline	26	1035
				Jane	16	1035
				Betsie	21	1035
				Daffie	11	690
				Caroline	?12	1035
				Isabella	8	690
				Emma	1	115
				Harriet	11	690
				No 19		13,800
Johnson, Saml.[505]	347	1500	Dr. Crk	Alf	25	1265
				John	23	1265
				Elick	20	1150
				Blair	17	1035
				Jerry	15	1035
				George	12	1035
				Mineve	2	230
				Ann	45	560
				Mariah	40	560
				Sue	18	1035
				Jane	17	1035
				Bill	15	1035
				Caroline	15	1035
				Avaline	1	115
				Sallie	12?	1035
				Adaline	6	460
				Cinda	3	230
				Liz	10	690
				No 18		14,805
Linebarger, David	100	700	Hoyle Crk	Pink	34	805
	100	300	Ridge Land	?Longa?	13	1035
				Alburtus	4	460
				Wade	3	230
				Harriet	27	1035
				Polly	14	1035
				Alice	6	460
				No 7		5060
Linebarger, J. R.	323	1900	S Fork	Bill	20	1150
				Alice	6	460
				No 2		1840
Linebarger, L.[506]	300	1200	S Fork	Berry	11	690
" "	212	1200	Olives Ford	Joe	10	690
				Harriet	54	345
				No 3		1725
" " as Adm M L	200	1200				
McLurd, R. L.	168	?900	Dr Crk	Hannah	11	690
				No 1		690
Moody, J.	32	100	Ridge			
Miller, J.	76	200				
Moore, Ann	369	1100				
Nims, F.[507]	584	6000	Duch Cr	Gilbert	22	1150
				Berry	28	1150
				Sampson	11	690
				John	7	460
				Lawrance	6	460
				Wm.	1	115

Taxable	Acres	Value	Location	Slave	Age	Value
				Wallace	1	115
				Ann	44	575
				Rose	44	575
				Mariah	26	1035
				Cinda	22	1035
				Louisa	20	1035
				Sallie	17	1035
				Sarah	17	1035
				Lizzie	8	690
				Margaret	2	230
				Mary	1	115
				No 17		11,500
Oates, James[508]	89	600	SF			
Pegram, E. L.				Harriet	17	1035
				No 1		1035
Rankin, S?ad[509]	270	1500		Green	46	805
				Sarah	21	1035
				Doll	4	230
				Laura	1	115
				No 4		2185
Rhyne, John[510]	622	3000	Fites Crk	Peg	50	?345
" "	126	400	Ridge	Phil	41	575
				West	26	1150
				Jess	17	1035
				Tom	14	1035
				Amzi	5	460
				Vanes	7	460
				Baby	1	115
				Caroline	29	1035
				Hannah	13	1035
				Harriet	20	1035
				Martha	15	1035
				Isabella	12	1035
				Alice	10	690
				Manda	8	690
				Catharine	3	230
				No 16		11,960
Rhyne, Jacob	121	1200				
Rankin, J. C.	212	1000		Burt	11	690
				Amanda	15	1035
				Easter	19	1035
				Harriet	1	115
				No 4		2875
Rhyne, David[511]	398	3500	S Crk	Ephraim	47	575
				Bill	30	805
				Adam	35	805
				Joe	15	1150
				Jud	33	805
				Alice	13	1035
				Tilda unsound	17	230
				No 7		5405
Rankin, J. D.[512]	913	6500		Dingo	56	115
	441	1800		?Herman	47	575
				Mose	44	575
				Fleet	44	575
				March	33	805
				A?lint	32	805
				Ransom	24	1150
				York	19	1150
				David	14	1035
				Pink	13	1035
				Bill	13	1035
				Amos	11	690
				Lee	4	460
				Abe	3	230
				Jake	2	230
				Candace	56	230

Appendix

Taxable	Acres	Value	Location	Slave	Age	Value
				Pauline ?USO.	44	230
				Margaret	42	575
				Liz Deficent	35	345
				Ann Def	31	460
				Cynthia	21	1035
				Liz	19	1035
				Eliza	23	1035
				Parth	18	1035
				Lena?	18	1035
				Jane	17	575
				Manda	12	1035
				Vina	8	690
				No 28		19,780
Rafter, Patrick[513]	86	800	S or T? Crk			
Rutledge, Alex[514]	171	1200	Dr Crk	Tom	14	1035
				Sam	11	690
				Jim	7	460
				Joe	4	460
				Caroline	30	805
				Lizzie	1	115
				No 6		3565
Rhyne, M. H.[515]	607	4500	F. Crk	Isaac unsd.	46	230
				David	29	1150
				Ephraim	10	690
				Will	6	460
				Sam	1	115
				Lila	35	805
				Evaline	32	805
				Mariah	25	1035
				Mary	8	690
				Ida	6	460
				Jane	4	460
				Alice	1	115
				No 12		7015
Rankin, J. P.	124	1000	S Crk	Charles	1	175
				B?ent	18	1035
				No 2		1150
Rankin, Richard[516]	335	2500	S Crk	Tom	50	345
" "	150	600	Cloninger tr	Bill	15	1035
" " Johns land	340	1800		Anderson	13	1035
				Jerry	7	460
				Mariah	44	575
				Minerva	34	805
				Sue	17	1035
				Sarah	15	1035
				Nancy	15	1035
				Adaline	13	1035
				Harriet	11	690
				No 11		9085
Rankin, J. R.[517]	310	3000	Dr Crk	Eph	44	575
				Bill	10	690
				George	10	690
				Dolph	2	115
				Mary	34	805
				Martha	32	805
				Harriet	16	1035
				Ann	16	1035
				Amanda	13	1035
				Peg	13	1035
				Emily	11	690
				Angeline	9	690
				Liz	7	460
				Rose Ann	6	460
				Martha Ann	1	115
				Mary	4	460
				No 16		10,695
Morris, Vincent[518]	64	250				

Taxable	Acres	Value	Location	Slave	Age	Value
Rankin, J B.	200	800	S Fork			
Rankin, Alex	130	700				
Rutledge, Wm.	57	300		Cudjo	45	805
" "	87	1000	D Cr	No 1		805
Rudisell, Heirs	900	1200	D Cr			
Rankin, Robt.[519]	183	1000				
" " for R. Alexander	229	1200		Louisa	28	1035
	280	700		No 1		1035
Rumfeldt, Isaac[520]	150	800				
Rishards, Wm.	273	1200		No 11		6670
				[no slaves listed by name]		
Smith & White ?L d.	320	1500				

Assessed out not Returned
Assessment of Land and Slaves for 1863=Woodlawn Com[pany]
[The following are in Woodlawn Company]

Taxable	Acres	Value	Location	Slave	Age	Value
Hovis, Absalom	167	700				
Moore, Ann	369	1100				
Mauney, Eph.	50	150				
Hoffman, Daniel?	?	2500				
Rhyne, Hugh	338	1800				
Jonas, Free	50	150				
McLurd. R. L. Agt				Boy	23	1142
				Genl?	22	1028
				Child	1	114
				No 3		2284
Shipp, Wm. T.[521]	837	5700	S or T. Crk	Mills Unsd.	46	345
	5	200		Henry	21	1150
				Joe	19	1150
				Tom	14	1035
				Levi	13	1035
				Ephraim	13	1035
				Richmond	9	690
				George	4	460
				Lizzie	34	690
				Lear?	23	1035
				Martha	16	1035
				Jane	14	1035
				Ann	12	1035
				Fanny	8	690
				May	1	115
				Susan	1	115
				No 16		12,650
Shipp, W. T.				Jane	20	1035
Guard Moore children				Adaline	15	1035
				Sarah	8	690
				No 3		2960
Scott, Abram	321	1700		Andy	24	1150
Duffy tr	170	500		Jim	22	1150
Cathy tr.	160	500		Tilman	20	1150
				Henry	?11	690
				Dick	10	690
				Jake	6	460
				Sol	3	230
				Lee	2	230
				Abe	1	115
				Juno	1	115
				Nancy infirm	42	000
				Nancy	3	230
				Phil	40	575
				Rachel	25	1035
				Betsey	24	1035
				Mary	22	1035
				Sopha	18	1035
				Mary ??	16	575
				Sue	6	690
				Harriet	3	230
				Lig?	1	115

Taxable	Acres	Value	Location	Slave	Age	Value
				No 21		12,535
Scott, Abram as				George	24	1150
Adm. Mrs. Moore				Sandy	32	1150
				Abe	17	1035
				Cephas	7	460
				Harriet	50	575
				Manda	40	575
				Eliza	36	805
				Caroline	17	1035
				Luce	17	1035
				Mary	7	460
				May	18	1035
				Baby	1	115
				Baby	1	115
				Baby	1	115
				Baby	1	115
				No 15		9775
Smith, Mary	125	500	F. Crk			
Smith, Jno B	75	500				
Sahms, Wm.	242	1200		Dos	28	1150
				Zimri	10	690
				Bill	8	690
				Isabella	10	690
				No 4		3220
" " for E. Martin				Hannah	14	1035
				Solomon	42	575
				No 2		1610
Smith, Lee	433	1800	S. Fork?	Albert	40	575
" " ~~Ridge tr~~	~~52~~	~~200~~		George	?18	1150
" "	~~25~~	~~40~~		No 2		1265
~~50~~	~~200~~					
Smith, Ben.	422	2500	S F	Alfred ??	26	460
Ridge	52	200		Kate	19	805
"	23	40		No 2		1265
"	50	200				
Smith, Robt.	484	2400				
Waggstaff, J. F.	100	700	S. Fork			
Agt for Grier	40	300				
Wilson, J. F.	223	700				
West, Ezekiel	221	500	D. C.			
West. Robt.	121	400	D. C.			
Johnston, Miss Mary				Jess	24	1150
				Ephraim	16	1035
				Harvey	13	1035
				Julius	8	690
				John	2	23
				Baby	1	115
				Vine	39	805
				Harriet	19	1035
				Frankey	10	690
				Sopha	6	470
				Patty	4	460
				Laura	2	230
				No 12		7935
Johnston, Miss Martha				Amos	13	1035
				George	11	690
				Abram	9	690
				Isam	8	690
				Bradley	5	460
				Elisabeth	31	805
				Emeline	27	1035
				Rose	25	1035
				Celia	2	230
				Baby	1	115
				No 10		6785

Tax Returns 1863

[The second section of the tax list was inconsistently formatted with numerous columns in the original, which varied by page. The author transcribed the taxables with identified items taxed beside their name. The transcripts found below include all eleven tax companies. Since acres, land value, town lots and number of slaves with their value were listed on the previous transcript, they are omitted from this list. Abbreviations for each item taxed is followed with the tax value and a semicolon. Items listed were transcribed as exactly as possible and some entries are ambiguous. The state and total tax follows individual listings. All money is in Confederate dollars with some variations. The categories listed include the following:] Acres Land; Value of Land; No of Town lots; Value of town lots; White Polls [wp]; No of Slaves; Value of Slaves; Solvent Debts due [solvent debts]; R R Capital[522]; Money or deposits on hand [cash]; State Bonds; County Bonds; Capital in Toll Bridges; Purchases of Cotton; Purchases of tobacco; R. R. Dividends due; Dogs over 2 [number]; Profits M. C. Goods & Woolen[523]; Profits on Leather; Profits on Iron; Money every S. Trade; Physicians Salary; Lawyers; Deadheads on R. R.[524]; Horses; Carriages; Mules; Studs and Jacks; Buying and Selling Slaves; Hotels; Toll Bridges & Ferrys; Gold Watches; Silver Watches; Pianos; Gold & Silver Plate Ware; Gold & Silver H Canes [gold or silver h cane]; Note Shavers; Pleasure Vehicles [pleasure v.]; Horses & Mules; Cattle; Other Livestock; Profits on Liquor; H & K Furniture[525]; Brandy Distilled [in gallons]; State or Co Tax; State Tax; Total Tax

Cherryville

Aderholdt, D.	6.40; 12.80
Aderholdt, M.	4.80; 9.60
Aderholdt, M. L.	cash 117; pleasure v. 75; brandy 13 gal; 2.52; 5.04
Black, Eph. Sen.	1 wp; solvent debts 800; cash 1000; 1 dog; gold watches 75; pleasure v. 75; note shaver 125; brandy 300; 6.82; 189.22
" as Admr of E. Evans	.80; 1.60
" as G O N B Anthony	solvent debts 237; .95; 1.90
Black, E. (Widow)	cash 507; brandy 240; 39.60; 72.91?
Black, S.	1 wp; 5.20; 10.40
Black, E. Senior	cash 537; pleasure v 50; 2.22; 4.44
Black, B.	1 wp; silver watches 75; 4.67; 9.35?
Black, Saml Sen.	cash 200; county bonds 512?; silver watches ?30; brandy 15; ?54.93; 109.84
" Gd Kisers H.	1.72; 3.45
" Agt E ?T Rutlege	.12; .24
Black, Thomas	7.49; 12.98
" Gd E Anthony	2.00; 4.00
Brown, James	2.40; 4.80
", R H	4.00; 8.00
Beam, J. F. & D.	3.60; 7.20
", John F	pleasure v 80; .80; 1.60
", Jno. T.	1 wp; 3.60; 7.20
Barber, Barbara	1.20; 2.40
Barnhill, Mary	.20; .40
", James	1 wp; 1.20; 2.40
Black, S. Jr	cash 300; brandy 22; 5.86; 11.72
", Gd M. Stroupe H	11.33; 22.67
Black, E. Jun	2.32; 4.64
Beam, Ann	2.50; 5.00
", Mary	.50; 1.01
Beam, Michael	pleasure v 50; gold watches 10; brandy 49; 23.36; 46.72
Blakely, Thos. F	1 wp; brandy 1½; 1.35; 2.70
Black, Daniel	brandy 20;
Black, Alf	gold watches 25; 2.25; 4.50
Collins, J M	.64; 1.28
Collins, Jno.	cash 20; .08; .16

Carpenter, James	1 dog; 10.00; 20.00
Conner, Wm.	.54; 1.08
Carpenter, B. M.	.89; 1.79
", Wm.	.42; .84
", Joshua	3.00; 6.00
Crouse, D.	.80; 1.60
Craft, Jno. P.	cash 145; 14.12; 28.25
Craft, M. J.	2.16; 4.32
Conner, E.	2.40; 4.80
Crites, H. J.	1.20; 2.40
Dellinger, Polly	.50; 1.00
", Peter	7.76; 15.52
", George as Exr P. D.	2.00; 4.00
", C.	2.40; 4.80
", Alfred	1 wp; 2.00; 4.00
", S.	.64; 1.28
", Michael	1 wp; 1.20; 2.40
Eaker, David	brandy 11; 1.10; 2.20
Eaker, Fanny C.	horses and mules 50; brandy 1½; 18.71; 37.42
", C.	4.00; 8.00
", David	1.20; 12.40
", Peter	brandy 4; .40; .80
Farries?, S.	2.00; 4.00
Faires, R. B. W.	1.40; 2.80
Fulton, J. W.	1 wp; cash 700; 4.00; 8.00
", J. B.	1 wp; cash 500; gold watches 100; 4.20; 8.40
Glascock, F. S.	1.00; 2.00
Homesley, Esther H.	brandy 40; 5.60; 11.20
Hallman, Jacob	1 wp; cash 56; 8.76; 17.52
Hallman, Ambrose	1 wp; 1.20; 2.40
Harrelson, Wm.	brandy 3; 4.64; 9.28
", W. O.	1 wp; 2.93; 5.86
", J. F.	silver watches 25; 2.80; 5.60
Homesly, A. B.	1 wp; brandy 112½; 2 dogs; 14.45; 30.90
Hoyle, J. M.	brandy 10; 4.20; 8.40
Hovis, George	18.14; 36.28
", George Jr.	1 wp; brandy 194; 20.60; 41.20
Harvey, J. N.	
Long, Barbara	.80; 1.60
Lawrence, T. H.	4.40; 8.80
Lusk, Joseph	solvent debts 900; cash 1200; buying & selling slaves 1400; gold watches 100; silver watches 25; pleasure v 50; 2 dogs; 17.65; 35.30
Lackey, James Adm	2.80; 5.60
Kendrick, J. L.	cash 60; 1.84; 3.68
McGinnis, J. J.	1 wp; solvent debts 757; cash 350; silver watches 15; pleasure v. 60; 21.45; 42.90
McGinnis, W. W.	solvent debts 1000; silver watches 55; pleasure v. 100; 1 dog; 10.75; 22.50
", " Gd Shell	solvent debts 408; 1.63; 3.26
Mauney, D.	5.80; 11.60
Mauney, Noah	1 wp; brandy 8; 2.00; 4.00
Morrison, B.	brandy 20; 3.38; 6.76
", Thos	1 wp; 1.20; 2.40
Neel, James	.90; 1.80
Putnam, L.	1.60; 3.20
Putnam, H.	.90; 1.80
Plonk, David	1 wp; cash 733; pleasure v 50; 9.50; 19.00
Reynolds, W	.03; .06
Reynolds, J.	.70; 1.40
Reynolds, Sally	brandy 21½; 2.15; 4.30
Reynolds, Martin	1 wp; 1.20; 2.40
Rudisill, J.	1.00; 2.00
", J. M.	brandy 194; 19.40; 38.80
", Wiley Ad PE	solvent debts 303; cash 173; 1.90; 3.80
", J. M. or J. ????	22.08; 44.16
Roberts, E. H.	cash 400; buying & selling slaves 1000; pleasure v. 100; 7.60; 15.20
Roberts, E. H. Admr. M. M.	cash 1100; brandy 50; 29.55; 59.10
Roberts, Jno H.	1 wp; solvent debts 500; cash 1000; gold watches 140; silver watches 35; 8.95; 17.90
Stroup, A. W.	1 wp; pleasure v. 158; brandy 20; 5.58; 11.16
", J. C.	cash 84; 3.53; 7.07

", C.	solvent debts 242; cash 386; 15.98; 31.96
", Barbara	brandy 6; 6.50; 13.00
", Abner	1 wp; 1.20; 2.40
", M. A.	solvent debts 36; .14; .29
Smith, H.	solvent debts 175; 1.48; 2.96
", J. R.	solvent debts 230; cash 884; county bonds 418;
", J. R. Geo? Mauney H.	solvent debts 90; .36; .72
", J. R. agt J. M.	cash 120; .48; .96
", David	pleasure v. 50; 5.24; 10.49
", David Agt C. Roberts	.40; .80
", David Agt J. Roberts	.40; .80
", David Agt W Ansly	.40; .80
", James	1 wp; 1.20, 2.40
Spake, Chrisopher	1 wp; 3.60; 7.20
Spake, S.	.80; 1.60
Summerour, H.	brandy 9; 7.56; 15.12
Shull, A.	1.60; 3.20
Sellars, Wm.	brandy 10; 5.36; 10.73
Sellars, Alf.	1 wp; brandy 2; 1.40; 2.80
Summit, Henry	1 wp; solvent debts 1200; cash 1150; studs and jacks 1/10; pleasure v. 650; brandy 400; ?130.23; 272.47
Taylor, E.	solvent debts 275; 1.90; 3.80
Whitworth, Wyoma	1.60; 3.20
Whitworth, Lydia	
White, Barbara	1.60; 3.20
Warlick, P. H.	1.40; 2.80
Warlick, Lydia	brandy 12; 1 dog; 4.40; 9.80
Warlick, S.	1.80; 3.60
Wacaster, Levi	.98; 1.92
Totals	$865.00 $1,736.00 6 dogs

Crowders Mountain

Adams, Jno H.	solvent debts 550; RR dividends 10; silver watch 15; gold & silver ware 25; pleasure v. 150; 55.57; 111.14
Anthony, Jas. C.	8.20; 16.40
Adams, Margaret	45.40; 90.80
Beattie, Francis	5.94; 11.88
", Wm.	2.00; 4.00
", Jas. O.	2.00; 4.00
Bell, Rachel R.	cash 240; 2.36; 4.72
Bell, Robert H.	2.20; 4.40
Boyce, E. E.	solvent debts 100; pleasure v. 100; 28.21; 56.42
Blackwood, Joseph	1 wp; solvent debts 204; 3.21; 6.83?
", Jane	1.40; 2.80
", Ann	1.40; 2.80
", Nancy	1.40; 2.80
Boyd, Robt. W.	pleasure v. 100; 47.57; 95.14
Bell, Eli	1 wp; 2.00; 4.00
Crawford, James	1 wp; solvent debts 500; county bonds 100; pleasure v. 65; 51.31; 102.62
Crawford, Jas. L.	1 wp; RR dividends 5; pleasure v. 75; 16.79; 33.58
", John O. Guard heirs ?	5.42; 10.85
", Wm. N.	.60; 1.20
Carroll, W. D.	1 wp; 7.32; 14.65
", Margaret	cash 140; 1.16; 2.32
", Sarah	cash 55; .22; .44
", Elisabeth	cash 27; .10; .21
Carson, Jos?. W.	2.80; 5.60
", Robt	cash 195; county bonds 100; silver watch 8; 4.66; 9.32
", Jas. M.	solvent debts 100; 6.20; 12.40
", " Exr T O C	2.20; 4.40
Crawford, M. A.	8.00; 16.00
", ", as Gd	4.37; 8.74
", Rachel J.	48.23; 96.47
Carson, Isabella	4.00; 8.00
Cobb, M. D.	solvent debts 500; cash 2000; 30.50; 61.00
Dickey, And. J.	1 wp; solvent debts 996; purchase of tobacco 200; RR dividends 5; brandy 150; 37.93; 75.86
", ", for Jas.	solvent debts 913; RR dividends 5; 13.55; 27.10

Davis, Mary J.	pleasure v. 75; .75; 1.50
Ferguson, Jas. Senr	14.45; 28.91
", Jas. Jr.	
Falls, Robt A.	1 wp; pleasure v. 50; brandy 20; profits on Liquor 450; 55.50; 111.00
Falls, Rebecca	5.40; 10.80
Falls, Wm.	solvent debts 400; pleasure v. 75; 15.09; 30.19
", " Agt Morrow	pleasure v. 50; 3.64; 7.29
Ferguson, Wm. M.	1 wp; solvent debts 100; cash 1000; pleasure v. 125; furniture 100; profits on liquor 300; 83.65; 167.50
Ferguson, Elis. J.	solvent debts 50; 3.40; 6.80
Ferguson, Jas. Jr.	1 wp; brandy 28; 5.80; 11.60
Ferguson, Thos Sen	solvent debts 550; cash 650; 14.00; 28.00
Ferguson, Milton	1 wp; cash 130; 2.52; 5.04
Ferguson, Thos W.	3.20; 6.40
Forbes, John H.	1 wp; brandy 12; 4.40; 8.80
Fronebarger, Lewis	6.00; 12.00
Foy, James	.48; .96
Falls, John R.	solvent debts 4059; cash 600; county bonds 100; studs and jacks 1/600; silver watch 15; pleasure v. 75; 93.51; 187.02
", Isabella	solvent debts 2757; cash 120; 11.51; 23.03?
Ford, Dr. J. W.	30.98; 61.97
Gamble, Robt F.	1 wp; cash 500; 11.00; 22.00
", A. J. by Robt	8.97; 17.94
?Henry, Thos	2.60; 5.20
Hill, Alex M.	4.80; 9.60
Hays, ? Mary?	.40; .80
Holland, Pris. R.	30.86; 61.93
Henderson, Wm.	2.00; 4.00
Hill, Z. S.	pleasure v. 60; 27.13; 54.27
Holland, W. R. Gd	12.42; 24.85
Hays, Wm. L.	1 wp; brandy 16; 2.80; 5.60
Lowrance, M. C.	2.40; 4.80
Love, Eliza E.	cash 250; 11.41; 22.83?
Love, Mary	4.20; 8.40
", " for S. & L. Estate	solvent debts 475; cash 275; 3.00; 6.00
", Naomi E.	15.45; 30.91
", Naomi	solvent debts 32; 1 dog;. 12; 1.25
", Jennet	cash 135; 6.62; 13.25
Love, Sarah	cash 735; pleasure v. 125; 8.21; 16.43?
", Mary A.	solvent debts 500; silver watch 10; 13.17; 26.34
", Mary (Widow)	3.67; 7.84
McCready, Jno	1.20; 2.40
", Wm.	1.20; 2.40
McNair, Enoch	9.70; 19.40
McClure, Jas. H.	17.60; 35.20
Mendenhall, Eli	solvent debts 1100; 9.20; 18.40
", " for J. H.	8.05; 16.10
McAlister, G. W.	pleasure v. 75; 3.95; 7.90
Oates, Wm.	8.54; 16.69
Obrian, Drucilla	.16; .32
Patterson, Wm.	.80; 1.60
Packard, Wm.	.60; 1.20
Petty, Chas. Q.	30.81; 61.62
Pearson, Wm.	2.00; 4.00
Parker, T. W.	silver watch 8; 1.28; 2.56
Parham, ?Martin?	silver watch 25; .25; .50
Revels, Gabriel	3.20; 6.40
", Stephen	1.20; 2.40
", Allen	1.20; 2.40
Service, S. T.	5.60; 11.20
Simmons, R. L.	3.08; 6.16
Torrence, Wm. W.	cash 100; 23.48; 46.97
", W. J.	1.20; 2.40
Wilson, L. & E. B.	2.71; 5.42
Wilson, Lawson	cash 2900, county bonds 300; RR dividends 10; silver watches 20; pleasure v. 100; furniture 50; 1 dog; 95.16; 191.33
", Edward	3.20; 6.40
Wilson, E. B.	cash 31; county bonds 800; RR Dividends 20; silver watches 15; 43.95; 87.90

", " Ad W?McLure?	cash 900; county bonds 600; 6.00; 12.00
", Saml. M.	3.94; 7.88
", Saml	2.00; 4.00
", William	cash 820; county bonds 100; cotton purchased 81; 10.00; 20.01
Whitesides, Edward	cash 893; pleasure v. 50; horses 1/60; 18.23; 36.42
", "Gd	cash 57; 3.03; 6.07
", Mary	2.00; 4.00
Wilson, J. J.	county bonds 500; 2.00; 4.00
Wier, W. O. Admr.	7.08; 14.77
Whitesides, Jno by E W	cash 186; .72; 1.49
", Mary & Marg.	cash 1332; 5.32; 10.65
", J. ?T.	1 wp; pleasure v. 65; 1.85; 3.70
Totals	$1,332.73 $2,667.57 2 dogs

Dallas

Abernathy, Starling	1.30; 2.60
Bell, John	cash 2800; 18.00; 36.00
Boyd, And.	1 wp; 1.20; 2.40
Barrett, E. S. for Keener	1 wp; Profits on M. leather 500; brandy 41; 24.10; 48.20
Brown, J. S.	horse 1/200; 2.40; 4.80
Best, Saml in Roberts Company	
Barrett, E S. For Phifer	6.40; 12.80
Beam, Col J.	.80; 1.60
Deck, Jonas	pleasure v. 50; furniture 1.00; 8.90; 1780
Cross, Tabitha	.40; .80
Costner, S. P.	1 dog; 15.52; 32.04
Clemmer, S. S.	cash 450; 11.61; 23.22
", Levi	cash 107; furniture 50; brandy 29; 7.32; 14.65
", Adam	11.40; 22.80
", Georges Est.	brandy 40; 50.88; 101.77
", Arabella	1.60; 3.20
Costner, M. H.	1 wp; cash 969; furniture 100; 21.10; 42.20
", " Ad J. Costner?	cash 457; 12.01; 24.00
?", E Costner?	cash 485; 1.94; 3.88
", Joseph	brandy 10; 3.20; 6.40
", Valentines heirs	10.00; 20.00
", M. H. for A.	10.20; 20.40
Cloninger, David	1.30; 2.60
", Jonas	2.20; 4.40
Costner, S. P. Adm	cash 1452; brandy 18; 7.60; 15.21
Fronebarger, Jac.	1 wp; cash 7000; pleasure v. 60; 72.62; 145.25
", " Guar W. F. Holland	cash 650; 18.14; 36.29
", " Adm E. H?urell [Murell?]	cash 1225; 4.90; 9.80
Ford, Amzi	silver watches 10; 3.40; 6.80
Fraley, Stephen	brandy 2; 2.20; 4.40
Featherston, J. B.	1 wp; 4.10; 8.20
Fite, J. W.	1 wp; pleasure v. 150; 2.70; 5.40
Friday, M. D.	1 wp; cash 180; furniture 118; brandy 8; 2 dogs; 15.27; 32.55
", " Ad J. Friday	cash 1085; 39.04; 78.08
", David	cash 30; furniture 300; brandy 10; 21.85; 43.71
", Elis. By M. D.	cash 1588; 15.08; 30.16
Flowers, Green	2.40; 5.80
Fronebarger, Ambrose	5.90; 11.80
Groner, Austin	2.00; 4.00
Gantt, Mary	16.72; 33.44
Gladden, Jno. J.	pleasure v. 100; furniture 100; 28.58; 57.16
Glenn, W. D.	1 wp; cash 1024; silver watch 30; 7.09; 14.19
Hoffman, David	6.20; 12.40
Hoffman, Daniel	county bonds 600; Hotel; pleasure v. 200; furniture 600; profits on leather 300; 1 dog; 87.58; 176.16
Holland, J. D. for E. B.	1 wp; cash 3485; gold watch 250; furniture 200; 23.64; 47.28
Holland, Robt	cash 1900; furniture 50; 27.17; 54.35
Holland, Franklin	cash 724; 2.89; 5.79
Hoyle, M. D.	cash 1859; pleasure v. 50; 7.93; 15.87
Hoyle, C W by J. C. S.?	cash ?5774; studs & jacks 1/15; gold watches 100; silver h cane 1; 172.29; 347.59
Hovis, Absalom	furniture 550; brandy 105?; 3 dogs; 13.30; 26.60

Holland, Robt for A. R.	6.40; 12.80
Jenkins, Joseph	cash 82; brandy 3; 4.62; 9.25
", Aaron	cash 1630; silver h cane 1; pleasure v. 10?; 10.82; 21.64
", Smith	cash 188; brandy 5; 7.65; 15.30
", William	pleasure v. 50; furniture 212; brandy 25; 1 dog; 53.75; 108.50
Jarrett, Saml.	cash 1000; silver watch 15; furniture 20; 14.40; 28.80
Jenkins, Eli	1.20; 2.40
", Harrison	2.00; 4.00
", Catharine	1.60; 3.20
", Berryman	1.50; 3.00
Kahnwieler, K.	1 wp; profits on leather 600; gold watch 2; 15.62; 31.24
Linebarger, Jonas	4.00; 8.00
", J. W.	pleasure v. 50; 5.10; 10.20
", Caleb	pleasure v. 50; 5.40; 10.80
", J. F. by H. Setzer	brandy 100; 16.00; 32.00
", Michael	4.40; 8.80
", " Agt S. J.	2.30; 4.60
", " Agt F. S. Hoffman	2.20; 4.40
Link, M.	4.40; 8.80
Long, And.	1 wp; purchases tobacco 108; pleasure v. 75; Brandy 3; 9.68; 19.36
Lewis, J. G.	cash 800; pleasure v. 50; 5.30; 10.60
", " Adm of Ann	cash 8000; 32.00; 64.00
", " Adm P. Fronebarger	cash 1000; 11.40; 22.80
Morris, W. G.	pleasure v. 60; 11.87; 23.74
Morris, Mary	2.40; 4.80
McAlister, H. C.	2.90; 5.80
Nathan, ?Myer	cash 7428; purchases tobacco 465??; 32.57; 65.14
Obian, Mrs. And.	5.00; 10.00
Pasour, Manassa	cash 579; brandy 4; 2 dogs; 32.02; 66.05
", " Exr	cash 490; 1.96; 3.92
", Saml	cash 110; pleasure v. 50; furniture 50; 4.74; 9.48
", Jac. A.	1 wp; brandy 5; 2.50; 5.00
", George J.	cash 150; furniture 200; brandy 15; 4.40; 8.80
", S. P.	cash 1100; 8.00; 16.00
", " Exr D P	cash 500; 2.00; 4.00
", Eli	1 wp; cash 5586; gold watch 35; pleasure v. 150; 19.79; 39.55
Peterson, J. R.	1 wp; silver watch 25; pleasure v. 50; furniture 100; 6.05; 13.10
", " for E. Jenkins	cash 115; .46; .92
Pegram, J. F.	1 wp; pleasure v. 75; 39.78; 79.57
", " M. M. Stowe heirs	cash 1800; furniture 600; 7.20; 14.40
", Mary	pleasure v. 200; 2.00; 4.00
", J. F. as Exr	43.32; 86.64
Plonk, Jacob Esqr	cash 14; "Cap in Toll Bridge" 25; furniture 30; 6.80; 13.60
", " Gd M. S. ?Samart	cash 583; 2.38; 4.66
", Mary C.	cash; 1.29; 2.59
Pasour, Hannah	4.00; 8.00
", George for Levi	1.40; 2.80
Pegram, J. F. for A. H. & Co.	.60; 1.20
Rhyne, Catharine	1.20; 2.40
Rhyne, Esli	purchases of tobacco 140; pleasure v. 60; brandy 27; 9.66; 19.32
", A. A.	cash 1000; brandy 18; 22.18; 44.37
", J. K.	1 wp; furniture 120; 6.68; 13.36
", Jac. M.	furniture 156; 1 dog; 55.20; 112.41
", Jos. K.	cash 582; studs and jacks 1/600; pleasure v. 75; on leather ?1200; furniture 50; 38.07; 76.15
", Christy	furniture 300; 35.62; 77.25
", Jac. Jr.	1 wp; brandy 15; 2 dogs; 2.70; 7.40
Robison, Nancy	5.40; 10.80
Rhyne, Dorcus	31.99; 63.98
", J. J. Est	20.60; 41.20
Rudisill, John	5.20; 10.40
Roberts, John H.	
Setzer, Henry	cash 4380; "Cap in Toll Bridge" 125; pleasure v. 100; furniture 210; 57.93; 115.86
", " Gd A S H	cash 172; 3.58; 7.17
Summit, L. M.	cash 700; pianos 1/150; furniture 300; profits on liquor 416; 61.66; 123.32
Stowe, Ferrie M.	15.05; 30.11
", LeRoy	silver h cane ?1; 64.57; 129.15
Smith, Andrew	1 wp; 5.20; 10.40

", Eli by C C W	1 wp; furniture 100; 4.90; 9.80
Sloan, Wm	1 wp; cash 2600; gold watches 150; gold h cane 1; physician 2000 [in column with silver cane]; furniture 200; 83.89; 167.78
Smith, J. C. for J. Rudisill	.70; 1.40
", D. B.	3.40; 6.80
Turbyfill, Jas.	1 wp; gold watch 100; 2.20; 4.40
Thornburg, Moses	1 wp; 1.84; 3.69
Thornburg, Daniel	RR Capital 41; furniture 219; brandy 55; 4 dogs; 16.98; 37.97
Withers, Susan	1.10; 2.20
", " for sons	3.20; 6.40
", ?W C	1 wp; 1.20; 2.40
", C. C.	1 wp; pleasure v. 75; furniture 100; 5.75; 11.50
", Wm.	cash 1437; pleasure v. 60; 6.34; 12.68
", E. H.	1 wp; cash 400; silver watch 15; 2.95; 5.90
", J. H.	1 wp; 1.20; 2.40
Wells, David	cash 229; 9.71; 19.43
", James	brandy 20; 2.00; 4.00
White, Jas. H.	cash 1785; pleasure v. 60; furniture 100; 57.05; 114.10
", " ? Gd Shtley?	cash 1000; 4.00; 8.00
", " ?for H. F.?	cash 100; silver watch 15; .55; 1.10
", T. S.	1 wp; 1.20; 2.40
", J. H. for White & ?Yrs?	6.00; 12.00
Withers, C. C. Adm	2.60; 5.20
Ward, Mary	6.88; 15.77
Dellinger, Alfred	.20; .40
Lewis, J. G. for D. ?Finger?	2.80; 5.60
Jenkins, Wm. Gd A. Shetley ?	cash 588; 2.35; 4.70
Totals	$1979.19 $3,975.38 Dogs Co tx

Duharts

Allen, Vincent	
Allen, ?Na L	2.60; 5.20
Armstrong, Matt.	1 wp; Studs and jacks 1/700; 14.30; 28.60
", John	1.30; 2.60
Abernathy, C. H.	6.00; 12.00
Anders, E. M.	1.50; 3.00
Bradley, ?Cailon	
Bradley, A. S.	cash 100; solvent debts 500; furniture 50; 21.80; 43.60
", J. W.	pleasure v. 70; furniture 10; 7.14; 14.28
", Eli H.	1 wp; 6.60; 13.20
", " for C. Rhodes	solvent debts 160; .64; 1.28
", Caleb	1 wp; 6.00; 12.00
", Albert for O. W. D.	4.10; 8.20
", " Exc Jas. D.	6.30; 12.60
Cox, Eli H.	1 wp; 5.20; 10.40
Capps, T. B.	
Cox, Thos	
Costner, Joe	
Cherry, John	2.30; 4.60
Clemmer, Jno Adm	5.60; 11.20
Davis, Jno. W.	1 wp; 2.60; 5.20
Dickson, W. S.	2.40; 4.80
", Jno. T.	3.80; 7.60
", Alex	3.40; 6.80
Ford, Jas, M.	1.90; 3.80
Ford, Alex	
", Frederick	
", Jas. H.	2.70; 5.40
Floyd, H. H.	1 wp; 3.70; 7.40
", " for John	9.20; 18.40
", Leroy	1 wp; solvent debts 300; 4.80; 9.60
", S. W.	1 wp; silver watch 20; 1.40; 2.80
Gaston, Rachel	1.50; 3.00
", Sarah	4.23; 8.46
", Adaline	1.40; 2.80
", John	
", " Gd ?Stowes heirs	
", Pink in South Point	

Gordon, John	22.57; 45.15
Gingles, Mary	1.20; 2.40
Grissom, J. F.	silver watch 12; 1.82; 3.64
Hanna, S. B.	pleasure v. 70; 2.70; 5.40
", Jas. H.	1 wp; silver watch 12; 1.32; 2.64
", Thos. M.	2.00; 4.00
", F. S.	
", Jas. M.	furniture 25; 5.42; 10.84
Holland, W. M. in Tanyd	
", L. M.	solvent debts 150; 3.60; 7.20
Hoffman, Jonas Guardian	1 wp; solvent debts 3260; 13.04; 26.08
Hoffman, Jonas Adm	solvent debts 7022; 28.08; 56.17
Houser, Abram	2.80; 5.60
Hoffman, Jonas	1 wp; solvent debts 6711; pleasure v. 50; furniture 50; 2 dogs; 46.92; 95.84
Hand, Uriah	1.20; 2.40
Helton, Milton	4.00; 8.00
Hoffman, Jacob	2 dogs; 7.60; 17.20
Hoffman, Miles	1 wp; cash 150; solvent debts 100; gold watches 50; pleasure v. 75; 2 dogs; 9.45; 20.90
Hoffman, Solomon	1 wp; cash 19; solvent debts 456; 8.09; 16.19
", Jno	12.15; 24.31
Jenkins, Jonas	1 wp; 2.70; 5.40
", Dan R.	1.30; 2.60
Leeper, Mary	2.00; 4.00
Love, R. C. G.	1 wp; solvent debts 410; 1 piano; pleasure v. 75; other livestock 250; 17.58; 35.16
", " as Gd	solvent debts 420; 1.68; 3.36
Linebarger, C. J.	1 wp; solvent debts 2750; pleasure v. 55; 1 dog; 57.66; 116.33
", L. J.	1 wp; gold watch 100; gold plated ware 40; pleasure v. 125; 1 dog; 49.86; 100.72
", Peter	solvent debts 100; 2.00; 4.00
", L & Co.	profits m. Cotton 15,000; 529.27; 1058.54
", Catharine	4.30; 8.60
Lay, W. B.	3.92; 7.84
", Jessee	studs and jacks 1/600; 7.40; 14.80
", C. H.	3.40; 6.80
McKee, Jemima	4.70; 9.40
Morrow, ?S. L. or T. L.	13.11; 26.22
McAlister, Joseph	1 wp; 1.20; 2.40
McCready, Elis.	1.60; 3.20
Murrell, Isaac	30.79; 61.58
", " ?Justus tr	3.20; 6.40
Mason, L A	1 wp; silver watches 35; pleasure v. 75; 58.29; 116.58
Noland, M. L.	3.20; 6.40
Perkins, Isaac	1.30; 2.60
Quinn, Jno. R.	1 wp; solvent debts 50; pleasure v. 50; 16.12; 32.25
Rhyne, Jonathan	1 wp; solvent debts 600; pleasure v. 60; furniture 50; 1 dog; 13.20; 27.40
", " Adm J. ?Shrp?	3.20; 6.40
", David	1.20; 2.40
", Jac. H.	cash 864; solvent debts 4740; pleasure v. 150; brandy 50; 3 dogs; 83.06; 169.12
", Daniel	cash 200; solvent debts 250; 15.27; 30.54
", Jac. A.	2.20; 4.40
", Eml.	3.10; 6.20
Ratchford, J. A.	4.60; 9.20
Rankin, A. N. ?Ro?	1.10; 2.20
Robison, Eli J.	1 wp; pleasure v. 90; 15.43; 30.87
Reed, Eliza	1.60; 3.20
Smith, Jas. D.	1 wp; solvent debts 1000; 14.60; 29.20
", " Gd	solvent debts 320; 1.28; 2.56
Service, Saml.	1.40; 2.80
Suggs, M. S.	1.20; 2.40
Stroup, Rebecca	2.80; 5.60
", Rufus	.80; 1.60
", Wesley	2.60; 5.20
Sahms, Wm.	1 wp; pleasure v. 65; 1.85; 3.70
Shannon, Hugh	5.00; 10.00
", James	5.00; 10.00
Spencer, Wm.	1 wp; 1.40; 2.80
Stowe, E. A.	1.37; 3.74
", Delphia	1.86; 3.72
", Logan	2.20; 4.40

", J. R. & S T?	3.60; 7.20
Selvy, Wm.	2.30; 4.60
Titman, Anthony	1 wp; 1 dog; 8.80; 17.60
", A. B.	25.35; 50.71
", " as Adm	1.94; 3.88
Whitesides, Wm.	4.60; 9.20
", Edward	2.40; 4.80
Wilson, Thos.	1 wp; cash 166; solvent debts 60; county bonds 200; silver watch 14; pleasure v. 50; 14.89; 29.78
", " Gd C. Whitesides	solvent debts 285; 1.14; 2.28
", " Gd J. F. Whitesides	solvent debts 322; 1.29; 2.58
", " Gd Priscilla	solvent debts 343; 1.37; 2.74
Williams, C. H.	4.40; 8.80
Totals	$1,384.47 $2,781.9[torn] 13 dogs

High Shoals

Aydlotte, Susan	11.98; 23.97
", R. K.	1 wp; solvent debts 450; pleasure v. 150; 1 dog; 4.42; 9.84
Arents, Jane Hrs	1.50; 3.00
Bynum, Martha	2.00; 4.00
Black, Vincent	furniture 25; 4.90; 9.80
Barron, B. B.	1 wp; gold watch 275; silver watch 75; pleasue v. 100; furniture 200; 160.77; 321.55
Bridgers, R. R.	241.10; 482.20
Bridges, Jno L	1 wp; gold watches 265; piano 1; pleasure v. 100; furniture 725; 1 dog; 261.71; 524.42
Cloninger, Michael	3.00; 6.00
", Elis. R.	cash 295; solvent debts 235; 17.43; 34.86
", Moses	cash 399; solvent debts 635; brandy 12; 16.24; 32.48
", Fanny	.80; 1.60
", Jonas S.	cash 102; solvent debts 646; pleasure v. ?75; 3.74; 7.49
Dellinger, Alfred	.80; 1.60
Friday, Ephraim	solvent debts 10,292; gold watch 75; piano 1; pleasure v. 75; furniture 50; 114.68; 229.37
Friday, Jno. N.	cash 255; solvent debts 201; pleasure v. 80; 86.91; 175.82
", Polly	solvent debts 300; 2.82; 5.64
", Elisabeth	brandy 1; 12.72; 25.45
", Michael	cash 600; solvent debts 2380; 56.57; 113.14
", Jacob W.	brandy 60; 2 dogs; 21.36; 44.72
", Jonas W.	1 wp; 1.20; 2.40
Gregory, S. B.	1 wp; silver watch 40; furniture 100; 15.42; 30.84
High Shoals Iron Co.	360.00; 720.00
" for Cook VA	29.97; 59.94
" for Dr. Wallace	16.84; 33.69
" for Dr. Gailard	7.45; 14.90
" Wid Sty?num	4.86; 9.72
Hovis, Adam	4.60; 9.20
", Philip	4.00; 8.00
", Jacob	.80; 1.60
", John	1 wp; 1.20; 2.40
Kistler, Lawson	.60; 1.20
Lineberger, J. D.	5.00; 10.00
", Eli	1.10; 2.20
Lanc?aster, John	1 wp; solvent debts 1726; 8.10; 16.21
Moore, Mary	cash 110; solvent debts 90; 15.70; 31.41
", Marg.	2.91; 5.83
", John C.	pleasure v. 50; 10.84; 21.69
", " for Ann	1.20; 2.40
Morris, Stephen	cattle 18; other livestock 60; 2 dogs; 6.31; 14.62
", " For Stroups hirs	cash 80; solvent debts 260; furniture 1; 1.46; 2.92
McGinnas, Jno A.	13.14; 26.28
", " as Exr. Rs Est	cash 1131; solvent debts 25; 4.62; 9.25
", " trustee for M. Smith	18.32; 36.66
Nance, Lawson	.40; .80
", John	1 wp; 1.20; 2.40
Oglisby, Sam O.	1.60; 3.20
Plonk, J. F.	1 wp; cash 500; solvent debts 538; purchasing tobacco 14; silver watches 30; pleasure v. 125; furniture 6; 2 dogs; 16.65; 35.50
Pasour, G. I.	1 wp; furniture 15; 4.70; 9.40
Peterson, C. J.	1 wp; silver watch 25; 3.35; 6.70
Powels, J. W. Est.	157.82; 315.65

Parker, J. J.	1 wp; 1.20; 2.40
Rutledge, Robt	silver watch 10; pleasure v. 65; other livestock 40; brandy 40; 19.55; 39.10
", James River Bend	
", Robt. Exr G. R.	cash 135; solvent debts 655; 3.16; 6.32
", A. R. agt R. R. C.	10.00; 20.00
Rhodes, Melchi	12.00; 24.00
", M & C	4.00; 8.00
", Caleb	cash 300; solvent debts 3300; toll bridges 121; furniture 105; 64.14; 128.28
", M. M.	solvent debts 1552; 6.20; 12.41
Rhyne, Solomon	27.54; 55.09?
", " heirs	4.80; 9.60
", H. M.	1 wp; silver watch 50; pleasure v. 150; 3.20; 6.40
Robison, Thos.	.60; 1.20
Smith, Mary	1.10;2.20
", David	1.20; 2.40
Summey, Elis.	cash 102; solvent debts 1998; pleasure v. 100; 24.81; 49.62
", Jonas	1 wp; 1.20; 2.40
Stroup, Caroline	.50; 1.00
", Bartlett	other livestock 53; 5.04; 10.09
", Benjamin	1.60; 3.20
", Jane	1.20, 2.40
", Hosea	1 wp; cash 8; 4.23; 8.46
", John D.	cash 127; solvent debts 256; 12.08; 24.17
", Nancy J.	cash 207; solvent debts 19; pleasure v. 50; 6.60; 13.20
", Israel R.	cash 350; solvent debts 720; pleasure v. 50; 13.98; 27.96
", Solomon	cash 40; ?cattle 3; other livestock 40?; 5.12; 10.24
", Wesley	silver watch 10; brandy 5; 3.76; 7.35
", And. J.	1 wp; cash 125; solvent debts 678; 4.41; 8.82
", ?Josh H.	?bank dividend 55?; silver watch 12; .34; .65
Sifford, D. M.	cash 186; silver watch 100; horses ?75?; 5.39; 10.79
Thomson, F. W.	13.45; 26.90
", L. E.	bank dividends 1500; cash 100; silver watch 80; piano 1; silver plating 51; pleasure v. 180; 60.58; 121.16
Weatherly, M. H.	1 wp; bank dividends 5506; silver watch 60; 23.82; 47.64
Williford, E.	1 wp; bank dividends 1?5?90; silver watch 50; pleasure v. 50; silver cane 1; 11.97; 23.95
Total	$2,106.44; $4,220.89 Dogs [no number given]

Roberts

Adams, Marg	1.20; 2.40
", Saml D.	.52; 1.05
Abernathy, ?St. G.	.80;1.60
Arrowood, Wm.	cash 852; bank dividends 375; silver watch 30; pleasure v. 50; 17.47; 34.94
", " for Marg.	8.79; 17.59
", B. F. by Wm.	solvent debts 226; silver watch 20; pleasure v. 50; 1 dog; 21.85; 50.71
Blackwood, Gideon	solvent debts 196; 57.86; 115.73
", Marg.	solvent debts 395; 1.58; 3.16
", Mary	solvent debts 278; cash 40; 1.27; 2.54
", Elis	solvent debts 308; 1.23; 2.46
Best, Saml	solvent debts 3857; state bonds 1060; pleasure v. 55; furniture 50; brandy 40; 2 dogs; 73.11; 148.23
", Michael	1 wp; pleasure v. 50; 1 dog; 10.30; 21.60
", A. J.	cash 150; 8.70; 17.40
Boggs, Jas. G.	1 wp; cash 2000; pleasure v. 225; profits on liquor 2000; 218.50; 437.00
Carpenter, L. B.	1.20; 2.40
Clemmer,S. J.	1.20; 2.40
Clark, Wm.	1 wp; 2.40; 4.80
", Adam	.48; .96
", J. W.	.53; 1.07
Deck, Peter	solvent debts 452; 7.80; 15.61
", " for Fall heirs	1.80; 3.60
Dickey, Alex	1 wp; cash 332; solvent debts 1484; RR dividends 100; 17.38; 34.76
", " for Jas.	solvent debts 157; 5.51; 10.63
Dameron, Geo	.60; 1.20
Eaker, Catharine	.90; 1.80
", Hiram	.40; .80
Fronebarger, Marg.	.60; 1.20
", John Senr	6.40; 12.80
", John Jr.	.10; .20

", Elis.	4.00; 8.00
", Jacob Senr.	2 dogs; 70.63; 143.26
", Jane	solvent debts 1081; 4.32; 8.65
Fulton, Jas. B.	3.84; 7.69
Ferguson, Thos. ?Senr	5.50; 11.00
", James	solvent debts 1427; pleasure v. 50; 13.00; 26.00
", William	4.00; 8.00
Falls, Robt Esq.	2.00; 4.00
Ford, Hiram	2.80; 5.60
Garrett, E W	1 wp; cash 8450; cotton 4439; gold watches 150; gold and silver plated 125; pleasure v. 150; 570.00; 114.01
Gamble, Joseph	cash 1332; 2 dogs; 37.54; 77.08
", " Gd	cash ?8187?; 32.75; 65.50
Gant, A. J.	1.20; 2.60
Garrett Brothers	427.96; 855.93
Garrett, R. H.	1 wp; 1.20; 2.40
Gaston, Jas. A.	1 wp; solvent debts 800; pleasure v. 58; 4.98; 9.96
Hester, Abram	1 wp; 1.20; 2.40
Herron, John	solvent debts 212; .84; 1.69
", "	2.44; 4.88
Hagar, George	.40; .80
", John	solvent debts 100; 10.40; 20.80
", Wm.	solvent debts 1214; pleasure v. 50; 15.83; 31.67
Holland, Frank	solvent debts 724; 6.39; 12.79
", Julius	1 wp; solvent debts 4635; 41.28; 82.57
Hovis, Jac. D.	pleasure v. 75; 3.95; 7.90
Huffstetler, John	1 dog; 2.80; 6.60
", H. B.	silver watch 20; pleasure v. 75; 1 dog; 8.55; 18.10
", " Adm C H	17.86; 35.73
", " Adm Hagers?	solvent debts 900; 3.60; 7.20
", Walter	.40; .80
Johnston, Dicey	3.20; 6.40
Kennedy, J. K.	1 wp; 2.00; 4.00
Kiser, George	2.00; 4.00
", Mary M.	4.00; 8.00
", Mary	1.58; 3.16
", Jacob	1 wp; cash 220; silver watch 25; 8.29; 16.58
", Zimiri?	pleasure v. 75; 4.05; 8.10
", Joseph	solvent debts 155; 1.58; 3.16
", Fanny (wid)	.60; 1.20
Long, Jos.	1 wp; 2.00; 4.00
", L. H.	2.70; 5.40
Love, Mary	2.04; 4.08
Leman, Wm.	1 wp; 1.20; 2.40
Mauney, Lawson	solvent debts 1024; pleasue v. 75; 23.03; 46.06
", Abe Sen	.08; .17
", Michael	solvent debts 57; 6.10; 12.20
", "	.22; .45
", John	solvent debts 314; studs and jacks 6.00; pleasure v. 100; profits from liquor 450; 54.88; 109.77
", Wiley	1 wp; pleasure v. 60; 3.80; 7.60
", Caleb	cash 164; 345 solvent debts; 3.23; 6.47
", Barbara	.60; 1.20
", Catharine	solvent debts 125; .50; 1.00
McKee, James	1 wp; solvent debts 120; silver watch 8; 3.36; 6.72
McNair, Jas.	solvent debts 165; county bonds 886; silver watch 35; 1 dog; 18.19; 37.40
McGill, Thos. P.	solvent debts 3245; pleasure v. 50; brandy 200; 60.40; 120.80
McGill, Wifes	11.54; 23.09
", Alex D.	11.20; 23.40
", John	5.60; 11.20
Murphy, Jno. E.	1 wp; solvent debts 800; silver watch 35; 4.75; 9.50
McGinnas, C. C.	1 wp; silver watch 10; 1.30; 2.60
McNair, Jas. Adm. Love Est.	solvent debts 3445; county bonds 742; 16.14; 33.49
", " for Whitesides	cash 41; .16; .33
Neill, Sarah W.	1.18; 2.37
", John W.	.14; .29
Oates, Thos. M.	2.30; 4.60
", Jas. B.	1 wp; silver watch 15; 7.15; 14.30

", John R.	4.40; 8.80
Ormand, Z. S.	5.16; 10.32
", Jno. J.	8.98; 17.96
", B. M.	1 wp; pleasure v. 85; 8.23; 16.46
", R. D.	pleasure v. 75; 1 dog; 4.28; 9.57
Pasour, Susan (wid)	1.32; 2.65
Parker, Hester	.40; .80
Price, Jno. J.	pleasure v. 90; 12.59; 25.19
Pool, J. N.	1 wp; 1.20; 2.40
Roberts, Jno. M.	1 wp; cash 2000; profits from leather 1500; silver watch 10; pleasure v. 150; 57.29; 114.59
Rhom, David	silver watch 18; 1.18; 2.36
Rudisill, Mary	solvent debts 200; 2.37; 4.74
Ramsour, S. A.	pleasure v. 125; 1 dog; 1.25; 3.50
Sellars, Abram	.96; 1.92
Stroup, Moses	solvent debts 859; county bonds 800; 17.41; 34.83
", Moses Jr.	solvent debts 365; silver watch 15; 1.61; 3.22
Smith, L. S.	1 wp; 1.20; 2.40
Service, Jas. W.	.60; 1.20
Thornburg, Jos	1 wp; solvent debts 204; county bonds 200; brandy 55; 13.12; 26.24
Thomas, Saml	solvent debts 223; 3.69; 7.38
Torrence, S. A.	solvent debts 2800; county bonds 500; gold watch 190; 33.16; 66.33
", " Adm	50.25; 100.50
", " Exr Love	solvent debts 530; county bonds 500; 4.12; 8.24
", " for Hugh	solvent debts 58; county bonds 500; 2.25; 4.46
Vandyke, Jas. A.	1.20; 2.40
White, Mary C.	solvent debts 424, county bonds 500; 14.16; 28.33
", Mary	solvent debts 534; pleasure v. 50; 14.26; 28.52
", Jas. F.	1 wp; profits on liquor 70; 16.86; 33.75
", Hannah J.	cash 50; .20; .40
", Robt. A.	cash 70; .28; .56
", Edw. M.	cash 140; .56; 1.12
", Sarah	cash 40; .16; .32
Wilson, Lawson K. M. G. M.	20.00; 40.00
White, J. A.	1 wp; 1.20; 2.40
Whitesides, Major	solvent debts 277; pleasure v. 50; 8.61; 17.23
", " for E. L.	solvent debts 1370; 5.48; 10.96
", Mary (wid)	4.80; 9.60
Whitworth, F. R.	studs and jacks 2/12; pleasure v. 75; 2 dogs; 68.75; 139.50
Kiser, Noah	.90; 1.80
", Margaret	.30; .60
", Elisabeth	.30; .60
", Barbara	.30; .60
", James	.30; .60
", Jane	.30; .60
", Philip	.30; .60
Totals	$1,944.68; $3,904.36

Rudisill

Aderholdt, David	cash 4554; pleasure v. 40; brandy 100; 40.02; 86.04
Alexander, Noah	cash 400; pleasure v. 80; brandy 3; 6.44; 12.89
Aderholdt, Eml.	1 wp; gold watch 75; pleasure v. 75; furniture 500; brandy; 4; 1 dog; 28.22; 57.44
Baker, Eli	1 wp; cattle 39?; brandy 20; 6.38; 12.76
Black, Alfred	.76; 1.52
", Saml Jr.	.30; .60
Beam, Peter	cash 1557; pleasure v. 50; brandy 2; 38.48; 76.96
Baker, allen	1.40; 2.80
Baker, Edward	brandy 85; 12.26; 24.52
Bolinger, D. W.	1 wp; tobacco sold 23; cattle 40; 1.45; 2.90
Crouse, Rufus	1 wp; 15.33; 30.66
Carpenter, A. G.	cattle ?130; 3.15; 6.30
Carpenter, Frederick Jr.	1 wp; cash 125; 3.55; 7.10
", John	cattle 15; 1.56; 3.12
", Alfred	cash 50; 2.00; 4.00
", Wm.	1 wp; cash 200; brandy 10; 1 dog; 5.00; 11.00
", Saml	4.00; 8.00
Carpenter, B. M.	10.48; 20.96
Carpenter, Fred. Sr	cash 1730; 36.22; 72.44

", " agt	4.40; 8.80	
", " as gd. ?MH & R	cash 1118; 4.47; 8.94	
", Ann as Guard C Carpenter heirs	cash 4?55; 5.82; 12.64	
", Henry	cash 105; 6.92; 13.84	
", Emanuel	cash 232; 3.13; 6.26	
", Abel	1 wp; 1.64; 3.28	
", Daniel	1 wp; 1.40; 2.80	
Carpenter, Joseph	1 wp; cash 500; pleasure v. 90; cattle 1–30; 20.82; 41.64	
", George	5.20; 10.40	
", Wm.	1 wp; cash 700; pleasure v. 50; 1 dog; 10.10; 20.20	
", Marcus	1 wp; cattle 1–75; 3.50; 7.00	
", " agt ?Rush	4.89; 9.78	
", Henry	1 wp; cash 420; brandy 100; 13.88; 27.76	
", Benjamin	1 wp; cash 2400; brandy 350; 45.80; 91.60	
", Caleb	cash 10; .79; 1.58	
", Absolom	brandy 4; cattle 1–8; .43; .86	
Costner, Amanda	.07; .14	
Crouse, David	3.79; 6.38	
Cathey, Francis	brandy 9; 1 dog; 8.60; 18.20	
Eaker, Christian	cash 2055; gold watch 100; furniture 100; brandy 50; 1 dog; 50.79; 102.58	
Eaker, Jesse	2.20; 4.40	
Eaker, Jacob	1.16; 2.33	
Evans, Edwd	1.92; 3.84	
", Agt M. Eaker	1.60; 3.20	
Gardner, Andrd	1.34; 2.69	
Hines, Daniel	cash 919; furniture 100; 17.01; 34.03	
", Henry	cash 220; .88; 1.76	
", George	cash 180; pleasure v. 100; 1.72; 3.44	
", Danl for S. Carpter	horse 1–200; 3.60; 7.20	
Hunt, George	cash 224; pleasure v. 60; 1.50; 3.00	
Havener, Jac.	1 wp; 2.00; 4.00	
Kiser, Philip	cash 410; ?cattle 1–40; 7.58; 15.16	
", Susan	5.60; 11.20	
", Jacob	1 wp; cash 50; brandy 82; 12.38; 24.77	
", Levi	cash 274; brandy 44; 1 dog; 13.09; 27.19	
", Hiram	cash 588; 2.35; 4.70	
", John	cash 168; furniture 50; 4.64; 9.29	
McBee, John	.80; 1.60	
Mauney, Abe Sen.	7.79; 15.58	
Mauney, Abe Jun.	1 wp; cash 400; brandy 20; cattle 1–56; 24.40; 48.80	
", Barbara	3.57; 7.02	
", Max.	cash 25; brandy 8; 6.22; 12.44	
", Lawson	cash 1000; ?cattle 1–152?; 7.00; 14.00	
", ?Lovina	cash 80; brandy 12; 6.12; 12.24	
", Susan	cash 42; .17; .34	
", Catharine	cash 177; .71; 1.42	
", Manuel	cash 324; 1.29; 2.59	
McLurd, John	4.00; 8.00	
Moore, James	1 wp; 1.20; 2.40	
Rudisill, Wiley	silver watch 10; pleasure v. 75; horses 150; furniture 130; brandy 200; county bonds 728; gold and silver plated 22; 61.84; 123.68	
", " for S. C's heirs	.60; 1.20	
", Jonas	studs 1/600; 32.65; 64.70	
", "	29.06; 58.12	
", E. A.		
", Emanuel	1 wp; pleasure v. 75; cattle 44; brandy 20; 1 dog; 7.32; 15.64	
", Mary	28.40; 56.80	
", Eli	11.04; 22.09	
", Pinckney	1 wp; 1.20; 2.40	
Summey, John	1 wp; brandy 16; 5.80; 11.60	
Shuford, Cynthia	29.44; 58.88	
", Wm.	cash 65; 2 [not listed]; .22; 2.32?	
Smith, Robt.	1.20; 2.40	
Senter, Jonas	1 wp; cattle 53	
Thornburg, Berry	1 wp; cash 100; brandy 5; 2.10; 4.20	
Taylor, Franklin	1 wp; 1.20; 2.40	
Vickers, Jno.	cash 258; 7.45; 14.86	
Williams, Jac.	1 wp; horses 135; 3.04; 6.08	

Wise, Ambrose	cash 356; pleasure v. 56; 2.17; 4.35
Williams, ?Marcus?	1 wp; 1.20; 2.40
Pasour, Saml.	1.10; 2.20
", John	3.60; 7.20
Total:	$796.25; $1,602.50

River Bend

Abernathy, Jas.	solvent debts 30; furniture 100; 1 dog; 27.38; 55.77?
", " Adm J. L. Alexander	cash 586; solvent debts 633; 2.53; 5.06
", " Adm Farrar	cash 184; solvent debts 730; 3.65; 7.31
", John P.	furniture 100; 24.32; 48.64
", M. Luther	15.82; 31.65
", D. M.	furniture 100; 1 dog; 24.85; 50.70
", Milton S.	2.80; 5.60
", Miles L.	2.80; 5.60
", Barbara	pleasure v. 300; furniture 50; 19.77; 39.55
", Miss Ann	13.31; 26.62
", Miss Bettie	solvent debts 275; 15.24; 30.49
", Wm. M.	1 wp; 1.20; 2.40
Armstrong, M. R.	cash 250; solvent debts 148; 4.79; 9.58
Broadaway, Wm.	1 wp; cash 51; solvent debts 192; pleasure v. 50; 42.38; 84.76
Burke, Monroe	1 wp; 2.80; 5.60
Bissell, E. H.	gold watch 50; furniture 100; 3.50; 7.00
Black, Jas. F.	pleasure v. 50; 3.70; 7.40
", Jas. L.	3.80; 5.60
Cansler, R. T.	1 wp; cash 496; pleasure v. 75; 1 dog; 22.15; 45.31
", Peter	cash 318; furniture 100; brandy 1 ½; 32.93; 65.87
Connell, David	cash 200; pleasure v. 50; 5.17; 10.34
", James	3.04; 6.08
", Martha	.70; 1.40
", Mary E.	cash 123; 1.19; 2.38
", Robt.	cash 324; 1.29; 2.59
Cox, Patrick	cash 848; solvent debts 300; gold watch 200; pleasure v. 60; furniture 100; brandy 36; 17.04; 34.08
", " Ad Jno.	cash 17; .06; .13
Cannon, Wm. F.	cash 800; silver watch 10; pleasure v. 50; 1 dog; 29.47; 59.?94
", W. Sidney	pleasure v. 50; 13.47; 26.95
", W. F. for S Jenkins	cash 622; solvent debts 365; 5.34; 10.69
", David E.	1 wp; 2.24; 4.48
Carpenter, Andrew	cash 2332; solvent debts 4668; pleasure v. 75; 96.18; 192.59
Clanton, Isaac	3.20; 6.40
", Lawson	2.00; 4.00
Cloninger, Wm.	1.60; 3.20
", Dan R.	1.40; 2.80
Derr, V.	furniture 500; 54.52; 109.05
", John H.	cash 172; 13.86; 27.72?
", Andrew J.	solvent debts 100; pleasure v. 100; 54.26; 108.52
Eddleman, Dicey	4.16; 8.32
", David F.	17.62; 35.25
Edwards, Wm.	cash 60; solvent debts 11; 3.28; 6.57
", Lewis	1 wp; pleasure v. 150; 6.00; 12.00
Farrar, Margaret	21.73; 43.47
", Nath. P.	2.49; 4.99
", John	1 wp; cash 150; silver watch 20; pleasure v. 50; 1 dog; 10.50; 22.00
Henderson, A. R.	1 wp; solvent debts 540; pleasure v. 50; 2 dogs; 54.49; 110.98
", Jas. A.	cash 4300; solvent debts 1007; pleasure v. 100; furniture 300; 76.42; 152.85
Henkle, Osborne	cash 581; solvent debts 707; 42.27; 84.54
", Hannah	1.40; 2.80
Handsell, Jno. P.	.60; 1.20
", Wm.	1 wp; 1.20; 2.40
Hart, Isabella	.20; .40
Holland, Sallie	cash 205; solvent debts 25; gold watch 50; pleasure v. 75; furniture 100; 7.28; 14.47
Hutchison, C. L.	4.00; 8.00
Johnston, S H	cash 1816; solvent debts 2544; county bonds 1200; silver watches 100; cotton 65; RR Dividend 525; plate and jewelry 225; piano 1; bank dividends 500; RR capital 1605; pleasure v. 250; furniture 1000; ?cattle 120; 226.83; 453.66
", Jno. R.	solvent debts 2190; county bonds 200; silver watch 100; pleasure v. 160; plate and jewelry 90; brandy 40; 1 dog; bank dividends 15; furniture 400; 117.72; 236.44

Johnston, James F.	38.80; 77.60
Jenkins, Sarah	.70; 1.40
Linebarger, Eli	pleasure v. 75; furniture 100; 41.93; 85.83
", " Trustee heirs?	solvent debts 380; 1.52; 3.04
", " Guard	solvent debts 27; .10; .20
Moore, J W	cash 300; solvent debts 1200; silver watches 75; pleasure v. 150; furniture 100; piano 1; 117.30; 234.60
McLean, W. B. Exr	cash 141; .56; 1.12
Mulligan, Jas.	3.20; 6.40
McCall, Jane	1.96; 3.93
McIntosh, J.[or T.] L.	.30; .60
", Wm.	1 wp; 4.32; 8.64
McDowell, R. J.[or T.]	120.64; 242.28
Pryer, Wiley	1.20; 2.40
Rutledge, James	solvent debts 400; furniture 200; 44.49; 88.98
Ryburn, And.	solvent debts 2318; silver watch 9; pleasure v. 75; 10.11; 20.22
Rumphelt, R. J. M.	1 dog; 1.00; 1.00
Rhyne, Michael	14.00; 28.00
Ransom, Ellen	.40; .80
Smith, M. A.	cash 100; 26.25; 52.50
Sadler, Henry	pleasure v. 50; 29.97; 59.94
Summerow, Ad.	16.98; 33.96
Sadler, Elisabeth	cash 716; 4.26; 8.52
Stroup, Caleb	1 wp; cash 158; silver watch 20; 3.43; 6.86
Sample, Wm.	6.40; 12.80
Tate, Thomas R.	cash 39,200; solvent debts 10,002; pleasure v. 900; cotton 178,840; profits 85,475; 5 dogs; gold watches 300; plate and jewelry 150; furniture 1000; 3429.52; 6864.04
", " as Gd	cash 2000; 8.00; 16.00
Underwood, Henry	cash 327; 265 ?money?; 16.28; 32.57
", Jacob	3.00; 6.00
Willis, S. S.	cash 13,000; solvent debts 280; pleasure v. 50; 65.62; 131.24
Total	$5,187.94; $10,390.88

South Point

Armstrong, J. L.	1 wp; 1 dog; 17.37; 35.75
", Arther	1 wp; silver watch 18; 2 dogs; 23.16; 48.33
", John M.	cash 525; 14.50; 29.00
", Elisabeth	14.43; 28.86
", Mathew Jr.	6.73; 13.47
Beattie, Robt. A.	11.85; 23.71
", Rufus J.	1 wp; cash 4966; 1 dog; 45.70; 92.41
", Saml.	cash 3500; 66.30; 132.61
", Smith	cash 1400; pleasure v. 50; furniture 50; 1 dog; 15.82; 32.64
", Jonathan	5.35; 10.71
", John W.	7.84; 15.69
", Wm.	silver watch 20; .20; .40
Berry, W. R.	1 wp; cash 230; 5.32; 10.64
Brandon, Rachel	21.78; 43.56
Bradley, Albert	1 wp; 2.40; 4.80
Craig, S. W.	36.89; 73.79
", " for A. Hoyles Est	cash 450; 1.80; 3.60
Craig & Co	cash 2300; 9.20; 18.40
Craig & Henderson	cash 1396; 5.58; 11.17
Caldwell, Sam C.	gold watch 150; 29.49; 58.99
", Joshua	1 wp; 1.20; 2.40
Dameron, John	9.65; 19.30
Ewing, Saml.	cash 7060; 57.72; 115.45
", Hugh Sen.	1.80; 3.60
", Hugh F.	1.80; 3.60
Finley, Robt. M.	2.80; 5.60
", W. G.	.80; 1.60
", S. S.	3.79; 7.59
", Jane	14.16; 28.33
Fite, Solomon	2.59; 5.18
", B. H.	1 wp; 1.20; 2.40
Groner, H. L.	4.00; 8.00
Glenn, Robts Est	cash 533; 22.29; 44.59
Gingles, Marg.	2.80; 5.60

Gullick, M. M.	pleasure v. 75; 65.32; 134.64
", J. N's Est.	2.00; 4.00
Gaston, Pink	1 wp; cash 500; 6.90; 13.80
", " for S Wrights Est.	.91; 1.82
Hanks, Wm.	silver watch 35; pleasure v. 50; 1 dog; 29.79; 60.58
", G. W.	1 wp; 9.77; 19.54
Henry, Robt.	10.92; 21.84
Hammel, Alex	pleasure v. 75; 3.95; 7.90
Hand, M. H.	silver watch 20; pleasure v. 105; 57.77; 115.55
", " Exr M. L.	collateral $1200 $600; 46.88; 93.76
", J. R.	1 wp; gold watch 100; pleasure v. 100; furniture 300; plate 100; 48.75; 97.50
", Jane	1.00; 2.00
Harrison, John	1 wp; 4.80; 9.60
Hand, M. H.	Gd M. Neagle 2.44; 4.89
Hall, Jas. D.	pleasure v. 50; 75.83; 151.66
", " for Kirkland	4.44; 8.88
Hislop, G. W.	cash 158; gold watch 100; silver h cane $\frac{1}{30}$; 2.10; 4.20
Henderson, A. L.	1 wp; cash 1140; silver watch 45; pleasure v. 100; 7.21; 14.42
Johnston, W. H.	cash 900; gold watch 75; brandy 27; 45.09; 90.18
Leeper, James	5.60; 11.20
", Andrew	14.48; 28.97
", " for J. ?Anthony	2.80; 5.60
", Naomi	40.29; 80.54
", Robt.	cash 100; 3.60; 7.20
Lonergan, Edward	silver watches 75; profits manufacturing 50; ferry 50; brandy 50; profit on liquor 400; 60.03; 120.06
", James Est.	16.00; 32.00
Lewis, James	1.60; 3.20
Linebarger, Manassah	1 wp; profits manufacturing 100; 6.45; 12.91
Long, Jno. R.	1 wp; 1.20; 2.40
McLure, ?Barmadus	1.20; 2.40
McLean, W. R.	silver watch 70; pleasure v. 35; profit manufacturing 50; 7.80; 15.60
", Marg. Est.	9.60; 19.20
", Robt. G.	profits manufacturing 75; furniture 50; 1 dog; 40.95; 82.90
McLean, John D	cash 22,484; silver watch 100; furniture 50; 2 dogs; 222.53; 447.07
Martin, Elisabeth	2.73; 5.47
", Milo	1 wp; cash 1900; pleasure v. 30; ?profits manufacturing cotton? 2000; furniture 50; 49.30; 98.60
McKee, Jas. D.	1.20; 2.40
", Wm.	30.98; 61.97
Mellon, G. W.	profits on manufacturing 150; furniture 150; 25.60; 51.20
McKee, G. O.	1 wp; brandy 30; 4.20; 8.40
Neagle, Andrew	28.44; 58.89
", Jno. E.	1 wp; profits on manufacturing 50; 33.04; 66.09
", Jno. P.	4.44; 8.88
", Jas. B.	33.66; 67.32
Neely, Jno.	29.26; 28.52
Neel, Andrew	1 wp; 1.20; 2.40
Pasour, D. R.	cash 530; silver watch 35; 2.47; 4.94
Ratchford, Jas.	? dog; 48.88; 99.76
", Robt. C.	cash 150; 11.80; 23.61
", Nancy	6.53; 15.06
", John	pleasure v. 50; 3 dogs; 28.57; 60.02
Reed, Wm.	cash 322; 55.44; 110.88
", Jas. W.	cash 500; 18.18; 36.57
", R. H. s Est.	cash 617; 2.46; 4.94
Rankin, W. B.	15.81; 31.63
", " Adm	
Rumphelat, H. W.	pleasure v. 50; 1 dog; 11.54; 24.08
Robison, Jas. W.	1 wp; 4.15; 8.30
Reynolas, John	1 wp; 1.20; 2.40
Sandifer, Philip	4.00; 8.00
Smith, Judith	5.60; 11.20
", Sarah	2.42; 4.84
Stowe, Wm. A.	13.80; 27.60
", L. W.	8.88; 17.77
", J. & E. B.	1 wp; silver watches 20; profits manufacturing 3500; 1 piano; silver cane 1; furniture 800; 1 dog; 943.16; 1887.33

", " for Taylor	12.66; 25.32
", " for Hines [or heirs]?	12.66; 25.32
", " ?Arendett?	7.68; 15.56
", Jasper gd Fords heirs	cash 5500; 22.00; 44.00
", Laura	13.84; 27.68
", M. G.	3.37; 6.74
", Eliza	5.27; 10.54
", C. Theodore	2.80; 5.60
Summer?, Mathew	cash 93; silver watch 20; .57; 1.15
Tucker, Alf	1 wp; cash 2600; 11.60; 23.20
Thomson, E. D.	2.12; 4.24
Wright, J. M.	cash 2700; silver watch 10; 41.74; 83.49
Wells, B. F.	cash 100; 62.62; 125.25
Waggstaff, Jno.	1 wp; silver watch 20; furniture 100; 5.20; 10.40
Webb, Hugh	1 wp; 1.20; 2.40
Ward, Rufus J.	1 wp; 1.20; 2.40
Wagstaff, J. F.	1.20; 2.40
Yarboro, Wm.	solvent debts?? 300; 468; 936
Totals	$2,980.33; $5,976.66

Tanyard

Adams, Wm.	.60; 1.20
Armstrong, John	1.60; 3.20
Berry, E. M.	note shaver 500; 5.30; 10.60
", E. Milton	1.20; 2.40
Brison, G. R.	solvent debts 40; 2.56; 5.12
", Jane A.	1.00; 2.00
", Wm.s children	1.00; 2.00
Brandon, Thos. L.	1 wp; 1 dog; 6.06; 13.12
Beard, Robt.	4.00; 8.00
", Jas. C. Est.	10.16; 20.33
", Emily	bank dividends 5; .10; .20
", S. F. D.	1.80; 3.60
Beattie, Wm.	2.80; 5.60
Brown, Elisabeth	.80; 1.60
Cook, Demsey	2.00; 4.00
Craig, R. H.	solvent debts 3000; cash 100; 8.89; 17.78
", Thos. N.	cash 400; 3.00; 6.00
Craig, John H.	1 wp; cash 1060; tobacco purchased 500; profits on leather 300; brandy 66; profits on liquor 40; 53.64; 107.28
", R. J.	1 wp; cash 40; tobacco purchased 165; 2.02; 4.04
", J. M.	1 wp; solvent debts 500; 3.20; 6.40
", William	10.13; 20.27
Clark, R. F.	3.60; 7.20
Combest, Wm.	1.00; 2.00
", Sarah J.	.50; 1.00
Clemmer, J. L.	2.00; 4.00
Clinton, Martha	8.58; 17.17
Choat, A. D.	3.40; 6.80
Detter, Andrew	cash 210; furniture 100; 19.23; 35.46
Dixon, A. C.	1 wp; 3.20; 6.40
Falls, A. J.	13.12; 26.24
", M. R.	solvent debts 550; gold watch 20; silver watch 10; pleasure v. 100; furniture 50; 3.70; 7.40
", Sarah	solvent debts 98; 20.27; 40.54
", Sarah L.	18.75; 37.57
", " as gd	solvent debts 945; 3.78; 7.57
Faires, E. M.	solvent debts 575; cash 425; tobacco purchased 1775; silver watches 20; pleasure v. 100; furniture 50; 37.00; 62.01
Featherstin, C. A.	30.50; 61.00
Ford, Isom	solvent debts 675; cash 75; pleasure v. 50; 6.30; 12.60
", Wm.	.20; .40
", Mary Ann	4.10; 8.20
Fewell, John J.	1 wp; 2.20; 4.40
", Jas. S.	1.00; 2.00
Glenn, J. Fs Est.	2.40; 4.80
", J. F. Senr.	silver watch 5; brandy 25; 6.15; 12.30
", E. M. Grd	pleasure v. 50; 4.80; 9.60

", E. M.	solvent debts 140; 1.06; 2.12
Gingles, Ruth	1.20; 2.40
", Dorcus	
", Charlotte	1.00; 2.00
Goble, Absolom	1.40; 2.80
Glenn, Mary ?L.	9.84; 19.68
Grier, Thos.	6.56; 13.13
Herdman, Rosana	1.00; 2.00
Henderson, W. A.	brandy 30; 1 dog; 5.00; 11.00
", Jonathan	1 wp; 1.20; 2.40
Hill, W. R.	3.60; 7.20
", Sarah	10.01; 20.03
Horseley, Richard	brandy 10; 2.20; 4.40
", Resin?	1 wp; silver watches 15; pleasure v. 50; 11.32; 22.65
Huffstetler, J. M.	1 wp; tobacco 129; 3.71; 7.43
", C. A.	1 wp; 4.00; 8.00
Holland, Melissa H.	cash 91; gold watches 50; 21.44; 42.88
", Nancy J.	cash 267; gold watch 50; 19.95; 39.91
", Wm. M.	furniture 50; ?1 lot 600; 33.96; 67.92
Holland, Wm R	1 wp; solvent debts 125; silver watches 15; pleasure v. 75; 66.81; 133.62
", " Gd J. Q. Holland	solvent debts 138; county bonds; 200; 9.43; 18.86
", M. C.	pleasure v. 75; 14.62; 29.24
", Mary	.40; .81
Hoffman, Levi	14.60; 29.20
Henry, Wallace	2.40; 4.80
Hope, Jas.	.40; .80
Jenksins, D A	1 wp; cash 2000; cotton 4500; pleasure v. 75; furniture 400; profits on liquor 200; 99.35; 198.70
", " for ?WRise	1 lot $600; .80; 1.60
Johnston, Marys Est.	1.20; 2.40
", Susans Est.	4.40; 8.80
", Wm.	tobacco 100; ?profits on liquor 25; 2.90; 5.80
Kincaid, J. R.	1 wp; cash 400; tobacco 526; 8.10; 16.21
Kendrick, Jas. M.	solvent debts 820; 3.28; 6.56
", M. L.'s Est.	2.80; 5.60
", Ellen	4.92; 9.85
", " as Gd	
", Jas. W.	2.40; 4.80
Linebarger, Es. Est.	2.00; 4.00
", Jacob	pleasure v. 50; ?profits on liquor 25; 46.80; 93.61
Lewis, J. J.	1 wp; tobacco 186; 9.50; 19.00
", Anns Est.	2.00; 4.00
Lockhart, Wm.	tobacco 75; 2.30; 4.60
Love, A. J.	2.00; 2.00
Moore, Walter Est.	2.80; 5.60
Mendenhall, N.	cash 3117; 17.36; 34.73
", Jno. J.	1 wp; cash 25; 7.30; 14.60
", Margaret	cash 1155; 5.64; 11.29
McCullough, J. F.	2.40; 4.80
", Vincent	1 wp; 2.30; 4.60
Massey, W. F.	1 wp; cash 400; tobacco 52; 7.00; 14.00
McDaniel, Elisha	1.60; 3.20
McAlister, Jane	1.00; 2.00
McArthur, C. R.	1 wp; 1.20; 2.40
Moore, Wm.	1 wp; tobacco 100; 1.60; 3.20
McAlister, Jenny	1.00; 2.00
Noland, Wm. M.	1 wp; 4.80; 9.60
Neagle, Dr. J. L.	1.40; 2.80
", Ann R.	2.00; 4.00
ODaniel, J. S. s Est.	2.00; 4.00
Parsley S. M.	1.00; 2.00
", David	1.00; 2.00
Pettus, Jas. T.	2 dogs; 15.49; 32.98
Quinn, Jas. Esqr	cash 3000; silver watch 15; 57.35; 114.71
", Tho. F.	pleasure v. 50; 6.09; 12.18
Ratchford, J. F.	3.50; 7.00
", Catharine Est.	4.00; 8.00
Ragan, D. F.	2.00; 4.00

", Jasper	.80; 1.60
Robison, S. C.	solvent debts 278; cash 710?; studs 6.00; pleasure v. 50; furniture 100; 23.12; 46.24
", Zimri	profits on leather 100; 5.60; 11.20
", Elam	1 wp; solvent debts 47; cash 50; 4.39; 8.78
", Mary A.	solvent debts 48; 1.79; 3.58
", Janes Est.	1.60; 3.20
", Harriet	1.60; 3.20
Riddle, J. B. F.	10.15; 20.30
", G. M. A. C.s Est.	4.00; 8.00
", Jane M.	solvent debts 6431; cash 40; gold watches 100; pleasure v. 250; furniture 100; 2 dogs; 27.08; 54.17
Stowe, Wm. T.	1 wp; gold watch 200; 63.13; 128.27
", Elisabeth	4.31; 8.62
", Nancy	2.60; 5.20
", Abram	brandy 10; 1 dog; 6.60; 14.20
", Jno s Est.	1.20; 2.40
", Theo B.	.80; 1.60
Smyer, J. F.	1 wp; solvent debts 1000; pleasure v. 50; livestock value 90; 1 dog; 36.83; 74.66
Stowe, Catharine	7.80; 15.60
Stroup, Maxwell	5.60; 11.20
Smith, J. W.	3.02; 6.05
", Elijah	2.00; 4.00
", Jas. W.	1 wp; 1.20; 2.40
Scott, E. N.	silver watch 15; .15; .30
Smith, David Est. by C J H	cash 270; 1.08; 2.16
Sandifer, Philip	4.00; 8.00
Torrence, Jno. C.	RR Dividend 10; pleasure v. 50; furniture 100; 13.50; 27.00
", Robt.	4.00; 8.00
", Harrison	2.40; 4.80
", Mary	solvent debts 712; RR dividends 10; pleasure v. 50; 31.31; 62.63
Wilson, Robt.	solvent debts 5054; cash 1900; pleasure v. 50; furniture 50; 99.82; 199.65
", J. F.	solvent debts 950; gold watch 50; 4.30; 8.60
", Wm. M.	solvent debts 870; 3.48; 6.96
", R. N.	solvent debts 850; 3.40; 6.80
", Edwin	.10; .20
", Robt. M.	solvent debts 5150; cash 1750; ?? RR Dividend 27; pleasure v. 100; furniture 200; 4 dogs; 99.67; 203.34
Wallace, Thos.	pleasure v. 50; 2.50; 5.00
", D. G.	pleasure v. 75; furniture 200; 9.13; 18.27
Warren, W. G.	1 wp; cotton 946; 19.21; 38.42
Walker, D. M.	3.00; 6.00
Holland, W. M. for Jane	1 wp; 1.20; 2.40
Totals	$1,423.00; $2,858.00

Woodlawn

Alexander, Nancy	9.12; 18.24
Abernathy, G. & Co.	10.80; 21.60
", C. W. agt. OW & Co	13.44; 26.88
", George	1 wp; 1.20; 2.40
", M.	1.38; 2.76
", M. C.	solvent debts 903; pleasure v. 75; 4.06; 8.72
", C. M.	1 wp; cash 150; solvent debts 76; 2.10; 4.21
", J. M.	1 wp; 1 dog; 1.20; 3.40
", Franklin	1 wp; 1.46; 2.93
Brevard, R. A.	2.80; 5.60
Bluford, Wm.	1.88; 3.76
Brinkley, Wm.	1 wp; 1.20; 2.40
Barnet, A. F.	1 wp; 1.20; 2.40
Clemmer, A.	2.40; 4.80
", John	3.20; 6.40
", Jonas	3.20; 6.40
Cannon, J. F.	solvent debts 550; 11.00; 22.00
", J. A.	3.60; 7.20
Dunn, Wm.	2.00; 4.00
Davidson, J. S.	gold watch 150; plate 53; pleasure v. 300?; cattle 3–187; 106.92; 213.84
Davenport, A W	cash 150; solvent debts 200; furniture 100; 77.14; 154.28
", Wm.	cash 500; solvent debts 930; pleasure v. 50; furniture 10; 14.26; 28.52
Ewing, S. R.	1 wp; pleasure v. 50; 3.70; 7.40

Fite, G. S.	cash 600; pleasure v. 50; furniture 100; 1 dog; 21.22; 43.44
", W. J.	1 wp; pleasure v. 100; 15.28; 30.56
", Henry	17.18; 34.36
Grier, Ann	5.90; 11.80
Gaston, Robt.	2.00; 4.00
", L. B.	1.60; 3.20
Hand, A. J.	1.20; 2.40
Hoffman, Caleb	1 wp; 12.00; 24.00
", Mary	2.30; 4.60
Hoover, Jacob	1 wp; solvent debts 670; 2 dogs; 6.28; 14.56
", Thos.	2.00; 4.00
Hanks, E.	34.36; 68.72
Hunter, C. L.	67.20; 134.40
Johnson, Saml.	2 dogs; 65.22; 132.44
Johnson, Mary	solvent debts 2000; R R Capital 3500; 53.74; 107.48
Johnson, Martha	cash 1220; solvent debts 1000; RR Capital 2700; 46.82; 93.64
Joy, James	1 wp; silver watch 25; 1.45; 2.90
Kelly, John agt Shilin?	solvent debts 132; .52; 1.05
Linebarger, David	24.24; 48.48
", Jonas R.	furniture 100; 15.36; 30.72
", L.	cash 182; pleasure v. 50; furniture 100; 1 dog; 18.72; 37.25
", " as Adm M. L.	4.80; 9.60
Lawing, Geo. A.	1 wp; 1.20; 2.40
Mooney, Ephraim	.60; 1.20
McLurd, R. L.	1 wp; cash 150; silver watch 20; solvent debts 500; 10.36; 20.72
", as Adm J. C.	solvent debts 800; 3.20; 6.40
", as Adm Mary	solvent debts 1000; 4.00; 8.00
Moody, J.	.40; .80
Miller, J.	.80; 1.60
Morris, Vincent	1.00; 2.00
Moore, Ann	4.40; 8.80
Nims, Fred	cash 600; gold watches 100; solvent debts 6000; pleasure v. 150; furniture 200; 1 dog; R R Capital 6000; 123.90; 248.80
Nims, Horace	gold watch 100; solvent debts 1500; 7.00; 14.00
Oates, James	cash 100; solvent debts 700; pleasure v. 50; 6.10; 12.20
Pegram, E. L.	cash 50; solvent debts 800; 7.54; 15.08
Rankin, Sidney	1 wp; solvent debts 100; 1 dog; 16.34; 33.68
Rhyne, John	solvent debts 1700; furniture 60; 68.48; 136.96
", Jacob	solvent debts 2256; 13.82; 27.65
Rankin, J. C.	1 wp; pleasure v. 50; 17.20; 34.40
Rhyne, D.	cash 690; solvent debts 2019; furniture 100; 46.85; 97.70
Rankin, J. D.	cash 200; solvent debts 4000; pleasure v. 100; furniture 150; 2 dogs; RR capital 200; 132.32; 266.64
Rafter, Patrick	silver watch 12; pleasure v. 50; 3.82; 7.64
Rutledge, Alex	pleasure v. 75; Deadhead 150 miles; 23.56; 47.12
Rhyne, M. H.	gold watch 50; pleasure v. 75; furniture 100; 1 piano; stud 10:00; 1 dog; 67.01; 35.02
Rankin, Joseph	8.60; 17.20
", Richard	cash 50; solvent debts 1600; furniture 55; 1 dog; 66.96; 134.92
", J. R.	pleasure v. 50; 2 dogs; 55.28; 112.56
", J. B.	solvent debts 70; 3.48; 6.76
", Alex	2.80; 5.60
Rutledge, Wm.	8.62; 17.24
Rudisills heirs	4.80; 9.60
Rankin, Robt.	silver watch 20; pleasure v. 50; 4.70; 9.40
", " agt R. Alex	11.74; 23.48
Rumphelett, Isaac	3.20; 6.40
Richards, Wm.	1 wp; silver watch 25; solvent debts 700; pleasure v. 100; 1 dog; 5.60; 11.20
", "	37.93; 76.86
Rhyne, Hugh	7.20; 14.40
McLurd, R. L. agt.	9.13; 18.27
Shipp, W. T.	solvent debts 1000; pleasure v. 250; furniture 150; bank ?cap? 14000; RR capital 400; county bonds 500; 1 piano; gold plate 30; 142.70; 285.40
" " as Gd	solvent debts 340; 13.00; 26.00
Scott, Abram	60.14; 120.28
", " as Admr	39.10; 78.20
Smith, Mary	2.00; 4.00
Smith, Jno. B.	2.00; 4.00
Sahms, Wm.	17.68; 35.36

", " as agt. E. Martin?	6.44; 12.88
Smith, Lee	silver watch 25; solvent debts 50; 2 dogs; 16.35; 34.70
", Ben	solvent debts 11; furniture 200; 17.66; 35.33
", Robt.	9.60; 19.20
", R. S.	1 wp; solvent debts 460; 3.04; 6.08
Tate, John	silver watch 25; solvent debts 14,256; 57.27; 114.54
Wilson, J. F.	1 wp; silver watch 18; pleasure v. 50; 4.68; 9.36
West, Ezekiel	2.00; 4.00
", Robt.	1.60; 3.20
Shipp & Davenport Exr of W? West	solvent debts 300; 1.20; 2.40
Totals [ambiguous]	$1,884.79; $3,787.60
Total Amt for state:	$21,884.89 Total Amt for County $22,016.89; Total $43,901.78

Tax List Details

In order to use the 1863 Gaston County Tax List most efficiently I created a number of charts to illustrate the data, learn from it, and communicate some intricacies. The following are a number of charts, whose data were gleaned from the tax list.

The following chart outlines each militia company (district) with the number of acres, the value of the acreage, the number of slave owners in each district (whites with slaves), and the number of slaves.

Company	# Acres	Valuation	Whites w/slaves	#slaves
Cherryville	14,895	$66,534	18	68
Crowders Mtn	18,561	$114,328	40	203
Dallas	25,276	$174,790	37	224
Duharts	19,584	$168,125	22	128
High Shoals	25,266	$167,130	31	432
River Bend	26,443	$288,990	39	375
Roberts	34,183	$142,408	38	250
Rudisill	12,317	$70,844	20	76
South Point	20,953	$184,364	64	422
Tanyard	21,364	$104,705	42	207
Woodlawn	27,766	$152,800	54	451
Total	241,530	$1,626,087	394	2,746

The total number of slave owners (394) is composed of the number of times they are listed as slaveholders in the tax assessment. The total number of slaveholders (372) does not duplicate separate ownership and is used to validate social class as listed in Chapter 1.

The following chart compares the companies in a number of categories by numerical order. They are ranked (1–11 with 1 being the highest) by the number of acres, the land valuation, the number of white slave owners, and the number of slaves.

Tax lists by # of acres	Valuation	# Whites w/ slaves	# slaves
1-Roberts	1-River Bend	1-South Point	1-High Shoals
2-River Bend	2-High Shoals	2-Woodlawn	2-South Point
3-Dallas	3-South Point	3-Tanyard	3-River Bend
4-High Shoals	4-Dallas	4-Crowders Mtn	4-Woodlawn
5-Woodlawn	5-Duharts	5-River Bend	5-Roberts
6-Tanyard	6-Roberts	6-Dallas	6-Dallas
7-South Point	7-Woodlawn	7-Roberts	7-Tanyard
8-Duharts	8-Crowders Mtn	8-High Shoals	8-CrowdersMtn
9-Crowders Mountain	9-Tanyard	9-Duharts	9-Duharts
10-Cherryville	10-Rudisill	10-Rudisill	10-Rudisill
11-Rudisills	11-Cherryville	11-Cherryville	11-Cherryville

The following charts further analyze the data using averages. The first chart provides the average acreage, average land valuation, and average number of slaves per slave owner by company. The data is derived by dividing the number of taxables into the total number of acres and acreage valuation in each tax company. Finally, the number of slave owners in each company is divided into the number of slaves to determine the average number of slaves owned in each company. The number in parentheses is the number of taxables in the list. The second chart illustrates by company the total slave valuation, average value per slave and per slave owner. The third chart ranks each company according to the three categories.

Average Acreage (Acres ÷ # Taxables)	Average Valuation (Valuation ÷ # Taxables)	Average # slaves to owners (# slaves ÷ # owners)
Cherryville (91) 164	731	3.8
C. Mtn (95) 195	1203	5.2
Dallas (109) 232	1604	6
Duhart (60) 326	2802	5.8
H. Shoals (97) 260	1908	13.9
River B (77) 339	3703	10
Roberts (109) 314	1306	6.8
Rudisill (66) 187	1073	3.6
S Point (95) 221	1941	6.7
Tanyard (135) 158	776	4.9
Woodlawn (82) 218	1210	8.3
Total (1017) 233	1563	7

Total Slave Valuation		Ave Value per slave[526]	Ave value per slave owner[527]
Cherryville	$45,277	$666	$2515
Crowders Mtn	$142,211	$701	$3646
Dallas	$177,978	$795	$4810
Duharts	$84,012	$656	$3819
High Shoals	$300,480	$696	$9693
River Bend	$266,101	$710	$7003
Roberts	$176,022	$704	$4757
Rudisill	$52,569	$692	$2503
South Point	$276,544	$655	$4390
Tanyard	$139,663	$675	$3325
Woodlawn	$249,989	$692	$5814
Total	$1,910,846	$696	$4887

Ranking: The following chart ranks each company in these three categories.

	Total Slave Valuation	Ave Value per slave	Ave Value per slave owner
Cherryville	11	9	10
Crowders Mtn	7	4	8
Dallas	5	1	4
Duharts	9	10	7
High Shoals	1	5	1
River Bend	3	2	2
Roberts	6	3	5
Rudisill	10	6	11
South Point	2	11	6
Tanyard	8	8	9
Woodlawn	4	6	3

The following chart communicates the taxes paid by each company and their rank (1–11) among themselves.

	State Tax	Total Tax	Rank
Cherryville	$865.00	$1,736.00	10
Crowders Mountain	$1,332.73	$2,667.57	9
Dallas	$1,979.19	$3,975.38	4
Duharts	$1,384.47	$2,781.9?	8
High Shoals	$2,106.44	$4,220.89	3

Roberts	$1,944.68	$3,904.36	5
Rudisill	$796.25	$1,602.50	11
	State Tax	Total Tax	Rank
River Bend	$5,187.94	$10,390.88	1
South Point	$2,980.33	$5,976.66	2
Tanyard	$1,423.00	$2,858.00	7
Woodlawn	$1,884.79	$3,787.60	6
Total State Tax: $21,884.89	Total Tax: $43,901.78	Total County Tax: $22,016.89	

An analysis of slavery is formulated in the following chart. It compares the 1850 Gaston County Census Slave Schedule, the 1860 Gaston County Slave Schedule, and the 1863 Gaston County tax list. The 1850 and 1860 federal census compiled slave data based upon gender and age categories by slave owner. There were 333 slave owners specifically enumerated in the 1850 census or about 4 percent of the population, who owned slaves or about 26 percent of the heads of household. In 1860 there were 364 slave owners, an increase of 31. The 1863 tax list included 372 total slave owners. The author used the source cited and counted the slaves by category. A chart illustrates the numerical breakdown of slave owners and the percentage of the total number of slave owners:

	1850	1860	1863
Persons owning one slave	84/25%	89/24%	91/24%
Persons owning 2–5 slaves	120/36%	126/35%	119/32%
Persons owning 6–10 slaves	71/21%	89/24%	91/24%
Persons owning 11–19 slaves	37/11%	48/13%	44/12%
Persons owning 20–30 slaves	12/3%	8/2%	13/3%
Persons owning more than 31 slaves	8[528]/3%	3[529]/1%	14/3%
Total slave owners	332	363	372

Percentage total does not equal 100% because of rounding.

On the same microfilm as the 1863 tax list and in another book, one may find the 1850 Gaston County tax lists. The author offers a summary of the 1850 tax lists as written in the source:

Amount of Taxes for Gaston County Year 1850

Town	Lots	Value	Land	Value	WP	BP	FBP*	Stud/V*
Dallas Company	31 T. Lots	5275	34,601	145,658	106	111		
Duharts Creek	3	?212	15945	37,740	68	28	1	1 300
Dutchmans Creek	9	920	20725	67,693	62	138		
Armstrongs Ford			18428	68,428	53	149		1 500
Fronebergers	3	277	20003	37,135	62	72		
Robinsons	2	458	19459	49,799	65	47		
Lourances	5	385	27734	108,511	59	83	1	
Hendersons	2		14945	59,725	48	101	1	1 500
Cloningers	4		8668	25,668	32	76		
Crouses	3	315	25,971	$55,274	90	54		2 350
Total Amount	61	7842	196479	650631	645	859	3	5 1650

*Other categories: Free Black Poll   Stud Horse   P Season   Int.

John H. Roberts   CCC [Clerk of County Court]

	On Lots	Land	[blank]	Stud Horse Tax
County Tax	$?630	$537?.59	304.56	$412 ½
Poor Tax	$3.92?0	$32581	$37600	$412 ½
School	$373.00	$260.65	$150.40	$412 ½[530]

The ten companies of 1850 compare to eleven 1863 companies. Apparently county officials maintained little consistency with company boundaries, names, or inhabitants over the years. Using my own research experience, I have postulated possible geographic congruency between the two tax lists. These comparisons are approximate since the districts increased by one company from 1850 to 1863.

1850	1863
Dallas	Dallas; Dallas Town; plus other lands
Duharts	Duharts
Dutchmans	River Bend
Armstrongs Ford	South Point
Froneberger	Roberts
Robinson	Tanyard
Lourances	High Shoals
Henderson	Woodlawn
Cloninger	parts of Woodlawn and River Bend
Crouses	Black/Cherryville and Rudisills

Gaston County Inflation

I created this chart to illustrate Civil War inflation. I used a number of sources: Jacob Froneberger Diary, David Schenck Diary, and *Carolina Watchman*. Some data are comparable and others are not. Where applicable I estimated the percentage of inflation for certain commodities. My daughter, Candace Hester, assisted me with the percent of increase. Other newspapers also list commodity prices during the war: *Western Democrat, The Bulletin, The Daily Bulletin,* and *North Carolina Whig*. You may access these sources for more information.

Jacob Froneberger Diary

	Oct 1861	Sept 1862	Sept 1863	Feb 1864	Oct 1864	Inflation %
Coffee	50 cts lb	$2 lb				300%
Sugar	25	50				100%
Shoes	2.50 pr	$10 pr				300%
Salt	8 sack	$12 bu	$35/50lb			
Calico	25 cts					
Corn	50 cts	125	$3 bu	$8 bu		1500%
Wheat	90 cts		$6 bu	$12 bu	$21 bu	2233%
Flour	$11 per 100lbs	$15				
Bacon	30					
Cotton cards	$8 pr		$50 pr			525%
Cotton yarn	$20/5lb	$40/5lb				50%
Coarse shirting		$2 yd				
Leather		$7/lb				
Cotton cloth			$5 yd			
Woolen jeans			$12 yd			
Pork			$1.15 lb			

David Schenck Diary

	Aug 1861	Oct 1861	Feb/Sept 1862	Jan 1864	Mar 1863	Percent
Yarn			30–35 ct lb	$18–30 bunch		
Shirting			30 ct/yd			
Jeans		75cts	$1.25	$10–20		2566%
Homespun dresses			50cts–75cts			
Sugar			40 cts	$4		900%
Flour	4.50–$5	$5–6	$20 barrel	$50–75	$50 barrel	1011%
Bacon		15–16 cts/ 20–25cts		35 cts/lb	75cts lb	400%
Beef		6 cts	4cts	10 cts/lb	50–60 cts	900%
Leather		60–65cts/ $5/$7 bunch	$1.25-$2/lb	$8–10		1566%
Cotton yarn						
Wool yarn		$2/lb	$10–12			500%
Sugar		15	60 cts			
Molasses		$3 gal				
Salt		$6	$10 bu	50–60 cts lb		

Corn 60–70 cts bu			$5–10	$3 bu	400%
Rice	3–5 cts				
Candles 25–30 cts lb/	45–50				100%

Aug 1861	Oct 1861	Feb/Sept 1862	Jan 1864	Mar 1863	Percent
Coffee 23 cts	25–40cts		$10		4247%
Calico	15–20cts		$7–7.50		4900%
Pork			1.50–2		
Cotton			$1–1.50 lb		
Butter			$2–3 lb		
Eggs			50cts–$1 doz		
Chickens			$1–1.50 a piece		
Paper pins			$2		
Soft fur hat			$50		
Coarse boots			$1–1.50		
Iron			75 cts lb		
Brandy or whiskey			$35–50 gal		
Negroes		$2000 "enormous"			

Carolina Watchman

Feb/Mar 1863	Apr 1863	Sept 1863			
Corn $3–4 bu		$4–5 bu			67%
Flour $42 bu	$25 bu	$27.50–40			
Apples/peaches		25cts doz			
Beef		40–50 cts			
Bacon		$1–1.50			
Butter		$1–1.25			
Candles		all any will pay			
Leather		$3–6 lb			
Iron		65–75 cts			
Nails		$1.25–1.50			
Eggs		40–50 cts doz			

Chapter Notes

Introduction

1. Gaston County Collection, List of Taxables 1863–1868, CR040.701.2, North Carolina Archives.
2. Previous sources on Gaston County include Cope and Wellman, *The County of Gaston*, 1961; Pruitt, *History of Gaston County*, 1939; and Ragan, *The History of Gaston County and Gastonia*, 2010.

Chapter 1

1. See Cope and Wellman, *The County of Gaston*, 68–69 and Ragan, *The History of Gastonia and Gaston County*, 97–103.
2. www.census.gov/prod/222/decennial.html/ North Carolina 1860(a)-10.pdf, accessed Aug 4, 2014.
3. The author identified German surnames based upon his own knowledge as a result of years of local and genealogical research.
4. *The Lincoln Courier*, Dec 22, 1846, 2; Feb 27, 1847, 2.
5. Ibid., March 1, 1847, 1, 2.
6. Ibid., June 12, 1847, 3; June 24, 1847, 3; Gaston's "Inspectors" included Mauneys, Samuel Black and ?James White?; Oates,' Andrew Love and John M'Carter; Stowe's, Larkin Stowe and John D. McLean; Costner's, Andrew Hoyle and J. H. White; Rhyne's, Richard Rankin and Daniel Rhyne; Aug 11, 1847, 2. Heller, *Dallas, North Carolina: A Brief History*, 31.
7. *The Lincoln Courier*, Oct 9, 1847, 3. Attendees selected Isaac Holland the chair and delegates included: "W. J. Wilson Esq., J. H. Holland, Dr. Wm. Sloan, Dr. L. A. Moore, James H. White, Samuel Torrence, M. C. Lowrance, Moses Cloniger, Col. S. N. Stowe, T. P. McGill Esq., B. F. Briggs, H. W. Fulenwider."
8. Gaston County Minute Docket, Feb, Oct Terms 1847, CRO40.301.1, NC Archives.
9. Cope and Wellman, *The County of Gaston*, 71. Gaston County Minute Docket, Feb, Apr Terms 1850, CR040.301.1, NC Archives.
10. Gaston County Minute Docket, Aug Term, 1850, Feb, Apr Term, 1851, CR040.301.1, NC Archives. *The Lincoln Courier*, June 6, 1851, 4.
11. Gaston County Minute Docket, Feb, Apr, Oct term 1855, CR040.301.1, NC Archives.
12. Cope and Wellman, *The County of Gaston*, 73, 76. Wilson was perennial Lincoln County Register of Deeds; Hoyl and Stowe were legislators. All possessed considerable wealth, prestige, and experience.
13. Gaston County Minute Docket, Feb, Oct term. 1856, CR040.301.1, NC Archives.
14. Gaston County Minute Docket, Aug term, 1857, CR040.301.1, NC Archives.
15. Gaston County Minute Docket, Oct term 1857, Apr term, 1858, CR 040.301.1, NC Archives.
16. Gaston County Minute Docket, Feb, May, Aug term, 1859, CR040.301.1, NC Archives.
17. See Chapter 2 for details.
18. *The Daily Bulletin*, Charlotte, Apr 14, Apr 22, May 12, May 28, July 4, July 13, Aug 12, 1861.
19. Ragan, *The History of Gastonia and Gaston County, North Carolina: A Vision of America at its Best*, 116, 123, 131, 139, 155. *Western Democrat*, May 28, 1861, Kings Mountain Grays, 3.
20. *Western Democrat*, Mar 19, 1861, A New Railroad Project; June 11, 1861, The Dallas and Kings Mountain Railroad, 2.
21. Military Collection, Civil War Collection, Quartermaster Dept, Misc Records 1861, #4, NC Archives.
22. Asheville Armory Ledger, LCHA, a copy in the hands of the author. Copy of an email from Kenny Simpson of NC Archives to Marshall Ramsey, Nov 6, 2013, and copy of a letter from W W Pearce, Capt. Ordinance [sic], to [Gov] Henry T Clark, Nov 7, 1861, places Ramsey's Journal into its proper context.
23. Asheville Armory Ledger, LCHA. The author identified the areas of his travels through his knowledge of surnames and identifiable persons listed in the journal.
24. Ibid.
25. NC Conf Citizen file, E. D. Ramsey, 3, 5, 6, www.fold3.com, accessed November 29, 2012.
26. Adjutant General Papers, Ledger 1861–1863, AG 25, p. 136, NC Archives, Raleigh; Asheville Armory Ledger, LCHA.
27. *The Daily Bulletin*, Feb 18, Feb 23, Feb 25, Feb 26, Feb 27, Mar 17, Mar 22, Mar 25, Apr 5, 1862.
28. *Western Democrat*, Sept 1, 1863, Militia Officers, 1; Exemption Granted, Melchi Rhodes Papers, Rubenstein Library, Duke University.
29. Jacob Froneberger Diary, Aug 15, 1864, Oct 30, 1864. Violet A. Sifford to Harriet McIntosh, Dec 4, 1864, Harriet R. McIntosh Papers.
30. *Carolina Watchman*, Feb 2, 9, 16, Mar 2, 3, Aug 10, 1863, 2.
31. *The Daily Bulletin*, Aug 15, Aug 20, Nov 8, Nov 5, Nov 12, Nov 15, Nov 18, Nov 24, 1862; Jan 21, Jan 23, Jan 26, Jan 28, Jan 29, 1863.
32. Melchi Rhodes Account Book, 1854–1859, Melchi Rhodes Papers, Duke University. Gladden and Bell, *The 1860 Census of Gaston Co., North Carolina*, 166, 192. Sherrill, *Annals of Lincoln County, North Carolina*, 366–367.
33. Melchi Rhodes Account Book. *The Daily Bulletin*, Wed, Nov 12, 1862.
34. North Carolina General Statutes, Private 1862–1863, Chapter 55, 68–69, book found at NC Archives Search Room and also online at http://ncgovdocs.org/guides/sessionlawslist.htm. Set tolls included: six horse wagon, 35 cents; five horse wagon, 30 cents; four horse wagon or coach, 25 cents; three horse wagon, 20 cents; two horse wagon, 15 cents; one horse wagon or cart, 10 cents; two horse carriage or buggy, 25 cents; one horse carriage or buggy, 20 cents; man and horse, 10 cents; horses or mules in

droves, two and a half cents each; for cattle, hogs, and sheep, 2 cents each. If anyone should "break through or pass over said bridge without stopping ... to pay the toll," they would be assessed $5 "for each offence."
35. Melchi Rhodes Account Book, Scan 84.
36. Ibid., Scan 78, 84, 85.
37. J C Whitson to Vance Aug 31, 1863, GP 168, Corr Aug 25–31, 1863, NC Archives.
38. Wiswall Papers, LCHA.
39. Guy R. Hasegawa, "'Absurd Prejudice': A. Snowden Piggot and the Confederate Medical Laboratory at Lincolnton," *North Carolina Historical Review*, Vol LXXXI, No 3, July 2004, 313–334. See also Guy R. Hasagawa and F. Terry Hambrecht, "The Confederate Medical Laboratories," *Southern Medical Journal*, Vol 96, No 12 (Dec 2003), 1221–1230. Gordon B. Mckinney, "Premature Industrialization in Appalachia: The Asheville Armory, 1862–1863," in *Civil War Collected Essays*, ed. Kenneth W. Noe and Shannon H. Wilson, 232–233, determined that many Unionists worked at the Armory to avoid military service. Joseph Carpenter of Gaston and others applied for claims and documented their employment at the Laboratory.
40. Civil War Collection, Quartermaster Dept, Misc Records, 1862 Folder #1, #7, NC Archives.
41. A R Homesly to Vance, Gov Papers, GP 170, Corr Oct 25–27, 1863, NC Archives. *Western Democrat*, Oct 27, 1863, Factory Burnt, 3.
42. *The Daily Bulletin*, July 7, 1862, Nov 8, 1862. *Western Democrat*, Apr 5, 1864, Cleveland Enterprise, 3. The Froneberger family of Gaston and Cleveland were related.
43. *The Daily Bulletin*, July 4, July 13, 1861. *NC Whig*, July 9, 1861, 2.
44. *The Daily Bulletin*, Feb 18, Feb 23, Feb 25, Feb 26, Feb 27, Mar 17, Mar 22, Mar 25, Apr 5, Aug 15, Aug 20, Nov 8, Nov 5, 1862.
45. See Chapter 2 for a further discussion of Governor's Vance's Proclamation, Jasper Stowe's response, and capitulation to the governor. *Carolina Watchman*, Feb 16, 1863, 1; Mar 3, 1863, 2.
46. *The Daily Bulletin*, Mar 3, Mar 24, 1863. A brief article appeared in the *Western Democrat* on Mar 31, 1863.
47. See www.bosticlincolncenter.com/background.htm, lincolnstudies.blogspot.com/2008/02/abraham-lincoln-enloe.html, www.abrahamlincolnonline.org/lincoln/education/father.htm, and Jerry A Goodnight and Richard Eller, *The Tarheel Lincoln: North Carolina Origins of "Honest" Abe*, 2003.
48. *Carolina Watchman*, Cotton Factory Burned, June 30, 1862, 4, quoted the *Raleigh Register*. The *Daily Bulletin*, Apr 1, 1863; *Western Democrat*, Apr 28, 1863, Promoted.
49. *The Daily Bulletin*, June 12, June 18, June 17, 1863.
50. *Carolina Watchman*, May 8, 1863, 2; June 29, 1863, 3.
51. *The Bulletin*, Mar 4, 1864.
52. *The Bulletin*, Apr 28, July 7, 1864.
53. *Daily Carolina Times*, June 28, July 11, Sept 28, 1864.
54. W. D. Glenn Diary, Feb 19, 23, 1865, L C Glenn Papers, #03052, Wilson Library, Southern Historical Collection.
55. [probably Violet Ann] to Harriet McIntosh, Mar 5, 1865, Harriet R. McIntosh Papers. This letter is most likely missing the signature page. I determined it was written by Violet Ann by comparing grammar and handwriting.
56. Ibid. Isabella Sifford to Harriet McIntosh, Mar 5, 1865, Harriet R. McIntosh Papers.
57. David Schenck Diary, February 1865, 37–38, the entry includes events into March.
58. Mary Chestnut, *A Diary from Dixie*, 344–356.
59. Isa Sifford to Harriet McIntosh, Apr 8, 1865, Harriet R. McIntosh Papers.
60. Jacob Fronbeger Diary, Feb 12, 1865.
61. Hartley, *Stoneman's Raid 1865*, Chapter 6, 7, 8, 9.
62. Charles E. Kirk, ed. *History of the 15th Pennsylvania Cavalry*, Capt. H. K. Weant, (1906), on Google Books, accessed Mar 15, 2014, 505–512.
63. Some Reminiscences of the Great Confederate War, Lewis Cass Payseur, transcribed by Mary Alice Beatty Carmichael in 2000 from an unknown newspaper, 1914, provided to the author by Greg Payseur, cited as L. Cass Payseur transcript.
64. Ibid. Kirk, ed. *History of the 15th Pennsylvania Cavalry*, William L Bratton, (1906) on Google Books, accessed Mar 16, 2014, 556–559. No local description of these events has been located. A similar event occurred at Lineberger's Woodlawn cotton factory on the South Fork.
65. Charles E. Kirk, ed., *History of the 15th Pennsylvania Cavalry*, Capt H. K. Weant, (1906), on Google Books, accessed Mar 15, 2014, 505–512. Hartley, *Stoneman's Raid 1865*, 310.
66. Hardy, *Civil War Charlotte: Last Capital of the Confederacy*," 63–64; Hartley, *Stoneman's Raid, 1865*, 320–324. W. D. Glenn Diary, April 18, 20, 1865, Glenn Papers, SHC.
67. Cope and Wellman, *The County of Gaston*, 95–96.
68. Jacob Froneberger Diary, May 14, 1865.
69. David Schenck Diary, March 16, The Fall of the Confederacy, June 7, 1865, 38–43.
70. I used copies of the Southern Claims made by Jason Harpe. Each can be accessed at www.fold3.com, Civil War, Southern Claims Commission, North Carolina, Gaston County.
71. David Schenck Diary, Fall of the Confederacy, June 7, 1865, 38–43. Hartley, *Stoneman's Raid, 1865*, 306–309, 336–338, and 350–351, discusses these issues.
72. Jasper Stowe, NC Citizen File, 8–9, www.fold3.com. Hardy, *Civil War Charlotte: Last Capital of the Confederacy*, 65–66.
73. Jacob Froneberger Diary, May 23, 1865.
74. W. D. Glenn Diary, May ?, 1865, Glenn Papers, SHC. Writing is very dim.
75. W. D. Glenn Diary, June 1, July 10, 1865, Glenn Papers, SHC.
76. Civil War Diary of Dr. Alonzo Garwood, Surgeon of the 28th Michigan Infantry, of the 1st Division of the 23rd Army Corps in charge of the Field Hospital, http://www.migenweb.org/michiganinthewar/infantry/diary.htm, May 20–June 22, accessed Sept 3, 2014, after being informed of this source by Jason Harpe and Bill Beam.
77. Escott, *Many Excellent People*, 3–5, 16–23. Another antebellum North Carolina social and economic class description was postulated by historian Guin Griffis Johnson, who identified a six tiered social structure. It was not used since the Escott model was more flexible and allows for easier interpretation to Gaston County statistics. See also Kruman, *Parties and Politics in North Carolina, 1836–1865*, 180–187 and Bynum, *Unruly Women*, 15–20.
78. Escott, *Many Excellent People*, 5–7, 12.
79. Ibid., 8–9.
80. Ibid., 9–10.
81. Ibid., 10–12.
82. Ibid., 15–19, 28–29, 5–7, 12.
83. Ibid., 22–24.
84. Landless white laborers were not systematically included in the tax list, and this number represents an estimation based upon the number of heads of household in 1860 minus the total number from the tax list.
85. Gaston County Tax List 1863–1868, CR040.701.2, NC Archives. The numbers of taxables listed by company does not equal the number of households listed in the census. For purposes of social class, the author combined persons with more than one slave entry. The number of slaveholders in 1863 was higher because of

multiple entries (See Appendix and Chapter 9).

86. Escott, *Many Excellent People*, 16–23.

Chapter 2

1. Cope and Wellman, *County of Gaston*, 66–69, 73. Stroupe, Stets, Wetmore, Crumbley, *Post Offices and Postmasters of North Carolina*, Vol. II (1996), 242.
2. See Cope and Wellman, *County of Gaston*, 67–72. The "donation" was actually a purchase agreement.
3. David Schenck Diary, Oct 31, 1857, online Folder 4, Vol 3, Scan 138.
4. *The Lincoln Courier*, March 1, 1847, 1, 2; June 24, 1847, 3.
5. Gaston County Minute Docket, Oct Term 1847, CR040.301.1, NC Archives.
6. Gaston County Minute Docket, Feb, Apr Terms 1848, CR040.301.1, NC Archives.
7. *The Lincoln Courier,* June 2, 1848, Entertainment at Dallas, Gaston County, N. C., 4.
8. Ibid., Sept 1, 1848, 3.
9. Gaston County Minute Docket, Feb, Oct Terms 1847; Feb, Aug, Oct Terms, 1849; Feb, Apr Terms 1850, CR040.301.1, NC Archives.
10. *The Lincoln Courier*, Mar 31, 1849, 4.
11. Gaston County Minute Docket, Aug Term, 1850, Feb, Apr Term, 1851, CR040.301.1, NC Archives.
12. Carpenter, Bell, Goodnight, *The Complete 1850 Gaston County Census*, 48–53. Gaston County, 1850 Tax List, Dallas Company, CR040.701.1.
13. *The Lincoln Courier*, Feb 1, 1851, 3, 4; Mar 8, 1851, 3, 4.
14. Ibid., June 6, 1851, 2, 3.
15. Gaston County Minute Docket, Sept term, 1851; Apr, Aug term, 1852; Aug term, 1853, CR040.301.1, NC Archives.
16. Gaston County Minute Docket, Apr, Aug, Oct terms, 1854; Feb, Oct term, 1856, CR040.301.1, NC Archives.
17. David Schenck Diary, June 25, 1857, online Folder 4, Vol 3, Scan 132.
18. David Schenck Diary, May 7, 1859, online Folder 4, Vol 3, Scan 178; July 4, 1859, Folder 4, Vol 3, Scan 184; July 22, 1859, Folder 4, Vol 3, Scan 185.
19. David Schenck Diary, Aug 1859, online Folder 4, Vol 3, Scan 194; January 1860, online, Folder 4, Vol 3, Scan 206.
20. Cope and Wellman, *The County of Gaston*, 203. Gladden and Bell, *The 1860 Census of Gaston Co.,* 152, 155.
21. Gladden and Bell, *The 1860 Census of Gaston Co.,* 157. See Hoffman, *Our Kin*, 95–96 for more information about him and his family.
22. Jacob Froneberger Diary, 1861. Gladden and Bell, *The 1860 Census of Gaston Co.,* 157.
23. Ibid., 152–157, Cope and Wellman, *The County of Gaston*, 203.
24. Gladden and Bell, *The 1860 Census of Gaston Co.,* 153–154, 157.
25. Ibid., 154.
26. Ibid., 152–157.
27. Ibid., 152–157.
28. An Act to Incorporate the Town of Dallas in Gaston County, Private Laws, 1862–63, Section 44, 4, book located at NC Archives.
29. Lesley, 447–449.
30. Cope and Wellman, *The County of Gaston*, 47, 58–59, 72–73.
31. Goodnight, Bell, and Carpenter, *The Complete 1850 Gaston County Census*, 186, 181.
32. Wm E. Rose to And. Hoyl et al., Gaston County Deed Bk 1: 55–58, 594–595; And. Hoyl, President of High Shoals Manufacturing to Philip Groot, Gaston County Deed Bk 1: 696–702; 2: 29–37.
33. Gladden and Bell, *The 1860 Census of Gaston Co.,* 193. J. Peter Lesley, 188.
34. 84 U.S. 44, 21 L.Ed. 570, 17 Wall. 44, OLCOTT v. BYNUM ET AL., *December Term, 1872,* provided to the author by Kathy Gunter Sullivan, Dec 10, 2012.
35. Gaston County Deed Bk 5: 395–399 and Bk 1: 696–702, Gastonia, and Lincoln County Deed Bk 42: 387–391, Lincolnton. Further documentation of the Wilkes dealings may be found at Gaston County Deed Bk 6: 120–124, Gastonia.
36. See also Gaston County Deed Bk 2: 1–2; 29–37; Bk 3: 18; Bk 2: 215 ½, Gastonia.
37. See Pruitt, *Abstracts of Deeds Lincoln Co, NC Books 45, 46, and 47 (1863–1874),* 32; Lincoln County Deed Bk 45: 256 for a land sale by the group. Apparently the deed was originally filed in Edgecombe County.
38. Robert Rufus Bridgers and John Luther Bridgers by H. C. Bridgers Jr., *Dictionary of North Carolina Biography,* ed. William S. Powell, Vol 1 A–C, 223–224. Blount-Bridgers House Docent Handbook December 2011, http://www.edgecombearts.org/BBH%20Docent%20Handbook%20-%20December%202011.pdf, accessed January 12, 2012.
39. B B Barron, Civil War, NC Conf Amnesty Papers, www.fold3.com, accessed Mar 13, 2014; 1860 Edgecombe County, NC census, Image #114, www.ancestry.com, accessed August 20, 2011.
40. The tax list incorrectly listed their last name as Bridges, a popular surname in present Cleveland and Rutherford County.
41. Gaston County Deed Bk 3: 402–403, Gastonia.
42. High Shoals Company, Civil War NC Conf Business File, www.fold3.com, 3, 13, 15, 17, 19, 21, accessed Jun 3, 2012.
43. High Shoals Company, Civil War NC Conf Business File, www.fold3.com, 5, 7, 9, 11, 21, 23, 25, 27, 29, accessed Jun 3, 2012.
44. High Shoals Company, Civil War NC Conf Business File, www.Fold3.com, accessed June 3, 2012.
45. J. H. Chapman to B. B. Barron Mar 7, 1864, T. D. Gay to High Shoals Jan 17, 1865, Folder #8, Rev. M. Bennette to High Shoals Iron Co Feb 24, 1864, Cicero Green to High Shoals Iron Co Sp 5, 1864, Folder #7, High Shoals Papers, LCHA.
46. Henry Moore to Col Wm Johnston June 13, 1864, J. C. Wolfe agt to Wm Johnston June 8, 1864, Folder #8, Andrew Baker & Co to High Shoals Iron Co Oct 18, 1864, and Nov 15, 1864, Alex Mcrae, Jr. & Co to High Shoals Co, Wilcox & Hand to R R Bridgers Oct 28, 1864, J. Thomas & Co to High Shoals Iron Co Nov 12. 1864, Folder #7, High Shoals Papers, LCHA.
47. J. H. Chapman to Barron Mar 7, 1864, Folder #8, Rev. M. Bennette to High Shoals Feb 24, 1864, J. Williford to Barron Dec 20, 1864, T. W. Dewey to Barron Aug 11, 1864, T. W. Do?? per R. Chapman to R R Bridgers Sept 9, 1864, Folder #7, High Shoals Papers, LCHA.
48. Henry Moore to Wm Johnston June 13, 1864, Waddell to Barron Nov 2, 1864, Folder #8, Daniel Finger note Aug 14, 1864, W. F. Carpenter note Aug 14, 1864, Receipt Columbia July 28, 1864, R R Bridgers & Co to North Carolina Rail Road Co June 30, 1864, R R Bridgers & Co to North Carolina Railroad Company, Sept 1863, Folder #7, High Shoals Papers, LCHA.
49. J. Williford to Barron Dec 20, 1864, Folder #7, Moore to Johnston June 13, 1864, Wolfe to Johnston June 8, 1864, Johnston to Gentlemen June 15, 1864, Folder #8, High Shoals Papers, LCHA.
50. Wm. Trelvar to R R Bridgers July 7, 1864, Folder #8, Dial to High Shoals July 28, 1864, Benj Oliver to Mr Bridgers Barron & Co July 27, 1864, T W Dewey to B B Barron Aug 11, 1864, Folder #7, High Shoals Papers, LCHA.
51. E O Elliott to R R Bridgers Dec 13, 1864, Folder #8, Robert Greenefield to High Shoals undated, T R Tate to High Shoals Iron Co Nov 28, 1864, Folder #7, High Shoals Papers, LCHA.
52. Wm. T. Worth? to High Shoals Iron Co July 2, 1864, Wm H. Jones to B B Barron July 29, 1864, Andrew Baker & Co to High Shoals Nov 15, 1864, W A Cook to High Shoals Co Sept 9, 1864, John B. Winthrop to

High Shoals Iron Co Nov 4, 1864, Folder #7, High Shoals Papers, LCHA.
53. Reference in McKean, 822–823, quoted *Richmond Daily Dispatch*, Oct 2, 1862, but the notice was not found at the following link: http://digitalcollections.wordpress.com/2007/03/02/richmond-daily-dispatch-1860-1865-university-of-richmond/.
54. Joshua Swift undated, E A Ellison to R Bridgers Aug 15, 1864, Wm L Kennedy to J L Bridgers Dec 20, 1864, Confederate States undated, Folder #8, B B Barron to T J Summer June 11, 1864, Barron to Col Palmer Nov 17, 1864, A W Woodfin to Barron Nov 22, 1864, Wm R Kennedy to Barron Dec 9, 1864, R R Bridgers to Bolin Dec 10, 1864, C. J. Brenizer to R Bridgers & Co. Feb 17, 1865, Folder #7, High Shoals Papers, LCHA.
55. Gaston County Deed Bk 3: 215; 225–227; 305–310. See also Gaston County Execution Docket, Superior Court, CR040.318.1, Fall Term 1861 and afterward for details of Briggs' bankruptcy.
56. Lesley, 188.
57. Goodnight, Bell, and Carpenter, *The Complete 1850 Gaston County Census*, 187, 177.
58. Gladden and Bell, *The 1860 Census of Gaston Co.*, 172, 164.
59. Gaston County Execution Docket, Superior Court, CR040.381.1, Fall Term 1861, Fall Term 1862, NC Archives.
60. Gaston County Deed Bk 3: 215, 225–227, 305–310, Gastonia. Oates was from Gaston, Homesley from Cleveland, and Baxter from Lincoln Counties. See also Gaston County Execution Docket, Superior Court, CR040.318.1, Fall Term 1861 and afterward for details of Briggs' bankruptcy.
61. Civil War NC Conf Citizen Papers, Garrett Brothers, 7, 3, 9, 11, 13 accessed June 3, 2012; Business File, JJ and FM Garrett, accessed June 3, 2012; Citizen File, J J Garrett, www.fold3.com, accessed June 3, 2012.
62. Lucy Penegar, "Woman of the House," unpublished booklet provided to the author, 43, 50–56.
63. North Carolina General Statutes, Private 1862–1863, Chapter 10, 13–18
64. See Chapter 1 for further information.
65. *Western Democrat*, June 4, 1861, J W Derr's Blast Furnace, 3; he advertised consistently in the paper throughout the war; Apr 14, 1863, Moulders Wanted, 2; Feb 23, 1864, Notice, 1; Mar 3, 1863, Vesuvius Furnace Iron Works, 4; July 7, 1863, Rehoboth Furnace, 3.
66. Goodnight, Bell, and Carpenter, *The Complete 1850 Census Gaston County, North Carolina*, 187.
67. Gladden and Bell, *The 1860 Census of Gaston Co.*, 166.
68. Ibid., 165.
69. *The Lincoln Courier*, Mar 31, 1849, 3.
70. "Background for Stowe's Factory," report by Coastal Carolina Research, Inc., 2009, provided to John Babington, copy provided to the author by John Russell. Stowe Family Account Book 1856–1874, Stowe Family Papers, Rubenstein Library, Duke University, Image 95 describes the mill "as it is" in the middle 1870s.
71. Stowe Account Book 1856–1874, Stowe Family Papers, Duke Unversity.
72. Gladden and Bell, *The 1860 Census of Gaston Co.*, 165.
73. Len Clemmer, "An Early Land Transaction on the South Fork of the Catawba River," *Footprints in Time* (Dec 2012), 174–178, in which Clemmer quoted estate papers, deeds, and Special Proceedings of Lincoln and Gaston County to document the creation of the mill. He communicated with the author concerning his research. See also Cope and Wellman, *The County of Gaston*, 67.
74. Ragan, *The History of Gaston County*, 212.
75. Goodnight, Bell, and Carpenter, *The Complete 1850 Gaston County Census*, 127–129. Gladden and Bell, *The 1860 Census of Gaston Co.*, 169–194.
76. Ibid.,130–134, in Mountain Island post office; 98–100, in Stowesville post office; 87–89, 92, Dallas and Erasmus post offices .
77. Gladden and Bell, *The 1860 Census of Gaston Co.*, 98–100.
78. Store Ledger 1857–1860, Stowesville, NC, Stowe Family Papers, Duke University.
79. Ibid.
80. Ibid.
81. Tate to Vance, Gov Papers, GP 160, Corr. Sept 11–20, 1862, NC Archives.
82. *Western Democrat*, July 7, 1863, 250 WOMEN, 2.
83. Civil War NC Conf Citizens File, Thomas R. Tate, www.fold3.com, 1–56, accessed on June 3, 2012. Private Collection, C W Garrett Papers, PC 1308–1309, NC Archives. I added the amounts listed. Most came from the Fold3 records, which interestingly did not have any record of Mountain Island Mill.
84. NC Conf Citizens File, Thomas R. Tate, 1–56, www.Fold3.com, accessed June 3, 2012. Military Collection, Civil War Collection, Quartermaster Department Papers, Miscellaneous Records 1860–1865, Folders 1861 #1, 1863 #1 and #2, NC Archives. Unfortunately the dates on the files do not match their contents. Most of the documentation for the purchases came from the NC Archives, which suggests that the Fold3 records, may omit significant numbers of records.
85. Civil War NC Citizen File, Thomas R. Tate, www.Fold3.com, accessed Aug 28, 2012.
86. *The Daily Bulletin*, Sept 2, 1863, Beautiful Cassimeres.
87. Civil War Collection, Miscellaneous Papers, 1861 Folder #1, NC Archives.
88. Civil War Collection, Quartermaster Dept., Misc Records, 1863, Folder #1, NC Archives.
89. Civil War NC Conf Citizens File, Jasper Stowe, www.Fold3.com, accessed Aug 30, 2012.
90. Civil War Collection, Quartermaster Dept, Misc Papers 1863, Folder #11, #12, #13, NC Archives. At least two entries may be duplicates.
91. Jacob Froneberger Diary March 20, 1863. *The Daily Bulletin*, Fri, Mar 10, 1863. *Western Democrat*, Mar 24, 1863, 3. Lineberger & Co to Vance, Gov Papers, GP 175, Corr Mar 15–17, 1864, and GP 176, Corr Apr 28–30, 1864, NC Archives. Civil War Conf NC Citizen File, J. L. Lineberger, www.Fold3.com, accessed August 28, 2012.
92. Treasurer & Comptrollers Papers, Military Papers, Cotton and Wool Account Book 1862–1865, #92, NC Archives. Since the list was at the beginning of the book, I assumed that it dated from 1862.
93. David Schenck Diary, Prices and Patriotism [1862] 248–249, Feb 26, 1862. Schenck did not specify which mill operation he observed.
94. *NC Whig*, November 5, 1861, Salt and Extortion 2, quoting from the *Fayetteville Observer*. *NC Whig*, September 17, 1861, Extortion, 2, copied from the *Clarendon Banner*. *NC Whig*, July 15, 1862, 1, 2. *The Daily Bulletin*, Nov 15, Nov 18, 1862.
95. *Carolina Watchman*, Jan 12, 1863, The Conscript Law and Cotton Factories 2. The Confederate Congress established a limit of 75 percent profit for cotton manufacturing, which Vance enforced.
96. Adjutant General Letter Book 1862–1864, AG44, 299, NC Archives.
97. Adjutant General Letter Book 1862–1864, AG44, 313–314, NC Archives.
98. *The Daily Bulletin* Charlotte, Jan 7, 1863, The Conscript Law and the Cotton Factories. Colonel M H Hand, Stowesville, Gaston County, supplied the article and it was signed by Jasper Stowe Stowesville, NC, Jan 5, 1863. It was reprinted in the *Carolina Watchman*, Jan 12, 1863, 2, and as Mr Stowe's Bill of Complaints, *The Standard*, Jan 21, 1863, 1.
99. *The Standard*, Jan 21, 1863, Mr Stowe's Bill of Complaints, 1. The

Standard article was reprinted in the *Carolina Watchman*, Jan 26, 1863, 3.
100. Adjutant General Letter Book 1862–1864, AG44, 332, NC Archives.
101. Minnie Stowe Puett, *History of Gaston County*, 186.
102. Robert A. Ragan, *The Textile Heritage of Gaston County 1848–2000*.
103. NC Conf Service Record, Jasper Stowe, 2, 3, www.fold3.com, accessed May 24, 2013. Puett, *History of Gaston County*, 185–187, Cope and Wellman, *The County of Gaston*, 92.
104. *Charlotte Observer*, May 23, 1902, a copy of which is located in the Stowe Family Papers, Perkins Library, Duke University.
105. *Western Democrat*, Mar 3, 1863, 3 quoting the Greensboro *Patriot* about other abuses.
106. Headdles were composed of hooks which the yarn was attached to, allowing the loom to weave, and the treadle, which was operated by foot, selected different yarn which made patterns and designs, from http://www.estherlederberg.com/EImages/Extracurricular/Cloth/Cloth%20Manufacture.html accessed, Sept 6, 2011.
107. *Carolina Watchman*, Dec 14, 1863, 3.
108. Hardy, *Civil War Charlotte: Last Capital of the Confederacy*, 23–39.

Chapter 3

1. Rufus W. Carson "Diary," Mar 4, 1908, John E. and Wylma H. Monteith Collection held in private hands, Stanley, NC. Carson wrote reminiscences in 1908 in a diary format.
2. Kenneth W. Noe, *Reluctant Rebels*, discussed later Confederate enlistees, while James M. McPherson, *For Cause and Comrades: Why Men Fought in the Civil War*, analyzed Union and Confederate enlistees. Both authors used contemporary letters instead of memoirs or regimental histories as more authentic than the later writings. McPherson estimated that 80 percent of Confederate soldiers could read and write, producing a marvelous resource for study.
3. This soldier was W. P. Cline of Catawba County, North Carolina.
4. Hoyle to his mother, April 29, 1862, Lemuel Hoyle Letters.
5. Hoyle to his mother, Sept 24, 1863, Lemuel Hoyle Letters.
6. David Schenck Diary, November 24 and 25, 1863, 266–267.
7. Hoyle to his mother, May 25, 1864, Lemuel Hoyle Letters.
8. Morris to wife, Nov 12, 1861, Apr 18, 1862, Morris Letters. McPherson, *For Cause and Comrades*, 93–94, describes this motivation as defending "home and hearth."
9. Morris to wife, Mar 27, 1863, Morris Letters.
10. Morris to wife, Apr 5, 1863, Morris Letters.
11. McPherson, *For Cause and Comrades*, 17–21.
12. Torrence to Dear Pa, July 20, 1861; to Miss Sarah P. Torrence, Dec 11, 1862; Dear Sister, June 8, 1862, *NCHR*, 479–480.
13. Jacob Dellinger to his father, Oct 18, 1861, F L Dellinger Correspondence.
14. J J Brown to wife, August 27, 1862, Brown Letters.
15. McPherson, *For Cause and Comrades*, 11, 79–80.
16. George L. Phifer, NC Conf Service Records, has two files online with the 1st Artillery and 49th Regiment, 2, 3, 6–7, www.fold3.com, accessed May 29, 2012.
17. Edward Phifer to Mother, Oct 19, 1862, Phifer Letter Transcriptions.
18. William L. Phifer and Edward X. Phifer, NC Conf Service Records, www.fold3.com, accessed May 29, 2012.
19. Edward Phifer to Mother, Nov 1, 1863; Minnie Gray to Edward Phifer, June 12, 1864; E. C. Phifer to Edward Phifer, June 20, 1864; Julia A. Patterson to My Dear Madam [Mrs. Phifer], June 24, June 28, 1864, Phifer Letter Transcriptions.
20. P. Frank Dellinger, NC Conf Soldier Records, www.fold3.com, accessed May 29, 2012, 1–14. P F Dellinger to H J Dellinger, to D H Dellinger, Mar 9, 1863; P. F. to Father and Family, Apr 10, 1863, D H Dellinger Correspondence.
21. Henry Huss to D H Dellinger, Mar 21, 1863; Robert F. Peck to Margaret, Feb 1, 1864; Thomas Howser to "Dear Cousin," Sept 5, 1864; see Daniel Dellinger to wife, Feb 18, 1864, D H Dellinger Correspondence. Official records indicate his service began June 1864, Daniel H Dellinger, NC Conf Service records, 1–2, www.fold3.com, accessed May 29, 2012.
22. Linebarger to his wife, May 1, 1863, Feb 20, 1864, Apr 28, 1864, "Letters of a Gaston Ranger."
23. Jacob Dellinger to his father, Oct 18, 1861, Sept 8, 1862; W B Brown to wife, Apr 4, 1862, F L Dellinger Correspondence.
24. Rufus W. Carson, NC Conf Service Records, 3, www.fold3.com, accessed May 29, 2012.
25. Senter to John Cloninger, Sept 16, 1863; Frances to Caleb, Apr 5, 1863, Senter Correspondence. Prior to his service Gaston Court Minutes listed Senter as a debtor a number of times, failing to have sufficient funds to pay his taxes. Gaston County, Execution Docket, Superior Court, CR040.318.1, Fall Term 1857, Spring Term 1858, Fall Term 1859, Spring Term 1860.
26. Davis to wife, June 19, Aug 17, 1863, Davis Correspondence.
27. M E Hanna to F S Hanna, Oct 30, 1862; William D Hanna to Dear Son, Nov 9, 1862; F S Hanna to Wife, Jan 25, 1863; Hanna to Caroline Hanna, June 20, 1863; Hanna to Wife, Sept 3–4, 1863, Hanna Papers.
28. Newton Sellers to his wife, Mar 3, 1864, to wife and Mr. Daniel Sellers, Apr 21, 1864, to wife, Apr 28, 1864, Newton Sellers Papers. Newton Sellers, NC Conf Service record, 9–10, www.fold3.com, accessed May 29, 2012.
29. Larkin Thornburg, "The Experience of a Seventeen Year Old Boy During the War Between the States," typescript copy at Gaston County Museum of Art and History, Dallas, and in the hands of the author.
30. McPherson, *For Cause and Comrades*, 98–100.
31. Morris to wife, Jan 7, Jan 27, 1862, Morris Letters.
32. Hoyle to Mother, July 29, Sept, Oct 23, 1861, Lemuel Hoyle Letters.
33. Hoyle to mother, Oct 1, Oct 11, Oct 27, 1863, Lemuel Hoyle Letters. Lemuel Hoyle, NC Confederate Service Records, 29, www.fold3.com, accessed May 29, 2012.
34. Hoyle to mother, May 7, May 25, June 5, June 22, Aug 22–23, Aug 29, 1864, Lemuel Hoyle Letters.
35. Hoyle to mother, Jan 9, Mar 11, 1865, Lemuel Hoyle Letters.
36. Torrence to Pa, July 20, Aug 31, 1861, to Pa and Sis, Sept 9, 1861, to Pa, Oct 30, 1861, to mother, Nov 17, 1861, to Mother, Mar 4, 1862, *NCHR*, 479–480; 481–482; 482–483; 484; 485–486; 490.
37. Senter to wife, May 3, Oct 23, Nov. 14, [undated letter], Dec 1, Dec 31, 1862; Feb 3, Feb 9, 1863, Senter Correspondence.
38. Senter to wife, Dec 3, 1863, Dec 4, 1863, Dec 18, 1863, Jan 1, 1864, Senter Correspondence.
39. P F Dellinger to D H Dellinger, June 8, June 22, Sept 15, Sept 25, 1862, D H Dellinger Correspondence; Hoyle to mother, Sept 9, Sept 23, Sept 25, Sept 29, 1862, Lemuel Hoyle Letters.
40. John Houser to D H Dellinger, Sept 27, 1862; George Rhyne to D H Dellinger, Oct 2, 1862; P F Dellinger to M A Rhyne, Jan 28, 1863, D H Dellinger Correspondence.
41. George M Rhyne, NC Conf Service Records, 5–7, 11–13, www.fold3.com, accessed May 29, 2012. Documentation differs on the date of his death from Jan 12–23 but it appears most likely that he died Jan 23.
42. J J to wife Christina, Aug 2, Aug 27, Dec 25, 1862; Jan 13, 1863; Lt. R. W. Carpenter to Mrs. Christina Brown, Apr 10, 1863, Brown Letters.

43. Carpenter Letters in private collection of Wade Carpenter, copy in possession of the author, Lawson Carpenter to Father, Dec 8, 1862. Carpenter died of disease.

44. Mary E. Sellers to her mother, Margaret E. Hagar, July 2, 1863, Sellers to wife, Apr 28, 1864, Newton Sellers Papers. David F. Eddleman, NC Conf Service Record, 15–16, 19, 21, 25, www.fold3.com, accessed May 29, 2012.

45. Linebarger to his wife, May 25, May 29, July 4, 1862; W I Stowe to Mrs. Linebarger, July 23, 1862; Linebarger to his wife, Nov 11, Nov 17, 1862, Apr 25, 1863, Jan 3, Feb 21, 1864, "Letters of a Gaston Ranger."

46. P. Nicholson to Mary Linebarger, May 25, 1864, B S Gaither to Henry Setzer, May 27, 1864, "Letters of a Gaston Ranger."

47. W. D. Glenn Diary, Jan 29, 1864, LA Glenn Papers, SHC.

48. Davis to wife, Aug 16, Oct 16, Oct 19, Oct 24, 1862; Wm R Barnet to Margaret M Davis, Oct 27, 1862; Wm R Barnet to T A Davis, Nov 30, 1862; Davis to wife, Feb 27, Mar 7, 1863, Davis Correspondence.

49. Davis to wife, June 5, July 3, July 31, Aug 6, Aug 17, Aug 27, 1863, Davis Correspondence.

50. Davis to wife, Sept 23, Nov 2, 1863, Davis Correspondence.

51. Elisabeth McNeely to Mrs. Mary Davis, Nov 5, 1864, Davis Correspondence.

52. Peter Dellinger to Uncle, July 9, 1861; J. R. Dellinger to father, Feb 23, 186?. The date appears to be 1861 but this is impossible. It may be 1863; Jacob Dellinger to his father, Oct 18, 1861; F W Dellinger to sister, Apr 14, 1864, F L Dellinger Correspondence.

53. B F Withers to J F Goodson Esq, May 5, 1862, Lucille Goodson Collection, LCHA; James H Hanna to Dear Cousin, Oct 14, 1862, Hanna Papers; Elizabeth Lineberger to husband, Dec 1862, "Letters of a Gaston Ranger."

54. F S Hanna to wife, Sept 18, 1862; M E Hanna to F S Hanna, Oct 30; Caroline to F S Hanna, Nov 5, Nov 19, 1862; Caroline Hanna and M E Hanna to F S Hanna, Dec 7, 1862; James H, E J, and May E Hanna to F S Hanna, Dec 10, 1862; F S Hanna to C. Hanna, Dec 14, 1862; F S Hanna to Wife, Jan 25, 1863, Hanna Papers.

55. F S Hanna to C Hanna, May 2, May 10, June 5, 1863, Hanna Papers. F S Hanna, NC Conf Service Records, 4–9, www.fold3.com, accessed May 29, 2012.

56. W. L. to Mother, July 8, 1862; to Dear Brother, Aug 30, 1863; Annie Peck to My Dear Friend, Oct 4, 1863, Phifer Letter transcriptions.

57. M E Lusk to Aunt Bettie Oct 1863; Frances Adams to My Dear Cousin, Oct 12, 1863, Phifer Letter transcriptions.

58. Edward Phifer to Mother, July 7, 1862, Jan, Feb 4,5, Feb 16, May 23, 1864; Minnie Gray to Edward Phifer, May 30, 1864; E. C. Phifer to Edward, June 20, July 8, 1864, Phifer Letter transcriptions.

59. Julia A. Patterson to My Dear Madam [Mrs. Phifer], June 24, June 2?, June 28, June 30, 1864; Wm. L. Lacy to Mrs. John F. Phifer, July 2, 1864; E. C. Phifer to Edward Phifer, July 8, 1864, Phifer Letter transcriptions.

60. Julia A. Patterson to My Dear Mrs. Phifer, June 11 [should be July 11], July 15, 1864, Phifer Letter transcriptions.

61. Senter to his wife, Aug 21, Sept 12, Sept 25, 1862, Jan 1, 1864, Senter Correspondence.

62. Hoyle to mother, Nov 6, Nov 10, 1862, Nov 22, Dec 3, Dec 13, Dec 18, 1862, Jan 30, 1863, Lemuel Hoyle Letters.

63. Morris to wife, May 5, 1862, Morris Letters.

64. Hoyle to mother, Nov 26, Dec 18, Dec 27, 1863; Jan 7, Jan 18, Mar 28, 1864, Lemuel Hoyle Letters.

65. Torrence to Mother and Sarah Priscilla Torrence, Jan 31; Torrence to Sister, Apr 12, 1863, NCHR, 505; 501–502.

66. Edney Hoover to Mary C. Hoover, Jan 11, 1864, Lincoln Times News, Wed Oct 26, 2011; Edney Hoover to Mary C. Hoover, Apr 19, 1864, Lincoln Times News, Wed Nov 23, 2011.

67. P F Dellinger to D H Dellinger, Aug 31, 1862; to Levi Wacaster, Dec 7, 1862, D H Dellinger Correspondence.

68. Sellers to his wife, Mar 3, 1864, Newton Sellers Papers.

69. Linebarger to wife, May 17, Nov 25, Nov 11, 1862, May 26, Aug 3, 1863; Feb 14, Apr 2, May 4, 1864, "Letters of a Gaston Ranger."

70. Hoyle to mother, Oct 10, 1862, Lemuel Hoyle Letters. Senter to wife, Sept 20, 1863, Senter Correspondence.

71. Morris to wife, Jan 29, Mar 20, 21, 1863, Morris Letters. Torrence to Pa, Jan 18, 1862; Torrence to Mother, Apr 12, 1863;Torrence to Mother and Affectionate Sister, May 7, 8, 1863, NCHR, 489, 504, 505–508.

72. Morris to wife, Apr 18, 1862; Mar 27, 1863, Morris Letters.

73. Morris to wife, Apr 15, 1863, Morris Letters.

74. F W to F L Dellinger, Jan 25, 1863, F L Dellinger Correspondence.

75. George Rhyne to D H Dellinger, Oct 2, 1862; D H Dellinger to wife, Nov 5, Nov 8, 1864, D H Dellinger Correspondence. Hoyle to his mother, Jan 30, 1863, Lemuel Hoyle Letters.

76. Hoyle to his mother, Mar 28, Apr 25, May 7, May 25, June 5, Oct 20, Oct 25, 1864, Lemuel Hoyle Letters.

77. Linebarger to wife, May 17, June 14, Dec 25, 1862, July 26, Aug 28, Sept 11, Sept 17, Oct 1, 1863, "Letters of a Gaston Ranger."

78. Linebarger to wife, June 3, July 4, Sept 11, Sept 23, 1862, "Letters of a Gaston Ranger."

79. Morris to wife, July 21, 1862, Morris Letters.

80. JJ Brown to his wife, Sept 28, 1862, Brown letters.

81. F W Dellinger to father and mother, brother and sister, Nov 5, 1862, F L Dellinger Correspondence.

82. Torrence to Mother, June 8, 1862; to Pa & Ma, July 14, 1862, NCHR, 494–495, 496–498.

83. Morris to wife, Sept 7, 1862, Morris Letters.

84. Jacob Dellinger to father, Sept 8, 1862, F L Dellinger Correspondence.

85. David Coon to Sister Barbara, Sept 28, 1862; to "Sister Bob," Nov 30, 1862, Dec 13, 1862, Coon, Yoder, and Killian Papers, LCHA.

86. Linebarger to wife, Nov 25, Dec 17, 1862, "Letters of a Gaston Ranger."

87. Torrence to Mother and Affectionate Sister, May 7, 8, 1863, NCHR, 505–508.

88. Letter fragment no date or names, D H Dellinger Correspondence.

89. Linebarger to wife, Feb 25, Apr 3, June 6, 1863, "Letters of a Gaston Ranger."

90. W. J. O Daniel to Mrs. Torrence, July 9, 1863, NCHR, 514–515.

91. W. J. O Daniel to Mrs. Torrence, July 9, 1863, to Mrs. Torrence, July 20, 1863, NCHR, 514–516.

92. W J O Daniel to Mrs. Torrence, August 10, 1863, NCHR, 516–517.

93. Hoyle to mother, July 12, 1863, Aug 1, 1863, Lemuel Hoyle Letters. In his company Hoyle reported 7 killed, 43 wounded, and 14 missing.

94. ?Seagle to "Dear Uncle," July 29, 1863, Coon, Yoder, and Killian Papers, LCHA.

95. Adolphus S. Coon to Dear Sister, Nov 18, 1863, July 30, 1864, Coon, Yoder, and Killian Papers, LCHA.

96. Cope and Wellman, The County of Gaston, 89. Puett, History of Gaston County, 203–204.

97. Linebarger to wife, July 5, July 10, 1863, "Letters of a Gaston Ranger."

98. Linebarger to father, Aug 3, 1863, "Letters of a Gaston Ranger."

99. Cephas Keener to Peter Keener and Daniel Finger, Oct 21, 1863, in hands of Fred Goodson and furnished to the author by Mark Goodson, his son. The family noted that Cephas Keener was later killed in the war.

100. Linebarger to wife, Mar 13, 1864, "Letters of a Gaston Ranger."

101. Hoyle to his mother, May 7, May 25, June 5, 1864, Lemuel Hoyle Letters.
102. Edney Hoover to Mary C. Hoover, May 16, 1864, *Lincoln Times News*, Wed Nov 30, 2011; Edney Hoover to Mary C. Hoover, June 5, 1864, *Lincoln Times News*, Wed Dec 7, 2011; Edney Hoover to Mary C. Hoover, June 27, 1864, *Lincoln Times News*, Wed Dec 14, 2011.
103. P L Boyd to Mis S Reinhardt, June 23, 1864, LCHA
104. H K to F L Dellinger, Aug 9, 1864, F L Dellinger Correspondence.
105. Peter Keener to Wife and Family, Oct 6, 1864, in hands of Fred Goodson and furnished to the author by Mark Goodson, his son.
106. Jas Fulton to Daughter Rachel Fulton, Jan 20, 1865, copy given to the author by Steve and Daphene Friday, a professor at Belmont Abbey College, on Jan 9, 2013.
107. D H Dellinger, NC Conf Service Records, 1-2, www.fold3.com, accessed 29, 2012.
108. Daniel Dellinger to wife, Feb 18, 1864, D H Dellinger Correspondence.
109. DH Dellinger to Frances, Oct 12, D H Dellinger to George Dellinger, Oct 27, D H Dellinger to Frances, Nov 3, Nov 8, 1864, D H Dellinger Correspondence.
110. D H Dellinger to Mrs. M. A. Rhyne, Nov 16, 1864; to Frances, Jan 19, 1865; to Family, Nov 27, 1864; to mother, [undated], D H Dellinger Correspondence.
111. D H Dellinger to Frances, Feb 1, Feb 22, 1865, D H Dellinger Correspondence.
112. Rufus W. Carson "Diary," Mar 4, 1908, John E. and Wylma H. Monteith Papers private collection.

Chapter 4

1. S H Williams to Vance Jan 4, Jan 6, 1864, Gov Papers, GP 173, Corr Jan 5-9, 1864, NC Archives. S H Williams, Conf Service Record, www.Fold 3.com, accessed September 6, 2012.
2. Senter to wife, May 22, 1862, Jan 8, Nov 1, Nov 12, Nov 16, Nov 22, 1863, Feb 9, 1864, Senter Correspondence.
3. Morris to wife, Dec 25, 1862, Morris Letters.
4. Morris to wife , Mar 29, Oct 21, 1863; Oct 20, Oct 24, Nov 27,1864, Morris Letters.
5. Daniel Dellinger to "Beloved Children," Sept 6, 1864, to wife, Sept 11, to Frances, Oct 29, 1864, to Frances, [undated], to Frances, Nov 3, to Family, Nov 27, 1864, DH Dellinger Correspondence.
6. Morris to wife, Feb 8, Oct 4, 5, 1862, Morris Letters.
7. Newton Sellers to wife and Mr. Daniel Sellers, Apr 21, 1864, Newton Sellers to wife, Apr 28, 1864, Newton Sellers Papers.
8. Linebarger to wife, Apr 18, Sept 15, Nov 25, 1862, to Dear Father, Jan 23, 1863, to wife, Feb 1, Feb 15, July 10, July 20, 1863, to father, Aug 3, 1863, to wife, Nov 1,1863, to father, Feb 20, 1864, to wife, Feb 21, 22, 1864, "Letters of a Gaston Ranger."
9. J J Brown to wife, Nov 30, Dec 25, 1862, Brown Letters.
10. Davis to his wife, [May 1862] two letters, May 25, 1862, two letters, June 10, to Richard Philbeck in the letter to his wife, Aug 31, to his wife, Oct 5, 1862, to his wife, Apr 16, to his wife, May 13, to his wife, June 19, to his wife, Aug 15,1863, Davis Correspondence.
11. F S Hanna to wife, Sept 18, 1862, Caroline to F S Hanna, Nov 5, Nov 19,1862, F S Hanna to C Hanna, May 10, 1863, Caroline Hanna to F S Hanna, Sept 16, 1863, Hanna Papers.
12. Mary C. Hoover to Edney Hoover, Feb 18, 1864, *Lincoln Times News*, Wed Nov 9, 2011; Edney Hoover to Mary C. Hoover, Mar 14, 1864, *Lincoln Times News*, Wed Nov 16, 2011.
13. Senter to "Dear Wife," May 22, June 23, Aug 24, Sept 12, 1862, Sept 30, May 15, Oct 17, Oct 30, 1863, Senter Correspondence.
14. Morris to wife, Sept 7, 1862, Morris Letters.
15. PF Dellinger to DH Dellinger, May 6, 1862, Wm W Haynes to D H Dellinger May 25, 1862, P F Dellinger to D H Dellinger May 16, 1862, D H Dellinger Correspondence.
16. Edney Hoover to Mary C. Hoover and to parents, Nov 12, 1863, *Lincoln Times News*, Wed Sept 14, 2011.Edney Hoover to Mary C. Hoover, Jan 3, 1864, *Lincoln Times News*, Wed Oct 5, 2011.
17. Morris to wife, Feb 8, 1862, Morris Letters.
18. Linebarger to Elizabeth C, May 17, July 4, Sept 11, Nov 11, 1862, to Dear Father, Jan 23, 1863, to wife, Feb 1, Feb 15, Feb 27, June 6, June 7, July 26, Oct 28, 1863, Mar 25, 1864, "Letters of a Gaston Ranger."
19. Senter to wife, Aug 24, 1862, Mar 3, Mar 24, May 20, 1863, Jan 7, Mar 6, Apr 27, 1864, Senter Correspondence.
20. P F Dellinger to D H Dellinger, Sept 15, 1862; D H Dellinger to P F Dellinger, Sept 20, 1862, Jan 4, 1863; P F Dellinger to D H Dellinger, Jan 28, 1863; Frances Dellinger to D H Dellinger, Sept 14, 1864; D H Dellinger to wife, Nov 10, 1864; Frances Dellinger to D H Dellinger, Jan 15, 16, 1865; D H Dellinger to Mrs. F. Dellinger, Jan 19, 1865, DH Dellinger Correspondence.
21. Hoyle to mother, June 7, 1861, Oct 10, Nov 6, 1862, Sept 8, 1863, Lemuel Hoyle Letters.
22. Morris to wife, Feb 10, Sept 24, Dec 28, 1862, July 29, 1864, Aug 27, 1863, Oct 20, 1864, Morris Letters.
23. Torrence to Mother, Aug 2, Aug 31, 1861; to Sis, Oct 31, 1861; to mother, Nov 17, 19, 1861; to Brother, Feb 9, 1863; to Mother and Affectionate Sister, May 7, 8, 1863; to Mother, June 17, 1863, *NCHR*, 480–481, 485–486, 502, 505–508.
24. J J Brown to Christina, Aug 8, Nov 30, 1862, Jan 13, 1863, Brown Letters.
25. Davis to wife, June 10, Oct 5, May 10, 1862, July 31, Oct 1, Dec 19, Dec 19, 1863, Davis Correspondence.
26. Frederick Dellinger to F W Dellinger, May 6, 1862; Henry to Father, Jan 9, 1865, F L Dellinger Correspondence.
27. F S Hanna to C. Hanna, Dec 14, 1862, to wife, Jan 29, May 10 May 10, May 18, 1863, Hanna Papers.
28. Edward Phifer to Mother, Nov 23, Dec 1862; W. L. Phifer to Mother, July 8, Oct 3, 1862, May 23, Aug 30, 1863; Edward Phifer to Mother, June 27, Oct 13, Oct 20, Oct 27, Nov 3, Nov 8, Dec 12, Dec 18, Dec 22, 1863, Jan 1864, Phifer Letter Transcriptions.
29. Linebarger to wife, Nov 17, Nov 25, 1862; Elizabeth C Linebarger to husband, Dec 1862, Linebarger to wife, Feb 1, Feb 15, May 1, July 26, Oct 28, Nov 26, 1863; to his father, Feb 20, 1864; to wife, Mar 25, 1864, "Letters of a Gaston Ranger."
30. Senter to wife, Aug 13, Dec 1, 1862, Senter Correspondence.
31. Morris to wife, Aug 19, Oct 4, Dec 6, 1862, Morris Letters.
32. Torrence to Pa, Aug 31, 1861; to Sis, Oct 31, 1861; to mother, Nov 17, 19, 1861; to Mother, Mar 19, 1862; to Sister, June 8, 1862, *NCHR*, 481–482, 485–486, 491–492, 496.
33. Hoyle to mother, Aug 21, 1861, Apr 9, Apr 29, May 9, 1862, July 12, 1863, Lemuel Hoyle Letters.
34. M L Holland to wife, no date given, McKean, Vol II, 655.
35. W. L. Phifer to Mother, July 8, 1862; Edward Phifer to Mother, Oct 4, 1862; W. L. Phifer to Mother, Dec 21, 1862; W. L. Phifer to Mother, May 23, 1863; W. L. Phifer to My Dear Brother [George], Aug 30, 1863; Edward Phifer to Mother, May 12, 1863; Edward Phifer to Mother, May 12, Nov 8, 1863; E. C. Phifer to Edward, Feb 16, 1864, Phifer Letter Transcriptions.
36. Brown to wife, Aug 27, Sept 28, 1862, Brown Letters.
37. Newton Sellers to wife, June 4, 1863, Apr 21, 1864, Newton Sellers Papers.
38. Peter Dellinger to Uncle, July 9, 1861; Jacob Dellinger to his father, Oct

18, 1861, F L Dellinger Correspondence.
39. Linebarger to wife, Aug 5, 1863, "Letters of a Gaston Ranger."
40. Edney Hoover to Mary C. Hoover and to parents, Nov 12, 1863, *Lincoln Times News*, Wed Sept 14, 2011; Edney Hoover to Mary C. Hoover, Oct 13, 1864, *Lincoln Times News*, Wed Dec 14, 2011.
41. Caroline to F S Hanna, Nov 5, Dec 7, 1862, Feb 15, Aug 30, 1863, Hanna Papers.
42. D H Dellinger to Frances, Oct 29, Oct 30, 1864, D H Dellinger Correspondence.
43. Davis to wife, two letters, May 25, July 25, July 30, 1862, Davis Correspondence.
44. David Coon to "Sister Bob," Nov 30, 1862, Dec 13, 1862, Coon, Yoder, and Killian Papers, LCHA.
45. F S Hanna to C. Hanna, Dec 14, 1862, F S Hanna to Wife, Jan 25, May 10, Aug 25, Aug 30, 1863, Hanna Papers.
46. Senter to wife, May 11, 1862, Mar 2, May 15, 1863, Senter Correspondence.
47. Edward Phifer to Mother, Jan 1864; E. C. P. to Ed Phifer, Jan 7 or 9, 1864; Edward Phifer to Mother, Feb 9, 1864; E. C. Phifer to Edward, Feb 16, 1864, Phifer Letter Transcriptions.
48. P F Dellinger to D H Dellinger, Jan 27, 1863, D H Dellinger Correspondence.
49. Hoyle to mother, June 7, 1862, Oct 1, Oct 11, Oct 27, 1863, Mar 28, Apr 25, Oct 20, 1864, Lemuel Hoyle Letters. Lemuel Hoyle, NC Conf Service Records, www.fold3.com, 29, accessed Sept 6, 2012.
50. Linebarger to wife, July 23, Dec 25, 1862, Feb 1, Feb 27, Oct 1, 1863; Linebarger to Jno. C. Pegram, Oct 7, 1863; Linebarger to wife, Jan 6, Jan 10, Feb 14, 1864, "Letters of a Gaston Ranger."
51. Edney Hoover to Mary C. Hoover, Jan 11, 1864, *Lincoln Times News*, Wed Oct 26, 2011. Newton Sellers to his wife, Mar 3, 1864, Newton Sellers Papers; J. R. Dellinger to father, Feb 23, 186?[3], F L Dellinger Correspondence.
52. Davis to wife, Aug 2, Aug 10, 1862, Davis Correspondence.
53. Edward Phifer to Mother, Sept 27, Oct 15?, Oct 20, 1863, Phifer Letter Transcriptions.
54. P F Dellinger to D H Dellinger, June 8, June 22, 1862, D H Dellinger Correspondence; M L Holland to wife, Aug 18, 1862, in McKean, 662; Lineberger to his wife, May 29, 1862, Elizabeth Lineberger to husband, Dec 1862, "Letters of a Gaston Ranger."
55. Undated *Gastonia Gazette* article; *Gastonia Gazette* article dated May 5, 1968, and "Frederick Washington Dellinger" summary from F L Dellinger Correspondence.
56. David Coon to "Sister Bob," May 23, 1862, Coon, Yoder, and Killian Papers, LCHA.
57. Linebarger to father, Aug 3, 1863, Jan 10, Mar 13, Mar 25, Apr 22, 1864, "Letters of a Gaston Ranger."
58. P F Dellinger to D H Dellinger, Jan 13, 1863, D H Dellinger Correspondence.
59. Hoyle to mother, Nov 22, 23, 1862, Lemuel Hoyle Letters.
60. Hoyle to mother, Jan 7, 1864, Lemuel Hoyle Letters.
61. Hoyle to mother, June 5, 1864, Oct 25, 1864, Lemuel Hoyle Letters.
62. Caleb to wife, Aug 9, 1862, Feb 24, 1863, Sept 16, Dear Cousin John Cloninger, Senter Correspondence.
63. Newton to wife, Arp 21, 1864, Newton Sellers Papers.
64. Hanna to wife, Sept 15, 1862, Sept 2, 1863, Hanna Papers. J J Brown to wife, Dec 25, 1862, Brown Letters.
65. Levi Wacaster to D H Dellinger, May 5, 1862; Henry Huss to D H Dellinger, Mar 21, 1863; Daniel Houser to D H Dellinger, Jan 14, 1864; Robert F. Peck to Margaret, Feb 1, 1864; D H Dellinger to his wife, Feb 18, 1864; Thomas Howser to Dellinger, Sept 5, 1864; Dellinger to wife, Sept 11, Nov 27, 1864; Noah Dellinger to D H Dellinger Jan 1, 1865; Dellinger to wife, Jan 27, 1865, D H Dellinger Correspondence.
66. Hoyle to mother, Nov 22, 1862, Apr 25, May 25, June 5, Sept 12, 1864, Lemuel Hoyle Letters.
67. Morris to wife, Jan 26, 1863; Ambrose Costner to "his sister," Feb 1, 1865, Morris Letters.
68. Torrence to Pa & Ma, July 14, 1862, *NCHR*, 496–498
69. Davis to wife, Sept 17, Sept 20, 1862; Wm R Barnett to Margaret M Davis, Oct 27, 1862; Davis to wife, Aug 27, Dec 19, Dec 22, 1863, Davis Correspondence.
70. Linebarger to wife, Aug 5, 1863, "Letters of a Gaston Ranger."
71. Em Houser to J R D, Apr 20, 1864, F L Dellinger Correspondence. David Coon to "Sister Bob," Dec 13, 1862, Mar 13, 1863, Dec 24, 1862, Coon, Yoder, and Killian Papers, LCHA.
72. Edney Hoover to Mary C. Hoover, Aug 13, 1863, *Lincoln Times News*, Wed Aug 10, 2011, Nov 19, 1863, *Lincoln Times News*, Wed Sept 21, 2011, Jan 3, 1864, *Lincoln Times News*, Wed Oct 5, 2011, June 27, 1864, *Lincoln Times News*, Wed Dec 14, 2011, accessed at LCHA.
73. Jas Fulton to Daughter Rachel Fulton, Jan 20, 1865, copy given to the author by Steve and Daphene Friday, a professor at Belmont Abbey College, on Jan 9, 2013.
74. E. C. Phifer to Edward Phifer, July 8, 1864, Phifer Letter Transcriptions.

Chapter 5

1. Drew Gilpin Faust, *Mothers of Invention*, and Victoria E. Bynum, *Unruly Women The Politics of Social and Sexual Control in the Old South* detail how the war reversed gender roles, adversely affected family life, and stressed husbands, wives, and children, and in John C. Inscoe, *Race, War, and Remembrance in the Appalachian South*, Chapter 7 addresses how mountain women coped with the war, Kindle edition.
2. 1860 Mecklenburg County census, Western Division, Image 96, www.ancestry.com, accessed Nov 7, 2012. Crow and Crow, *1850 Lincoln County Census*, 42, House #342. Bynum, *Marriage Bonds of Lincoln and Tryon Counties, North Carolina*, 86.
3. These letters may be found at Harriet R. McIntosh Papers, PC.1847, Private Collections, NC Archives, and will be sourced using date and correspondents. The familial relationships of some but not all have been established.
4. Bettie Little to Harriet McIntosh, Feb 2, 1864, Harriet R. McIntosh Papers.
5. Isa Little to Harriet McIntosh, June 25, July 7, 1862, Bettie Little to Harriet McIntosh, Mar 20, Sept, 1864, Harriet R. McIntosh Papers.
6. Elmina L. McIntosh to Alexander McIntosh, Sept 12, 1864, Harriet R. McIntosh Papers.
7. Bettie Little to Harriet McIntosh, Oct 9, 1864, Harriet R. McIntosh Papers.
8. Violet A. Sifford to Harriet McIntosh, Dec 4, 1864, Harriet R. McIntosh Papers.
9. Elmina L. McIntosh to Harriet McIntosh, Dec 13, 1864, Harriet R. McIntosh Papers. Isaac L. McIntosh, NC Conf Service Record, www.fold3.com, accessed Sept 6, 2012. The files also included records of a John L. McIntosh, who was captured at Gettysburg. Cottage Home was a post office in eastern Lincoln and Gaston Counties.
10. Elmina L. McIntosh to Harriet McIntosh, Jan 15, 1865, Cousin Violet Ann to Harriet McIntosh, Jan 22, 1865, Harriet R. McIntosh Papers.
11. [probably Violet Ann] to Harriet McIntosh, Mar 5, 1865, Harriet R. McIntosh Papers. This letter is most likely missing the signature page. I determined it was written by Violet Ann by comparing grammar and handwriting.
12. Bettie Little to Harriet McIntosh, Feb 12, Mar 12, May 14, 1865, Harriet R. McIntosh Papers.

13. Violet Ann to Harriet McIntosh, June 3, 1865, Harriet R. McIntosh Papers.
14. Isabella Little to Harriet McIntosh, June 25, 1862, Bettie Little to Harriet McIntosh, Nov 17, 1863, D B Brown to Harriet McIntosh, Dec 27, 1864, Harriet R. McIntosh Papers.
15. Chas H Newbold to Harriet McIntosh, June 20, Chas H and Jennie Newbold to Harriet McIntosh, Aug 14, 1865, Harriet R. McIntosh Papers.
16. W. L. Phifer to Mother, Dec 21, 1862, Edward Phifer to Mother, Jan, 1864, Phifer Letter Transcriptions.
17. E. C. P. to Ed Phifer, Jan 7 or 9, 1864, Edward Phifer to Mother, Apr 15, 1864, Phifer Letter Transcriptions.
18. Edward Phifer to mother, May 29, May 19, May 23, 1864, Minnie Gray to Edward Phifer, May 30, 1864, Phifer Letter Transcriptions.
19. Minnie Gray to Edward Phifer, June 12, 1864, Phifer Letter Transcriptions.
20. Gladden and Bell, *The 1860 Census of Gaston Co.,* Vestal's Ford Post Office, House #1260, 142. Belinda J. Morris to Harriet McIntosh, Mar 9, 1859, Harriet R. McIntosh Papers.
21. Belinda J. Morris to Harriet McIntosh, Apr 15, 1859, Jan 25, Feb 25, 1860, Harriet R. McIntosh Papers.
22. Isabella Little to Harriet McIntosh, June 25, 1862, R W Little to Harriet McIntosh, Jan 11, 1862, Harriet R. McIntosh Papers.
23. Bettie Little to Harriet McIntosh, Oct 25, Nov 17, 1863, Feb 2, Mar 20, June 5, Sept, 1864, Harriet R. McIntosh Papers.
24. W. D. Glenn Diary, Nov 7, 1864, Glenn Papers, SHC, probably Mrs. William Groves Morris.
25. Elmina L. McIntosh to Alexander McIntosh, Sept 12, 1864, Harriet R. McIntosh Papers.
26. Bettie Little to Harriet McIntosh, Nov 6, 1864, Harriet R. McIntosh Papers.
27. Violet A. Sifford to Harriet McIntosh, Dec 4, 1864, Elmina L. McIntosh to Harriet McIntosh, Jan 15, 1865, Cousin Violet Ann to Harriet McIntosh, Jan 22, 1865, [probably Violet Ann] to Harriet McIntosh, Mar 5, 1865, Harriet R. McIntosh Papers.
28. Aunt Elmina McIntosh to Harriet McIntosh, Mar 20, 1865, Harriet R. McIntosh Papers.
29. Bettie Little to Harriet McIntosh, May 14, 1865, Harriet R. McIntosh Papers.
30. Violet Ann to Harriet McIntosh, June 3, 1865, Harriet R. McIntosh Papers.
31. [unknown] to Harriet McIntosh, July 6, 1865, Harriet R. McIntosh Papers. The letter may have been written by Bettie Little as it resembles her handwriting.
32. W. L. Phifer to Mother, Nov 5, Dec 21, 1862, Edward Phifer to Mother, Aug 8, 1863,Phifer Letter Transcriptions.
33. Minnie Gray to Edward Phifer, May 30, 1864, June 12, 1864, Phifer Letter Transcriptions. The party was most likely hosted by Mrs. Jasper Stowe in their Lincolnton home.
34. Jennie to Mr. Phifer [Edward], Oct 21, 1863, Edward Phifer to Mother, Sept 27, 1863, Phifer Letter Transcriptions.
35. *Western Democrat,* Dec 22, 1863, The Concert at the Lincolnton Female Seminary, 3.
36. Bettie Little to Harriet McIntosh, Oct 9, 1864, Harriet R. McIntosh Papers.
37. Violet A. Sifford to Harriet McIntosh, Dec 4, 1864, Harriet R. McIntosh Papers.
38. Elmina L. McIntosh to Harriet McIntosh, Jan 15, 1865, [probably Violet Ann] to Harriet McIntosh, Mar 5, 1865, Bettie Little to Harriet McIntosh, May 14, 1865, Isa Sifford to Harriet McIntosh, Apr 8, 1865, Harriet R. McIntosh Papers.
39. Violet Ann to Harriet McIntosh, June 3, 1865, Harriet R. McIntosh Papers.
40. D H Dellinger to P F Dellinger, Aug 31, 1862, D H Dellinger Correspondence.
41. Frances Dellinger to D H Dellinger, Nov 20, 1864, D H Dellinger Correspondence.
42. Jacob Froneberger Diary, June 27, Sept 27, 1864.
43. D H Dellinger to George Dellinger, Oct 27, 1864; D H Dellinger to Family, Nov 27, 1864; Frances to D H Dellinger, Dec 26, Dec 28, 1864, D H Dellinger to Frances Dellinger, Jan 27, 1865; D H Dellinger to F. Dellinger and family, Feb 1, 1865, D H Dellinger Correspondence.
44. Morris to wife, Apr 18, Sept 28, Dec 23, 1862; Mar 15, Apr 15, 1863, July 7, 1864, Morris to companion, Feb 5, 1865, Morris Papers.
45. Davis to wife, Apr 5, 1863, Davis to wife, May 26, 1863, Davis Correspondence.
46. Morris to wife, Oct 9, 1864, Dec 11, 1864, Morris Papers; Davis to wife, June 11, 1863, Davis Correspondence.
47. Senter to wife, [undated] 1862, Sept 30, 1862, May 15, Oct 17, 1863, Senter Correspondence.
48. W. C. Wolfe to Pheobe L. Wolfe, Oct 11, 1864, copy of the letter given to the author by Steve Huffstetler, Bessemer City, NC. As a descendant, Huffstetler provided me family and historical information about Wolfe.
49. Davis to wife, May 25, July 30, 1862, Mar 7, May 26, June 19, 1863, Davis Correspondence.
50. Belinda J. Morris to Harriet McIntosh, Feb 25, 1860, Harriet R. McIntosh Papers.
51. Elmina L. McIntosh to Alexander McIntosh, Sept 12, 1864, Cousin Violet Ann to Harriet McIntosh, Jan 22, 1865, Harriet R. McIntosh Papers.
52. Morris to wife, Dec 28, 1862, Apr 15, 1863, Sept 8, 1863; Morris to wife, Jan 28, July 29, 1864, Morris Papers. L L Morris to A Costner, Sept 24, 1863 copy in possession of Daniel Wilson, Dallas, NC.
53. Jacob Froneberger Diary, Oct 2, 1864.
54. E. C. Phifer to Edward, Feb 16, 1864, Minnie Gray to Edward Phifer, June 12, 1864, Phifer Letter Transcriptions.
55. Frances to D H Dellinger, Dec 26, 1864, Frances to D H Dellinger, Dec 28, 1864, D H Dellinger Correspondence.
56. D H Dellinger to wife, Dec 29, 1864, D H Dellinger to Frances Dellinger, Jan 27, 1865, D H Dellinger Correspondence.
57. Thomas Davis to Margaret and Children, Aug 13, 1862, to Margaret, Sept 27, 1862, to wife, Apr 5, 1863, two letters, to wife, May 10, 1863, to wife, July 31, 1863, to wife, Aug 23, 1863, to wife, Oct 1, 1863, Aug 15, 1863, Davis Correspondence.
58. Brown to his wife, Dec 25, 1862, Brown Letters.
59. Jas Fulton to Daughter Rachel Fulton, Jan 20, 1865, copy given to the author by Mike and Daphene Friday, a professor at Belmont Abbey College, on Jan 9, 2013.
60. Senter to wife, Feb 13, 1864, Senter Correspondence.
61. *The Daily Bulletin*, Ladies Relief Society, May 8, 1862, 2.
62. Gaston County Court of Pleas and Quarter Sessions of April Sessions 1861, Jacob Froneberger Papers, supplied to the author by Corinne Puett Giannitrapani. There are no County Court Minutes at the NC Archives during the Civil War.
63. Gaston Court Minutes, Jacob Froneberger Papers.
64. Paul Escott, "Poverty and Governmental Aid in Confederate North Carolina," *North Carolina Historical Review*, Oct 1984, 462–480 details the creation of a welfare system for needy soldier families.
65. Civil War Records 1864–1923, Civil War—Aid to soldier's wives and widows, CR060.920.2, Lincoln County Records, NC Archives.
66. Ibid.
67. Catharine Wortman to Gov Vance Mar 27, 1863, Gov Papers, GP 163, Corr Mar 26–28, 1863, NC Archives.
68. Morris to wife, Dec 28, 1862, Mar 15, Mar 29, 1863, Morris Letters.
69. F S Hanna to C Hanna, May 2,

1863, F S Hanna to C Hanna and Albert Bradley, Aug 25, 1863, Caroline Hanna to F S Hanna, Sept 16, 1863, Hanna Papers.
70. J J Brown to his wife, Sept 18, Sept 28, Dec 25, 1862, Brown Letters.
71. Linebarger to Capt. Jno. C. Pegram, Oct 7, 1863, Linebarger to wife Oct 28, 1863, Jan 3, Jan 6, Jan 10, Feb 21, Mar 25, Feb 22, Apr 4, Apr 22, 1864, Elizabeth to James Wellington Linebarger, May 17, 1864, "Letters of a Gaston Ranger."
72. Senter to Dear Wife, Dear Aunt, May 31, 1864, Senter Correspondence.
73. Morris to wife, Feb 10, Apr 10, Apr 13, Apr 18, 1862, Morris Letters.
74. Morris to wife, April 25, May 5, 1862, Morris Letters.
75. Jacob Froneberger Diary, Nov 28, 1861, Oct 12, 1862. Pegram was Froneberger's father-in-law and Ormand was his sister.
76. Ibid., June 27, Aug 15, 1864.
77. Ibid., May 14, 1865.
78. E. C. Phifer to My Dear Son, Edward, Apr 21, 1864, Phifer Letter Transcriptions.

Chapter 6

1. Bynum, *Unruly Women*, 129.
2. *NC Whig*, September 17, 1861, Extortion, 2, copied from the *Clarendon Banner*, November 5, 1861, Salt and Extortion 2, quoting from the *Fayetteville Observer*, February 11, 1862, Another Call for Volunteers, Distilling Corn, 2; April 1, 1862, Remember, Notice, 2; April 8, 1862, Notice, 2.
3. *The Daily Bulletin,* Apr 24, 1862.
4. *NC Whig*, July 15, 1862, 1, 2.
5. David Schenck Diary, Prices and Patriotism [1862] 248–249. Hoyle to mother, Sept 9, Sept 23, Sept 25, Sept 29, 1862, Lemuel Hoyle Letters.
6. *The Daily Bulletin*, Nov 28, 1862
7. See Chapter 2 for an extensive discussion of this issue.
8. *Western Democrat*, Mar 24, 1863, copied from the *Standard*, 2.
9. *Carolina Watchman*, Mar 23, 1863, 2; *Western Democrat*, Mar 24, 1863, The Women Helping Themselves, 3.
10. Bynum, *Unruly Women*, 125–130, 133–134. *Western Democrat*, Apr 7, 1863, 3.
11. *Carolina Watchman*, Apr 6, 1863, Address to the People of N Carolina by Gov. Z. B. Vance, 2.
12. *Carolina Watchman*, Apr 6, 1863, Address to the People of N Carolina by Gov. Z. B. Vance, 2 Apr 27, 1863, A Proclamation, 3; May 4, 1863 Important item, 1.
13. *The Daily Bulletin*, Apr 1, 1863, Letter from Columbia, also May 6, 1863 From Western North Carolina, an editorial bemoans speculators and extortionists. *Carolina Watchman*, May 4, 1863, 1.
14. Daniel Hoffman to Vance Apr 16, 1863, Jas. H. Carson to Vance, Apr 16, 1863, Gov Papers, GP 164, Corr. Apr 15–18, 1863, NC Archives.
15. *Carolina Watchman*, Apr 27, 1863, 2.
16. *The Daily Bulletin*, June 16, 1863, From Western North Carolina.
17. Andrew Parker to Vance, Gov Papers, GP 172, Corr Dec 15–20, 1863, NC Archives. Bynum, *Unruly Women*, 123–124.
18. Froneberger Diary, [?Sept 1862], Sept 21, 1863.
19. Froneberger Diary, Feb 14, June 6, Sept 27, 1864.
20. W. D. Glenn Diary, Nov 4, 1864, Glenn Papers, SHC.
21. David Schenck Diary, April 25, 1863, 257–258.
22. Ibid., November 24 and 25, 1863, 266–267.
23. Ibid., December 12, 1863, 267–268.
24. Ibid., January, January 22, 1864, 6: 4–7.
25. Ibid., January, Gold—Negroes, January 1865, 6: 34–36.
26. See *The Daily Bulletin* for some examples: Mar 25, Apr 15, July 22, Aug 24, 1862.
27. Rodney Steward, *David Schenck and the Contours of Confederate Identity*, Knoxville: University of Tennessee Press, 2012, Chapter 3.
28. Steward, *David Schenck*, 45–54. The recent publication of Dr. A. B. Pruitt, *Minutes of Confederate District Court North Carolina District 1861–1863*, details some of the Receiver's activities but was received late in the project and has not been utilized. Schenck is referenced in the index numerous times.
29. Gaston County Deed Bk 3: 378–379, Gaston Courthouse, Gastonia, NC.
30. Gaston County Deed Bk 4: 156, Gaston Courthouse, Gastonia, NC.
31. Steward, *David Schenck*, 49–61.
32. McCurry, *Confederate Reckoning*, 278.
33. Ibid., 278. Yearns and Barrett, *North Carolina Civil War Documentary*, 93.
34. *The Daily Bulletin* Charlotte, Apr 18, Apr 17, Apr 22, Apr 24, Apr 10, 1862. *NC Whig*, July 1, 1862, Holden's Tactics, 2.
35. Davis to wife, June 10, 1862, [May 1862], two letters, Davis Correspondence. Senter to wife, May 22, June 23, 1862, Senter Corrrespondence. Hoyle to mother, Mar 16, 1864, Lemuel Hoyle Letters.
36. John H. Roberts to Vance, June 25, 1863, Gov Papers, GP 166, Corr June 23–27, 1863, NC Archives.
37. Caroline to F S Hanna, Nov 5, 1862, Hanna Papers. Morris to wife, Sept 28, 1862, Morris Letters.
38. *Carolina Watchman*, Mar 9, 1863, 3.
39. James H. White to Vance, January 18, 1864, Governor's Papers, GP 173, Corr. Jan 15–19, 1864; Dr. Goode to Vance Mar 20, 1863, Gov. Papers, GP 163, Corr. Mar 19–21, 1863; J. H. McIntosh to Vance Apr 2, 1863, Gov Papers, GP 164, Corr. Apr 1–5, 1863; W. O. Harrelson to Vance Dec 1, 1863, Gov Papers, GP 164, Corr. Dec 1–4, 1863, NC Archives.
40. Bynum, *Unruly Women*, 130–134. Drew Gilpin Faust, *Mothers of Invention*, discusses the changing roles of southern women because of the war.
41. Jacob Froneberger Diary, Feb 14, June 6, Aug 15, Dec 18, 1864; Feb 12, 1865.
42. W. D. Glenn Diary, Nov 3, 1864, LA Glenn Papers, SHC.
43. D H Dellinger to wife, Nov 5, 1864, D H Dellinger Correspondence.
44. Civil War Records, Southern Claims Commission, Disallowed or Approved, North Carolina, Gaston County, filed by name, www.fold3.com. Fortunately Jason Harpe of Lincoln County Historical Association made copies of the papers for Gaston County and provided them to the author, who also used them online.
45. Escott, *Many Excellent People: Power and Privilege in N. C. 1850–1900*, 3–15. Escott specifically studied Caldwell, Randolph, and Alamance Counties. See Chapter 1 for Gaston socio-economic classes.
46. For data, I used Gladden & Bell, *The 1860 Census of Gaston Co.*, which included the Slave Schedule, Lincoln County 1860 census and Slave Schedule at www.ancestry.com, accessed Dec 4, 2012, since one person lived in Lincoln County in 1860 and moved to Gaston to make his claim, and the Gaston County 1860 census and Slave Schedule at www.ancestry.com, when I wanted to verify the data. I never identified Nancy S. Falls.
47. *The Standard*, Aug 5, 1863, Public Meeting in Gaston County.
48. Jacob F. Plonk Claim, N C Southern Loyalist Claims, Approved, www.fold3.com, accessed August 28, 2011.
49. Austin Groner, NC Southern Loyalist Claims, Barred and Disallowed, Gaston, www.fold3.com, accessed Aug 28, 2011.
50. Linebarger to wife, Feb 14, 1864. "Letters of a Gaston Ranger."
51. Aaron Jenkins, NC Southern Loyalist Claims, Barred and Disallowed, Gaston, www.fold3.com, accessed Aug 28, 2011.
52. Michael Cloninger, NC Southern Loyalist Claims, Barred and Dis-

allowed, Gaston, www.fold3.com accessed Aug 28, 2011.

53. W. O. Harrelson to Vance Jan 20, 1863, Gov Papers, GP 161, Corr Jan 20–24, 1863, NC Archives.

54. Ann E. Leonhardt, NC Southern Loyalist Claims, Barred and Disallowed, Lincoln, 17, www.fold3.com, accessed Aug 28, 2011. Ann E. Leonhardt was a daughter of Jacob Carpenter and sister to the brothers. She insisted in her loyalist claim that her husband never served in the Confederate army either. Originally the Leonhardt (Linhart) family was pacifist German Brethren (Dunker).

55. Jacob M Carpenter, NC Confederate Service Records, 2–4, 7, 17, 29, 21, 13–14, www.fold3.com, accessed Aug 28, 2011. See Carpenter, *Carpenters A Plenty*, 103–105 for transcriptions of the letters.

56. Jacob M Carpenter, NC Confederate Service Record, 24, P H Carpenter, NC Confederate Service Records, 11, 12, www.fold3.com, accessed Aug 28, 2011.

57. Henry Summitt to Vance June 15, 1863, Gov Papers, GP 166, Corr June 15–17, 1863, NC Archives.

58. W. O. Harrelson to Vance Jan 20, 1863, Gov Papers, GP 161, Corr Jan 20–24, 1863, NC Archives.; Carpenter, *Carpenters A Plenty*, 31–33, 36, 60.

59. Hoffman, *Our Kin*, 72–73.

60. Ibid., 72–74. Efforts to locate his service record failed.

61. Ibid., 74.

62. Jonas Hoffman, NC Southern Loyalist Claims, Barred and Disallowed, Gaston, www.fold3.com accessed Dec 4, 2012. The statements of Eli Pasour and C. C. Withers, who were listed as witnesses to prove his union loyalty are missing from the file. Both were witnesses for numerous Gaston Loyalist Claims.

63. Hoffman, *Our Kin*, 502–503; 4–5.

64. Yearns and Barrett, *North Carolina Civil War Documentary*, 93–111.

65. Ibid., 94–100, various reasons for desertion are discussed.

66. Senter to his wife, Oct 23, 1862; Feb 9, 1863, May 15, 1863, May 20, May 23, 1863, Senter Correspondence.

67. Frances to Caleb Senter, April 5, 1863, Vincent Barnett to Frances Senter, May 22, 1863, Senter Correspondence.

68. Senter to John Cloninger Dear Cousin, Sept 16, 1863, Senter to wife, Sept 23, 1863, Senter Correspondence.

69. F S Hanna, NC Conf Service Records, 2, www.fold3.com, accessed, Dec 4, 2012.

70. M E Hanna to F S Hanna, Oct 30, Nov 5, 1862, Hanna Papers.

71. F S Hanna to C. Hanna, Dec 14, 1862, Jan 25, 1863, F S Hanna to Caroline Hanna, June 5, June 20, 1863, Hanna Papers.

72. F S Hanna to C Hanna and Albert Bradley, Aug 25, 1863, F S Hanna to Dear Wife, Aug 30, 1863, Hanna Papers.

73. F S Hanna to Wife, Sept 3–4, 1863, Hanna Papers.

74. F S Hanna, NC Conf Service Records, 7, 8, 9, www.fold3.com, accessed Dec 4, 2012.

75. Caroline Hanna to F S Hanna, Sept 16, 1863, Hanna Papers.

76. F S Hanna, NC Conf Service Records, 6, www.fold3.com, accessed Aug 4, 2012.

77. Larkin Thornburg Typescript, 18.

78. Ibid., 1, 18–19.

79. Ibid., 18.

80. Newton Sellers, NC Conf Service record, 9, www.fold3.com, accessed May 29, 2012.

81. Newton Sellers to wife, June 4, 1863, Newton Sellers Papers. Newton Sellers, NC Conf Service record, 10, www.fold3.com, accessed May 29, 2012.

82. Mary E. Sellers to her mother, Margaret E. Hagar, July 2, 1863, Newton Sellers to his wife, Mar 3, 1864, Newton Sellers Papers.

83. Newton Sellers to wife and Mr. Daniel Sellers, Apr 21, 1864, Newton Sellers Papers.

84. Newton Sellers to wife, Apr 28, 1864, Newton Sellers Papers.

85. Newton Sellers, NC Conf Service Record, 8, www.fold3.com, accessed May 29, 2012.

86. Newton Sellers to wife and Mr. Daniel Sellers, Apr 21, 1864, Newton Sellers Papers.

87. Jacob L. Workman, NC Conf Service Records, 1–17, www.fold3.com, accessed May 29, 2012. There is also a James L. Workman whose records are mixed together. Jacob L. was in Company K, 11th NC Regiment.

88. Jacob Kiser, NC Conf Service Records, 9–21, www.fold3.com, accessed May 29, 2012.

89. Jacob L. Workman to N. A. H. Workman Feb 28, 1864, transcribed by Helen Whisnant on Apr 9, 2012, from the original held by Daphine Peach. The letter was part of a Civil War exhibit at the Gaston County Art and History Museum, Dallas.

90. Jacob L. Workman, NC Conf Service Records, 1–17, www.fold3.com, accessed May 29, 2012.

91. Morris to wife Dec 6, 1862, Mar 4, 1863, Mar 20,21, 1863, Morris Letters.

92. Senter to wife, Oct 30, 1863, Senter Correspondence.

93. Senter to wife, Nov 1, Nov 16, Nov 22, 1863, May 1 and 2, 1864, Senter Correspondence.

94. Morris to wife, Apr 5, June 29, 1863, Morris Letters.

95. Linebarger to wife, Sept 11, Dec 5, 1863, Linebarger to Father, Feb 20, 1864, C Q Petty to Linebarger, Oct 19, 1863, Linebarger to wife, Apr 28, 1864, "Letters of a Gaston Ranger."

96. Davis to wife, May 11, Sept 23, 1863, Davis Correspondence.

97. *Carolina Watchman*, Feb 2, 1863, 3; Feb 9, 1863, 3; May 18, 1863, 3; May 25, 1863, 3;

98. James McLure to Vance June 16, 1863, Gov Papers, GP 166, Corr. June 15–17, 1863, NC Archives.

99. James M. McLure, NC Conf Service Records, 11, 7, 8, 16, www.fold3.com, accessed May 29, 2012.

100. Barlett Nixion to Vance Oct 23, 1863, Gov Papers, GP 170, Corr. Oct 20–24, 1863; D. F. West to Vance Oct 15, 1863, Gov Papers, GP 170, Corr. Oct 10–15, 1863, NC Archives.

101. J. W. M. Abernathy to Vance Nov 4, 1863, Gov Papers, GP 171, Corr. Nov 4–9, 1863, NC Archives.

102. L. E. Thompson to Vance Oct 3, 1863, Gov Papers, GP 170, Corr Oct 1–5, 1863, NC Archives.

103. James H. White to Governor Vance Apr 13, 1863, Governor's Papers, GP 164, Corr. Apr 10–14, 1863, NC Archives. Eli Rudisell, also known as Jonas Eli Rudisill, NC Confederate Service Records, www.fold3.com, accessed June 4, 2012.

104. Wm. T. Shipp to Vance Aug 28, 1864, Gov Papers, GP 179, Corr Aug 25–28, 1864, NC Archives.

105. Jacob Froneberger Diary, Sept 27, 1864.

106. Marshall Ramsey Jr., John Jacob Cornwell typescript, June 2009, 5, 6, 9–10, 15, a copy in possession of the author.

107. Ramsey, Cornwell typescript, 10–24. Ramsey also quotes liberally from Michel Tucker Butts, *Galvanized Yankees on the Upper Missouri*.

108. Ramsey, Cornwell typescript, 10. US Records of Confederate Prisoners of War 1861–1865, Images 4, 6, 7, 9, 12, 13, 15–18, 21–25, 27, 30 , 32, 37, 41, www.FamilySearch.org accessed Nov 17, 2013, citing NARA microfilm publication M598.

109. US Records of Confederate Prisoners of War 1861–1865. The Lincoln County enlistees included Henry Brotherton, William Ballard, George Avery, Abraham Aker, Albert M. Nixon, John J. Cornwell, Lewis Elmore, John F. Goodson, W H Green, John Holbrook, Jefferson M Hager, Green A. Hager, William P. Hawkins, William S. Kids, Philetas Moore, and Daniel Sain. The Cleveland County enlistees included William P. Bingham, William Elmore, Joel Hoyle, Robert G. Kiser, M. M. Leng?, James P. Martin, General M. Neal, John H. Peeler, Henry N. Revel, and Hiram J. White.

110. Ramsey, Cornwell typescript, 24–27.

111. Hoyle to mother, Sept 1, 1863, Lemuel Hoyle letters.

Chapter 7

1. Charles B. Dew's *Apostles of Disunion Southern Secession Commissioners and the Causes of the Civil War*, describes the campaign by Deep South politicians to influence votes in favor of secession.
2. *Western Democrat*, Jan 8, 1861, Public Meeting, 3. See also *Western Democrat*, Dec 18, 1860, 2, for a similar organization in Catawba County.
3. *Western Democrat.*, Mar 26, 1861, Lynched, 1.
4. Ibid., June 11, 1861, Mob Law, 1.
5. *NC Whig*, May 21, 1861, Hung by a Mob, 2.
6. *Western Democrat*, May 21, 1861, Hanging at Shelby, N. C., 2.
7. John Huffstetler, Southern Loyalist Claims, Barred and Disallowed, Gaston, www.fold3.com, accessed Aug 28, 2011. Three of his sons served in the Confederate army, one volunteered and the other two were conscripted.
8. He appears as "E. M. Robinson" on the 1860 Gaston census next to David Wells, on whose land he lived, at House #498 Crowders Mountain Post Office. His name may be Elkanah, a biblical name.
9. Elhanan W. Robinson, Southern Loyalist Claims, Barred and Disallowed, Gaston, www.fold3.com, accessed Aug 28, 2011.
10. *The Daily Bulletin*, Apr 10, 1862. *NC Whig*, April 1, 1862, Remember, Notice, 2; April 8, 1862, Notice, 2.
11. Mobley, *"War Governor of the South" North Carolina's Zeb Vance in the Confederacy*, 76–77, 83–86.
12. Justices to Gov Vance Mar 16, 1863, Gov Papers, GP 163, Corr Mar 15–18, 1863. His name is given as Hugh and Hua and as Lyttle and Little in various records.
13. Brotherton, *Lake Norman Piedmont History*, provided to the author by Greg Little, 17.
14. Ibid., 18.
15. *Western Democrat*, Apr 7, Broke Jail, 3, Apr 14, $100 Reward, 3; Apr 21, 1863, Arrested, 3.
16. Lincoln County Minute Docket Superior Court 1858–1869, Special Term 1863, CR060.311.4, NC Archives. Jurors included mill owner John F. Phifer, a Hoke, two Ramsours, John Coulter, three Carpenters, a Summey, a Heafner, a Shrum, and a Dellinger.
17. Lincoln County Minute Docket Superior Court 1858–1869, Special Term 1863, CR060.311.4, NC Archives. *Western Democrat*, Apr 28, 1863, Sentenced, given to the author by Jason Harpe.

18. Brotherton, *Lake Norman Piedmont History*, 17, 20. Mobley, *Zeb Vance*, 76–77, 83–86 discusses the law and the Lyttle case.
19. Supreme Court Papers, State v. William Cody, 60NC197, (June 1864), Case 8670; Lincoln County, Criminal Action Papers, CR060.326.9, 1862–1865, NC Archives. The trial testimony is located in both files and both copies are difficult to read.
20. Lincoln County Minute Docket Superior Court 1858–1869, Fall Term 1863, CR060.311.4, NC Archives.
21. Supreme Court Papers, State v. William Cody, 60NC197, (June 1864), Case 8670. Lincoln County Minute Docket Superior Court 1858–1869, Special Term Feb 1, 1864, CR060.311.4, NC Archives.
22. *The Bulletin*, Wed. Apr 27, 1864 ran an advertisement for their capture.
23. Lincoln County Minute Docket Superior Court 1858–1869, Fall Term 1864, CR060.311.4. Lincoln County Criminal Action Papers, CR060.326.9, 1862–1865, NC Archives.
24. Gaston County Superior Court Minute Docket 1847–1869, CR040.311.1, NC Archives.
25. W. D. Glenn Diary, Nov 16, 1864, LA Glenn Papers, SHC.
26. *Western Democrat*, Nov 29, 1864, Gaston, 3.
27. W. D. Glenn Diary, Dec 3, 16, 1864, LA Glenn Papers, SHC. Jacob Froneberger Diary, December 18, 1864.
28. L. Cass Payseur Transcript.
29. Lincoln County State Docket, Superior Court 1851–1869, CR060.321.3, NC Archives.
30. L. Cass Payseur Transcript.
31. 1860 Gaston County Census, House #265, 30. William Cody/Coday, NC Confederate Service Record, Image 1–14, Joseph Carpenter, NC Confederate Service Records, Image 1–7, www.fold3.com accessed Aug 28, 2011. Numerous Joseph Carpenter service records required aligning his age, location, and service. Adjutant General's Papers, Adjutant General Letter Book 1862–1864, AG44, 224. Carpenter, *Carpenters A Plenty*, 262–263
32. Gaston County Minute Docket, Fall Term 1859, CR040.301.1, NC Archives.
33. *Western Democrat*, Mar 10, 1863, Barn Burnt, 3, Mar 24, 1863, North Carolina Items, 3.
34. David Schenck Diary, August 13, 1863, 263.
35. L L Morris to A Costner, Sept 24, 1863, copy in possession of Daniel Wilson. The tax list assessed Joseph K. Rhyne of Dallas Company for land, cash, a carriage, leather, and furniture.

36. *Western Democrat*, Nov 24, 1863, Deserters and Tories, 3.
37. Anna B. Walker to Miss Mary Torrence Dec 25, 1863, L. A. Glenn Papers, Subseries 1.2, 1863–1864, Folder #22, SHC. The tax list assessed Alexander Dicky for land and "Tos. J. McGill" for land and two slaves both in Roberts Company.
38. *Western Democrat*, Dec 14, 1863, Deserters, 1; Sept 22, 1863, Trouble at Home, 1; Jan 12, 1864, Another Robbery, 3.
39. D F Ramsaur to unnamed, Aug 24, 1863, Linda Bell Collection, LCHA.
40. *Western Democrat*, June 9, 3; June 16, 1863, Runaways, 3.
41. *Western Democrat*, Sept 8, Deserters, 1, Tory Raid in the Mountains, 2, Sept 22, 1863, Trouble at Home, 1.
42. *Western Democrat*, Mar 1, The Raid Into Macon County, NC, 1; Mar 8, Murder Violence and Treason, 1; Apr 26, From Western North Carolina, 3; Mar 15, 3; May 31, Look Out, 3; June 28, 1864, Look Out for Them, 3.
43. P L Boyd to Mis S Reinhardt, June 23, 1864, LCHA. 1860 Gaston County census, www.ancestry.com, Image 163, House #1249. Bynum, *Lincoln County Marriage Bonds*, 22. 1870. Gaston County census, www.ancestry.com, Image 37, House #230; 1880 Lincoln County census, www.ancestry.com, Ironton Twp., Image 28–29, House #553, accessed Aug 28, 2011.
44. *Western Democrat*, July 12, Another Tory Raid, 2; Deserters in Yadkin, 1; Murder in Davie, 2; Aug 2, Tories and Deserters Captured, Deserter Caught, 2; Aug 23, Trouble in Wilkes, 1, Outrages of Deserters and Tories, 3; Aug 30, Suspension, 3; Sept 27, Raid into Mitchell County, 1; Oct 11, The Home Guard, Homicide in Cabarrus, 3; Nov 1, Superior Court, 3; Nov 8, Outrages by Deserters, Escaped From Jail, 3; Nov 15, 1864, A Fight in Wilkes, 1.
45. G. F. Good to Vance Apr 14, 1864, Gov Papers, GP 176, Corr Apr 15–19, 1864, NC Archives.
46. Lincoln County Minute Docket Superior Court 1858–1869, Fall Term 1864, CR060.311.4, NC Archives.
47. *Western Democrat*, Dec 27, 1864, The Home Guard; 3; Jan 24, 1865, Deserter Killed, 2.
48. Lincoln County Minute Docket Superior Court 1858–1869, Mar 4, 1865, CR060.311.4, NC Archives.
49. Drucilla O'Brian, NC Southern Loyalist Claims, Barred and Disallowed, Gaston, www.fold3.com, accessed Aug 28, 2011.
50. W. D. Glenn Diary, Jan 13, 1865, LA Glenn Papers, SHC.
51. Nancy S. Robinson, NC Southern Loyalist Claims, Barred and Disallowed, Gaston, www.fold3.com, accessed Aug 28, 2011.

52. See Bynum, *Unruly Women* and *Long Shadow of the Civil War* for similar abuse of Unionist females.
53. *Western Democrat*, Aug 25, 1863, An Act To Punish Aiders and Abettors of Deserters, 2; Gaston County, Superior Court Minute Docket, CR 040.311.1, NC Archives.
54. Lincoln County, Superior Court Minute Docket, CR060.311.4; Adjutant General's Office, Home Guard Letter Book, 1863–1865, AG52, 290, NC Archives.
55. Lincoln County, Miscellaneous Papers, CR060.928.2 Criminal Action Papers Concerning harboring deserters, NC Archives.
56. Gladden and Bell, *The 1860 Census of Gaston Co.*, House #1265, 143.
57. Linebarger to wife, Sept 11, 1863, "Letters of a Gaston Ranger."
58. William T. Auman and David D. Scarboro, "The Heroes of America in Civil War North Carolina," *The North Carolina Historical Review*, Vol LVIII, No 4, October 1981, discusses the organization, stating that about 10,000 southerners belonged and that the group had its origin in the North Carolina Quaker Belt.
59. Allen Diehl Albert, ed., *History of the Forty-Fifth Regiment of the Pennsylvania Veteran Volunteer Infantry, 1861–1865*, 365–366 accessed at http://books.google.com/books?id=Js2CAAAAIAAJ&pg=PA362#v=onepage&q&f=false on November 30, 2011. J. H. Marsh, Southern Loyalist Claims, Barred and Disallowed, Lincoln, images 24–29, www.fold3.com, accessed Aug 28, 2011. Image 32 confirms Marsh's membership in the Heroes of America.
60. Auman and Scarboro, 345.
61. *Carolina Watchman*, May 25, 1863, 2; Aug 24, 1863, 3; Yearns and Barrett, *North Carolina Civil War Documentary*, 101–102; *Western Democrat*, June 23, 3; Aug 25, 2; Sept 1, 1.
62. Shelton Laurel was a massacre of Unionists and deserters by the Madison County, NC Home Guard. Other atrocities included torture of wives and children of deserters or Unionists. See Bynum, *Unruly Women*, 144, 148–150.
63. *Western Democrat*, Sept 1, 1863, Militia Officers, 1; Mar 17, 1863, Headquarters, 3; Mar 1, 1864, An Act in Relation to the Militia and a Home Guard for Home Defence, 1; Apr 26, 1864, Enrolling Notice, 3; Oct 11, 1864, The Home Guard for Gaston, Lincoln, Cleveland, 3.
64. Adjutant General's Papers, Roster of the Militia of North Carolina 1861–62, 1864, AG 129, 470–473, NC Archives, enumerate the Gaston County records with pages 286–289 for Lincoln, 402–409 for Cleveland, and 398–401 for Catawba.
65. Adjutant General's Office, Letter Book 1862–1864, AG44, 607, NC Archives.
66. Hand to Mendenhall, Sept 2, Sept 23, 1862, Mendenhall Papers, LCHA.
67. Hand to Mendenhall, Dec 4, 1862, June 27, July 16, Aug 2, 1863, May 18, 1864, Mendenhall Papers, LCHA.
68. Hand to Mendenhall, Dec 4, 1862, [undated probably Feb 1863], Wm R Scott to Mendenhall, Aug 13, 1864; Scott to A L Henderson, May 18, to Mendenhall, May 20, 1864, Mendenhall Papers, LCHA.
69. Adjutant General's Office, Letter Book 1862–1864, AG44, 205, NC Archives. Hand to Mendenhall, May 22, Dec 1, 1863, Mendenhall Papers, LCHA. The May 22 letter listed the following deserters from Co H, 37th Regt as to be arrested: "M L Holland, H F Ewing, John Thomason, W E Featherston, B S Reynolds, J L M Clemer, Laban Canedy, Saml Canley, L L Clemer, Jesse Elmore, J W Ferguson, Levi Hovis, N A Reynolds, J F Rachford, J Whitesides, Saml Hanna, Caleb Reynolds, Joseph Black, ?Junps Beam, David Brown."
70. Adjutant General's Office, Letter Book 1862–1864, AG44, 354; W. O Harrelson to Vance Mar 18, 1864, Gov Papers, GP 175, Corr May 18–22, 1864, NC Archives.
71. Wm. T. Shipp to Vance, Dec 15, 1863, GP 172, Corr Dec 15–20, 1863, NC Archives.
72. Hand to Mendenhall, Sept 6, Sept 24, 1864, Mendenhall Papers, LCHA
73. Larkin Thornburg typescript, 5–6.
74. Hand to Mendenhall, Oct 23, 1862, Mar 23, July 16, 1863, Mendenhall Papers, LCHA.
75. Hand to Mendenhall, Oct 22, Dec 1, 1863, Mendenhall Papers, LCHA.
76. A L Henderson to Mendenhall, Nov 12, 1864, Mendenhall Papers, LCHA. Adjutant General's Office, Letter Book 1862–1864, AG44, 517, 539, NC Archives.
77. Adjutant General's Office, Letter Book 1862–1864, AG44, 508, NC Archives. Plonk had died.
78. Hand to Mendenhall, July 16, 1863, Mendenhall Papers, LCHA.
79. Adjutant General's Office, Letter Book 1862–1864, AG44, 181, 274; Home Guard Letter Book, 1863–1865, AG52, 607, 260, Letter Book 1862–1864, AG44, 501, NC Archives.
80. Adjutant General's Papers, Adjutant General Letter Book 1862–1864, AG44, 165, 289, 299, 324, 358, 379, 542, 575, 576, NC Archives.

Chapter 8

1. Cope and Wellman, *The County of Gaston*, 66–69.
2. Kruman, *Parties and Politics in North Carolina 1836–1865*, Chapter 8. Escott, *Many Excellent People: Power and Privilege in North Carolina, 1850–1900*, 15–23. Gaston County social class was examined in Chapter 1.
3. See Escott and Chapter 1 for a fuller discussion of Escott's social class delineations and how his parameters apply to Gaston County.
4. Gaston County Minute Docket CR040.301.1, NC Archives.
5. Ibid.
6. Ibid.
7. Cope and Wellman, *The County of Gaston*, 62–64.
8. Ibid., 57.
9. Goodnight, Bell, and Carpenter, *The Complete 1850 Census of Gaston County*, 26, 128, 187, 180.
10. Gladden and Bell, *The 1860 Census of Gaston Co.*, 187, 121, 152.
11. James H. White to Vance October 10, 1863, Governor's Papers, GP 170, Corr. Oct 10–15, 1863, NC Archives.
12. Goodnight, Bell, and Carpenter, *The Complete 1850 Census of Gaston County*, 48, 128, 146; Gladden and Bell, *The 1860 Census of Gaston Co.*, 116, 186.
13. Goodnight, Bell, and Carpenter, *The Complete 1850 Gaston Census*, 115, 174, 1, 136, 185; Gladden and Bell, *The 1860 Census of Gaston Co.*, 70, 54. Carpenter, *Carpenters A Plenty*, 269–270.
14. David Schenck Diary, Aug 5, 1858, online, Folder 4, Vol 3, Scan 159.
15. Kruman, *Parties and Politics in North Carolina 1836–1865*, Chapter 8. Escott, *Many Excellent People: Power and Privilege in N. C. 1850–1900*, 10–28.
16. Kruman, *Parties and Politics in North Carolina 1836–1865*, 189–194. Escott, *Many Excellent People: Power and Privilege in N. C. 1850–1900*, 29–36.
17. Kruman, *Parties and Politics in North Carolina 1836–1865*, 219–221.
18. David Schenck Diary October 1, 1860, 179–180.
19. Ibid., 1860, 180–181.
20. David Schenck Diary, 1860, online Scan 225, 226, 227; 1860, 184–185.
21. Ibid. General Assembly Session Records, Nov 1860-Feb 1861, Elector's Votes for President and Vice President, NC Archives.
22. *Western Democrat*, Nov 13, 1860, Gaston County Hurrah for Gaston, 3.
23. David Schenck Diary 1860, 180, 185, 186.
24. Ibid., March 18, 1861, 191, 192.
25. David Schenck Diary, February 1, 1861, 190.

26. See Kruman, *Parties and Politics in North Carolina 1836–1865*, Chapter 8; Yearns and Barrett, *North Carolina Civil War Documentary*, 4–17; John C. Inscoe and Gordon McKinney, *The Heart of Confederate Appalachia: Western North Carolina in the Civil War*, Chapter 6, Kindle edition.
27. See Dew, *Apostles of Disunion*, Chapter 1 and 2.
28. *The Daily Bulletin*, December 4, 1860. The newspaper incorrectly identified him as M. R. Hand. *Western Democrat*, Dec 11, 1860, Public Meeting in Gaston, 3.
29. *The Daily Bulletin*, December 4, 1860. *Western Democrat*, Dec 11, 1860, Meeting in Lincoln, 1.
30. *Western Democrat*, Jan 1, 1861, Meeting in Cleveland County, 2.
31. *The Daily Bulletin*, Jan 23, 1861; see also *Western Democrat*, Jan 1, 1861, Public Meeting in Lincoln, 2.
32. *Western Democrat*, Jan 1, 1861, Public Meeting in Lincoln, 2.
33. Ibid., Jan 22, 1861, Meeting in Gaston County, 2.
34. Ibid., Jan 22, 1861, Lincolnton, 3.
35. *The Daily Bulletin*, Thurs Jan 31, 1861, Public Meeting at Castenia Grove, N. C.
36. *Western Democrat*, Feb 5, 1861, Public Meeting, 1.
37. Kruman, *Parties and Politics in North Carolina 1836–1865*, 200–205.
38. *Western Democrat*, Feb 19, 1861, Candidates for Convention, 3; Mar 5, 1861, Delegates, 3.
39. David Schenck Diary March 18, 1861, 190–192.
40. General Assembly Session Records, Nov 1860-Feb 1861, Votes Pro and Con for Convention and for Delegates, NC Archives.
41. Kruman, *Parties and Politics in North Carolina 1836–1865*, Appendix B, 273–276.
42. *Western Democrat*, Mar 12, 1861, The Result, 3; *The Daily Bulletin*, Charlotte, Mar 22, 1861.
43. *NC Whig*, March 19, 1861, 2.
44. *Western Democrat*, Mar 26, The Southern Rights Convention, 3; Mar 19, 1861, Southern Rights Meeting, 3.
45. David Schenck Diary, March 1861, 192–193; Kruman, *Parties and Politics in North Carolina, 1836–1865*, 214–215.
46. *Western Democrat*, Apr 9, 3; Apr 16, 1861, 3.
47. Ibid., Apr 30, 1861, Lincoln County Southern Rights Association, 3.
48. David Schenck Diary, May 15, 1861, 194.
49. *NC Whig*, April 23, 1861, 2.
50. *Western Democrat*, May 7, 1861, Candidates, 3.
51. David Schenck Diary, August 16, 1861, 37–38.
52. Kruman, *Parties and Politics in North Carolina, 1836–1865*, 231–233; Steward, *David Schenck*, 40–41.
53. *NC Whig*, July 1, 1862, Holden's Tactics, 2.
54. Ibid., July 15, 1862, 1, 2; May 13, 1862, The Governorship, 2; May 20, 1862, 2.
55. David Schenck Diary, August 1862, 240–241.
56. *The Daily Bulletin*, Aug 18, 1862.
57. General Assembly Session Records, Nov-Dec 1862, Box 3, Governor's Election's Returns (Alamance-Iredell), NC Archives.
58. General Assembly Session Records, Nov-Dec 1862, Box 3, Certificates of Election—Senate, NC Archives. David Schenck Diary, August 1862, 240–241.
59. Excerpts of Vance's speech in Mobley, *"War Governor of the South" North Carolina's Zeb Vance in the Confederacy*, 33.
60. David Schenck Diary, August 1862, 240–241.
61. Mobley, *Zeb Vance*, 46–71. The Tithing Law collected 10 percent of citizen goods and commodities.
62. Ibid., 44–45. Escott, *Many Excellent People Power and Privilege in North Carolina, 1850–1900*, 45.
63. *The Standard*, Aug 5, 1863, www.Ancestry.com, accessed May 27, 2011, originally sent to the author by Jill Byers.
64. Ibid., Aug 5, 1863.
65. Ibid., "Public Meeting in Gaston County."
66. *Western Democrat*, Aug 25, 1863, 2. *Carolina Watchman*, Aug 24, 1863, 3, and *Western Democrat*, Aug 18, 1863, mentioned the meeting without details.
67. *Western Democrat*, Aug 25, 1863, 2. The Grand Jury consisted of John H. Adams Foreman, Jacob Underwood, Andrew A Leeper, John N Friday, J P Abernathy, Jos K Rhyne, Thos Hoover, Sol Hoffman, Bartlett Stroup, Wm Wilson, Henry M Rhyne, Monroe Burke, Wm D Carroll, Eli E Cox, Jonas Jenkins.
68. Ibid., The Programme Changed, 3.
69. David Schenck Diary, August 13, September 11, 1863, 263–265.
70. *Carolina Watchman*, July 27, 1863, 1, 2.
71. Morris to wife, Mar 4, 1863, Morris Papers; Mobley, *Governor Vance*, 44–45.
72. *Carolina Watchman*, Aug 31, 1863, 1, 2
73. *The Daily Bulletin*, Aug 19, 1863.
74. *Carolina Watchman*, Sept 14, 1863 "Mob Violence in Raleigh," 2, quoted the Raleigh *Progress*.
75. *Carolina Watchman*, Sept 14, 1863, 2, 3.
76. Ibid., Sept 21, 1863, "From *Progress* Sept 11," 2.
77. Newton Sellers to wife, Apr 28, 1864, Newton Sellers Papers.
78. *Carolina Watchman* Aug 31, 1863, "Circular To Voters of the Eighth Congressional District of North Carolina," 3; Oct 19, 1863, 3; Nov 9, 1863, "The Election"; Nov 23, 1863, "The Election in the 8th District," 3. Kruman, *Parties and Politics in North Carolina*, 252–253.
79. Edward Phifer to Mother, Nov 21, 1863, Phifer Letter Transcriptions. *Daily Bulletin*, Nov 10, Nov 19, 1863.
80. *Daily Bulletin*, Aug 29, Nov 10, Nov 19, 1863.
81. Kruman, *Parties and Politics in North Carolina*, 240–241; Mobley, *Zeb Vance*, 108–110.
82. Kruman, *Parties and Politics in North Carolina*, 231, 242–243.
83. J C Whitson to Vance Aug 31, 1863, GP 168, Corr Aug 25–31, 1863, NC Archives.
84. David Schenck Diary, February 19, March 26, 1864, 6: 7–10.
85. *Western Democrat*, Feb 9, 1864, Gaston County, 3.
86. Mobley, *Zeb Vance*, 117, 124–125. Kruman, *Parties and Politics in North Carolina*, 251–252, 259, 262, 264, 265.
87. James H. White to Vance, January 18, 1864, Gov Papers, GP 173, Corr. Jan 15–19, 1864, NC Archives.
88. John C. Inscoe and Gordon B. McKinney, *The Heart of Confederate Appalachia Western North Carolina in the Civil War*, 158–160, Kindle edition.
89. K. J. Kenedy to Vance Feb 29, 1864, Gov Papers, GP 174, Corr. Feb 28–18, 1864, NC Archives.
90. W. O Harrelson to Vance Mar 18, 1864, Gov Papers, GP 175, Corr May 18–22, 1864, NC Archives.
91. *Western Democrat*, May 17, 1864, Grand Jury of Lincoln County, 3. Jurors signing included C L Hunter Foreman, M Shitle, H Cansler, P Kistler, G S Ramseur, Wm P Connel, Allen Alexander, Phillip Hovis, J Helderman, J G Armstrong, M Carpenter, H H Wilkinson, George Coon, John Lackey, Adam Towry, Daniel Finger, Absalom Brown, Thomas Wells.
92. *Western Democrat*, June 7, 1864, Governor Vance, 3.
93. Petition to Vance April 30, 1864, Gov Papers, GP 176, Corr. Apr 28–30, 1864, NC Archives. Others signing include J. F. Pegram, Liet. Wm. R. Scott, Wm. Jenkins, Thos. Wilson, M D Glenn, R C G Love, A. L. Henderson, Henry Setzer, James H. White, J. Lusk, Eli Berry, Wm. Arrowood, John C. Smith, Jacob Plonk, J. P. Sellers, D. W. Froneberger.
94. Jacob Froneberger Diary, June 6, 1864.
95. Minnie Gray to Edward Phifer, June 12, 1864, Phifer Letter Transcriptions.

96. J. L. Miller to Vance June 1, 1864, Gov Papers, GP 178, Corr. June 1-4, 1864; W. C. Lee to Vance June 18, 1864, Gov Papers, GP 178, Corr June 15-24, 1864, NC Archives.

97. J C Anthony to uncle J W Carson, July 31, 1864, John and Wylma Monteith Papers.

98. Senter to wife, March 31, 1864, Senter Correspondence.

99. David Schenck Diary, August 20, 1864, 19.

100. Kruman, *Parties and Politics in North Carolina*, 265.

101. General Assembly Session Records, Nov-Dec 1864, Box 2, Governor's Election Returns, NC Archives.

102. *Western Democrat*, Aug 9, 1864, Legislature, 3.

103. W D Glenn Diary, November 29, 1864, L A Glenn Papers, SHC.

104. *The Daily Bulletin*, March 23, 1865, Public Meeting in Gaston, citizens to collect supplies included Capt. A. L. Henderson, W. M. Johnson, Jacob Lineberger, Robert Wilson, John H. Adams, E. B. Wilson, Thomas Wilson, J. L. Lineberger, J. Froneberger, Wm. Jenkins, Joseph Gamble, Samuel A. Torrence, E. Aderholdt, Wiley Rudisill, Joseph Lusk, and J. Stroup.

105. Mobley, *Zeb Vance*, 170, quoted Vance to David L. Swain, Sept 22, 1864, Vance Papers, Private Collection, NC Archives.

106. General Assembly Session Records, Nov-Dec 1865, Box 2, Certificates of Election—House; Certificates of Election—Senate, NC Archives. *Daily Carolina Times*, Oct 31, Nov 3, 1865.

107. *Daily Carolina Times*, Oct 31, Nov 3, 1865.

108. General Assembly Session Records, Nov-Dec 1865, Box 2, Governor's Election Returns, NC Archives. See also Inscoe and McKinney, Chapter 6, for a discussion of mountain political dissent and peace initiatives.

Chapter 9

1. Cope and Wellman, *County of Gaston*, 71. Gaston County, Tax List, 1847-1860, CR040.701.1, NC Archives. The 1850 tax districts with majority black polls were Dallas, Dutchmans Creek, Armstrongs Ford, Fronebergers, Lourances, Hendersons, and Cloningers.

2. Gladden and Bell, *The 1860 Census of Gaston Co.*, 195. Cope and Wellman, *County of Gaston*, 76 gives the total number of slaves as 2,199 and 360 slave owners.

3. www.census.gov/prod/www/decennial.htm/northcarolina1860(1)-10.pdf, accessed Aug 18, 2014.

4. The number 394 is the number of separate slaveholders listed. In Chapter 1, duplicate listings are combined for a total of 372 to create a more accurate portrait of social class in Gaston County.

5. The author mathematically compiled the data from the tax list.

6. Gaston County Minute Docket, CR040.301.1, NC Archives. I examined Feb Term 1847 through Aug Term 1860 for analysis with additional discussion in Chapter 8.

7. Cope and Wellman, *The County of Gaston*, 66-71. See the 1860 Gaston County census for their trades.

8. Rudolph Young, "Iron Station Roots of an African American Community in Lincoln County, North Carolina," unpublished typescript in hands of the author.

9. "Background for Stowe's Factory," report by Coastal Carolina Research, Inc, 2009, provided to Mr. John Babington, copy provided to the author by John Russell, speculates that slaves may have worked in the mill.

10. See the Appendix for charts illustrating the comparisons.

11. "Onetime Citizen Carpenter Fought In Thirty Battles," *Kings Mountain Herald*, which quoted a *Gastonia Gazette* article of February ?, 1935, a copy of the article is in possession of the author.

12. "A Bit of History" quoted in Carpenter, *Carpenters A Plenty*, 354-355.

13. John Huffstetler, Southern Loyalist Claims, Barred and Disallowed, Gaston, www.Fold3.com, accessed Aug 28, 2011. He resided in Roberts District in northwestern Gaston County.

14. Larkin Thornburg, "The Experience of a Seventeen year Old Boy During the War Between the States," copy in possession of the author and at the Gaston County Museum of Art and History.

15. See David Goldberg, *America Aflame How the Civil War Created a Nation*, for a thorough consideration of racism in both north and south, which Goldberg contends was facilitated by evangelical Christianity.

16. David Eddleman owned slaves but only one letter survived.

17. Morris to wife, Apr 5, 1863 and numerous other letters, Dec 25, 1862, Jan 26, Mar 15, 1863; Ambrose Costner to sister, July 19, 1862, Morris Letters.

18. A Costner to Sister Dec 16, 1864, copy in possession of Daniel Wilson.

19. Hoyle to mother, Sept 9, Sept 23, Sept 25, Sept 29, 1862; Jan 18, Jan 23, 1864, Lemuel Hoyle Letters.

20. Lemuel Hoyle letters and Phifer Letters Transcripts were examined for this analysis.

21. Bell, *1870 Gaston County Census*, House #110, #112, #113, 100-101. Morris was at House #113.

22. Ibid., House #332, 81, with "W. W." at House #331, same page. Other blacks headed households nearby but none can be identified from the tax list. Margaret's age was probably incorrectly enumerated in either the census or the tax list.

23. David Schenck Diary, Oct 1858, online, Folder 4, Vol 3, Scan 165; Steward, *David Schenck*, 47, 62.

24. Morris to wife, Mar 15, 1863, Morris Letters; Gladden and Bell, *The 1860 Census of Gaston Co.*, House #1237, 139, 192.

25. B F Withers to J F Goodson Esq, Feb 12-15, 1862, Goodson Collection, LCHA.

26. *The Daily Bulletin*, Aug 12, 1861, Aug 15, Aug 20, Nov 8, Nov 5, 1862, Sept 2, 1863.

27. *The Bulletin*, Mar 4, 1864, *The Daily Bulletin*, Feb 17, Mar 3, Mar 10, 1865; David Schenck Diary January, Gold—Negroes, January 1865, 6: 34-36.

28. Joshua Swift undated, E A Ellison to R Bridgers Aug 15, 1864, Wm L Kennedy to J L Bridgers Dec 20, 1864, Confederate States undated, Folder #8, B B Barron to T J Summer June 11, 1864, Barron to Col Palmer Nov 17, 1864, A W Woodfin to Barron Nov 22, 1864, Wm R Kennedy to Barron Dec 9, 1864, R R Bridgers to Bolin Dec 10, 1864, C. J. Brenizer to R Bridgers & Co. Feb 17, 1865, Folder #7, Iron Station Papers, LCHA.

29. Harriett Spake to Mr. Spake, Jan 9, 1865, D H Dellinger Correspondence.

30. *Western Democrat*, Dec 20, 1864, Notice, 2.

31. The three sources include: http://nationalhumanitiescenter.org/pds/maai/enslavement/text1/wlbost.pdf, WPA Narrative of W. L. Bost, 1937, accessed November 17, 2012, cited as WPA Narrative of W. L. Bost. http://memory.loc.gov/cgibin/ampage?collId=mesn&fileName=111/mesn111.db&recNum=357&itemLink=r%3Fammem%2Fmesnbib%3A@field%28DOCID%2B@lit%28mesn%2F111%2F354350%29%29, WPA Narrative of Sarah Gudger, 193, accessed February 21, 2013, cited as WPA Narrative of Sarah Gudger. "A PenPicture of Wesley Mauney—an Ex-Slave," 1933, typescript in possession of the author, cited thusly.

32. WPA Narrative of W. L. Bost.

33. WPA Narrative of Sarah Gudger.

34. WPA Narrative of W. L. Bost.

35. WPA Narrative of Sarah Gudger.

36. Gladden and Bell, *The 1860 Census of Gaston Co.*, House #177, 20. Cope and Wellman, *The County of Gaston*, 70. Carpenter, *Carpenters A Plenty*, 551-552. Goodnight, Bell, and Carpenter, *The Complete 1850 Census of Gaston County, North Carolina*, 129.

37. "A PenPicture of Wesley Mauney—an Ex-Slave."
38. Ibid.
39. Copy of document in hands of the author, Dr. Ed Anthony Collection.
40. Copy of undated document in hands of the author, *ibid.*
41. 1860 Spartanburg County, SC Northern Division Slave Schedule, Image 29, Thomas Little; 1860 Spartanburg Co census Northern Division, Image 204–205, House #1402, www.ancestry.com, accessed, May 2, 2013.
42. WPA Sarah Gudger Interview.
43. WPA Interview of W. L. Bost.
44. WPA Sarah Gudger Interview.
45. Lincoln County, Lists of School Children, 1845–1846, CR060.926.2, NC Archives, copy provided to the author by Rachel Eichemeyer.
46. WPA Interview of W. L. Bost.
47. Robert Carpenter, "Salem Lutheran and United Church of Christ: A Story of Faith and Peace," unpublished manuscript. The author has personal knowledge of Old St. Pauls Lutheran Church and Macpelah Presbyterian Church. All three churches were constructed prior to the Civil War and still stand (2015). Salem and Macpelah are in Lincoln County; St. Pauls is in Catawba County.
48. "A PenPicture of Wesley Mauney—an Ex-Slave," 9–10, 16–18.
49. WPA Interview of W. L. Bost.
50. Ibid.
51. Ibid.
52. WPA Sarah Gudger Interview.
53. "A PenPicture of Wesley Mauney—an Ex-Slave," 8.
54. Ibid., 6.
55. Ibid., 2.
56. WPA Interview of W. L. Bost.
57. 1860 Catawba County Slave Census, Image 1, www.Ancestry.com, accessed November 17, 2012.
58. WPA Interview of W. L. Bost.
59. "A PenPicture of Wesley Mauney—an Ex-Slave," "Random Notes from Uncle Dewey Maceo Mauney," 134.
60. Rudolph Young, "African American History at the Bend of the River Catawba," undated and un-paginated typescript in possession of the author, printed by the *Trans-Catawba African American Genealogical and Historical Association.*
61. A PenPicture of Wesley Mauney—an Ex-Slave," "Naomi Amelia Wellmon Mauney," 2.
62. Michael Dean Richardson, Benjamin Russell Hanby, *The Secret Service: the field, the dungeon, and the escape,* American Pub Co, 1866, 444, accessed Dec 13, 2012, at http://books.google.com/books?id=vRgPAAAAYAAJ&source=gbs_navlinks_s.
63. 1850 Gaston County Slave Schedule, 1860 Gaston County Slave Schedule, www.ancestry.com, accessed Aug 14, 2012.
64. Bell, *The Population Schedule of the Ninth Census of the United States 1870,* 1–267.
65. Bell, *Gaston County North Carolina 1880 Census,* 1–316, data calculated by the author.
66. 1860 Lincoln County census, Image 23, House #266; 1860 Lincoln County Slave Schedule, Image 4, www.ancestry.com both accessed Nov 21, 2012. Gladden and Bell, *The 1860 Census of Gaston Co.,* House #1137, 128. Rudolph Young stated the familial connection of the Demps family in "The Free Black Population," unpublished typescript.
67. Rudolph Young, Logan Johnson, "Iron Station Roots of an African American Community in Lincoln County, North Carolina," unpublished typescript in hands of the author. Philbeck and Turner, *Lincoln County Wills,* #321.
68. Jonas W. Derr 1881, Lincoln County Wills, CR060.801.8, NC Archives.
69. 1870 Lincoln County census, Union Township, House #86, Image 12, www.ancestry.com, accessed May 2, 2013.
70. Rachel K. Eickemeyer, "The Descendants of Pinkney and Harriet Mauney of Lincoln County, North Carolina," unpublished typescript provided to the author by Ms. Eickemeyer.
71. Ibid., 1–35.
72. Ibid., 4–11.
73. Victoria E. Bynum, *The Long Shadow of the Civil War Southern Dissent and its Legacies,* 1–2, 10–11, 13–14, 97, 105, 117–135.
74. Puett, *History of Gaston County,* 185.
75. 1860 Gaston County Slave Schedule, Scan 13; 1870 Gaston County Census, House #395, Scan 61, 1880 Gaston County Census, House #112, Scan 11, www.ancestry.com viewed March 1, 2014.
76. Stowe Family Account Book, Duke University.
77. *The Bulletin,* July 7, 1864.
78. Allen Diehl Albert, ed., *History of the Forty-Fifth Regiment of the Pennsylvania Veteran Volunteer Infantry 1861–1865,* Williamsport, Pa: Grit Pub Co, 1912, 363–368 accessed at http://books.google.com/books?id=Js2CAAAAIAAJ&pg=PA362#v=onepage&q&f=false on November 30, 2011. J. H. Marsh, Southern Loyalist Claims, Lincoln, www.fold3.com/. Marsh's claim is stated on images 24–29. Image 32 confirms Marsh's membership in the Heroes of America. Kensler plantation would be Cansler plantation and Wizewell was Whiswall, the paper manufacturer at Hokeville/Laboratory. The soldiers called the owner of the cotton factory "Wm. I. Hoke."
79. Richardson, Hanby, *The Secret Service,* 420–431, 441–445.
80. "Reminicences of the Civil War by Col. R. N. Wilson Dictated to a member of the Gastonia Chapter U. D. C.," and other material, including a copy of Jerry Wilson's pension application, provided by Lynda Hancock to the author. North Carolina Confederate Pension Applications 1885–1953, www.familysearch.org, accessed June 26, 2013.
81. "A PenPicture of Wesley Mauney—an Ex-Slave," 1933, 8. WPA Interview of W. L. Bost.
82. Richardson, Hanby, *The Secret Service,* 441–446.
83. 1860 Gaston County Slave Schedule, Image 1, 2, 3, www.fold3.com, accessed Dec 4, 2012.
84. Gladden and Bell, *The 1860 Census of Gaston Co.,* 172, 173, 179–181, 184, 188.
85. Ibid., 158–163.
86. Carpenter, Bell, and Goodnight, *The Complete 1850 Gaston County Census,* 131–133.
87. See Bynum, *Unruly Women* for more information.
88. Ibid., 88–90, 99–100. Gaston County Minute Docket, CR040.301.1, NC Archives.
89. 1860 Gaston County census Slave Schedule, www.fold3.com, accessed Feb 25, 2013. Carpenter, Bell, and Goodnight, *The Complete 1850 Gaston County Census,* 127–130.
90. Gladden and Bell, *The 1860 Census of Gaston Co.,* House #387, 44, 164. Rudolph Young, "African American History at the Bend of the River," Revels, typescript in author's possession. 1850 Rutherford County census, image 93, House #628, www.ancestry.com, accessed June 8, 2014
91. Gladden and Bell, *The 1860 Census of Gaston Co.,* House #940, 105. Rudolph Young, "African American History at the Bend of the River," The Free Black Population, typescript in author's possession. Gaston County Roads and Bridge Records—Petitions Concerning Roads 1859–1888, CR040.925.1, NC Archives; also printed in *Footprints in Time,* Dec 2012, 179–186.
92. Rudolph Young, "African American History at the Bend of the River," includes a brief history of the Brooks family, typescript in author's possession. Gladden and Bell, *The 1860 Census of Gaston Co.,* House #350, #351, 40. 1860 Cleveland County census, Scan 31, House #210, www.ancestry.com, accessed Nov 20, 2012. Young in the source describes a court case involving Sarah Brooks, who fought being enslaved.

93. Rudolph Young, "African American History at the Bend of the River," Revels.
94. Gladden and Bell, *The 1860 Census of Gaston Co.*, 152–157.
95. Lee Hunter (free person of color), Gaston County Estates 1839–1971, CR040.508.71, NC Archives.
96. Ibid. No vouchers or notes have been located in his estate file to determine the sources of his debts.
97. 1850 Mecklenburg Co census, Image 4, House #33, www.ancestry.com, accessed Nov 25, 2012.
98. 1860 Gaston County census, image 117–118, House #907, www.ancestry.com, accessed June 29, 2014.
99. David Schenck Diary 1860, 167–169. Gaston County Superior Court Minute Docket, CR040.311.1, NC Archives.
100. Gladden and Bell, *The 1860 Census of Gaston Co.*, Mortality Schedule, 163.
101. Mobley, *Zeb Vance*, 220–221, quoted from Mary Bayard Devereux Clarke, "Autobiography of the Hon. Zebulon B. Vance, Coped from the Original Notes in His Own Handwriting" 1868, manuscript in possession of Mary Moulton Barden.

Appendix

1. Possibly David Adderholt at House #146 GC 1860 census, 16, White Pine PO.
2. Lick Fork is a small creek which is located in the extreme northwestern corner of Gaston County, northwest of Cherryville. It flows into Muddy Fork of Buffalo Creek.
3. Possibly Michael Adderholt, House #54, GC 1860 census, 6, Craigville PO.
4. Indian Creek is a major creek which rises in present Catawba County and flows into the South Fork River near Long Shoals. Part of the creek flows along the present Gaston-Lincoln County line.
5. Possibly Ephraim Black at House #1 GC 1860 census, 1, Craigville PO
6. Muddy Fork flows into Buffalo Creek and is located in the extreme northwestern portion of Gaston County west of Cherryville.
7. Beaverdam Creek flows into the South Fork River between Long and High Shoals. It is located in northern Gaston County and runs west to east.
8. Possibly Benajah Black at House #70 GC 1860 census, 8, White Pine PO.
9. Possibly Samuel Black House #193 GC 1860 census, 22, White Pine PO.
10. Possibly House #52 GC 1860 census, 6, Criagville PO.
11. See House #64 GC 1860 census, 7, Craigsville PO.
12. Possibly House #76 GC 1860 census, 8, White Pine PO.
13. See House #138 GC 1860 census, 15, White Pine PO.
14. Beaverdam Creek.
15. Possibly Bennett Carpenter at House #187 GC 1860 census, 21, White Pine PO.
16. Possibly House#149 GC 1860 census, 16, White Pine PO.
17. Possibly House #49, GC 1860 census, 6, Craigville PO.
18. Possibly Christy Eaker House #142 GC 1860 census, 16, White Pine PO.
19. See House #126 GC 1860 census, 14, White Pine PO.
20. Possibly S. S. Glapcock? House #11 GC 1860 census, 2, Craigville PO.
21. Possibly Walker Faris House #203 GC 1860 census, 23, White Pine PO.
22. See House #35, GC 1860 census, 4, Craigville PO.
23. See House #199 GC 1860 census, 22, White Pine PO.
24. Possibly J. F. Hoyle at House 34 GC 1860 census, 4, Craigville PO.
25. Possibly George Hovis at House #78 GC 1860 census, 9, White Pine PO.
26. See House #135 GC 1860 census, 15, White Pine PO. He was listed as Sheriff.
27. See House #57 GC 1860 census, 7, Craigville PO.
28. See House #119 GC 1860 census, 13, White Pine PO.
29. Possibly Abner Stroup at House #3 GC 1860 census, 1, Craigville PO.
30. Possibly J. C. Stroup at House #10 GC 1860 census, 2, Craigville PO.
31. Possibly Christopher Stroup, House #2 in 1860 Gaston County census, 1, Craigville PO.
32. Possibly Samuel Spake, House #18 GC 1860 census, 3, Craigville, PO.
33. Henry Summit is credited as being an early settler of present Cherryville. See House #123 GC 1860 census, 13, White Pine PO.
34. See House #23, GC 1860 census, 3, Craigville PO.
35. See House #400 GC 1860 census, 45, Crowder Creek PO.
36. See House #371 GC 1860 census, 42, King Mtn PO.
37. Crowders Creek heads south of present Bessemer City and running through Gaston County and entering the Catawba River in South Carolina.
38. See House #436 GC 1860 census, 49, Crowders Creek PO.
39. Possibly William C. Beaty at House #431 GC 1860 census, 49, Crowders Creek PO.
40. See House #444 GC 1860 census, 50, Crowders Creek PO.
41. Possibly Robert Bell at House #441 GC 1860 census, 50, Crowders Creek PO.
42. See House #397 GC 1860 census, 45, Crowders Creek PO.
43. See House #466 GC 1860 census, 53, Crowders Mtn PO.
44. See House #467 GC 1860 census, 53, Crowders Mountain PO.
45. Possibly Robert Boyd House #424 GC 1860 census, 48, Crowders Creek PO.
46. See House #429 GC 1860 census, 49, Crowders Creek PO.
47. Possibly James Crawford House #384 GC 1860 census, 43, Crowders Creek PO.
48. See House #474 GC 1860 census, 53, Crowders Mtn PO.
49. See House #378 GC 1860 census, 43, Crowders Mtn PO.
50. Possibly A. Jackson Dickey at House #425, 48, Crowders Creek PO.
51. See House #439 GC 1860 census, 50, Crowders Creek PO.
52. See House #442 GC 1860 census, 50, Crowders Creek PO.
53. Possibly James Ferguson at House #437 GC 1860 census, 50, Crowders Creek PO.
54. Possibly either House #414 or House #421 GC 1860 census, 47–48, Crowders Creek PO.
55. Possibly J. Harvey Forbes at House #394 GC 1860 census, 45, Crowders Creek PO.
56. See House #374 GC 1860 census, 43, Crowders Mtn PO.
57. Possibly Robert Gamble at House #460 GC 1860 census, 52, Pleasant Ridge PO.
58. Possibly Martin Lowrance at House #390 GC 1860 census, 44, Crowders Creek PO.
59. See House #386 GC 1860 census, 44, Crowders Creek PO.
60. Possibly John McCreedy at House #464 GC 1860 census, 52, Crowders Mtn PO.
61. Possibly William McCreedy at House #462 GC 1860 census, 52, Pleasant Ridge PO.
62. See House #491 GC 1860 census, 55, Crowders Mtn PO.
63. See House #412 GC 1860 census, 47, Crowders Creek PO.
64. Possibly George McAlister at House #492 GC 1860 census, 55, Crowders Mtn PO.
65. See House #418 GC 1860 census, 47, Crowders Creek PO.
66. Kings Mountain is located in southeastern Gaston County and runs as a ridge with Crowders Mountain. Both mountains are also in South Carolina.
67. Possibly Charles Petty at House #405 GC 1860 census, 46, Crowders Creek PO.
68. See House #478 GC 1860 census, 54, Crowders Mtn PO.
69. Probably Gabriel Revels House

#387 GC 1860 census, 44, Crowders Creek PO.
70. Possibly Samuel Service House #470 GC 1860 census, 53, Crowders Mtn PO.
71. Inherited the William Joseph Wilson House which still stands.
72. Possibly Ezra B. Willson at House #392 GC 1860 census, 44, Crowders Creek PO.
73. See House #472 GC 1860 census, 53, Crowders Mtn PO.
74. See House #473 GC 1860 census, 53, Crowders Mtn PO or House #493 Crowders Mtn PO.
75. See House #430 GC 1860 census, 49, Crowders Creek PO.
76. See House #479 GC 1860 census, 54, Crowders Mtn PO.
77. Possibly Wm. W. Torrence at House #413 GC 1860 census, 47, Crowders Creek PO.
78. Kettle Shoals is a small creek which rises east of Pasour Mountain and flows into the South Fork River north of Dallas.
79. See House #510 GC 1860 census, 57, Dallas PO.
80. See House #1297 GC 1860 census, 146, Dallas PO.
81. See House #1296 GC 1860 census, 146, Dallas PO.
82. Big Long Creek runs the length of Gaston County. It rises near the Cleveland County line and runs into the South Fork River near Spencer Mountain.
83. See House #1080 GC 1860 census, 121, Dallas PO.
84. See House #1084 GC 1860 census, 122, Dallas PO.
85. Little Long Creek runs just north of Big Long Creek. It rises northwest of Dallas and runs into Big Long Creek at Spencer Mountain.
86. Possibly George Clemmer at House #1388 GC 1860 census, 156, Dallas PO.
87. Possibly Joseph Costner at House #1335 GC 1860 census, 151, Dallas PO.
88. See House #1339 GC 1860 census, 151, Dallas PO.
89. See House #721 GC 1860 census, 81, Dallas PO.
90. See House #515 GC 1860 census, 58, Dallas PO.
91. See House #1325 GC 1860 census, 149, Dallas PO.
92. Kettle Shoals, north of present Dallas and flows into South Fork River.
93. Possibly Elizabeth Friday House #1330 GC 1860 census, 150, Nail Factory PO.
94. See House #1087 GC 1860 census, 122, Dallas PO.
95. See House #755 GC 1860 census, 84, Dallas PO.
96. See House #501 GC 1860 census, 56, Dallas PO.

97. See House #306 GC 1860 census, 34, Crowders Mtn PO.
98. See House #1347 GC 1860 census, 152, Dallas PO.
99. Catawba Creek rises in present Gastonia and runs into the South Fork River just north of the NC-SC line.
100. See House #502 GC 1860 census, 56, Dallas PO.
101. See House #303 GC 1860 census, 34, Dallas PO.
102. Ambiguous: Original was 4-8 with the letters "A" over the 4 and "P" over the 8.
103. Son of "Rich" Andrew Hoyl. Lived at the Hoyle Historic Homestead. He was a deaf mute. See House #1094 GC 1860 census, 123, Dallas PO.
104. See House #735 GC 1860 census, 82, Dallas PO.
105. See House #505 GC 1860 census, 57, Dallas PO.
106. See House #500 GC 1860 census, 56, Dallas PO.
107. See House #1359 GC 1860 census, 154, Dallas PO.
108. See House #1294 GC 1860 census, 146, Dallas PO.
109. Possibly Drucilla O'Brien at House #1393 GC 1860 census, 157, Dallas PO.
110. See House #1305 GC 1860 census, 147, Dallas PO.
111. See House #1302 GC 1860 census, 147, Dallas PO.
112. See House #1346 GC 1860 census, 152, Dallas PO.
113. See House #1302 GC 1860 census, 147, Dallas PO.
114. Possibly Jessee R. Peterson at House #1336 GC 1860 census, 151, Dallas PO.
115. See House #1298 GC 1860 census, 146, Dallas PO.
116. See House #730 GC 1860 census, 82, Dallas PO.
117. Possibly A. Alex Rhyne at House #1372 GC 1860 census, 155, Dallas PO.
118. Possibly John J. Rhyne and wife Dorcas at House #726 GC 1860 census, 81, Dallas PO.
119. Possibly John J. Rhyne House #726 GC 1860 census, 81, Dallas PO.
120. See House #511 GC 1860 census, 57, Dallas PO.
121. W. G. Morris lived north of Dallas. His home still stands north of the North Gaston High School campus. See House #1343 GC 1860 census, 152, Dallas PO.
122. See House #718 GC 1860 census, 80, Dallas PO.
123. See House #609 GC 1860 census, 68, Chesnut Oak PO.
124. See House #1345 "Physician" living with Jacob F. Pegram GC 1860 census, 152, Dallas PO.
125. See House #1090 GC 1860 census, 122, Dallas PO.

126. See House #736 GC 1860 census, 82, Dallas PO.
127. See House #1368 GC 1860 census, 155, Dallas PO.
128. See House #1352 GC 1860 census, 153, Dallas PO.
129. James H. White lived on Big Long Creek west of Dallas just off White and Jenkins Road. White operated a grist mill, served a number of years as state representative and senator, and was also instrumental in the creation of Gaston County. See House #1077 GC 1860 census, 121, Dallas PO.
130. See House #1387 GC 1860 census, 156, Dallas PO.
131. See House #171 GC 1860 census, 19, White Pine PO.
132. Tax List for persons owning land in Town of Dallas (delineated by town lots).
133. Possibly Jacob F. Pegram at House #1345 GC 1860 census, 152, Dallas PO.
134. The town lot is written as 15 over 1. Subsequent town lots are written the same way but it is unclear what it means. The valuation of this lot was 3,000.
135. Most likely a store which originally belonged to "Rich" Andrew Hoyl.
136. The following entries were written in two columns. It is unclear but assumed that the second column is simply a list of town lots with the owner. I wrote the transcription as it appears on the original.
137. Possibly S. Peter Pasour at House #1354 GC 1860 census, 153, Dallas PO.
138. The Eli Pasour House still stands on the Dallas Court Square.
139. See House #1365 GC 1860 census, 154, Dallas PO.
140. Possibly John G. Lewis at House #1355 GC 1860 census, 153, Dallas PO.
141. See House #1397 GC 1860 census, 157, Dallas PO.
142. See House #1360 GC 1860 census, 154, Dallas PO.
143. See House #1395 GC 1860 census, 157, Dallas PO.
144. This town lot of Daniel Hoffman is most likely the Hoffman Hotel, which still stands and houses the Gaston County Museum of Art and History.
145. See House #1394 GC 1860 census, 157, Dallas PO.
146. Possibly Mathus Armstrong at House #770 GC 1860 census, 86, Dallas PO.
147. Duharts Creek rises in present Gastonia, runs through commercial properties at Eastridge Mall, Gaston Mall, and Franklin Square. It runs into the South Fork River near present Cramerton.
148. Possibly Elias M. Anders at

House #634 GC 1860 census, 71, Chesnut Oak PO.
149. Possibly Alexander Bradley at House #516 GC 1860 census, 58, Dallas PO.
150. Possibly Joseph Bradley at House #604 GC 1860 census, 68, Chestnut Ridge PO.
151. See House #524 GC 1860 Census, 59, Dallas PO.
152. See House #751 GC 1860 census, 84, Dallas PO.
153. Possibly Oliver Davis at House #518 GC 1860 census, 58, Dallas PO.
154. Possbily William Dixon at House #644 GC 1860 census, 72, Catawba Creek PO.
155. See House #815 GC 1860 census, 92, Erasmus PO.
156. See House #832 GC 1860 census, 93, Erasmus PO.
157. See House #818 GC 1860 census, 92, Erasmus PO.
158. Possibly James Hanna at House #629 GC 1860 census, 70, Chesnut Oak PO.
159. See House #529 GC 1860 census, 59, Chesnut Oak PO.
160. See House #530 GC 1860 census, 59, Chesnut Oak PO.
161. Possibly L. M. Holland at House #534 GC 1860 census, 60, Chesnut Oak PO.
162. Possibly William R. Holland at House #645 GC 1860 census, 72, Catawba Creek PO.
163. Possibly Mary Holland at House #646 GC 1860 census, 72, Catawba Creek PO.
164. See House #626 GC 1860 census, 70, Dallas PO.
165. See House #927 GC 1860 census, 104, Stowesville PO.
166. See House #760 GC 1860 census, 85, Dallas PO.
167. See House #653 GC 1860 census, 73, Catawba Creek PO.
168. See House #758 GC 1860 census, 85, Dallas PO.
169. R. C. G. Love became a major cotton manufacturer after the Civil War.
170. Possibly Caleb Linebarger at House #958 "Merchant" GC 1860 census, 108, Woodlawn PO.
171. Possibly J. Logan Linebarger at House #957 "Manufacturer" GC 1860 census, 107, Woodlawn PO.
172. Woodlawn, also called the Pinhook, Cotton Mill was operated by the Lineberger family near present Lowell.
173. Possibly William Lay at House #619 GC 1860 census, 69, Dallas PO.
174. See House #754 GC 1860 census, 84, Dallas PO.
175. Possibly Coatsworth Lay at House #1066 GC 1860 census, 119, Dallas PO.
176. See House #740 GC 1860 census, 83, Dallas PO.
177. See House #753 "Keeper of poor" GC 1860 census, 84, Dallas PO.
178. Possibly James Quinn at House #535 GC 1860 census, 60, Chesnut Oak PO.
179. See House #618 GC 1860 census, 69, Dallas PO.
180. See House #609 GC 1860 census, 68, Chesnut Oak PO.
181. Possibly Daniel W. Rhyne at House #625 GC 1860 census, 70, Dallas PO.
182. See House #623 GC 1860 census, 70, Dallas PO.
183. See House #631 GC 1860 census, 71, Chesnut Oak PO.
184. Possibly Mary L. Suggs at House #635 GC 1860 census, 71, Chesnut Oak PO.
185. See House #632 GC 1860 census, 71, Chesnut Oak PO.
186. See House #766 GC 1860 census, 86, Dallas PO.
187. See House #525 GC 1860 census, 59, Dallas PO.
188. See House #523 GC 1860 census, 59, Dallas PO.
189. Possibly Jessee and Susannah Aydlotte at House #1118 GC 1860 census, 126, Dallas PO.
190. See House #1279 GC 1860 census, 144, Nail Factory PO.
191. Brevards Station was the railroad depot at present day Stanley.
192. Co-owner of High Shoals Iron Works.
193. Co-owner of High Shoals Iron Works.
194. Possibly Michael Cloninger at House #1128 GC 1860 census, 127, Stanley Creek PO.
195. Hoyles Creek rises in Lincoln County and flows through northeastern Gaston County into the South Fork River between Stanley and Dallas.
196. Possibly John Derr at House #1136 GC 1860 census, 128, Stanley Creek PO.
197. See House #1273 GC 1860 census, 144, Nail Factory PO.
198. See House #1262 GC 1860 census, 142, Vestels Ford PO.
199. Possibly Mary Friday at House #1275 GC 1860 census, 144, Nail Factory PO.
200. See House #1330 GC 1860 census, 150, Nail Factory PO.
201. See House #1273 GC 1860 census, 144, Nail Factory PO.
202. Possibly Jacob Friday at House #1276 GC 1860 census, 144, Nail Factory PO.
203. High Shoals Iron Company owned land from High Shoals to Bessemer City at one time. The company also owned slaves separately from the owners of the iron works.
204. Railroad land probably refers to the railroad line which ran from Stanley (then Brevard's Station) to Lincolnton.
205. See House #1126 GC 1860 census, 126, Dallas PO.
206. See House #1252 GC 1860 census, 141, Vestals Ford PO.
207. Possibly Jacob Plonk at House #1277 GC 1860 census, 144, Nail Factory PO.
208. See House #1261 GC 1860 census, 142, Vestals Ford PO.
209. Vestals Ford was located on the South Fork River near present Philadelphia Lutheran Church.
210. See House #1270 GC 1860 census, 143, Vestals Ford PO.
211. See House #1269 GC 1860 census, 143, Vestals Ford PO.
212. Brevard Station is present day Stanley.
213. See House #1096 GC 1860 census, 123, Dallas PO.
214. See House #1264 GC 1860 census, 142, Vestals Ford PO.
215. See House #1255 GC 1860 census, 141, Vestals Ford PO.
216. See House #1254 GC 1860 census, 141, Vestals Ford PO.
217. See House #1257 GC 1860 census, 142, Vestals Ford PO.
218. Possibly Frank W. Thompson at House #1266 GC 1860 census, 143, Vestals Ford PO.
219. See House #1209 "Physician" GC 1860 census, 137, Castanea Grove PO.
220. Stanley Creek rises in northeastern Gaston County and flows into Dutchmans Creek.
221. See House #1238 1860 census, 139, Cottage Home PO.
222. Leepers Creek rises in eastern Catawba County and combines with Killians Creek to create Dutchmans Creek in northeastern Gaston County.
223. Possibly David M. Abernathy at House #1238 GC 1860 census, 139, Cottage Home PO.
224. Dutchmans Creek is created in northeastern Gaston County from Leepers and Killians Creek and it flows into the Catawba River in present Mt. Holly.
225. Possibly John B. Abernathy at House #1240 GC 1860 census, 140, Cottage Home PO.
226. See House #1246 GC 1860 census, 140, Vestels Ford PO.
227. See House #1241 GC 1860 census, 140, Cottage Home PO.
228. The Plank Road connected Lincolnton and Charlotte and ran approximately with present Highway 16.
229. See House #1213 GC 1860 census, 137, Castanea Grove PO.
230. See House #1244 GC 1860 census, 140, Vestels Ford PO.
231. See House #1228 GC 1860 census, 138, Castanea Grove PO.
232. See House #1187 GC 1860 census, 134, Mountain Island PO.

233. Riverbend refers to the pronounced bend in the Catawba River north of present Mt. Holly.
234. See House #1236 GC 1860 census, 139, Castanea Grove PO.
235. See House #1195 GC 1860 census, 135, Mountain Island PO.
236. See House #1197 GC 1860 census, 136, Mountain Island PO.
237. The Andrew Carpenter House still stands and is locally and Nationally designated an historic property. See House #1143 GC 1860 census, 128, Stanley Creek PO.
238. See House #1131 GC 1860 census, 127, Stanley Creek PO.
239. See House #1133 GC 1860 census, 127, Stanley Creek PO.
240. Possibly Valentine Derr at House #1134 GC 1860 census, 127, Stanley Creek PO.
241. See House #1136 GC 1860 census, 128, Stanley Creek PO.
242. See House #1219 GC 1860 census, 138, Castanea Grove PO.
243. Widow of Peter Eddleman, Revolutionary War veteran and famed cabinetmaker.
244. See House #1237 GC 1860 census, 139, Cottage Home PO.
245. See House #1211 GC 1860 census, 137, Castanea Grove PO.
246. See House #1212 GC 1860 census, 137, Castanea Grove PO.
247. See House #1200 GC 1860 census, 136, Mountain Island PO.
248. Possibly Andrew Henderson at House #1191 GC 1860 census, 135, Mountain Island PO.
249. See House #1188 GC 1860 census, 135, Mountain Island PO.
250. See House #1215 GC 1860 census, 137, Castanea Grove PO.
251. See House #1235 GC 1860 census, 139, Castanea Grove PO.
252. Possibly John Hansel at House #1132 GC 1860 census, 127, Stanley Creek PO.
253. See House #1231 GC 1860 census, 139, Castanea Grove PO.
254. Possibly Lafayett Hutchinson at House #1144 GC 1860 census, 129, Stanley Creek PO.
255. Possibly Sidney H. Johnston "Physician" at House #1224 GC 1860 census, 138, Castanea Grove PO.
256. See House #1218 GC 1860 census, 138, Castanea Grove PO.
257. Timberland was used to produce charcoal for the iron furnaces.
258. See House #1203 GC 1860 census, 136, Mountain Island PO.
259. Possibly John W. Moore at House #1222 GC 1860 census, 138, Castanea Grove PO.
260. See House #1156 GC 1860 census, 130, Mountain Island PO.
261. Possibly Blair and Elizabeth McGee at House #1151 GC 1860 census, 129, Stanley Creek PO.
262. See House 1196 GC 1860 census, 135, Mountain Island PO.
263. See House #1233 GC 1860 census, 139, Castanea Grove PO.
264. See House #1232 GC 1860 census, 139, Castanea Grove PO.
265. See notation at House #1227 GC 1860 census, 138, Castanea Grove PO.
266. Killians Creek rises in eastern Catawba County and flows into Leepers Creek to create Dutchmans Creek in northeastern Gaston County.
267. Possibly Wiley Prior at House #1230 GC 1860 census, 139, Castanea Grove PO.
268. See House #1135 GC 1860 census, 128, Stanley Creek PO.
269. Possibly Milton Smith at House #1139 GC 1860 census, 128, Stanley Creek PO.
270. See House #1150 GC 1860 census, 129, Stanley Creek PO.
271. Possibly Celeb Stroup at House #1243 GC 1860 census, 140, Cottage Home PO.
272. Thomas Tate owned and operated Mountain Island Cotton Factory on the Catawba River, the first cotton mill in the county. See House #1183 GC 1860 census, 134, Mountain Island PO.
273. See House #1217 GC 1860 census, 137, Castanea Grove PO.
274. See House #1205 GC 1860 census, 136, Mountain Island PO.
275. See House #1184 GC 1860 census, 134, Mountain Island PO.
276. See House #371 GC 1860 census, 42, Kings Mtn PO.
277. Crowders Creek.
278. Long Creek.
279. See House #322 GC 1860 census, 36, Old Furnace PO.
280. See House #486 GC 1860 census, 55, Crowders Mtn PO.
281. See House #301 GC 1860 census, 34, Dallas PO.
282. See House #289 GC 1860 census, 33, Dallas PO.
283. Possibly A. Jackson Best at House #311 GC 1860 census, 35, Dallas PO.
284. Beaverdam Creek.
285. See House #261 GC 1860 census, 29, Old Furnace PO.
286. Possibly either Levi, Lemuel or Lewis Clemmer at House #s 271, 272, 273 GC 1860 census 31, Old Furnace PO.
287. See House #226 GC 1860 census, 25, Old Furnace PO.
288. See House #268 GC 1860 census, 30, Old Furnace PO.
289. Possibly James W. Clark House #264 GC 1860 census, 30, Old Furnace PO.
290. See House #316 GC 1860 census, 36, Old Furnace PO.
291. See House #372 GC 1860 census, 42, Kings Mountain PO.
292. See House #256 GC 1860 census, 29, Old Furnace PO.
293. See House #255 GC 1860 census, 29, Old Furnace PO.
294. Possibly John Fronabarger at House #287 GC 1860 census, 33, Dallas PO.
295. See House #180 GC 1860 census, 20, Dallas PO.
296. Possibly Jacob Fronabarger at House #288 GC 1860 census, 33, Dallas PO.
297. See House #324 GC 1860 census, 36, Old Furnace PO.
298. See House #370 GC 1860 census, 42, Kings Mountain PO.
299. See House #307 GC 1860 census, 35, Crowders Mtn PO.
300. The Garrett brothers moved from Edgecombe County to Gaston and purchased the iron works, iron and gold mining operations of B. F. Briggs.
301. Kings Mountain tract.
302. Crowders Mountain tract.
303. Yellow Ridge was a very productive gold and iron mine.
304. See House #223 GC 1860 census, 25, Old Furnace PO.
305. See House #231 GC 1860 census, 26, Old Furnace PO.
306. See House #246 GC 1860 census, 28, Old Furnace PO.
307. See House #217 GC 1860 census, 24, Old Furnace PO.
308. See House #254 GC 1860 census, 29, Old Furnace PO.
309. Possibly Lawson Long House #251 GC 1860 census, 28, Old Furnace PO.
310. See House #258 GC 1860 census, 29, Old Furnace PO.
311. Possibly House #260 GC 1860 census, 29, Old Furnace PO.
312. See House #259 GC 1860 census, 29, Old Furnace PO.
313. See House #250 GC 1860 census, 28, Old Furnace PO.
314. See House #235 GC 1860 census, 26, Old Furnace PO.
315. See House #232 GC 1860 census, 26, Old Furnace PO.
316. See Thomas J. McGill at House #236 GC 1860 census, 27, Old Furnace PO.
317. See House #225 GC 1860 census, 25, Old Furnace PO.
318. See House #484 GC 1860 census, 54, Crowders Mtn PO.
319. See House #480 GC 1860 census, 54, Crowders Mtn PO.
320. See House #483 GC 1860 census, 54, Crowders Mtn PO.
321. See House #237 GC 1860 census, 27, Old Furnace PO.
322. The Ore Bank was a productive iron mine, which was jointed operated by members of the Ormand family.
323. Chestnut Ridge was a small hill located northeast of present Kings Mountain.

Chapter Notes—Appendix

324. See House #219 GC 1860 census, 25, Old Furnace PO.
325. See House #234 GC 1860 census, 26, Old Furnace PO.
326. See House #218 GC 1860 census, 24, Old Furnace PO.
327. See House #270 GC 1860 census, 30, Old Furnace PO.
328. See House #1323 GC 1860 census, 149, Dallas PO.
329. See House #489 GC 1860 census, 55, Crowders Mtn PO.
330. See House #239 GC 1860 census, 27, Old Furnace PO.
331. Possibly Joshua Vandike at House #286 GC 1860 census, 32, Dallas PO.
332. Possibly House #238 GC 1860 census, 27, Old Furnace PO.
333. Possibly House #228 GC 1860 census, 26, Old Furnace PO.
334. Kings Mountain Gold Mine was a corporation which existed for a number of years. It was a profitable operation and owned by the Wilson family during the period studied.
335. See House #245 GC 1860 census, 28, Old Furnace PO.
336. See House #326 GC 1860 census, 37, Old Furnace PO.
337. See House #493 GC 1860 census, 55, Crowders Mtn PO.
338. Possibly Feynel Whitworth at House #488 GC 1860 census, 55, Crowders Mtn. PO.
339. See House #312 GC 1860 census, 35, Crowders Mtn. PO.
340. See House #146 GC 1860 census, 16, White Pine PO.
341. See House #170 GC 1860 census, 19, White Pine PO.
342. See House #145 Emanuel Adderholt GC 1860 census, 16, White Pine PO.
343. Mountain Branch creek is currently known as the Sulfur Mine Branch and runs north of Pasour Mountain, flowing into the South Fork River at High Shoals.
344. See House #192 GC 1860 census, 22, White Pine PO.
345. See House #139 GC 1860 census, 15, White Pine PO.
346. Beaverdam Creek.
347. See House #109 GC 1860 census, 12, White Pine PO.
348. See House #158 GC 1860 census, 18, White Pine PO.
349. See House #167 GC 1860 census, 19, White Pine PO.
350. Possibly Bennett Carpenter House #187 GC 1860 census, 21, White Pine PO.
351. See House #166 GC 1860 census, 19, White Pine PO.
352. See House #148 GC 1860 census, 16, White Pine PO.
353. See House #1313 GC 1860 census, 148, Dallas PO.
354. See House #1315 GC 1860 census, 148, Dallas PO.
355. Possibly House #155 GC 1860 census, 17, White Pine PO.
356. See House #1320 GC 1860 census, 149, Dallas PO.
357. Christian Eaker was a justice of the peace and his home still exists but is in poor repair. See House #142 GC 1860 census, 16, White Pine PO.
358. See House #106 GC 1860 census, 12, White Pine PO.
359. See House #102 GC 1860 census, 11, White Pine PO.
360. See House #153 GC 1860 census, 17, White Pine PO.
361. See House #176 Phillip Kizer GC 1860 census, 20, Dallas PO.
362. See House #150 GC 1860 census, 17, White Pine PO.
363. See House #1312 GC 1860 census, 148, Dallas PO.
364. See House #151 GC 1860 census, 17, White Pine PO.
365. Abraham Mauney Sr. and his slaves did the brick work for most of the buildings in Dallas like the courthouse, jail, and Hoffman Hotel. Wesley Mauney was born and returned here after emancipation. Abraham Mauney's home still stands. See House #177 GC 1860 census, 20, Dallas PO.
366. See House #179 GC 1860 census, 20, Dallas PO.
367. Possibly House #156 GC 1860 census, 17, White Pine PO.
368. Possibly John McBee House #175 GC 1860 census, 20, White Pine PO.
369. Possibly House #140 GC 1860 census, 15, White Pine PO.
370. Possibly House #188 GC 1860 census, 21, White Pine PO.
371. See House #189 GC 1860 census, 21, White Pine PO.
372. See House #152 GC 1860 census, 17, White Pine PO.
373. Possibly Linthy Shuford House #160 GC 1860 census, 18, White Pine PO.
374. See House #1314 GC 1860 census, 148, Dallas PO.
375. See House #1304 GC 1860 census, 147, Dallas PO.
376. See House 162 GC 1860 census, 18, White Pine PO.
377. See House #168 GC 1860 census, 19, White Pine PO.
378. Possibly Jonas Center House #174 GC 1860 census, 20, White Pine PO.
379. See House #864 GC 1860 census, 97, South Point PO.
380. Possibly House #984 GC 1860 census, 110, Woodlawn PO.
381. See House #973 GC 1860 census, 109, Woodlawn PO.
382. See House #975 GC 1860 census, 109, Woodlawn PO.
383. See House #977 GC 1860 census, 109, Woodlawn PO.
384. See House #709 GC 1860 census, 79, South Point PO.
385. See House #974 GC 1860 census, 109, Woodlawn PO.
386. Possibly S. W. Craig at House #863 GC 1860 census, 97, South Point PO.
387. See House #848 GC 1860 census, 95, Stowesville PO.
388. See House #710 GC 1860 census, 80, South Point PO.
389. See House #996 GC 1860 census, 111, Woodlawn PO.
390. See House #992 GC 1860 census, 111, Woodlawn PO.
391. Possibly Hugh Ewing at House #967 GC 1860 census, 108, Woodlawn PO.
392. Possibly Robert Finley at House #711 GC 1860 census, 80, South Point PO.
393. See House #986 GC 1860 census, 110, Woodlawn PO.
394. Possibly Harvey Groner at House #918 GC 1860 census, 103, Stowesville PO.
395. See House #970 GC 1860 census, 109, Woodlawn PO.
396. See House #856 GC 1860 census, 96, Stowesville PO.
397. See House #917 GC 1860 census, 103, Stowesville PO.
398. See House #915 GC 1860 census, 103, Stowesville PO.
399. See House #872 GC 1860 census, 98, Stowesville PO.
400. See House #978 GC 1860 census, 110, Woodlawn PO.
401. See House #869 GC 1860 census, 97, South Point PO.
402. See House #857 GC 1860 census, 96, Stowesville PO.
403. Possibly James D. Hall at House #990 GC 1860 census, 111, Woodlawn PO.
404. Carpenter was probably his occupation.
405. See House #849 GC 1860 census, 96, Stowesville PO.
406. See House #988 GC 1860 census, 111, Woodlawn PO.
407. See House #900 GC 1860 census, 101, Stowesville PO.
408. See House #912 GC 1860 census, 102, Stowesville PO.
409. See House #993 GC 1860 census, 111, Woodlawn PO.
410. Possibly William R. McLean at House #905 GC 1860 census, 101, Stowesville PO.
411. See House #708 GC 1860 census, 79, South Point PO.
412. See House #715 "Physician" GC 1860 census, 80, Dallas PO.
413. Probably Catawba Creek and River.
414. See House #919 GC 1860 census, 103, Stowesville PO.
415. See House #894 GC 1860 census, 100, Stowesville PO.
416. See House #867 GC 1860 census, 97, Stowesville PO.
417. See House #871 GC 1860 census, 98, South Point PO.

418. See House #870 GC 1860 census, 97, South Point PO.
419. Possibly Willaim Reid at House #925 GC 1860 census, 104, Stowesville PO.
420. Possibly James W. Reid at House #924 GC 1860 census, 104 Stowesville PO.
421. See House #963 GC 1860 census, 108, Woodlawn PO.
422. See House #876 "manufactor" GC 1860 census, 98, Stowesville PO.
423. Stowesville Cotton Factory was the third cotton mill established in the county.
424. See House #876 GC 1860 census, 98, Stowesville PO.
425. Possibly John Wright at House #847 GC 1860 census, 95, Stowesville PO.
426. Possibly Burell Wells at House #971 GC 1860 census, 109, Woodlawn PO.
427. Possibly William B. Yarborough at House #921 GC 1860 census, 103, Stowesville PO.
428. See House #837 GC 1860 census, 94, Erasmus PO.
429. See House #702 GC 1860 census, 78, Erasmus PO.
430. It is unclear whether C. C. stands for Catawba Creek or Crowders Creek since both are listed in this company.
431. Possibly George Bryson at House #584 GC 1860 census, 65, Erasmus PO.
432. See House #694 GC 1860 census, 78, Erasmus PO.
433. Possibly William Bryson at House #704 GC 1860 census, 79, Erasmus PO.
434. See House #703 GC 1860 census, 79, Erasmus PO.
435. Possibly James C. Beard at House #674 GC 1860 census, 76, Erasmus PO.
436. Possibly William C. Beaty at House #431 GC 1860 census, 49, Crowders Creek PO.
437. See House #698 GC 1860 census, 78, Erasmus PO.
438. See House #765 GC 1860 census, 86, Dallas PO.
439. Possibly Laban Clemmer at House #678 GC 1860 census, 76, Erasmus PO.
440. See House #845 GC 1860 census, 95, Stowesville PO.
441. See House #561 GC 1860 census, 63, Pleasant Ridge PO.
442. Possibly Alfred Dixon at House #643 GC 1860 census, 72, Catawba Creek PO.
443. Possibly Elias M. Faris at House #546 GC 1860 census, 61, Pleasant Ridge PO.
444. See House #688 GC 1860 census, 77, Erasmus PO.
445. See House #587 GC 1860 census, 66, Erasmus PO.
446. See House #685 GC 1860 census, 77, Erasmus PO.
447. See House #687 GC 1860 census, 77, Erasmus PO.
448. Possibly John F. Glenn at House #695 GC 1860 census, 78, Erasmus PO.
449. See House #686 GC 1860 census, 77, Erasmus PO.
450. See House #675 GC 1860 census, 76, Erasmus PO.
451. Possibly M. C. and Dorcas Gingles at House #682 GC 1860 census, 76, Erasmus PO.
452. See House #589 GC 1860 census, 66, Erasmus PO.
453. Possibly William A. Henderson at House #557 GC 1860 census, 62, Pleasant Ridge PO.
454. Possibly William Hill at House #553 GC 1860 census, 62, Pleasant Ridge PO.
455. See House #841 GC 1860 census, 94, Stowesville PO.
456. Possibly Caleb Huffstetler at House #551 GC 1860 census, 62, Pleasant Ridge PO.
457. See House #649 GC 1860 census, 73, Catawba Creek PO.
458. See House #671 GC 1860 census, 75, Catawba Creek PO.
459. See House #645 GC 1860 census, 72, Catawba Creek PO.
460. See House #646 GC 1860 census, 72, Catawba Creek PO.
461. Possibly David A. Jenkins at House #570 GC 1860 census, 64, Pleasant Ridge PO.
462. See House #579 GC 1860 census, 65, Pleasant Ridge PO.
463. Possibly Elenor Kendric at House #679 GC 1860 census, 76, Erasmus PO.
464. See House #572 GC 1860 census, 64, Pleasant Ridge PO.
465. Possibly Judson Lewis at House #831 GC 1860 census, Erasmus PO.
466. Possibly Ann Lewis at House #581 GC 1860 census, 65, Pleasant Ridge PO.
467. See House #850 GC 1860 census, 96, Stowesville PO.
468. See House #393 GC 1860 census, 44, Crowders Creek PO.
469. See House #596 GC 1860 census, 67, Catawba Creek PO.
470. Possibly Foenaw Massey at House #565 GC 1860 census, 63, Pleasant Ridge PO.
471. Possibly Elisha McDonald at House #662 GC 1860 census, 74, Catawba Creek PO.
472. See House #697 GC 1860 census, 78, Erasmus PO.
473. Possibly Esther O'Daniel at House #542 GC 1860 census, 61, Chestnut Oak PO.
474. Possibly Samuel Pessley at House #696 GC 1860 census, 78, Erasmus PO.
475. Possibly James Pettis at House #582 GC 1860 census, 65, Erasmus PO.
476. Possibly James Quinn at House #535 GC 1860 census, 60, Chestnut Oak PO.
477. See House #840 GC 1860 census, 94, Erasmus PO.
478. See House #655 GC 1860 census, 73, Catawba Creek PO.
479. See House #652 GC 1860 census, 73, Catawba Creek PO.
480. See House #654 GC 1860 census, 73, Catawba Creek PO.
481. Possibly Joseph F. Riddle at House #571 GC 1860 census, 64, Pleasant Ridge PO.
482. See House #567 GC 1860 census, 63, Pleasant Ridge PO.
483. Possibly John C. Torrance at House #537 GC 1860 census, 60, Chesnut Oak PO.
484. See House #597 GC 1860 census, 67, Catawba Creek PO.
485. See House #684 GC 1860 census, 77, Erasmus PO.
486. Possibly William G. Warren at House #586 GC 1860 census, 66, Erasmus PO.
487. Possibly Monroe Abernathy at House #954 GC 1860 census, 107, Woodlawn PO.
488. See House #1071 GC 1860 census, 120, Dallas PO.
489. See House #1062 GC 1860 census, 119, Stanley Creek PO.
490. Possibly John F. Cannon at House #1055 GC 1860 census, 118, Stanley Creek PO.
491. The home of A. W. Davenport still stands north of Mt. Holly and is a designated local historic property. Possibly A. Wesley Davenport at House #1039 GC 1860 census, 116, Mountain Island PO.
492. See House #1155 GC 1860 census, 130, Mountain Island PO.
493. Possibly Hugh Ewing at House #964 GC 1860 census, 108, Woodlawn PO or Samuel R. Ewing at House #992, 111, Woodlawn PO.
494. See House #1002 GC 1860 census, 112, Woodlawn PO.
495. Possibly George Fite at House #1001 GC 1860 census, 112, Woodlawn PO.
496. Possibly William J. Fite at House #1000 GC 1860 census, 112, Woodlawn PO.
497. Fites Creek rises in central eastern Gaston County and flows east into the Catawba River near present Mt. Holly.
498. See House #1114 GC 1860 census, Stanley Creek PO.
499. See House #1031 GC 1860 census, 115, Woodlawn PO.
500. Taylor's Creek rises in central eastern Gaston County and flows west to east into Dutchman's Creek near present Mt. Holly.
501. Possibly Jack Hand at House

#1035 GC 1860 census, 116, Mountain Island PO.
502. See House #1038 GC 1860 census, 116, Mountain Island PO.
503. Possibly May Hoffman at House #1005 GC 1860 census, 112, Woodlawn PO.
504. See House #1059 GC 1860 census, 118, Stanley Creek PO.
505. See House #1046 GC 1860 census, 117, Stanley Creek PO.
506. Possibly Lewis Linebarger at House #994 GC 1860 census, 111, Woodlawn PO.
507. Possibly Frederick Nims at House #1036 GC 1860 census, 116, Mountain Island PO.
508. See House #1074 GC 1860 census, 120, Dallas PO.
509. Possibly Sidney Rankin at House #1146 GC 1860 census, 129, Stanley Creek PO.
510. See House #1021 GC 1860 census, 114, Woodlawn PO.
511. See House #1033 GC 1860 census, 115, Mountain Island PO.
512. Possibly John D. Rankin at House #1047 GC 1860 census, 117, Stanley Creek PO.
513. See House #1014 GC 1860 census, 114, Woodlawn PO.
514. Possibly Alexander Rutledge at House #1049 GC 1860 census, 117, Stanley Creek PO.
515. Moses H. Rhyne's home still stands just west of Mt. Holly. See House #997 GC 1860 census, 111, Woodlawn PO. His store still stands in Dallas on the Courthouse Square.
516. See House #1051 GC 1860 census, 118, Stanley Creek PO.
517. Possibly James R. Rankin at House #1149 GC 1860 census, 129, Stanley Creek PO.
518. See House #1148 GC 1860 census, 129, Stanley Creek PO.
519. See House #1006 GC 1860 census, 113, Woodlawn PO.
520. See House #948 GC 1860 census, 106, Stanley Creek PO.
521. See House #1025 GC 1860 census, 115, Woodlawn PO.
522. Rail Road capital or stock in railroad companies.
523. Profits Manufactured Cotton or Woolen goods.
524. Persons allowed to ride the rails free.
525. Probably Household and Kitchen Furniture.
526. Slave valuation divided by the number of slaves.
527. Slave valuation divided by the number of slaveholders.
528. Goodnight, Bell, and Carpenter, *The Complete 1850 Census of Gaston County, North Carolina*, 127–130. The author counted the slaves into slave owning categories and completed the mathematical calculations.
529. Gladden & Bell, *1860 Gaston Co Census*, 169–195.
530. Gaston County Collection, Tax List, 1847–1860; 1863–1868, CR040.700.1, NC Archives.

Bibliography

The bibliography is divided into two sections: primary and secondary sources. Within the primary sources are manuscripts in private hands, in archives and repositories within which I separate the major archival locations, in printed works, newspapers, and internet. Secondary sources include books, periodical articles, internet, and unpublished materials. A goal of the project was to bring together an expansive collection of local, regional, state, and national sources. Another goal was to access previously unpublished and uncirculated primary source manuscripts held in private hands. Many new sources have been discovered, and as a result of this project some are now held by the Lincoln County Historical Association. I am aware of two other major Civil War era sources which I was unable to access: the diary of James W. Reid and the war letters of Marion Legget Holland. Reid's diary is in private hands, remaining unavailable to the public, and the Holland letters at one time were at the Gaston County Museum of Art and History, where they cannot now be located. Both sources would add to the portrait. Certainly other sources remain in attics, lock boxes, file cabinets, and old furniture drawers. It is my hope that others may make their papers available to be placed in archives or to get photocopied or microfilmed so that their story may be told.

Primary Sources

Manuscripts in Private Hands

Dr. Ed Anthony Collection. Gastonia, NC.

F. L. Dellinger Collection. Held in private hands and provided to the author by Mike Stroupe.

J. J. Brown Letters. Held in private hands, copies and typescripts provided to the author by Elizabeth Carpenter. Lincolnton, NC.

Jacob Froneberger Diary. Copies provided to the author by Corinne Puett Gianitrapani of West Chester, Pennsylvania.

Jacob L. Workman Letter. In the hands of Daphine Peach of Dallas, NC. Transcribed by Helen Whisnant and permission given by Daphine Peach.

Jas. Fulton Letter. Provided to the author by Steve and Daphne Friday. Daphne is a professor at Belmont Abbey College.

John E. and Wylma H. Monteith Collection. Provided by Mr. and Mrs. Monteith, Stanley, NC.

Keener Letters. In the hands of Fred Goodson and Mark Goodson, his son, furnished copies of originals to the author, of Gastonia, NC.

Lawson Carpenter Letter. In the hands of Wade Carpenter, Jr. of Lincolnton, NC. Copy provided to the author.

Lewis Cass Payseur. "Some Reminiscences of the Great Confederate War." Unknown newspaper, 1914, probably in Lancaster County, SC. Transcribed by Mary Alice Beatty Carmichael, 1975–1985, of Birmingham, AL. Provided to the author by Greg Payseur, of Shelby, NC.

"Reminiscences of the Civil War by Col. R. N. Wilson Dictated to a member of the Gastonia Chapter U. D. C.," and other material, including a copy of Jerry Wilson's pension application. Provided to the author by Lynda Hancock of Gastonia, NC.

Thomas Davis Correspondence. Copies provided to the author by Steve Huffstetler of Bessemer City, NC. These documents were posted on the internet but could not recently be accessed.

W. C. Wolfe Letter. Copy given to the author by Steve Huffstetler of Bessemer City, NC.

William Groves Morris Papers. In hands of Danny Wilson of Dallas, NC.

Manuscripts in Archives or Repositories

Rubenstein Library, Duke University, Durham, NC. Melchi Rhodes Account Book, 1854–1859, Melchi Rhodes Papers.

Stowe Family Papers. Stowe Family Account Book, 1856–1874.

Stowe Family Papers. Store Ledger, 1857–1860, Stowesville, NC.

Lincoln County Historical Association, Lincolnton, NC

A. C. Wiswall Papers.
Asheville Armory Ledger.
Boyd to Reinhard.
Caleb Senter Civil War Letters. Copies of original letters at the LCHA.
Coon, Yoder, and Killian Family Papers.
Daniel Haynes Dellinger Papers. Larry Philip Leonard Collection.
Edward W. Phifer Papers. Southern Historical Collection, UNC-CH. Transcriptions of letters from these papers are located at the LCHA.
Hanna Papers.
High Shoals Iron Works Papers. Lincoln County Library Collection.
Linda Bell Collection.
Lucille Goodson Collection.
Mendenhall Papers.

North Carolina Department of Archives and History, Jones Street, Raleigh

Adjutant General Letter Book 1862–1864. AG44.
Adjutant General Papers. Ledger 1861–1863, AG 25.
Adjutant General's Office. Home Guard Letter Book, 1863–1865. AG52.
Adjutant General's Papers. Roster of the Militia of North Carolina 1861–62, 1864, AG 129.
Gaston County Collection. Court of Pleas and Quarter Sessions Minute Docket, CRO40.301.1.
Gaston County Collection. Gaston County Execution Docket, Superior Court, CR040.318.1
Gaston County Collection. Gaston County Superior Court Minute Docket 1847–1869, CR040.311.1
Gaston County Collection. Lee Hunter (free person of color), Gaston County Estates 1839–1971, CR 040.508.71.
Gaston County Collection. Tax List, 1847–1860; 1863–1868, CR040.701.1, CR040.701.2.
General Assembly Session Records. Nov. 1860-Feb 1861, Elector's Votes for President and Vice President; Votes Pro and Con for Convention and for Delegates.
General Assembly Session Records. Nov-Dec 1862, Box 3, Governor's Election's Returns (Alamance-Iredell); Certificates of Election—Senate.
General Assembly Session Records. Nov-Dec 1864, Box 2, Governor's Election Returns.
General Assembly Session Records. Nov-Dec 1865, Box 2, Certificates of Election—House; Certificates of Election—Senate; Governor's Election Returns.
Governor's Papers. Zebulon B. Vance.
Lincoln County Collection. Civil War Records 1864–1923. Civil War—Aid to soldier's wives and widows, CR060.920.2.
Lincoln County Collection. Lincoln County Criminal Action Papers 1862–1865, CR060.326.9.
Lincoln County Collection. Lincoln County Minute Docket Superior Court 1858–1869, CR060.311.4.
Lincoln County Collection. Lincoln County State Docket, Superior Court 1851–1869, CR060.321.3.
Lincoln County Collection. Lists of School Children, 1845–1846, CR060.926.2, copy provided to the author by Rachel Eichemeyer.
Lincoln County Collection. Miscellaneous Papers, CR060.928.2, Criminal Action papers Concerning Harboring Deserters.
Lincoln County Collection. Wills, CR060.801.8, NC Archives.
Military Collection. Civil War Collection, Quartermaster Dept., Misc. Records.
Military Collection. Civil War Collection, Quartermaster Department Papers, Miscellaneous Records 1860–1865.
North Carolina Supreme Court Papers, State v. William Cody, 60NC197 (June 1864), Case 8670.
Private Collection, C. W. Garrett Papers, PC1308–1309.
Private Collection. Edward W. Phifer Jr. Collection 1789, 1842–1895, 1934, PC1368.1.
Private Collection. Harriett R. McIntosh Papers, PC1847.
Treasurer & Comptrollers Papers. Military Papers, Cotton and Wool Account Book 1862–1865, #92.

Southern Historical Collection, Wilson Library, University of North Carolina at Chapel Hill, Chapel Hill

David Schenck Papers, 1849–1917, 00652. http://www2.lib.unc.edu/mss/inv/s/Schenck,David.html
L. A. Glenn Papers, 03052.
Lemuel J. Hoyle Papers, 04746, also in private hands of Marshall Ramsey, Jr. of Columbia, SC, who shared them with the author.
Nims, Rankin, and Spratt Family Papers, 04255.
Phifer Family Papers, 02726-z.
William Groves Morris Papers, 03626-z.

Other Locations

Gaston County Deeds. Register of Deeds. Gaston County Courthouse, Gastonia, NC.
"Letters of a Gaston Ranger," which includes transcriptions of letters, copy located at Brevard Station Museum, Stanley, NC.
Lincoln County Deeds. Register of Deeds, Lincoln County Courthouse, Lincolnton, NC.
Newton Sellers Papers. Copies of originals provided to the author by Gaston County Museum of Art and History, Dallas, NC.
"A PenPicture of Wesley Mauney—an Ex-Slave." 1933, typescript in possession of the author.
Thornburg, Larkin. "The Experience of a Seventeen Year Old Boy During the War Between the States."

Typescript, copy at the Gaston County Museum of Art and History and in the hands of the author.

US Supreme Court Case, 84 U.S. 44, 21 L.Ed. 570, 17 Wall. 44, Olcott v. Bynum et al., December Term, 1872, provided to the author by Kathy Gunter Sullivan.

Printed Primary Sources

An Act to Incorporate the Town of Dallas in Gaston County. North Carolina General Statutes. Private Laws, 1862–63, Section 44, 4. North Carolina Archives, Raleigh.

Bell, Linda. *Gaston County North Carolina 1880 Census*. Charlotte, NC: AlphaGraphics, 1998.

_____. *The Population Schedule of the Ninth Census of the United States, 1870, Gaston County, North Carolina*. Self-published, February 14, 1992.

Bynum, Curtis L. *Marriage Bonds of Lincoln and Tryon Counties, North Carolina*. 1929, repr. Catawba County Historical Association and Lincoln County Historical Association, 1962.

Chestnut, Mary. *A Diary from Dixie*. Ed. Isabella D. Martin and Myrta Lockett Avary. New York: Appleton, 1905. Kindle edition.

Gladden, Donald, and Linda A. Bell. *The 1860 Census of Gaston Co., North Carolina*. Privately published, 1992.

Goodnight, Libby, Linda Bell, and Robert C. Carpenter. *The Complete 1850 Census of Gaston County, North Carolina*. Ozark, MO: Yates, 1985.

North Carolina General Statutes. North Carolina Archives, Raleigh.

North Carolina General Statutes, Private 1862–1863. North Carolina Archives, Raleigh.

Kirk, Charles E., ed. *History of the 15th Pennsylvania Cavalry*. 1906. Google Books.

Lesley, J. Peter. *The Iron Manufacturer's Guide to the Furnaces, Forges and Rolling Mills of the United States*. New York: John Wiley, Publishers, 1859; repr. Nabu Public Domain Reprints.

Monroe, Haskell. "The Road to Gettysburg: The Diary and Letters of Leonidas Torrence of the Gaston Guards." *North Carolina Historical Review* (October 1959): 478–517.

Pruitt, Dr. A. B. *Abstracts of Deeds Lincoln Co, NC Books 45, 46, and 47 (1863–1874)*. Self-published, 2011.

Pruitt, Dr. A. B. *Minutes of Confederate District Court North Carolina District, 1861–1863*. Self-published, 2014.

Philbeck, Miles S., Jr., and Grace Turner. *Lincoln County North Carolina Will Abstracts, 1779–1910*. Self-published, 1986.

Newspapers

The Bulletin (Charlotte, North Carolina). Microfilm at Atkins Library, University of North Carolina at Charlotte, ANOC5.

Carolina Watchman (Salisbury, North Carolina), 1832–1898. http://exhibits.archives.ncdcr.gov/newspaper/included.html.

Charlotte Observer (Charlotte, North Carolina). Extant newspapers in collections or owned by the author.

The Daily Bulletin (Charlotte, North Carolina). Microfilm at Atkins Library, University of North Carolina at Charlotte, AND32.

Daily Carolina Times (Charlotte, North Carolina). Microfilm at Atkins Library, University of North Carolina at Charlotte, AND325.

Gastonia Gazette (Gastonia, North Carolina). Extant newspapers in collections or owned by the author.

Kings Mountain Herald (Kings Mountain, North Carolina). Extant newspapers in collections or owned by the author.

The Lincoln Courier (Lincolnton, North Carolina). http://www.digitalnc.org/newspapers/lincoln-courier-lincolnton-nc/.

Lincoln Times News (Lincolnton, North Carolina). Copies of soldier letters accessed in the files at Lincoln County Historical Association, Lincolnton.

Mountain Eagle (Shelby, North Carolina). Microfilm at North Carolina Archives, ShMISC-1.

North Carolina Whig (Charlotte, North Carolina). http://www.digitalnc.org/newspapers/north-caroliana-whig-charlotte-nc/.

The Standard (Raleigh, North Carolina). http://search.ancestry.com/search/db.aspx?dbid=6639.

Western Democrat (Charlotte, North Carolina). http://www.digitalnc.org/newspapers/western-democrat-charlotte-n-c/.

Internet Primary Sources

Albert, Allen Diehl, ed. *History of the Forty-Fifth Regiment of the Pennsylvania Veteran Volunteer Infantry 1861–1865*. Williamsport, PA: Grit, 1912, 365–366. http://books.google.com/books?id=Js2CAAAAIAAJ&pg=PA362#v=onepage&q&f=false.

Bost, W. L. WPA Narrative, 1937. http://nationalhumanitiescenter.org/pds/maai/enslavement/text1/wlbost.pdf.

Garwood, Dr. Alonzo. Civil War Diary. Surgeon of the 28th Michigan Infantry, of the 1st Division of the 23rd Army Corps in charge of the Field Hospital, May 20-June 22, 1865. http://www.migenweb.org/michiganinthewar/infantry/diary.htm.

Gudger, Sarah. WPA Narrative, 1937. http://scholar.lib.vt.edu/vtpubs/mountain_slavery/sarah.pdf.

North Carolina Confederate Service Records. Citizen Files, Business Files, Amnesty Papers, Southern Claims Commission, accessed at www.fold3.com.

Richardson, Michael Dean, and Benjamin Russell Hanby. *The Secret Service: The Field, The Dungeon, and the Escape*. American Pub Co, 1866, 444. Accessed Dec. 13, 2012, at http://books.google.com/books?id=vRgPAAAAYAAJ&source=gbs_navlinks_s.

U.S. Census. www.census.gov/prod/www/decennial.htm/northcarolina1860(1)-10.pdf.

Secondary Sources

Books

Bridgers, H. C. Jr. "Bridgers, Robert Rufus" and "John Luther Bridgers." *Dictionary of North Carolina*

Biography, ed. William S. Powell, vol. 1, A-C. Chapel Hill: University of North Carolina Press, 1979.
Brotherton, Ken. *Lake Norman Piedmont History*. Self-published, 1993. Provided to the author by Greg Little.
Butts, Michel Tucker. *Galvanized Yankees on the Upper Missouri*. Clarksville, TN: Austin-Peay University Press, 2003.
Bynum, Victoria E. *The Long Shadow of the Civil War: Southern Dissent and its Legacies*. Chapel Hill: University of North Carolina Press, 2010.
_____. *Unruly Women: The Politics of Social and Sexual Control in the Old South*. Chapel Hill: University of North Carolina Press, 1992.
Carpenter, Robert C. *Carpenters A Plenty*. Baltimore, MD: Gateway, 1982, repr. 1993.
Cope, Robert F., and Manly Wade Wellman. *The County of Gaston: Two Centuries of a North Carolina Region*. Gaston County Historical Society, 1961.
Dew, Charles B. *Apostles of Disunion: Southern Secession Commissioners and the Causes of the Civil War*. Charlottesville: University of Virginia Press, 2001.
Escott, Paul D. *Lincoln's Dilemma: Blair, Sumner, and the Struggle Over Racism and Equality in the Civil War Era*. (A Nation Divided: Studies in the Civil War Era). Charlottesville: University of Virginia Press, 2014. Kindle edition.
_____. *Many Excellent People: Power and Privilege in North Carolina, 1850–1900*. Chapel Hill: University of North Carolina Press, 1985.
Faust, Drew Gilpin. *Mothers of Invention: Women of the Slaveholding South in the American Civil War*. Chapel Hill: University of North Carolina Press, 1996.
Gallagher, Gary W. *The Confederate War*. Cambridge, MA: Harvard University Press, 1997.
_____. *The Union War*. Cambridge, MA: Harvard University Press, 2011.
Goldberg, David. *America Aflame: How the Civil War Created a Nation*. New York: Bloomsbury, 2011.
Goodnight, Jerry A., and Richard Eller. *The Tarheel Lincoln: North Carolina Origins of "Honest" Abe*. Hickory, NC: Tarheel, 2003.
Hardy, Michael C. *Civil War Charlotte: Last Capital of the Confederacy*. Charleston, SC: History, 2012.
_____. *North Carolina in the Civil War*. Charleston, SC: History, 2011.
Hartley, Chris J. *Stoneman's Raid, 1865*. Winston-Salem, NC: John F. Blair, 2010.
Heller, Kitty Thornburg. *Dallas, North Carolina: A Brief History*. Charleston, SC: History, 2013.
Hoffman, Laban Miles. *Our Kin*. 1915, repr. Gaston County Historical Society, Baltimore: Genealogical, 1968.
Kruman, Marc W. *Parties and Politics in North Carolina, 1836–1865*. Baton Rouge: Louisiana State University Press, 1983.
Inscoe, John C. *Race, War, and Remembrance in the Appalachian South*. Lexington: University Press of Kentucky, 2008.
Inscoe, John C., and Gordon McKinney. *The Heart of Confederate Appalachia: Western North Carolina in the Civil War*. Chapel Hill: University of North Carolina Press, 2000. Kindle edition.
McCurry, Stephanie. *Confederate Reckoning: Power and Politics in the Civil War South*. Cambridge, MA: Harvard University Press, 2010.
McKean, Brenda Chambers. *Blood and War at My Doorstep: North Carolina Civilians in the War Between the States*, vol. I. N.p.: Xlibris, 2011.
_____. *Blood and War At My Doorstep: North Carolina Civilians in the War Between the States*, vol. II. N.p.: Xlibris, 2011.
McKinney, Gordon B. "Premature Industrialization in Appalachia: The Asheville Armory, 1862–1863." In *Civil War in Appalachia: Collected Essays*, ed. Kenneth W. Noe and Shannon H. Wilson. Knoxville: University of Tennessee Press, 2004.
McPherson, James M. *For Cause and Comrades: Why Men Fought in the Civil War*. Oxford: Oxford University Press, 1997.
Mobley, Joe A. *"War Governor of the South" North Carolina's Zeb Vance in the Confederacy*. Gainesville: University Press of Florida, 2005.
Noe, Kenneth W. *Reluctant Rebels*. Chapel Hill: University of North Carolina Press, 2010.
Puett, Minnie Stowe. *History of Gaston County*. Charlotte, NC: Observer, 1939.
Ragan, Robert Allison. *The History of Gastonia and Gaston County, North Carolina: A Vision of America at its Best*. Charlotte, NC: Loftin, 2010.
_____. *The Textile Heritage of Gaston County, 1848–2000*, Charlotte, NC: R.A. Ragan, 2001.
Sherrill, William L. *Annals of Lincoln County, North Carolina*. Charlotte, NC: 1937, repr. Baltimore: Regional, 1972.
Steward, Rodney. *David Schenck and the Contours of Confederate Identity*. Knoxville: University of Tennessee Press, 2012.
Stroupe, Vernon S., Robert Stets, Ruth Y. Wetmore and Tony L. Crumbley. *Post Offices and Postmasters of North Carolina*, vol. II. Charlotte: North Carolina Postal History Society, 1996.
Trotter, William R. *Bushwackers! The Mountains*. Winston Salem, NC: John F. Blair, 1989.
Yearns, W. Buck, and John G. Barrett. *North Carolina Civil War Documentary*. Chapel Hill: University of North Carolina Press, 1980, repr. 2002.

Periodicals

Auman, William T., and David D. Scarboro. "The Heroes of America in Civil War North Carolina." *The North Carolina Historical Review*, Vol. LVIII, No. 4 (Oct. 1981).
Clemmer, Len. "An Early Land Transaction on the South Fork of the Catawba River." *Footprints in Time* (Dec. 2012), 174–178.
Escott, Paul. "Poverty and Governmental Aid in Confederate North Carolina." *North Carolina Historical Review*, Vol. 61 (Oct. 1984), 462–480.
Hasegawa, Guy R. "'Absurd Prejudice': A. Snowden Piggot and the Confederate Medical Laboratory at Lincolnton." *North Carolina Historical Review*, Vol LXXXI, No. 3 (July 2004), 313–334.

Hasagawa, Guy R., and F. Terry. Hambrecht. "The Confederate Medical Laboratories." *Southern Medical Journal*, Vol. 96, No. 12 (Dec. 2003), 1221–1230.

Internet Sources

www.abrahamlincolnonline.org/lincoln/education/father.htm.

www.ancestry.com.

Blount-Bridgers House Docent Handbook December 2011, http://www.edgecombearts.org/BBH%20Docent%20Handbook%20-%20December%202011.pdf.

www.bosticlincolncenter.com/background.htm.

www.familysearch.org.

http://www.estherlederberg.com/EImages/Extracurricular/Cloth/Cloth%20Manufacture.html

lincolnstudies.blogspot.com/2008/02/abraham-lincoln-enloe.html

Unpublished Manuscripts, Papers, Essays or Research

"Background for Stowe's Factory." Report by Coastal Carolina Research, Inc., 2009, provided to John Babington, copy provided to the author by John Russell.

Carpenter, Robert C. "Salem Lutheran and United Church of Christ: A Story of Faith and Peace." Manuscript in hands of the author and Lincoln County Historical Association.

Eickemeyer, Rachel K. "The Descendants of Pinkney and Harriet Mauney of Lincoln County, North Carolina." Provided to the author by Ms. Eickemeyer

Penegar, Lucy. "Woman of the House." Booklet provided to the author.

Ramsey, Marshall, Jr. Cornwell Typescript, copy given to the author.

Young, Rudolph. "African American History at the Bend of the River Catawba." Undated, unpaginated typescript in possession of the author, printed by Trans-Catawba African American Genealogical and Historical Association.

_____. "Iron Station Roots of an African American Community in Lincoln County, North Carolina." Typescript in hands of the author.

_____. "Revels." In "African American History at the Bend of the River." Typescript in author's possession.

Index

Aaron 215–216, 224
Abba/Abby 239, 241
Abe 198, 205, 238, 243, 245–246, 253, 255–256
Abernathy, Ann 222, 270
Abernathy, A.W. 154
Abernathy, Barbara 222, 270
Abernathy, Bettie 222, 270
Abernathy, C.M. 275
Abernathy, Coleman H. 116, 157, 210, 263
Abernathy, C.W. 250, 275
Abernathy, D.M. 222, 270
Abernathy, Franklin 275
Abernathy, G., & Co 250
Abernathy, George 275
Abernathy, Green 92
Abernathy, James A. 142, 221, 270
Abernathy, J.M.W. 125, 275
Abernathy, John P. 222, 270
Abernathy, M. 250, 275
Abernathy, M. Luther 221, 270
Abernathy, M.C. 275
Abernathy, Miles L. 222, 270
Abernathy, Milton S. 222, 270
Abernathy, R.H. 131, 137
Abernathy, ?St. G. 266
Abernathy, Starling 209, 261
Abernathy, Starling G. 228
Abernathy, Wm. M. 270
Able 239
Abram/Abraham 219, 228, 231, 237, 256
Adai 230
Adam 199, 208, 217–218, 227, 249, 253
Adams, Frances 64
Adams, Jennie 96
Adams, Jno. H. 199, 259
Adams, Marg. 199, 228, 259, 266
Adams, Saml. D. 228, 266
Adams, Wm. 137, 245, 273
Adeline 100, 197–198, 202, 205–206, 211–212, 221, 227, 230–231, 236, 239–240, 242–244, 251–252, 254–255
Adelphia/Addelph 218, 181
Aderholdt David 196, 234, 257, 268
Aderholdt, Eml 234, 268
Aderholdt, M. 196, 257
Aderholdt, M.L. 257
Aderholdt, Noah 234, 268

Adolph 236
Aggy 211–212
Alberry 251
Albert/us 205, 208, 218, 225–226, 229, 237, 244, 247, 250, 252, 256
Albertine 208
Aleann 230
Alex/Alexander 197, 200, 202, 225
Alexander, A.T. 154
Alexander, James T. 172
Alexander, J.L. 270
Alexander, J.P. 12
Alexander, Nancy 250, 275
Alexander, R. 255
Alexander, S.E. 154
Alexander, W.H. 137
Alfred 202, 205, 214, 223, 225, 230, 243, 245, 249, 252, 256
Alice/Alace 206, 209, 212–213, 216, 221–222, 224–225, 231, 233, 238, 242, 252–254
Alicia 231
A?lint 253
Allen 215–216, 230, 235
Allen, ?Na L. 263
Allen, Vincent 263
Alse? (Alex) 202
Alsey 229
Aly 198
Amanda 203, 209, 211, 213, 220–221, 224–225, 237–238, 247, 250–251, 253–254
Ambrose 212
Amma 230
Ammon 39
Amos 206, 217, 244, 253, 256
Amy 220, 226, 250
Amzi 203, 207, 209, 224, 241, 249, 253
Ancell 242
Anders, E.M. 210, 263
Anderson 200–201, 230, 248, 254
Anderson, Rev. Monroe 97
Andrew 199
Andrews, Mr. 68
Andy 198, 203, 208, 211–212, 218, 225, 239–243, 247–248, 251, 255
Angeline 218, 254
Anise? 211
Ann/a 198–199, 201–203, 205–207, 209, 211–212, 215, 217, 219–226, 228, 230–231, 234, 236–237, 239, 241, 243–245, 249, 251–255

Anthony 199, 209, 241, 249
Anthony, E. 197, 257
Anthony, J.C. 199, 162, 259
Anthony, John P. 132
Arents, Jane 265
Arents, Jonas 214
Armstrong, Arther 237, 271
Armstrong, Elisabeth 237, 271
Armstrong, Jno. L. 237
Armstrong, John 237, 240, 245, 263, 271, 273
Armstrong, Mathew, Jr. 210, 237, 263, 271
Armstrong, M.R. 222, 270
Arrowood, B.F. 228, 266
Arrowood, Marg. 228, 266
Arrowood, William 139, 228, 266
Arther/Arter 216, 218, 233, 249
Ashley 215
Augustus 218, 226, 241
Austin 216, 227, 250
Avaline 252
Aydlotte, R.K. 265
Aydlotte, Susan 214, 265

Baby 251, 253, 256
Baily? 237
Baird, Jas. C. 245
Baird, Robt. 245
Baird, S.F.D. 245
Baker, Allen 235, 268
Baker, Andrew 38
Baker, Edward 28, 235, 268
Baker, Eli 234, 268
Ballard, Mr. 182
Barbara 197, 205, 218, 236
Barber, Barbara 197, 257
Barnet, A.F. 275
Barnet, William R. 61
Barnett, Thomas R. 90
Barnett, Thomas W. 119
Barnhill, James 257
Barnhill, Mary 197, 257
Barrett, Elisha S. 139, 154, 204, 261
Barrett, Maggie 99
Barringer, D.M. 148
Barron, B.B. 36–38, 173, 214, 221, 265
Bart 237
Bartlett 227

313

Bat 214
Batey 212
Baxter, Peter Z. 18, 40, 77, 136
Beam, Ann 197, 257
Beam, D.F. 136
Beam, Col. J. 50, 210, 261
Beam, J.F. & D. 197, 257
Beam, Jno. T. 197, 257
Beam, John F. 257
Beam, Mary 257
Beam, Michael 197, 257
Beam, Peter 235, 268
Beard, Emily 273
Beard, Jas. C. 273
Beard, Robt. 273
Beard, S.F.D. 273
Beattie, Franas/Francis 51, 200, 210, 259
Beattie, Jas. O. 200, 259
Beattie, John W. 237, 271
Beattie, Jonathan 237, 271
Beattie, Rufus J. 214, 237, 271
Beattie, Saml. 237, 271
Beattie, Smith 237, 271
Beattie, Wm. 200, 245, 259, 271, 273
Beaty, Robert 10, 30, 237, 271
Beauregard 213
Becca 217
Bell, Cephas 74
Bell, Eli 200, 259
Bell, John 148–149, 204, 261
Bell, Rachel R. 200, 259
Bell, Robert H. 200, 259
Benen 232
Ben/jamin 197, 200, 203, 206, 212, 215–217, 224, 231, 233–235, 243–246, 250–251
Bennette, M. 38
B?ent 254
Beny 203
Berry 212, 252
Berry, E. Milton 245, 273
Berry, E.M. 245
Berry, W.R. 238, 271
Best, A.J. 229, 266
Best, Michael 229, 266
Best, Saml. 229, 266
Bethphage Lutheran 97
Betsey/Bet/Betty 201, 204, 206, 215–218, 220, 223, 226–227, 233–234, 248, 251–252, 255
Beula 230
Bill/y 76, 131–132, 196, 199, 201–202, 205–206, 208, 214, 216, 220–222, 224, 226, 228, 232, 242, 249, 251–254, 256
Biney 235
Bissel/Bessel, Ed. H. 186, 222, 270
Black, Alfred 235, 257, 268
Black, Benaga 142, 197, 257
Black, Daniel 257
Black, E. Jun. 197, 257
Black, E. Senior/Widow 197, 257
Black, Eph. Sen. 196, 257
Black, Janie 197
Black, Jas. F. 222, 270
Black, Jas. L. 222, 270
Black, S. 257
Black, Saml. Jr. 197, 235, 257, 268
Black, Samuel/Sen./Esqr. 12, 197, 204, 229, 235, 257

Black, Thomas 197, 257
Black, Vincent 214, 265
Blackwood, Ann 200, 259
Blackwood, Elis 266
Blackwood, Gideon 266
Blackwood, Jane 200, 259
Blackwood, Joseph 200, 259
Blackwood, Marg. 266
Blackwood, Mary 266
Blackwood, Nancy 200, 259
Blair 252
Blakely, Thomas F. 139, 257
Blount, Thomas 37
Bluford, Wm. 250, 275
Bob 199, 205–206, 216, 222–223, 225, 228, 230, 232–233, 239, 243, 246, 250–251
Boger, Sarah 180
Boggs, Jas. G./Jos. G. 229, 266
Bolinger, D.W. 268
Bolivar 208
Bonapart 240
Boo 207
Boon 216
Booth, John Wilkes 87
Borders, Jacob 113
Bordley, Thomas 31, 50
Boss 197
Bost, Jonas 174–175, 178, 184
Bost, Joseph 41
Bost, W.L. 174–179, 182–184
Boy 217, 255
Boyce, E.E. 28, 200, 259
Boyd, And 261
Boyd, P.L. 73, 135
Boyd, Robert 28, 200, 259
Brad 228
Bradley 256
Bradley, Albert 139, 238, 263, 271
Bradley, Alexander 130
Bradley, A.S. 210, 263
Bradley, B.G. 63
Bradley, ?Cailon 263
Bradley, Caleb 210, 263
Bradley, Eli 139, 210, 263
Bradley, Elis. 50, 210
Bradley, Jas. D. 263
Bradley, J.W. 116, 157, 210, 263
Bradley, Miss Margia 100
Bradshaw, Pride 135
Bragg, Gov. 148
Brandon, Rachel 238, 271
Brandon, Thomas R. 139
Brandon, Thos. L. 245, 273
Breckenridge, John C. 22, 147–149, 153
?Bretis 214
Brevard, Robert A. 17, 53, 94, 250, 275
Brevard Station 11, 116, 125, 186, 195
Bridgers/Bridges, J.L. 36–38, 41, 216, 265
Bridgers/Bridges, R.R. 36–38, 41, 160, 215, 265
Briggs, Benjamin F. 11, 31, 35, 39–42, 183, 194
Briney 231
Brinkley, Wm. 275
Brison, G.R. 245, 273
Brison, Jane A. 245, 273
Brison, Wm. 245, 273

Broadaway, Wm. 181, 222, 270
Broadfoot 104
Brooks, Jerry 185
Brooks, Leroy 185
Brooks, Sarah 186
Broomhed, J. 137
Brown, Bedford 148
Brown, Christina 60, 81
Brown, D.B. 93
Brown, Elisabeth 245, 273
Brown, James 197, 257
Brown, J.J. 52, 54–55, 60, 68, 78, 81, 85, 89, 100, 102
Brown, J.L. 204
Brown, Margaret 62
Brown, Mary 197
Brown, R.H. 197, 258
Brown, W.B. 56
Brown, William 126
Browning, James 135
Bruce 238, 240
Bryant, Magga 95
Bryant, Mrs. 129
Burke, Monroe 222, 270
Burt 208, 253
Burton, Frank 104
Buster 221
Bynum, Albert A. 124
Bynum, John 92
Bynum, Martha 214, 265
Bynum, Rufus 116
Bynum, Victoria E. 181
Bynum, William P. 19, 36, 62, 99, 131–133, 138, 159, 164
Byrd, O.P. 123
Bytha 231, 237

Cab or Cub 214
Caharine 206
Caid? 248
Cain 208
Caldwell, Joshua 271
Caldwell, Sam C. 238, 271
Caleb 200, 205
Call 223
Calvin 198, 201–202, 216, 228
Camilla 242
Can 236
Candace 208, 245, 253
Cannon, David E. 223, 270
Cannon, E. 197
Cannon, J.A. 250, 275
Cannon, J.F. 250, 275
Cannon, William 197
Cannon, William S. 139, 223, 270
Cannon, Wm. F. 223, 270
Cansada 206
Cansler, Henry 9, 131, 150
Cansler, Jacob 78
Cansler, Peter 222, 270
Cansler, Richard T. 10, 222, 270
Capps, T.B. 263
Caroline 198, 200, 202, 206–207, 212, 215, 217, 219–220, 225–226, 230–231, 234, 238–241, 247, 252–254, 256
Carpenter, Abel 235, 269
Carpenter, Absolom 269
Carpenter, A.G. 235, 268
Carpenter, Alfred 235, 268
Carpenter, Andrew 170, 223, 270

Carpenter, Ann 235, 269
Carpenter, Benjamin 269
Carpenter, B.M. 197, 235, 258, 268
Carpenter, Caleb 269
Carpenter, Daniel 117, 170, 235, 269
Carpenter, Emanuel 235, 269
Carpenter, Frederick 146, 170, 235, 268-269
Carpenter, Frederick, Jr. 235, 268
Carpenter, George 235, 269
Carpenter, Henry 235, 269
Carpenter, Jacob 83, 117
Carpenter, Jacob Mauney 117
Carpenter, James 28, 197, 258
Carpenter, J.L. 235
Carpenter, John 235
Carpenter, Joseph 129, 132-134, 181, 235, 269
Carpenter, Joshua 197, 258
Carpenter, Lawson 60
Carpenter, L.B. 229, 266
Carpenter, Marcus 235, 269
Carpenter, Marquis L. 139
Carpenter, Nancy 133
Carpenter, Peter Hoke 117
Carpenter, P.W. 60
Carpenter, Saml. 235, 268
Carpenter, Wm. 197, 235, 258, 268-269
Carroll, Elisabeth 259
Carroll, Margaret 259
Carroll, Mary 200
Carroll, Sarah 259
Carroll, W.D. 200, 259
Carry 201, 220
Carson, Isabella 201, 259
Carson, James 53, 259
Carson, Jas. M. 201
Carson, Jos?/Jas. W. 200, 259
Carson, Martha A. 201
Carson, Rachel J. 201
Carson, Robt. 200, 259
Carson, R.W. 162
Carson, Rufus 53, 57, 74
Carson, T.O.C. 259
Carter, Ran 78
Caser/Ceaser 212, 244
Casiner, J.W. 18
Cass or Cap 208
Catawba County 7, 9, 13, 17, 35, 41, 111, 139, 144-145, 153, 156, 158, 163, 165, 174
Cate 206
Catharine 200, 227, 237, 247, 250-251, 253
Cathey, Francis 235, 269
Caty 197
Cauble, Ephraim 16
Celia 238, 256
Cephas/Cephe/Cephaus 202, 206-207, 211, 218, 220, 222-223, 256
Cern 224
Certen 231
Chambers 248
Chambers, Mansfield 35, 186
Chancellorsville, Battle of 70, 81, 117, 133
Chapman, J.H. 38
Charinsa? 216
Charity/Charty 216, 243
Charles/Charley 172, 200, 203-206, 209, 211, 216, 218-219, 222, 224, 226-227, 229, 233, 238, 240, 242, 247-248, 254
Charlotte 7, 12, 19, 21-22, 48, 59, 75, 95, 106-107, 112, 122-123, 129-130, 134-135, 148, 150, 154-155, 159, 203-204, 206, 213, 217, 223, 236, 241, 249
Chaudins 226
Cherry 224, 231
Cherry, John 210, 263
Cherryville 21, 52, 62, 82, 114, 158, 162, 195
Chestnut, Mary 19
Chila 205, 247
Child 220, 233-234, 245, 255
Childs, Eben 63
Childs, L.D. 18-19, 42, 63, 108
Chloe 245
Choat, A.D. 245, 273
Chole 209, 215
Christman, S.R. 46
Christy 203
Cicero 217
Cinda 199-200, 203, 245, 247, 250, 252-253
Clanton, Isaac 223, 270
Clanton, Lawson 223, 270
Clara 212, 217, 225, 235, 239
Clark, Adam 229, 266
Clark, Dorcas 185
Clark, Eliza 185
Clark, J.W. 229, 266
Clark, R.F. 245, 273
Clark, Wm. 28, 229, 266
Clarke/Clarky 212, 227
Clarrisa 215
Clay 197, 222, 224
Clem 205, 218
Clem, Sarah 185-186
Clementine 198
Clemmer, A. 250
Clemmer, Adam 205, 261
Clemmer, Andrew 42, 275
Clemmer, Arabella 205, 261
Clemmer, George 34, 50, 205, 210, 261
Clemmer, J.L./L.J. 229, 245, 273
Clemmer, John 42, 210, 250, 263, 275
Clemmer, Jonas 250, 275
Clemmer, Levi 204, 261
Clemmer, Lewis 31, 34, 50
Clemmer, L.L. 204
Clemmer, S.J. 266
Clemmer, S.S. 261
Clemmer, Valentine 42
Cleveland County 7, 9, 13, 16, 35, 53, 59, 61-62, 99, 102, 107, 109, 111-113, 117, 122, 126, 129, 135-136, 138-139, 145, 149-151, 153, 156, 158, 163, 165, 194
Clim 220
Clinton, Martha 245, 273
Cloah/Cloa 206, 233
Cloda 244
Cloninger, Adam 9
Cloninger, Dan/David R. 223, 270
Cloninger, David 204, 261
Cloninger, Elis R. 217, 265
Cloninger, Fanny 217, 265
Cloninger, Frances 75
Cloninger, Jacob 141
Cloninger, Jonas 139, 204, 261, 265
Cloninger, Michael/Mike 116, 217, 265
Cloninger, Moses 217, 265
Cloninger, Wm. 223, 270
Cob, J.A. 172
Cob, J.A. 172
Cobb, M.D. 201, 259
Cody, William 132-134
Coleman 225
Collins, J.M. 197, 257
Collins, Jno. 257
Columbus 204, 234
Combest, Sarah J. 245, 273
Combest, Wm. 245, 273
Comfort 212
Conley, Anna/Ada 93, 96
Connell, David 222, 270
Connell, James 222, 270
Connell, Martha 223, 270
Connell, Mary E. 223, 270
Connell, Robt. 270
Connelly, Mr. 63
Conner, E. 258
Conner, William 86, 258
Conscription 13-14, 46, 112-114, 116-117, 119-120, 122-123, 125-126, 134, 137, 139, 141, 158
Constantine 239
Cook, Demsey 245, 273
Cooly 226
Coon, Adolphus S. 52-55, 70-71
Coon, David 52-55, 69-71, 85, 87, 90
Coon, Henry 69
Cooper 228
Cooper, Emily 186
Cornelia 226, 228
Cornelius 216
Cornwell, John Jacob 126-127
Costar/Costner, Jacob B. 126
Costner, A. 261
Costner, Aaron 17
Costner, Amanda 269
Costner, Ambrose 89, 99, 103, 134, 138, 150, 164-165, 171, 204
Costner, C. 209
Costner, E. 261
Costner, Henry 104, 204
Costner, Jacob/J. 31, 103, 172, 204, 261
Costner, Joe/Joseph 204, 261, 263
Costner, J.P. 205
Costner, Louisa 98
Costner, Manda 235
Costner, M.H. 261
Costner, Randall 76, 166-167, 172
Costner, S.P. 261
Costner, Valentine 204, 261
Costner, Zimri 17, 124
Cotton factory 18, 42-49, 106-107
Coulter, John 150
Cox, Eli H. 210, 263
Cox, Jno. 270
Cox, Patrick 223, 270
Cox, Thos. 263
Craft, Jno. P. 197, 258
Craft, M.J. 28, 197, 258
Craig, Alex 135

Craig, A.S. 135
Craig, J.M. 273
Craig, John H. 245, 273
Craig, R.H. 245, 273
Craig, R.J. 273
Craig, S.W. 10, 238, 271
Craig, Thos. N. 245, 273
Craig, William 245, 273
Craig and Co. 271
Craig and Henderson 271
Crawford, Jas./Jas. L. 200, 259
Crawford, John O. 200, 259
Crawford, M.A. 259
Crawford, Rachel J. 259
Crawford, Wm. N. 200, 259
Cricy 227
Crites/Critz, H.J. 198, 258
Crittendon, J.J. 152
?Critty 207
Cross, Tabitha 209, 261
Crouse, D./David 28, 197, 235, 258, 269
Crouse, Rufus 235, 268
Crow, Festus 186
Cudjo 255
Cylva 212
Cynthia 254
Cyrus 204, 207, 237, 241

Daffie 252
Dallas 1, 9–10, 19–23, 30–35, 41, 48–51, 67, 75, 83, 92, 95, 97, 99, 103, 109–110, 113–116, 121, 126, 129–130, 133, 137, 139, 141, 144–145, 148, 150, 160–162, 169–170, 172, 185–186, 195, 213, 243, 250
Dalton, Jane 13
Dameron, George 28, 229, 266
Dameron, John 238, 271
Daniel/Dan 200, 214–217, 223–225, 227–228, 235–236
Danse 215
Dare 203
Darky 245
Dave 171–172, 197, 200, 228, 241–242
Davenport, A.W. 8, 27, 30, 117, 146, 154, 156, 251, 275
Davenport, Wm. 251, 275
David 212, 216, 236, 242, 253–254
Davidson, J.S. 250
Davis 249
Davis, Jefferson 22, 124, 141, 156–158, 164
Davis, John W. 28, 210, 263
Davis, Margaret 62
Davis, Mary J. 260
Davis, O.W. 210
Davis, Robert 125
Davis, Thomas Allen 52, 57, 61–62, 78, 82, 85, 87, 90, 98–100, 112, 124
Davison, J.S. 27, 275
Deb 245–246
Deck, Jonas 209, 261
Deck, Peter 229, 266
Delia 226, 231
Delila 238
Della 230
Dellinger, A. 198
Dellinger, Alfred 217, 258, 263, 265
Dellinger, Alj. 51, 210
Dellinger, Asalger? 92

Dellinger, C. 198, 258
Dellinger, Daniel Haynes 52, 56, 60, 73–74, 77, 79–80, 85, 89, 97, 100, 114, 189
Dellinger, F. Wash 62, 67, 69, 82, 87
Dellinger, Frances 80, 97, 100
Dellinger, Frederick Lineberger 52, 54–56, 62, 82, 85
Dellinger, George 73, 80, 97, 198, 258
Dellinger, H. 39
Dellinger, Henry K. 73, 82
Dellinger, Jacob 53–55, 62, 69, 85
Dellinger, J.F. 87
Dellinger, J.R. 86
Dellinger, Michael 258
Dellinger, Minnie Cobb 87
Dellinger, M.L. 92
Dellinger, Noah 89
Dellinger, P. Frank 56, 60, 66, 74, 79–80, 86–87
Dellinger, Peter 62, 85, 198, 258
Dellinger, Polly 198, 258
Dellinger, S. 198, 258
Delphia/Delph/Delphina 204, 207, 218, 227, 231
Dennis 220
Derr, A.J. 180, 223, 270
Derr, Frances 180
Derr, Jane 180
Derr, John H. 223, 270
Derr, Jonas W. 41, 180
Derr, Valentine 154, 223, 270
Desertion 2, 14–15, 53, 62, 93, 106–128, 133–138, 140–144
Detter, Andrew 245, 273
Dial, M.C. 38
Dicey/Dice 199, 220, 229
Dick 212, 214–215, 220, 224, 227, 230, 241, 244, 250, 255
Dick, R.B. 164
Dickson, Alex 210, 229, 263
Dickson, Jno. T. 210, 263
Dickson, W.S. 210, 263
Dicky, Elick 134, 266
Dicky, Jas. 259, 266
Dicky/Dickey, And. J. 201, 259
Dilcey/Dilsey 208, 212, 214
Dilsa 240
Dinah 202, 215, 237, 239, 241, 244, 251
Dine 202
Dingo 253
Dixon, A.C./A.S. 245, 273
Dixon, E. 151
Dixon, John 137
Diza 227
Doctor 233
Doll 222–223, 253
Dolly 218
Dolph 254
Dorcus 218, 238, 242
Dorsey 231
Dos 256
Douglas, Stephan A. 148–149
Draft *see* Conscription
Draper 221
Drucilla 251
Dudley 220, 222
Du?ffy 204
Dunn, Wm. 251, 275

Durett? 242
Durham, C.C. 150

Eaker, C. 198, 258
Eaker, Catharine 229, 266
Eaker, Christian 10, 30, 235, 269
Eaker, D. 126
Eaker, David 28, 198, 258
Eaker, Fanny C. 258
Eaker, Hiram 229, 266
Eaker, Jacob 235, 269
Eaker, Jesse 126, 235, 269
Eaker, M./Mary 235, 269
Eaker, Peter 258
Eaker, S.C. 198
Easter 219–220, 230, 253
Eddleman, David 60, 171–172, 224, 270
Eddleman, Dicey 224, 270
Eddleman, W.P. 227
Edgecombe County 15, 36–37, 39–41, 160, 167–168, 183
Edith 231
Edmond 220, 222, 225
Edney 200
Edow 218
Edward/Edd 217, 220, 239–240
Edwards, Lewis 224, 270
Edwards, Thomas H. 11
Edwards, Wm. 30, 224, 270
Edwin 197
Edy 214
Eickemeyer, Rachel K. 180
Elam/Elan 237, 250
Elenr 224
Eli/Elias 199, 202, 211, 218, 225, 233
Elick 240
Elick 252
Elie 228
Elijah 220
Elisabeth 207, 212–213, 222, 230, 246, 250, 256
Elite 23–29, 52, 144–146
Elitha 218
Eliza 209, 212–213, 216–217, 219–220, 225, 237–238, 240, 242, 243, 245, 254, 256
Ellen 227, 229, 232, 234, 248
Ellice 214
Ellis 216
Ellis, Governor 147, 150, 153
Ellison 39
Ells 240
Elmina 205–206, 218, 224, 235–236, 239–240, 249
Elvey/Elvy 216, 219, 223
Elvira J. 201, 206, 226, 241
Elzy 207
Em 236
Emancipation Proclamation 72, 89, 130, 178
Emauel 219
Emeline 204, 208, 213, 215, 225, 227, 240, 256
Emily 216, 231, 254
Emma 208, 223, 235, 241, 252
?Engal 231
Enloe, Abraham 17
Ensly, Wm. 199
Ephraim/Eph. 197, 212, 217, 226, 237, 242, 248, 253–255, 256

Esau 242
Escott, Paul D. 23–25, 101, 114, 144
Esther 209, 215, 225, 234, 237, 240, 244, 248
Etta 240
Eurre? 220
Evaline 229, 250, 254
Evans, Edwd./E. 235, 257, 269
Evans, M. 197
Ewing, Hugh F. 238, 271
Ewing, Hugh Sen. 238, 271
Ewing, Samuel L. 108, 238, 271
Ewing, S.R. 251, 275
Ezekiel 211–212
Ezra 201, 204

Faires, Elias M. 11, 246, 273
Faires/Farris, R.B.W. 198, 258
Falls 233
Falls, A.J. 245, 273
Falls, Isabella 260
Falls, John R. 260
Falls, M.R. 273
Falls, Ola 201
Falls, R. 87
Falls, Rebecca 201, 260
Falls, Robert A. 139, 201, 260, 267
Falls, Sarah 245, 273
Falls, Sarah L. 245, 273
Falls, William 151, 201, 260
Fan 204, 237
Fanny 198, 209, 211, 214–215, 217, 221, 228–230, 231–233, 246, 250, 255
Farrar, John 224, 270
Farrar, Margaret , 224, 270
Farrar, Nath. P. 224, 270
Farres?/Farries, S. 198, 258
Farrier 197
Farrow, John 139
Fayette 221, 226
Featherstin, C.A. 246, 273
Featherston, J.B. 205, 261
Fed 202, 217, 245
Female 221
?Fenton 215
Ferguson, Elis J. 201, 260
Ferguson, James Sen. 201, 230, 260
Ferguson, James/James, Jr. 10, 201, 230, 260, 267
Ferguson, Milton 201, 260
Ferguson, Ola 201
Ferguson, Thomas J. 10, 267
Ferguson, Thos. Sen. 201, 260
Ferguson, Thos. W. 201, 260
Ferguson, William M. 150, 201, 230, 267
Fewell, Jas. S. 246, 273
Fewell, John J. 246, 273
Fields 215
Finger, D. 263
Finger, John 126
Finley, Jane 238, 271
Finley, Robt. M./Robt. W. 238, 271
Finley, S.S. 238, 271
Finley, W.G. 238, 271
?Fisher 215
Fite (or Tite) 200, 203, 204–205
Fite, B.H. 271
Fite, G.S. 251, 275
Fite, Henry 251, 276

Fite, J.W./W.J. 209, 251, 261, 276
Fite, Solomon 238, 271
Fleet 253
?Flora 246
Flora 203
Florence 207
?Flory 206
Flowers, Green 205, 261
Floyd, H.H. 28, 210, 263
Floyd, J.L. 246
Floyd, John 210, 263
Floyd, Leroy 263
Floyd, S.W. 263
Forbes, John H. 201, 260
Ford, Alex 263
Ford, Amzi 30, 33, 50, 205, 246, 261
Ford, Frederick 263
Ford, Hiram 230, 267
Ford, Isom 246, 273
Ford, Jas. H. 210
Ford, Jas. M. 210, 263
Ford, John 263
Ford, Dr. J.W. 260
Ford, Mary Ann 246, 273
Ford, Wm. 246, 273
Fosit, Mr. 68
Fox, Rev. A.J. 97
Foy, James 260
Fraley, Stephen 205, 261
France 219
Frances 205–206, 218, 226, 231, 235–236, 245, 248
Frank 131–132, 198–199, 202, 215–217, 221–223, 225, 227, 233–235, 237, 239, 242–243, 251
Frankey 225–226, 256
Franklin 211
Free blacks 23–29, 139, 141, 165–168, 180, 184–188
French 218
French, Geo. J. 21
Friday, Charlie 172
Friday, David 205, 261
Friday, Elisabeth 205, 217, 261, 265
Friday, Ephraim 10, 26, 30, 217, 246, 265
Friday, Harriet 172
Friday, J. 261
Friday, Jacob W. 217, 265
Friday, John 205
Friday, John N. 26, 50, 205, 210, 265
Friday, Jonas W. 265
Friday, Marion D. 139, 141, 205, 261
Friday, Michael 217, 265
Friday, Polly 217, 265
Frone 209
Froneberger, Ambrose 205, 261
Froneberger, C.A. 69
Froneberger, D. 16, 234
Froneberger, Danl. 130
Froneberger, Elis 229, 267
Froneberger, Jacob 10, 12, 14, 20, 22, 28, 33, 45, 50–51, 75, 97, 99, 101, 104, 109–111, 114, 126, 133, 139, 162, 205–206, 210, 229, 261, 267, 280
Froneberger, Jane 267
Froneberger, John, Jr. 229, 266
Froneberger, John, Senr. 229, 266
Froneberger, Lewis 104, 260

Froneberger, Marg. 229, 266
Froneberger, Paul 9–10, 32–33, 51, 130, 147, 210, 262
Froneberger, Rufus 104
Fry, Joseph 41
Fulenwider, Col. H. 176
Fulenwider, H.W. 123
Fulenwider, John 35
Fulenwider, Robert 56, 64
Fulton, James 52, 73, 90, 100, 267
Fulton, J.B. 230, 258
Fulton, J.W. 258
Fulton, Rachel 73, 100

Gaither, B.S. 61
Gamble, A.J. 260
Gamble, Andrew Jackson 176
Gamble, Ann 176
Gamble, John 176
Gamble, Joseph 230, 267
Gamble, Robt. F. 260
Gant, A.J. 230, 267
Gantt, Mary 209, 261
Gardner, Andred 235, 269
Garrento/Garnto/Gurentto, Nath. T. 126
Garrett, Charles W. 40
Garrett, E.W. 267
Garrett, Francis M. 40–41
Garrett, Isaac W. 40
Garrett, J.J. 41
Garrett, Joseph C. 40
Garrett, Richard H. 40, 267
Garrett Brothers 39–42, 169, 183, 194, 230, 267
Garwood, Alonzo 23
Gaston, Adeline 210, 263
Gaston, Jas. A. 267
Gaston, John 263
Gaston, Larkin B. 10, 276
Gaston, Pink 210, 263, 272
Gaston, Rachel 210, 263
Gaston, Robt. 246, 251, 276
Gaston, Sarah 210, 263
Gaston County Courthouse 9, 30–31, 132–133, 148–149
Gay, T.D. 38
Genl? 231, 255
Gentry see Elite
George 176, 199–200, 202–203, 206, 208–209, 212, 215–218, 220, 222, 224, 226–229, 231–234, 237–238, 240–244, 246–249, 251–252, 254–256
Georgiana 228
German 8–9
Gettysburg, Battle of 70–72, 81, 159, 162
Gev 202
Gilbert 202, 249, 252
Giles 200, 212, 233, 241
Gill 208
Gillam, Alvin 20
Gilly 204
Gingles, Charlotte 246, 274
Gingles, Dorcus 246, 274
Gingles, Mrs. M./Mary 100–101, 211, 264
Gingles, Marg. 238, 271
Gingles, Ruth 246, 274
Ginney 206

Girl 223
Gladden Jno. J. 206, 261
Glascock, F.S./S.S. 198, 258
Glenn, E.B. 246
Glenn, E.M. 273
Glenn, John F. 32, 246, 273
Glenn, Mary L. 246, 274
Glenn, Robt. 238, 271
Glenn, W.D. 19, 21–23, 61, 95, 110, 114, 133, 137, 164, 261
?Glosea 231
Go 227
Goble, Absalom 246, 274
Goode, Dr. B.F. 80, 113, 136
Goodman 67
Goodson, J.F. 62
Gordon, John 210, 264
Grace/Gracy 202–204, 214, 226, 231, 237
?Gragel 219
Grand 217
Granny 243
Grant, General Ulysses 88, 164
Granville 213, 237
Gray, Mary 44
Gray, Minnie 94, 96, 99, 162
Green 208, 211, 216, 223, 226, 238–239, 241, 243, 246, 250–251, 253
Green, Cicero 38
Gregory, S.B. 218, 265
Grief or Gruf 217, 220, 224
Grier 215
Grier, Ann 251, 276
Grier, Thomas 36, 246, 274
Grigg, J. 82
Grissom, J.F. 264
Grisson 211
Groner, Austin 32–33, 50, 116, 137, 209, 261
Groner, H.L. 238, 271
Groot, Philip 36–37
Gudger, Sarah 174–179, 183–184
Gullick, J.N. 239, 272
Gullick, Milton 27, 183, 238, 271
Gus 222
Gustus 205

Hager 267
Hager, George 231, 267
Hager, James 92
Hager, John 231, 267
Hager, Thomas 92
Hager, Wm. 232, 267
Hagia? 231
Hainey, Timothy 129
Haley 199, 203, 248
Hall 247
Hall, Jas. D. 240, 272
Hall, Solomon 178
Hallman, Ambrose 258
Hallman, Jacob/Jack 198, 258
Hammel, Alex 239
Hammel, Alex 272
Hammerskold, C.J. 14, 131
Hamp 249
Hand, A.J. 276
Hand, Jack 251
Hand, James Rufus 139, 239, 272
Hand, Jane 240, 272
Hand, M.L. 272
Hand, Moses H. 27, 46–48, 133, 139–142, 146, 150, 187, 239–240, 272
Hand, R.J. 32
Hand, Uriah 211, 264
Handsell, Jno. P. 225, 270
Handsell, Wm. 270
Hanks, E. 251, 276
Hanks, G.W. 239, 272
Hanks, Wm. 239, 272
Hanna, Caroline 63, 78, 85, 102, 113, 120–121
Hanna, Franklin S. 5, 29, 52, 57–58, 62–63, 78, 82, 85–86, 88–89, 102, 119–122, 264
Hanna, James M. 10, 62, 116, 121, 146, 151, 157, 211, 264
Hanna, Jas. H. 264
Hanna, M.E. 62
Hanna, S.B. 211, 264
Hanna, Thomas M. 28, 211, 264
Hannah 200–201, 205, 215, 217, 224–226, 229–231, 236, 238–239, 241, 243, 246–249, 251–253, 256
Hany 203
Hardy 230
Hardy, Michael C. 49
Harrelson, J.F. 198, 258
Harrelson, W.O. 17, 113, 117, 140, 162, 198, 258
Harrelson, Wm. 198, 258
Harretta 215
Harriet 100, 171–173, 197–204, 208, 211, 218, 221–224, 227, 233–234, 239–241, 243–246, 248–256
Harris 217
Harris, Adolphus P. 31
Harris, Robert 113
Harrison 215
Harrison, John 240, 272
Harry 200, 219–220, 223, 230, 232, 245–246
Hart, Isabella 225, 270
Hartwell 222
Harvey 256
Harvey, J.N. 29, 258
Hasley 215
Havener, Jac 269
Haynes, William W. 79
Hays, ?Mary? 260
Hays, Wm. L. 260
Haywood 231
Heafner, Jacob 55
Heath, Robert R. 111, 131, 136
Helen 226
Helton, Milton 211, 264
Hemings, Sally 179
Hemphill, William 175
Henderson 226
Henderson, A.L. 140, 142, 272
Henderson, Andrew R. 12, 139, 173, 224, 270
Henderson, C.C. 142, 150
Henderson, Jas. A. 224, 270
Henderson, Jonathan 274
Henderson, W.A. 246, 274
Henderson, Wm. 260
Henkel, Rev. P.C. 67–68
Henkle, Hannah 225, 270
Henkle, Osborne 224, 270
Henny 242
Henrietta 240
Henry 202, 208, 212, 214–216, 218–220, 223–228, 234, 236, 241, 243–244, 246, 250, 255
Henry, Robt. 239, 272
?Henry, Thos. 260
Henry, Wallace 247, 274
Herbert 215, 224
Herdman, Rosana 246, 274
Herman 253
"Heroes of America" 138
Herron, John 231, 267
Hester, Abram 267
Hester, Candace 280
Hettie/Hetta 199, 244, 250
Hewet, Moses 41
Hida 209
High 225
High Shoals 18, 30–31, 35–42, 94, 133, 160, 167, 169–170, 173, 179, 183, 194, 218–219, 265
Hill 216
Hill, Alex M. 260
Hill, John F. 17
Hill, Sarah 246, 274
Hill, W.R. 246, 274
Hill, Z.S. 260
Hilliard/Hillyard 214, 244
Hillory 204
Hill's Chapel 96
Hines 216
Hines, Daniel 235, 269
Hines, George 123, 269
Hines, Henry 269
Hin?on 214
Hiram 172
Hisber? 216
Hislop, G.W. 272
Hister 203
Hobbs, Alfred 137
Hobbs, Susannah 137
Hoffman Hotel 10, 33, 108, 169
Hoffman, Caleb 251, 276
Hoffman, Daniel 32–33, 50–51, 108–109, 186, 206, 210, 247, 255, 261
Hoffman, David 207, 261
Hoffman, Fred 124
Hoffman, F.S. 262
Hoffman, Jacob 211, 264
Hoffman, J.H. 135
Hoffman, John 211, 264
Hoffman, Jonas 10, 43, 104, 118, 211, 264
Hoffman, Levi 247, 274
Hoffman, L.M. 118
Hoffman, Mary 276
Hoffman, May 251
Hoffman, Miles 211, 264
Hoffman, S.H. 116, 157
Hoffman, Solomon 211, 264
Hogan 241
Hoke, John 100
Hoke, John F. 9, 42, 63–64, 164
Hoke, General Robert F. 158
Hoke, W.J. 18, 154, 182
Hokeville 12, 16, 42, 138, 182, 195
Holbrook, Allison 138
Holbrook, Mahala 138
Holden, W.W. 47, 106, 112, 118, 126, 155–161, 163–165
Holland, E.B. 33, 206, 261

Holland, Frank 232, 261, 267
Holland, I. 8, 30
Holland, Jane 51, 275
Holland, Jas. M. 264
Holland, J.D. 172, 206, 261
Holland, Jesse 9, 30–31
Holland, J.Q. 247, 274
Holland, Julius 51, 206, 232, 267
Holland, L.M. 264
Holland, Mary 211, 247, 274
Holland, M.C. 206, 274
Holland, Mrs. M.C. 101
Holland, Melissa H/M. 246, 274
Holland, M.L. 52, 63, 84, 87, 211
Holland, M.M. 211
Holland, Miss N.J. 100, 274
Holland, Nancy J. 211, 246
Holland, Pris. R. 260
Holland, Mrs. R.F. 100
Holland, Robert 10, 206–207, 261–262
Holland, Sallie 225, 270
Holland, S.D. 34
Holland, W.F. 206, 261
Holland, Wm. M. 10, 50, 246, 264, 274–275
Holland, Wm. R. 211, 247, 260, 274
Holly 219
Home guard 12, 14, 47–48, 134–142
Homesley 198
Homesley, A.B. 13, 16, 136, 198, 258
Homesley, A.R. 40, 46, 172
Homesley, Esther H. 258
Hoover, Edney 72, 78–79, 85, 86, 90
Hoover, Jacob 251, 276
Hoover, John 251
Hoover, Mary C. 78
Hoover, Thomas 276
Hoovey, Aaron E. 36
Hope, Christy 137–138
Hope, James 18, 247, 274
Hope, Prudence 138
Hope, Thomas 138
Horace 228
Horsley, Resin? 246, 274
Horsley, Richard 246, 274
Houser, Abram 211, 264
Houser, Daniel 89
Houser, Em. 90
Houser, Isaac 13
Houser, John 60
Houston 219
Hovis, Absalom 206, 255, 261
Hovis, Adam 219, 265
Hovis, Francis 137
Hovis, George/George, Jr. 198, 258
Hovis, Jac. D. 232, 267
Hovis, Jacob 219, 265
Hovis, John 29, 265
Hovis, Mary 137
Hovis, Philip 219, 265
Howser, Thomas 56, 89
Hoyl 206
Hoyl, Andrew 8–10, 26, 30–31, 33, 51, 144
Hoyle, Caleb Wilfong 10, 26, 183, 206, 261
Hoyle, Eli 30
Hoyle, J. 198
Hoyle, J.M. 258
Hoyle, Jonas 87

Hoyle, Lemuel 5, 52–53, 56, 59–60, 65–67, 70–72, 81, 84, 86, 88–89, 107, 112, 127, 154, 159, 171–172, 191
Hoyle, M.D. 261
Hoyle & Co. 209
Hubbard 227
Huffstetler 77
Huffstetler, C.H. 267
Huffstetler, C.A. 246, 274
Huffstetler, H.B. 232, 267
Huffstetler, J.W. 246
Huffstetler, J.M. 274
Huffstetler, John 130, 170, 232, 267
Huffstetler, Walter 232, 267
Hull, G.W. 136
Hullet, Caleb 123
Humphrey 226, 241
Hunt, George 269
Hunter, C.L. 27, 252, 276
Hunter, Eliza 187
Hunter, Jane 187
Hunter, Lee 186–187
Hunter, Rush 187
Hunter, Sylvia 187
Huss, David 60
Huss, Henry 56, 89
Hutchison, C.L. 225, 270

Ida 224, 238, 254
Ike 206–207, 223
Infant 208, 212, 214, 216–220, 229, 232, 239, 242, 244
Inflation 106–111, 280
Inlow, Abraham 17
Ione 206
?Ireal 217
Iron and gold 35–42
Isaac 197, 200, 205, 214, 216, 219–220, 225, 227, 229, 231, 239–240, 243, 251, 254
Isabella/Isabel 211, 217, 222, 229, 240–242, 252–253, 256
Isam 214, 217, 228, 239, 256

Jack 197, 201, 214, 218, 220, 238, 243–244
Jackson, Thomas Jefferson "Stonewall" 18, 70
Jacob 202, 212–213, 231, 236–238, 243
Jake 196, 199, 207, 226, 229, 231–232, 245, 253, 255
James 208, 210–212, 218, 223–224, 227, 230, 233, 252
Jane/ie 171–172, 199–200, 205–206, 211–215, 217, 220, 222–223, 226–227, 230, 232–233, 236–240, 242–243, 245–247, 249, 251–252, 254–255
Jarrett, Samuel 12, 51, 157, 207, 210, 262
Jasper 219, 227, 237–240, 243
Jcheck 201
Jeff/rey 202, 206, 218, 234, 251
Jefferson 213
Jefferson, Thomas 179
Jemima 227
Jenkins, Aaron 116, 207, 262
Jenkins, Berryman 28, 207, 262
Jenkins, Catharine 207, 262
Jenkins, Dan R./Daniel 211, 264

Jenkins, David A. 116, 118, 138, 146, 152, 164, 247, 274
Jenkins, E./Eli 207, 262
Jenkins, H. 116, 157
Jenkins, Harrison 207, 262
Jenkins, J.C. 154
Jenkins, Jonas 211, 264
Jenkins, Joseph 207, 262
Jenkins, Saml. 225
Jenkins, Sarah 225, 271
Jenkins, Smith 76, 207, 262
Jenkins, Wm. 207, 262–263
Jenks, O.B. 142
Jenny 200, 208–209, 215, 222, 245, 248
Jerry 182, 215–226, 228, 249, 252, 254
Jess/e 199, 212, 219, 224, 235, 253, 256
Jilius 218
Jim/my 201, 203, 205–208, 216, 218, 220–221, 223–225, 228–230, 232, 235–236, 240–244, 247, 249–251, 254–255
Jimbo 226
Jink 225
Jinny/Jinna 100, 212, 224, 233, 239, 246–247
Joab 251
Joana 237
Joe 199, 201–202, 206–208, 211–212, 215–216, 218, 222–223, 225–226, 229–230, 240–241, 247, 251–255
John 202–204, 206–209, 211, 213–215, 218–219, 222, 226–231, 236, 239, 241–244, 249, 251–252, 256
Johnson, Amos 180
Johnson, President Andrew 165
Johnson, B.J. 131, 138
Johnston, Derr 180
Johnston, Dicey 232, 267
Johnston, James F. 225, 271
Johnston, Jenny 11
Johnston, Jno. R. 225, 270
Johnston, Marg. 247
Johnston, Martha 173, 256, 276
Johnston, Mary 173, 256, 274, 276
Johnston, Samuel C. 139, 252, 276
Johnston, S.H./Dr. S.X. 26, 146, 151–155, 173, 225, 270
Johnston, Susan 247, 274
Johnston, William 155, 274
Johnston, Wm. H. 10, 240, 272
Jonah 239
Jonas 243
Jonas, Free 185, 255
Jones, Wm. H. 38
Jordan 243
Joseph 212, 217, 221, 237, 244
Josiah 199
Joy, James 276
Jud/a 209, 253
Jude 247, 251
?Judy 216
Julia 212, 223, 233–235, 250
Julian 197, 221
Julius 239, 241, 246, 256
July 218, 226
Junea 216
Junius 223
Juno 224, 255

Kahnwieler, K. 207, 262
Kate 204–205, 207, 209, 229, 241, 251, 256
Keener 215
Keener, Cephas 72
Keener, David 72
Keener, Peter 72, 73
Keeve 201
Kelly, John 276
Kendrick, Ellen 247, 274
Kendrick, Jas. M. 274
Kendrick, Jas. W. 247, 274
Kendrick, J.L. 258
Kendrick, M.L. 247, 274
Kendrick, S.L. 198
Kenedy, K.J. 161-162, 267
Kennedy, J.R. 232
Kennedy, William L. 39, 173
Kensler (Cansler) 182
Kincaid, Jas. 151
Kincaid, J.R. 247, 274
King 247
King, Adolphus 180
King, Charley 180
King, Manirva 180
Kings Mountain Gold Mine 41, 169, 234, 268
Kirkland 240
Kiser, Barbara 234, 268
Kiser, Elisabeth 234, 268
Kiser, Fanny 232, 267
Kiser, George 232, 267
Kiser, Hiram 269
Kiser, J. 229
Kiser, Jacob 123, 232, 236, 267, 269
Kiser, James 234, 268
Kiser, Jane 234, 268
Kiser, John 237, 269
Kiser, Joseph 232, 267
Kiser, Levi 236, 269
Kiser, Margaret 234, 268
Kiser, Mary 267
Kiser, Mary M. 232, 267
Kiser, Noah 234, 268
Kiser, Philip 234–236, 268–269
Kiser, Susan 269
Kiser, Zimri 82, 232, 267
Kisiah/Kissy 236, 246
Kistler, Lawson 219, 265
Kit/ty 208, 228
Kizer or Kiza 226
Kruman, Marc 160

Laben/Labe 198, 206–207, 212, 236, 251
Laboratory 15–16, 138, 182, 195
Lackey 224
Lackey, James 198, 258
Ladies Relief Society 100–101
Lafayette 228
Lambert 250
Lancaster, John 29, 265
?Landa 241
Lander, Mr. 99
Lander, Samuel 112
Lander, William 41, 112, 152–154, 159–160
Landless whites 23–29, 116, 144, 171
Laney 220
Lany, Barbara 198
Lark/Larkin 239, 242, 248

Latta 210
Laura 203, 208, 212, 220–222, 226–228, 242, 253, 256
Lavinia 220
Lawing, George A. 276
Lawing, J.J. 31, 137
Lawrence 216, 252
Lawrence, L.H. 101
Lawrence, T.H. 258
Lawson 197, 199–200, 204–205, 222, 227, 236, 238, 240, 250
Lay, A.T. 135
Lay, C.H. 116, 212, 264
Lay, Jesse 116, 212, 264
Lay, W.B. 116, 157, 212, 264
Lay, William 140–141
Leah 202, 209, 215–216, 224, 227, 231, 244
Leander/a 197, 203, 229, 249
Leanorah 224
Lear 255
Lebo 243
Lee 207, 225, 236–237, 245, 247, 253, 255
Lee, Colonel 67
Lee, General Robert E. 58–59, 74, 164
Lee, W.C. 162
Leeper, Andrew 240, 272
Leeper, J. Anthony 272
Leeper, James 240
Leeper, Mary/May 211, 239, 264
Leeper, Naomi 240, 272
Leeper, Robt. 272
Leman, Wm. 267
Lena 239, 254
Leonhardt, Mary 100
Lepsey 202
LeRoy 216, 247, 249
Lesley, J. Peter 35, 39
Lett/Letty 245, 247
Levi 217, 220, 228, 255
Lewis 199, 202–203, 206, 214–215, 220, 224, 227, 230, 232–233, 245, 250–251
Lewis, J.J. 247, 274
Lewis, Ann 247, 262, 274
Lewis, James 241, 272
Lewis, John G. 12, 33, 51, 74, 150, 154, 209–210, 234, 262–263
Lewis, Mr. 86, 89
Liberty 216
Lig 255
Lila 209, 254
Limbrick 238
Lincoln, Abraham 17, 22, 87, 107, 130, 148–150, 152, 158, 187
Lincoln County 7–8, 12, 14, 17–18, 30, 41, 43, 53, 55, 62, 87, 91, 97, 101, 111, 117, 124–127, 131–132, 135–140, 142, 144–145, 148–156, 158, 160, 163–165, 172, 180, 194
Lincolnton 20, 23, 30–32, 41, 59, 63–65, 82, 84, 93, 96, 99, 110, 131, 135, 150, 152, 162, 182, 185
Lincolnton Female Seminary 96
Linda/Linda or Sinsa 200, 206, 222–223, 229, 231
Lineberger, Caleb J. 43, 205, 211, 262, 264
Lineberger, Catharine 211, 264

Lineberger, D., & Co. 226
Lineberger, David 252, 276
Lineberger, Eli 219, 225, 265, 271
Lineberger, Elizabeth 62, 87, 102–103
Lineberger, Ephraim 247
Lineberger, Es. 274
Lineberger, F.L. 205
Lineberger, Jacob 247, 274
Lineberger, James Wellington "Willie" 5, 52, 56, 60, 66–70, 72, 77–80, 83, 85–87, 90, 102–103, 116, 124, 138, 205, 262
Lineberger, J.D. 219, 265
Lineberger, J.F. 262
Lineberger, John L./L.J. 43, 205, 212, 264
Lineberger, Jonas R. 205, 252, 262, 276
Lineberger, L. 252
Lineberger, L./ L. & Co 212, 264, 276
Lineberger, L.J. 205
Lineberger, Lewis 43
Lineberger, Manassah 241, 272
Lineberger, Margaret 205
Lineberger, Mary 61
Lineberger, Michael 205, 262
Lineberger, M.L. 276
Lineberger, Peter 211, 264
Lineberger, Robert F. 139
Lineberger, S.J. 262
Liner? 232
Link, M. 205, 262
?Linzy 207
Lip 239
Litha 222
Little, Arch 92
Little, Bettie 92–96
Little, Isabella 91–94
Little, John E. 93
Little, R.W. 94
Little, Thomas 175–176
Little/Lyttle, Hugh/Hua 131–132
Livingston 242
Liz/Lez 222, 226, 230, 239, 241, 252, 254
Lizzie/Lize 207, 211, 215, 222, 225, 227, 229, 231, 235, 243, 247–248, 251, 253–255
Lockhart, Wm. 247, 274
?Loge 223
Lolan 228
Lonegren, Edward 14, 31, 241, 272
Lonegren, James 31, 241, 272
Long, Andrew 28, 51, 137, 207, 210, 262
Long, Barbara 258
Long, Isabella S. 203
Long, John R. 44, 272
Long, Jos. 232, 267
Long, L.H. 267
Long Shoals 15–16, 42, 195
Longa 252
Longstreet 240
?Lop 223
Lottie 229, 233
Louis 211–212, 214, 220
Louisa 211–212, 214, 220, 229–230, 240–241, 249, 253, 255
Love 203, 214

Index

Love, A.J. 247, 274
Love, Andrew 8, 30
Love, Eliza E. 260
Love, Jennet 203, 260
Love, L.H.? 232
Love, Mary 203, 232, 260, 267
Love, Mary A./M.A. 203, 260
Love, May 203
Love, Naomi 260
Love, Naomi E. 203, 260
Love, Robert C.G. 139, 211, 264
Love, Sarah 203, 260
Love, S.W. 50–51
Lovelace, Allison 44
Lovelace, Bolivar 44
Lovinia 227
Lowe, Isaac 132
Lowrance, L.H. 198
Lowrance, M.C. 260
Luce 237, 244, 256
Lucin? 222
Lucinda 200, 227, 233–234, 238
Luckey 207–208
Lucy 206, 208, 214–215, 219–221, 230–232, 234, 238, 240, 242–243
?Luff 248
Lula 216
Lusk, Joseph 130, 147, 198, 258
Lusk, M.E. 63
Luther 218
Lydia 207, 228
Lyle 249
Lyn 236

Mack 198, 209, 220, 226, 228
Madison 220
Mag/Mage 206, 226, 234, 239, 241–242
Magdeline 208
Mahala 200, 221, 236
Major 200
Male 221
Malvina 231
Man 219
Manda 214, 220–221, 229, 232, 253–254, 256
Manuel 210, 225, 246, 252
Marces/cus 205, 252
March 235, 253
Margaret 200–204, 209, 213, 217, 220–222, 224–225, 227, 229–230, 235, 239–240, 242, 247–251, 253–254
Mariah 200, 202, 214, 218–219, 223, 229–231, 237, 242, 246, 252–254
Marian 225
Marion 248
Mark 199, 214
Marks, J.G. 10
Marsh, James H. 138, 182
Marshall 218, 223, 240
Martha 196, 203, 209, 214–215, 222, 224–225, 229–231, 234, 236–237, 239, 242–244, 250–251, 253–255
Martin 197, 207, 217–218, 221
Martin, E. 276
Martin, Elisabeth/E. 241, 256, 272
Martin, J. 210
Martin, J.G. 46
Martin, Milo 272
Martin, W.M. 91

Mary/Maria/Mary Jane 199–200, 205, 207–209, 211–214, 218–219, 221–226, 230–231, 233–234, 236, 238–244, 246–247, 250–256
Mason, L.A. 9–10, 18, 32, 35, 164, 212, 264
Massey, Freno 142
Massey, Green 137
Massey, Washington F. 139, 248, 274
Massey, W.G. 17–18
Mat/Matt 206, 220
Mathew 200, 244
Matilda 197, 231
Matty 228
Mauney 50
Mauney, Abe Jun. 236, 269
Mauney, Abraham 169, 175–176, 179, 181, 195, 232, 236, 267, 269
Mauney, Barbara 236, 267, 269
Mauney, Caleb 232, 267
Mauney, Catharine 267, 269
Mauney, D. 198, 258
Mauney, Dewey Maceo 179
Mauney, Eph. 256
Mauney, Harriet 180
Mauney, John 232, 267
Mauney, Lawson 232, 236, 267, 269
Mauney, ?Lovina 236, 269
Mauney, Manuel 267, 269
Mauney, Max 236, 269
Mauney, Michael 232, 267
Mauney, Naomi 174
Mauney, Noah 258
Mauney, Pinkney 180–181
Mauney, Priscilla 176
Mauney, Samuel 176, 179
Mauney, Susan 232, 269
Mauney, Wesley 167
Mauney, Wesley 4, 167, 174–179, 181–184, 195
Mauney, Wiley 232, 267
Maxwell, Dr. J.S. 152–153
May 199, 206, 214, 255–256
May, George 96
McAlister, Jane 248, 274
McAlister, Jenny 274
McAlister, Joseph 264
MCalister, Smith 75
McAllister, G.W. 203, 260
McAllister, H.C. 207, 262
McArthur, C.R. 274
McArthur, E.A. 9
McArver 213
McBee, John 236, 269
McBee, V.A. 150
McCall, Jane 226, 271
McCorkey, L. 41
McCorkle, M.L. 164
McCready 212
McCready Elis 264
McCready/McGrady, Jno. 203, 260
McCready/McGrady, Wm. 203, 260
McCullough, J.F. 248, 274
McCullough, Vincent 248, 274
McDaniel, E.B. 135
McDaniel, Elisha 248, 274
McDowell, Robert 26, 226, 271
McEntire 111–112
McGee, Elizabeth 226
McGill, Alex D. 233, 267

McGill, Jackson 134
McGill, John 233, 267
McGill, Thos. P. 233, 267
McGill, Tos. J. 233
McGill, Wife 233, 267
McGinnis, C.C. 267
McGinnis, John A. 219, 265
McGinnis, John J. 139, 198, 258
McGinnis, W.W. 142, 198, 258
McIntosh, Alexander 91–92, 95
McIntosh, Elmina 92, 95–96, 99
McIntosh, Harriet R. 5, 19, 91–97, 99
McIntosh, Isaac 92, 226
McIntosh, J.H. 113
McIntosh, Melinda/Belinda 91
McIntosh, William 92
McKee, Green O. 139, 272
McKee, Jas. D./L. 232, 241, 267, 272
McKee, Jemima 213, 264
McKee, William 147, 150–152, 226, 241, 272
McLain, William R. 186–187, 241, 272
McLean, John D. 26, 146, 183, 241, 272
McLean, Jos. 241
McLean, Margaret 241, 272
McLean, Robt. G. 241, 272
McLean, Dr. William B. 152, 271
McLelland, John 32
McLurd, Jas. H. 203
McLurd, J.C. 276
McLurd, John 32, 236, 269
McLurd, Mary 276
McLurd, R.L. 252, 255, 276
McLure, ?Barmadus 241, 272
McLure/McClure, James 124, 260
McNair, Enoch 203, 260
McNair, James 10, 232, 267
McNeely, Elizabeth 62
McPherson, James F. 53–54, 58
Mecklenburg County 21, 26–27, 35, 49, 91, 111, 152–156, 158, 163, 186–187
Melinda 201
Melissa 212
Mellon, G.W. 242, 272
Melvina 216
Mendenhall, Eli 139–142, 203, 260
Mendenhall, J.H. 260
Mendenhall, Jno. J. 247, 274
Mendenhall, Margaret 248, 274
Mendenhall, Nathan 28, 247, 274
Mera 209
Mexican War 8
Mice 220
Michael, W.H. 18, 154
Michaels, A.E. 31
Middle class 23–29, 52, 116, 118, 144–146, 172
Mike 198, 212, 219
Mila 221
Mile?/Miles 200, 202–203, 208, 213, 225, 227, 234, 238, 242, 245, 251
Miliard 231
Militia *see* Home guard
Millen, Alexander 44
Miller 251
Miller, J. 252, 276
Miller, J.L. 162

Miller, Jno. T. 150
Millie 197, 200, 208–209, 214, 216–217, 220–221, 224, 227, 233–234, 239, 245–246
Mills/Mils? 223, 241, 255
Milton/Milt 198, 209, 218, 228
Mima 230
Minder?/Minda/Mindra 213, 225, 233
Minerva 211–212, 240, 252, 254
Mingo 203, 222
Minor 203, 246, 249
Minta/Minty 211, 244
Miram/Miraim/Miriam 211, 215
Missouri 197, 211
Moderwell, Erastus Cratty 21
Mollie 199, 201, 248
Molton, R.A. 17
Monroe 205, 214, 221–222, 224–225, 236, 240, 247–248
Moody, J. 252, 276
Mooney, Ephraim 276; *see also* Mauney
Moore, Ann 219, 252, 255, 265, 276
Moore, Henry 38
Moore, Jas. C. 134, 269
Moore, John C. 219, 265
Moore, J.W. 26, 226, 271
Moore, Marg. 219, 265
Moore, Mary 219, 265
Moore, Mrs. 256
Moore, Walter 247, 274
Moore, Wm. 274
Morning 214
Morris 200, 208, 247–248, 252
Morris, Amos 10, 32
Morris, Belinda 94, 99
Morris, Caroline 94
Morris, Lee 166
Morris, Louisa Costner 76, 95, 134, 166, 195
Morris, May/Mary 50, 210, 262
Morris, Stephen 219, 265
Morris, Vincent 254, 276
Morris, William Groves 4, 28, 40, 52–54, 56–58, 65–72, 75–77, 79, 81, 84, 89, 97–99, 102–104, 113, 123–124, 134, 158, 164–166, 171–172, 184, 191, 195, 207, 262
Morrison 224
Morrison, B. 198, 258
Morrison, J. 198
Morrison, Thos. 258
Morrow, S.L. or T.L. 212, 264
Mose/Moses 203, 205, 211, 213, 219, 223, 231, 234, 240, 253
Mosteller, George 42
Mott or Moll 223
Mountain Island Cotton Mill 17, 21, 26, 42–49, 168–169, 194
Mulinix, L. 48
Mulligan, Jas. 226, 271
Murphey, Jno. E. 267
Murrell, Isaac 116, 212, 264
Murrell, William 187
Musk 218
Myma 241

Nail Factory 94; *see also* High Shoals
Nance, Cleben 59
Nance, John 29, 265
Nance, Lawson 219, 265
Nancy/Nan/Nance 199, 201, 205, 212–213, 215, 217–218, 221, 223–224, 229–230, 232, 238, 240–244, 247, 254–255
Nantz, John 92
Nash 215
Nat 222, 230
Nathan 206, 215, 217
Nations, M/Myer 10, 262
?Nay 235
Neagle, Andrew 242, 272
Neagle, Ann R. 248, 274
Neagle, Jas. B. 242, 272
Neagle, J.L. 28, 248, 274
Neagle, Jno. E. 242, 272
Neagle, Jno. P. 242, 272
Neagle, M. 240, 272
Neal/Neill 200, 223, 238–241, 243
Ned 209, 211, 213, 216, 226, 232, 235, 237, 247
Neel, Andrew 272
Neel, James 198, 258
Neely, Jno. 242, 272
Negro 228
Neill, John W. 233, 267
Neill, Sarah W. 233, 267
Nelly 197, 249
Nelson 206
Nercis 220
Nerla 216
Nerve 244
Newbold, Charles H. 93
Newt./Newton 245, 249
Nicholas (Nichols), John 44
Nicholson, Rev. P. 61, 68
Nims, Fred 252, 276
Nims, Horace 276
Ninerva 216
Niney/Nina 216, 231
Ninif? 215
Nixon, Bartlett 125
No 202
Noah 236, 242
Noe, Kenneth 53, 58
Noland, M.L. 213, 264
Noland, Dr. W.W./Wm. M. 151, 248, 274
Nolen, James 32
Nora 226
Norol 220
Novel 244

Oates, James 253, 267, 276
Oates, James H. 31
Oates, John R. 233, 268
Oates, Samuel R. 18, 40, 172
Oates, T.M.A. 16, 233, 267
Oates, Wm. 203, 260
Oats, James B. 130, 233
O'Brian, Drucilla/Mrs. And. 137, 203, 260, 262
O'Brian, John 137
Obrian, Widow 207
O'Daniel, J.S. 248, 274
O'Daniel, W.J. 70
Odom, J.B. 164
Off 249
Oglisby, Sam O. 219, 265
Olive 212, 224
Oliver 231
Olly 222
Olmstead, Fanny 93–94
Olney Presbyterian Church 100–101
Ormand, B.M. 268
Ormand, Jno. J. 233, 268
Ormand, Lizzie 104
Ormand, Robert D. 12, 233, 268
Ormand, Z.S./T.S. 233, 268
Osborne, Judge 133
Oscar 220, 241
Owen 216
Ozier 225

Packard, Wm. 203, 260
Palmer, William J. 20–23, 133
Pamela 215
Paper mills 15–16, 42
Parham, ?Martin? 260
Parham, Wm. 136
Paris 242
Parker, Andrew 109
Parker, Hester 233, 268
Parker, J.J. 266
Parker, T.W. 260
Parsley, David 274
Parsley, S.M. 274
Parth 254
Pasour, D.R./D.P. 262, 272
Pasour, Eli 10, 34, 50, 115, 262
Pasour, George 207, 262
Pasour, G.I./George J. 219, 262, 265
Pasour, Hannah 207, 262
Pasour, Jac A. 207, 262
Pasour, John 236, 270
Pasour, Levi 207, 262
Pasour, Manassa 207, 262
Pasour, Saml. 207, 237, 262, 270
Pasour, S.P. 33, 50, 207, 262
Pasour, Susan 233, 268
Patsey 201, 204, 213, 217, 227
Patterson, Julia A. 56
Patterson, Wm. 203, 260
Patty 234, 256
Paul 241
Pauline 254
Payseur, Lewis Cass 20–21, 133
Peace movement 114, 116, 121–122, 156–161, 163
Pearson, Judge 157
Pearson, Wm. 203, 260
Peck, Annie 63
Peck, Robert F. 56
Peel 217
Peg/gy 199, 214, 224, 234, 253–254
Pegram, E.L. 253, 276
Pegram, Jacob F. 12, 33, 41, 50, 83, 146, 209, 262
Pegram, Mary 262
Pegram, M.P. 48
Pegram, Sue 99
Pegram, William W. 33
Pegram, Winchester 32–33, 104
Penegar, Lucy 49
Perkins, Isaac 213, 264
Perlina 212
Perry 221, 224
Peter 204, 211–212, 222, 229–230, 237–238, 243, 245, 249–250
Peterson, C.J. 265
Peterson, J.R. 207, 262

Index

Petre 204
Pettus, Jas. T. 248, 274
Petty, Charles Q. 11, 17, 182, 203, 260
Phebe/Pheby 202, 217
Phifer, E.C. 63-64, 82, 85, 90, 96, 104
Phifer, Edward X. 52, 55-56, 63-64, 83-87, 90, 93-94, 96, 104, 159, 162, 171-172
Phifer, George 52-53, 55, 63-64, 83-84, 86, 90, 93
Phifer, J. 204
Phifer, John F. 19, 46, 52, 55-56, 64-65, 83
Phifer, M.L. 204
Phifer, Mamie 93
Phifer, William L. 55, 63-64, 82, 84, 90, 93, 95, 171-172
Phil/Philip 220, 253, 255
Philbeck, Richard 78
Phillips, Frederick 36
Phillis 200-202, 207, 213, 215, 242-243, 249
Piggot, A. Snowden 16
Pink/Pinckney 198, 200, 205, 208-209, 212, 222, 236, 247, 251-253
Pixley, N.H. 12, 16, 46
Plonk, David 198, 258
Plonk, Jacob 15, 30-31, 113, 213, 262
Plonk, Jacob F. 9, 116, 219, 265
Plonk, Mary C. 262
Plonk, Philip 140, 142
Polly 217, 227, 234, 250, 252
Pool, J.N. 268
Pool, John 164
Porter 213
Powell, Joseph A.W. 36-38, 219, 265
Prier, Jno. J. 233
Prince 211, 223, 226, 245
Prince, Robert 186
Priscilla 203, 225, 227
Prudy 226
Pryer, Wiley 227, 271
Puett, Minnie Stowe 48, 181
Pursley, David 248
Pursley, S.M. 248
Putnam, H. 198, 258
Putnam, L. 198, 258

Quince 224
Quinn, James 9, 150, 248, 274
Quinn, Jno. R. 213, 264
Quinn, Tho. F. 248, 274

Rabb, James 186
Rachel 200, 203, 213, 215, 225, 233, 236-237, 246-247, 255
Rafter, Patrick 254, 276
Ragan, Daniel F. 147, 157, 187, 248, 274
Ragan, Jasper 248, 274
Railroad 9, 12, 41
Raleigh 62, 89, 47, 112, 141, 159, 164
Ramsaur, D.F. 135
Ramseur, C.H. 142
Ramsey, E.D. 12-13
Ramsey, James D. 159-160, 165
Ramsey, Marshall, Jr. 126
Ramsey, Mrs. David 102

Ramsom, Ellen 271
Ramsour, Caleb 134
Ramsour, Elisha 41
Ramsour, Jacob 41
Ramsour, J.H. 130
Ramsour, S.A. 268
Randall 54, 76, 103-104, 166, 171-172
Randolph 149
Rankin, Alex 255, 276
Rankin, A.N. ?Ro? 264
Rankin, Ellen 227
Rankin, J.B. 255, 276
Rankin, J.C. 253, 276
Rankin, J.D. 27, 50, 129, 146, 253, 276
Rankin, Jonas 185
Rankin, Joseph 276
Rankin, J.P. 254
Rankin, J.R. 254, 276
Rankin, Macon 187
Rankin, R. Alex 276
Rankin, Rebecca 213
Rankin, Richard 10, 28, 30, 50, 129, 144, 146, 150, 154, 254, 276
Rankin, Robert 255, 276
Rankin, S?ad 253
Rankin, Samuel 12
Rankin, Sib 129
Rankin, Sidney 276
Rankin, W.A. 18
Rankin, W.B. 272
Rankin, William Rufus 11, 243
Ransom 253
?Rariah? 202
Rasbourn 215
Ratchford 213
Ratchford, Catharine 248, 274
Ratchford, J.A. 264
Ratchford, Jas. 272
Ratchford, J.F. 248, 274
Ratchford, John 243, 272
Ratchford, Joseph 242
Ratchford, Miss M.E. 100
Ratchford, Nancy 243, 272
Ratchford, Robt. C. 243, 272
Rebecca 200, 219
Red 231
Reed, Eliza 213, 264
Reed, R.H. 272
Reed, William 10, 243, 272
Reegal? 231
Reid, David 17
Reid, James W. 150, 243, 272
Reinhardt, Mis S. 73, 135
Reinhardt, W. 235
Rena 235
Rener 232
Renolas, John 272
Reuben/Ruben 204, 206, 216, 230, 235, 246
Revels, Absalom 185
Revels, Allen 260
Revels, Ann 185
Revels, Boo 135
Revels, Elias 185
Revels, Gabriel 167, 185, 203, 260
Revels, Hiram Rhodes 185
Revels, Stephen 260
Reynolas, B. 198
Reynolds, J. 258
Reynolds, Martin 258

Reynolds, Sally 258
Reynolds, W. 198, 258
Rheinhour, Franklin D. 41
Rhett 239
Rhine 202
Rhodes, Caleb 10, 15, 37, 50, 210, 220, 266
Rhodes, M. & C. 229, 266
Rhodes, Melchi 10, 14-15, 37, 41, 220, 266
Rhodes, M.M. 266
Rhody/Rhoda 205, 213, 225, 246, 250
Rhom, Catharine 186, 262
Rhom, David 233, 268
Rhom, Isaac 130
Rhom, Jacob 31
Rhyne, A.A. 207, 262
Rhyne, Catharine 51
Rhyne, Catherine 210
Rhyne, Christy 208, 262
Rhyne, D. 276
Rhyne, Daniel 213, 264
Rhyne, David 253, 264
Rhyne, Dorcus 207, 262
Rhyne, Eml. 213, 264
Rhyne, Esli 78, 208, 262
Rhyne, George 60, 67
Rhyne, H.M. 266
Rhyne, Hugh 255, 276
Rhyne, J./J.J. 207, 262, 264
Rhyne, Jac A. 213, 264
Rhyne, Jac H. 208, 264
Rhyne, Jac M. 207, 262
Rhyne, Jacob/Jac., Jr. 253, 262, 276
Rhyne, J.K. 207, 262
Rhyne, John 253, 276
Rhyne, Jonathan 10, 213, 264
Rhyne, Joseph 134
Rhyne, Joseph K. 78, 207, 262
Rhyne, Josh Marcus 135
Rhyne, J.R. 77
Rhyne, Mary Ann Dellinger 74, 97
Rhyne, Michael 227, 271
Rhyne, Moses H. 12, 28, 33-34, 42, 50, 208-209, 254, 276
Rhyne, M.S. 113
Rhyne, Solomon 220-221, 266
Richard 202
Richards, William 14, 221, 255, 276
Richie 227
Richmond 60, 62, 64, 67, 69, 72-73, 88-89, 255
Riddick 216
Riddle, G.M.A.C. 248, 275
Riddle, Jane M. 248, 275
Riddle, J.B.F. 248, 275
Rilty 209
Rinda/Rinah 204, 243
Rine? or Rene 204
Robert/Rob 215, 231, 239, 242, 248, 249, 252
Roberts, C. 199
Roberts, E.H. 199, 258
Roberts, J. 199
Roberts, J.A. 136
Roberts, John H. 18, 31-33, 113, 130, 157, 164, 208, 258, 262
Roberts, John M. 18, 139, 233, 268
Roberts, J.W. 175, 177
Roberts, M.M. 199

Roberts, Priscilla 178
Robinson, Elhanan W. 130
Robinson, Nancy S. 137, 207, 262
Robison, A. 137
Robison, Elam 248, 275
Robison, Eli J. 248, 264
Robison, Harriet 248, 275
Robison, Jane 275
Robison, Jas. W. 248, 272
Robison, Mary A. 248, 275
Robison, S.C. 248, 275
Robison, Thos. 221, 266
Robison, Zimri 248, 275
Romulus 224
Ron 207, 216
Rose 211, 216, 225-227, 233-234, 244, 250, 253-254, 256
Rose, William E. 31, 36
Roseman, Robert 113
Roswell 200
Roxana 203, 212, 217, 222, 238-239, 244
Roy 205
Rudisill, E.A. 236, 269
Rudisill, Eli 123, 125, 236, 269
Rudisill, Emanuel R. 139, 269
Rudisill, J. 198, 258, 263
Rudisill, Jacob 113, 123
Rudisill, J.M. 198, 258
Rudisill, John 50-51, 209, 262
Rudisill, Jonas 59, 236, 269
Rudisill, Mary 233, 236, 268-269
Rudisill, Pinckney 269
Rudisill, S.C. 269
Rudisill, Wiley 236, 258, 269
Rudisills, heirs 255, 276
Rufe 232
Ruff 198
Ruffin, Thos. 148
Rufus 201-202, 206, 211, 218-219, 225, 235-236, 242, 245, 252
Rumpelett, Isaac 255, 276
Rumpfelt, Hezekiah 10
Rumphelat, H.W. 243, 272
Rumphelt, R.J.M. 271
Russel 243
Ruth 216
Rutledge, Alexander 129, 254, 276
Rutledge, A.R. 220, 266
Rutledge, James 219, 227, 266, 271
Rutledge, Robt. 220, 266
Rutledge, Wm. 51, 210, 255, 276
Rutlege, E.T./E.J. 199, 257
Ryburn, And. 271

Sabra 230
?Sack 219
Sadler, Elisabeth 227, 271
Sadler, Henry 227, 271
Sahms, William 21, 256, 274, 276
Salina 211, 222
Sallie/Sallay 204, 216, 218, 223-224, 226, 240, 250-253
Sam/Samuel 197, 199, 200, 202, 206, 208, 212, 216, 218, 221, 227, 230, 233-234, 236, 238-241, 243-244, 246-247, 249, 251, 254
?Samart, M.S. 262
Sammons, R.L. 203
Sample, Wm. 227, 271
Sampson 238, 246, 250, 252

Sandifer, Philip 245, 272, 275
Sandy 202-203, 256
Sarah 171-172, 200-201, 205-208, 212, 217-218, 226, 230, 232, 235, 237-241, 243-244, 246-247, 251, 253-255
Sarvel? 233
Saryan 197
Saylor 221
Saylor, E. 199
Scales, A.W. 148
Schenck, David 19, 22, 30, 32, 46, 53, 103, 107, 110-112, 134, 147-151, 153-155, 158, 160-161, 163, 165, 172-173, 176, 187, 189, 280
Scott 242
Scott, Abram 27, 146, 183, 255-256, 276
Scott, E.N. 275
Scott, William R. 140-141
Seagle, Daniel 150
Seapock, Peter 132
?Sefe 205
Sela 222
Selina 243
Sellars, Alf. 259
Sellars, Wm. 199, 259
Sellers, Abram 233, 268
Sellers, Eli 58, 122
Sellers, J.P. 44
Sellers, M. 198
Sellers, Mary E. 60
Sellers, Newton 5, 52, 58, 66, 77, 85-86, 88, 122, 159
S?elly 199
Selvy, Wm. 213, 265
?Senah 239
Senter, Caleb 4, 52, 57, 59, 65-66, 75-76, 79-80, 84, 86, 88, 98, 100, 103, 112, 119-120, 122-124, 163, 191
Senter, Frances 119
Senter, Jonas 237, 269
Sepp 239
Service, Jas. W./Jos. W. 233, 268
Service/Sarvice, Saml. 213, 264
Service, S.T. 203, 260
Setzer, Alex 221
Setzer, George 41
Setzer, Henry 9, 15, 52, 61, 208, 221, 262
Shamm 236
Shannon, Hugh 213, 264
Shannon, James 213, 264
Shelby 9, 13, 16, 20, 22-23, 117, 129, 135, 150, 162
Sherell, Leanadas 137
Sherill 237
Sherman, William T. 19-20, 22, 164
Sherrill, Mary 138
Shetley, A. 263
Shilo Church 102
Shipp, William T. 18, 27, 101, 126, 134, 139-141, 146, 164, 255, 276
Shuford, Cynthia 269
Shuford, Sidney A. 176, 236
Shuford, Wm. 269
Shull, A. 199, 259
Sidney/Sid 205, 214, 217, 224-225, 229-230, 241
Siena 101
Sifford, D.M. 221, 266

Sifford, Isabella 19, 96
Sifford, Mry 94
Sifford, Violet Ann 19, 92-93, 95-97
Silas 216, 236
Sill/er 217, 231, 250
Silvey 205, 217, 226
Simmons, R.L. 260
Simon 226, 237, 240
Sinda 231
Singleterry, Mr. 97
Sipp 219, 239, 242
Skelton, Dr. 104
Slaves/slavery 23-29, 52, 110, 128, 135, 139, 142, 145, 149, 151, 154, 165-188, 190, 277-279
Sloan, Dr. William 18, 31, 33, 36, 41, 104, 116, 123, 126, 138-139, 146, 148, 151-153, 158, 160, 165, 189, 208, 263
Smart 240
Smith 220, 235
Smith, Andrew 199, 262
Smith, Ben 256, 277
Smith, David 221, 259, 266, 275
Smith, D.B. 50, 209, 263
Smith, Dr. 65
Smith, Elijah/Eli 208, 249, 263, 275
Smith, H. 199, 259
Smith, James 259
Smith, Jas. D. 213, 264
Smith, Jas. W. 275
Smith, J.C. 263
Smith, J.H. 135
Smith, Jno. B. 256, 276
Smith, John 139
Smith, J.R. 199, 259
Smith, Judith 243, 272
Smith, J.W. 249, 275
Smith, Leander 139
Smith, Lee 256
Smith, L.S. 268
Smith, M. 265
Smith, M.A. 227, 271
Smith, Mary 199, 221, 256, 266, 276
Smith, Noah 126
Smith, Robt. 236, 256, 269, 277
Smith, R.S. 277
Smith, Sarah 243, 272
Smyer, J.F. 275
Snorance 217
Solomon 236, 241, 255-256
Sopha/ie/Sofe 203, 212-213, 223, 227, 230, 255-256
Spake, Christopher 199, 259
Spake, Harriet 173
Spake, Philip 97
Spake, S. 199, 259
Sparks, M.R. 135
Spencer, Wm. 213, 264
Spree 220
Stanford 234
Stanhope 240
Stanley, Governor 161
Stansill, J.F. 159
Starling 241-242
Stephen/Steve 199, 217, 228, 241
Stephens, Alexander 187
Steward, Rod 111
Stewart 216, 219, 232
Stiles 234

Stone, J.P. 135
Stoneman's Raid 19–21
Stowe 263
Stowe, Abram 249, 275
Stowe, (C.) Theo(dore) B. 244, 249, 273, 275
Stowe, Catharine 249, 275
Stowe, Delphia 213, 264
Stowe, E.A. 213, 264
Stowe, Edwin B. 181
Stowe, Mrs. E.L. 101
Stowe, Elisabeth 248, 275
Stowe, Eliza 244, 273
Stowe, Ferrie M. 209, 262
Stowe, J. & E.B. 10, 27, 42–49, 168, 173, 243–244, 272–273
Stowe, Jasper 8, 14, 22, 27, 31, 33, 42–49, 106, 112, 154, 181, 213, 273
Stowe, J.F. 249
Stowe, Jno. 249, 275
Stowe, Jordan 181
Stowe, J.R. 213
Stowe, J.R. & S.T. 265
Stowe, Laben 104
Stowe, Larkin 8–10, 30, 42, 144
Stowe, Laura 244, 273
Stowe, Leroy 172, 208, 243–244, 249, 262
Stowe, Logan 213, 264
Stowe, L.W. 272
Stowe, Maj. L.W. 139
Stowe, M.M. 262
Stowe, M.G. 244, 273
Stowe, Mrs. 96
Stowe, Nancy 249, 275
Stowe, Samuel N. 18
Stowe, Tom 167, 181
Stowe, Vina 181
Stowe, W.I./J. 61, 100, 244, 248
Stowe, William A. 18, 243, 272
Stowe, Wm. T. 275
Stowesville 27, 42–49, 74, 139, 168–169, 173, 181, 195
Stroup, Abner 259
Stroup, And. J. 266
Stroup, A.W. 199, 258
Stroup, B. 199
Stroup, Barbara 259
Stroup, Bartlett 221, 266
Stroup, Benjamin 221, 266
Stroup, C. 199, 259
Stroup, Caleb 227, 271
Stroup, Caroline 221, 266
Stroup, Hosea/Hozy 94, 221, 266
Stroup, Israel R. 221, 266
Stroup, Jane 221, 266
Stroup, J.C. 199, 258
Stroup, John D. 221, 266
Stroup, ?Josh H. 266
Stroup, M.A. 259
Stroup, Maxwell 249, 275
Stroup, Moses 94, 233, 268
Stroup, Moses, Jr. 268
Stroup, Nancy J. 221, 266
Stroup, Rebecca 213, 264
Stroup, Rufus 213, 264
Stroup, Solomon 221, 266
Stroup, Wesley 213, 221, 264, 266
Sucky/Suck 215, 239
Sue/Suse 222–223, 226, 239, 251–252, 254–255

Suggs, M.S. 213, 264
Summer?, Mathew 273
Summerow, Ad. 271
Summerow, David 227
Summerow, H. 199, 259
Summers, Bonnie Mauney 181
Summey, Elis 221, 266
Summey, John 236, 269
Summey, Jonas 266
Summitt, Henry 32, 117, 199, 259
Summitt, Lawson M. 10, 33, 172, 208, 262
Sumner, B.H. 154
Susan 100, 202, 206, 208, 214, 216, 218
Susan/nah 231, 240, 242, 249, 251, 255
Syl? 208
Syler 240
Sylvanus/Silvanus 221, 247
Sylvy/Sylva/Silva 238–241, 244, 248

Tait 252
?Talby 234
Tate, John 17, 42, 45, 277
Tate, Thomas R. 10, 14, 26, 42–49, 168, 227, 271
Tavis 227
Tax list 1850 279
Taylor 223, 240
Taylor, E. 259
Taylor, Franklin 269
Teder 248
Temp 214
Texann 220
Theodore 222
Thomas 210–211
Thomas, Saml. 233, 268
Thompson, F.W. 221, 266
Thompson, Leonard E. 41, 111–112, 125, 148, 152, 154, 157, 172, 187, 221, 266
Thompson, Mr. 95
Thomson, E.D. 244, 273
Thornburg, Berry 269
Thornburg, Daniel 263
Thornburg, Jos. 233, 268
Thornburg, Larkin 5, 58, 121–122, 140–141, 170–171
Thornburg, Moses 121, 263
Thornton 212
Thurmond, Strom 179
Tiddy, William 14
Tilda/Tildah 202, 204, 217, 253
Tilman 255
Tim 219
Tiny 217
Tish 250
Titman, A.B. 213, 265
Titman, Anthony 213, 265
Titus 220, 229
Toll bridge 14–16, 37, 41, 48
Tom/Thomas 172, 199, 202, 206, 208, 214, 216, 218, 223, 225–226, 228, 233–234, 237–241, 243, 248–251, 253–255
Toney 219, 230, 233
Toney, J.W. 150
?Took 216
Torrence, Harrison 249, 275
Torrence, Hugh 268

Torrence, Jno. C. 249, 275
Torrence, Leonidas 52–54, 59, 65–66, 69–71, 81, 84, 90, 171
Torrence, Miss M.A. 100
Torrence, Margaret 172
Torrence, Mary 249, 275
Torrence, Robt. 249, 275
Torrence, S.A. 233, 268
Torrence, William 249
Torrence, William J. 139, 260
Torrence, William W. 172, 204, 260
Tracy, Dr. J.W. 151
Trial 226
Trifena 214
Tucker, Alf 273
Tucker, A.M. 44
Tucker, Mary 44
Turbyfill, Jas. 263
Turner 214, 224, 247

Underwood, Emma 228
Underwood, Henry 228, 271
Underwood, Jacob 228, 271
Unionists 2, 22, 128, 136, 142, 149, 152–153, 158, 160–161, 163–164

Vance, Zebulon B. 1, 3, 14, 16–18, 45–48, 75, 102, 107–109, 113, 117, 119, 124–125, 130–131, 136, 138, 140, 155–164, 187
Vandik, James 122, 234, 268
Vanes 253
Venie/Vena 209, 251
Vergo 216
Vestel's Ford 14–15, 135
Vice 202
Vickers, Jno. 237, 269
Vine/Vina 201, 206, 209, 223, 225, 235, 237–238, 244, 248, 251, 254, 256
Violet 206, 208, 211, 215, 221, 224, 226, 229, 233, 238, 243, 246, 248

Wacaser, G.M. 136
Wacaster, Levi 89, 199, 259
Wade 207, 218, 229, 243, 252
Wagstaff, J.F. 256, 273
Wagstaff, Jno. 244, 273
Walker 199, 202, 230, 248
Walker, D.M. 250, 275
Wallace 197, 209, 221, 236, 238, 253
Wallace, D.G. 244, 275
Wallace, Mary 44
Wallace, Thomas 249, 275
Walt?/Walter 218, 223
Ward, Mary 99, 209, 263
Ward, Rufus J. 273
Warlick, Lydia 199, 259
Warlick, P.H. 199, 259
Warlick, S. 199, 259
Warren 248–249
Warren, Dr. 61
Warren, W.G. 250, 275
Wash/ington 214–216, 230, 240
Watt, Mel 179
W.C. & R. Rho. 220
Weatherly, M.H. 266
Webb 252
Webb, Elizabeth 44
Webb, Hugh 273
Webster, John 176

Wellman, Naomi 178
Wells, B.F. 244, 273
Wells, David 152, 208, 263
Wells, James 263
Wesley 228, 230, 237
West 214, 227, 239, 249, 253
West, D.F. 125
West, Ezekiel 256, 277
West, Robt. 256, 277
West, W. 277
Whig Party 9–10, 144, 148–149, 155, 190
White, Barbara 199, 259
White, Edw. M. 268
White, Hannah J. 268
White, Henry F. 146, 263
White, J.A. 268
White, James Hillhouse 4, 11, 28, 30, 113, 117, 125, 144–145, 154, 156, 161–162, 195, 208, 263
White, Jas. F. 234, 268
White, John B. 146
White, Mary 234, 268
White, Mary C. 234, 268
White, Robt. A. 268
White, Sarah 268
White, Thaddeus 146, 263
White, Thomas H. 138
White & Young 208
Whitehurst, Jake 39
Whitesides, C. 265
Whitesides, Edward 12, 204, 213, 261
Whitesides, E.L. 268
Whitesides, J.F. 265
Whitesides, John 261
Whitesides, J.T. 261
Whitesides, Major 234, 268
Whitesides, Marg. 261
Whitesides, Mary 204, 234, 261, 268
Whitesides, Priscilla 265
Whitesides, Wm. 213
Whitley, Mrs. 95
Whitson, J.C. 16, 160
Whitworth, F.R. 234, 268

Whitworth, Lydia 259
Whitworth, Wyoma/Nyoma 199, 259
Wier 204
Wier/Weer, Alexander 51, 146, 152, 204
Wier, B.A. 50
Wier, W.O. 204, 261
Wilbert 250
Wilburn 213, 237
Wilkes, Charles 36
Will/William/Wm. 212, 215, 218–219, 223–224, 226–227, 240, 250–252, 254
Williams, C.H. 214, 265
Williams, Jac. 269
Williams, Jacob 237
Williams, Marcus 270
Williams, S.H. 75
Williams, Dr. T. 150
Williford, E. 221, 266
Willis 214, 225, 228, 231
Willis, S.S. 228, 271
Wills 198
Willy/Willie 220, 218, 224, 230
Wilmington 60, 63, 70, 118, 120–121, 141, 162
Wilson 245
Wilson, E.B. 26, 41, 204, 249, 260, 275
Wilson, Edward 260
Wilson, Edwin 204
Wilson, Jerry 182
Wilson, J.F. 256, 275, 277
Wilson, J.J. 261
Wilson, L. & E.B. 203, 260
Wilson, Lawson 12, 26, 41, 183, 195, 203, 234, 260, 268
Wilson, Robert M. 275
Wilson, Robert Newton 52, 182, 275
Wilson, Robert W. 249
Wilson, Robt. 214, 249, 275
Wilson, Saml. M. 204, 261
Wilson, Samuel 13, 204, 261
Wilson, Thomas 213, 265

Wilson, William/William M. 204, 261, 275
Wilson, William Joseph 8–10, 26, 30, 41, 144, 195
Wince 220
Winn 223
Winner? 220
Winny 230, 234
Winthrop, John B. 39
Wise, Ambrose 270
Wiswall 16, 182
Withers 209
Withers, B.F. 62, 172
Withers, C.C. 209, 263
Withers, E.H. 263
Withers, J.H. 263
Withers, M.R. 209
Withers, Susan 208, 263
Withers, W.C. 263
Withers, Wm. 263
Wolfe, J.C. 38
Wolfe, W.C. 62, 99
Woman 219
Woodlawn Mill 21, 42–49, 168–169, 195
Workman, Jacob L. 123
Workman, Nancy 123
Worth, Jonathan 165
Worth, Wm. T. 38
Wortman, Catharine 102
Wright, J.M. 244, 273
Wright, S. 244, 272
Wyatt 246
Wyche, Mrs. 64
Wylie/Wiley 238, 249

Yarboro, Wm. 245, 273
Yates 111–112
Yeomen 23–29, 52, 116, 144, 147, 171
York 202, 233, 253
Yorkville/York 12, 41
Young, Rudolph 179–180, 185–186

Zenas 237–238, 252
Zenith 233
Zimri 248, 256

www.ingramcontent.com/pod-product-compliance
Lightning Source LLC
Chambersburg PA
CBHW081538300426
44116CB00015B/2671